Medical Services; Pathology

HISTORY OF THE GREAT WAR

BASED ON OFFICIAL DOCUMENTS

MEDICAL SERVICES

PATHOLOGY

EDITED BY

Major-General Sir W. G. MACPHERSON, K.C.M.G., C.B., LL.D.,

Major-General Sir W. B. LEISHMAN, K.C.M.G., C.B., F.R.S., LL.D.,

and

Colonel S. L. CUMMINS, C.B., C.M.G., LL.D.

LONDON:
PRINTED & PUBLISHED BY HIS MAJESTY'S STATIONERY OFFICE.
To be purchased through any Bookseller or directly from H.M. STATIONERY OFFICE
at the following addresses: Imperial House, Kingsway, London, W.C.2, and
28 Abingdon Street, London, S.W.1; York Street, Manchester;
1 St. Andrew's Crescent, Cardiff; or 120 George Street, Edinburgh.

1923.

Price, £1 1s. Net.

CONTENTS

LIST OF COLOURED PLATES.

(6986)   Wt. 10080/Ps20436   5/23   Harrow   G 51.

CONTRIBUTORS TO THE VOLUME ON PATHOLOGY

ADAMI, J.G., C.B.E., M.D., F.R.S., Colonel C.A.M.C. (Reserve of Officers); A.D.M.S. to D.G.M.S., Canadian Contingent.

Influenza.

ANDREWES, Sir F. W., O.B.E., M.D., F.R.C.P., F.R.S., Major R.A.M.C.(T.F.).

The Pathology and Bacteriology of Tetanus.
Bacillary Dysentery.

BALFOUR, Andrew, C.B., C.M.G., M.D., B.Sc., F.R.C.P.E., Lieut.-Colonel R.A.M.C.(T); Member of the Advisory Committee, Eastern Mediterranean, 1915–16; President of the Advisory Committee, Mesopotamia, 1916–17; Member of the Medical Mission, Expeditionary Force, East Africa, 1917.

Typhus Fever.

BRADFORD, Sir J. Rose, K.C.M.G., C.B., C.B.E., D.Sc., M.D., F.R.C.P., F.R.S., Major-General A.M.S.(T); Consulting Physician, B.E.F. France.

Acute Infective Polyneuritis.

CUMMINS, S. L., C.B., C.M.G., M.D., LL.D.(N.U.I.), Colonel A.M.S.

Tetanus in its Statistical Aspects.
Tuberculosis.

DOBELL, Clifford, F.R.S.

Amœbic Dysentery. (With Col. D. Harvey).

DUNN, J.S., M.A., M.D., Brevet-Major R.A.M.C.(T).

War Nephritis. (With Col. R. Muir).

FLEMING, Alex., M.B., B.S., F.R.C.S., Captain R.A.M.C.(T).

Infection of Wounds by Microbes other than spore - bearing Anaërobes. (With Major W. H. Tytler).

GOADBY, Sir K. W., K.B.E., M.R.C.S., L.R.C.P., D.P.H.(Cantab.); Hon. Bact. Specialist, Royal Herbert Hospital, Woolwich; Member of Tetanus Advisory Committee.

Latent Sepsis in Wounds.

GORDON, Mervyn H'., C.M.G., C.B.E., M.A., B.Sc., M.D., Lieut.-Colonel R.A.M.C.(T); Member of Army Pathological Advisory Committee; Consulting Bacteriologist for Cerebro-spinal Fever, and Officer in Charge of the Central Cerebro-spinal Fever Laboratory.

Cerebro-spinal Fever.

HARVEY, D., C.M.G., C.B.E., M.D., Lieut.-Colonel (temp. Colonel) R.A.M.C.; Deputy Director of Pathology, War Office; Vice-Chairman, Army Pathology Advisory Committee.

Amœbic Dysentery. (With Prof. C. Dobell).

JAMES, S. P., M.D.(Lond.), M.R.C.S., L.R.C.P. (Lond.); Lieut.-Colonel I.M.S.; A.D.M.S. Sanitation, Mesopotamian Expeditionary Force.

Encephalitis Lethargica.

KEITH, Sir Arthur, M.D., C.M., LL.D., F.R.S., F.R.C.S., Conservator of the Royal College of Surgeons.

The War Office Collection of Pathological Specimens. (With Prof. S. G. Shattock).

CONTRIBUTORS TO THE VOLUME ON PATHOLOGY

LEDINGHAM, J. C. G., C.M.G., M.A., D.Sc., M.B., Ch.B., F.R.S., Lieut.-Colonel R.A.M.C.(T) ; Consulting Bacteriologist, Mesopotamia ; Member of Medical Advisory Committee in Mediterranean.
Diarrhœa and Enteritis.

LEISHMAN, Sir W. B., Knt., K.C.M.G., C.B., M.B., C.M., F.R.C.P., F.R.F.P.S., LL.D., F.R.S., K.H.P., Major-General A.M.S. ; Director of Pathology, War Office.
Organization of the Pathological Service.
The Enteric Fevers.

McNEE, J. W., D.S.O., M.D., D.Sc., M.R.C.P. (Lond.) ; Major R.A.M.C. (T.), Assistant Adviser in Pathology, First Army, B.E.F., France.
Trench Fever.

MUIR, Robert, M.D., Sc.D., F.R.S., Lieut.-Colonel R.A M.C.(T.F.).
War Nephritis. (With Major J. S. Dunn).

ROBERTSON, Miss M., M.A.
Bacteriology of Anaërobic Infection.

SEMPLE, Sir David, D.Sc., M.D.(R.U.I.), Lieut.-Colonel R.A.M.C.(R.P.) ; Director-General Public Health Dept., Egypt, 1913–18.
Gingivitis and Vincent's Angina.

SHATTOCK, S. G., F.R.C.S., F.R.S.
The War Office Collection of Pathological Specimens. (With Sir Arthur Keith).

STOKES, Adrian, O.B.E., D.S.O., M.D., F.R.C.S.I., Captain R.A.M.C.(T).
Gas Gangrene.
Spirochœtal Jaundice.

TYTLER, W. H., B.A., M.B. (Toronto), Major, C.A.M.C.
Infection of Wounds by Microbes other than Spore - bearing Anaë-robes. (With Capt. A. Fleming).

WRIGHT, Sir Almroth, Knt., K.B.E., C.B., M.D., D.Sc., F.R.S., Colonel R.A.M.C.(T) ; Consultant Physician, B.E.F., France.
The Physiology of Wounds.

Note.—(T) means temporary commission. (T.F.) means Territorial Force commission.

ABBREVIATIONS

A.A.M.C.	.. ..	Australian Army Medical Corps.
A.D.M.S.	.. ..	Assistant Director of Medical Services.
A.T.S.	.. ..	Antitetanic Serum.
C.A.M.C.	.. ..	Canadian Army Medical Corps.
C.S.F.	.. ..	Cerebro-spinal Fever.
D.G.A.M.S.	..	Director-General, Army Medical Service.
D.G.M.S.	.. ..	Director-General of Medical Services.
D.M.S.	.. ..	Director of Medical Services.
G.H.Q.	.. ..	General Headquarters.
I.M.S.	.. ..	Indian Medical Service.
M.R.C.	.. ..	Medical Research Council.
N.Z.M.C.	.. ..	New Zealand Medical Corps.
P.M. ..	.. ..	Post Mortem.
R.A.M.C.	.. ..	Royal Army Medical Corps.
R.N. ..	.. ..	Royal Navy.
R.N.V.R.	.. ..	Royal Naval Volunteer Reserve.
T.A.B.	.. ..	Mixed Typhoid and Paratyphoid Vaccine.
T.V. ..	.. ..	Typhoid Vaccine.
U.S.A.	.. ..	United States Army.

PREFACE.

THE volume on Pathology is the final volume of the series of volumes dealing with the diseases, surgery and hygiene of the war, as distinct from the volumes on the general history, which are concerned with the administration, organization and strategical and tactical employment of the medical services in the various campaigns, and the volume on statistics and epidemiology, the data for which are in the hands of the Ministry of Pensions. Many of the contributions to the present volume have a more individual character than those in the preceding volumes, since they deal largely with the personal researches and investigations of their respective authors into the pathological problems of disease and of wound infection, and into the employment of sera and bacterial vaccines. There is, for example, recorded in it the individual work of Sir Almroth Wright at Boulogne; of Colonel J. G. Adami, Sir Frederick Andrewes, Professor Clifford Dobell and Dr. Mervyn Gordon in the United Kingdom; of workers such as Majors Stokes, Shaw Dunn and McNee in mobile laboratories in the field; and of others who contributed individually to throw light upon the pathology of wounds and disease.

The chapter on the War Office Collection of Pathological Specimens was originally intended to be of much wider scope than that presented. The difficulty, however, of preparing an account of the more important specimens at present conserved in the Museum of the Royal College of Surgeons was so great that, in order to avoid delay in the publication of the volume, this chapter deals only with the general organization of the collection and the arrangements made by the War Office for its conservation.

Much valuable assistance in the preparation of this volume has been given to the Editors by Colonel D. Harvey, the Deputy Director of Pathology at the War Office. Acknowledgments are also due to Professor W. G. MacCallum, the Medical Research Council, the *Lancet*, the Oxford Medical Publications, and Messrs. Constable & Co., for permission to reproduce various illustrations which have already appeared in their publications.

January 1923.   W. G. M.

CHAPTER I.

THE organization of pathological work during the war was similar to that of most other branches of military activity, inasmuch as, from small beginnings, it had to expand to meet growing needs and to adapt itself continually to ever-changing requirements. Thanks to the splendid support of civil pathologists and bacteriologists it was possible to keep abreast of the situation in most theatres of war and, in general, to maintain this service at a very high level of efficiency.

The subject includes a description of the organization of the pathology work in the regular army as it existed at the outbreak of hostilities; the organization of this work in the field during the war; the general character of the work which fell to the pathological department in the field; and the organization at home during the war.

The Organization of Pathology and Bacteriology in the Army before the War.

The importance of pathology to the army, both in peace and in war, was by slow degrees becoming recognized in the years preceding the war, but it was very far from having reached a point satisfactory either to those engaged in it or to those who realized its great importance in connection with the diagnosis, treatment and prevention of disease. The need for any centralized organization and direction of this branch of medical work had not been admitted, and such control as existed was vested, under the Director-General, in respect of different portions of its work, in no less than three subdivisions of the medical department of the War Office, which were concerned respectively with personnel, with medical and professional matters and with equipment. Matters of a technical nature were referred either to the Army Medical Advisory Board or to the staff of the Royal Army Medical College. Proposals to reorganize this work in a manner more in accord with its importance had not been accepted.

As it existed in 1914 the organization may be described briefly under the headings of (a) personnel and training, (b) work under peace conditions, and (c) organization for war.

B

Personnel and Training.—All officers of the Royal Army Medical Corps were required to go through a three months' course of instruction at the Royal Army Medical College on entering the Service.   In this course an important place was occupied by the subject of pathology, which was taught both by systematic lectures and by practical work in the laboratories.   At this course, known as the Junior Course, it was endeavoured to supplement the bacteriological knowledge acquired by the young officer at his medical school so as to fit him to deal with ordinary problems of bacteriological diagnosis, particularly in connection with such conditions as he was most likely to encounter in military hospital work and in connection with tropical disease.   The course, which went hand in hand with similar systematic and practical instruction in hygiene and with systematic lectures on the diagnosis and treatment of tropical disease, aimed at making the officer self-reliant and competent to carry out efficiently the major part of the routine work of laboratory diagnosis.

On taking up their duties in commands at home and abroad subsequent to this junior course most of these officers had the opportunity, of which a number availed themselves, of gaining further practical experience in the subject at the hospital or other laboratories in their stations, by working in these laboratories either voluntarily or as part of their duty.

Some years later in their service all captains of the R.A.M.C. were required to go through the "Senior" course of instruction at the Royal Army Medical College, in order to qualify for promotion to the rank of major.   The average service of the officers forming such senior classes was about nine or ten years, and all had done at least one tour of foreign service. The portion of this course devoted to pathological instruction was partly of the nature of a "refresher" course, but a number of subjects, both by lecture and in the laboratory, were dealt with in fuller detail, and a higher standard was expected at the examination.   The duration of this senior course in pathology was three months.

Finally, in accordance with the approved system, every officer who went through the above senior class was given the option of selecting a special professional subject in which to undergo further instruction, with a view to trying to attain in it the high standard necessary to qualify as a specialist in that subject.   Among those open to him was bacteriology. Of each senior class, then, a few officers each session having chosen this subject were given a further course of three months' instruction in advanced bacteriology in all its branches, in protozoology, helminthology and the preparation and standardization of sera and vaccines.

If successful in the examination held at the end of this course the officer was registered as a specialist in bacteriology, and, if subsequently employed as such, was entitled to the modest sum of 2s. 6d. a day in supplement of his pay.

By this system it resulted that, while every officer had to attain a definite standard of knowledge of ordinary clinical pathology and bacteriology, a certain number, averaging six or seven a year, reached the grade of specialist after a further period of three months' advanced instruction.

From the date of introduction of this system in 1903 to that of the outbreak of war fifty-nine officers of the R.A.M.C. had qualified as specialists in bacteriology and of these the majority were still on the Active List.

Prior to the war there were only eight specialist appointments authorized at home and three abroad, though efforts were being made to obtain authority for others, and in consequence the majority of officers possessing this qualification were employed in other lines. Naturally, also, a number of those who qualified among the earliest batches had, in 1914, attained a seniority which entitled them to employment in administrative work or in charge of important hospitals or other units.

Stated briefly, the supply of trained pathologists in the Corps was in 1914 more than sufficient to staff the few authorized appointments, but the majority of those not employed in pathology had attained a seniority which would inevitably preclude their being counted upon for laboratory work in the event of any war involving general mobilization.

Special arrangements were made for the training of suitably qualified R.A.M.C. orderlies as laboratory attendants, and volunteers from the various companies of the R.A.M.C. were, at regular periods, formed into classes which attended at the Royal Army Medical College for a course of training lasting nine months and comprising instruction in the methods not only of the pathological but also of the hygiene laboratory. At the end of this course the passing of a theoretical and practical examination, of the standard laid down in the regulations, entitled the candidate to the grade of qualified laboratory attendant, carrying a small addition to pay and, conditional on good service and the passing of later examinations, to promotion within this grade up to the rank of staff-sergeant.

A few senior appointments to warrant rank were open to first-class men at the Royal Army Medical College, but such had in addition to be fully qualified in the other branches of Corps work.

At the outbreak of war approximately fifty men were employed in laboratory work at home and abroad, while a small number had passed to the Reserve and would be available on mobilization. What has just been said as to the officers available for pathology work on mobilization applies also to the non-commissioned officers and men specially trained for the work of laboratory attendant; while there were more than enough for peace duties there were far too few for the needs of a fighting force of any size. Many who had qualified in former years had by reason of their efficiency and seniority been promoted to non-commissioned ranks too high to allow of their employment as ordinary laboratory attendants.

In the various commands pathological laboratories, equipped on an adequate but far from luxurious scale, were attached to and usually situated within the principal military hospitals of the command. All pathological material requiring expert examination from out-stations was sent to these laboratories. Routine work of the ordinary clinical pathological nature was supposed to be dealt with locally, and in hospitals of any size this was usually performed by one of the medical staff, in addition to his other duties. Unfortunately, as so often happens even in the present day, far too much simple routine work of this nature, such as urine examinations, blood-counts, and so on, was passed on to the central laboratory, whose pathologist in consequence was often swamped with routine examinations which every army medical officer had been trained to carry out for himself. In spite of this handicap many of these laboratories were centres of vigorous research work and many valuable additions to pathological knowledge have emanated from them.

Behind this admittedly slender structure of pathological organization lay the pathological department of the Royal Army Medical College, which always endeavoured to maintain the closest possible touch with the officers in charge of command and station laboratories. Each was of the greatest possible assistance to the other. The College obtained valuable pathological material from laboratories at home and abroad which, in their turn, aided in many ways in furthering the enquiries and researches occupying the attention of the central body.

On the other hand, the pathologist serving in a more or less isolated area was able to consult the College staff and to send difficult or doubtful material to them for confirmation or for further investigation.   The staff of the College had, in addition, the great advantage of frequent and close association with the pathologists of the various metropolitan institutions and schools of medicine, a privilege of which they endeavoured to take every possible advantage.

It remained for the war itself to demonstrate the importance of the services which modern pathological knowledge was in a position to offer in aid of the common aim—the maintenance of the health of the troops and the effective treatment of the sick and wounded.   In spite of the comparatively recent experience of the South African War no essential increase or change in the scale of establishment of pathologists had been introduced and all that was laid down was that each general hospital of 1,040 beds should include in its equipment a well-appointed bacteriological laboratory and that this should be placed in charge of one or of two officers detailed as bacteriologists.   Two trained laboratory attendants were to be attached to the hospital for duty in the laboratory.

The Organization of Pathology in the Field during the War.

It has already been said that no central pathological organization existed in peace nor had one been contemplated in war establishments.   Like other branches of the Service, when the need came an organization gradually evolved itself, more or less adequate for the needs that had to be met.   Failing any pre-arranged system of sufficient elasticity to meet the complex needs of forces operating at a distance and under climatic conditions which varied from those at Archangel to those on the Equator, the War Office limited itself to the provision of personnel and equipment, leaving it to the medical directorate of the force in question to employ these to the best advantage. Although there were certain disadvantages in this, in practice it worked fairly satisfactorily.   Obviously the conditions for successful working were rooted in the personalities of the administrative medical officers of the force, and of the bacteriologists concerned, and in the degree to which each appreciated the importance of the respective duties and responsibilities of the other.   That this understanding was so often and so fully realized is a tribute to the truly British quality of adaptability, since such mutual appreciation could scarcely have been taken for granted in the case, for instance, of bacteriologists fresh from the freedom of civil employment and of administrative officers not perhaps fully cognizant of the military value of modern bacteriology.

In field forces operating at a great distance from the home base a large degree of autonomy in matters of pathological organization was not only inevitable but in many ways advantageous. It was only in technical matters that it is to be regretted that there was a lack of central organization.

Except in the smallest of the expeditionary forces, where the bacteriologists attached to the principal hospital advised the administrative medical officer, if and when he was consulted, it sooner or later became obvious that, whatever position or title might be locally conferred upon him, an experienced Adviser in Pathology was required. Although the larger and older established sanitary organization frequently included in its personnel regular officers competent to give such advice, and sometimes qualified as specialists in bacteriology as well as in hygiene, where this was not the case the want was soon felt of someone who would accept the grave responsibility for the technical advice often required in matters of considerable military importance.

This need was met in various ways, either by asking for an experienced military or civilian bacteriologist to be sent out as " senior bacteriologist," or by having such an officer attached to a local Medical Advisory Committee, as in the case of Egypt, Gallipoli and Palestine.

British pathology has reason to be proud of the response which was made to the urgent demands for bacteriologists, whether for executive or advisory work, and heavy as these demands became they were always met, and there was scarcely a home laboratory which did not send the bulk of its staff, and often its chief, to serve wherever the call lay. Scarcely less credit attaches to the few who remained to serve the needs of the armies at home, of the many thousands of sick and wounded in home hospitals, and to do double and treble routine work for those who had gone overseas. Apart from its value, no more strenuous and unremitting labour fell to any group of medical officers than to the bacteriologists. While the pressure upon the surgeon, the physician, or the administrator might indeed be almost unbearable at times, it was at least intermittent. On the other hand, the work of the bacteriologist was never done.

Appointments to the posts of bacteriologists of general hospitals on mobilization were made by the Director-General's staff at the War Office from such regular specialists as were available, and afterwards from temporarily commissioned officers who had had experience in bacteriology. The supply of the first class was very soon exhausted as, with a few exceptions, the services of the regular specialist class were soon claimed in other directions, their places having to be filled either by another member of the staff of the hospital, if a qualified man was available, or by the posting of a temporarily commissioned officer to the unit. Of all the regular officers who had qualified as specialists in bacteriology before the war no more than four remained at this work by the time the campaign was six months old, and those only because it was recognized that their special knowledge of some branch of bacteriology made them indispensable. This was regrettable in many ways, but it could not be gainsaid that priority of claim attached to the urgent need for experienced medical officers in charge of field units. Nor can the Corps grudge, it can only lament, the death of two brilliant young bacteriologists in Captains Rankin and Fry—the former being awarded a posthumous V.C. for his gallantry in action, while the latter was a victim of his devotion to duty during the notorious typhus outbreak at Wittenberg after his capture by the enemy.

The conditions prevailing during the earlier weeks of the war in France were not such as to permit any full development of bacteriological work. The retreat from the Belgian frontier and the consequent and frequent changes in the location of headquarters and of medical units were naturally inimical to such development, and it was not until military conditions became somewhat more stabilized that the larger medical units, such as general hospitals, stationary hospitals and isolation hospitals were fully opened and began to work in all their branches. The first hospital laboratories to open were those of No. 2 and No. 4 General Hospitals at Havre and Versailles respectively.

As a result of the early fighting anxiety was caused by the unexpected prevalence among the wounded of tetanus, gas gangrene, and the graver forms of sepsis, and as many technical points in connection with these conditions had to be enquired into and dealt with, Colonel Sir William Leishman, Expert in Tropical Diseases on the Army Medical Advisory Board, was directed to join the expeditionary force on 3rd October 1914,

and was attached in an advisory capacity to the staff of the
D.M.S. of the force, at that time Surgeon-General T. P. Wood-
house : from then until April 1918, when he was relieved
by Colonel S. Lyle Cummins, he remained the responsible
adviser of the Director-General of the Medical Services,
British Forces in France, in all matters connected with
pathology and with the employment of sera and vaccines.   A
few months later the designation of " Adviser in Pathology "
was attached to the post and it was determined that, while
immediately responsible to the Director-General, he should be
located at the headquarters of the D.M.S. Lines of Communication, and attached to the staff of that officer. Authority was
given for his making such visits and inspections as might be
called for, and the administrative medical heads of each army
and of the principal bases, as these became established, were
authorized to consult him on technical matters.

As the size of the force and the complexities of the medico-
military situation increased, the scope of the duties of the
Adviser in Pathology naturally expanded in proportion.
Though far from exhaustive the following list will give some
idea of the main lines of work devolving on him in the year
1917 :—

1. Adviser in pathology to the expeditionary force.
2. Member of the Advisory Board of the Director-General, Medical
    Services, G.H.Q.
3. Chairman of research committees on trench fever and on nephritis.
4. Inspection of all mobile and hospital laboratories, at the front and on
    the lines of communication.
5. Co-ordination of the work done in the laboratories.
6. Recommendations on appointments to the charge of laboratories.
7. Advice on the installation and equipment of new laboratories.
8. Distribution of laboratories and pathologists to meet local emergencies.
9. Advice to medical store department on laboratory equipment, reagents,
    apparatus, etc.
10. Advice on all matters relating to the supply and employment of sera
    and vaccines.
11. Advice on tropical and parasitic diseases in native troops and labour
    contingents.
12. Collaboration with the A.D.M.S. (Sanitation) in the control of in-
    fectious disease.
13. Collection and analysis of returns relating to enteric fever and tetanus.
14. Reports to the D.G.M.S., G.H.Q. and to the D.G.A.M.S., War Office.
15. Arrangements for the collection of pathological specimens.
16. Member of the Inter-Allied Sanitary Commission, Paris.
17. Member of the Inter-Allied Surgical Conference, Paris.
18. Liaison with the pathological work of the armies of the Allies.

As the work increased an assistant was allotted to the
Adviser in Pathology, a post held in France first by
Major A. B. Smallman and later by Captain Graeme Gibson,

who died at Abbeville of influenzal pneumonia in 1919 when engaged upon an important research into the ætiology of this disease.

The need for delegation of part of the duties of supervising and co-ordinating the work of the laboratories became manifest towards the end of the war, and authority was given for the appointment of an Assistant Adviser in Pathology to each army and to each of the principal bases. These officers did not cease to hold charge of their respective mobile and hospital laboratories, but acted in addition as local advisers to their Ds.M.S. and superintended the working of the other laboratories in their area, under the general direction of the Adviser in Pathology.

The system outlined above of the organization of pathology in France was in its principal features reduplicated in the other expeditionary forces, with modifications adapted to the local conditions and to the size of the force concerned. At first the responsibility for the advisory duties was not in specialist hands but either in those of the senior officer of the sanitary service or, as in the case of the operations in Gallipoli, Egypt, Salonika and Mesopotamia, in those of an advisory medical and sanitary committee composed of distinguished civil experts.

Laboratories.

The laboratories were of three classes :   (1) mobile bacteriological laboratories ; (2) hospital laboratories ; and (3) research laboratories.

Mobile Bacteriological Laboratories.—The history of the origin and development of these units is one of considerable interest and has been well described by Lieut.-Colonel A. C. H. Gray,* who himself had charge of one of the earliest which was sent to France. Their employment in close touch with the front-line forces had been contemplated as a practical proposition for an expeditionary force prior to the war, and in particular had been advocated in an able thesis by Colonel S. L. Cummins. Although none had been authorized or organized on mobilization it was not many weeks before the need for such units was increasingly felt and a request for them was sent to the War Office. Colonel Cummins, who was at that time on the headquarters staff of the force, supplied in outline the kind of equipment which the situation called for, and prompt steps were taken to supply this need. With the helpful collaboration of Lieut.-Colonel C. J. Martin and his

---

* *Journ. of R.A.M.C.*, 1922, Vol. xxxviii, p. 323.

colleagues of the Lister Institute, a suitable motor was found, originally fitted as a motor caravan, and this was purchased, dismantled and equipped as a mobile laboratory in a short space of time.   The Lister Institute also lent the services of one of the most competent of their staff in the person of Major S. R. Rowland, who, in addition to his high technical proficiency, had a good knowledge of motors.   This officer was placed in charge of the new laboratory and took it over to France, where he was joined by Major A. Stokes, and where, as No. 1 Mobile Bacteriological Laboratory, it played a most prominent part in the early pathological history of the war. It was one of the particularly sad incidents of the campaign that Major Rowland did not live to reap the certain credit and probable rewards which should have fallen to him for his splendid work.   He died in 1917 from cerebro-spinal meningitis contracted in the course of his duties.

This first mobile laboratory proved excellent as regards its medical equipment and its working facilities, but its great weight and size were inconvenient and unsuited to the roads and the mud of Flanders.

The next was presented to the War Office by an anonymous donor and known as the " Princess Christian Motor Laboratory "; it was taken out to France by Major A. C. H. Gray and was soon followed by a third in charge of Captain J. W. McNee.   An illustrated account of these was published in the *Lancet* of 23rd January 1915.   They too, however, were reported to be rather overweighted by the equipment so that it was decided that all the later patterns should be mounted as lorries and not as cars.   The most important change consequent on this decision was that the laboratories were now running on solid tyres instead of on twin pneumatics, as was the case with the earlier type.   Fortunately the apprehensions that this might prove disastrous to the more delicate parts of the equipment proved groundless, and the fact that extraordinarily few breakages occurred during transits across rough country roads, fields and so on, speaks well both for the care with which the fittings were designed and for the trouble which the staff of the laboratories took in packing.

As to the equipment itself, this was designed to make the laboratory completely independent and to allow of the carrying out of all ordinary bacteriological operations—cultural, chemical and microscopical.   With this in view, autoclaves, steam sterilizers, incubators, centrifuges and all customary apparatus were provided, and much ingenuity was displayed in the design and fixing of these, both as regards the distribution of weight and the conservation of space adequate for the workers when the laboratory was open. In general it may be said that they answered their purpose admirably and that this was abundantly proved by the character and volume of the work performed in them.

It was never contemplated that the bacteriologist in charge should consider himself bound to limit himself to the restricted space furnished by the motor lorry, and in the majority of instances, at all events when the unit was stationary for some time, advantage was taken of some neighbouring building, hut, or even tent, to dismount a portion of the equipment and to carry out at any rate a part of the work in this annexe. It says much, however, for the general planning of the laboratories that some of the officers in charge preferred to carry out the whole of the work in it, even when supplementary accommodation could, if desired, have been obtained.

The question was raised on several occasions during the war as to whether this mobile, self-contained laboratory, with its obviously narrow accommodation, was the most suitable form in which to supply to the forward line and the casualty clearing stations the bacteriological assistance needed in so many directions. It was not infrequently suggested that it would have been preferable to carry the whole equipment, packed in suitable boxes, in ordinary lorries, to be indented for when required, and to utilize in all cases a building or hut for the installation of the laboratory. On the face of it there was something to be said for such a suggestion, and no doubt more equipment could in this way have been carried and greater comfort and elbow-room obtained for the workers, but it was decided to retain them for the reason that great military importance attached to the fact that these units should be really mobile, not only in name but in fact. That they should be so was perhaps rather forgotten by their critics who saw the war drag on with a movement of the lines, forwards and backwards, of only a few miles in the year. Those responsible, however, could not afford to take the risk of partially diminishing their mobility, knowing that trench warfare might at any time change into a war of movement, and in 1918 the army in France experienced such changes, having to deal with rapid movements both of retreat and of advance.

It was during these periods that the advantages of compactness and independent mobility must have become manifest even to those who were sceptical before. For example, in the German offensive before Amiens in the spring of 1918 every mobile bacteriological laboratory attached to the armies involved got away in a few hours without the loss of a test tube, and indeed in some cases were able to salve portions of the equipment of casualty clearing stations which had been abandoned to the enemy with all their costly outfit. In such an emergency it would have been chimerical to have expected empty wagons to have been placed at the disposal of the unit, even if time had been available to pack up the equipment. Not only did they get away promptly when the orders came, but in a very few hours after reaching the place to which they had been directed they were open again and doing useful and important work.

Again, on the final advance, the mobile laboratories were able to keep well in touch with the advanced medical units, and give all the help in the treatment of the wounded and the diagnosis of infectious disease which they had been accustomed to furnish during the period of trench warfare.

Although completely equipped for making their own culture media, etc., the laboratories were not intended to carry more material than would suffice for some weeks' work when thrown entirely on their own resources, and reserves of all they could require were maintained in the depots of medical stores. The bulk of these materials was kept in one of the large base depots which served as a feeder to the advanced depots, and on the latter the laboratories indented for the necessary renewals of their expendable material, the replacement of worn or broken equipment and for any special apparatus or reagent which they might require and which was not included in the regular equipment. This system worked well, and although at times certain reagents or stains might be difficult to obtain, the War Office spared no effort to supply the laboratories with everything they could reasonably need. Any matters of doubt in this connection were referred to the Adviser in Pathology.

In the official "War Establishments" which appeared in the course of the campaign it was laid down that two officers should be attached to each mobile laboratory, but in view of the shortage of medical officers this rarely took effect, and the great majority were worked single-handed. Here and there it was possible, at times of stress, to attach a second bacteriologist to a laboratory as a temporary measure, but only in three instances in France were there exceptions to this rule—Nos. 1, 3 and 5 Mobile Laboratories had usually two, in view of the importance and the amount of the bacteriological work in the areas to which they were posted. Had it been possible the full establishment would more often have been provided, not only to lessen the strain of the very responsible work falling to the bacteriologist, but for the reason that the laboratories which had the good fortune to have more than one bacteriologist were able at times to supplement their routine work by researches which proved of immense value to the army and added very considerably to scientific knowledge. While every bacteriologist endeavoured to further the many important enquiries to which the war gave rise, either as part of a general plan or on his own initiative, this was naturally more fruitful where two or more men could work together.

During the war twenty-five mobile bacteriological laboratories were supplied to armies overseas, as follows :—

France	18
Salonika	3*
Egypt	3
East Africa .. .. `..`	1*

* These were " pack " laboratories.   The remainder were motor laboratories.

Naturally, the employment of motor laboratories presupposes a country provided with roads, for where roads cease the motor laboratory stops. In such cases provision was made for the bacteriological service of the force by having a modified equipment packed in cases of size and weight suitable for pack transport on mules or for carriage by native porters. The three units sent to Salonika and the unit sent to East Africa were of this nature.

Still smaller units, usually to meet some special situation, were organized under local arrangements, being equipped either from the bacteriological laboratory of a general hospital or from the depots of medical stores. For instance, in Palestine a number of small malaria diagnosis units were organized by Captain Manson-Bahr, and did excellent practical service, while in Mesopotamia the needs of the large force scattered over a great area with difficult communications were met by the provision of a well-planned scheme of field laboratories varying in size from small units capable only of doing clinical diagnosis work to the large central laboratory at Baghdad which could undertake work of any kind.

The practical difficulties of carrying out laboratory work in the field were encountered in their most acute form in the Gallipoli operations, where many causes combined to hamper the work of the bacteriologists, not the least being the frequent loss of urgently needed equipment through the sinking of transports, and in East Africa, where the transport difficulties were immense, everything having to be carried by porters through the jungle.   In both instances the limitations imposed upon the amount of bacteriological help in diagnosis are reflected in the returns for infectious diseases from these areas.

Hospital Laboratories.—The armies were well provided with hospital laboratories from the first.   A well-equipped bacteriological laboratory was an integral part of every general hospital of 520 beds, and the details of this equipment, which was held in mobilization stores, had been subject to frequent revision by the War Office in consultation with the staff of the Royal Army Medical College, so that it contained all that was needful for the employment of most modern bacteriological methods. One bacteriologist was authorized in the establishment of the hospital and very rarely was more than one available even when such general hospitals expanded, as they subsequently did, to 1,040 and more beds, when the authorized establishment was increased to two.

The smaller hospital units known as stationary hospitals had no bacteriological staff or equipment allotted to them' but some of these units became so large and dealt with cases of disease or wounds of such a nature that they too had eventually to be equipped with laboratories.   Fortunately the elasticity of the system, or, to put it otherwise, the fortunate absence of rigidity, made it easy to deal with such cases in accordance with the needs of the situation, and equipment on practically the same scale as a general hospital was promptly supplied when the necessity was realized and sanction had been obtained.

The number of general hospitals supplied by the War Office with medical stores and despatched overseas to the various forces was 122, but this does not complete the tale as there was in addition a number of both general and stationary hospitals equipped and staffed by the Australian, Canadian, South African and New Zealand Governments, Indian hospitals furnished by the Indian Government and sent wherever Indian troops were serving, and finally a few voluntary hospital units provided by such bodies as the British Red Cross and St. John Ambulance Association, or through the munificence of individuals or corporate bodies.   Many of them brought with them well-equipped laboratories and trained pathologists.

As an illustration of the size to which the laboratory problem had grown the following figures may be quoted, referring to the situation at the end of 1917 in the British Armies in France :—

	Hospital Units.	Pathologists.
General hospitals	35*	38
Stationary hospitals ..	21	19
Canadian general hospitals ..	4	5
Canadian stationary hospitals	6	4
Australian general hospitals	3	2
New Zealand general hospitals	1	—
South African general hospitals	1	1
Native labour contingent hospitals	5	1
Indian general hospital	1	—
Voluntary hospitals ..	8	5
	85	75

* Six of these were staffed by American medical officers.

At that time there were also in France fifteen mobile bacteriological laboratories employing seventeen officers and these, with the Adviser in Pathology and his assistant and three officers employed in the Boulogne Research Laboratory under Colonel Sir Almroth Wright, gave a total at that date of ninety-seven pathologists.

It has not been possible to obtain figures of similar detail in the case of the other expeditionary forces.

As an illustration of the extent to which the army was indebted, to the civil profession, to the Colonies and to the United States Army for the pathological service, it may be added that, at the time the above figures were recorded, only four out of the total of ninety-seven were regular officers of the R.A.M.C.

In the case of some of the medical units included in the above list the special nature of their work called for a certain amount of modification, both in the equipment provided and in the scale of personnel which it was endeavoured to maintain. These were the units which acted as infectious disease hospitals, such as Nos. 14 and 25 Stationary Hospitals and also the large venereal disease hospital—No. 39 General—at Havre. In these cases the volume of diagnostic work was always heavy and at times almost overwhelming, but the laboratory staff of these important units never allowed it to get beyond their control and even contrived to add largely to the new knowledge which was one of the medical fruits of the war.

In view of the number of medical officers engaged in laboratory work and of the difficulty with which the general medical needs of the armies could be met in the closing stages of the war, it was frequently discussed whether economies of personnel might not be effected by instituting a system of central laboratories in the large hospital bases in France. After careful consideration, however, it was decided to maintain the unit system as long as this could be done, chiefly on the grounds that it was felt that the work was certain to lose much of its value once the pathologist was practically divorced from personal touch with the patient and with the medical officer in charge of the case. Such, it was realized, would have been an inevitable result of the suggested change. Further, weight was properly attached to the fact that at times of pressure or emergency the professional services of the hospital pathologists were always at the disposal of the officer commanding the hospital and at such times they gave much needed assistance in performing orderly duty, dressing wounds, administering anæsthetics and so on, until the relaxation of the tension permitted the resumption of their ordinary occupations.

Research Laboratories.—No provision had been contemplated in the war establishments for the installation of central laboratories, to be devoted to research problems and freed from the burden of the routine duties falling on the pathologists attached to hospitals or mobile laboratories. In this, as in so many other directions, a lesson was learnt, and there is reason to hope that such laboratories will be provided in future establishments. It was always hoped, and indeed confidently anticipated, that the pathologists engaged in the various authorized bacteriological units would have opportunities from time to time to engage in enquiries connected with the needs of the sick and wounded and this proved to be the case. Some of the most valuable of the scientific advances in medical knowledge came from the individual labours of men working in mobile or hospital laboratories. However, the new medical and surgical problems which the progress of the war brought to notice demanded fundamental researches beyond the powers of individuals, whose first duty lay in meeting the daily needs of the physicians and surgeons of the area their laboratory served. The situation was met in several ways, and although it would no doubt have simplified matters considerably if the War Office had adopted the principle of establishing central or research laboratories, at a suitable site, in connection with each field force of sufficient importance, still, much research work was undertaken and yielded good results.

In France the British forces had the advantage from an early date of the personal help of Colonel Sir Almroth Wright, who joined it, technically, as one of the first of the consultant physicians sent out by the War Office. Starting from very small beginnings in the buildings at Boulogne occupied by No. 13 General Hospital, he established by degrees what was essentially a research laboratory, devoted in the main to the study of the pathology and treatment of wounds. He was assisted for varying periods by a number of his former colleagues and assistants from his institute in St. Mary's Hospital, and from this centre emanated a large part of the new contributions to pathological knowledge on such subjects as wound pathology and bacteriology, and on the causation, prevention and treatment of gas gangrene.

Research work on other subjects was usually organized by the formation of an *ad hoc* committee of enquiry, who enlisted the services of pathologists specially qualified in the particular lines of research required and who held meetings from time to time to draw up programmes of research and make the necessary arrangements for their effective conduct. Instances of these were the enquiries carried out in France in connection with pyrexia of uncertain origin and trench fever, war nephritis, surgical shock and influenza. In some of these, most valuable collaboration was furnished by colleagues of the American Army Medical Services, while the inter-allied meetings of experts in hygiene, pathology and surgery which took place frequently in Paris were also most helpful and stimulating.

Much work of fundamental importance was also carried out at home in connection either with war hospitals or in the pathological laboratories of the universities and medical schools. Every effort was made by medical officers to avail themselves of the new knowledge and experience thus gained, while they did not hesitate to apply to the laboratories for help in the investigation of problems which it was beyond their own capacity to solve under war conditions.

The Medical Research Committee.

On the outbreak of war this young organization, now the Medical Research Council, at that time a part of the machinery of the National Health Insurance scheme, found the majority of its plans for research either gravely hampered or altogether interrupted. With the approval of the authorities it decided to devote a large part of its energies and, if necessary, of the funds at its disposal to the purpose of the medical needs created by the military situation in what was clearly a national emergency. It promptly offered to the War Office its large research institute at Hampstead which it was on the point of equipping and opening, and this was used as a military hospital throughout the war ; it also offered the services of such of its research staff as remained available for the carrying out of any enquiries which might be referred to it by the War Office.

The liaison between the British Expeditionary Force and the Medical Research Committee was always very intimate, since the Adviser in Pathology to the forces in France was himself a member of the Committee, and this liaison was still further strengthened at a later date by the appointment of Lieut.-Colonel T. R. Elliott as the executive representative of the Medical Research Committee in France. Colonel Elliott, who later became consultant physician for the Boulogne Base, was instrumental in carrying through on behalf of the Committee a number of measures which proved of great value, not only to the cause of pathology, but also to the general medical and surgical necessities of the force. For example, the organization of a system by which it became possible for those who had treated cases in their early stages to ascertain particulars of the ultimate results was successfully carried into effect and filled a blank which could not apparently be provided for by any modifications in the existing official statistical machinery. In no branch was the assistance of the Medical Research Committee of greater volume and importance than in pathology, and without the whole-hearted support which the Committee was in a position to give, and did give, the record of pathology for the war might have been a very modest one and far from worthy of the high position held by British pathology. Full details of the assistance thus given to the War Office are recorded in the Annual Reports of the Medical Research Council for the years 1914-1920, but the debt which pathology owes to the Medical Research Council and to its Secretary, Sir Walter Fletcher, cannot be measured or forgotten.

Among the lines on which the Medical Research Committee gave their services the following may be specially mentioned :—

Training of Protozoologists.—In connection with the diagnosis of amœbic dysentery, a disease which gave rise to a good deal of anxiety in the Eastern theatres of war, a demand arose for expert protozoologists, qualified to undertake the necessary microscopical examinations. The Committee arranged with the War Office for the recruitment of a number of protozoologists, and placed the services of Professor C. Dobell, the head of their department of protozoology, at the disposal of the War Office for the purposes of the necessary special training in this branch of science. After a practical course of instruction under Professor Dobell the protozoologists were posted to the forces in question, and both there and at the special dysentery centres at home their services were of the greatest value to the army.

Publication of Special Reports.—Few measures were so immediately and directly valuable as the diffusion of the newly acquired experience gained in the progress of the campaign and of the results of special researches. The Medical Research Committee undertook this work on a large scale and arranged for the publication and wide circulation of such of these special reports as were not of a confidential nature. Those of them bearing on matters of pathological or bacteriological interest were highly appreciated by the army pathologists, more particularly as many of the reports were too detailed and too lengthy to be admitted to the columns of the more accessible medical journals.

In addition to the above, they undertook the compilation and editing of an extremely valuable Medical Supplement to the Monthly Summary of news from the Foreign Press, published by the War Office. In this, by enlisting the assistance of technical experts, they published *précis* of all items of medical news appearing in the allied, neutral and enemy Presses, including items of pathological interest, and sent monthly to each expeditionary force sufficient copies to allow of their distribution to every medical unit. The value of this could hardly be over-estimated in view of the natural difficulties for men serving in the field to obtain access to current medical literature.

Supply of Standard Agglutinable Cultures.—As soon as the importance of these was recognized for the accurate diagnosis of the enteric fevers, and in lesser degree of bacillary dysentery, the Medical Research Committee provided substantial assistance towards the organization and upkeep of what has now become known as the Standards Laboratory at Oxford University. Here, under the guidance of Professor G. Dreyer, Major Ainley Walker and Captain Gardner, the preparation and standardization of these cultures on a large scale were commenced and an organization built up for their direct supply to all pathological units indenting for them directly or through the usual official channels. The importance of this service may be gathered by a reference to Chapter IX of this volume, where it will be seen how large a part the Dreyer agglutination method played in the diagnosis of enteric fevers.

Preservation and Collection of Museum Specimens.—Invaluable assistance was given by the Medical Research Committee to the organization of the measures necessary to ensure that the extremely important specimens collected by surgeons and pathologists, illustrative of the effects of wounds and of disease, should be treated in such a way as to preserve their value in a permanent form and should be sent home as rapidly as possible for final mounting and disposal. By collaboration between the War Office, the Medical Research Committee, and the army pathological organization this difficult matter was eventually placed on a thoroughly satisfactory footing, and a happy solution of the problem of what to do with them on arrival in England was obtained through the generosity of the Royal College of Surgeons, who agreed to their being received at their museum and sanctioned the services of Sir Arthur Keith, Professor Shattock and Mr. C. F. Beadles in the supervision of their final mounting and classification. The magnificent collection now on view in the Museum of the Royal College of Surgeons is a tribute to the thoroughness of this organization and constitutes a valuable and permanent record of the effects of the various weapons and lethal agents used in the war.

Finally, mention should be made of the fact that the Committee promptly recognized how greatly the value of many professional reports and papers would be enhanced by skilled illustration, and they enlisted for this purpose the services of Mr. A. K. Maxwell, who proceeded to France and gave his assistance wherever it was required. The beautiful figures in natural colours and in black and white which illustrate so many of the articles which appeared during and after the war in current medical literature testify to the general manner in which advantage was taken of this exceptional opportunity.

Nature of Work performed by Pathological Laboratories.

Any attempt at a full account of the work done in these numerous laboratories, scattered literally over the world, would be out of place. A brief account, however, of the general nature of the work which fell to the mobile and hospital laboratories may be of interest.

The Mobile Laboratories.—By far the larger portion of the routine in the mobile laboratories was in connection with the constant warfare against the infectious diseases whose bacterial cause is known. The examination of material from suspected cases of enteric fever, dysentery, diphtheria, cerebro-spinal meningitis and influenza was usually a daily task, and often a very heavy one. In the case of diphtheria and cerebro-spinal meningitis, the occurrence of a case involved in addition the examination of material from a number of contacts, although it may be said that the labour expended in this direction often appeared of doubtful value. It was almost invariably the opinion of the officer in charge of a mobile laboratory that if satisfactory results were to be obtained from these examinations it was essential that he should himself visit the case and take the specimens. Material collected by others was all too often taken or packed in such a manner as to make its useful examination futile. Although this naturally curtailed very considerably the time available for actual work in the laboratory this was never grudged, for it was the constant practice, at least in France, to encourage in every possible manner the closest relationship between bacteriologist, patient and the physician or surgeon. To this end approval was given to the representations made that to every mobile laboratory should be allotted a small motor-car to take the pathologist between the medical units and his laboratory. In France this was absolutely essential, as the area served by each laboratory was very large and the ground could not have been covered in any other way. Motor bicycles with side-car attachments were tried at first but proved inadequate.

A large amount of what may be termed minor bacteriology and clinical pathology had also to be performed, such as the examination of sputum and urine and the making of blood-counts. Efforts were made to relieve the laboratories of some of this work, which was well within the competence of many of the officers on the medical divisions of casualty clearing stations, but with little effect.

Autopsies and the collection and disposal of suitable museum specimens also formed part of the duties of the officer in charge of a mobile laboratory, as well as the frequent preparation of autogenous vaccines and advice as to their administration.

The amount of work in connection with wound pathology varied with the degree of activity in the sector but was sometimes very heavy, including the investigation of blood, pus, joint fluids and fluids from serous cavities for the presence of septic organisms. This was a particularly responsible and delicate kind of work, for upon the results often depended the surgeon's decision as to operation.

With the writing up of records, the telegraphing and reporting of the results of his examinations to the units concerned, the furnishing of reports called for from division, corps, army or general headquarters, it will be seen that the average day of the officer in charge of a mobile laboratory was a strenuous one. It was, however, full of interest and variety, and there was never any difficulty in obtaining excellent men to fill these charges.

When an action was in progress, the bacteriologist, acting under instructions, offered his help to the staff of the casualty clearing stations to which he was attached.

The Hospital Laboratories.—The work here was in many respects similar to that performed in the mobile units, but differed chiefly in there being less of the work connected with the detection of infectious diseases and the examination of contacts and more of the work in connection with wounds. As severe cases were detained longer in the general and stationary hospitals than in casualty clearing stations, it was possible for the bacteriologist to see more of them and to follow their progress more closely. The surgeon and the pathologist here worked in more intimate touch than was usually possible in the forward areas, and this association was particularly valuable in the later stages of the war, when qualitative and quantitative bacterial studies of a particular wound were of importance in relation to questions of secondary suture. Examinations of the cellular and bacterial content of pleuritic and synovial fluids were also more frequent in general hospitals, and the results had an important bearing on the surgical treatment. Opportunities were also more favourable here for carrying out systematic bacteriological control in connection with new methods of dressing or in the testing of alternative antiseptic applications, and much valuable work is on record in this connection.

An additional duty which at times fell upon the pathologist of general hospitals was the training of new laboratory attendants. The supply of trained men, even from civil sources, soon failed to equal the demand, and it was necessary for the armies to train selected recruits, as they had done in peace, and many keen and competent men were turned out in this way, acquitting themselves well in the official examination and doing good work in the laboratories to which they were subsequently posted.

Of especial value was the work of Lieut.-Colonel C. J. Martin, A.A.M.C. at Rouen Base. This officer, after a period of service in Egypt and Palestine, became the officer in charge of the laboratory of No. 25 Stationary Hospital at Rouen, as well as consultant bacteriologist to the Australian Expeditionary Force and an assistant adviser in pathology. His laboratory became a centre to which all the pathologists in the numerous hospitals in and around Rouen turned for advice and assistance, and from which emanated many valuable observations on bacillary dysentery, influenza and other diseases.

At Etaples, a central mortuary was established under the supervision of Captain T. H. G. Shore, R.A.M.C., whose careful pathological work was of great benefit to the medical officers of the hospitals in the vicinity.

Organization of Pathological Work in Home Commands during the War.

As will have been gathered from the account of the peace organization of this subject, the few pathologists employed in the commands were dispersed upon mobilization, in consequence of the urgent need for every available trained officer and man. Such reinforcements as were available from officers and men recalled to the colours were inadequate even to fill the posts in the expeditionary force. Special arrangements had therefore to be made to meet the growing needs of the home garrison and of the large mass of men under training. Further, it was not many weeks before the never-ceasing stream of sick and wounded began to pour into the home hospitals, a stream whose volume and rate of flow increased steadily as the armies overseas grew in numbers and in military activity.

The bacteriological service was associated with the organization of the territorial force general hospitals, each of which had eventually a bacteriologist on its establishment, and had a small laboratory equipment allotted to it. In the majority of instances, however, such general hospitals were formed either in or in close connection with existing civil hospitals, or with the medical schools of the universities. These had already well-equipped laboratories and a highly trained staff, and in the majority of instances the services of these existing

institutions were utilized, the pathological staff either acting
in an honorary capacity or being given commissions in the
Territorial Force or temporary commissions in the R.A.M.C.
From many points of view this was an admirable arrangement,
and some of the most valuable pathological work done during·
the war came from the staff of these general hospitals. As
the voluntary and other hospitals increased in numbers and
in size, the smaller units came to be grouped around a larger
one for administrative reasons, and as this larger unit, usually
a general hospital, was most frequently utilizing one of these
pre-existing laboratories, these were further employed in most
commands to serve the bacteriological needs of the smaller
affiliated units. This system had the merit of economizing
both laboratories and pathologists, and as the number of sick
and wounded in home hospitals increased, this became a
compulsory economy, for the simple reason that the supply
of qualified and available men was exhausted. Fortunately,
in many instances, the services were secured of women bacteriologists, who rendered admirable and devoted work to the
army. At the same time, had it been possible to do so, a
greater amount of decentralization of the pathological work
would, in certain directions, have been advantageous. Every
pathologist will admit that he can be of more help to the
surgeon or physician if he can himself see the patient, or at
least can discuss his case with the officer who is treating him.
The alternative of merely carrying out some routine tests on
material known by a number, and collected under unknown
and possibly unsuitable conditions, is frequently a most
unsatisfactory procedure for all concerned.

General questions relating to the organization of these
hospital laboratories were dealt with by the various branches
of the Director-General's department at the War Office, while
advice and guidance on technical matters were obtained
partly from the Army Sanitary Committee, which continued
to sit during the war, and partly from Lieut.-Colonel D. Harvey,
the officer in charge of the Army Vaccine Department at the
Royal Army Medical College.

Later in the war the Director-General appointed a Pathological Committee, under the chairmanship of Surg.-General
Sir David Bruce, which acted in an advisory capacity and
suggested problems for research.

The need for further co-ordination of the pathological work
at home also led to the appointment in 1917 of Colonel Sims
Woodhead as Inspector of Laboratories, who threw himself

with characteristic enthusiasm into the toilsome work of visiting and reporting upon the laboratories scattered throughout the United Kingdom.

Finally, in April 1918, the Adviser in Pathology with the armies in France was recalled to act in a similar capacity at the War Office.

Organization for Special Investigations.

As the war progressed certain problems involving special pathological organization presented themselves in connection with the prevalence, or feared prevalence, of various medical or surgical affections. In these cases the organization of the appropriate means of control was, under the general control of the Director-General, entrusted either to some expert pathologist, specially qualified in the particular subject, or to a group of pathologists associated in an *ad hoc* committee. A short account of the more important of these organizations may be given, but for details reference should be made to the chapters dealing with the subjects in question, either in this volume or in those devoted to the diseases and surgery of the war.

Tetanus.—The unexpected prevalence of tetanus as a complication of wounds, especially in the earlier months of the war, gave rise to considerable anxiety and it was soon realized that some special organization was required to ensure not only that the condition should be recognized at the earliest moment but that the most recent expert information as to the best means of prevention and of treatment should be available for all medical officers in charge of the wounded. Such an organization was effectively established through the advice and direction of a War Office Tetanus Committee, under the chairmanship of Surg.-General Sir David Bruce. In addition to suggesting and co-ordinating important experimental investigations in some of the large laboratories, the Committee drew up from time to time pamphlets of instructions dealing with the prevention, recognition and treatment of the disease, which incorporated the most recent knowledge on all these points. These pamphlets were circulated widely by the War Office and were of the greatest possible assistance to medical officers, the majority of whom, naturally, had little or no personal experience of the disease. In addition, they secured the appointment in various important centres of especially experienced pathologists as tetanus officers to the area. The necessary orders were issued that, on the appearance of any suspicious symptoms in a wounded man, telegraphic information should immediately be sent to this tetanus officer, who promptly visited the case and advised the officer in charge on its treatment.

The Committee also drafted a " tetanus case-sheet " which had to be completed for every case, and undertook the analysis of these sheets when rendered at its termination. Thanks to the carefully thought out " questionnaire " on these case-sheets, a most valuable record was obtained of the current experience on such points as the early symptomatology of the condition, the dosage and the frequency of administration of prophylactic antitoxin, the best mode of administration and the results of its therapeutic application. As a result of the Committee's analysis of these returns, and of others collected in the armies in the field, the instructional pamphlets were revised and re-published on several occasions, and the medical service of the army was thus kept up to date on the latest advances in knowledge of the management of tetanus in a way which would hardly have been possible under any other system.

Enteric Fevers.—The natural fear of possible epidemics of enteric fever arising either among the great mass of troops under training, or among the civil population, emphasized the necessity for very special precautions. These were elaborated by the War Office in accordance with the advice of their own experts on this subject and were issued in the form of Army Council Instructions, which defined the procedure to be adopted in dealing with the different branches of the subject. These Army Council Instructions dealt, for example, with the administration of prophylactic vaccines, defining the periods at which inoculations and re-inoculations should be carried out in soldiers who volunteered for them, the system of recording the inoculations, and the precautions to be observed in carrying them out. Others were concerned with the administrative measures necessary to secure the segregation of the sick, and eventually, their aggregation, when fit to travel, in certain enteric convalescent depots. Others again, of a more technical nature, defined the minimum bacteriological standards to be observed in the laboratory tests required both for accuracy of differential diagnosis and for the detection and the determination of the disappearance of the carrier condition. The greatest importance was rightly attached to the latter and no efforts were spared to obviate the potential dangers consequent on the discharge of an undetected or an uncured carrier to civil life or back to the fighting line. In this the War Office worked hand in hand with the Ministry of Health, who were always notified of the discharge of any soldiers from the army as " chronic carriers " in order that the local medical officer of health might be informed and the needful precautions taken to prevent the spread of infection among the man's family or his neighbours. Instances did occur where small outbreaks were traced to such cases but they were gratifyingly rare and it is probable that this was to some extent consequent upon the careful individual instruction given to every invalided carrier as to the nature of his condition and the personal precautions which it was essential for him to practise.

Dysentery.—Very similar problems presented themselves in connection with dysentery, of which, at some periods, large numbers of convalescents and chronic cases were admitted from overseas to home hospitals. Both amœbic and bacillary forms had to be dealt with and in certain directions called for differential measures. Here, too, the organization of these measures was undertaken by the War Office, fortified by expert advice, and followed administrative lines similar to those instituted in the case of the enteric fevers. This was particularly the case with bacillary dysentery, where similar principles of segregation and collection into dysentery hospitals, and eventually into a dysentery convalescent depot at Barton-on-Sea, were put into force, while Army Council Instructions dealing with the detection and disposal of bacillary carriers were drawn up and issued. In this instance also the discharge of convalescents or of chronic carriers to furlough or to civil life was notified to the local medical officer of health through the Ministry of Health.

The case of amœbic infection, however, presented special features and, in a sense, special difficulties, chiefly in connection with the long period required for effective treatment and the disposal of cases which continued to pass cysts of *Entamœba histolytica*. The experience of the war brought to light new and interesting facts, especially in relation to this form of dysentery, some of which added considerably to the administrative difficulties in dealing with the cases. Rules which, in the earlier part of the war, were framed upon existing knowledge, required, at a later stage, revision in important details. To advise upon these a War Office Dysentery Committee was formed in the summer of 1918, under the chairmanship of Colonel Sir William Leishman, and included experts in both bacteriology and protozoology. The conclusions of this Committee appeared in the form of memoranda on bacillary and amœbic dysentery respectively, and were the basis for the revised Army Council Instructions on the management and disposal of these cases. The armistice lessened the urgency of the need for these new measures, but did not lessen the great value of the information on which they were framed.

The assistance given by the Medical Research Council in the training of protozoologists under Professor Dobell has already been mentioned and was helpful in providing expert laboratory skill in the areas at home and abroad where it was most required.

Cerebro-spinal Meningitis.—The epidemic spread of this disease in parts of the British Isles in 1915-16 caused considerable concern and it soon became clear that this situation also demanded a specially organized laboratory service, in supplement of the existing hospital service. This was called for by reason of the technical nature of the diagnostic tests required, the need for special culture media and for specially prepared diagnostic sera. The War Office, with the advice of the Army Sanitary Committee, approved of the establishment of a central cerebro-spinal fever laboratory at the Royal Army Medical College—later accommodated in the laboratories of Westminster Hospital—where Lieut.-Colonel Mervyn Gordon undertook not only the direction of the required research work and the preparation and distribution of media and agglutinating sera but, in addition, gave short courses of instruction to groups of hospital pathologists in the most recent methods of cultivating and " typing " the various strains of meningococci. These officers, on returning to their hospital or district laboratories, acted as specialists in dealing with cases and contacts of the disease. The country was divided for the purpose into administrative areas, and if suitable laboratories did not already exist in them such were provided.

This laboratory organization has been described in detail by Colonel R. J. Reece in Volume II. of the Hygiene of the War, and the more strictly pathological side in the present volume by Colonel Gordon.

Trench Fever.—What was required in connection with this newly described disease was not so much any special organization of or within the pathological service as new knowledge of its nature and of the mode of its causation. A very important part of the required knowledge was obtained through the series of researches instituted and carried out at home by a War Office Committee on Trench Fever, of which Surg.-General Sir David Bruce was chairman. The story of the remarkable researches into the nature and ætiology of this newly observed disease has been told in the volumes on the Diseases and Hygiene of the War, but it may be added that the independent nature of the enquiries conducted in France by the American Commission, working at the British Hospital at St. Pol, and those organized by the War Office Committee combined to ensure a rapid solution of the important question of the mode of spread of the disease by the body-louse.

Material for Pathological Work.

Towards the end of the war the work in all pathological laboratories was hampered by the increasing difficulty of obtaining the commoner experimental animals, which were often unprocurable even at greatly enhanced prices, the ordinary breeders of rabbits and guinea-pigs having mostly disappeared or gone out of business. Difficulties were also encountered in rearing them in small laboratories in numbers sufficient for the routine needs. This became eventually so serious a matter that arrangements were made for the establishment of a small number of local breeding centres to serve the needs of all the laboratories in a given district. This proved economical and satisfactory.

Another scheme of centralized production was the subject of discussion and negotiation at the time of the armistice, namely, the central preparation of culture media. For this purpose it was proposed to take over a portion of a certain factory and to establish in it, under the charge of a competent bacteriologist, the equipment necessary for the mass production of the more usual culture media, with a view to their distribution on demand to the various laboratories scattered over the country. Peace put an end to the negotiations, so there is no experience to record as to how such a scheme would have worked. It appears a little doubtful whether it would have effected the desired economies and whether it might not have interfered to some extent with the effective working of the laboratories.

The branch of the Director-General's establishment concerned with the supply of material had heavy calls made upon it to meet the requirements of the laboratories in all parts of the world in the matter of equipment, apparatus, reagents, and so on. It is common knowledge how dependent this country had become on the enemy countries for much essential material of this kind, and how difficult it was at first during the war to obtain satisfactory substitutes.   No efforts were spared by the officers in charge of this branch to meet all these requirements as fully and as promptly as possible, and had it not been so, the work of every laboratory abroad, and many at home, would have been gravely hampered.

The laboratories of the Royal Army Medical College remained open throughout the war, and one of its busiest sides was the Army Vaccine Department, which had to expand greatly to cope with the huge demands for protective vaccines.   This department, which was throughout in charge of Lieut.-Colonel D. Harvey, was responsible for the preparation and issue of the following quantities of vaccines for the use of the troops.   The figures will give some idea of the unremitting labour and the heavy responsibility which fell to the officer in charge and to his colleagues.

Quantities of the principal prophylactic vaccines issued from the Vaccine Department of the Royal Army Medical College, 4th August 1914—31st July 1919.

Vaccine.	C.cm.
Typhoid (T.V. & T.A.B.)	25,068,271
Cholera	8,507,749
Influenza	1,806,325
Plague	390,910
Dysentery (Gibson's Sero-Vaccine)	99,225

Although large reserves of typhoid vaccine were available on the outbreak of the war it would not have been possible to meet all the demands which crowded on one another in the first two or three months had it not been for the generous assistance of the Lister Institute and of the Inoculation Department of St. Mary's Hospital.   Each of these laboratories prepared large quantities of " T.V." for the College, employing the same strains and the same technique, and thus enabled it to meet all requirements until its own machinery had been multiplied to a sufficient extent.

The College was also responsible for the issue of all sera, and this became a formidable part of its daily work.   These sera, principally tetanus and diphtheria antitoxins and dysentery serum, were almost entirely purchased under contract from various sources, but the College had to deal with innumerable questions in connection with their standardization and employment.

In other spheres of its activity—and they were many—the Royal Army Medical College was greatly helped, and on many occasions, by sister institutions in London and elsewhere, which spared neither time nor trouble if they could aid the common cause through their knowledge or with the resources at their disposal.

CHAPTER II.

THE PHYSIOLOGY OF WOUNDS.

IN any complete dissertation on the physiology of wounds the physiology and histology of trauma and wound repair, the physiology and chemistry of shock, and above all the reaction of the wound to bacterial infections and to the therapeutic methods employed in combating those infections, would have to be considered.

This chapter deals almost exclusively with the last of these subjects, but it may none the less be useful to note what points under the first two headings would properly come up for consideration.

Under the heading of the *physiology and histology of trauma and wound repair*, the histological responses to trauma, the production of granulation tissue and callus, the formation of new bone and connective tissue, and, finally, the growth of new epithelium and the healing over of the wound should come under consideration. And there should also come under discussion not only the histology of the aseptic but also that of the septic wound. No important contribution to these questions would appear, however, to have been made in the course of the war, and they need not be considered here.

Further, in connection with the physiology of repair there would appropriately come up for consideration the procedures of skin and bone grafting and the suture of the wound. These subjects, involving as they do questions of surgical technique, have already been dealt with in the volumes on the Surgery of the War. Suture of the wound must, however, in view of its bearing on the treatment of bacterial infection, come under consideration here.

Under the heading of the *physiology of shock* there would have to be discussed that instantaneous collapse which follows in quite exceptional cases upon the traumatic ictus; and, again, that delayed form of collapse which almost regularly supervenes when the severely wounded man is exposed to cold; when the circulation in a limb is cut off by a tourniquet; when, instead of being immobilized, a fractured limb is subjected to succussions during transport; and when the patient is placed under an anæsthetic which sends down his blood-pressure. This so-called secondary shock—which killed in the course of the war perhaps as many of the wounded as sepsis, and which kills practically all who die of operations in times of peace and in civil practice—is almost certainly a chemical as distinguished from a nerve shock, the poisons which come into operation here being almost certainly acid metabolic products, elaborated in exæmic muscle.* The general physiology and treatment of shock has already been dealt with in the volumes on the Surgery of the War.

It is therefore not specially considered here, except in so far as it is linked up with the development of gas gangrene. In connexion with this it may be premised that the chemical conditions which are provided by exæmia of muscle exactly satisfy the requirements and consequently favour the development of the gas gangrene bacillus.

That wound sepsis and saprogenous infections—by which are meant septicæmia, tetanus, gas gangrene and such-like—were going to constitute the great medical tragedy of the war was appreciated quite at the beginning by those who carefully pondered the condition of the wounded arriving at the base. The Director-General, Sir Alfred Keogh, in October 1914, concisely summed up the medical situation thus: " We have in this war gone straight back into all the septic infections of the Middle Ages."

It may here be useful to describe succinctly the state of things that prevailed in the hospitals at the base in the early months of the war.

Every wound—one may say every wound, for there was hardly an exception—was very heavily infected, and presented, each according to its type, the features summarized below :—

(1) *Avulsing wounds, i.e.,* wounds produced by the avulsing of great pieces of flesh.—In these the originally naked surface of the wound was coated with black and stinking sloughs, while the trough was occupied by a putrid and almost fæcal-looking discharge in which every kind and variety of microbe was pullulating.

(2) *Perforating and fracturing wounds, i.e.,* wounds in which the projectile had in its passage encountered bone and broken this to pieces.—Of these wounds there were two varieties. In the one the fragmented bone had been blown clean out, leaving an irregularly crateriform wound of exit, at the bottom

---

* Wright and Colebrook, " On the acidosis of shock and suspended circulation" (*Lancet*, 1st June, 1918) ; *also* " Technique of the Teat and Capillary Glass Tube " (Constable, London, 1921), Chap. vii, " Clinical Appendix on Acidosis and Acidæmia."

of which were pockets between the muscles and extensive fissures in the fractured bone. In the other the explosive impact had hollowed out in the interior of the limb a cavity of quite irregular contour with blind passages running in between the muscles, the cavity being cut off, or to all intents and purposes cut off, from the exterior by hernia of muscle, supplemented in some cases by a valvular closing over of the skin. Such valvular closure was the result of the limb being at the moment of wounding in the flexed position, and being afterwards in bed brought into the extended position.

In both varieties of the perforating and fracturing wound the cavity contained fragments of bone, pieces of projectile, portions of clothing, frayed ends of muscle and such-like, all these lying embedded in a corrupted pus in which every conceivable microbe was luxuriantly growing.

(3) *Sutured amputation wounds.*—In these the dead spaces left by the bringing together of the flaps were filled with a putrid discharge in which there was a luxuriant mixed bacterial growth.

(4) Lastly, there were what may be described as *implunging wounds*, *i.e.*, wounds produced by nearly spent pieces of shell or shrapnel. The projectile, together with the clothing it carried in, was here implunged into the soft parts, and these had closed round the foreign body, leaving no encompassing cavity or communication with the exterior.

In all these different types of wound the infection had in practically every instance extended beyond its focus of origin. Streptococcal invasions of the encasing tissues were all but universal, and diffuse cellulitis was specially frequent in unopened implunging wounds, this being no doubt due to the microbes being here implanted directly into connective tissue or muscle instead of, as in other types of wounds, into a cavity extraneous to the tissues.

Not infrequently these streptococcal infections of the tissues had led on to septicæmia.

Tetanus, also, was of frequent occurrence, and it occurred in connexion with all the different types of wounds.

Even more ghastly were the numerous cases of gas gangrene. The form of gas gangrene which in the early days of the war came most conspicuously under observation was that in which the infection spread up the limb in the subcutaneous tissue, manifesting itself first in a rusty or dull purplish mottling, then in œdema with fine gaseous crepitation. This ended in a leaden blue discoloration of the skin; and on this livid background

were large sagging bullæ filled with a black hæmorrhagic
fluid peopled with gas gangrene bacilli. In these bullæ there
was often a production of gas and this floated and moved
about in the fluid after the fashion of a bubble in a spirit level.

The other form of gas gangrene, that in which the infection
is deep-seated and travels up in muscles, had at this time
not yet been recognized. But cases of that form of invasion
often presented themselves—the injured limb becoming hard,
glistening white, and cold as marble, and death always
followed. Frequently the gas gangrene infection had its
focus of origin in heavily infected perforating and fracturing
wounds, or amputation wounds that had been sutured. But
injuries which cut off the arterial supply of the muscles of
the calf of the leg, and bruises which disorganized the capillary
circulation in large areas of muscle, and implunging wounds
which, of course, would produce similar interference with the
circulation, were those that gave most frequent occasion to
gas gangrene infection.

What was intellectually distressing in connexion with all this
septic disaster was that the edifice built up by Lister and his
successors and by the confident dogmata of surgeons seemed
here to lie in ruins. It is indubitable that if before the outbreak
of the war a concensus of surgical opinion had been taken on the
question as to whether grave and universal infection of wounds
was in prospect, it would, in view of the experience gained in
the South African War and in the accident wards of civil
hospitals, have been confidently asserted that such sepsis
was a thing that belonged to the past. It is not, therefore, a
matter for surprise that when septic infection became rampant
the idea occurred that some sinister unknown agency must
with the outbreak of the war have come into operation.

It took time to surmount that illusion; but little by little it
became clear that what was presenting itself in war wounds
was only what regularly presents itself in cases of accident
in the wilds; and of course not only there, but wherever
lacerated wounds are abandoned to themselves. What was
actually occurring was only what was bound to happen in
the medical situation then existing. The military position in
the first months of the war was such that only the most urgent
operative procedures, such as the amputation of shattered limbs,
could be undertaken at the front. Practically all the wounds—
and it must be remembered that war wounds are from their
very nature bound to be grossly infected wounds—had to be
sent down unoperated upon to the base.

That this postponement of operation was the direct cause of the sepsis was established beyond doubt as soon as it became possible to make different medical dispositions. A new era began when, following the example of the French army, the casualty clearing stations, whose appointed function it had been to evacuate the wounded, were fully equipped as surgical hospitals. From that time on, except in times of great pressure, all wounds which required operative treatment were operated upon as soon as the patient was brought in from the field. The wound was laid open and was cleansed and resected. That is to say, the foreign matter was turned out, the devascularized tissues which would have necrosed and formed sloughs were excised, and drainage-tubes were inserted. In fact the wound was, so far as operative procedures can achieve this, placed in a satisfactory physiological condition. After the adoption of these measures putrid wound infections became, relatively speaking, rare and the incidence of saprogenous diseases, such as gangrene and tetanus, was greatly reduced.

Preliminary Research into the Physiology of Wounds.

This general survey may serve as an introduction to an account of the research work on septic infection of wounds undertaken during the war in the Research Laboratory at Boulogne. To arrive at an understanding of the procession of events in infected wounds not only those initial and terminal events which come to the cognizance of the senses and impress themselves on clinical observation, but also all those intermediate events which escape clinical observation, and are therefore commonly ignored, must be brought into the field of view. To obtain information with respect to these intermediate events special laboratory methods have to be devised and exploited.

In setting down what has been learned by these methods with respect to bacterial infections of wounds it will be well to commence with the simplest kind of wound and then go on to septic infections of greater complication.

A certain preliminary physiological foundation must first be laid down. Part of that foundation will consist of facts which are of common knowledge, part of new fundamental facts discovered in the course of the war and not yet familiar.

The facts of common knowledge are first that microbes are destroyed by phagocytosis and intracellular digestion in leucocytes; and secondly, that the blood fluids, although the current conceptions here are very nebulous, possess a certain bactericidal power.

New Data concerning the Blood Fluids.

Of the new facts which are essential for the understanding of the processes of septic infection the most important is that the microbes found in wounds can be distributed into two classes—a class of *serophytes* and a class of *sero-saprophytes*. Serophytes can grow and multiply in the unaltered blood fluids. Sero-saprophytes can support life and multiply only in what may provisionally be called "corrupted" blood fluids.

The evidence on this question is clear and simple. Any mixture of microbes is taken, such, for example, as is obtainable from a putrid septic wound, or from the intestinal contents.

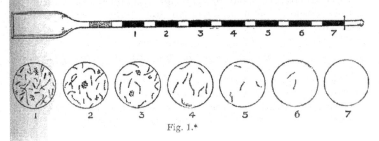

Fig. 1.*

One unit volume of this is then aspirated into the distal portion of a capillary tube; then (making in this way a "wash and after-wash" culture) a series of separate unit volumes of normal serum is drawn into the capillary stem, and the tube is then placed in the incubator. In the first and heaviest implanted volumes of serum there will be obtained a mixed culture of serophytic and non-serophytic microbes; in the intermediate and more lightly implanted volumes, as a rule only a culture of staphylococcus and streptococcus with occasionally a diphtheroid microbe; and in the distal unit volumes, a pure cultivation of streptococcus (Fig. 1). This quite invariable result shows that the staphylococcus and streptococcus grow better than any other microbes in the blood fluids and lymph. Further proof of this is obtained by attaching a small cupping apparatus—"lymph leech"—to the

---

* This and other figures are taken from Wright, "Technique of the Capillary Glass Tube" (Constable, London, 1921).

non-disinfected walls of a putrid septic wound.   There will—
despite the fact that there will here have been implanted all
manner of microbes—then be obtained in the fluid drawn into
the belly of this lymph leech, a culture°consisting entirely of
serophytes, and often a pure cultivation of streptococcus (Fig. 2).

Leaving out of regard for the moment what further can
be learned from this experiment, attention may be focussed
on two great general principles: *first*, on the principle that
serophytic microbes, and only serophytic microbes, will be
capable of growing in the clean and wholesome wound; *secondly*,
on the principle that of all the organisms found in the putrid
wound only the serophytic organisms, and in particular the

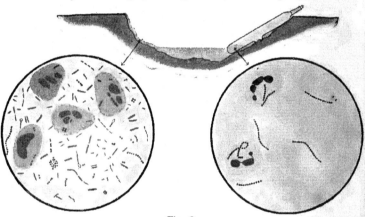

Fig. 2.

streptococcus, will be capable of invading the blood-stream.
That none of the saprophytic organisms can invade the blood-
stream, will, of course, hold good only so long as the blood
fluids remain " uncorrupted."

For the explanation of these facts that only serophytes can
grow in the wholesome wound and that only these can invade
the blood-stream, one must look primarily to the antitryptic
power of the blood fluids.   It has long been known, but it has
not been appreciated, in connexion with resistance to bacterial
infection, that the blood fluids have the power of neutralizing
digestive ferments; that, put more briefly, they have an
antitryptic power.

In the course of the researches summarized in this chapter
it suggested itself with respect to this antitryptic power that

it must constitute an important element of anti-bacterial defence, for reflection showed that microbes in the blood would, for their nutriment, be bound to depend on such digestive action as they might be able to exert upon the food-elements around them ; and that with that power abolished they must starve, just as starvation would follow if a man were deprived of his digestive enzymes. The obvious way of putting the inference that the antitryptic power of the blood inhibited microbic growth to the proof was to make graduated additions of trypsin (using inactivated trypsin in the control experiments) to the serum. When the experiment in question is made it comes out quite clearly that additions of trypsin favour the growth of streptococcus in the serum. For example, with complete neutralization of the antitryptic power of the serum, a 6,000-fold increased growth of streptococcus* has been obtained. Further, it comes out clearly that *pari passu* with the blunting off of the antitryptic power the serum becomes an eminently favourable medium for all the different varieties of sero-saprophytic organisms. To this must be added that the bactericidal and opsonic power of the serum is, as increasing doses of trypsin are introduced into the serum, first reduced and then completely abolished.

The application of these facts to the physiology of the wound appears when they are related to the facts that leucocytes furnish a tryptic ferment, and that leucocytes which have ingested microbes furnish this in more abundance, and that this ferment is discharged when the leucocytes disintegrate or are artificially broken down. The view that antitryptic power is an important element in the mechanism of defence wins support also from the fact that when the antitryptic power of the blood is increased, as it regularly is in the wounded,† the growth of serophytic organisms in the serum is correspondingly restricted.

Further experiments showed how it is that serophytes manage, in spite of the antitryptic power of the serum, to grow out in it into colonies. When staphylococci or streptococci

---

* In the case of staphylococcus implantations no increased growth is achieved by adding trypsin to the serum. This, no doubt, stands in relation with the fact that the staphylococcus secretes a very potent tryptic ferment.

† In the case of the severely wounded the antitryptic power may be as much as fourfold the normal, this increase being already well marked within twenty-four hours after wounding. A similar increase of anti-tryptic power comes under observation also after inoculations of bacterial vaccines. (Wright, "Conditions which Govern the Growth of the Gas Gangrene Bacillus in the Dead and Living Organism," *Proc. Roy. Soc. Med.*, 1917, vol. x.)

are implanted into ordinary blood-plasma obtained by simple centrifugalization of the blood or into recalcified citrated plasma, and such implanted plasma is, before it clots, filled into a capillary tube or into such a "slide cell" as is shown in Fig. 3, then each colony—and this is specially conspicuous in the case of staphylococcus—digests the fibrin which is in immediate contact with it, hollowing out for itself in this way a cavity in the clot. And as the colony grows the clear halo around it grows bigger and bigger.

It is thus shown that serophytic microbes can, by a secretion of trypsin, overcome the antitryptic power of the serum and obtain for themselves nutriment by the digestion of the proteins of the blood fluids. With this the question as to how serophytic microbes succeed in growing out in the blood would appear to be solved.

There are, however, certain other points remaining; and it

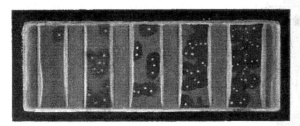

Fig. 3.

will facilitate the discussion of these and also of a number of others which will come up in connexion with the pathology and treatment of bacterial infections to make use of an apparatus of new technical terms. It will be convenient to speak of the normal blood, and also of the normal blood fluids (for these, as has been seen, have a certain power of protecting themselves against bacterial invasion), as possessing *phylactic* power. When the blood or blood fluids have been deprived of that power, they may be termed *ecphylactic*. When they have by immunization received an access of phylactic power, they may be called *epi-phylactic*. Finally when phylactic elements are transported into an ecphylactic focus, the term *kataphylaxis* may be employed or the agent may be termed a *kataphylactic agent*. Now making use of these terms it will be appreciated that when trypsin is introduced into and mixed with serum the entire fluid is rendered *pro tanto* ecphylactic. Where, as in the experiments reported above, the staphylococcus is implanted sparsely into the plasma, the whole medium is not rendered ecphylactic; but instead a certain number of ecphylactic foci—foci in which the microbes can henceforward grow unrestrained—are established.

The rôle played in pathology by the ecphylactic focus and the necessity of taking this into account in the treatment of all bacterial infection will gradually become clear. It will be sufficient here to bring out two points.

If after the microbes had been implanted the blood fluid had been kept in continual motion instead of being allowed to come to rest, the tryptic ferment of the microbes would have been dispersed through the medium and so frittered away, and the ecphylactic conditions required for free growth of the microbes would not have been realized. And, again, in the circumstances, the implanted microbes, instead of being exposed to the antibacterial action of only that fraction of serum which immediately encompasses them, would have been exposed to that of the entire volume of blood fluids.

It is thus seen that stagnant, as distinguished from actively streaming blood fluids must be more liable to become infected.

The next point has application to kataphylactic treatment. Consideration will show that if after growth had already started perpetually renewed supplies of antitryptic serum could be transported into the foci of bacterial growth the ecphylactic conditions there initially established would, little by little, be abolished and microbic growth would have been arrested.

All that has been said above with regard to the rôle of the blood fluids in hindering or favouring infection may be summarized in the form of two general physiological principles :—

(1) The natural uncorrupted blood fluids are competent to keep saprophytic microbes at bay and to preserve the wound against putrid infections, but these uncorrupted blood fluids will, when they collect in the wound, furnish a favourable nutrient medium for serophytic bacteria.

(2) Additions of trypsin, such as are furnished by the disintegration of leucocytes, corrupt the wound discharges and convert these into an ideal cultivation medium for serophytic and sero-saprophytic organisms indiscriminately.

From these physiological generalizations emerge two broad therapeutical principles for the treatment of wounds :—

(1) Where there is a putrid and unwholesome wound—in

other words, a wound with sero-saprophytic infection—the proper treatment will be to flush it with fresh wholesome blood fluids.

(2) Where there is a clean and wholesome wound—in other words, a wound with a purely serophytic infection—fresh and active leucocytes must be brought into the wound, and these must be provided with the conditions which are essential to their efficient functioning. To that end the physiology of the leucocyte must be carefully studied.

New Data relating to the Physiology of the Leucocyte.

The most important of the physiological properties of the leucocyte are : (a) its very active spontaneous motility ; (b) its power of emigrating from the capillaries ; (c) its stereotropism ; (d) its chemotactic attractions and repulsions ; (e) its power of ingesting and destroying by intracellular digestion microbes that have been prepared for phagocytosis and digestion by the opsonic and protryptic * action of the serum ; and (f) its power of excreting under appropriate stimuli bactericidal substances which kill microbes of various species exposed to their chemical influence. Further, there comes into consideration, in connection with the leucocyte, the fact that it sets free trypsin when it disintegrates.

The bald proposition that the leucocyte is motile fails to bring before the mind any adequate conception of its activity. How far the current conception falls below actuality can be realized by proceeding as follows :—A drop of blood is placed on a glass slide, is allowed to clot, and is then incubated in a moist chamber at blood temperature for twenty to thirty minutes. The clot is now shaken off, the loose red corpuscles are washed off under a tap, and the drop fixed and stained. It will now be seen, on examination under the microscope, that the area of the slide upon which the blood was deposited is occupied by an almost continuous sheet of leucocytes which have emigrated from the clot and have flattened themselves upon the glass in every condition of active movement (Fig. 4).

As this emigration takes place upon almost every kind of surface, the influence of chemotactic stimuli cannot here come into operation ; and the obvious inference is that in this experiment nothing more has been done than to provide the leucocytes with what they require for locomotion—fixed points to which they can make fast and then haul upon. Such points

---

* S. R. Douglas, *Proc. Roy. Soc.* B. 1916, Vol. lxxxix.

of attachment are provided by the strands of fibrin in the blood clot. To these fibrin strands the leucocytes will, in obedience to their stereotropism, attach themselves and along these they will find their way to the surface of the slide. Arrived there, they will flatten themselves out so as to come in contact with a maximum area of solid surface; and then, finding at their disposition everywhere on the slide and the under-face

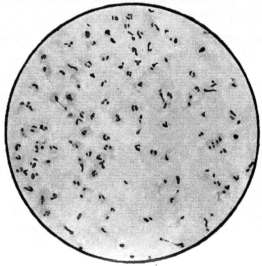

Fig. 4.

of the clot firm points of attachment, they will in the exercise of their propensity for spontaneous movement haul themselves about from place to place.

There are two other points which should be appreciated. The less important may, as directly linking itself on here, be taken first. Inspection shows that practically all the leucocytes found in these emigration films are polynuclear. The poly-nuclear leucocyte has in the matter of locomotion two advan-tages over the mononuclear. It can, owing to the subdivision of its nucleus, make its way out through the capillary wall. And, again—and it is this that comes into consideration here—it can travel much faster. Proof of this is obtained by the following procedure: Blood is filled into an emigration tube*

---

* Wright, "Technique of the Teat and Capillary Glass Tube."

and is then centrifugalized.   The red corpuscles are thus carried to the bottom ; there are ranged upon the top of these the polynuclear leucocytes, and over these again the large and

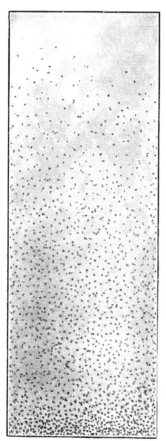

small mononuclear leucocytes, while the upper half of the tube is occupied by a clear plasma which presently sets into a clot. When an emigration tube containing such centrifuged blood is placed in the incubator the leucocytes immediately begin to transport themselves into the vacant clot, crawling up the trellis of fibrin. In the first half hour the mononuclear leucocytes, which being disposed at the top have the advantage of the start, are in advance ; but soon the polynuclears, coming forward through the ranks of the mononuclears, take the lead. After that they forge steadily ahead, leaving the mononuclears further and further behind.

The second and more important point relates to the behaviour of leucocytes freely suspended in fluid. These, because they have no fixed points to anchor themselves to and haul upon, cannot transport themselves from place to place. In a moving fluid they are swept along by the current; in a quiescent fluid they sink to the bottom (Fig. 5).

Fig. 5.

That leucocytes cannot transport themselves in pursuit of microbes through a fluid medium is of vital importance in the treatment of wounds, for it teaches that a wound which contains any appreciable amount of effusion is a wound which cannot be sterilized by leucocytic agency. Given an effusion of serum, serophytic microbes will always find opportunity for cultivating themselves out of reach of the leucocytes.

The fact that leucocytic movements can be influenced and directed by chemotactic stimuli must next be taken into consideration.

When comparative experiments are made, imposing blood on the one hand on a clean glass surface and on the other on

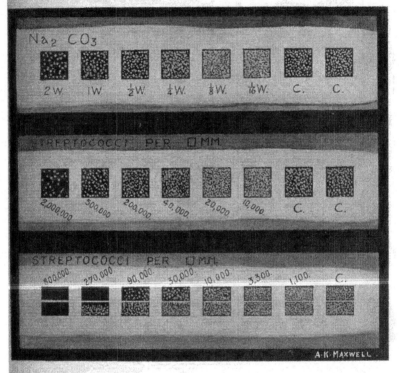

Fig. 6.

surfaces which have been coated with microbic suspensions, it is found that leucocytes emigrate in larger numbers on to surfaces which are lightly implanted with bacteria, and that they are repelled from heavily implanted surfaces. Illustration of this is furnished in Figures 6, 7 and 8.

Coming now to the consideration of the bactericidal effect exerted by leucocytes, perhaps the most instructive single experiment is the following. For it the following articles are required : (a) a piece of glass tubing about $2\frac{1}{2}$ in. in length and $\frac{1}{2}$ in. internal diameter, and sealed off and rounded at the end ; (b) a glass lath, (i.e., rectangular slat of cover-glass or microscopic slide) cut to such dimensions as to fit loosely into the tube ; and (c) an agar plate whose surface has been evenly implanted with a culture of staphylococcus or streptococcus. The lath is introduced into the tube, blood is then filled in,

and this is immediately centrifugalized so as to carry down the red corpuscles, and to give a stratified layer of leucocytes at the top of this and plasma above. With the lath left in position, the tube is now incubated for half an hour or more. On removing the lath from the clot and washing off the red blood corpuscles with serum, a dense band of leucocytes will be found on each face, firmly attached to midway down the glass. One face of the lath is now wiped clean, and the other is now imposed on the implanted surface of agar and pressed down gently so as to get rid of superfluous serum. The plate is now incubated, and the result is then as shown in Fig. 8. It will be seen that the entire surface of the agar is covered with a continuous sheet of microbes, except only where the leucocytes have come into operation. There the agar remains clear, and if the lath is now removed from the agar and the leucocytes fixed and stained, they will be found full of ingested microbes. This shows that leucocytes, when placed in good physiological conditions, can within the limits of their range of locomotion, completely sterilize an infected surface.

Fig. 7.

There is still one further fact about the leucocytes of which cognizance must be taken. This is that leucocytes can kill microbes not only by the familiar way of phagocytosis and intracellular digestion, but also quite apart from any ingestion by setting free bactericidal elements which directly attack the microbes.

This conclusion is forced upon us when, instead of a leucocyte-covered lath bathed in serum, one which has been thoroughly washed in physiological salt solution is imposed on the implanted agar. There is then precisely the same area of sterilization as before. Now, as staphylococci and streptococci are never ingested except in the presence of serum, and as examination of the lath shows that in this case there is no appreciable phagocytosis, the inference is clear that leucocytes can kill not only by phagocytosis and intracellular digestion, but also by chemical attack exerted extracellularly. Again, inasmuch as this sterilizing action is obtained only with living

Fig. 8.

leucocytes and not with leucocytes which have been killed by drying, it is clear that the extracellular killing of microbes here in question is due not to a *post mortem* escape of bactericidal elements from the leucocytic body, but to active excretion which is elicited when the living leucocyte is subjected to an appropriate stimulation.

The fact that leucocytes can in two several ways bring about the destruction of microbes has in connection with the treatment of bacterial disease generally far reaching importance, but the fact of chief concern here is that the imposition of a leucocyte-covered lath on an infected surface is in its essence the same procedure as the suture of an infected wound. In other words, what is of concern here is that if in the suture of the wound the conditions realized in these *in vitro* experiments are achieved, the same satisfactory sterilizing results will be obtained. Consideration further shows that if the experiments with leucocyte-covered laths are to serve as a model in suturing operations it is clear that there must come into application in the wound blood fluids of the same quality as those of the normal blood, and leucocytes in the same proportionate numbers and as freshly derived from the blood as are brought into operation in the *in vitro* experiments. Again, it will be essential that the leucocytes shall be provided with the same facilities of access to the microbes as they have under a lath. That means that there must not be left between the walls of the sutured wound any pockets of serum in which the microbes are safe from leucocytic attack. And lastly—but this is a condition which does not, in connection with suture, require to be specially emphasized—the leucocytes must be as effectively protected against desiccation as in the above experiment.

One further and final point must receive attention. This relates to the fact that leucocytes, and more particularly leucocytes which have ingested bacteria, contain within them a store of trypsin ; and that this is set free when the leucocyte dies and is broken down artificially. A simple way of demonstrating the setting free of this trypsin is the following :—An ordinary microscopic slide is taken, and at either end a buttress is made of two superposed slats cut from a thick microscopic slide and coated with vaseline. Upon these buttresses another slide is then placed. Into the "slide-cell" thus formed about 100 c.mm. of blood drawn from the finger are introduced, care being taken in filling to bring the blood in contact with both the roof and the floor of the slide cell so that it may run together into a column stretching from the upper to the lower slide. The slide cell is now placed in a moist chamber and incubated for about an hour. In this way a copious emigration of leucocytes from either end of the blood column is obtained. The cell is next pulled to pieces and the clot and loose red blood corpuscles washed off under a flowing tap, and the slides then dried. Next—and by this means the leucocytes which have been killed, but not disintegrated by desiccation are broken down—a drop of physiological salt solution is imposed on them, and this is then concentrated and evaporated to dryness in the incubator. This operation may be repeated, adding a drop of water to the leucocytic film and re-evaporating.

The two slides, each with its disc of disintegrated leucocytes, are now disposed so that the one disc shall lie immediately over the other. Then the slide-cell is reconstructed, but this time for each supporting buttress only a single thin slat of cover-glass dipped in vaseline is used. The cell is then filled with recalcified citrated plasma. The citrated plasma is obtained by mixing with blood drawn from the finger one-tenth of a 5 per cent. solution of citrate of soda and then centrifuging. The plasma which is pipetted off is then, to restore its coagulability, recalcified by adding 0·25 per cent. of calcium chloride cryst. After filling in the plasma the ends and sides of the slide cell are sealed with melted paraffin, and it is then placed in the incubator for a number of hours. A digestion of the clot, commencing in the area occupied by the disintegrated leucocytes and spreading out from thence to the periphery, is now obtained.

The fact that the disintegrating leucocyte sets free trypsin—here rendered manifest by the digestive action exerted on the clot—is of general pathological significance. In relation to wounds, the setting free of trypsin from the leucocyte prepares the way for sero-saprophytic infections; for it corrupts the discharges, and converts these into a favourable nutrient medium for all microbes without distinction. Again, the setting free of trypsin is responsible for the erosion which is seen at the mouth of every discharging sinus and on every wound surface which is not re-dressed at very frequent intervals. To the action of trypsin is due also that erosion in the depth of the wound which leads, when large vessels course in the neighbourhood, to secondary hæmorrhage. Lastly, the separation of sloughs is in every case the work of trypsin set free from leucocytes, and it will be seen later that by employing a procedure essentially similar to that by which trypsin was set free in the experiment described above, the separation of sloughs can be very much accelerated.*

A certain scientific foundation has now been laid and this must serve as a basis to the study of the physiology of the infected wound. It will be convenient to take up first the study of the wholesome granulating wound.

* In view of the fact that secondary hæmorrhage will not again be referred to in this chapter, attention may perhaps be called to the fact that the presence of trypsin in the depth of the wound can readily be detected by collecting a little of the pus on a tampon of cotton-wool and introducing this into a little hypercalcified milk (milk with an addition of ½ per cent. calcium chloride) warmed to 50°C. Clotting of this milk shows the presence of tryptic ferment. (Wright, "Technique of the Teat and Capillary Glass Tube," Chap. vii. App. 2, and Chap. xii, Sect. 13.)

The Wholesome Granulating Wound.

This is a wound in which there are antitryptic blood fluids, and in consonance with this a purely serophytic infection. Further, upon the encasing walls there is a protective coating of granulation tissue, and superficial to this a film of leucocytes which is being constantly reinforced by fresh emigration from the capillaries in the vascular granulation tissue. The evolution of events which occur in this type of wound has been carefully studied by Dr. A. Fleming, employing a technique modelled upon that employed in the lath experiments already described.

In this case impression cultures were made by applying a cover-glass to the surface of the wound and then transferring this directly or after desiccation to an implanted or unimplanted surface of an agar plate. When transferred to the agar without delay the leucocytes of the discharge come into operation living, and the culture obtained may be designated a " bio-pyo-culture." When, before implantation on the agar, the leucocytes are allowed to desiccate, the culture obtained may be called a " necro-pyo-culture."

For the observations in question the point of departure selected was the moment after the wound had been thoroughly syringed out with physiological salt solution. The first fact brought to light was that syringing is a procedure which carries away from the surface of the wound all the larger formed elements, in other words, all the leucocytes; but leaves behind many of the smaller elements—the microbes. When a cover-glass is applied to the surface of a syringed wound and is then fixed and stained, and examined by the microscope, leucocytes are found to be absent and only microbes are seen. And when a cover-glass from the wound is imposed upon an agar plate and incubated, the implanted microbes grow out in full number into colonies.

A cover-glass applied to the surface of the wound three to eight hours afterwards gives a very different picture. Large numbers of freshly emigrated leucocytes are found and interspersed among these a few scattered microbes; and when bio-pyo-cultures are made, in other words, when the leucocytes of the pus are placed in favourable external conditions, they attack and kill the microbes and complete sterilization is effected.

Pyo-impressions made later show that the pus is, as it lies in the wound, gradually losing its antibacterial power; and at the expiration of twenty-four hours there is on the surface of the wound a rapidly increasing population of microbes.

The whole cycle of events here described is made manifest to the eye in Fig. 9.

Certain further material points were brought out by Dr. Fleming's researches.

(1) The first of these is that active leucocytes, such as are obtained from a wound which has been syringed out three

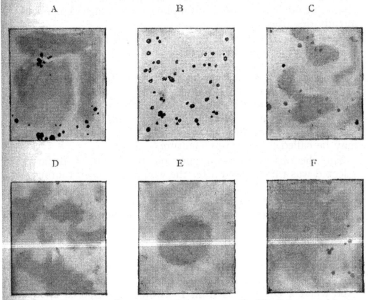

Fig. 9.—Pyo-impression cultures from a wound : (A) before washing; (B) immediately after washing with physiological salt solution ; (C) 1½ hours after ; (D) 4 hours after ; (E) 8 hours after ; (F) 24 hours after.

hours before, are competent to destroy not only the microbes contained in the pus but also extraneous microbes in large numbers. This is seen when leucocytes collected from the wound are imposed upon agar previously implanted with microbes (Fig. 10).

(2) Another practically important point has reference to the case where there is an excess of serum in the wound discharges. When a cover-glass is imposed on such a pus serum will be expressed and will dispose itself in the form of a ring round

the leucocytic disc. Such serophytic microbes as have been carried beyond the reach of the leucocytes will grow out here, forming a ring of colonies. Fig. 11, A, shows such a circlet of

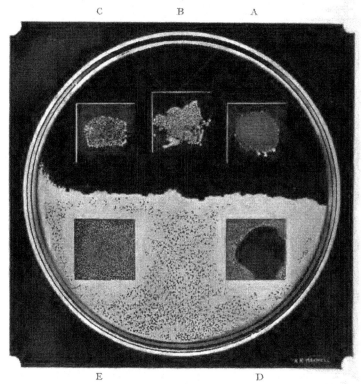

Fig. 10.—Pyo-impression preparations made from a "clean" wound : (A) pus imposed directly upon sterile nutrient agar; (B) the same pus dried; (C) the same pus heated to 48° C; (D) the same pus imposed directly upon nutrient agar heavily implanted with staphylococcus; (E) the same pus heated to 48° C. and similarly implanted.

colonies. Where, as was done in the case of the preparation in Fig. 11, B, a sample of pus is stirred up in a drop of serum, colonies of serophytic microbes come up all over the field except in the islands of pus.

(3) If before making a pyo-impression culture, the pus is allowed to dry, or is heated above 46° C., the thermal death-point of the leucocytes, its bactericidal power is abolished.

This is shown by the fact that colonies of serophytic microbes now come up thickly in the substance of the pus (Fig. 10, B, C, and E, and Fig. 12).

The therapeutic lesson already learned from the lath experiments—the lesson that the proper way of sterilizing an infected surface is to cover it in and turn leucocytes loose upon it—is by the data set forth above reinforced and supplemented.

The study of pyo-impression cultures brings out the subsidiary but very important facts that so long as the wound remains open the infection is never extinguished, and that washing and dressing impose only a temporary restriction

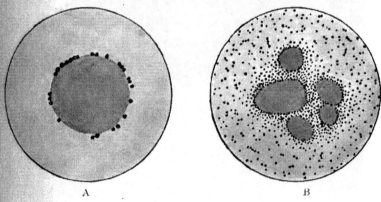

A   B

Fig. 11.—Bio-pyo-cultures from a "clean" wound: (A) pus as obtained from wound ; (B) the same pus mixed up with serum.

upon bacterial growth, and that the infection begins again to make progress so soon as the leucocytes succumb to the unfavourable external conditions encountered in the wound.

This cycle of events here described is uninfluenced by any application of antiseptics. In point of fact the effect of antiseptics is in general pernicious. They may by their negative chemotactic action hinder the emigration of leucocytes. They may coagulate the albumen of the tissue elements and of the discharges, forming a glaze over the walls of the wound which will mechanically confine the microbes and prevent also the emigration of leucocytes and the outflow of wholesome fluids into the wound. Again, antiseptics may by exerting an irritant action bring into the wound an excessive quantity of serum. Or again, they may reduce the antitryptic power of the blood fluids and by so doing convert this into a more favourable nutrient medium for all kinds of microbes. Important illustration of all these points is furnished by Dr. A. Fleming in a paper on " The Action of Chemical and Physiological Antiseptics in the Septic Wound."*

Nor, again, can the cycle of events above described be influenced by the exhibition of vaccines. Vaccines cannot be of service when the leucocytes are unprovided with shelter and facilities for locomotion and the external conditions are such that the blood fluids must, by the setting free of leucocytic trypsin very quickly be corrupted.

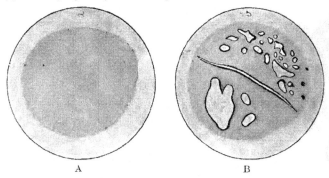

A   B

Fig. 12.—Impression cultures made (A) with pus, with anaërobic gas-forming organisms, taken directly from the wound, and (B) the same pus heated to 46° C.

The proper principle when dealing with a wholesome wound is to *close in order to sterilize, instead of using antiseptics with a view to closing.* In connexion with this therapeutic principle the following points may be emphasized :—

(1) The procedure here enjoined is that which Nature herself employs. She extinguishes the wound infection only by closing the wound.

(2) There is in the *modus operandi* of closure employed by Nature one outstanding defect. The epithelium grows in only very slowly from the edges of the wound. In consequence of this dilatory ingrowth the bacterial infection will in extensive bounds persist for indefinitely long periods, with the result that contracting scar tissue takes the place of the normal epithelial covering.

(3) By artificial closure, whether by actual suture, by drawing together of the edges by strapping, or by skin

* Brit. Jl. of Surgery, Vol. vii, No. 25, 1919.

grafting, the wound is promptly sealed, with the result that the bacterial infection is rapidly extinguished and the formation of scar tissue is avoided.

The physiological technique of the suturing operation sums itself up in the case of the wholesome granulating wound in the following :—

(a) The wound will be in the best condition for operation three or four hours after it has been washed out with physiological salt solution.

(b) An endeavour must be made to avoid leaving any pockets or dead spaces, and as far as possible to prevent any effusion into these. The best way of securing this will be to apply firm compression.

(c) The preparatory employment of antiseptic applications will, in view of what has been said above, be definitely contraindicated.

(d) Vaccines also may be ruled out as unneccessary if the operation can be properly conducted. But they may perhaps find useful application in those cases where it is difficult to secure accurate apposition of the walls of the wound. For by the agency of vaccines both the antitryptic and bactericidal power of the blood fluids may be increased, and that being so, it should be possible to some extent to keep in check bacterial growth in pockets of serum.

The Foul Wound with Putrid Infection.

There will, of course, be all kinds of differences in degree among the wounds that fall into the category of corrupt wounds. There will be (a) the lightest form, the neglected granulating wound where the discharges have by postponement of dressing been allowed to become tryptic, and a slight sero-saprophytic infection has supervened. There will be (b) such extravagantly putrid wounds as have been described at the beginning of this chapter. There will be (c) quite recent wounds where the infection is in the initial stage and which will, if they go untreated, develop into definitely putrid wounds.

It will be remembered that the special features of definitely putrid wounds are the following :—The walls of the wound cavity are formed by naked tissues ; the cavity contains a putrid pus in which every kind of microbe is pullulating ; the infection has penetrated into the walls ; and these are covered with gangrenous sloughs. It will also be remembered that these wounds fall into two classes. Where the wound cavity has laid open to the air and where drying has closed the superficial capillaries the necrosis produced by bacterial infection will have been supplemented by that due to the shutting off of the blood supply. Where the cavity is cut off from the exterior there will be a profounder invasion of the surrounding tissues and a more aggravated bacterial intoxication of the system.

Surgical science as it existed before the war provided for the treatment of these cases only a very meagre armamentarium of therapeutic measures. For wounds leading into abscess cavities it prescribed only that they should be freely laid open, should be provided with drainage-tubes, and should be syringed out with antiseptics. For the slough-covered open putrid wound it prescribed only syringing with antiseptics.

That the free laying open of the wound achieved its main object cannot be doubted. It constantly staved off impending gangrene, and arrested to some extent that progressive invasion of the encasing tissues which ultimately leads to septicæmia. Over against this must be set the fact that all operative procedures upon infected tissues, carry in their train risks from excessive auto-inoculation. In particular this applies to that preliminary routine which during the war was committed to the theatre orderly. Very vigorous ablutions and antiseptic applications and the careless casting loose of limbs from the splints under the anæsthetic must often have conveyed into the blood and lymph-stream formidable quanta of bacteria and bacterial products.

Passing to the therapeutic measures employed for holding in check the septic process in the wound, it is subject to no dispute that the syringings with antiseptics and the traditionary devices for draining which surgical science provides proved inefficacious as applied to the putrid septic wound. Day after day one saw the wounds so treated fill up with the same quantity of putrid pus, and this pus contained exactly the same pullulating population of microbes.

There was thus in connexion with putrid suppurating wounds a therapeutical problem urgently pressing for solution, a problem which was before the war, and is perhaps even now deliberately put out of sight. In that problem the following points stood out quite clearly : (a) the insertion of drainage-tubes is, as a device for securing effective drainage, absolutely futile ; (b) antiseptics applied in the wound are quite incapable of accomplishing what is demanded of them ; (c) an extravagant pullulation of microbes such as occurs in the putrid wound is inexplicable except on the basis of some defect in the discharges.

(a) With regard to drainage, consideration shows that its true object and end should be (i) to drain away from the cavity of the wound and the surrounding infected tissues the corrupted fluid which provides a good nutrient medium for microbes, and (ii) to drain into the infected tissues and wound cavity uncorrupted fluids derived from the blood. In other words the proper conception of drainage is arrived at when it is regarded as a kataphylactic operation whose object it is to abolish ecphylactic conditions, and bring the phylactic powers of the blood into action upon the infecting microbes. Now the drainage-tube itself does nothing beyond providing a channel of exit through which the discharges can escape when the cavity of the wound is full to overflowing, or when the outflow is favoured by gravity. But even when the wound opens downwards there will always remain behind on the walls of the cavity a slime of discharge, and that will prevent the infected surface of the cavity and the infected tissues below coming back to a wholesome condition.

It will appear later that effective drainage, which is in the treatment of putrid septic wounds absolutely essential, can in point of fact be quite simply achieved.

(b) Coming next to the consideration of the disappointing results of antiseptics applied in the wound, there is for these a very simple explanation. All antiseptics have, in addition to those chemical properties which have won them their title, and are published from the housetops, also other chemical properties about which the advocates of antiseptics say as little as possible. All antiseptics, not excluding those which are specially belauded as operative in serum, enter into chemical combination with proteins other than those contained in bacterial protoplasm. Those antiseptics which are dyestuffs also combine chemically with the fabrics which are used as dressings for the wound. In consequence of these vagrant chemical affinities antiseptics are efficacious only when brought into contact with microbes which are suspended in watery fluids or else lie high and dry, naked to chemical attack. Or, putting this in the inverse way, it may be said that antiseptics are quenched, in other words, they lose their power of entering into lethal chemical combination with microbes when they are introduced into or imposed upon albuminous fluids or applied to albuminous surfaces; and, as pointed out by Fleming, the same thing happens when antiseptics which are also dyestuffs are brought into contact with cotton or linen dressings.

The point specially important to appreciate is that antiseptic syringings can never extinguish an infection in pockets filled with pus or serous effusion.   This is brought out very clearly by the instructive experiments of Fleming, made with "artificial wounds," consisting of test tubes drawn out at their inferior end into hollow spikes, in imitation of the diverticula of war wounds.   These were filled with serum, implanted with fæcal material, and then incubated.   After twenty-four hours the contents were evacuated.   The tube was then filled with antiseptic and re-emptied several times.   It was then refilled with sterile serum and reincubated.   After twenty-four hours it was as heavily infected as before.   In the next experiment the " artificial wound " was " re-dressed " in precisely the same

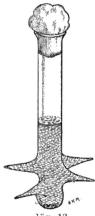

fashion, except only that here the antiseptic was, on the first re-dressing, left in the wound for one hour; on re-dressing the next day for three hours; and on the subsequent day, at the third re-dressing, for twenty-four hours.   In each case the sterile serum became heavily infected.   And in comparative experiments, in which in one set of tubes physiological salt was employed for washing out the tube, and in other sets of tubes eusol, Dakin's solution, $2\frac{1}{2}$ per cent. carbolic acid, brilliant green, and flavine respectively, the final results were precisely similar.   And, again, precisely similar results were achieved when the conditions of the experiment were varied by employing for the serum culture, instead of a tube with recesses,

Fig. 13.

a plain tube into which there had been introduced a pledget of asbestos wool to do duty as a foreign body.

The lessons of these experiments are clearly that infected fluid can never, by ordinary mechanical means, be effectually evacuated from a recessed wound or a tissue or fibre, and that the microbes that lie in recesses or interspaces occupied by an albuminous fluid are by this completely sheltered from the attack of antiseptics.   And these experiments further teach us that it is futile to hope for any effective washing out of a recessed wound or infected tissues, or for any sterilization of recesses and interspaces by the agency of antiseptics unless we can find a solution which has the power of drawing into itself albuminous fluids, and which will at the same time itself be drawn into such fluids.

(c) The final point made in criticism of the treatment applied to putrid wounds was that the rapid pullulation of microbes in these and the polymorphic character of the infection ought immediately to have made it clear that here the conditions are so favourable to the microbes that no application of antiseptics could by any possibility be effective. The moment this was appreciated it was seen to be essential to ascertain whether the patient's blood fluids were vitiated in the source or whether they became vitiated only as they lay in the wound. An experiment already incidentally referred to, the experiment in which a "lymph leech" is applied to the walls of the wound, definitely resolved this question. The details of the experiment are as follows :—An ordinary stout-walled test-tube is taken and a hole blown in the wall about half-way down to serve as a mouth, and the upper end is then drawn out into a convenient

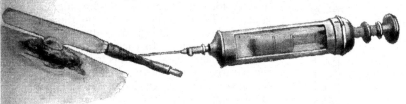

Fig. 14.

nozzle. A short length of rubber tubing sealed at one end with a little piece of glass rod is then fitted to this. The needle of a syringe is now passed through the wall of the rubber tubing and the mouth of the lymph leech is then applied to the wall of a putrid septic wound which has been emptied of pus. A vacuum is now created in the interior by drawing out the piston of the syringe. The needle is withdrawn, and the lymph leech is left clinging to the walls of the wound. After a period of hours, when the cavity of the wound has filled up again with putrid discharge, the belly of the lymph leech contains only a clear fluid. Specimens of the pus and of the fluid from the lymph leech are now taken and microscopic preparations made from each. The difference between the two will be seen on glancing at the insets to Fig. 2. In the specimen of the discharge from the cavity of the wound there is a teeming population of microbes and disintegrated leucocytes. In the specimen from the belly of the lymph leech there is practically a pure cultivation of streptococcus. There are also wholesome leucocytes in small numbers.

The facts learnt from this experiment are : (a) that the lymph
when tapped off from the walls of the wound is uncorrupted ;
(b) that it is only after effusion and by the agency of corruptive
influences operative in the wound that the lymph is converted
into a nutrient medium in which every putrefactive microbe
flourishes unrestrained ; and (c) that these corruptive influences
can be overborne by providing a sufficient indraught of lymph
into the wound cavity.

It will be seen that there is here the basis for an effective
treatment of sero-saprophytic infections of wounds. All

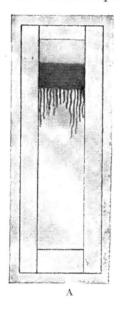 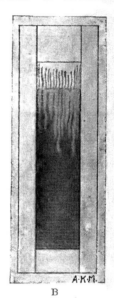

A   B

Fig. 15.

that is required is to flush the wound with wholesome lymph.
A variety of different agencies can effect this. (a) Direct
negative pressure may be employed, as in the experiment
with the lymph leech. (b) There can be applied to the walls
of the wound any solution which induces active hyperæmia.
(c) Recourse may be had to passive hyperæmia. And, lastly,
(d) there can be applied in the wound any solution which
has a power of drawing into itself an albuminous fluid. From
the point of view of convenience and easy regulation this will
be the easiest of all the methods.

Now salt solutions of appropriate strengths have in relation to albuminous solutions very interesting and for the purpose here in view very important faculties.*   They very energetically draw albuminous solutions into themselves, and are by reciprocal action drawn into albuminous fluids.   This "intertraction" is very strikingly made manifest to the eye when there is introduced into a plane-walled cell† first a 5 to 7 per cent. solution of sodium chloride (Fig. 15).   With this the cell is to be filled more than half full.   Upon this heavier salt solution is to be superimposed a little serum coloured with watery eosin and upon the top of this a stratum of water.   Then, directing attention to the dividing line between the serum and salt, one sees—appearing almost instantly—active mass movements of intertraction, with characteristic appearances which may be denoted "pseudopodial interpenetration."   These are manifestations of a down-draught of the lighter supernatant serum into the heavier subjacent salt solution, and of updraught of salt solution into the serum, and by this process of mixture, which is subsequently reinforced and supplemented by ordinary diffusion, there is in a comparatively short time achieved, as shown by the uniform distribution of the eosin, a completely equable mixture of the stratified saline and albuminous solutions.   While these active movements of indraught and mixture are in progress below where the serum and salt solution come together, the upper frontier, that where the serum is in contact with water, remains almost absolutely quiescent.   Here there comes into operation only that very slow and quite familiar process of interpenetration known as diffusion.

The attractive power exercised by salt solution upon serum which is manifested to the eye in the above experiment is capable of being turned to good account in connexion with the putrid septic wound.   Here is an agency which can establish genuine drainage.   The salt solution will aid in ablution, inasmuch as it will draw out serum from the recesses of the wound and the interstices of infected tissues.   It will also function as a kataphylactic agent, producing that indraught of wholesome serum into the wound cavity which is required for the abolition of the sero-saprophytic infection.   The most

---

* Wright, *Proc. Roy. Soc. B.*, 1921, Vol. xcii; Schoneboom, *Proc. Roy. Soc. A.*, Vol. ci, 1922.

† The plane-wall cell employed for this experiment is easily made by taking a couple of glass microscopic slides, separating them by passing down from one of the narrower ends of the apposed slides a loop of stout cord or wire, and then immersing the three other sides in turn into a mixture of resin and beeswax, afterwards of course withdrawing the loop.

suitable solutions of salt for employment in wounds will be solutions of $2\frac{1}{2}$ to 5 per cent. sodium chloride. Solutions weaker than $2\frac{1}{2}$ per cent. possess too little drawing power, and concentrated solutions act as escharotics—even 5 per cent. solutions give considerable pain when applied to tender new-formed skin at the edges of wounds. They may also, when kept long applied to unbroken skin, produce irritation and a pustular staphylococcic infection. But these incidental evil effects can all be guarded against by applying to the skin surfaces a protective covering of vaseline.

From the above it is apparent that by applying 5 per cent. salt solution a putrid infection lurking in the diverticula of wounds can be abolished. But in addition to this there is, as we have seen, another feature to be regarded. The surface of the putrid wound is coated with sloughs, and there is in these sloughs—just as there is infected foreign matter such as clothing or a sequestrum of dead bone—an ecphylactic focus which will prevent the re-establishment of wholesome conditions and the healing of the wound. The next task must accordingly be to consider how to get rid of the sloughs.

The physiological agency Nature here employs is tryptic digestion, the trypsin for this purpose being provided by the disintegration of leucocytes. Upon this device therapeutics may profitably be modelled. Where there is a thin layer of desiccated slough, such as is formed when the skin only has been torn off and the subcutaneous tissue has been exposed to desiccation, an efficient method will be to apply strips of lint soaked in trypsin. But in the ordinary case where there is a thick necrotic layer a superficial application of trypsin will be quite inadequate, and the proper course will be to bring into application trypsin in the depth of the slough. In connexion with this it will be remembered that leucocytes set free trypsin when subjected to the action of strong salt solutions; and also that when strong salt solutions are brought into application upon albuminous solutions the albumen is carried into the saline solution and the salt into the albuminous solution. If, therefore, a 5 per cent. salt solution is applied to a slough, albuminous fluids will pass out from its interstices, and salt solution will pass in and will come into operation on the leucocytes held fast in its tissue. Trypsin will then be set free and the strands which hold together the necrotic material, and those also by which it is attached to the tissues beneath, will be eaten through and the entire slough will be disintegrated and cast loose.

Two quite simple experiments confirm these conclusions :— (1) Two test-tubes are filled with white of egg leaving room in each above for a cotton-wool plug, and the albumen is then coagulated by immersion in boiling water. Two cotton-wool plugs, soaked in a non-tryptic pus, are then introduced into the test-tubes, and these are inverted into beakers, one containing 0·85 per cent. and the other 5 per cent. salt solution. All this is now placed in the incubator and examined after twenty-four hours. The results will then be as shown in Fig. 16.

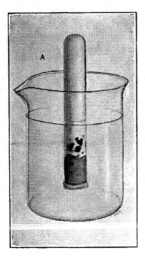 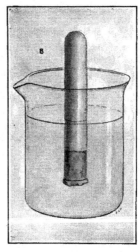

Fig. 16.

It will be seen that while in the tube immersed in physiological salt solution very little has happened, in the other tube the white of egg has been extensively tunnelled by digestion.

(2) In the second experiment an attempt is made to imitate more closely the conditions obtaining in a slough-covered wound. Two beakers are taken, filled to a depth of 2 or 3 cm. with egg albumen, and this is coagulated by immersion in boiling water. A little uncoagulated white of egg, left over for the purpose, is then poured on the surface. Two discs of lint which will lie comfortably in the beakers are now taken and, with the nap turned uppermost, imposed on the coagulated white of egg. Then by again immersing the beakers in boiling water the discs of lint are luted down

firmly upon this foundation. This lint, which is to do duty
as an artificial slough, is covered with pus, a non-tryptic pus
being chosen, and the same quantum of pus being employed
in each beaker. Then into one of the beakers some 5 per cent.
salt solution is poured, and into the control beaker the same
quantity of physiological salt solution. The beakers are then
incubated for an hour or more. After that enough water is
added to the first beaker to reduce considerably the concentration of the salt, and to the other the same quantity of
physiological salt solution. The beakers are now replaced in
the incubator, and then the progress of events watched by
examination at frequent intervals. It will then be seen that
comparatively soon the artificial slough in the beaker with the

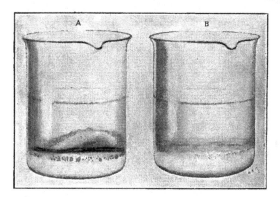

Fig. 17.—In beaker (A) is shown the loosening of the
artificial slough, and the digestion of the subjacent hard-
boiled white of egg, which is obtained by treatment of the
superjacent pus with 5 per cent. salt solution. In beaker
(B) is shown the much smaller amount of digestion
obtained by treatment of the pus with 0·85 per cent.
salt solution.

5 per cent. salt solution becomes loosened from its foundation,
while the other remains for a long time firmly attached.

The results here obtained *in vitro* are in full concordance
with those actually obtained in the wound. When 5 per cent.
salt solution is applied the sloughs are very rapidly cleaned
off, and with this the conversion of the putrid wound into a
clean and wholesome wound is completed. It must be clearly
understood that with this the utility of the 5 per cent. salt
solution treatment is exhausted. From this time forward,

except only in the case of a recurrence of the sero-saprophytic infection, the wound must be treated in accordance with the therapeutic principles applicable to clean wounds.

We may pass now from the terribly putrid wound, that which has been left for days without surgical recision, to the less heavily infected wound. In dealing with this type of wound very signal successes, attracting general attention in the early middle period of the war, were obtained in the hospital at Compiègne under the direction of Alexis Carrel. As important questions of principle, and in particular the issue of the efficacy of antiseptics, are here in question, it will be well to consider carefully the treatment adopted by him.

The facts that have to be regarded are the following :— (a) Owing to the propinquity of Compiègne to the firing line the patients were received for treatment before the infection of their wounds had made much progress ; (b) recision and surgical cleansing of the wounds was very carefully carried out ; (c) that done, the wounds were at frequent and regular intervals flushed with Dakin's fluid—this, which is a solution of hypochlorites, being carried down into the recesses of the wound by a system of tubes. To this flushing with Dakin's fluid the therapeutic successes achieved in the hospital were attributed. It was, in other words, assumed that the employment of a suitable bactericidal agent and its application in a suitable manner were the essential elements in the successful treatment of infected wounds.

One must here consider, first, whether the factor of proximity to the front and that of early and careful recision and cleansing did not, in connexion with the successes achieved, come heavily into account ; secondly, whether the mere mechanical lavage did not also count for much ; and, lastly, whether Dakin's fluid, though employed in the capacity of a bactericidal agent, does not really owe its therapeutic virtues to the physiological reaction it exerts on the wound.

With regard to the rôle played by early and careful recision and cleansing of the wound, it will suffice to hark back to the fact that as soon as surgical hospitals were established behind the firing line and emphasis was laid on early recision and surgical cleansing of the wound, putrid infections became rare. And it may perhaps be added that as soon as the influence of such early surgical intervention was fully appreciated the interest excited by Carrel's results and the vogue of his treatment quickly passed away.

With regard to the frequent and efficient lavage secured by

Carrel's procedures it is obvious *a priori* that such lavage must in the treatment of wounds always be of great importance, and there is unanimity among those who have had to deal with wounds requiring frequent laborious and painful re-dressing that the methods of lavage elaborated by Carrel are extremely valuable.

Passing now to the vital issue as to whether Dakin's fluid, which is the essential element in Carrel's treatment, is thera-peutically valuable by reason of its possessing bactericidal properties or by reason of its possessing other properties dis-tinct from this but valuable in the wound, one's judgment must evidently be guided not by the *a priori* views but by the results of direct experimental enquiry. Such experimental enquiry into the bactericidal and physiological effects of applica-tions of Dakin's fluid to wounds has been made by Fleming.* His investigations establish that Dakin's fluid loses all bactericidal potency within five minutes after its introduction into the wound, and further that applications made to the surface of a clean wound do not, even when repeated hourly for four hours, in any way diminish the population of microbes. To this may be added that the microbic population found on a clean wound treated with Dakin's fluid does not differ with respect to either character or number from that found on clean wounds treated only with salt solution. It is not without significance that under either treatment only sero-saprophytic microbes are eliminated, and only serophytic microbes are found to survive.

The experiments of Fleming have further shown that applications of Dakin's fluid induce increased effusion, this effusion manifesting itself not, as when 5 per cent. salt solution is applied, immediately, but only after the lapse of a certain latent period. The effusion here in question is accordingly produced not by the forces of "intertraction" but by the active congestion. That Dakin's fluid induces hyperæmia is of course familiar to those who have seen the bright coral-red granulations of wounds treated by hypochlorites, or have witnessed the troublesome irritation which develops on the circumjacent skin when hypochlorite solutions are employed in excessive strength.

The facts brought out here establish that it will, in every case where a beneficial result is attributed to antiseptic treatment, be logically necessary to show that the results cannot be ascribed to a beneficial physiological reaction pro-duced in the wound. Thus, for example, in those oft-cited cases of Lister in which undiluted carbolic acid was successfully

* *Loc. cit.*

employed in the treatment of compound fractures, the possibility of successes of this kind being due to a kataphylactic pouring out of lymph must be taken into account. A profuse pouring out of lymph was in point of fact a very striking feature in connexion with those war wounds which were treated with undiluted carbolic acid, and such profuse outpouring is also specifically mentioned by Lister in connexion with his cases.

Gas Gangrene Infection.

The treatment of putrid infections leads by a natural transition to the consideration of gas gangrene and tetanus, for these are interlinked with the putrid wound infections by the fact that they develop only when ecphylactic conditions prevail in the wound and only, at any rate in the case of gas gangrene, when the fluids at the seat of implantation are profoundly altered.

Dealing first with gas gangrene, the key to its understanding lies in the study of the requirements and conditions of life of the microbe. In connexion with these the fact which has most impressed itself on the bacteriologist and the surgeon, is that the microbes which produce gas gangrene—the *Bacillus welchii* and its close congeners the *Bacillus œdematiens* and the *Bacillus fallax*—are anaërobic microbes. But exaggerated importance has been attached to this; and the erroneous assumption that the microbe could grow only under anaërobic conditions led at the outset of the war to quite futile methods of treatment. For example, oxygen was injected into the affected parts on the notion that infection might thus be prevented from spreading. That such practice lacked scientific foundation is clear when it is remembered that Tarozzi had already shown long before the war that, when pieces of animal tissue are added to bouillon, vigorous cultures of the gangrene bacillus can be obtained in open tubes. Confirmation of these findings of Tarozzi was obtained every day during the war, the bacillus of gas gangrene being often found growing luxuriantly in open wounds.

Instead of pursuing that theme let us turn our attention to a fundamental guiding principle in pathological and therapeutic research. In connexion with all infections, whether they are septicæmic infections or wound infections, or special saprogenous infections such as gas gangrene and tetanus, the facts which, above all other facts, require to be sought out are those which relate to the growth of these pathogenetic microbes in the blood fluids.

In connexion with each species of pathogenetic microbe it should be determined first whether it can grow in the unaltered blood fluids, and, if the microbes fail to grow in these, what are the influences which can convert the blood fluids into a medium which will be favourable to its growth.

In the course of the researches undertaken during the war* it was ascertained that the bacillus of Welch will not grow in normal serum until enormous implantations, implantations of the order of 20,000,000 microbes per cubic centimetre, are arrived at; but it has to be appreciated, as having a general application, that if very much smaller numbers are implanted, and if the infection is subsequently concentrated by gravitation or centrifugalization, a culture is obtained in those regions of the serum where the implantation is sufficiently enriched—in other words, the microbes grow in the lower part of the tube. And, again, if as a preliminary to implanting into serum the gas gangrene microbes are inserted into a fabric, they will develop in those interstitial pockets in which there is the required concentration of microbes in the unit volume of serum. This clearly accounts for the cases in which infection proceeds from a piece of infected clothing implanted into the tissues by the projectile.

Experiments of this kind undertaken with normal serum were, in view of what had been elicited with respect to sero-saprophytic infections generally, followed up by implantations of the gas gangrene bacillus into serum of artificially reduced antitryptic power. In this medium, very luxuriant cultures were obtained from quite small implantations; and the gas gangrene bacillus was found to grow also in aërobic conditions. Here, of course, is an explanation of the microbe of gas gangrene being very often found growing freely in open putrid wounds.

It was plain, however, that the faculty of growing freely in sera of reduced antitryptic power did not furnish the key to the explanation of the special features of gas gangrene infection. And reflection after a time led to the finding of something that was special to the gas gangrene bacillus. It suggested itself, on considering the fact that the microbe elaborates acid when it cultivates itself in serum, and on relating this with the "avalanche growth" of the culture, that the blunting of the supervening alkalinity of the serum by the growing microbe might possibly be the factor which provided for the gas

---

* Wright, "Conditions that govern the growth of the bacillus of gas gangrene in artificial culture media in the blood fluids *in vitro* and in the dead and living organism." *Proc. Roy. Soc. of Medicine*, 1917, vol. x, pp. 1–32.

gangrene bacillus favourable conditions of growth. Experiment
showed that this is so, and that it is a matter of practical
indifference whether the alkalinity of the serum is reduced by
an addition of mineral or lactic acid or by exposure to carbonic
acid. The optimum addition of acid was found to be that
which just neutralizes or just falls short of neutralizing
the medium.

Here, then, was perhaps a key to the problems of gas
gangrene infection. To take those problems in order :—

(1) The first problem arises in connection with the facts
discovered by Welch. It was left an enigma by Welch why
the gas gangrene bacillus injected into the blood-stream produces no infection in the living rabbit, while, if the animal is
killed immediately after injection and kept warm, there will
be obtained in a very few hours a teeming blood culture which
distends the whole corpse with gas and converts the liver into
a foaming mass. This paradoxical result stands in relation to
the fact that the alkalinity of the blood is, when the corpse is
kept warm, rapidly reduced by an influx of lactic acid from
the muscles. That here is the circumstance upon which the
success of the bacterial implantation pivots is shown by the
fact that the multiplication of the microbe in the corpse
commences as soon as the alkalinity of the blood is sensibly
reduced, and then gains speed like an avalanche, going faster
and faster as the alkalinity of the blood is progressively reduced.

Proof that there is here a true nexus of cause and effect is
obtained by varying the procedure.* If instead of giving first
the intravenous injection and then killing and incubating the
animal, the animal is first killed and successive samples of
blood are now from time to time withdrawn from the corpse
and implanted with the bacillus, the rate of growth and the
luxuriance of the cultures increase with the reduction of blood
alkalinity, while at the same time successful cultures are
obtained from smaller and smaller implantations of the bacillus.
Lastly, if the intravascular injection of Welch's bacillus is
preceded or followed up by one of bicarbonate of soda, the
growth of the microbe in the dead animal is postponed.

(2) The key to the problem of the post-mortem invasion of
the blood found, a whole series of clinical problems also are
unlocked. There is *first* the problem as to why gas gangrene
takes origin in connexion with muscle ; *secondly*, as to why it
so often develops after the application of a tourniquet, and in
the muscles of the calf after a lesion of the posterior tibial

* Wright, *loc. cit.*

artery; *thirdly*, why it is so frequently associated with trench foot, and implunging wounds, and wounds where there is extensive bruising by the agency of pebbles and grit driven in by explosions; *fourthly*, why gas gangrene so often develops in the wounded who have lain out in the cold, in those who are affected with shock, and, if one can in such matters trust to impressions, in those suffering from exhaustion after extreme muscular effort.

Each and all of these problems find quite simple resolution when it is remembered that muscle elaborates and sets free lactic acid not only when it enters into rigor mortis, but also whenever its oxygen supply fails or becomes inadequate. Now this will happen under three different sets of conditions :—

(1) It will happen, in the first place, when the blood supply to a muscle or set of muscles is interfered with. The interference may result from an arterial lesion—for example, a lesion to the principal artery of a limb, or to an artery which, like the posterior tibial, is the exclusive source of supply to a group of muscles ;—or from artificial compression of the vessels ; or from an extensive lesion of the capillary circulation such as results from bruising and implunging wounds ; or, lastly, from interference with the circulation such as results from long exposure to wet and cold.

(2) Again, the oxygen supply to the muscles will be interfered with when, as in shock, there is a general collapse of the circulation ; for when the blood-pressure sinks away the peripheral arteries carry no blood and the muscles are by consequence starved of oxygen.

(3) Lastly, when excessive demands are made upon the muscular system the supply of oxygen will, despite the fact that the blood-vessels are intact and the general blood-pressure is maintained, be unable to keep pace with the chemical requirements of the muscles.

Accordingly, under all these three different sets of conditions a local acidosis will be established in muscle, and where there is instead of a quite restricted myogenic acidosis a general acidosis of muscle such as is associated with shock, there will inevitably, as soon as this excess of acid is conveyed into the blood stream, supervene an acidæmia. This myogenous or shock acidæmia, as it may be termed, will prepare the way for the growth of the bacillus of Welch in the blood, in other words, for the development of a gas gangrene septicæmia.

It has been seen in the above how the soil is, by the generation of acid in muscle, prepared first for the local invasion by the gas gangrene bacillus, and afterwards for the secondary septicæmia. But the microbe can establish itself without assistance from myogenous acid. It can, when other circumstances are favourable, pave its own way. It has already been seen that the gangrene bacillus, when sufficiently heavily implanted, will furnish a culture even in normal serum, elaborating acid, and establishing by this conditions more favourable to its growth. In precisely the same way the gas gangrene bacillus can, if sufficiently heavily implanted, establish itself in the subcutaneous tissues or elsewhere, and the local infection and production of acid, when allowed to proceed unchecked, can without help afforded by myogenous acid render the blood acidæmic and so prepare the way for a blood infection.*

.But for the most part the events in gangrene are much more intricately interwoven than has as yet appeared, for the gas gangrene bacillus, when it pullulates in the body, produces a characteristic toxæmia. Beginning quite abruptly with vomiting, this leads rapidly to a collapse of the circulation, which makes the undertaking of any operative procedures impossible. The pulse at the wrist becomes impalpable, the face turns an ashen grey, the hands, feet, and after these the entire limbs, tip of the nose, forehead and cheeks become cold as stone, while the mental faculties for the most part remain quite intact, and then death—as is its wont in other acidæmias, and notably in scurvy—comes quietly and without warning given. For example, one may look away from the patient for a moment and then, on turning round, find him dead. It will be clear that the toxæmic collapse and shock here in question will, like every other form of collapse and shock, cut off the oxygen supply from the muscles, thus engendering a myogenic acidæmia. After that if the circulation is brought back that will lead, as in other cases of shock, to an absorption of myogenous acid into the blood, and, if the focus of infection has not in the meantime been extirpated, in addition to a larger absorption of gas gangrene toxins. With these points made clear, the treatment of gas gangrene may next be considered.

Nothing need be said here about the local surgical treatment except that, when extirpation has to be left incomplete—where, for example, it has proved impossible to resect the whole of the infected muscle, or where a limb has been amputated and the gangrene infection has already spread on to the trunk, or,

---

* Wright, *loc. cit.*, Charts I-VI.

again, where it has been impossible to get enough covering without including in a flap a doubtful patch of skin—it will be urgently necessary to supplement the treatment by efficient drainage, *i.e.*, by drawing out the corrupt lymph from the infected tissues, and drawing into these tissues from the blood-vessels a lymph, in which the gas gangrene bacillus cannot grow. In cases like the above-mentioned, and also wheresoever incisions are made with the idea of providing drainage, applications of a 5 per cent. salt solution will render useful service. They will in the case of incisions prevent these becoming lymph-bound, and will provide that copious kataphylactic flushing with wholesome lymph which is required.

With regard to general constitutional treatment of gas gangrene, the choice of this must clearly be contingent on the interpretation placed upon the symptoms. In other words, the treatment selected will depend upon whether the symptoms are ascribed predominantly to the acidæmic process, or predominantly to special toxins elaborated by the gas gangrene bacillus, or to both these elements conjointly and to an approximately equal extent.

There is room here for frank differences of opinion on these questions, and the situation is as follows. When the train of reasoning set out above, and also inference from clinical observation, had led to the conclusion that there was an acidæmic factor in gas gangrene toxæmia, and when it had been verified by titrations of the blood alkalinity that the patient's collapse and enfeeblement go hand in hand with the intensity of the acidæmia, the conclusion was inevitable that whatever else might be done or left undone, it was essential to combat the acidæmia. Accordingly, intravenous injections of 4 per cent. bicarbonate of soda were resorted to.* The benefit obtained by these injections is one of those things that are subject to no dispute ; and there is, in the domain of medicine, probably nothing more dramatic than what happens when a gas gangrene patient who is in a state of complete collapse, and who may be panting in air-hunger, receives an injection of alkali. He will often within a very short time sit up in bed and smoke, read a newspaper, and call for food : in short, he is brought into a condition in which he is easily able to endure the administration of an anæsthetic and an extirpation operation. But—and this point cannot be too strongly insisted upon—the patient will, in default of proper treatment,

* Wright, *loc. cit.* Table III, and Wright and Fleming, " Further Observations on Acidæmia in Gas Gangrene," *Lancet*, 1918, Feb. 9th.

after a time almost inevitably relapse, such relapse being due to the resorption of a fresh quantity of myogenic acid and (if in the meantime the focus of infection has not been extirpated) also of microbe-elaborated acid and toxins. Such relapse is best forestalled by the oral administration of lactate of soda, the lactate of soda being administered in doses of 8 grm. every three hours until such time as the body is saturated with alkali and the urine rendered alkaline.

The surprising therapeutic efficacy of bicarbonate of soda injections creates a doubt as to whether specific toxins, other than acids, come much into account in the causation of the collapse. The toxæmia of gas gangrene infection has, however, by many investigators been envisaged from an entirely different point of view from that here maintained, and these observers see here a perspective in which acidæmia plays no part, and the toxins of the gas gangrene bacillus attract to themselves all the attention. In their judgment the goal of endeavour in the treatment of gas gangrene must be to place at the disposal of the surgeon an antitoxic or antibacterial serum.

In connexion with this question it will suffice to note that the anti-gangrene sera which have been prepared by French scientists and employed in the French army have been very favourably reported upon. But it is not even certainly known with respect to these whether the action exerted upon the patient is antibacterial or antitoxic; or whether—and this is in view of the large volume of serum employed and its insertion into the site of infection—the sera act simply as any kataphylactic introduction of wholesome blood fluids would act. In the British army, the results obtained with anti-gas-gangrene sera were negative. Here, as in the French army, experiential and statistical methods were employed, instead of direct observation of the effects obtained on the patients' blood.

Tetanus.

While the special study of tetanus lay outside the sphere of research here summarized, it may not be unprofitable to indicate the important problems which here still await solution. Before all others it will be of import to determine, for this has a very important bearing on prophylaxis, whether the tetanus bacillus can grow in the unaltered or only in corrupted blood fluids. For clearly, if, as the clinical facts suggest, the tetanus belongs, like the gas gangrene bacillus and so many other microbes, to the class of the sero-saprophytic microbes, it will then be a denizen only of foul wounds and ecphylactic foci, and tetanus will occur only in such conditions as prevailed at the outset of the war; and, if that is the case, it becomes a matter for consideration whether injections of antitetanic serum might not have been discarded with advantage in those cases where there was opportunity for the early and careful recision of wounds.

On the Forestalling of Infection in War Wounds and on the Physiological Principles which should here come into application.

The surgery of war wounds, that is to say, of wounds where there are mangled and devascularized tissues and an implant-ation of bacteria, may be summarized in three general principles :—

(1) All devascularized parts must be resected, and this should be done with the least possible delay.

(2) When the devascularized parts have been resected steps must be taken to deal with the infection left in the wound and to prevent fresh infection.

(3) When the surgical cleansing and recision of the wound has to be postponed, steps must be taken to prevent, so far as possible, the development of infection in the devascularised tissues.

The rationale of these principles briefly is as follows :—

(1) The amputation of lacerated limbs, and of limbs whose main artery has been severed, is of course dictated by the consideration that infected animal tissues when cut off from their blood supply fall a prey to gangrene and provide an ecphylactic region in which microbes can grow without restraint. And immediate amputation is required because microbic growth commences without any delay. In conformity with this, not even under the pressure of events at the outset of the war, were wounded limbs sent down to the base unamputated.

In the recision and surgical cleansing of wounds the very same principles come into application. The surgeon here resects all those tissues which the projectile has lacerated, and which, since they have been deprived of their anti-bacterial defence, will become infected sloughs. Here also, if putrid infection and gas gangrene are to be forestalled there must be no delay. But at the same time, inasmuch as delay does not here as in the case of the mangled limb mean inevitable death, resection and surgical cleansing can, but of course only under penalty, be postponed or even omitted. As has already been seen at the outset of the war, the wounded were sent down to the base unoperated, and this was also the case afterwards, whenever after extensive military operations the medical units at the front were congested. The penalty that has to be paid for this is the development of gas gangrene in a certain proportion, and of putrid wound infections in nearly 100 per cent. of the severely wounded.

(2) When the devascularized parts have been resected there remain naked surfaces, and where the flaps have after amputation or after excision of tissues been loosely brought together there is also a wound cavity which fills up with effusion. On these naked tissues and in this effusion if proper measures are not taken microbes will establish themselves. To prevent this, steps must be taken to prevent desiccation—for desiccation closes down the capillary circulation and prevents the emigration and the functioning of leucocytes. Further, by bringing the walls of the wound everywhere in close contact, the leucocytes must be given free access to every part of the surface. Again, by bringing the walls of the wound in close contact, all dead spaces where serum might accumulate, must be obliterated. For accumulations of serum provide a nutrient medium for serophytes and a safe refuge from the leucocytes.

All this can be achieved by primary suture of the wound, but this procedure will not everywhere be applicable. For example, it may be impracticable to effect adequate cleansing of the wound; or there may not be sufficient skin covering available; or again the gap in the tissues may be of too large dimensions or too irregular to permit of its surfaces being accurately brought together.

Here it may parenthetically be observed that where the gap left by the resection operation is of immoderate size, suture may in certain cases be made feasible by resort to some artificial filling. Fillings of fat have sometimes been employed; and in the latter part of the war a filling of paraffin, bismuth and iodoform, proposed by Rutherford Morison as an antiseptic filling, was extensively employed. The faults of that particular filling were that the material though intended to operate as an antiseptic, was itself not sterile; and that it contained in the bismuth and the iodoform definitely poisonous elements.

Where primary suture is impracticable, the resected and surgically cleansed wound should, pending resort to secondary suture, be treated on essentially the same principles as the clean granulating wound: that is to say, the wound should always, as soon as the emigrated leucocytes cease to operate effectively against the microbes, be cleansed with physiological salt solution, and if sero-saprophytic microbes should put in an appearance, these should be eliminated by short applications of a 5 per cent. salt solution.

(3) Where, owing to stress of circumstances, resection and surgical cleansing of the wound have to be postponed, treatment should aim at preventing, as far as possible, the development of putrid infection in the devascularized tissues. What the French call a *pansement d'attente*—a *retardative* or *inhibitory* dressing—is then required.

At the outset of the war the ordinary but not clearly formulated notion about a retardative dressing was that it might be any kind of antiseptic dressing. Afterwards, when in view of the condition of the wounded arriving at the base it had been realized that all the ordinary kinds of antiseptic dressing were useless as inhibitory dressings, the accepted idea for improving them was to employ more and more concentrated antiseptics, and when, again, these more concentrated antiseptics proved unavailing it was suggested that viscid and very slowly soluble antiseptic pastes should be filled into the wounds. Those who witnessed the outbreak of gas gangrene cases which occurred in connexion with wounds choked with these pastes may well be said to have seen something of the savage revenge that Nature can take when fundamental physiological principles are flouted.

In reality, as suggested in a memorandum which was circulated in the war, what is really required is a *kataphylactic* dressing. Such a dressing would in the case of widely open wounds be gauze or lint soaked in 5 per cent. salt solution. backed with further dressings soaked in saturated 35 per cent. salt solution, and over these protective material. In the case of wounds with only small external openings, tubes might be introduced and through these 5 per cent. salt solution carried down repeatedly into the wound.

Such kataphylactic dressings might also with advantage be employed not only for the prevention of putrid infections in the devascularized tissues of the unresected wound, but also as a travelling dressing for wounds that have after resection and surgical cleansing to be transported from one hospital to another. They would prevent the desiccation of the wound and its invasion by sero-saprophytic microbes.

In conclusion, it may be pointed out that this question of retardative and travelling dressings, which has suffered from much neglect by reason of the fact that in this war surgical hospitals were established close behind the lines, is bound in future wars to make good its claim to attention. In wars of movement, and even in stationary wars in all times of pressure, there will only be one way of staving off putrid wound infections and gas gangrene and tetanus, and that will be by using an efficient retardative dressing.

CHAPTER III.

GAS GANGRENE.

A T the outbreak of the war, gas gangrene was a surgical complication of wounds which was known as a rare civilian disease with an uncertain ætiology. The experience of the South African War had not led military surgeons to foresee the possibility of a large number of cases and little was known of its treatment, or the prognosis, when cases occurred. In the early fighting around Mons and in the subsequent retreat there were not many cases, probably on account of the fine weather, open warfare, and the fact that many of the severely wounded could not be evacuated. It was not recognized as a complication of the first importance until the advance to the Marne and the fighting on the Aisne had allowed of the greater proportion of the wounded being continuously observed. At this period there were probably more cases of gas gangrene than at any subsequent time, and it is estimated by competent surgeons that it occurred in 10 to 12 per cent. of the wounded. The cause of this high incidence is probably to be found in several factors : first, the unknown danger of the condition and the comparative ignorance of its surgical prophylaxis ; second, the slow evacuations; and thirdly, the unexpected numbers of wounded, which led to the overcrowding of the evacuating units and the consequent delay in surgical intervention. In the middle of September 1914, the Army Medical Service realized the importance of the condition, and Dr. Weinberg, of the Pasteur Institute, was asked to see some of the cases. This was the beginning of his brilliant researches in the field of the pathogenic anaërobes.

Early in October the army moved to Flanders, and immediately Sir Anthony Bowlby and Sydney Rowland set out to investigate the condition. Their first work was to eliminate the possibility of the disease being a hospital infection. This point having been settled in the negative, it became of importance to ascertain and eliminate the predisposing causes.

The clinical phenomena are sufficiently described in the surgical volumes.* The factors bearing on the ætiology and the pathology of the disease, as elucidated during the war, are dealt with here.

---

* "Surgery of the War," Vol. I, Chap. vi.

Gas gangrene may be defined as a spreading necrosis of tissue, generally muscle tissue, with the formation of œdema and gas. As a result of the spreading necrosis, the muscle undergoes a variety of changes which are evidenced by variations in the colour and contractility of the tissue.

Ætiology.

The local conditions of the soil appear to influence the incidence. In the South African War, where there was a hot, dry climate and a sandy soil, the disease was rare ; on the Italian front and at Gallipoli gas gangrene was far less frequent than on the Western front, where the fighting was mainly on highly cultivated and fertile land.

There is also reason to believe that the prevailing weather has an influence on the incidence of the disease. During wet cold weather more cases occur than in dry cold weather or dry warm weather ; it is the prevalence of mud and the infiltration of the clothing with soil that is of importance in this connection.

The condition of the man when he receives his wound is also of moment. Men exhausted by a long march, hunger and cold, or those who are tired as a result of the long period of duty in the trenches or worn out from the results of the stress of a bombardment, are more likely to be the subjects of gangrene than troops who are fresh and well fed.

The type of the wound and the missile causing it are of importance. Deep wounds with much destruction of tissue and with no opportunity for drainage are those in which gangrene is almost certain to set in. Superficial wounds were not often the site of gangrene and deep wounds in which there was opportunity for free drainage of the discharge were less likely to be affected.

Wounds in which a large vessel is injured or severed or in which the blood supply is interfered with in any way, by extravasation of blood, by bruising of the tissues, or by pressure of a fragment of bone, are all favourable to the development of pathogenic anaërobes. The retention of a foreign body of any kind, whether it be the missile, or pieces of clothing carried in by it or particles of soil, will predispose a wound to gangrenous change. Large pieces of shell or bomb are more dangerous than bullets.

Certain areas of the body were soon recognized as being the favourite sites for the occurrence of gas gangrene. The buttock was probably the commonest of these, then the calf and the hamstrings. On the other hand, the trunk as a whole was a relatively rare situation for gas gangrene. It was never seen to occur in the scalp. The neck and the erector spinæ were rarely affected. The blood supply of the part was probably the most important ætiological factor. When an artery was severed or tied, especially a large artery, gangrene might confidently be expected. When the blood supply was interfered with by any other cause, whether by a tourniquet, by tight bandages, by ill-fitting splints, by extravasation of blood, or by exsanguination of the patient, gangrene was a probable complication.

The surgical factor in the disease is of the first importance. While early in the war the incidence was high—10 to 12 per cent. of the wounded, as already noted—in 1918 in a series of 40,000 wounded from two army fronts only 400 cases of gangrene were recorded. This change was no doubt due to many improvements, but probably to none so much as to the better understanding of the disease by the surgeons. When all wounds were opened, cleaned and drained the incidence decreased, but it was not until complete excision of wounds became a standard method of procedure that gangrene really ceased to be a serious menace. What may be called a surgical prophylaxis had been established, devitalized tissue was removed and a healthy surface left; a limb that experience had taught would be certainly useless and a danger to life, if gangrene supervened, was amputated before the onset of the process. Towards the end of hostilities the cases in which gangrene occurred were those in which the patient was suffering from such grave shock as to preclude surgical intervention, or those in which loss of blood from a severed vessel rendered the patient's resistance negligible.

Delay was also reduced to a minimum as the war progressed. Any form of delay in establishing the surgical prophylaxis predisposed to gangrene. This might be caused by large numbers of wounded, difficulties in collection and evacuation, long distance to the loading point and bad or congested roads The time factor when an infection is established is probably of greater importance in gas gangrene than in any other disease. It is difficult to determine when a wound infected with anaërobes becomes a gangrenous wound. A very large proportion of wounds are infected with anaërobic organisms, which may multiply in the wound but need not necessarily invade undamaged tissue. When the organisms merely proliferate in a wound and live on the dead tissue which has resulted from the passage of the missile and do not invade and destroy healthy tissue, gas gangrene cannot properly be said to have occurred. A case of gas gangrene might therefore be defined as one in which the tissues not already damaged by the passage of a projectile are invaded by organisms and death and putrefaction of previously undamaged tissue begins.

The incubation period of gas gangrene may vary between extreme limits. Definite gangrene with gas issuing from the wound and with a spreading œdema has been seen within five hours of the trauma, while, on the other hand, there are many recorded cases of gangrene having set in weeks or even months after receipt of the original wound. These latter cases have often been associated with some fresh operative procedure.

Varieties of the Disease.

There may be simple anaërobic infection of a wound in which the discharge is sanious and malodorous, the muscle slowly degenerating without any active invasion of undamaged tissue. This condition has been frequently mistaken for true gas gangrene during the war.

Sometimes an abscess in which gas develops will form around a small deeply imbedded projectile, and when the former is opened the odour is found to be typical of gas gangrene. The abscess contains pus, gas and necrotic tissue, but this form of gas gangrene is not dangerous and does not often give rise to the acutely spreading type.

The disease may be confined to a group of muscles without spreading to neighbouring groups ; for instance, the extensors of the foot may be affected or in the arm the triceps without any other muscle being invaded. Again, there may be massive gangrene of all the muscles of a limb ; this is most common when the main artery has been destroyed. Any of these types may be the starting point of a fulminating gangrene in which the rapidity of the process is terrifying. In these cases death may supervene within a few hours.

Pathology.

The starting point of gangrene is generally a wound, though definite metastatic cases have been described. The wound is infected by the passage of the missile with its accompanying layer of clothing or by particles of soil carried in with it. Damaged and dying muscle, with its blood supply impaired, makes an ideal ground for anaërobes, the available oxygen being probably quickly absorbed by the dying tissue. The organisms multiply and produce their specific toxins which diffuse through the neighbouring tissues in the œdema fluid collected around a focus of anaërobic infection, and the toxins devitalize more muscle, preparing a way for the spread of the bacteria. A localized focus thus develops into a widespread area of anaërobic infection, and along with the growth of the organisms goes the death and putrefaction of the tissue.

The production of œdema is a most striking characteristic of gas gangrene ; it has led some of the Continental authors to call the disease "gazœdème." The collection of œdema fluid always precedes the gangrenous change and organisms can be demonstrated in the fluid at levels where no gangrenous change has taken place in the muscle. The death and disintegration of the muscle is a later development and follows in the path of the œdema and bacterial invasion. Gas bubbles in the œdema fluid are seen when the process has become advanced ; they are generally not evident at the advancing edge of the fluid but are more obvious near the origin of the infection. The fluid spreads very rapidly in the subcutaneous tissues, and when the tension becomes great, it is common for it to form bullæ in the skin, which are generally hæmorrhagic and often contain the anaërobe causing the gangrene in a comparatively pure state. Without entering into the discussion as to whether gas gangrene is or is not a disease of muscle, it may be said that it is essentially a disease of muscle though theoretically it may arise in the absence of muscle tissue.

The changes in the muscle and skin have been described by Wallace. Pallor due to swelling of the deeper tissues is the first change noted in the skin ; this is succeeded by a dirty yellow discoloration, followed by the appearance of purple-red patches which become, as it were, more cyanotic. At this stage the œdema fluid which is flooding the deeper tissues may break through and produce the bullæ mentioned above. The purple discoloration is followed by yellow and then green changes with signs of liquefaction.

In the muscle colour changes are also present, brown or almost black and liquefying muscle being seen at the origin of the infection, and then a succession of colour changes from yellowish-red to purple and light red, and then to the normal muscle tint.

The microscopic appearance of the muscles is shown in the microphotographs. Figs. 1 and 2 have been taken from sections made by Professor J. Shaw Dunn from human tissue, while Figs. 3 to 12 are from rabbit's muscle and are shown as they confirm the appearances described by Shaw Dunn and McNee in human tissue. The first change in the muscle is a shrinking of the fibre and, as it were, a coagulation of the fibrils, the staining reaction of the fibre becomes more intense and it shrinks away from the enclosing sheath. In a normal fibre cut in cross-section there is a fragmentation of the

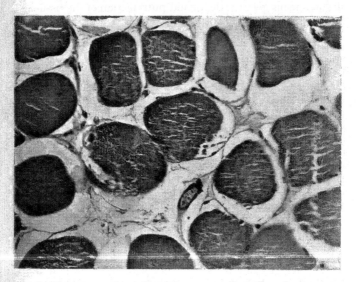

Fig. 1.—Human muscle at the extreme spreading edge of a gangrenous process. One fibre shows degeneration, apparent coagulation and shrinking from the sheath. The other fibres show the normal striation which occurs when muscle is cut in cross section.

protoplasm which is almost constantly present ; this fragmentation disappears and the fibre when cut in cross-section appears to be a homogeneous mass as soon as it is affected by the necrotic process. It is possible that the fibre is separated from its sheath by the spread of the œdema fluid, and it is sometimes possible to demonstrate œdema fluid in the space between the sheath and the muscle-fibre, near the spreading edge of the gangrene. At the periphery of the degenerating process the nuclei of the sheath are generally visible and have not lost their staining reaction, but as the process becomes more

advanced they lose this reaction.   On examination, the changes
in the fibres farther from the spreading edge become more
striking ; there is fragmentation of the fibres and what one
must believe to be early liquefaction.   The bacteria are
found around the fibres and in the space between the sheath
and the contracted fibre ; where the process is more advanced
the organisms begin to invade the fibres and grow within them.

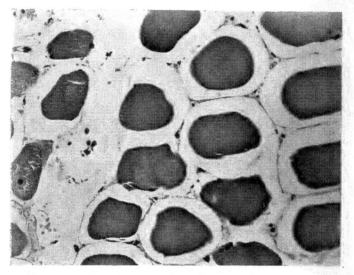

Fig. 2.—Section from the same piece of muscle nearer the site of the gangrene.
All the fibres have the appearance of coagulation and have separated from their
sheath.   The nuclei are still staining well.   Slight evidence of œdema fluid in
the space between the fibre and the sheath.

The process probably varies with the type of infection, and
the changes in colour and discoloration of the skin probably
also depend on the organisms that are causing the process.
    Distribution of the Organisms in the Body.—The bacteria
proliferate in the wound in very great numbers, and can
be seen in stained films and in sections of the muscle.   The
organisms can be demonstrated in the tissues well in advance
of the apparent gangrenous process.   The findings naturally
depend on the type of infection and the rapidity of the spread.
In infections with *Bacillus welchii* or *Vibrion septique* the
number of organisms is enormous ; on the other hand, in

some of the infections with *Bacillus œdematiens* the number of organisms is trivial in comparison with the lesions produced.

The question of the invasion of the blood stream is one of considerable difficulty. In *Vibrion septique* infection the blood stream may be invaded at an early period of the disease, and positive blood cultures have been obtained twenty-four hours before death and even in one case in which the patient recovered after an amputation, though his blood stream was invaded at the time of operation. Blood infection is common

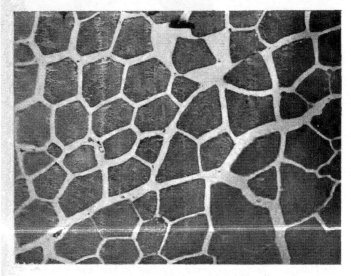

Fig. 3.—Normal rabbit muscle in cross section. The fibres show the same fragmentation in section as in the human fibres.

in *Vibrion* infections and probably it occurs at an earlier period of the disease than in the other types of infection. There is not, however, sufficient statistical evidence to state this as a fact. In *B. welchii* infection invasion of the blood stream is a late event and in some cases really terminal. Positive blood cultures have been obtained twelve and eight hours before death, but generally it is not until the last hour or two of life that blood culture is positive. During the last few hours it is, however, the rule. *B. œdematiens* is less common in the blood stream than either *B. welchii* or the *Vibrion septique*, and when it does occur it is generally terminal. *B. fallax* was obtained in blood culture on two occasions, once in a man forty-eight hours before death and in the other case as a terminal event. The reported cases of metastatic gas gangrene would make it probable that invasion of the blood stream is more common than is supposed. In most of the reported cases *B. welchii* has been found in the secondary focus.

Laboratory Diagnosis.

Laboratory diagnosis in its essentials is a question of recognizing the particular variety or varieties of pathogenic

Fig. 4.—Normal rabbit muscle in long section. Nuclei and cross striation well seen. Variable intensity in the staining of the fibres.

anaërobe which are germinating in the wound, in the muscle, or in the spreading edge of the œdema fluid. This has been the subject of an enormous amount of work and a not inconsiderable amount of controversy. The isolation of anaërobes in a pure state is a matter of great technical difficulty and the time taken precludes the use of the information gained being of practical value. In order to achieve any degree of success from the serum treatment of gas gangrene an early diagnosis of the main pathogenic anaërobes present is essential, and to obtain this information with rapidity and some degree of certainty the following procedure was found to be satisfactory in practice. It has been shown that animals protected with the specific antitoxins of the pathogenic anaërobes will survive inoculation with the corresponding live culture ; this holds good for mixed cultures and mixed

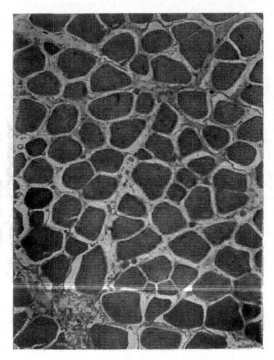

Fig. 5.—Rabbit muscle, early gangrenous change. Fibres have lost the fragmentation, become separated from the sheath, nuclei have failed to stain and there is evidence of œdema between sheath and fibre.

antitoxins as well as for pure strains. The practice, therefore, has been to inoculate a series of animals with a mixture containing antitoxin and emulsion of the muscle, œdema fluid, or fluid from the bullæ. A series of six animals is taken for one case, white mice being used to replace guinea-pigs if the latter are not available. One is inoculated with the material alone, one with the material and a suitable dose of *B. welchii* antitoxin, one protected with *Vibrion septique* antitoxin, one with *B. œdematiens* antitoxin, one with *B. welchii* and *Vibrion septique* antitoxin, and finally one with *B. welchii* and *B. œdematiens* antitoxin. The results can generally be read within about twelve hours ; for example, the animal protected against *B. welchii* and the *Vibrion septique* survives and the rest are dead. A Welch-vibrion mixed gangrene is assumed and the case is treated accordingly. When animals cannot be procured in sufficient quantities two will suffice—one protected against *B. welchii* and one against *B. welchii* and *Vibrion septique.*

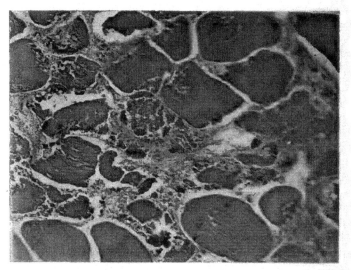

Fig. 6.—Rabbit muscle.   More advanced stage.   Œdema and early liquefaction of the muscle.

If both animals die it is probably a *B. œdematiens* gangrene, if neither die it is probably a *B. welchii* gangrene, and if the animal protected against *B. welchii* alone dies it is probably a *Vibrion septique* gangrene. There is the objection that from one part of a wound one may demonstrate one pathogenic anaërobe and in another part another variety of pathogenic anaërobe may be predominant. This objection will, however, arise in every form of diagnosis, whether cultural or serological. Considerable importance is, of course, attached to the area from which the sample is taken for inoculation into the animals ; tissue from the actively spreading edge of the gangrene, the fluid from the œdema at this site, and especially the fluid in bullæ, should be selected.

The examination of films is of limited value but is sometimes useful. It is occasionally possible to recognize the " bladder " and " citron " forms of the vibrion in a wound exudate and

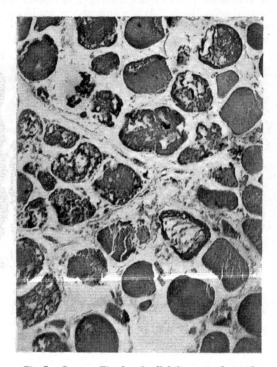

Fig. 7.—Same as Fig. 6, only slightly more advanced.

one may hazard a provisional diagnosis of a vibrion gangrene. In three out of nine cases in which the vibrion was incriminated the forms have been seen, twice in fluid from the wound and once in fluid from the bullæ. Films showing nothing but thick, short Gram-positive rods with very few sporing organisms suggest a Welch gangrene. It is rarely possible to determine the identity of *B. œdematiens* in films from a wound. The cultural diagnosis is long and full of pitfalls. *B. welchii* is easily cultivated, almost universally present in cases of gangrene, and is readily recognized by its colonies on plates grown in anaërobic conditions and its reaction on milk. Its presence should be presumed in all cases of gangrene and the attention of the bacteriologist should be directed to the detection of the other pathogenic anaërobes. *Vibrion septique* may be recognized by plating, but will more often be missed, and the only good method for its detection is animal

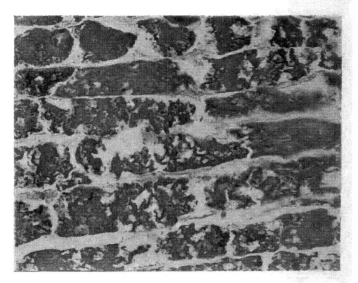

Fig. 8.—Long section of rabbit muscle.   Very advanced change.

inoculation.   The same applies to *B. œdematiens;* it may be obtained in culture by various methods, but none are so reliable as its isolation from the heart's blood or gelatinous œdema fluid of an inoculated animal.

An indication of the infection can be gained from the type of the œdema fluid and the appearance of the muscles. *Vibrion septique* produces a definite red change in the muscles and a rose-red œdema fluid full of organisms which may show definite motility. *B. œdematiens* generally produces a white, glairy, sticky œdema in which organisms often cannot be demonstrated. *B. welchii* infections are often associated with a bronzing of the skin and a brown or yellow discoloration of the muscles.

Serotherapy.

The treatment of the condition is essentially surgical, but there is definite evidence that much may be achieved in the future with the aid of antitoxic sera. It was not until the early months of 1918 that antitoxic sera were used by the British army, though they had been used by the French army surgeons for some time in a limited number of cases. In the winter of 1918, Major Bull of the United States army brought with him from America a small stock of *B. welchii* antitoxin, which

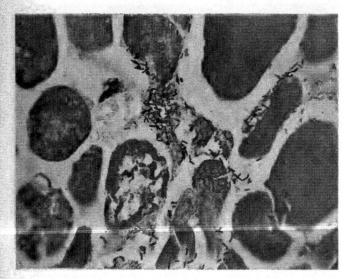

Fig. 9.—Moderately advanced change. The organisms are seen in the œdema fluid around the fibres. One fibre suggests liquefaction.

was used in a few experimental cases on the British front. It became evident that the serum was useful in certain cases, but that to obtain more general successes it would be necessary to use a serum which also contained antitoxins for the other pathogenic anaërobes. In April 1918 some serum was provided by Messrs. Burroughs & Wellcome for experimental use which contained *B. welchii* and *Vibrion septique* antitoxin. The titre of this serum was not high and the difficulties met with in its preparation were considerable. Greater quantities of serum were available throughout the summer and autumn months, but in none of these was the

titre as high as the manufacturers had hoped to obtain. The
results obtained with these sera were not striking but held out
the definite hope that with sera of greater potency and with
a better knowledge of the best means of administration they
would be of value.

In a few cases the results were so striking as to leave no
reasonable doubt that they were due to the serum treatment.
On the whole, however, the results were disappointing, perhaps
from lack of knowledge as to dosage and the best route of

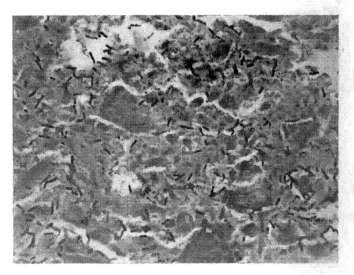

Fig. 10.—Structure completely lost.   Organisms stained in what appears to
be a mass of degenerating muscle and œdema fluid.

administration. The disease untreated is susceptible to such
unexpected developments that it is very difficult to judge
results.

For example, a man, apparently moribund, with a completely
gangrenous thigh and with gaseous œdema spreading up his
flank and obvious in the axilla, has been seen to recover
from the infection and survive an amputation of the thigh
performed some days later. In view of cases of this nature
it is always difficult to judge correctly the results of any line
of treatment, especially as the disease does not lend itself to
control experiments.

The treatment with serum should be instituted as early as possible and should be regarded rather as an aid to surgical treatment than as a treatment in itself. The surgeon may be assisted by the limitation of the spread of an infection which is in an early stage or in limiting the spread of an infection which it is surgically impossible to eradicate. For instance, after the removal of a group of gangrenous muscles the surgeon may fear the recurrence of the process in a neighbouring group, and in this case antitoxic sera may be of use in saving further

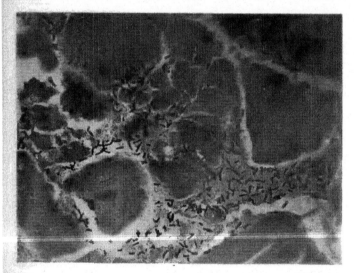

Fig. 11.—Organisms beginning to invade the degenerate muscle fibres.

removal or destruction of tissue. Or a large vessel may have to be tied in an infected wound and the condition thus made suitable for a violent fulminating gangrene. In this case the local infiltration of the tissues with antitoxic sera may save the limb. Consequently it is recommended that the serum should be given to all wounded men in whom there is gross injury to muscle, to all cases in which a large vessel is severed, to all cases who have been partially exsanguinated, and to all cases who are admitted in such a state of shock that they have to be allowed time to resuscitate before any operation is possible. In the first instance the serum given should be polyvalent with the weight thrown on *B. welchii* antitoxin.

In the event of expert bacteriological assistance not being available, the mixed serum should be continued, but in the event of a bacteriological diagnosis being possible the future treatment should be guided by the findings. In view of the almost invariable presence of *B. welchii*, it would never be safe to exclude *B. welchii* antitoxin at any time.

The value of monovalent sera is upheld by French authors and they are probably right. The route of administration is also of considerable importance ; the absorption of sera from

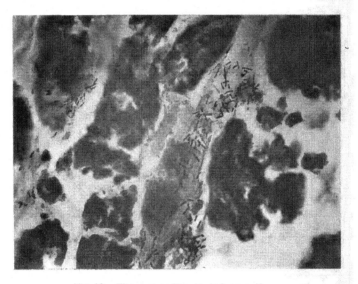

Fig. 12.—The same as Fig. 11, in long section.

the subcutaneous tissue is too slow. In cases of established gangrene, therefore, the serum should be administered intravenously and in large quantities. If the serum is well diluted in saline at the commencement (1 : 100) and the injection carried out slowly, the risk of anaphylactic shock is greatly diminished. The serum should also be used locally by injections into the muscles around the focus and by instillation into the gangrenous focus, as in the majority of cases the site of the gangrene is outside the reach of antitoxin circulating in the blood-stream. The points of injection of the serum may be so chosen as to set up a " barrage " between the spreading gangrenous process and the normal tissue. The injections should be repeated at frequent intervals, every few hours intravenously and at every dressing or operation locally. It is important to remember, however, that no serum treatment will replace surgical treatment. The object in view in treating a patient with antitoxic sera should be either to limit the spread of the process before or after operation or to render a deeply intoxicated patient a subject on whom surgical intervention may be attempted with some hope of success.

Prophylaxis.

In the summer of 1918 a considerable experiment on the serum prophylaxis of gas gangrene was attempted under the direction of Colonel S. L. Cummins, Adviser in Pathology to the British Army in France. Antitoxin for *B. welchii* was introduced into the anti-tetanic serum which was being used as a routine prophylactic for all the wounded. This serum was marked "A.T.S. & W." and was issued to alternate divisions over a large part of the front. The divisions lying between those to whom this special serum had been issued continued to use the ordinary A.T.S. The field medical cards of the wounded were marked at the time of injection "A.T.S. & W." or "A.T.S. & O.," as the case might be, and careful records were kept at the casualty clearing stations and base hospitals of the incidence of gangrene in both groups. The results of this experiment are given in the following table prepared by Colonel Cummins :—

	Number of Men.	Cases of Gangrene.	Deaths.	Morbidity per 1,000.	Mortality per cent. of cases.
Front Area.*					
A.T.S. & W.† ..	9,484	119	26	12·54	21·84
A.T.S. & O.‡ ..	13,303	156	38	11·72	24·35
At the Base.					
A.T.S. & W. ..	15,740	43	5	2·73	11·62
A.T.S. & O. ..	23,792	92	21	3·86	22·82

The experiment demonstrates what would naturally be expected, that the number of cases occurring in the casualty clearing stations was not influenced and that the incidence at the base was probably diminished. The period between

* Reports from casualty clearing stations to 20th September, 1918.
† A.T.S. & W. = antitetanic serum and antitoxin for *B. welchii*.
‡ A.T.S. & O. = ordinary antitetanic serum.

the administration of the prophylactic serum and the recording of the presence of gangrene at a casualty clearing station would often be a matter of only a few hours, and also those cases which had been lying out, or whose evacuation had been delayed owing to military conditions, and in whom the gangrenous process had probably begun at the time of the injection of the serum, are included in the casualty clearing station records. On the other hand, the mortality in cases arising in base hospitals was reduced by about 50 per cent. It must also be remembered that only one of the pathogenic organisms was prophylactically dealt with in this series.

It is consequently believed that in prophylaxis the most promising results in the use of antitoxic sera for gas gangrene will be obtained. For this purpose a combined antitoxin should be available, which should contain antitoxin for tetanus, *B. welchii, B. œdematiens* and *Vibrion septique.* The titre of the serum should be as high in antitoxic units as it is possible to make it. The serum should be used as soon as possible after the wound has been inflicted ; it should be injected intramuscularly and, in the severely wounded, locally as well.

This should be regarded as a normal routine for all wounded, and when the patient is admitted to the casualty clearing station the case should again be considered with a view to the possible occurrence of gangrene, and if the surgeon thinks it advisable a further series of injections of the prophylactic serum should be made at the time of operation.

It is further suggested that all men who are admitted to the resuscitation wards should receive further injections, as should also all men with severed vessels or in whom the vessels are tied at operation.

CHAPTER IV.

BACTERIOLOGY OF ANAËROBIC INFECTIONS.

ANAËROBIC bacteria have been the subject of a considerable amount of study from the time of Pasteur's epoch-making discovery, in 1861, of organisms able to live in the absence of free oxygen; nevertheless, no department of bacteriology presented a more unsatisfactory or confusing body of knowledge when the moment came to turn the available information to practical account. Excellent work had been done by many investigators, more notably by Pasteur, Koch and Gaffky, Gohn and S. Sachs and Novy, working with *Vibrion septique* and malignant œdema; and by Welch, Fraenkel, Achalme and Veillon, working with *Bacillus welchii*. *B. chauvoei* had been studied by Chauveau, Kitisato, Grassberger and Schattenfroh, Leclainch and Vallée, and others. Tissier and Martelly had made valuable contributions to the whole subject in their interesting work on the putrefaction of meat, and von Hibler had made an attempt to classify and describe the pathogenic anaërobes in his monograph of 1908. In spite of the value of much of this pioneer work, the peculiar difficulties inherent in the study of the anaërobes produced extremely conflicting results so that the literature abounded in contradictions and obscurities.

The extreme urgency of the problem which arose in 1914 with the occurrence of many cases of gas gangrene and the wealth of material available, brought about a fresh study of the whole group, as a result of which many of the obscurities have been cleared up and a substantial agreement in all the matters of any serious importance has been reached by a number of independent workers in France, England and America. This mass of experience was embodied in a report to the Medical Research Committee (No. 39), which in conjunction with the valuable monograph of Weinberg and Séguin, " La Gangrène Gazeuse," may be said to afford a statement of the question of the anaërobic infection of wounds as it stood in 1919 at the end of the war. It is possible, therefore, as the outcome of the researches of many individual investigators, to give a brief account and a classification of the anaërobes concerned in the infection of war wounds which expresses a general consensus of experience and opinion.

H

The explanation of the earlier conflict in the results of highly competent investigators is due to the great technical difficulties in obtaining the anaërobes in pure cultures. This is the bitter experience of every worker in this field of investigation, and it is only by the clear and frank recognition of this that any useful contribution can be made to the study of the anaërobes.

Anaërobes infecting Wounds.—Among the relatively long list* of anaërobes that are found infecting wounds a distinction may be drawn between those liable to set up gas gangrene with symptoms of generalized intoxication and those whose presence causes only local infection but whose action may be contributory to the conditions of gas gangrene and tetanus. It must be borne in mind that the number of the organisms not definitely pathogenic is very considerable and that they may be present in any combination. They may seriously affect the local conditions, especially in gangrenes of late occurrence and in the heavy anaërobic infections described in the previous chapter, which do not proceed to an acutely spreading gangrene. Anaërobes, including *B. tetani* and all the highly pathogenic species, may be recovered from wounds which are in good condition and in which there are no signs of gangrene or tetanus. This saprophytic method of existence within the wound, while not in itself a serious condition, may give rise at any time to acute gas gangrene or tetanus. It is to infections of this nature that late gas gangrene supervening upon surgical treatment is probably due.

(1) *Organisms immediately concerned with Gas Gangrene.*

B. welchii—Migula 1900. (Synonyms: Bacillus of Achalme, 1891; *B. aerogenes capsulatus*, Welch and Nuttall, 1892; *B. phlegmonis emphysematosae*, E. Fraenkel, 1893; *B. perfringens*, Veillon and Zuber, 1898; *B. enteritidis sporogenes*, Klein, 1895.)

Vibrion septique — Pasteur and Joubert, 1877. (Synonym: *B. oedematis maligni*, Koch, 1881.)

B. œdematiens—Weinberg and Séguin, 1915.

B. fallax—Weinberg and Séguin, 1915.

B. histolyticus—Weinberg and Séguin, 1916.

B. egens—Stoddard, 1919.

B. tumefaciens—Wilson.

---

* It is not claimed that the list here given is absolutely exhaustive in the case of the non-pathogenic bacteria; it does, however, give all the pathogenic anaërobes recognized and isolated and all the non-pathogenic types found with any frequency.

(2) *Anaërobes infecting Wounds whose Action may be contributory to the condition of Gas Gangrene.*

B. *sporogenes*—Metchnikoff, 1908.

B. *parasporogenes*—(Type XII of McIntosh, 1917).

B. *tertius*—Henry, 1917. (Rodella's Bacillus III, von Hibler's Bacillus IX.)

B. *cochlearius*—Douglas, Fleming, and Colebrook. (Type III C of McIntosh, 1917.)

B. *tetanomorphus*—(Type IX entitled B. *pseudotetanus* of McIntosh and Fildes.)

B. *aerofetidus*—Weinberg and Séguin, 1916.

B. *bifermentans*—Tissier and Martelly, 1902.

B. *sphenoides*—Douglas, Fleming, and Colebrook.

B. *multifermentans tenalbus*—Stoddard, 1919.

The classification and the cultural characters of the species here named are set out in the following extract from Report 39 of the Medical Research Committee :—

" Morphology.

The first subdivision is based upon morphology and the next upon cultural reactions. The production of characteristic toxins is a quality which is valuable in classification where available, and serological reactions form a final series of distinctions which may or may not be of specific value.

The anaërobes may be divided into three groups upon their morphology :—

(a) Organisms with oval spores which are central or subterminal in position.

(b) Organisms with oval spores which are strictly terminal in position.

(c) Organisms with spherical spores which are strictly terminal in position

Cultural Characteristics.

Further divisions can be made upon cultural reactions, such as the capacity for decomposing protein, carbohydrates, and alcohols.

All organisms have a certain capacity for attacking proteins and splitting sugars, but these characters have to be sufficiently marked to be readily appreciable under the test-tube conditions of artificial cultivation, and have to be somewhat arbitrarily defined for the purposes of classification.

In the case under consideration proteolytic characters are judged by the capacity of liquefying coagulated serum and gelatine. In working with the anaërobes the gelatine test has been used in the special manner first employed by Runeberg, and differs from that generally employed in bacteriology. Owing to the unsatisfactory amount of growth of the anaërobes obtained at 25° C., the inoculated gelatine stab is incubated at 37° C. for forty-eight hours under anaërobic conditions, thereafter it is cooled by being placed in a beaker of cold water and the reading taken. In the case of the saccharolytic organisms the fermentation is recognized by a definite capacity for producing acid or acid and gas in sugar-containing media.

Subsections based upon these characters can be arranged as follows :—

A. Organisms showing proteolytic and saccharolytic properties.

B. Organisms showing proteolytic properties only.

C. Organisms showing saccharolytic but no proteolytic properties.

D. Organisms showing no obvious proteolytic or saccharolytic properties.

Subsection A would be subdivided into :—

A1. Organisms predominatingly proteolytic with, however, a restricted but definite capacity of fermenting certain carbohydrates.

A2. Organisms predominatingly saccharolytic possessing, however, in addition, slight proteolytic properties as shown by the liquefaction of gelatine.

The criterion in accordance with which an anaërobe is here classified as a predominatingly proteolytic organism is the capacity to produce liquefaction of coagulated serum.

The accompanying table shows the arrangement of the organisms classified in these terms.

CLASSIFICATION.

Morphology	Both proteolytic and saccharolytic properties.		Slight proteolytic but no saccharolytic properties.	Saccharolytic but no proteolytic properties.	Neither saccharolytic nor proteolytic properties.
	Proteolytic properties predominating. Coagulated serum and gelatine are liquefied.	Saccharolytic properties predominating. Serum not liquefied; gelatine liquefied.	Serum not liquefied. Gelatine liquefied.	Neither serum nor gelatine liquefied.	Neither serum nor gelatine liquefied.
Central or subterminal spore.	B. sporogenes. B. histolyticus. B. aerofetidus. B. bifermentans. —	B. welchii. Vibrion septique. B. chauvoei. B. oedematiens. B. botulinus.	— — — —	B. fallax. B. butyricus. B. multifermentans tenalbus. —	— — — —
Oval terminal spore ..	—	—	—	B. tertius.	B. cochlearius.
Spherical terminal spore.	—	— —	B. tetani. —	B. tetanoides. B. sphenoides.	— —

TABLE OF THE CHARACTERS OF THE ANAËROBES ISOLATED FROM WOUNDS.

Name.	Motility.	Spores.	Surface Colony.	Colony in Agar shake.	Cultural Reactions in				Animal Reactions.	Remarks.
					Milk.	Meat.	Coagulated Serum.	Gelatine.		
B. sporogenes.	+	Oval: central or subterminal. Spores are readily formed in all media; they are very resistant to heat.	Woolly colony with tangled filaments at the periphery.	Opaque woolly colony.	Precipitation of casein which is later digested.	Gas: blackening; digestion with very putrid odour.	Liquefaction.	Liquefaction.	Not pathogenic for laboratory animals: large doses may produce local necrosis: a few strains are said to be pathogenic for guinea-pigs.	Non-specific toxic products are produced in culture media.
B. parasporogenes.	+	As for B. sporogenes.	Round and opaque. Occasionally the margin shows woolly filaments later.	Opaque colonies lenticular or irregular.	As for B. sporogenes	.	.	}	Not pathogenic for laboratory animals.	
B. histolyticus.	+	Oval; usually subterminal. Spores are readily formed in all media.	Flat, delicate colonies with crenated edges.	Arborescent coral-like colonies, with fine woolly ends to the branches.	Digested.	Digested. Tyrosin crystal produced.	Liquefied.	Liquefied.	Strains vary in pathogenicity. Pathogenic strains produce hæmorrhagic liquefaction of the soft parts of the limb injected; death occurs in 24 to 48 hours.	Specific toxin produced.
B. aerofœtidus.	Slight.	Oval and subterminal. Spores are not readily formed in any medium.	Round, transparent, with feathery processes.	Small irregular masses.	Clot and gas in 24 to 48 hours, later, a certain amount of digestion.	Putrid odour; medium becomes red then blackens.	Liquefied.	Liquefied.	Not pathogenic.	

TABLE OF THE CHARACTERS OF THE ANAËROBES ISOLATED FROM WOUNDS—cont.

Name.	Mo-tility.	Spores.	Surface Colony.	Colony in Agar shake.	Cultural Reactions in					Remarks.
					Milk.	Meat.	Coagulated Serum.	Gela-tine.	Animal Reactions.	
B. bifer-mentans.	±	Spores are usually central but may also be subterminal. They are readily formed in all media.	Round or crenated.	Lenticular or irregular but without filamentous outgrowths	Precipitation of casein which is later digested.	Gas: blackening; digestion with putrid odour.	Liquefied.	Lique-fied.	Not pathogenic.	Morphology is characteristic. Stout rod often growing in chains. The spores do not distend the rod.
B. welchii.	—	Large oval with slightly flattened ends; central or subterminal. Spores formed only in sugar free media rich in protein, such as coagulated serum, alkaline egg fluid and casein broth.	Round with smooth edges.	Opaque and lenticular.	Stormy fermentation: very rapid clotting with evolution of gas; clot torn with gas: acid reaction.	Gas: pink colour: sharp butyric acid odour; no blackening.	Not lique-fied: spores formed; filaments and in-volution types occur.	Lique-fied.	Pathogenic for guinea-pigs, pigeons and mice: less so for rabbits. Spores not formed in the animal; no long filaments on surface of liver. Many strains are of low pathogenicity.	Produces a specific soluble toxin.
Vibrion septique.	+	Spores are formed readily in all media: they are central or subterminal.	Delicate and faintly opalescent: round sometimes with indented or crenated edges.	Semi-transparent with fern-like branchings.	Acid and clot: some gas may be formed: slow reaction, 3 to 6 days.	Gas: pink colour which fades later: no blackening.	Not liquefied: variations in morphology—citrons, navicular types, club-shaped forms, &c. may be developed.	Lique-fied.	Pathogenic for guinea-pigs, pigeons, rabbits, and mice: long threads are formed on the peritoneal surface of the liver. Citron and navicular types, &c. may be seen in the tissues post mortem.	Produces a specific soluble toxin.
B. chau-voei.	+	Spores are formed readily. They are central or subterminal.	Delicate round or with spreading indented edges.	Colony small composed of minute club-like filaments.	Acid: clot in 3 to 6 days: some gas may be evolved.	Gas: pink colour which fades later: no blackening.	Not lique-fied: navicular forms, &c. may be developed.	Lique-fied.	Pathogenic for mice and guinea-pigs: rabbits are relatively insusceptible: long filaments are not formed on the peritoneal surface of the liver. Navicular types may be seen in the tissues post mortem.	Distinguished from Vibrion septique by sugar reactions, specific agglutinins and specific soluble toxin.

TABLE OF THE CHARACTERS OF THE ANAËROBES ISOLATED FROM WOUNDS—cont.

Name.	Motility.	Spores.	Surface Colony.	Colony in Agar shake.	Cultural Reactions in				Animal Reactions.	Remarks.
					Milk.	Meat.	Coagulated Serum.	Gelatine.		
B. œdematiens.	Only motile under strictly anaerobic conditions.	Spores formed in all media: oval with slightly flattened ends: central or subterminal.	Flat and inclined to be confluent, growing out in finger-like processes.	Transparent snow-flake colonies, sometimes with more opaque centres.	Acid after 4 to 6 days. Slight clotting after some weeks.	Gas: no blackening; pink colour at first, then bleached.	Not liquefied.	Liquefied.	Pathogenic for mice, guinea-pigs, and pigeons; produces gelatinous oedema. Does not usually form spores in animal body, no long filaments on liver.	Produces specific soluble toxin.
B. botulinus.	+	Spores are formed but not readily: they are oval and subterminal.	Flat, round, or irregular.	Semi-opaque, bi-convex, or kidney-shaped: older colonies may send out irregular projections.	No change in medium, growth is scanty and may fail.	Poor growth: medium is improved by addition of glucose: no blackening.	Not liquefied.	Liquefied.	Pathogenic for laboratory animals.	Produces specific soluble toxin. This organism is difficult to cultivate upon artificial media. Growth occurs between 18°C. and 35°C.
B. fallax.	+	Spores are not formed readily, but do occur in small numbers in meat and coagulated serum: they are oval and subterminal.	Round or crenated and slightly granular, occasionally containing a bubble.	Lenticular or irregular.	Acid: clot after 3 to 7 days.	Gas: pinkish colour; no blackening.	Not liquefied.	Not liquefied.	When recently isolated some strains are pathogenic for guinea-pigs, the pathogenicity disappears upon cultivation.	This organism is sometimes recovered from the blood of the patient in cases of gas gangrene. Produces a soluble toxin.
B. butyricus.	+	Oval spores usually central, but may also be subterminal.	Flat and irregular in shape.	Irregular or lenticular.	Firm acid clot in 24 hours.	Gas: no blackening.	Not liquefied.	Not liquefied.	Not pathogenic.	
B. multifermentans tenalbus.	+	Spores are central or subterminal.	Round with slightly irregular edges.	Irregular or lenticular colonies are opaque.	Acid and clot.	Gas: no blackening.	Not liquefied.	Not liquefied.	Not pathogenic.	

TABLE OF THE CHARACTERS OF THE ANAËROBES ISOLATED FROM WOUNDS—*cont.*

Name.	Motility.	Spores.	Surface Colony.	Colony in Agar shake.	Cultural Reactions in				Animal Reactions.	Remarks.
					Milk.	Meat.	Coagulated Serum.	Gelatine.		
B. tertius.	— or only very faintly motile.	Spores formed readily: they are oval and strictly terminal.	Round and opalescent with slightly crenated edges. May be granular when older.	Irregular or lenticular: opaque.	Acid and later, clot.	Gas; no blackening.	Not liquefied.	Not liquefied.	Not pathogenic.	This organism is actively saccharolytic which distinguishes it from *B. cochlearius.*
B. cochlearius.	+	Spores are formed but not readily: they are oval and strictly terminal.	Round or slightly crenated glass-clear colonies.	Lenticular.	No change.	Little gas; no blackening.	Not liquefied.	Not liquefied.	Not pathogenic.	Growth is not prolific in pure culture.
B. tetani.	+	Spherical and strictly terminal.	Flat and delicate with projections growing out at the edges.	Branching and flocculent.	No change.	Gas; no blackening.	Not liquefied.	Liquefied.	Pathogenic.	Produces a specific soluble toxin.
B. tetanoides.	+	Spherical and terminal.	Flat with slightly crenated edges.	Irregular but do not grow out into branches.	No change.	Gas; no blackening.	Not liquefied.	Not liquefied.	Not pathogenic.	
B. sporoides.	+	Spherical and terminal when fully developed.	Round, usually with smooth edges.		Acid and sometimes a soft clot.	Little gas; no change in colour.	Not liquefied.	Not liquefied.	Not pathogenic.	There is a characteristic wedge-shaped appearance in the sporing state.

It will be noted that for the sake of greater completeness and for purposes of comparison *B. chauvoei*, *B. botulinus* and *B. butyricus* have been included, although they are not apparently found in wounds. *B. chauvoei* has been described from wounds in man in Germany, but there is some doubt as to whether the organism is really *B. chauvoei* or *Vibrion septique*. *B. chauvoei* was never recovered from wounds in France by either British or French workers, although diligent search was made for it.

The methods of dealing bacteriologically with conditions presenting the possibility of such a number of different organisms depends upon a sound and flexible technique and a clear understanding of the significant reactions of the various types. A good method of anaërobic culture is essential, but this was achieved in practice by the most varied means including the original deep stab culture used by the earliest workers in this section of bacteriology. Any method or apparatus which produces good conditions of anaërobiosis can be used with success.

Surface culture on serum agar slopes or plates combined with growth in chopped meat medium or in Tarozzi tubes (*i.e.*, broth with a piece of fresh tissue) forms a good starting point. The results so obtained have to be replated repeatedly and controlled in every way that the ingenuity of the worker can suggest, and recourse may be had to differential heating of sporing cultures, animal passage through normal animals or through those protected with immune sera and to growth upon selective media. The strain finally obtained should be grown out several times in succession on a range of media that will reveal the important cultural characteristics. The range found useful and upon which the classification is based consists of the following :—

Milk.

Meat. (This medium must be autoclaved with the greatest care.)

Coagulated serum.

Gelatine.

The sugar media made by adding 1 per cent. of the requisite sugar to Coles' casein broth are also useful in certain cases. Vigilant care is required in the attempt to obtain pure cultures, and a critical attitude towards a supposedly pure culture is necessary.

In dealing with wound material there are certain useful indications of which advantage should be taken. In rapid

I

cases of gas gangrene arising shortly after the occurrence of the wound the anaërobic flora is less complex than in cases occurring at a later period. The saprophytic types are less prevalent in these early acute conditions and if the sample is taken from the spreading edge of the gangrene or from bullæ, a direct and immediate plating on to serum agar slopes may, in favourable cases, reveal the more important organisms which are actually causing the gangrene. The material should also be grown in meat, and blood cultures may be made in this medium. In the hands of an experienced worker, cultural methods will very generally disclose the responsible anaërobes in material of this kind taken under suitable conditions from the actual edge of the gangrene, but none of these purely cultural methods are sufficiently rapid to be of any practical service to the surgeon in the really urgent choice of the antisera to use after the initial polyvalent dose. The method described in the previous chapter should be used whenever possible.* It has been proved to be of great value under field conditions, and also in the laboratory it is a rapid and efficient means of orientation when an unknown culture or material containing pathogenic anaërobes from any source is brought for examination. This method is also of great assistance in sifting out the various anaërobes contained in earth, etc.

The following are the salient features of the more important types of infective anaërobes :—

B. welchii.—This organism is extremely prevalent in wounds, often without producing any serious disturbance ; on the other hand, it may occasion acute gangrene with general symptoms of intoxication. It is so frequently present that it would rarely be safe to consider that *B. welchii* is absent from a gangrene in which the prime causal agent was *Vibrion septique* or *B. œdematiens* (see p. 90). *B. welchii* is non-motile, it grows with great rapidity in culture media, and produces considerable quantities of gas and acid in the presence of any fermentable sugar. The organism does not form spores in media containing sugar and such cultures are apt to die in the course of a few days. Spores are formed in protein media free from sugar.

Guinea-pigs, pigeons, and mice are susceptible to infection, but rabbits offer considerable resistance ; they can, however, be infected with massive doses. The pathogenicity of individual strains varies within wide limits, many being of very low virulence for laboratory animals. Washed bacilli suspended

---

* *See* Chapter III, pp. 87 and 88.

in saline are non-pathogenic. This is due to the fact that they are deprived of the soluble toxin contained in the broth in which the bacteria have been grown; the toxin causes necrotic changes in the tissues which enable the organisms to proliferate. It must be remembered that the inoculation of cultures of the anaërobes into animals does not repeat the conditions of natural infections. In nature the organisms are introduced in the form of spores, and their power of proliferation is dependent upon a very complex series of conditions. Ultimately

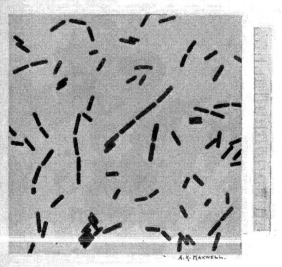

Fig. 1.—*B. welchii.* Film preparation, 18-hour-old culture on alkaline egg.

the anaërobic organism produces its toxins in the living body, and so brings about a state of affairs that can be compared with the experimental infection but the initiation of the process is fundamentally different.

The lesions produced in guinea-pigs by the inoculation of a lethal dose of a living culture of *B. welchii* (0·1 to 1 c.c., according to virulence and condition of culture) into the muscles of the thigh are as follows: An extensive œdema occurs within a few hours of the injection, which may spread over the whole abdomen and into the axillary region. The animal usually dies within twenty-four to forty-eight hours, but occasional spontaneous recoveries do occur even with doses which are lethal for the majority of animals of the same weight. Sublethal doses produce lesions of greater or less severity from which the animals recover.

Post-mortem examination shows an extensive œdema slightly blood-stained, sometimes containing oily droplets. There may be some gas in the tissues, and the muscles affected have the appearance of being digested. They are soft and friable in consistency and of a pale pink colour. The bacteria invade the tissues and may be found in great numbers even in situations considerably removed from the site of inoculation.

Vibrion septique.—The morphology of this organism shows a wide range of forms according to the conditions of culture.

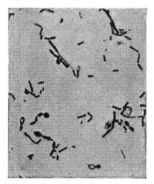

Fig. 2.—*Vibrion septique.* 48 hours' growth on serum agar. (x 1,000.)

Fig. 3.—*Vibrion septique.* Smear from peritoneum of mouse. (x 500.)

In addition to the rods with or without central or subterminal spores, such types as deeply staining bulb-like forms often growing in short chains, bladder-shaped individuals and "citron" or "navicular" types may be found. These last are pale citron or boat-shaped bodies with deeper staining points at one or both extremities. These various appearances may be seen in films made directly from infected tissues, blister fluid, etc.

Pigeons, guinea-pigs, mice, rabbits, and dogs are all susceptible to infection with *Vibrion septique.* If a lethal dose (0·01 to 0·5 c.c., according to virulence and condition of culture) of a living culture of *Vibrion septique* is injected into the muscles of the thigh of a guinea-pig, the animal dies in twelve to twenty-four hours with symptoms of œdema and gas in the tissues.

Spontaneous recovery in guinea-pigs which have become infected with *Vibrion septique* does not occur. Sublethal doses produce no symptoms whatever.

The *post-mortem* appearances consist in an extensive blood-stained œdema, gas is developed in the areolar tissue around the affected muscles and pockets of gas are found in the groin and axilla. The muscles involved show a very deep red colour; there is no putrid odour. The bacteria proliferate

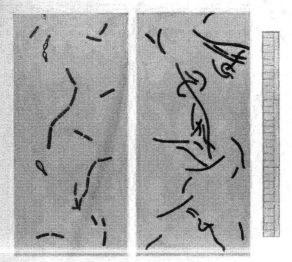

Fig. 4.—*B. œdematiens.*
Egg broth culture.

Fig. 5.—*B. œdematiens.*
From surface colony.

actively and may be found in very large numbers in the muscles and exudates. The peritoneal surface of the liver shows long snake-like filaments which are of diagnostic importance.

B. œdematiens.—This organism which was discovered by Weinberg and Séguin in cases of gas gangrene is closely allied to the *B. œdematis maligni II*, described by Novy in 1894. It is a large rod frequently curved, and forms spores which are large and slightly flattened at the ends.

Guinea-pigs, rats, mice, and rabbits are all susceptible to infection. In guinea-pigs a spreading gelatinous œdema is produced and death occurs within twenty-four to forty-eight hours. After death the muscles at the site of inoculation are red. There is as a rule very little gas in the tissues. The œdema is extensive and gelatinous ; it is usually quite colour-less, but if the infection has proceeded very rapidly it may be coloured a faint pink. The bacteria may be found at the site of inoculation but do not invade the œdema fluid and tissues to anything like the extent found in infections with *B. welchii* and *Vibrion septique*.

B. histolyticus.—This organism has not been described as wholly responsible for any case of gas gangrene, but its action has been recognized by Weinberg and Séguin as a serious factor in certain cases, and its capacity for digesting living tissue is so striking that it is more justly ranged among the pathogenic anaërobes than among the purely saprophytic forms. The cultures autolyze very early and observations

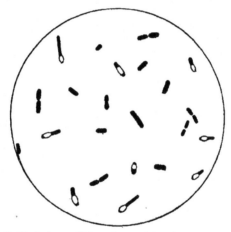

Fig. 6.—*B. histolyticus.*   16 hours' growth in alkaline meat.   (x 1,500.)

and experiments with this organism should be carried out after fourteen to eighteen hours' growth. The strains vary in pathogenicity for guinea-pigs, some producing serious lesions involving the actual digestion and diffluence of the tissues of the injected limb and culminating in the death of the animal, while other strains produce only transitory effects and are very slightly pathogenic.

B. fallax.—This organism occurs in infected wounds, and is found in certain cases of gas gangrene. Some of the strains are pathogenic for laboratory animals when first isolated but fail to produce any symptoms after further cultivation.

B. egens.—There is some doubt as to whether this is really a separate species. It has been found that *B. welchii* antiserum will protect a susceptible animal (guinea-pig) against this organism. The tendency is to consider it a *B. welchii* strain with a feeble capacity for fermenting carbohydrates.

B. tumefaciens.—The account of this organism is not perfectly clear. *B. œdematiens* antiserum even in quite small doses (0·01 c.c.) neutralizes its toxic and pathogenic action in susceptible animals. It is improbable that it is a new species ; one can hardly avoid the suggestion that the pathogenic element is *B. œdematiens*, the cultural discrepancies being due to impurity in the strain.

Of the saprophytic bacteria, *B. sporogenes* should be noted because of its all-pervasive character ; it is present in a very large proportion of all war wounds. It is a serious contributory factor in certain gangrenes and in heavy anaërobic infections, and in laboratory experience its presence is found to increase the pathogenicity of the pathogenic anaërobes, notably of *B. welchii*. The non-specific growth products of this species are found to be toxic. The filtered fluid from a six to seven day culture in chopped meat

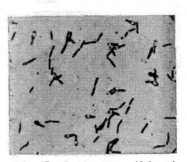

Fig. 7.—*B. sporogenes.* 48 hours' growth on agar (x 1,000.)

medium, injected into the peritoneum of guinea-pigs in doses of 1 c.c. and upwards, according to the nature of the strain used, will cause immediate symptoms of intoxication followed by death. If the animal does not succumb in the course of the first few minutes it recovers completely. Barger and Dale considered that this toxic substance was a volatile poison probably of the nature of an ammonium base. McIntosh and Fildes, as a result of a series of experiments, suggested that ammonium sulphide which is produced in considerable quantities in cultures of *B. sporogenes* was probably of importance in producing the symptoms.

B. sporogenes is of particular importance in the bacteriology of the anaërobes as it is the most frequent and most troublesome contaminator of anaërobic cultures. It is present to begin with in nearly all the material from which any anaërobe can be cultivated, it is extraordinarily tenacious of life, and its capacity for slow proliferation without becoming obviously manifest for long periods renders it difficult to detect. It grows over a very large range of temperature and has a remarkable capacity for entering into close microbic associations with a number of different organisms. These mixed cultures may behave with the most deceptive stability for months. This organism has indeed been the source of much of the confusion existing in regard to the cultural characters of many of the anaërobic species.

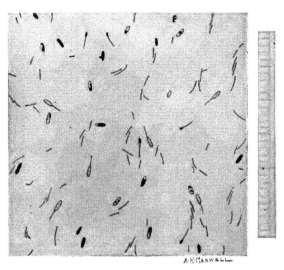

Fig. 8.—*B. tertius.*   5-year-old colony on alkaline egg agar.   (x 1,300.)

B. tertius is remarkable because of its frequent presence in wounds, and on account of its striking appearance.

B. cochlearius is interesting as a very frequent contaminator of tetanus cultures, and on account of the great difficulty of isolating it in pure culture.

B. tetanomorphus resembles *B. tetani* closely in morphology but is entirely without toxic effect and differs from it in cultural characters; it is found in frequent association with *B. tetani*.   *B. bifermentans* in the non-sporing state bears a morphological resemblance to *B. welchii*.   *B. multifermentans tenalbus* was only rarely found in wounds, but it is of particular interest in showing a morphological resemblance to *Vibrion septique*; it is a non-pathogenic organism.

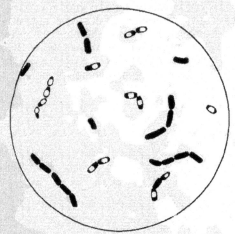

Fig. 9.—*B. bifermentans.* 48-hour growth on meat medium. (x 1,500.)

Serological Reactions.

Agglutinins.—Agglutinins may be called forth in the blood of rabbits by the intravenous injection of bacteria belonging to most of the anaërobic species; notable exceptions are, however, *B. welchii* and *B. tertius.* A great deal of interesting information can be obtained from the study of agglutination reactions of anaërobes, but as a practical means of diagnosis the method is not applicable for a number of reasons. In the first place, in the case of many organisms, such as *Vibrion septique*, *B. tetani* and *B. sporogenes* the agglutination reactions are ultra-specific and the species subdivide into serological groups. With *Vibrion septique* only cultures in a satisfactory state of purity are agglutinable. Some species, notably *B. œdematiens*, appear only to be agglutinated by the homologous serum, and in the case of this organism there is a marked tendency to auto-agglutination. The agglutination reaction has to be taken on its merits in the case of each species. In general it may be said that positive results are of value in a rapid diagnosis, but a negative result requires such an amount of critical investigation to arrive at a decision as to whether it is the outcome of an ultra-specific serological reaction, an impure culture, or a specifically different agglutinin, that the test is unsuitable for practical purposes of routine diagnosis.

Antitoxic Sera.—During the course of the war anti-toxic sera were made against *B. welchii, Vibrion septique, B. œdematiens* and *B. histolyticus.* These sera proved to be of service in treating cases of gas gangrene, as already noted,* but in any attempt to assess their therapeutic value it must be understood that the samples actually used had not attained the full titre possible and that the whole work was still very incomplete at the conclusion of the war. It will be seen that the amount of protection demonstrable by laboratory experiment compares not unfavourably with that of the well-established antitoxic sera such as *Diphtheria* and *Tetanus.*

The workers responsible for the production of these sera were Weinberg and Séguin, who worked with *B. welchii, Vibrion septique, B. œdematiens* and finally with *B. histolyticus* ; Bull and Pritchett in America, who made notable advances in obtaining a *B. welchii* antiserum ; McIntosh and O'Brien, who worked at the production of antibacterial sera ; and Henry, who finally obtained a dry *B. welchii* toxin. Owing to the practical difficulties of manufacture the sera actually used were for the most part antitoxic, but the laboratory tests carried out with the anti-bacterial sera were very promising.

Toxins and Antitoxins.—*Bacillus welchii* produces a soluble toxin which may be obtained from sixteen to twenty-four cultures in 0·2 per cent. glucose broth, or glucose broth containing muscle or muscle extract. The method of preparing the medium, reaction, etc., have an important bearing upon the strength of toxin obtained. Still more important is the toxin-producing capacity of the individual strain of the organism selected. Different strains vary very greatly in regard to this capacity. The soluble toxin obtained by filtration is destroyed by heating to 70° C. for thirty to sixty minutes ; it is non-dializable. The toxin has been dried by Henry using a method of double precipitation : firstly, by a two-third ammonium saturation and secondly by alcohol.

B. welchii produces a diffuse low-power toxin ; with a good example the minimum lethal dose of the filtrate is 0·1 c.c. for a 20-gm. mouse inoculated intramuscularly. Bull and

---

* Chapter III, p. 91 *et seq.*

Pritchett used pigeons and obtained a minimum lethal dose of the filtrate of 0.3 c.c. These two figures are just about equivalent to each other. Henry, by drying and redissolving the toxin, has been able to obtain solutions containing from 50 to 250 minimum lethal doses for mice per cubic centimetre. The toxin is hæmolytic and produces œdema and necrosis at the site of inoculation ; introduced intravenously into rabbits, death occurs in two to two and a half hours with symptoms of respiratory disturbance, muscular tremors, paresis, diarrhœa and hæmaturia.

An antitoxic serum can be produced in horses by the repeated inoculation of graded doses of toxin. The unit of measurement of the potency of the serum actually used in England is twice the amount of antitoxin required to neutralize two minimum lethal doses of toxin for a 20-gm. mouse. Sera have been produced containing 5,000 of these units. A guinea-pig can be protected against quantities of living culture in excess of an invariably lethal dose* by being injected up to seven days previously with 3 c.c. of antitoxic serum of a titre of about 1,000 units per cubic centimetre. If the living culture and the antitoxic serum are injected simultaneously after being in contact for thirty minutes at the temperature of the laboratory 0.01 c.c. of serum will prevent infection.

Vibrion septique produces a soluble toxin which is contained in the filtrate of glucose broth cultures, of chopped meat cultures, or of flasks of broth into which pieces of the fresh liver taken aseptically from guinea-pigs or rabbits infected with the organism have been dropped. The pieces of liver serve as inoculum and also assist in the production of anaërobiosis. All the cultures tested were found to develop equally potent toxins ; long subculture upon artificial media does not appear to alter this character in any way. The initial reaction of the medium is, however, of the greatest importance and failure to produce toxin of any value is generally due to an unsuitable reaction. A hydrogen-ion concentration of about 7.6 to 8.0 appears to be the most suitable reaction for the production of toxin. In the presence of glucose the best results were obtained after twenty to twenty-four hours' growth ; in the absence of glucose it takes about forty-five hours' growth to reach the optimum toxin production.

---

* A lethal dose of a living culture is notoriously an erroneous conception ; nevertheless, with organisms of this nature where the accompanying toxin plays so large a part in infection, experience with an individual culture admits of a fairly accurate estimation of a lethal dose.

The toxin of *Vibrion septique* is of the diffuse order ; it causes œdema and local necrosis but does not produce death with regularity when injected subcutaneously or intramuscularly into mice or guinea-pigs. Intravenous injection of 0·1 or 0·5 c.c. of toxin into rabbits produces death in three to fifteen minutes with symptoms of cardiac and respiratory disturbance, convulsions and paralysis. A delayed reaction in which death occurs after three to twenty-four hours takes place with lesser doses. The rapid reaction producing death in three to fifteen minutes can be used as a means of testing antitoxic sera ; the delayed reaction is unsuitable for this purpose as it is difficult to adjust the dose and individual animals show a variable resistance. In practice the rabbit is unsuitable to use for the large number of tests required in manufacturing the sera and in England the following method is made use of instead. It is found that 0·05 c.c. of toxin injected intramuscularly into a mouse produces a recognizable œdema. The test dose of toxin used is ten times this amount, *i.e.*, 0·5 to 1 c.c., according to the strength of the toxin. The relation of the minimal œdema-producing dose in mice to the intravenous lethal dose in rabbits is approximately such that ten times the minimal œdema-producing dose is equal to three minimum lethal doses intravenously for the rabbit. The unit of measurement of the *anti-Vibrion septique* serum is the amount of antitoxin which, when placed in contact with ten minimal œdema-producing doses of toxin, will prevent the appearance of any lesion whatsoever in the mice injected with the mixture.

A serum containing 10,000 such units per cubic centimetre can be made. Protection against infection with living cultures can be afforded to experimental animals as in the case of *B. welchii* with doses of serum adjusted according to the titre.

B. œdematiens grown in meat medium or in broth for six to ten days develops a toxin which, after filtration, produces death in mice upon the intramuscular injection of quantities from 0·0025 to 0·0002 c.c. The toxin acts after a latent period of twelve to forty-eight hours. The toxin is very fragile and deteriorates with the passage of time, exposure to light and air and fluctuations of temperature. It is preserved with a minimum of loss when stored *in vacuo* in the dark at the temperature of the ice-chest. The serum is prepared by the intramuscular injection of carefully graduated doses of filtered toxin into horses.

The unit of measurement introduced by Weinberg at the

Pasteur Institute when he first made the serum is that quantity of serum which when placed in contact with 100 minimum lethal doses will neutralize the toxin and prevent the death of the animal (mouse). A serum containing 20,000 such units per cubic centimetre can be made.

A serum has been made against *B. histolyticus* by Weinberg. The toxin can be demonstrated in very young cultures, fourteen hours, but is destroyed by the changes that take place upon further incubation of the culture. It is extremely difficult to filter this toxin with success as it is apt to be retained in the filter-candle. The toxin produces death in rabbits when injected intravenously, and this effect can be prevented when the toxin is mixed with the serum produced by injecting the toxin into horses. The serum proved useful in certain cases but it has not been further developed.

The sera actually supplied to the British army were made by the Wellcome Physiological Research Laboratories under conditions of the greatest difficulty. The successful production of high titre sera on a large scale is dependent upon the correct adjustment of a great number of different factors which in the case of the new sera all required investigation. The urgent demand for the anti-gas gangrene sera was met as rapidly as possible but the final high titre sera were not available until just before the armistice.

The following table shows the titre of some of the sera which were finally produced.

Highest Titres in Anti-gas Gangrene and Anti-tetanus Sera.

	Monovalent horses.					Divalent horses.					Trivalent horses.		
T.	1,000	—	—	—	300	600	500	—	—	400	300	200	200
V.	—	10,000	—	—	1,000	—	—	2,000	10,000	300	300	1,000	3,000
W.	—	—	1,000	—	—	1,000	2,080	4,000	3,000	500	1,000	1,000	100
E.	—	—	—	20,000	—	—	—	—	—	—	—	—	—

Figures represent units per cubic centimetre. Vertical columns represent single bleedings of a horse.

T.= Tetanus ; the unit is ten times the amount protecting against 100 minimum lethal doses of a certain toxin.

V.= *Vibrion septique* ; the unit is the amount protecting against 10 minimal œdema-producing doses of a certain toxin.

W.= Welch ; twice the amount protecting against 2 minimum lethal doses of a certain toxin.

E.= Œdematiens ; the unit is the amount protecting against 100 minimum lethal doses of a certain toxin.

A complete bibliography is published in No. 39 of the Special Report Series of the Medical Research Council, 1919. The list is a particularly long one and is consequently unsuitable for reproduction here.

CHAPTER V.

INFECTION OF WOUNDS BY MICROBES OTHER THAN SPORE-BEARING ANAËROBES.

WHILE the widespread investigation of wound infections which was carried out during the whole period of the war added greatly to our knowledge of the biological evolution of a septic wound, yet no great advances have been made in the methods of classification or in the definition of the specific characters of the aërobic bacteria concerned.

The most important progress has been the general recognition of the important part played by *Streptococcus pyogenes* as a cause of death of the patient or delayed healing of the wound, and even this advance was delayed till the later years of the war, largely because attention had up to then been diverted by the more obvious and seemingly more urgent problem of anaërobic infection and gas gangrene. The greater part of the literature concerning aërobic infections in the war is made up of data regarding the frequency and time of occurrence of the various types.

The Origin and Course of Infection.

Primary Infection.—The variety of the bacterial types found in the primary wound infection, and the diversity of their grouping, might seem evidence of haphazard infection from various sources. The important pathogenic species, however, form a comparatively small group, one or other member of which plays the dominant rôle in every infection, and these are all types which are traceable to an origin from the human or animal body. The important pathogenic aërobes of the primary wound infection are streptococci, staphylococci and coliform bacilli. Most of the species, as Fleming pointed out in 1915, are fæcal types, but all are types which may be found on the soldier's skin, and most of them in manured soil. To these two sources of infection, skin and soil, the unprotected wound is constantly exposed, and it is certain that they play a very important part in providing the bacterial invaders, but it is impossible at present to apportion the relative responsibility of the two sources as regards aërobic infection.

Levaditi and Delrez have studied the skin flora of the normal soldier, and have found all the important pathogenic aërobes, including *Streptococcus pyogenes*. These authors consider the rôle of the skin in wound infection to be capital, and they find that conditions of warfare favour the spread of certain organisms among groups of soldiers, so that each group may have its characteristic skin flora. They found, for instance, that Belgian soldiers behind the lines showed *S. pyogenes* in 12 per cent., while among the men in the trenches, and even among those who had left them a month previously, the figure was 62 per cent. They also believe that racial factors play a part, the English in their area showing *S. pyogenes* in 56 per cent. of wounds as against 19 per cent. among the Belgians and French. Läwen and Hesse found that *Staphylococcus aureus* was more frequent in wounds of the hairy parts, where this organism is most common normally. They consider that the pyogenic cocci in general come from the skin.

The importance of soil which has been heavily contaminated by intestinal bacteria of human or animal origin is well known in the study of anaërobic infection, but what part it plays as an origin of aërobic infection is less clear. Sacquépée, for instance, believes that both anaërobes and aërobes come from infected soil. Many of the pathogenic aërobes are present in manured soil, and Houston and McCloy found *S. faecalis* almost constantly in mud from the boots of wounded men on arrival at a base hospital. *S. pyogenes*, on the other hand, seems less likely to persist apart from the body.

The primary infection of the wound from the practical standpoint may be considered as that present at the time of the patient's entry into the most advanced surgical operating unit, as a rule after at least ten or twelve hours have elapsed since the infliction of the wound. Nearly all the bacteriological examinations on which knowledge of primary infection is based have been made at this stage, and experience has shown that earlier examinations give incomplete information. Further, the primary surgical operation is the most important dividing point in the early history of the wound, since the attempt is made to eliminate the bacterial infection present.

Examination within the first six to eight hours has given irregular and often negative results. Beebe quotes French observers in general as believing that it is impossible to find bacteria microscopically in a bleeding wound at this stage. He has himself obtained cultures from a few cases after four hours, and Läwen and Hesse got positive cultures in 67 in a series of 70 wounds, many of which were less than two hours old. It is general experience, however, that up to about eight hours the bacteria are held in check by the freshly exuded blood, and are present in such small numbers that cultural results are at best incomplete. At ten to twelve hours the infection has greatly increased, and cultures give a fairly accurate picture of the bacterial flora, though Tissier and his colleagues lay down the period from the fourteenth to eighteenth hours as the time when cultures should be made to determine the presence of the streptococcus.

The primary flora may consist of anaërobes and aërobes or of aërobes alone, rarely, if ever, of anaërobes alone. Tissier states that pure anaërobic infection does not occur. The number of aërobic types which are found with any considerable frequency is not large, though a great variety of saprophytic species occurring each in a very small percentage of cases has been recorded. Table I represents the findings of Stokes and Tytler in a series of wounds, averaging about twelve hours old.

TABLE I.

(a)   The Incidence of various Aërobic Bacteria in 165 Wounds, averaging about Twelve Hours after Wounding.

	Number.	Percentage.
Negative	23	13·9
Hæmolytic streptococci	30	18·2
Non-hæmolytic streptococci	64	38·8
Staphylococcus aureus	23	13·9
Staphylococcus albus	80	48·5
Micrococcus tetragenus	22	13·3
Diphtheroid bacilli	12	7·2
Gram-negative bacilli	38	23·0
Gram-negative cocci	15	9·0
Gram-positive, spore-bearing bacilli	59	35·7

(b)   The Incidence of Streptococci in 365 Wounds at the same stage.

	Number.	Percentage.
Negative, for streptococci	207	56·6
Hæmolytic streptococci	54	14·8
Non-hæmolytic streptococci	104	28·6

Note.—As the object of these examinations was to determine the presence of the hæmolytic streptococcus, it is probable that a certain number of non-hæmolytic strains were missed in series (a) which the more thorough examination of series (b) would have shown.

The general course of infection, as described by the numerous writers on the subject, may be briefly reviewed. Up to the tenth or twelfth hour the aërobes develop more rapidly than the anaërobes, and are represented chiefly by cocci. The commonest are the *Streptococcus faecalis* or *Enterococcus*, and the staphylococci. The *Streptococcus pyogenes* is found in about 15 per cent. of wounds at this stage, and coliform bacilli with about the same frequency. After the twelfth hour, according to Sacquépée, the anaërobes commence rapid development, and by the thirteenth to seventeenth hours take the lead. He explains the delayed development of the anaërobes by their arrival in spore state, and the occasional early fulminating cases of gas gangrene by infection with vegetative forms.

At twenty-four hours both aërobes and anaërobes are well established, and both increase progressively, though the development of the former may be masked, for practical determination, by the enormous numbers of anaërobes. This condition, in the unexcised wound, continues for about three days, and then, if the spread of infection has become limited, the anaërobes commence a steady decrease in numbers, and tend to disappear by the seventh to tenth day. The evolution of the aërobic flora is less constant, but in general their progressive increase brings them level with the anaërobes by the fourth day, according to Tissier. The aërobic species are still those of the primary infection, the pyogenic cocci, and bacilli of the *B. coli* or Friedländer type, along with various saprophytes. One or other of the more pathogenic types dominates the picture, most commonly *Staphylococcus aureus*, one of the hæmolytic white staphylococci, or *Streptococcus faecalis*, but when the *Streptococcus pyogenes* is present it is clearly dominant.

This primary aërobic flora has usually reached its maximum by the fourth or fifth day, and from that time gradually decreases, but the decrease is slower and less regular than with the anaërobes, and the course varies according to which types are dominant. The organisms which have the power of invading living tissue persist, while the defensive forces of the body, increasing in activity in response to the stimulus of infection, soon eliminate the less resistant types unless they are protected by conditions in the wound from the action of fresh serum and leucocytes. Thus the *Streptococcus pyogenes*, which grows well in fresh serum and readily invades healthy tissue, outlasts all the other primary invaders, and at whatever stage it gains entry tends to remain the dominant organism up to the time of healing. The power of invading living tissue is shared by the *Staphylococcus aureus* and some species of *Staphylococcus albus*, and accordingly these types are found persisting for considerable periods. The less pathogenic *Streptococcus faecalis* and the various saprophytic cocci have little invasive power and are disappearing by the end of the first week unless the conditions permit of a continued saprophytic existence.

, At the end of the first week the primary aërobic infection has begun to diminish and to be replaced by the various organisms which constitute the secondary infection. At this stage the growth of the granulation tissue has begun and the surface is covered with a layer of stale serum containing many dead leucocytes, which provides a soil on which saprophytes may grow with comparative freedom. Thus *B. pyocyaneus, B. proteus, B. fluorescens* and other types of coliform organisms are found flourishing at this stage.

Secondary or Hospital Infections.—Just as in the primary infection so in the secondary infection which occurs in practically every wound, a small group of organisms constantly appears, and again these are mainly cutaneous and fæcal types. The most frequent secondary invaders are diphtheroid bacilli, *B. pyocyaneus,* and *B. proteus,* while *B. coli, Streptococcus pyogenes* and *Staphylococcus aureus* usually also appear some days or weeks after the wounded man's admission to hospital.

By " hospital " infections in this connection are meant those infections which are not part of the primary infection but which develop during the stay of the patient in hospital. They may occur in three ways :—

(1) The microbes may gain access to the wound from the surrounding skin which is included under the same dressing, or from contamination of the wound or dressing with the patient's own fæces.

(2) The wound may become contaminated with air-borne microbes during some temporary disturbance of the dressing.

(3) The microbes may be introduced owing to some want of care on the part of the surgeons or nurses, who either carry the infection from one patient to another in the course of treating the wounds, or who hand on to the patient a microbe with which they themselves are infected.

Hospital Auto-infections.—On the skin of a healthy man there are to be found many staphylococci, many diphtheroid bacilli (including the acne bacillus, which is probably the most common bacillus on the skin) and a certain number of streptococci. In wounds it is uncommon to see *Staphylococcus aureus* as a part of the primary infection, but it was seldom that a wound persisted for any length of time without being infected with this microbe. It is probable that it gained access to the wound from the patient's own skin in the majority of cases. It was very common to see in patients, who had a copious discharge which kept the surrounding skin sodden or who were being treated with wet dressing, many small pustules around the wound, and the microbe in these pustules was invariably a staphylococcus.

Diphtheroid bacilli also were very common in wounds in the later stages, and as these are normal inhabitants of the skin it is likely that in most cases they were contaminations from the surrounding skin.

Bacillus coli infections in all probability arose in many cases by direct spread from the patient's own fæces. Many of the wounds were in close proximity to the anus, and many were obviously contaminated with fæces. This does not explain all the *B. coli* infections, however, as many occurred in wounds which should not have had fæcal contaminations, and it is very doubtful if wounds of the thigh, which were very liable to fæcal contamination, were more often infected with *B. coli* than were others of the same nature elsewhere where fæcal contamination should not have occurred.

Air-borne Infections.—This method of infection was probably very uncommon for two reasons; firstly because the wounds were covered with dressings except for short intervals, and secondly because in cases where the air of hospital wards had been carefully examined very few microbes of high pathogenicity were found.

Infection carried by means of the Surgical Attendant.—It has long been recognized that certain infections are very easily carried from one patient to another in the same ward. In the pre-antiseptic and pre-bacteriological days the infection which was best known in this connection was that of the bacillus of blue pus (*B. pyocyaneus*) which manifested itself to the surgeon in the blue colour which it imparted to the dressings. Another infection which was known and feared was erysipelas, which manifested itself in no mistakable manner. There are others, however, which are just as readily conveyed from one patient to another in a hospital ward, but which do not obtrude themselves on the notice of the surgeon.

The occurrence of *Streptococcus pyogenes* on the skin has been dealt with and it is probable that many of the secondary infections with this organism were derived from the patient's own skin. On the other hand, it has been clearly shown by Sir Almroth Wright that streptococcus is the most serophytic of all the microbes found in wounds, *i.e.*, it can grow with the greatest freedom in the unaltered serum, so that it should be most easily carried from one patient to another by want of care on the part of the attendant. In most cases, however, its access to a wound does not lead to any dramatic change in the condition, and it remains unnoticed, except by bacteriological examination, unless some serious complication such as erysipelas or septicæmia develops. The readiness with which erysipelas may be carried to other patients in the same ward has long been known and has led to cases of this nature being isolated from other surgical cases even up to the present day. Erysipelas is merely one manifestation of the same streptococcus which was to be found in practically every serious wound at some period, so that the danger which wounded men ran of being infected from their neighbours in the hospital ward should not be minimized. To avoid the danger of this hospital infection with streptococcus some of the French surgeons isolated all wounds which contained *Streptococcus pyogenes* from the other surgical cases, and this procedure seems to be the most reasonable method of dealing with the problem.

One of the best instances of hospital infection in the war was published by Fitzgerald and Robertson. They found that of 67 wound cases arriving in Toronto between 20th May and 7th June, 1917, true diphtheria bacilli were recovered in 40. It was found that one of the nurses attending these men had a slight wound in her finger from which *B. diphtheriae* was isolated, and there can be little doubt that this infection of the finger played a large part in the abnormal prevalence of *B. diphtheriae* in this batch of wounded men.

The temporary infections with *B. pyocyaneus*, *B. coli* and *B. proteus* which were so commonly seen in extensive wounds were probably in large part carried from one patient to another. Fortunately they were of little importance. It was not uncommon to cultivate all the cases in a ward and find only one or two who had, say, *B. proteus*, and then to find when the wounds were cultivated a few days afterwards that they were all infected with this organism.

The mode of entry of the secondary invaders has been dealt with under " hospital infections." Their nature can be seen by reference to Tables II and III and by a comparison of these with Table I. Table II is compiled from results obtained at a base hospital in France, and Table III from a hospital in England.

In addition to the organisms noted in these tables, various non-pathogenic cocci and bacilli were occasionally found.

A study of these tables shows that in the later stages of the wound three types of microbe predominate, namely, streptococci, staphylococci and diphtheroid bacilli, with occasional superadded infections of one or other of the types of *B. coli*, *B. proteus* or *B. pyocyaneus*. In these late infections the streptococci are nearly all of the pyogenes type and the staphylococci nearly all "aureus." Both of these are comparatively seldom represented in the primary infection, and both were the most persistent of all the microbes, and did not disappear until the wound was practically healed.

TABLE II.

Common Types of Bacteria, other than the Spore-bearing Anaërobic Bacilli found in. Wounds at a Base Hospital in France.

Time since infliction of wound.	No. of wounds examined.	Strepto- cocci.	Staphylo- cocci.	Coliform bacilli.	Diphtheroid bacilli.
1 to 7 days..	127	102	40	37	9*
8 to 20 ,, ..	56	51	16	18	21
Over 20 ,, ..	27	24	19	19	16

* Some of these bacilli were obligate anaërobes.

TABLE III.

Common Types of Bacteria, other than the Spore-bearing Anaërobic Bacilli found in 54 Wounds examined in a Hospital in England.

Organism.	On admission to hospital.	At any period during stay in hospital.
Streptococcus	48	53
Staphylococcus	33	45
B. pyocyaneus	8	23
B. proteus	19	29
B. coli type	19	29
Diphtheroid bacilli	34	43

Influence of Surgical Treatment.

The above description of the evolution of the infection in a wound applies to wounds treated as they were in the earlier years of the war. The practice introduced later, of excision and suture of the wound, profoundly modified the course of the infection. In the successful excision and suture the infection was brought abruptly to an end, partly by the mechanical removal of some of the infecting bacteria, partly by the removal of the damaged tissues, which were incapable of overcoming even the smallest infection, and partly by bringing healthy tissues into close apposition by suture, so that the protective forces of the body could act to advantage on the microbes which were left and destroy them. Even where the suture was not completely successful the usual result was that the primary infection was eliminated with the exception of *Streptococcus pyogenes* and possibly staphylococcus. Where the wound was excised and for some reason was not sutured the primary infection only attained minor importance, and at the end of three or four days the flora of the wound resembled closely that of a wound two or three weeks old. The secondary infection of such a wound, however, would be exactly the same as that of a wound which had not been excised.

Characters of the Non-sporing Anaërobic and the Aërobic Bacteria found in Wounds.

Non-sporing Anaërobic Bacteria.—A number of varieties of non-sporing obligate anaërobic bacteria has been described by various observers. These have consisted of both bacilli and cocci. Wright and Fleming have described a slender Gram-positive bacillus which was present in the early stages of suppurating wounds under the name of the " wisp " bacillus, from its arrangement in small " wispy " bundles. This bacillus could be seen in very large numbers in the pus from a considerable proportion of the wounds. It grew in small transparent colonies on agar or glucose agar. It was an obligate anaërobe. It fermented glucose with much acid production. Further than that its characters were not worked out.

Fleming in 1915 and Cottet in 1918 described as of frequent occurrence an anaërobic streptococcus. As will be seen later a number of streptococci were obligate anaërobes when isolated from the body but they soon became educated to grow in the presence of air. There were, however, streptococci which through many generations remained obligate anaërobes and which differed in certain respects from the ordinary *Streptococcus pyogenes* of the wounds. These will be referred to again in discussing the streptococci.

Douglas, Fleming and Colebrook isolated from certain wounds, cocci which under the microscope were seen to arrange themselves into typical tetrads. Some of these grew copiously like staphylococci and others in small grey colonies more like streptococci. Some of them also rapidly became acclimatized to aërobic conditions, while others remained through many generations obligate anaërobes.

Fleming isolated from the blood of one wounded man a Gram-negative bacillus which grew only under the strictest anaërobic conditions. This bacillus grew in very small colonies on glucose agar, and in culture it exhibited very great pleomorphism, the elements ranging in size from small coccoid forms to long swollen threads extending across half the field of the microscope.

It is clear, therefore, that anaërobic non-sporing bacteria were not uncommon in the wounds, but comparatively little work was done with them. This was probably due to the difficulty experienced in isolation and subsequent cultivation— the viability of all these microbes seems to be very limited— and also to the belief which most bacteriologists held that they were saprophytes and of no real importance in the wound. It is a commentary on the attitude of bacteriologists to this class of bacterium that in the final report of the Committee upon Anaërobic Bacteria and Infections there is no mention of the non-sporing anaërobic bacteria.

Spore-bearing Aërobic Bacteria.—These were commonly found in the wounds in the early stage. They rapidly disappeared, and were only rarely found in properly treated wounds after suppuration had been established. For the most part they belonged to the *B. mesentericus*, *B. subtilis* and *B. mycoides* groups, and were of importance only because in films from the discharges they simulated in appearance the spore-bearing anaërobic bacilli. Two varieties, *B. tetanoides* and *B. pseudo-tertius*, deserve more special mention, as they were little recognized before the war and because their similarity to important anaërobic types is very striking.

B. tetanoides has been noted as occurring in wounds by many observers. It exactly resembles *B. tetani* morphologically, so that it is impossible to say from the simple microscopic examination of the discharge whether the true *B. tetani* is present or its aërobic saprophytic double. It is motile and ciliated. It gives bluish colonies with flowery prolongations when grown aërobically on agar. It is feebly proteolytic and does not ferment any of the test sugars. It must not be confused with an anaërobic non-pathogenic bacillus closely resembling *B. tetani* and described in the final report of the Committee on Anaërobic Bacteria as *B. tetanomorphus*.

B. pseudo-tertius, described by Fleming, bears the same relation to the *B. tertius* as *B. tetanoides* bears to *B. tetani*. In appearance it is exactly like its anaërobic double. It is Gram-positive, motile and grows on ordinary media both aërobically and anaërobically. The colony on agar resembles that of *Bacillus tertius* closely, being small and transparent with slightly irregular edges. It has no demonstrable proteolytic characters and does not liquefy gelatin, but is very strongly saccharolytic, fermenting glucose, lactose, saccharose, dextrin, starch, salicin, mannite and glycerin, with the formation of acid and a small quantity of gas.

Staphylococci.—In the recently inflicted wound staphylococci were frequently found, the white varieties being much more common than the yellow at this stage (Table I).   In the later stages, on the other hand, *Staphylococcus aureus* was often seen, and the white types, many of which are probably pure saprophytes, were rarer.   The typical yellow variety was a secondary invader of considerable importance, and the severe infections were always associated with much tissue necrosis, but generalized infection was rare.

The staphylococci form a loosely defined group and probably represent more than one variety of bacteria.   A series of strains isolated during the course of the work reported by Tytler and Stokes, and subcultured repeatedly during two or three months, showed great variety in the appearance of the growth on solid media, and further not infrequently showed change on subculture.   Of 100 strains originally white, 20 developed pigment after one or more subcultures.   The microscopical appearances varied in all degrees from the typical irregularly grouped spherical cocci to tetrad formation as well developed as in the true *M. tetragenus*.   The more typical yellow strains usually showed spherical cocci, but otherwise there was no constant relation between gross and microscopical characters.

TABLE IV.

203 *Strains reported as Staphylococci tested on Blood-agar.*

Organism.	No. of strains.	Hæmolysis.		
		Definite.	Slight or doubtful.	None.
(a) *Staphylococcus aureus*—				
Typical	41	41	0	0
Atypical group I	9	0	2	7
„ „ II ..	20	0	7	13
Miscellaneous atypical strains	10	3	1	6
(b) *Staphylococcus albus*—				
Typical	111	84	12	15
Atypical group III ..	12	2	3	7

Note.—Atypical groups I, II and III are strains which had gross characters distinct enough to suggest that they were separate varieties. Groups I and II were probably saprophytes which had no true place among the staphylococci. Group III was the previously recognized type of white staphylococcus in which the growth on agar is dense chalky white with a surface like that of unglazed porcelain.

Table IV shows the action of these strains on blood, as tested in pure culture on blood-agar plates. Hæmolytic power has been suggested as a criterion of pathogenicity, but from the frequency with which it occurs even among the white strains it seems probable that it is not reliable evidence on this point.

Streptococci.—This group of microbes is by far the most important of all the non-sporing bacteria found in wounds and was responsible for almost all the deaths from sepsis in the later stages of wound infection.

The literature of the streptococcal group of microbes was very voluminous before the war and it has been very sensibly increased since 1914, but the classification of these organisms still remains very unsatisfactory. In the early days of bacteriology attempts were made to classify them by means of the length of the chains. Thus arose the names *S. longus* and *S. brevis.* Later they were divided into hæmolytic and non-hæmolytic, depending on their action on blood. Later still the sugar fermentation tests were used to differentiate them and the names *S. pyogenes, S. faecalis, S. salivarius* and so on were given to different groups. More recently the fermentation tests combined with the action on blood have been used as a means of differentiation. While this is probably the best it is yet very unsatisfactory, and with Holman's classification, which is the most widely accepted, it is found that there have to be placed in the same category streptococci of characters widely different in respects other than those used in the classification. The great importance given to the action on blood has in the later years of the war led to very different types of streptococci being grouped together under the name of *Streptococcus haemolyticus,* and referred to, especially in American literature, as if they were the same or closely allied organisms. It is true that in the hæmolytic group of streptococci are included most of those which cause acute infections, but there were very definite differences between the types found in wounds and those isolated from the chest in, for instance, influenzal pneumonia.

Of the streptococci which were encountered in wounds two types were fairly distinct, namely, *Streptococcus pyogenes* and *Streptococcus faecalis.* These may be discussed in some detail.

S. pyogenes, in war wounds, as in civil practice, is the most dangerous of all the pyogenic microbes met with and it was the cause of nearly all the septicæmic conditions occurring in the later stages of wound infections. Its importance has been emphasized by nearly all the writers on wound infections. Tissier especially drew attention to this question and elaborated the theory that the streptococcal infection was not only dangerous in itself but opened the way for the spore-bearing anaërobes and so was the forerunner of gas gangrene. Fleming and Porteous, working at No. 8 Stationary Hospital in 1918, obtained 49 positive blood cultures, and of these 44 were pure cultures of *Streptococcus pyogenes*. Of the others, two were *B. welchii*, one *B. œdematiens*, and two staphylococci. These cultures were all made from men with septic compound fractures of the femur, and the results show the enormous preponderance of *S. pyogenes* in generalized infections. This is in exact correspondence with what is found in civil practice.

In films from the discharges of wounds, *Streptococcus pyogenes* occurs in pairs or in chains which are usually seen to be made of pairs of cocci. Very frequently the cocci are intracellular and in all stages of disintegration. In cultures on solid medium the cocci are frequently seen only in pairs and very short chains and it is sometimes difficult in such cultures to determine microscopically whether the microbe is a streptococcus. In broth, however, or other fluid medium it grows out into long chains. In young cultures the individual cocci are rounded or flattened on their adjacent sides, in sharp contrast to *S. faecalis*, in which the cocci are elongated in the direction of the chain. In older cultures there is great variation in the size and shape of the cocci. They may become elongated, pear-shaped, or almost bacillary in form. Frequently, even in five or six hour broth cultures, there are to be seen in the chains one or two very much swollen individuals.

Streptococcus pyogenes grows well on all the ordinary culture media, but the growth on Douglas trypsin digest medium is very much more copious than it is on media made with meat extract and peptone. The colonies are greyish, up to 2 mm. in diameter, with a very slightly irregular margin and a definite dark area in the centre when seen by transmitted light. In broth it grows in woolly masses which settle to the bottom or adhere to the sides of the culture tube, leaving the supernatant broth clear.

On gelatin growth occurs slowly at 20° C. without liquefaction. There is no liquefaction of coagulated serum or egg.

In milk it usually produces acid and a firm clot which later contracts and expresses a clear whey. The clotting of milk by *S. pyogenes* is, however, variable, and it has been shown by Fleming and Porteous that it depends to some extent on the calibre of the tube used in the test. The smaller the tube used the quicker is the clotting, and there may be a definite clot in a small tube when even after long incubation there is no clot evident in a wide tube.

Usually it produces acid in glucose, lactose, saccharose and salicin, but not in mannite, raffinose and inulin. About 12 per cent. of the strains, however, ferment mannite. Apart from this the mannite and the non-mannite fermenters are identical morphologically, culturally and serologically.

All strains develop a hæmolysin in culture. S. pyogenes seems to differ from the hæmolytic streptococci found in the chest in cases of broncho-pneumonia and also from the hæmolytic streptococci found in the mouth in that, although they lake unaltered blood cells, they have no action on hæmatin. When planted on boiled blood medium, therefore, S. pyogenes does not change the colour, whereas most of the other hæmolytic streptococci rapidly change the colour to a greenish-yellow.

S. pyogenes usually dies out in a month or less on agar or in broth, but it can be kept alive for a long time on Dorset's egg medium or the minced meat medium such as is used for the growth of anaërobes.

In order to isolate S. pyogenes an agar plate, preferably grown anaërobically, usually suffices. It prefers, in general, anaërobic conditions, and when first isolated a certain number of strains will grow only in the absence of oxygen, although they can be readily acclimatized to aërobic conditions.

The best method of plating is to incorporate the infected material in about 5 c.c. of blood-agar at 45° C. and then to pour this in a thin layer over the surface of an ordinary agar plate. In this way there is a sufficient thickness of medium for the cocci to flourish and there is not so thick a layer of blood as to obscure the hæmolytic action, which is much more evident when the colony is in the substance of the agar than when it is merely on the surface.

When organisms like B. proteus are present the easiest method of isolation of the streptococci is by Wright's method of pyo-sero culture. He has shown that streptococci grow in unaltered human serum very much more readily than do the other microbes found in wounds and in the later dilutions of the infected material grown in this way a pure culture of streptococci may be obtained.

Douglas and Colebrook have shown that broth containing

active trypsin is superior to ordinary or glucose broth as a method of blood culture. A quarter of a cubic centimetre of trypsin (Allen & Hanbury's) is added to 5 c.c. of broth and the tubes are incubated to see that they are sterile. Then 1 c.c. of blood is added to each tube. In such a medium it has been found that growth occurs with a smaller implantation and is noticeable earlier than when plain broth is used.

Another method which has given very good results is to put 2 or 3 c.c. of blood into sufficient sterile distilled water to lake it. This diluted blood clots slowly and there is sufficient time to carry it from the bedside to the laboratory and deal with it before clotting occurs. The laked blood is added to 15 c.c. of melted agar at 45° C. and poured into a Petri dish. This method has the additional advantage of giving the number of microbes in the circulating blood. In generalized streptococcal infections following septic wounds the number of cocci in the blood was usually under 100 per cubic centimetre and often only one or two colonies developed from a cubic centimetre of blood. The number may, however, rise as high as 4,000 colonies per cubic centimetre. It has also been found that Robertson's meat medium, such as is used for the growth of anaërobes, gives better results than does plain broth in the cultivation of streptococci from the blood and this medium has the advantage that not only will it yield a culture of the streptococci which are indifferent to oxygen but also of those which are at first strict anaërobes as well as any obligate anaërobic bacteria which may be present.

Douglas, Fleming and Colebrook found that the serum of a rabbit which had been immunized with one strain of S. pyogenes from a wound would agglutinate up to titre all the strains of this organism. The agglutination reactions were the same whether the strain tested was one which fermented mannite or not.

Anaërobic Streptococci. — In 1915 Fleming described an anaërobic streptococcus as being of frequent occurrence in wounds. It was found in 9 out of 12 wounds taken at random. In 1918 Cottet found a true anaërobic streptococcus in 10 out of 33 wounds.

This streptococcus was difficult to isolate as it always occurred in association with S. pyogenes and the colonies of the two were identical. It grew in long chains, and in old cultures there were very marked involution forms; it did not clot milk and gave no change of colour on neutral red egg medium (S. pyogenes always gave a bright red colour). In shake or stab cultures in glucose-agar growth only occurred in the depths. One strain carried through many generations maintained its true anaërobic characters. Apart from its failing to produce a red colour on neutral red egg medium this coccus very closely resembled S. *pyogenes*.

Streptococcus faecalis.—The literature regarding this organism is somewhat confusing in that the term has been applied loosely to several different streptococci. The name S. *faecalis* was given by Andrewes and Horder to a streptococcus commonly found in the fæces which had certain definite characters, but it has been loosely applied to all large oval short-chained streptococci which grow copiously on the ordinary medium. In the French literature, Burnet and Weissenbach refer to this organism as the enterococcus, a name which, however, is not so limited as is the S. *faecalis* and includes all the organisms found in fæces which resemble in their morphology and growth the true S. *faecalis*.

Andrewes and Horder defined it as a short-chained streptococcus which fermented lactose, saccharose, mannite and salicin but not raffinose or inulin and did not hæmolyze blood, and it is well to restrict the name to streptococci with these characters, except that more recent research has shown that the inulin fermentation is not a constant character.

S. *faecalis* is part of the primary infection of wounds and was very commonly found in large numbers in the first few days after the wound was inflicted. After the first week, however, it gradually disappeared and only comparatively rarely was present in the older wounds. Thus, Douglas, Fleming and Colebrook found it in only 7 cases out of 61 on arrival in England, whereas S. *pyogenes* was present in nearly every case.

S. *faecalis* is a large oval coccus generally occurring in pairs although in glucose broth culture, especially when grown anaërobically, it may grow out into chains of ten or more elements. It is present in the intestinal contents of man and animals and is very commonly found in manured soil. Houston and McCloy, as already stated, recovered it on every occasion from mud scraped from the boots of wounded men on their arrival at a base hospital.

S. *faecalis* grows well on all the ordinary media. On peptone agar it grows in a small colony resembling that of S. *pyogenes*, but on Douglas' tryptic digest agar its growth more nearly resembles that of staphylococcus. In broth it produces an even turbidity. It ferments lactose, saccharose, mannite and salicin but not raffinose. Some strains ferment

inulin and others do not. Some strains also rapidly liquefy
gelatin and coagulated serum or egg. Although classed as an
aërobe it prefers anaërobic conditions and some strains when
first isolated are obligate anaërobes. One of its most striking
characters is its great resistance to adverse circumstances.
It lives for a very long time in culture without replanting.
It will resist heating to 55° C. for half an hour, and often it
will even resist a temperature of 80° C. for ten minutes. Its
growth is not inhibited by ox-bile. Houston and McCloy have
used heating at 55° C. for half an hour as a means of isolating
the organism, and Weissenbach has employed glucose peptone
water to which has been added one-tenth of its volume of ox-bile.
In this medium *S. faecalis* grows well, while *S. pyogenes*
is completely inhibited. Animals inoculated with a vaccine
of this organism develop agglutinins, and researches conducted
since the war have shown that serologically there are different
races of *S. faecalis*.

Little need be said regarding other streptococci found in
wounds, as the work done during the war has added nothing to
our knowledge of them. Malone and Rhea, however, made
the interesting observation that in penetrating chest wounds it
was common to find streptococci of the type normally found
in the respiratory tract.

Coliform Bacilli.—Many varieties of these bacilli have been
isolated from wounds at all stages, but, in general, infections
with these are more common in the later stages of the wounds.
Stokes and Tytler found that 23 per cent. of wounds contained
these bacilli on admission to a casualty clearing station. Their
incidence in the later stages can be gauged from the following
table compiled from figures given by Stewart working in Leeds,
and Fleming working in Boulogne.

TABLE V.

Time after infection.	Number of cases investigated.		Percentage incidence of coliform bacilli.	
	Stewart.	Fleming.	Stewart.	Fleming.
Under 7 days	17	127	41	29
8 to 20 ,, ...	47	56	42	32
Over 20 ,, ...	58	27	74	70

From this table it is obvious that infection with these bacilli
is largely secondary. The infection is frequently very transitory
and it was noticed that one coliform bacillus may disappear

and its place be taken by another of a different type. With few exceptions they seem to be passing saprophytes which do not really infect the wounds but which gain access and proliferate in the discharge until such time as the conditions favourable to their growth have ceased.

Some experiments by Wilson are very instructive in connection with coliform infections. He planted a clean wound copiously with a living culture of *B. coli* isolated from the intestine of the same patient and then observed the fate of the organisms. He found that nearly all had disappeared in twenty-four hours and at the end of forty-eight hours they could not be seen in films or recovered in culture.

A full description of the coliform bacilli found in wounds is given by Matthew J. Stewart.

B. pyocyaneus. — The war has not added much to the knowledge of this organism. Its incidence in wounds varied much in different wards of the same hospital and in different hospitals, but in general it appeared to be more frequent the longer the man remained in hospital.

The colour produced by different strains varied from almost jet black to a very pale green. Some strains hardly produced any colour in culture.

While in many cases this microbe existed in the wound as a saprophyte there is no doubt that it sometimes exercised a definite pathogenic effect. In many cases the infection was very transitory.

B. proteus.—The incidence of this microbe was very like that of *B. pyocyaneus*. When present it obtruded itself on the bacteriologist by spreading over the culture and obscuring everything else. Like *B. pyocyaneus* it was at times merely a saprophyte, but that in many cases it was really causing an infection was shown by the fact that the sera of patients frequently agglutinated the bacillus. A full description of the morphological, cultural and serological characters of *B. proteus* found in wounds is given by Douglas, Fleming and Colebrook.

Gram-negative Cocci.—These were present in some wounds at the beginning and they were also to be found in some in the later stages. Some of these Gram-negative cocci, and especially those found in the earlier stages of the wound, were strict anaërobes and similar to certain Gram-negative cocci which can be isolated from the fæces.

One variety found in the later stages was an obligate aërobe. It was somewhat larger than a staphylococcus, non-motile,

and apart from a certain number of diplococcal forms, showed
no special arrangement. It grew readily on agar, forming large
white round colonies with a dull surface. It fermented glucose
with the formation of acid but did not attack any of the other
sugars.

Wilson and Steer made use of this organism for growing
anaërobic bacilli in symbiosis without any other anaërobic
precaution.

Micrococcus tetragenus.—Stokes and Tytler, in 165 recent
wounds, 17 times isolated organisms which were believed to
represent the true *M. tetragenus* of Gaffky. On the blood-
agar plates they showed fine translucent, greyish colonies,
seldom more than 1 mm. in diameter, and usually surrounded
by a green halo in the underlying medium. In almost every
case they were picked as streptococci, but under the microscope
showed well-marked tetrads. On the agar slope the growth
was thin and translucent, and resembled that of a *Streptococcus
faecalis,* being perhaps a little less luxuriant. None of the
strains produced hæmolysis on blood-agar. It was not possible
to confirm the diagnosis by animal inoculation.

Tetrad formation was commonly seen among species which
showed the characteristic growth of staphylococcus, and on
this account reports of the occurrence of *M. tetragenus*
are most unreliable.

Diphtheroid Bacilli.—Bacilli of this type are very common
in the later stages of wound infection, and have generally been
regarded as saprophytes and of little importance. Fitzgerald
and Robertson reported that out of 67 cases arriving in Toronto
between 20th May and 7th June, 1917, true diphtheria bacilli
were recovered in 40. These bacilli were identified both by
cultural and inoculation tests. In some cases, but not in all,
the wounds showed the characteristic diphtheritic membrane.
The extraordinary prevalence of this infection was partly
explained by the fact that one of the nurses who was dressing
these men had a slight wound in the finger from which *B.
diphtheriae* was isolated, as noted above.

Fitzgerald and Robertson's report led to an investigation
of the diphtheroid bacilli in wounds in some of the Canadian
hospitals in England, the results of which were published by
Adami and others. Out of 306 cases investigated there were
found in 4 bacilli which had the morphological and cultural
characters of true diphtheria bacilli, and of these 4, 2
were found to be pathogenic to animals, producing the lesions
characteristic of the Klebs-Loeffler bacillus.

Reports have been published from various areas that in a certain small proportion of wounds bacilli could be isolated apparently identical with *B. diphtheriae*, although in many cases there was no clinical sign of the presence of such a bacillus.

Anaërobic diphtheroid bacilli are not uncommon in the early days of the wound. In the later stages of the wound masses of diphtheroid bacilli were frequently to be seen in the pus, but when this was planted out in the ordinary way a very scanty growth resulted. It is possible that many of these were anaërobic and of the type of the " acne bacillus." This bacillus would not appear on a plate from the pus grown aërobically, nor would it appear on a plate incubated anaërobically for the usual time (twenty-four to forty-eight hours), hence there would be every chance of its being missed in the cultures. This bacillus also is one of the most common on the skin of the patient and its growth is encouraged by the presence of some serous fluid, so it is very likely that it would infect the open wounds.

Aërobic diphtheroid bacilli were extremely common in the wounds in the later stages, but there is little evidence that they were anything but saprophytes. Their characters have been observed and recorded by Adami and others and by Douglas, Fleming and Colebrook, and for these reference might be made to the original papers or to the Report of the Committee on the Anaërobic Bacteria and Infections.*

Infection after the Wound has Healed.

The ultimate healing of the wound, that is, the closing of the integument over it, must not be taken as a sure and certain sign that the microbes which were responsible for the sepsis have completely disappeared.† Time and again it has been brought home to the surgeon that they may remain in a quiescent condition in the scar tissue, so that when an operation is performed at a later date involving this scar tissue it is not uncommon to get an infection of the operation wound with streptococci, staphylococci, *B. welchii*, *B. tetani*, or other organism. It might be argued that it was a fresh infection in the case of the common suppurative organisms such as the streptococcus, but this could not be so with organisms such as *B. welchii* or *B. tetani*, which are unknown as infections of operation wounds in modern times. Bacteriological investigations of the scar tissue, also, have revealed the presence of these organisms months after the healing of the wound.

---

* M.R.C. Special Report Series, No. 39.   † See Chap. VI.

Influence of the Aërobic on the Anaërobic Infection.

It is a function of aërobic bacteria that they can make use of, and indeed prefer, the free oxygen dissolved in the medium and contained in the air above. It can easily be shown by fitting a vaseline plug above a broth culture of an aërobic bacterium, such as one of the diphtheroid group, that the oxygen is absorbed and the vaseline plug is drawn down the tube. In some cases the whole of the oxygen will be absorbed from the air above the culture.

It can easily be seen, therefore, that the aërobic bacteria in their growth in a wound may have a powerful effect in making the conditions favourable for the pululation of the obligate anaërobic bacteria. Methods have long been in use for growing anaërobic bacteria in symbiosis with *B. subtilis*, and during the war Wilson and Steer made use of an aërobic Gram-negative coccus for the same purpose.

Many experiments were made before the war showing the influence which aërobic bacteria had on the anaërobes. In 1889 Roger showed that an inactive strain of *Vibrion septique* could be rendered pathogenic for a rabbit by injecting it in association with *B. prodigiosus*. In 1893, Vaillard and Rouget stated that tetanus spores would grow out in the tissues when they were injected with aërobic bacteria which protected them against phagocytosis, and much other work has been done along these lines. It was the common experience during the war that gaseous emphysema could be produced in animals with a much smaller dose of *B. welchii* if it is combined with some other organism, either anaërobic or aërobic.

Tissier has attributed the spread of the primary anaërobic infection of wounds to the action of the associated aërobes, especially streptococci.

Douglas, Fleming and Colebrook have studied the question of bacterial symbiosis *in vitro* and they have found that all the common aërobes found in wounds have the power of stimulating the growth of the common anaërobes. Not only does the anaërobe grow more quickly in association with the aërobe but in some cases growth was obtained with an implantation one million times smaller than was necessary when the anaërobe was grown alone. They found also that the stimulation of growth was as marked when the cultures were grown under strict anaërobic conditions as when semi-anaërobic conditions obtained. They found also that the growth of *B. welchii* was stimulated when planted in association with the other anaërobes, and in some cases a mutually symbiotic effect was observed when the different anaërobes were grown together. It was noticed also that the diphtheroid bacilli had a powerful stimulant action on the growth of streptococci. It is clear from the work which has been done in this connection that symbiosis between the aërobic and anaërobic bacteria or between the different aërobic bacteria may play an important part in the establishment of serious infections with one or other of these, such as in the case of gas gangrene or generalized streptococcus infection.

BIBLIOGRAPHY.

Adami & others	Combined Enquiry into the Presence of Diphtheria and Diphtheroid Bacilli in wounds.	Canad. Med. Assoc. Jl., 1918, Vol. viii, pp. 769–85 : *and* Bull. of the Canadian Army Med. Corps, 1918, Vol. i, p. 33.
Andrewes & Horder	A Study of Streptococci Pathogenic for Man.	Lancet, 1906, Vol. ii, pp. 708, 775, 852.
Beebe	Wound Bacteriology	War Medicine (American Red Cross), 1918–19, Vol. ii, No. 6, p.1023.
Burnet & Weissenbach	Classification des Streptocoques	Bull. de l'Inst. Pasteur, 1918, Vol. xvi, pp. 657 and 697.
Cottet	Note sur les streptocoques dans les plaies de guerre : fréquence des streptocoques anaérobies.	Compt. Rend. Soc. de Biol., 1918, Vol. lxxxi, p. 6.
Douglas & Colebrook	On the Advantage of using a Broth containing Trypsin in making Blood Cultures.	Lancet, 1916, Vol. ii, p. 180.
Douglas, Fleming & Colebrook.	Studies in Wound Infections	M.R.C. Special Report Series, No.59, Lond., 1920.
,,	Studies in Wound Infections : on the Question of Bacterial Symbiosis in Wound Infections.	Lancet, 1917, Vol. i, p. 604.
Fitzgerald & Robertson.	Report of an Outbreak of Diphtheric Wound Infection among Returned Soldiers.	Journal Amer. Med. Assoc., 1917, Vol. lxix, p. 791.
Fleming	On the Bacteriology of Septic Wounds.	Lancet, 1915, Vol. ii, p. 638.
,,	The Aërobic Infections of War Wounds	M.R.C. Special Report Series No. 39, Lond., 1919, p. 70.
Fleming & Porteous	On Streptococcal Infections of Septic Wounds at a Base Hospital.	Lancet, 1919, Vol. ii, p. 49.
Gross & Tissier	Indications des sutures primitives et secondaires des plaies de guerre, d'après les données de bactériologie.	Bull. et Mém. de la Soc. de Chirurgie, 1917, Vol. xliii, p. 1498.

Holman .. .. The Classification of Strepto-   Jl. Med. Research,
              cocci.   1916, Vol. xxxiv,
                                               p. 377.
Houston & McCloy .. The Relation of the Enterococcus Lancet, 1916, Vol. ii,
              to " Trench Fever " and   p. 632.
              Allied Conditions.
Lâwen & Hesse .. Bakterienbefunde bei frischen Münch. med. Woch-
              Kriegsschussverletzungen und   enschr, 1916, Vol.
              ihre klinische Bedeutung.   lxiii, p. 688.
Levaditi & Delrez .. Sur l'origine cutanée des strepto- Compt. Rend. de
              coques adaptés dans les plaies   l'Acad. des Scien-
              de guerre.   ces, 1917,Vol.clxv.
                                                p. 444.
Malone & Rhea .. Studies on Streptococci re-   Jl. Path. and Bact.
              covered from Sick and   1918–19, Vol. xxii,
              Wounded Soldiers in France.   p. 210.
Roger .. .. Quelques effets des associations Compt. Rend. Soc.
              microbiennes.   de Biol., 1889, Vol.
                                               xli, p. 35.
Sacquépée .. .. La flore initiale habituelle, et Compt. Rend. Soc.
              la flore de passage dans la   de Biol., 1918,Vol.
              gangrène gazeuse.   lxxxi, p. 526.
     ,, ... Études bactériologiques sur les Jl. de Physiol. et
              plaies de guerre.   Pathol. Générale,
                                               1917–18, Vol. xvii,
                                               p. 621.
Stewart .. .. A Study of the Coliform Organ- Jl. of Hygiene, 1917–
              isms infecting the Wounds of   18, Vol. xvi, p.291.
              War.
Stokes & Tytler .. Primary and Delayed Primary Brit. Jl. Surg., 1918–
              Suture of Gunshot Wounds.   19, Vol. vi, p. 92 ;
                                               Bacteriological
                                               Report, p. 111.
Tissier .. .. Recherches sur la flore bactér- Bull. de l'Acad. de
              ienne des plaies de guerre.   Méd., 1916, Vol.
                                               lxxvi, p. 337 ; and
                                               Ann. de l'Inst.
                                               Pasteur, 1916,Vol.
                                               xxx, p. 681. Ibid.,
                                               1917, Vol. xxxi,
                                               p. 161.
     ,, ... Application de données bacterio- Bull. de l'Inst. Pas-
              logiques à la chirurgie de   teur, 1918, Vol.
              guerre. (Review).   xvi, p. 273.
Vaillard & Rouget .. Note au sujet de l'étiologie de Ann. de l'Inst. Pas-
              Tétanos.   teur, 1893, Vol. vii,
                                               p. 755.
Weissenbach.. .. Un bon caractère différentiel Compt. Rend. de la
              entre le streptocoque pyogène   Soc. de Biol.,1918,
              et l'entérococque.   Vol. lxxxi, p. 559.
Wilson .. .. The Phagocytic Response to the   Brit. Med. Jl., 1918,
              Introduction of Bacteria into   Vol. i, p. 533.
              Clean Wounds.
Wilson & Steer .. Points in the Technique em- Ibid., 1918, Vol. ii,
              ployed in the Isolation and   p. 568.
              Cultivation of Anaërobic Bac-
              teria.
Wright .. .. An Address on Wound Infec-   Ibid., 1915, Vol. i,
              tions.   pp. 625, 665, 720,
                                               762.

CHAPTER VI.

LATENT SEPSIS IN WOUNDS.

LATENT sepsis may be defined as the existence of virulent bacteria in the tissues unaccompanied by clinical signs of their presence. Chronic suppuration may co-exist, but the organisms found in the discharges are not those which remain latent in the deeper tissues. During the earlier part of the war, as soon as wound cases which had partially or completely healed came up for subsequent operation, readjusting deformities and other surgical treatment, it was found that, despite the greatest precautions of modern surgery, a certain number of wounds submitted to re-operation developed acute inflammation, with or without suppuration, and for the most part within twenty-four hours, and that associated with the local disturbance in the wound severe constitutional disturbance supervened, signalized by hectic fever and signs of generalized infection. At first such "flares" were attributed to failure in the asepsis of the operation, the surgeon invariably blaming his technique when such untoward symptoms arose ; but it was observed that even healed wounds subjected to simple massage showed the same tendency to light up after manipulation, that a stiff joint such as the knee in fractured femur cases might become the seat of active suppuration as the immediate result of simple passive movements, especially if a wound had pre-existed in the immediate vicinity of the joint. As a result of these "flares," as they have been termed, following upon operation and simple movement massage, investigation has brought to light the fact that the bacteria which infected so large a proportion of the wounds remain latent in the wounded but healed tissues for very long periods, and that when disturbed they may become active again and give rise to severe and even fatal infection. In some instances a foreign body, such as a bullet or a portion of shell case, has been present in a healed cavity. The following cases illustrate this.

Case 1.—Wounded June 1918, compound fracture of femur at junction of middle and upper third. March 1919, healed with the exception of a small sinus at the site of injury. Knee-joint somewhat stiff with disuse. Sinus excised and wound sutured. Knee-joint bent 10° to increase movement. Twenty-four hours later, rigor, and temperature rose to 103° F. Two days later, incision into thigh, swelling of knee-joint, which was opened and found full of pus on the seventh day after the first operation. Four weeks later, the temperature remaining up and the condition of the case being desperate, the leg was amputated at the knee-joint.

Case 2.—Wounded April 1918. Femur—compound fracture. April 1919, some necrotic bone and a small metal fragment removed on the 342nd day after injury. On the fourth day after operation the temperature had reached 105° F., the whole thigh was œdematous and red, but there were no bullæ and no evidence of gas in the tissues. Streptococci were present in the urine, but absent from the blood. Bacteriological examination at the time of operation—metal fragment embedded in semi-gelatinous fluid in a cavity in the bone.

Bacillus welchii, B. sporogenes, B. tertius group and streptococci (anaërobic) were isolated from the fluid surrounding the metal fragment.

Penhallow reports a case of " flare " due to latent gas infection in a healed wound seventy-five days after injury. *B. welchii* was isolated from the tissues two days after the operation.

The presence of latent bacteria in wound tissues does not always give rise to suppuration or constitutional disease even when operations are performed, in fact, probably not more than 50 per cent. of such cases "flare," even though metallic fragments surrounded by gelatinous material containing anaërobic bacteria are discovered.

Slade and Laus found 4 out of 15 bullets removed to be sterile and 16 out of 27 shell fragments, all from healed wounds. Fronnin found 3 out of 20 encapsuled shell fragments were sterile.

The following case is illustrative of the prolonged period during which organisms may remain latent and yet not give rise to disease when disturbed :—

Case 3.—The man was wounded in the early part of the war in 1914 by a rifle bullet which lodged in the neck of his right femur : the wound healed and he returned to duty, the bullet remaining *in situ*. In October 1918 he was again wounded but in another part of the body (shoulder). He had complained of discomfort in his right thigh for some time before the second wound, and, therefore, when in hospital he requested that an operation should be performed to remove the foreign body from the femur. The bullet was removed and a bacteriological examination carried out. Two types of anaërobic bacilli were isolated from this bullet—the *B. sporogenes* and a round-end-sporing bacillus belonging to the *tertius* group. *B. welchii* was not present and no organisms of the coccal group were found. The patient made an uninterrupted recovery, no local suppuration ensued and no constitutional disturbance.

A large number of other cases, of which the above is an example, can be cited in which foreign bodies remaining in the tissues and completely healed over retain the infection for periods up to and exceeding four years (see Table III).

Latent infection is not confined to foreign bodies such as metal fragments and clothing, but may persist in fragments of bone and bony tissue. The following is an illustrative case and may be quoted as a typical example of the cases included in Tables II, III and IV, which give the incidence of bacteria demonstrated as present in bone injuries for long periods after the original wound.

Case 4.—Compound fracture of the tibia ; first bacteriological examination on the fourth day after wounding ; a small perforating wound in the anterior surface of the middle of the tibia and two large exit wounds in the calf. There was no pus, but on stethoscopic examination, gas infiltration was recognized ; the wound was widely opened up and during the operation cultivations and tissue for histological examination were obtained. *B. welchii, Vibrion septique, B. sporogenes* and *B. tertius* group were demonstrated in the cultures. The microscope showed early signs of gas infiltration, but much blood infiltration due to diapedesis as well as rupture of the vessels. Proliferation of the connective tissue was in progress and very few polymorphonuclear cells were found. The muscle bundles showed the irregular staining and other features, common to early gas infiltration. Very few organisms could be found in the sections, even after prolonged search. The patient made an uninterrupted but slow recovery. Another bacteriological examination was made on the 668th day after injury, of a fragment of bone removed from the cavity which had granulated and healed over. *B. sporogenes* was demonstrated in addition to streptococci. *B. sporogenes* was present in each examination, six of which were made at intervals up to the hundredth day, when the patient was transferred to an auxiliary hospital, and the seventh and last examination on return to the main hospital.

The presence of various anaërobes belonging to one of the four classes already cited, namely, *B. welchii, B. sporogenes, Vibrion septique* and the group of round-end-sporing bacilli, *B. tertius*, in which group probably *B. tetani* is included, has been demonstrated in completely healed wounds after periods varying from 100 to 1,825 days.

Histological examination of many healed wounds reveals evidence of gas infiltration of the tissues having accompanied or immediately followed the original wound, although no clinical signs of such disease were present. Fig. 3 shows wounded tissue after a period of thirty-two days and the active repair taking place in gas infiltrated tissue, whilst Fig. 4 shows, thirty-nine days after wounding, the typical appearances of replacement of muscle-fibre damaged by gas infection, although the clinical signs were absent. In the completely healed wound, where the whole of the muscle-fibre has been replaced by irregular fibrous tissue, the demonstration of old gas infection is not so easy, but the masses of fibrous tissue running in between the normal muscle have a characteristic appearance, and point to previous disruption of the muscle bundles followed by cell infiltration.

Bacterial Incidence in Wounds.

In order to approach satisfactorily the question of latent sepsis, it is essential first of all to study the character and percentage infection for all types of unhealed and recent wounds

and then to compare these results with the bacteriological
findings in healed wounds. The series of 1,472 cases in which
observations on this point were made form three categories,
according to the time which had elapsed from the receipt of
the wound to the date of the bacteriological examination.
The first period is from one to fifteen days, the second from
sixteen to fifty days, and the third more than fifty days after
the original injury. In the examination of the cases the routine
method of examination adopted was by (1) film preparations
from the discharge stained by Gram and Giemsa's methods ;
(2) cultivations from the depths of the wound, (a) aërobic—agar,
glucose formate broth, (b) anaërobic—minced meat and litmus
milk. The anaërobic cultures were incubated in a special
anaërobic jar in an atmosphere of hydrogen, after preliminary
exhaustion with an air-pump. The cultures were examined
and Gram-stained films made at intervals of one, two, three
and eight days, the routine methods adopted in the recognition
of the organisms being those laid down in the Special Report
on Anaërobes issued by the Medical Research Council. In the
film preparations the presence of streptococci, free spores or
sporing bacilli, Gram-positive bacilli and Gram-negative
bacilli were noted. In the cultivations the growth of streptococci aërobically and anaërobically were noted and the presence
of four groups of anaërobes determined—*B. welchii*, *B.
sporogenes*, *B. tertius* group and other anaërobes. Of the 1,472
wounds examined, 671 were investigated in from one to fifteen
days of injury.

Table I gives the percentage incidence of the six groups of
organisms as determined by cultivation as well as the organisms
seen in the film preparations of the wound discharge, and the
percentage incidence in " All wounds " is contrasted with those
of one to fifteen days.

The presence of spores in the wound discharges was recorded
in 9 per cent. of the 671 cases examined one to fifteen days
after injury. Dean and Mouat recorded spores in 2 out of
18 cases (11 per cent.) examined between September 1914 and
June 1915. Actual spores were not so frequent as Gram-
positive large bacilli (28 per cent.). Goadby's series of 1,472
cases in Table I comprise wounds examined during the whole
period of the war, and it is important to recall that the
percentage of wounds with spores in the discharges progressively
declined toward the later period from 12 per cent. in 1915,
to 6 per cent. both in 1916 and 1917, and 2 per cent. in 1918.
The incidence of Gram-positive bacilli in wound discharges

also diminished from 37 per cent. in 1915 and 36 per cent. in 1916 to 28 per cent. in 1917 and 20 per cent. in 1918. This diminution was no doubt due to early excision of an increasing proportion of the wounds during 1918. On comparing " All wounds " with the cases examined one to fifteen days after wounding in Table I, certain organisms, especially *B. tertius* group and streptococci, are found more frequently in the " All wound " series than in the more recent wounds (one to fifteen days). Bone injuries show a higher bacterial infection percentage than the all wound series, especially the compound and comminuted fractures. The flora of bone injuries is of primary importance in latent sepsis.

TABLE I.

Percentage Incidence of certain Organisms in all Types of Wound.

	1,472 cases.	671 cases.
	All wounds.	1 to 15 days after injury.
Gram-stained films of wound discharge—		
Spores free or in bacilli..	6 per cent.	9 per cent.
Streptococci	25 ,,	66 ,,
Gram-positive bacilli	28 ,,	28 ,,
Gram-negative bacilli	25 ,,	27 ,,
Aërobic and anaërobic cultivations—		
Aërobic streptococci	48 ,,	46 ,,
Anaërobic streptococci	75 ,,	60 ,,
B. welchii	29 ,,	37 ,,
B. sporogenes	32 ,,	32 ,,
B. tertius group (round and oval end spores)	29 ,,	11 ,,
Other anaërobic bacilli	20 ,,	24 ,,

From the 1,472 cases a group has been specially selected comprising injuries in which compound comminuted fracture of large bones had occurred at the original wounding. The bacteriological examinations of these cases are given in Table II; the relative frequency percentage of the various organisms in every case is higher for the " bone injuries " than for " all wounds."

With the exception of streptococci, the one to fifteen-day wounds of bone show a higher infection-rate than those examined at a later period. In wounds generally, therefore, there appears an increase of streptococcal infection in the older wounds, but while a comparison of Tables I and II shows an increased percentage of streptococci in the later examined wounds, there

is a diminution in the number of anaërobic bacilli, except in
the *tertius* group in Table I. Anaërobic streptococci in these
tables implies the development of streptococci in the anaërobic
cultivation tubes, often without corresponding growth in the
aërobic cultivations (60 per cent. as against 75 per cent.).
The proportional percentage incidence of the organisms
scheduled in the two groups is seen to be somewhat similar.
In 100 open wounds two to twenty-two days after injury,
Henry found anaërobes in 72 per cent., *B. welchii* in
66 per cent. and *B. sporogenes* in 48 per cent., while in an
analysis of 210 cases, Fleming found *B. welchii* in 34 per
cent. and streptococci in 90 per cent. eight to twenty days
after wounding. To elucidate still further the question of
reinfection or persistent infection of wound tissues the cases
of "bone injury" were scrutinized and those selected in which
a second bacteriological examination had been made at least
fifty days subsequent to the first, both examinations having
been made during surgical operations, the first examination
within fifteen days of injury. In many of the cases the last
bacteriological examination was made after more than a year's
interval from the first. One hundred and nine cases were so
examined and are given in Table III. The first examination
in every case was made during one to fifteen days after injury.
The bacterial groups are similar to those in Tables I and II,
and the tables are therefore strictly comparable.

TABLE II.

*Percentage Incidence of certain Organisms in Wounds complicated with
Compound Comminuted Fracture of Bone.*

	387 cases—all examinations.	96 cases—1 to 15 days after wound.
Gram-stained films of wound discharge—		
Spores free or in bacilli..	12 per cent.	18 per cent.
Streptococci	31 ,,	50 ,,
Gram-positive bacilli	32 ,,	51 ,,
Gram-negative bacilli	31 ,,	35 ,,
Cultivations—		
Aërobic streptococci	65 ,,	61 ,,
Anaërobic streptococci	79 ,,	75 ,,
B. welchii	35 ,,	53 ,,
B. sporogenes	38 ,,	49 ,,
B. tertius group (round and oval end spores)	31 ,,	42
Other anaërobic bacilli	20 ,,	28

TABLE III.

Persistence of certain Organisms in Bone Wounds.

109 Cases.	Films from Discharge.				Cultivations.					
					Aërobic.		Anaërobic.			
	Spores.	Strepto-cocci.	Gram-positive bacilli.	Gram-negative bacilli.	Strepto-cocci.	Strepto-cocci.	B. welchii.	B. sporo-genes.	B. tertius group.	Other anaërobic bacilli.
1st examination (1 to 15 days after injury)	11	36	39	30	68	74	35	34	38	18
1st and 2nd examinations (at least 50 days later) ..	7	7	8	7	35	60	12	10	11	1
Last examination only ..	1	10	5	16	22	17	11	16	12	7

TABLE IV.

Persistence of certain Organisms in 113 Cases of Healed Wounds not previously Examined.*

113 Cases.	Films from Discharge.				Cultivations.					
					Aërobic.	Anaërobic.				
	Spores.	Strepto-cocci.	Gram-positive bacilli.	Gram-negative bacilli.	Strepto-cocci.	Strepto-cocci.	B. welchii.	B. sporo-genes.	B. tertius group.	Other anaërobic bacilli.
1st examination at time of operation	—	—	—	—	29	57	15	42	27	—

* Including closed cavities with metal fragments, nerve operations and excision of joints.

TABLE V.

*Persistence of certain Organisms in 671 Cases of Open Wounds.**

671 Cases.	Films from Discharge.				Cultivations.					
					Aërobic.	Anaërobic.				
	Spores.	Strepto-cocci.	Gram-positive bacilli.	Gram-negative bacilli.	Strepto-cocci.	Strepto-cocci.	B. welchii.	B. sporo-genes.	B. tertius group.	Other anaërobic bacilli.
1st examination (1 to 15 days after injury)	9	66	28	27	46	60	37	32	11	24

* Flesh wounds and those involving bone examined.

M

A somewhat significant fact emerges from Table III. It will be seen that a certain proportion of the wounds examined show a different flora at the two examinations, but that the number of wounds showing the presence of the same organism at both examinations is roughly one-third among the sporing anaërobic bacilli and more than two-thirds with streptococci of anaërobic habit. Further, about two-thirds of the anaërobes apparently disappear, but less than a quarter of the anaërobic streptococci. These wounds were all so far healed—the majority completely —that the surgeon deemed operative procedure safe.

Two other series of figures are included in Tables IV and V for comparison, (1) a series of 113 cases of healed wounds in which the first bacteriological examination was made at the time of operation, and (2) the series of 671 cases " all wounds " from Table I examined one to fifteen days after injury (first examination only). It may be considered, therefore, that the whole of the organisms in the " closed cavity cases," and the organisms in the second and third divisions of the 109 cases were " latent," in that there were no clinical symptoms of their presence, and yet cultivations obtained under strict precautions during the operations gave luxuriant growths demonstrating the vitality of the sequestered bacteria.

Histology of Latent Infection.

Healed wound tissues frequently give unmistakable evidence of healed gas infection and it is demonstrable that the splitting of the soft tissues near the original wound by gas distension greatly contributed to the persistence of bacteria in the wound.

Figs. 1 and 2 are of muscle tissue removed from a wound on the twelfth day of injury ; there were no clinical signs of gas infection. Fig. 1 shows unmistakable separation of the muscle bundles and irregular staining of the tissue. Fig. 2, taken a few fields away from Fig. 1 of the same specimen, shows commencing replacement of the muscular fibres, which will ultimately become obliterated by fibrous replacement tissue.

Figs. 3 and 4 are muscle tissue from a wound on the thirty-second day after injury and show the infiltration of the gas-distended muscle bundles by round-celled infiltration ; the transverse section shows the relationship of the disrupted bundles, while the longitudinal section gives a clear picture of the infiltration. Figs. 5 and 6 are high-power magnifications ($\times$ 1,000) of the two previous sections, and show the bacteria present in the tissue.

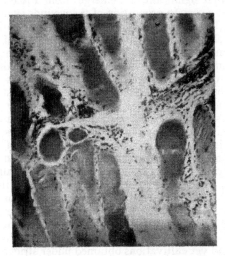

Fig. 1.—Muscle removed at operation twelve days after wounding (shell fragment). Separation of muscle bundles, irregular staining of muscle tissue, commencing repair after mild gas infiltration. Stained hæmatoxylin and eosin. (x 150.)

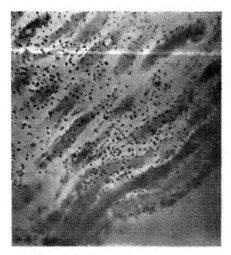

Fig. 2.—Muscle tissue, same specimen as Fig. 1, a short distance farther from the actual injury, partial destruction of muscle structure and replacement commencing

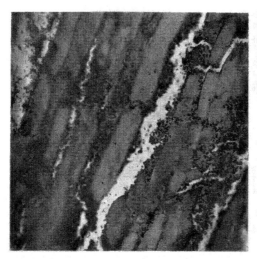

Fig. 3.—Muscle tissue removed from wound of hand on thirty-second day after injury by shell fragment ; longitudinal section, repair of gas infiltrated tissue.

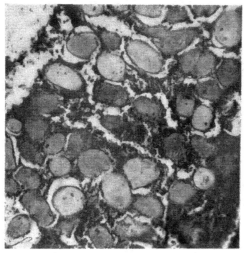

Fig. 4.—Muscle tissue removed from wound of hand on thirty-second day after injury by shell fragment ; transverse section, repair of gas infiltrated tissue.   Stained hæmatoxylin and eosin.   (x 150.)

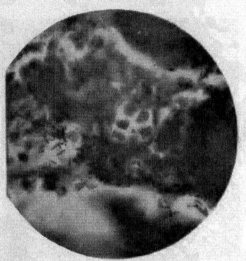

Fig. 5.—A portion of Fig. 3, highly magnified, showing organisms in tissue.

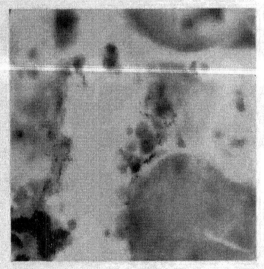

Fig. 6.—A portion of Fig. 4, highly magnified, showing organisms in tissue and active phagocytosis. Stained Gram-Weigert. (x 1,000.)

The histology confirms the bacteriological findings in respect to the soft tissues. In the case of bony injuries the correlation is more difficult. The specimens of bony tissue generally available were mainly sequestra and portions of bone in the immediate vicinity of chronic suppuration of latent infection which were removed at operation. It was noted that cultivations made from bone cavity gave a more luxuriant growth from the sequestrum or from the tissue underneath the granulation tissue lining the cavity than from the granulation tissue of the cavity or from the pus present in the cavity. Some idea of the mechanism of infection in these cases is

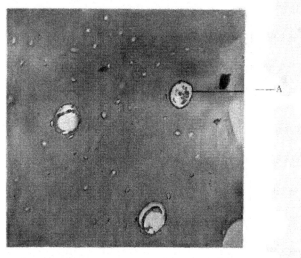

Fig. 7.—Hard sequestrum removed from cavity wall in fractured femur 180 days after injury: unaltered bone structure with Haversian canals: one at "A" plugged with cellular material. Stained Gram-Weigert. (x 150.)

suggested by Figs. 7, 8, 9 and 10, which are portions of a sequestrum removed one hundred and eighty days after the original injury. The sequestrum was hard and white and firmly adherent to the surrounding bony wall of the cavity, of which it apparently formed a part. The low-power photograph (Fig. 7) shows that the bone structure is partially intact but that the Haversian systems are prominent. The Haversian systems were found in some cases blocked, Fig. 8 being the high-power photograph of the blocked canal in Fig. 7.

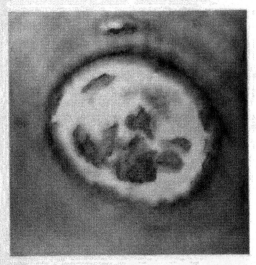

Fig. 8.—Haversian canal at "A" (Fig. 7), highly magnified, showing cellular plug in canal containing bacteria. Stained Gram-Weigert. (x 1,000.)

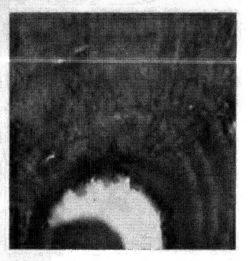

Fig. 9.—Wall of Haversian canal from Fig. 7, showing structure and canaliculi. Stained hæmatoxylin and eosin. (x 1,000.)

An examination of the cells in this canal shows bacteria present and it appears probable that contributions to latent infection are made by organisms remaining sequestered in the Haversian canals of bone into which they enter before coagulation has taken place.   Figs. 9 and 10 are from the same sequestrum and show well-marked staining and enlargement of the canaliculi of the bone.   Fig. 9 is stained by hæmatoxylin-eosin, whereas Fig. 10 is stained by Gram-Weigert and shows in the canaliculi dark masses which on examination leave no doubt that they are bacteria, although partially disintegrated.   Figs. 11 and 12

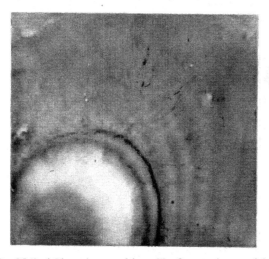

Fig. 10.—Wall of Haversian canal from Fig. 7; organisms and bacterial debris in canaliculi.   Stained Gram-Weigert.   (x 1,000.)

are portions of the end of a previously amputated tibia, excised *post mortem.* This case, after remaining quiescent, developed a serious and fatal septicæmia following a blow on the end of the healed amputated limb.   Streptococci were obtained from the blood and from the urine, and Fig. 12, a high-power photograph, shows the organisms present in the matrix of the cancellous bone.   Fig. 13 is a portion of a soft sequestrum removed from a femur three hundred and seventy-two days after injury, and shows the remains of bacteria present in some of the cellular tissue ; whilst Fig. 14 is a portion of hard sequestrum removed from another fractured femur two years

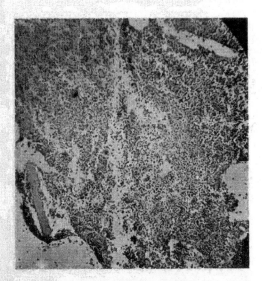

Fig. 11.—Cancellous bone from end of amputated tibia (gas infection), removed *post mortem* 246 days after wound.   Patient died of streptococcal septicæmia.   Cancellous bone, low power,   Stained hæmatoxylin and eosin. (x 150.)

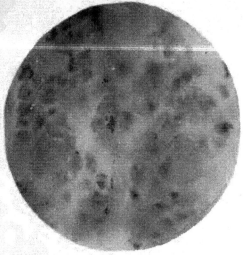

Fig. 12.—Same case as Fig. 11.   High power cocci *in situ* in tissue. Stained Gram-Weigert.   (x 1,000.)

subsequent to the date of injury, showing organisms still
present in the depths of the tissue. The histological examination
of the bony tissue, therefore, fully supports the bacteriological
findings.

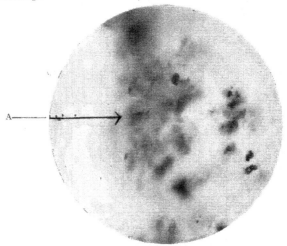

Fig. 13.—Soft sequestrum removed from cavity in fractured femur (shell
wound) 374 days after injury. A large Gram-positive bacillus is seen
encapsulated at " A." Stained Gram-Weigert. (x 100)

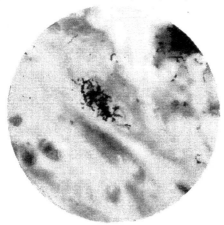

Fig. 14.—Hard sequestrum removed from cavity in fractured femur (shell
wound) two years subsequent to primary wound. Organisms *in situ*.
Stained Gram-Weigert. (x 1,000.)

Clinical Evidence of Latent Infection.

Clinical evidence of "flares" occurring in healed wounds may be referred to finally. Two temperature charts have been selected as they both show "flares" occurring in the same patient upon different occasions. Chart I is a record of two

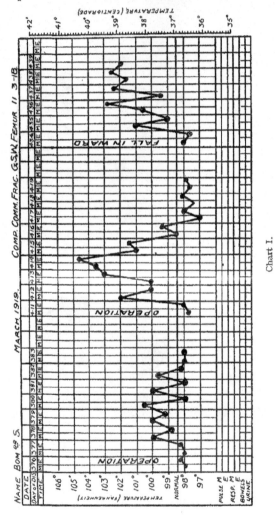

Chart I.

separate operations, each of which was followed by an acute temperature reaction and general signs of blood infection. The last temperature reaction was determined by a slight injury due to a fall in the ward ; no abrasion was caused yet the blow³⁄₂₄ was followed by a rigor and suppuration in the knee-joint.

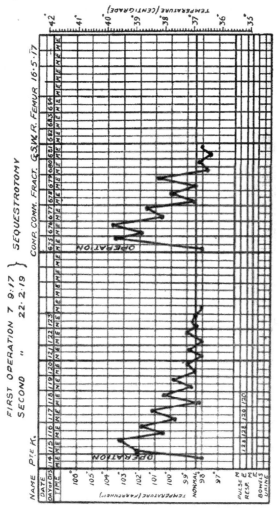

Chart II.

Chart II shows two attacks of acute temperature reaction occurring at an interval of two years in the same case. These two cases are typical of a very large number of " flares " following operation or massage and illustrate the rapidity with which the reactions followed the disturbance of latent organisms. The organism causing these " flares " has in almost every case proved to be a streptococcus, sometimes, but not invariably, hæmolytic. *Streptococcus faecalis* was isolated in the two cases of which the temperature charts are given.

Table VI is a record of 169 cases of subsequent operations ; the primary wounds were healed or partially healed. These cases are divided into two series—those which received three doses of prophylactic vaccine previous to the operation being performed ; the other series " control " cases selected by the surgeon as satisfactory controls. Of the immunized cases, 23 per cent. had a temperature rise of over 100° F., as compared with 65 per cent. of the non-immunized cases. The vaccine administered was a polyvalent streptococcal vaccine containing *B. pyogenes, S. angeosus, S. faecalis* and *S. mitis*,* these organisms being the most common types in cases of " flare " subsequent to operation. This series of cases was carried out in one hospital ;† the cases were all operated on by one surgeon, who selected the control cases. The control and test cases received the same surgical treatment, dressing, etc., and were nursed in the same wards, the only difference being the preliminary administration of the vaccine. The results were so satisfactory that a large-scale experiment was attempted, and it was sought by means of specially devised cards to carry out a general and widespread investigation of the value of prophylactic vaccine. The result of this enquiry was unsatisfactory ; from the record cards returned there appeared to be very slight advantage in favour of the vaccine cases, but by no means as striking as that in the series quoted. It has been impossible to follow the matter up further, but the very striking results obtained when the cases were carefully controlled and the surgical procedure comparable warrant a more extended trial.

Latent infection is, therefore, in some measure a phase of persistent infection, yet the examination of histological preparations of sinuses leading to sequestra and the bacteriological examination of such sinuses, compared with the bacteriology of the sequestra and tissues removed from bone

* The streptococci were typed by the method suggested by Holman.
† Royal Herbert Hospital, Woolwich.

TABLE VI.

Temperature Reactions* of Immunized and Non-immunized Cases.

No. of cases in group.	Type of operation.	Immunized Cases.						Non-immunized Cases.					
		No. of immunized cases.	Temp. 100°F.	Temp. 101°F.	Temp. 102°F. and over.	No. with temp. reaction.	No. with no reaction.	Non-immunized cases.	Temp. 100°F.	Temp. 101°F.	Temp. 102°F. and over.	No. with temp. reaction.	No. with no reaction.
	Healed wounds												
29	Operations on nerves, suture or freeing from scar tissue	2	1	—	—	1	1	27	10	3	—	13	14
10	Metal fragments in bone	3	—	—	—	—	3	7	—	1	1	2	5
4	Bone-grafting	3	2	—	—	2	1	1	—	1	—	1	—
2	Excision of joints	—	—	—	—	—	—	2	1	1	—	2	—
5	Bone-plating	2	1	—	—	1	1	3	—	1	2	3	—
4	Reamputations	2	1	—	—	1	1	2	1	—	—	1	1
2	Tendon operation	2	2	—	—	2	—	—	—	—	—	—	—
1	Empyema healed	1	—	—	—	—	1	—	—	—	—	—	—
	Unhealed wounds												
47	Femur sequestrotomy	15	1	2	—	3	12	32	3	9	8	20	12
23	Tibia ,,	15	2	1	—	3	12	8	2	2	4	8	—
10	Humerus ,,	8	—	—	1	1	7	2	—	1	1	2	—
7	Radius-ulnar ,,	6	1	—	—	1	5	1	—	—	1	1	—
25	Other cases (flesh wounds excised and sutured. Foot, hand, etc.)	13	1	1	—	2	11	12	2	4	4	10	2
169		72	12	4	1	17	55	97	19	23	21	63	34

* The temperature reactions are grouped in three classes—100° F., 101° F., 102° F., occurring within the first six days of the operation.

cavities, have demonstrated that the pus rarely contains the organisms which are discoverable in the deeper layers, even when careful preliminary cleansing of the external wound is performed and material is obtained from the depths of a sinus.

It may therefore be stated as a general conclusion that the wounds of the war, owing to their early infection with large numbers of organisms of the anaërobic class, were predisposed by the incipient gas infiltration of the tissues to the persistence of organisms in the wounded tissues. Such organisms became shut off in the deeper tissues and remained latent for long periods ; exactly how long is by no means clear, but periods of as long as five years have already been demonstrated. It is natural that the persistence of such infections should be accompanied from time to time with an exacerbation of the original infection following operative procedure, but it is remarkable that the actual numbers of " flares," as already defined, should have been so small. Thus, in 119 consecutive secondary operations, of which particulars were obtained at the Royal Herbert Hospital, 47 per cent. gave rise to clinical symptoms of temperature and constitutional disturbance, while 53 per cent. showed no such signs. Some of the " flares " arising after operation have been of a serious and even fatal nature.

BIBLIOGRAPHY.

Bond	..	.. The Recrudescence of Local Sepsis in Completely Healed Wounds.	Brit. Med. Jl., 1915, Vol. ii, p. 467.
Dean & Mouat		.. The Bacteria of Gangrenous Wounds.	Jl. of R.A.M.C.,1916, Vol. xxvi, p. 189.
Elliott & Henry		.. Chylo-hæmothorax from Wounds involving the Thoracic Duct.	Lancet, 1917, Vol. i, p. 872.
Fleming	..	.. On the Bacteriology of Septic Wounds.	Lancet, 1915, Vol. ii, p. 638.
Goadby	..	.. An Enquiry into the Natural History of Septic Wounds.	Lancet, 1916, Vol. ii, pp. 89, 585, 851.
,,	..	.. The Bacterial Flora of War Wounds.	Brit. Med. Jl., 1918, Vol. i, p.581.
,,	..	.. Latent Infection of Healed Wounds.	Lancet, 1919, Vol. i, p. 879.
Penhallow	..	.. Latent Gas Bacillus Infection in a Healed Bullet Wound.	Lancet, 1916, Vol. i, p. 866.

CHAPTER VII.

TETANUS IN ITS STATISTICAL ASPECTS.

A N examination of the records of former wars brings to light one fact that has an important bearing upon the examination of evidence for or against the success of prophylactic measures. It is, that the incidence of tetanus in pre-serum days varied within very wide limits in different campaigns, the variations being apparently unconnected with the relative efficiency of the medical services concerned, with the use of this or that measure of prevention or treatment, or with any other factor within human control. Exact records are not available as to the numbers of cases during the Peninsular battles but it is well known that, in spite of the excellence attained by the surgeons of the British army under the inspiration of McGrigor, tetanus carried off hundreds of our wounded. Again, Rutherford Alcock in his " Notes of the Medical History and Statistics of the British Legion of Spain," published in 1838, records 17 cases of tetanus in 1,351 wounded, an incidence of 12·5 per 1,000. Sir George Ballingall in his " Outlines of Military Surgery " (1838) calculated that the number of tetanus cases amongst the wounded of armies was about 1 in 79. Longmore in his " Gunshot Injuries " (1895) quotes Demme to the effect that tetanus occurred in 10 per 1,000 of the wounded in the Italian hospitals in 1859. Nor was the disease confined to land warfare. Sir Gilbert Blane, quoted by Sir George Ballingall, states that the number of wounded in the naval action of April 1782 in the West Indies was 810, of whom 20, or about 26 per 1,000, were attacked by tetanus, 17 dying of the disease.

In some of the great wars that came later in the last century there seemed to be a decided drop. The official medical history of the British forces in the Crimean war records but 2 cases of tetanus per 1,000 of wounded. The surgical history of the American Civil war shows an incidence of 2 per 1,000 also, and the German statistics of 1870-71 record 3·5 cases of this disease per 1,000.

Finally came a series of wars, the South African campaign, the Nile expedition, the Russo-Japanese war, in which tetanus seemed to have vanished completely, or almost completely, from the catalogue of military diseases, and perhaps there was a tendency to attribute this fact to the more modern methods of surgical treatment, which were meeting with such success in hospital practice in civil life. A little reflection would have sufficed to disturb this optimistic attitude of mind. Longmore had noted that " not a single case of tetanus occurred among the British troops during the New Zealand war, between the years 1863 and 1867." Yet it can hardly be claimed that the surgery in such an expedition and at such a time could have approached modern standards. " There do not appear to have been any cases of tetanus among the large number of gunshot wounds which were treated in the hospitals of Paris on the occasion of the insurrectionary outbreak of 1848; at any rate, there were not sufficient to attract notice."

In the Franco-German war itself, while, as stated, the incidence of tetanus worked out at $3 \cdot 5$ per 1,000 over the whole area of operations during the war, there were marked local variations on either side of this mean, variations that could not be explained by differences in surgical procedure in the different formations of such a highly standardized machine as the German army. At Metz, for instance, tetanus cases amounted only to $1 \cdot 6$ per 1,000, while in the northern theatre the incidence was 11 per 1,000. The true explanation of this variation came with the discovery of the tetanus bacillus by Nicolaier in 1885. The factor of prime importance is the presence of the spores of this bacillus in the soil of the battle area and their introduction into the wound. The presence of these spores in the soil is in its turn largely a question of the degree of admixture with the dung of horses and cattle, the spores being numerous in highly cultivated and well-manured ground and rare in desert spaces or uncultivated land. The mere fact of cultivation, however, or even of heavy manuring, is not in itself sufficient. In the Russo-Japanese war, battles were fought in zones of intensive cultivation on ground manured with both human and horse manure, yet there was practically no tetanus. It must be assumed that in this area either the intestines of man and animals were free from tetanus bacilli or that the climatic or other conditions were such that the spores could not persist in the soil in appreciable numbers. The immunity of the troops from the disease is in itself practically a proof that the tetanus spores were rare or absent in the area of military operations. It is clear that the distribution of this organism over the world's surface is very irregular. In those countries where it is a common saprophyte in the intestines of domestic animals and where the environment is such as to favour the conservation of spores in the soil, tetanus will tend to be of common occurrence amongst the wounded in war.

If it be true, then, that the one essential factor in the endemiology of tetanus is the presence of tetanus spores in the soil of the battle area and that the distribution of this organism over the world is subject to marked variation, then the war of 1914–18, with its far-flung battle-line extending east and west, north and south, might have been expected to provide marked contrasts of tetanus incidence in its different theatres.   It may be said at once that the incidence of tetanus, outside French and Belgian territory, was insignificant.

Only seven cases of the disease occurred in Mesopotamia during the whole period of operations.   Six cases are reported from Gallipoli, all in patients with " trench feet."   In Italy, during 1918, there were but three admissions for tetanus in British hospitals.   Only four cases are known to have occurred in Salonika, according to Crisp English and Kelly.   No information as to tetanus in Egypt is available, from which it may be inferred that there was not enough of this disease to attract attention in that country and Palestine.   As in the Franco-German war of 1870–71, so on the Western front in 1914–18, it was especially in the northern theatre of operations that tetanus presented a serious problem, demanding constant watching, constant record, and a system of prophylaxis founded on the modern conception of the disease.   It is possible that the " favouring " action of calcium salts in the soil, alleged by Cramer and Bullock to facilitate the establishment of tetanus germs introduced into wounds, may help to explain the high incidence of this complication in the northern part of France, where a chalky soil is the rule.

Although many records of the incidence and mortality of tetanus amongst the British during the war have already been published, these have suffered to some extent from the fact that they have tended to deal with the question from the point of view of those who worked at the disease in home territory on the one hand, or of those engaged in collecting information in France on the other.

Sir David Bruce, in the elaborate series of reports which he published, was obliged to confine his statistics to the figures available in England, and his incidence-rates were necessarily based on the numbers of wounded reaching home hospitals. Although these rates give a good general idea of what actually occurred, there is an appreciable factor of error due to the dilution of the wounded by those arriving from theatres of war in which tetanus was rare or absent. And, again, the men suffering from minor wounds, which were capable of being dealt with in the medical units in the front area, who returned direct to their units on discharge from casualty clearing stations or field ambulances, could not be taken into account. The records, published by Sir William Leishman and his co-workers, of wounds from the battle areas suffered, too, in being partial records, based chiefly on the cases of short incubation, since the slow-developing cases tended to occur after the patients had been invalided to home hospitals. The object of the present summary is to combine, as far as possible, all the cases that arose as a result of the military operations in France and Belgium, whether they developed in England or at the front.

Incidence of Tetanus.

Sir David Bruce gives for England a total of 1,458 cases. The published records for France are not quite continuous. Sir William Leishman records 179 cases up to July 1915, and 160 cases from July to October 1916. There are no published records to fill in the gaps, but as tetanus was a notifiable disease in France the tables kept up by Colonel Beveridge, the A.D.M.S. (Sanitation), at General Headquarters, give an approximation to the numbers that arose in the periods not covered by the published reports. These tables show that 28 cases were reported from August to December 1915. The same tables give a total of 148 cases from January to June 1916. From this time onwards, the reports of the Adviser in Pathology at General Headquarters afford reliable information, thanks to the system of records introduced by Sir William Leishman. Taking all these figures together, it is possible to arrive at what must be a fair approximation to the actual case incidence in hospitals in the war area. The cases, so estimated, work out at a total of 1,071. Adding these numbers to those given by Sir David Bruce, it would appear that there were 2,529 cases of tetanus as the result of the fighting in France and Belgium. It is safe to attribute all these cases to the fighting in France without the risk of grave error as the time taken in transferring wounded from other theatres to England was so long as to cover the incubation period even of " modified " tetanus, in all but exceptional cases, and it is known that tetanus was practically absent from the areas of battle in the Eastern and Mediterranean theatres of war. Official figures give the total wounded, less gassed, on the Western front as 1,710,369, so that the incidence of tetanus in those wounded on that front during the whole war amounts to 1·47 per 1,000. It may perhaps be pointed out that this figure shows but little improvement on that of the American Civil war or the Crimean war (2 per 1,000), or that it compares badly with many campaigns of recent and ancient times. But it must be remembered that the fighting was taking place in an area already notorious for its danger, an area in which the German troops had recorded an incidence of 11 cases per 1,000 of wounded in 1870–71. And, again, in no previous war and in no other theatre were the combatants exposed to wounding by projectiles of so terrible a character, and to conditions so well calculated to ensure earth contamination of wounds, or that tended so greatly to hamper the early collection of casualties from the scene of injury. The true measure of the success of the prophylactic methods is to be found, not in a comparison with other wars but in the contrast between the earlier months of the war on the Western front and subsequent periods of the operations in the same area.

Tetanus Incidence by Months.—The incidence per 1,000 for each month of the war is set forth in Chart I. This record, while approximating in the main to that of Bruce, differs from it in that it is based on the combined monthly incidence in the hospitals both in France and England, and that it is calculated not on the wounded arriving in England but on the numbers of wounded, less gassed, actually occurring in each month in France and Belgium. It will be remarked that, while Bruce's diagram shows an incidence of 3·7 only for August 1914, the addition of cases in France brings the total incidence in that month to 8·5 per 1,000, thus removing what had appeared an inexplicable contrast with the following month. The numbers for the early part of 1915, based on the tables of the A.D.M.S. (Sanitation), are certainly below the true numbers as they are from "disease notifications" only, an unreliable source of information when fighting is severe, and are not founded on "case sheets" like the subsequent records. Still, it may be taken that the fluctuations shown are on the whole fairly correct. A curious difference from Bruce's diagram is found in the high incidence now brought to light in the early months of 1916. Some of this increase may perhaps be due to the tetanus of "trench feet," which was probably common during the months in question. It is to be noted that nearly half the total cases in France in

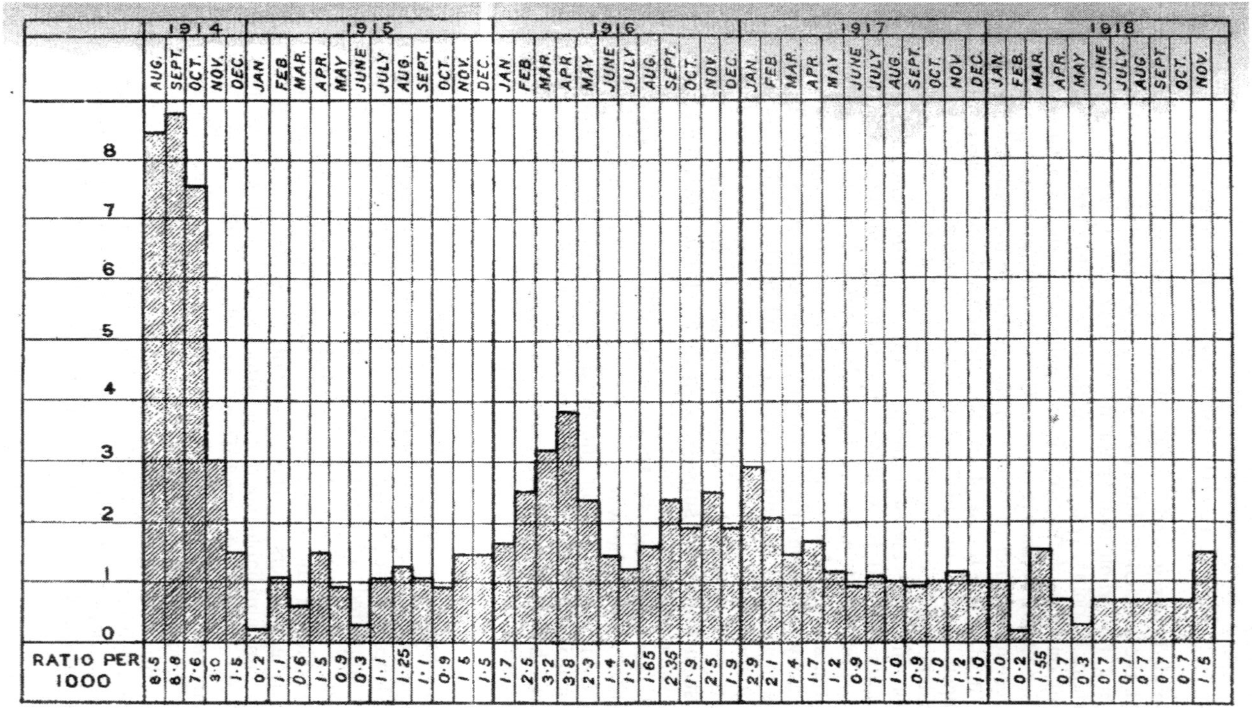

CHART I.—RATIO PER 1000 OF CASES OF TETANUS TO TOTAL WOUNDED (LESS GASSED).

Year	Month	Ratio per 1000
1914	AUG	8·5
	SEPT	8·8
	OCT	7·6
	NOV	8·0
	DEC	1·5
1915	JAN	2·0
	FEB	1·1
	MAR	0·6
	APR	1·5
	MAY	0·9
	JUNE	0·3
	JULY	1·1
	AUG	1·25
	SEPT	1·1
	OCT	0·9
	NOV	1·6
	DEC	1·5
1916	JAN	1·7
	FEB	2·5
	MAR	3·2
	APR	3·8
	MAY	2·3
	JUNE	1·4
	JULY	1·2
	AUG	1·65
	SEPT	2·35
	OCT	1·9
	NOV	2·5
	DEC	1·9
1917	JAN	2·9
	FEB	2·1
	MAR	1·4
	APR	1·7
	MAY	1·2
	JUNE	0·9
	JULY	1·1
	AUG	1·0
	SEPT	0·9
	OCT	1·0
	NOV	1·2
	DEC	1·0
1918	JAN	1·0
	FEB	0·2
	MAR	1·55
	APR	0·7
	MAY	0·3
	JUNE	0·7
	JULY	0·7
	AUG	0·7
	SEPT	0·7
	OCT	1·0
	NOV	1·5

RATIO PER 1000

8 7 6 5 4 3 2 1 0

796.100/30.4964/502 1500.10.22

December 1916 were from this cause and have consequently been deducted from the total in estimating the incidence in relation to wounded in that month.   It is probable that some such deduction ought to be made for the wet and trying months of the winter of 1915–16, but in the absence of reliable information it is thought better to let the totals stand.   Another element may perhaps enter into this question.   The Fourth Army was formed and moved into the Somme area in February 1916.   Here this army had to occupy ground containing an excessively high proportion of chalk, over which no severe fighting had yet taken place, and where much land was still under relatively undisturbed cultivation.   It is at least possible that in these factors some explanation of the rise in tetanus incidence may be found.   ·Whatever may be the cause, it is a remarkable fact that the case incidence in the early months of 1916 reaches a higher level than at any other period subsequent to 1914.   From the spring of 1917 onwards to the end of the war the incidence continues steadily low and is remarkably free from fluctuations.   The regularity of the record is broken only by the two apices that follow the heavy fighting of March and November 1918, when the evacuation of wounded was disorganized owing to the rapid moves of casualty clearing stations during the retreat and subsequent advance, with consequent interference with surgical technique.

Mortality in Tetanus.

In former wars tetanus appears to have been an almost universally fatal disease, the case mortality usually being about 85 per cent.   Sir Gilbert Blane is said by Ballingall to have had a death-rate of 85 per cent., or 17 deaths in 20 cases, after a naval engagement.   Dr. Rutherford Alcock recorded 15 deaths in 17 cases, or 88·2 per cent., in the British Legion in Spain.   Demme is quoted by Longmore to have had 85 deaths in 92 cases in the Italian campaign of 1859, a death-rate of 92·4 per cent.   More important figures, because they are based on larger numbers, are those of the American Civil war and the Franco-German war of 1870–71, in which the mortality was 89·3 per cent. in 505 cases and 90 per cent. in 350 cases respectively.

In the total of 2,529 cases already mentioned as having occurred in the wounded in the British hospitals on the Western front in 1914–18, there were 1,254 deaths, amounting almost exactly to 50 per cent.   This number, though it compares very favourably with any previous record, is certainly an over-statement. The wounds in which tetanus arose were often of a terrible severity, and it is beyond question that many of the deaths attributed to tetanus were in reality due to the wounds themselves, the resultant shock, gas gangrene, or sepsis. Still, it is impossible to sort out correctly all the factors contributing to a fatal termination in the recorded cases ; consequently all patients reported as dying while suffering from tetanus have been included as deaths from that disease.

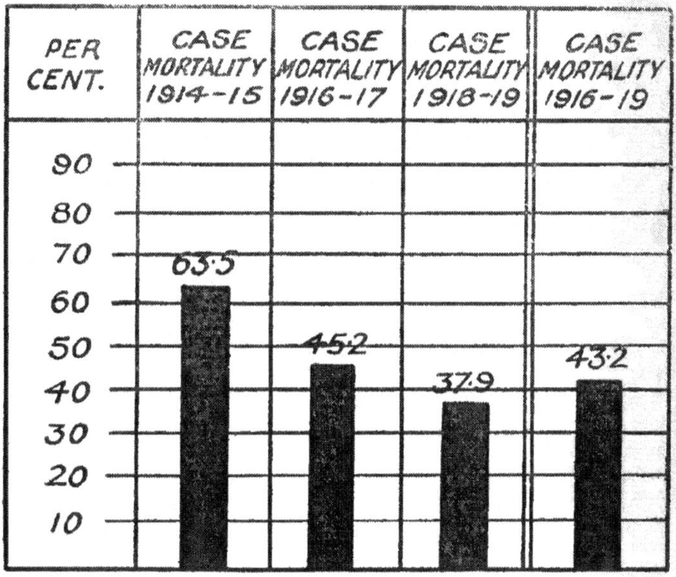

PER CENT.	CASE MORTALITY 1914-15	CASE MORTALITY 1916-17	CASE MORTALITY 1918-19	CASE MORTALITY 1916-19
90				
80				
70	63·5			
60				
50		45·2		43·2
40			37·9	
30				
20				
10				

Chart II.—Illustrating reduction in case mortality in tetanus during the war.

In this figure, too, are included the deaths over the whole period of the war, but as will be shown directly, the case mortality was much greater during the early months than during any subsequent period.

This gradual reduction in case mortality was a marked feature in the reports from the office of the Adviser in Pathology in France and also in those by Sir David Bruce in England. As was to be expected, the mortality-rates in home hospitals were always considerably lower than in hospitals in France, owing to the former dealing to a greater extent with the late cases and with groups of patients in which the disturbing factor of death from hæmorrhage, shock and acute sepsis was much less operative. It is not possible to obtain completely reliable figures of the mortality at all periods of the war for the cases occurring in France, some of the records used in computing the gross mortality being estimates only. The published records from France are reliable, but deal with irregular periods which, while illustrating the character of the mortality in the cases dealt with, do not fall into definite yearly series. For this reason annual mortality-rates for France, similar to those published for England by Sir David Bruce, have not been compiled. To get an idea of the real fall in mortality in all cases from the Western front, the published records only have been used and have been sorted into two-yearly periods. The result is given in Chart II. In the last column, the mortality from 1916 to 1919 is given, and is seen to be as low as 43·2 per cent., showing that when the period of insufficient prophylaxis is excluded, the death-rate from tetanus had been reduced to about half that recorded in previous wars. That this very satisfactory diminution in the death-rate was largely due to the almost universal use of anti-tetanic serum as a measure of prophylaxis will be shown later, but it is desirable before entering upon this question to discuss the non-specific factors that have had a bearing on mortality in tetanus.

Non-specific Factors influencing Mortality in Tetanus.—The large number of multiple wounds was a feature of the war, owing no doubt to the extensive use of high explosive shells, bombs and grenades. Sir David Bruce records the occurrence of 576 multiple wounds with a mortality of 176, and 882 single wounds with 325 deaths. Table I gives an analysis of 632

TABLE I.

Mortality and Incidence as regards Position of Wound in Cases of Tetanus.

Site of Wound.	632 Cases of Tetanus in British Hospitals in France.				
	No. of Cases.	Incidence per cent.	Recovered	Died.	Case Mortality per cent.
Multiple wounds ..	284	45·0	86	198	69·8
Single wounds ..	348	55·0	122	226	64·9
Head, neck and face..	18	5·1	8	10	55·5
Trunk	66	18·9	10	56	84·8
Upper extremity ..	76	21·8	23	53	69·6
Lower extremity ..	188	54·2	81	107	56·9

TABLE I.—*continued.*

Site of Wound in cases of single Wounds.	880 Cases of Tetanus in Home Hospitals.				
	No. of Cases.	Incidence per cent.	Recovered	Died.	Case Mortality per cent.
Head, neck and face..	29	3·3	24	5	17·2
Trunk	135	15·2	80	51	37·8
Upper extremity ..	236	26·7	132	101	43·3
Lower extremity ..	480	54·4	303	171	36·1

Site of Wound.	505 Cases of Tetanus in the American Civil War.				
	No. of Cases.	Incidence per cent.	Recovered	Died.	Case Mortality per cent.
Head, neck and face..	21	4·1	1	20	95·2
Trunk	55	10·9	5	50	90·9
Upper extremity ..	137	27·2	18	119	86·8
Lower extremity ..	292	57·8	30	262	89·7

cases of tetanus in British hospitals in France, with 284 multiple wounds, of which 198 died. In the same table is given an analysis of 505 cases of tetanus in the American Civil war, and Sir David Bruce's analysis of single wounds in cases arising in home hospitals during the war. Several points of interest arise in studying this table. The enormous excess of the mortality-rate in all types of wounds in the American Civil war is at once apparent, showing that the factor of difference, whatever it may have been, is equally operative in wounds of all situations. While the mortality in hospitals in France is greater in all types than that in England, it will be noticed that the difference is particularly marked in wounds of the trunk. This fact lends point to the remark previously made as to the factor of error underlying statistics of mortality in tetanus cases, especially in the cases of short incubation treated in the hospitals in France. The excessive death-rate, in the French series, from wounds of the trunk is explicable in terms of the danger of all penetrating wounds of the chest, abdomen and spine. That these three types of wounds all showed a very high rate of mortality will be seen on examining Table II., in which the same series of 632 cases in France is analysed in greater detail. In the latter table, too, where the accidental wounds are separated from those due to weapons of war, an interesting point comes to light. It is seen that

TABLE II.

A further Analysis of Mortality in relation to Position of Wounds in 632 Cases of Tetanus—France, 1916–18.

Nature of Wound.	Tetanus in Battle Wounds.			Tetanus in Accidental Wounds.			Tetanus in all Wounds.			Deaths per cent.
	Total.	Recd.	Died.	Total.	Recd.	Died.	Total.	Recd.	Died.	
Multiple wounds ..	282	85	197	2	1	1	284	86	198	69·8
Head and neck	15	7	8	3	1	2	18	8	10	55·5
Non-penetrating of trunk	29	4	25	1	1	—	30	5	25	83·3
Penetrating of chest ..	25	4	21	—	—	—	25	4	21	84·0
Penetrating of abdomen	11	1	10	—	—	—	11	1	10	90·9
Upper extremity :										
Shoulder and arm ..	30	9	21	2	1	1	32	10	22	68·7
Forearm	7	1	6	1	—	1	8	1	7	87·5
Hand	10	4	6	26	8	18	36	12	24	66·6
Lower extremity ·										
Buttocks and thigh ..	84	31	53	—	—	—	84	31	53	63·0
Knee	20	10	10	2	1	1	22	11	11	50·0
Leg	50	20	30	3	3	—	53	23	30	56·6
Ankle	4	2	2	—	—	—	4	2	2	50·0
Foot	12	6	6	13	8	5	25	14	11	44·0
Total ..	579	184	395	53	24	29	632	208	424	67·0

accidental wounds of the hand proved much more fatal than accidental wounds of the foot. This is probably due to the fact that foot injuries, by making walking painful, compel the sufferer to seek treatment, while wounds of the hand if slight tend to be ignored and the chances of an early prophylactic inoculation are thus diminished. Reverting to Table I, it is of interest to note how closely similar is the distribution of wounds leading to tetanus in the war with that in the American Civil war. In all three analyses, the wounds of the lower extremity represent over 50 per cent. of all single wounds, and the percentages of the wounds of other situations closely correspond.

Clinical Types of Tetanus.—The War Office Tetanus Committee classified cases of tetanus into six clinical types as follows :—

Ai. Trismus the earliest symptom. With complete closure of jaws developing within twenty-four hours after onset of the symptoms.
Aii. Trismus the earliest symptom. With complete closure of jaws developing after twenty-four hours from onset.
Aiii. Trismus the earliest symptom. With incomplete closure of jaws.
B. Trismus occurring after other symptoms of tetanus have shown themselves.
C. General tetanus without trismus.
D. Local tetanus.

This classification was only adopted in France at a comparatively late stage of the war and consequently the material for a complete analysis of the cases arising in that country is lacking. Sir David Bruce has analysed the cases in home hospitals in this connection and a similar analysis of the cases in French hospitals in 1918 has been published by Colonel S. L. Cummins. In order to deal with tetanus on the Western front as a whole, the percentages in these two analyses have been combined. The relative incidence of each type is given in

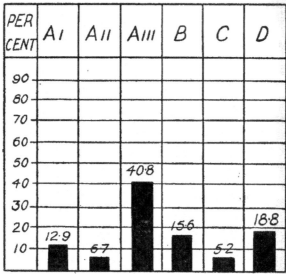

Chart III.—Percentage of incidence of each type of tetanus. Combined figures for England and France.

Chart III and the relative mortality-rates in Chart IV. It will be seen at once that Type Aiii was the commonest variety in the cases analysed and that this type was, with the exception of local tetanus, the least fatal type of the disease. In the types characterized by complete trismus coming on early, the death-rate was so high as to be comparable to the general tetanus death-rate in former wars. At the same time, even these severe types were much less fatal in hospitals in England than in the hospitals in France, showing that cases of late development tended to run a more favourable course. It is a point worthy of note that no case of local tetanus proved fatal in home hospitals, while of 35 cases so classified in France,

8 died, a mortality of 22 per cent.   This difference probably depends on the fact that there were no tetanus inspectors to standardize classification in France.   It is probable that, had these cases been examined by an expert, they would have been placed in some other class.   It seems fairly safe to assume that uncomplicated " local tetanus " is never fatal.   It is an interesting fact that so large a number as 50 cases of general

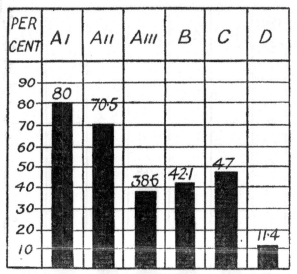

Chart IV.—Percentage tetanus mortality by types.   Combined figures for England and France.

tetanus without trismus arose in home hospitals and 10 in France.   The mortality in these atypical cases was relatively high.

The Interval between Date of Injury and Onset of Tetanus in relation to Mortality.—Ballingall quotes Sir J. McGrigor, to the effect that "if tetanus does not occur for 22 days from the date of the wound, the patient is safe."   While the experience of later wars, fully borne out by recent observations, has demonstrated that this opinion is not by any means in strict conformity with the facts, still the remark may be quoted as indicating that in old wars as well as in new ones, a long interval between the injury and the onset of symptoms is all in favour of the patient.   The surgeons in the American Civil war concluded that " the later the occurrence of tetanus after injury, the better was the chance of recovery." Charts V and VI from the articles by Sir David Bruce and Colonel Cummins respectively, show that, both in the hospitals in England and in France, the mortality-rates fell steadily as the time after wounding increased. Perhaps the best evidence as to this inverse relation between mortality and incubation is to be found in an article by Captain F. Golla, a member of the Tetanus Committee, from which Charts VII and VIII are

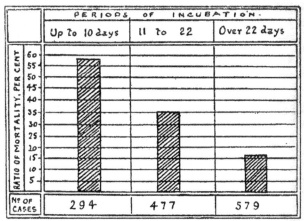

Cha V.—Tetanus in home hospitals. Relation between incubation period and case mortality. (Bruce.)

Chart VI.—Tetanus in hospitals in France. Relation between incubation period and percentage mortality. (Cummins).

here reproduced.   It is manifest, from the records illustrated in these diagrams, that any factor leading to the lengthening of the incubation period will make for a diminution in the death rate from tetanus.   These considerations lead to the necessity for a more detailed consideration of the whole question of the " incubation period " of tetanus in the late war.

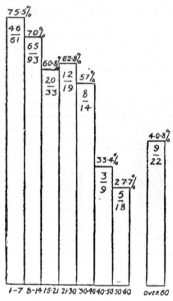

Chart VII.—Mortality of initial trismus cases in English and French hospitals.

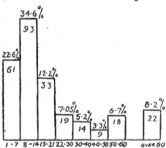

Chart VIII.—Incubation of initial trismus cases in British wounded—England and France 269 cases.   Inverse relation of incubation period to case mortality.
(F. Golla).

The Incubation Period.

Chart IX represents a frequency curve of the incubation periods of all cases up to the forty-fifth day after wounding, for which records exist, in hospitals in France and England during the war. It will be seen that, while there is a rapid ascent in the curve to the seventh day, the highest peak is reached on the eleventh day after which, with the exception of one apex on the fourteenth day, the curve falls gradually

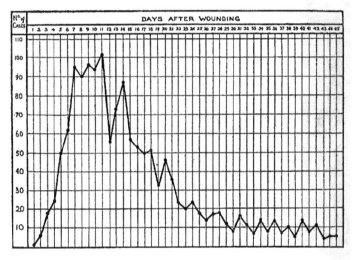

Chart IX.—Incubation periods of 1499 cases of tetanus in France and England. All cases with incubation periods greater than 45 days have been omitted. In addition to those in the chart, 264 cases varied from 46 to 831 days. (Bruce.)

until it ceases to be of sufficient interest to reproduce in diagrammatic form. But although the numbers on any one day cease at about the forty-fifth day to be significant, it is important to notice that the total of cases occurring later than the forty-fifth day was considerable, amounting to 264 cases.

In Chart X, the actual numbers of cases occurring on each day up to the twenty-fifth after wounding, have been reduced to percentages of the whole number within that period, and it has thus been possible to obtain curves, illustrating the differences between the periods of incubation in tetanus cases in the late war and in the American Civil war. A glance at the chart

will show that the largest number of cases occurred on the
eighth day in the American Civil war, or three days earlier
than in the British army in France.   It will be seen, too, that
the British incubation period curve lies consistently below
that of the American Civil war up to the eleventh day, after
which, with one drop on the twelfth day it remains consistently
above it.   The columns to the right of the chart indicate that

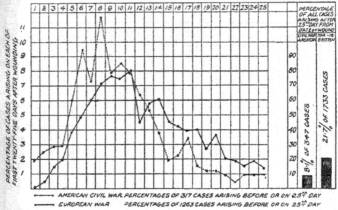

Chart X.—Comparison between incubation periods in American Civil War and
European War, 1914–18, British forces in France.

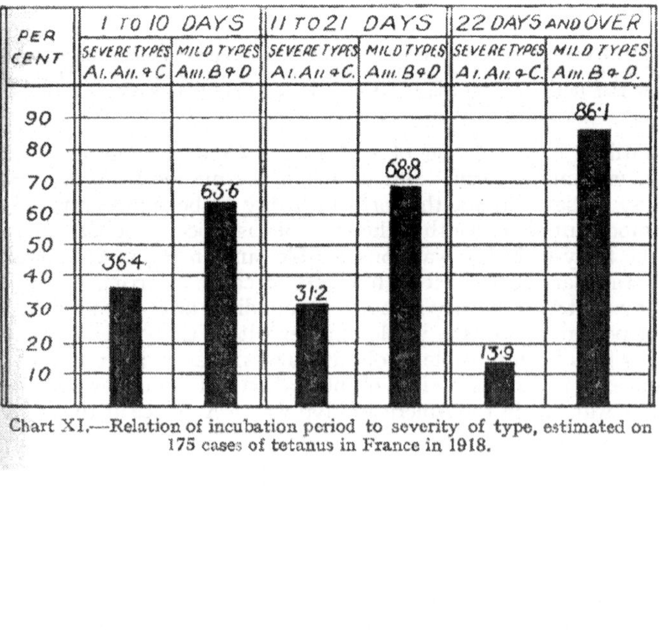

Chart XI.—Relation of incubation period to severity of type, estimated on
175 cases of tetanus in France in 1918.

only 8·1 per cent. of the American cases had a longer incubation period than twenty-five days, while 21·7 per cent. of British cases occurred after that day.   It has already been pointed out that the lengthening of the incubation period goes hand in hand with a lessened case mortality, and it is beyond question that there is an inverse relation between these two elements.

To ascertain whether, apart from its influence on mortality, the lengthening of the incubation period had any actual influence on clinical type, the records of 175 cases occurring in France in 1918 were examined and the result is shown in

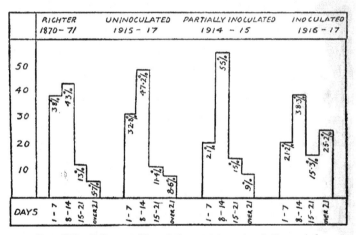

Chart XII.—Influence of inoculation on tetanus incubation periods.

Chart XI.   Here it is seen that there is a steady diminution in the percentage of the severer types, Ai, Aii, and C, and a steady increase of the milder types, Aiii, B and D, as the incubation period increases.

In Chart XII are compared graphs representing the percentages of cases of varying incubation period in the Franco-German war, in non-inoculated British troops in the war of 1914–18, in the partially inoculated British troops in 1914 and 1915, and finally in the British army in 1916 and 1917, when prophylactic inoculation was almost universal.   It will be observed that, while the graph for the non-inoculated men in the 1914–18 war conforms closely to that for the German troops in 1870–71, the graph for the inoculated cases takes a totally different form, owing to the fact that the cases of rapid onset are greatly reduced, while those showing a longer incubation period than twenty-one days are proportionally more numerous.   The conclusion seems inevitable that the prophylactic inoculation was the factor leading to an increase of the incubation period.

The Prophylactic Use of Antitetanic Serum.

Owing perhaps to the fact that recent experience in the South African and Russo-Japanese wars had suggested that tetanus was unlikely to be an element of great importance in modern military operations, the provision of prophylactic serum was made on a small scale, designed to cover its use only in severe wounds of a type specially liable to be complicated by tetanus infection.   The first few weeks of the war sufficed to show that, in the French and Belgian areas of operations at least, every wound was a potential portal of entry for the spores of the tetanus bacillus, and great efforts were made by the War Office to provide serum on a sufficient scale to ensure a prophylactic inoculation to every wounded man.   So successful were these efforts, that by the end of November ample provision was available at the scene of operations.

With the exception of a few hundred doses purchased in Paris early in the war, all the serum used in the British Expeditionary Force was derived from English and American sources and was standardized in terms of the " United States unit."   On this system, one-tenth of a unit of antitoxin is just sufficient to save a standard guinea-pig for four days from the " official test dose " of one hundred minimum lethal doses of toxin, or, in other words, one unit of antitoxin neutralizes one thousand minimal lethal doses of toxin.   The serum for prophylactic use was issued in glass phials each containing 10 c.c., representing 1,500 units of antitoxin.   It was usual to administer to each patient one-third of the contents of a phial, or 500 units, and this was the dose recommended throughout the war by the War Office Tetanus Committee.   In 1916 the Director-General of Medical Services in France issued a circular recommending that, in all wounds involving injury to vessels or to bone and in all lacerated wounds, a larger dose of 1,000 units was desirable.   In many instances, medical officers acting on their own initiative gave half a phial or 750 units as their routine dose.   Every effort was made to administer antitoxin as soon after wounding as possible.   The exact details were in the hands of the Assistant Directors of Medical Services of the divisions, but it may be said that in nearly all cases the first dose was given at the field ambulance and an entry to this effect was made on the field medical card, the amount given being stated.   These cards were examined at the casualty clearing stations, and when no entry was found a prophylactic dose was there given.   In June 1917 instructions were given that four prophylactic inoculations should be given at intervals of seven days and every effort was made to conform to this instruction both in France and England.   In June 1918, on the recommendation of the Adviser in Pathology in France, the initial dose for prophylaxis was raised to 1,500 units in the hope that this measure might, by prolonging the period of high antitoxin concentration in the blood, still further reduce the incidence of tetanus.   The termination of the war in the following November prevented the accumulation of sufficient statistics to justify any conclusion as to the wisdom of this larger inoculation, but it is held by Sir David Bruce that nothing is to be gained by inoculation of more than 500 units if the repeated doses can be ensured to the patient during his evacuation and after arrival in home territory.

Effect of the Prophylactic Inoculation.—Though the area over which fighting took place was well known to be highly charged with tetanic infection, the whole picture of tetanus was definitely more benign than in former wars.   Not only was the incidence much lower than what had prevailed in the same districts in previous campaigns but the mortality was reduced by half, the incubation period prolonged and the clinical types greatly modified in the direction of a lessened severity.   While it is certain that a gradually improving surgical technique contributed materially to these satisfactory results, it is certain, too, that a factor of inestimable importance was the universal use of antitoxin as a prophylactic agent. As has already been pointed out, the incidence of the disease in the early months of the war was over 8 per 1,000 wounded, a figure which compares with that noted in the northern theatre in the Franco-German war of 1870–71.   During these early months, little or no antitetanic serum was available. With the issue of serum on an adequate scale in October and November, the incidence dropped rapidly and reached a very low level by December 1914.   The close association of this drop with the increased supply of serum is illustrated in Chart XIII.   From 1914 onwards, the almost constant use of antitetanic serum eliminates any satisfactory non-inoculated control group with which to draw comparisons.   Certain cases, more especially of accidental wounds, went without the inoculation, but while the total numbers of wounded are known and the incidence statistics can be based on these figures, there is no record of the numerous cuts, scratches and abrasions that went unrecorded and for which no serum was given, and so the incidence of tetanus in terms of non-inoculated accidental wounds cannot be expressed.   From one source only can any reliable information be derived beyond that provided in Charts I and XIII.   For some time no definite orders existed for the use of prophylactic serum in trench foot and the majority of

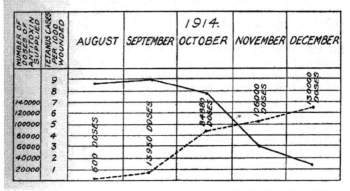

 = TETANUS INCIDENCE PER 1000 WOUNDED.

 = SUPPLY OF ANTITOXIN SENT TO FRANCE MONTHLY.

Chart XIII.—Illustrating fall in tetanus incidence as supply of antitoxic serum increased, 1914.

these cases went unprotected.   In December 1917 the Director-General of Medical Services in France issued an order that serum should be given to all cases of trench foot, and the results were at once apparent in a dramatic fall in the incidence of tetanus in cases of this kind.   This drop in case incidence, occurring in mid-winter at the very time when trench foot was most prevalent, is illustrated in Chart XIV.   Another point which, though less significant, is still worthy of attention in this connection is to be found in Chart I, where it is seen that, while there was marked fluctuation of the tetanus ratio in 1915 and 1916 and in the early months of 1917, the incidence became much more regular and on a lower level for the rest of the war. The order for the administration of repeated prophylactic inoculations was issued in June 1917, and so coincides exactly with the fall of the tetanus incidence to about 1 per 1,000. Although, as has been pointed out, other elements came into consideration to explain the irregularities of incidence in 1916 and 1917, this exact correspondence of a drop in incidence with the commencement of multiple inoculations is very suggestive.

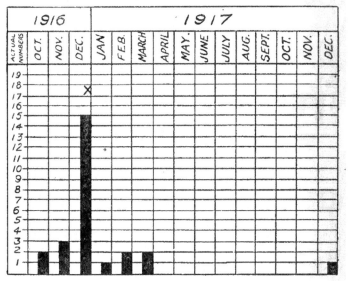

Chart XIV.—Tetanus in trench foot cases, 1916–18.

N.B.—Orders for prophylactic inoculation of all cases of trench foot were issued at the end of December 1916, as indicated by X.

While it is difficult owing to the absence of a satisfactory " control " group to compare incidence in inoculated and non-inoculated patients, it is a simple matter to compare mortality-rates in these two classes. In France, during the latter half of 1916, the whole of 1917 and during 1918 up to the armistice, there were 520 cases in wounded persons in which it can be shown by reliable records that prophylactic inoculation was given. Of these 345 died, a mortality-rate of 66·5 per cent. In the same period there were 160 cases in non-inoculated persons, with 115 deaths, or 71·8 per cent. But a serious fallacy enters into these figures, as many of the non-inoculated cases were in patients with accidental cuts, abrasions and scratches in which the deaths from ancillary causes, such as shock, severe sepsis and hæmorrhage, were altogether absent. If instead of the total number of non-inoculated cases only those in which the injuries were war wounds are taken, it is found that in 72 such cases there were 60 deaths, or a mortality of 83·3 per cent.   These numbers, set out in Table III, afford

TABLE III.

Rate of Mortality in Protected and Unprotected Tetanus Cases in War Wounds.

	No. of Cases.	Recovered	Died.	Mortality per cent.
France (1916, 1917 and 1918)				
Protected	520	185	345	66·5
Unprotected	72	12	60	83·3
England (Sir D. Bruce)				
Protected	899	676	203	22·5
Unprotected	559	260	298	53·3

an interesting comparison with the figures for home hospitals recorded by Sir David Bruce.   In the latter, while the mortality in both groups is much lower than in France, the mortality in the protected group is very much below that in the non-protected cases, a point of importance, as here the error introduced by shock, sepsis, and so on is much less operative owing to the greater lapse of time since wounding.   Nor was it only on the gross mortality that the effects of antitoxin were seen. In Tables IV and V the effect of time of inoculation on the mortality is given for cases in France and in England, and it is seen that on the whole the mortality is greater where the interval between wounding and inoculation is prolonged.

TABLE IV.

The Effect of Time of Inoculation on Mortality.
In Home Hospitals.

Prophylactic Inoculation.	No. of Cases.	Recovered	Died.	Mortality per cent.
On day of wound	611	467	144	23·5
One day after wound	140	111	29	20·7
Two days after wound	106	79	27	25·4

TABLE V.

The Effect of Time of Inoculation on Mortality.

In Hospitals in France.

Prophylactic Inoculation.	No. of Cases.	Recovered	Died.	Mortality per cent.
Inoculation within 24 hours ..	269	99	170	63·2
Inoculation later than 24 hours..	69	16	53	76·7

Chart XV points to a reduction in case mortality with increase of the number of prophylactic doses. While none of these differences are large, they all tend in the same direction and the

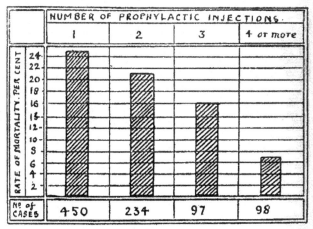

Chart XV.—The effect of one or more prophylactic inoculations on the death-rate. (Bruce.)

cumulative result amounts to a strong argument for the effect of prophylactic administration of serum in lessening the mortality in tetanus. It has already been shown how the prolongation of the incubation period is accompanied by a lower mortality, and it has been claimed that any factor tending to increase the period of incubation will tend to lower the mortality at the same time. Chart XVI, taken from the records of Sir David Bruce, shows clearly that the period of incubation is definitely prolonged by the use of prophylactic inoculations, and it is therefore justifiable to claim that in this way, too, antitetanic serum lessens the case mortality.

Closely bound up with this part of the problem is the action of the serum in modifying the clinical type in the direction of a decrease in severity. "Local tetanus" on anything like a large scale was unknown in previous wars, and was hardly ever met with in the early months of the war of 1914–18. Its occurrence as a common phenomenon in war is a new feature and can only be explained by the introduction of some new and benign factor into the circumstances influencing the severity of the disease. It may be claimed with confidence that this

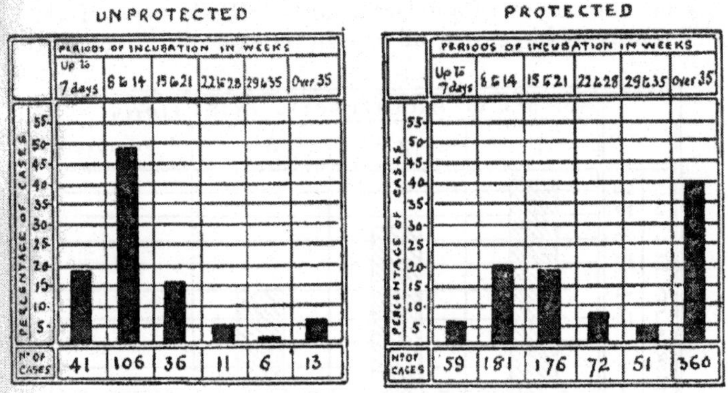

Chart XVI.—Comparison of the period of incubation in protected and unprotected. (Bruce.)

new factor has been the universal use of antitetanic serum. While giving full weight to the importance of efficient surgery in ameliorating the severity and diminishing the mortality of tetanus, more especially when excision of wounds is practised as in the latter part of the war, neither this nor any other factor can be so closely associated with a diminution of incidence, severity and mortality, and with a prolongation of the incubation period, as can the administration of antitoxic serum. The high value of this method of prophylaxis would appear to be the outstanding fact of the history of tetanus in the European war of 1914–18.

BIBLIOGRAPHY.

See Bibliography at the end of Chapter VIII.

CHAPTER VIII.

THE PATHOLOGY AND BACTERIOLOGY OF TETANUS.

THE experience of the war has advanced our knowledge of the pathology and bacteriology of tetanus in many directions. Apart from the fact that serum prophylaxis of all wounded men constituted a vast experiment in which laboratory results on animals have been confirmed and amplified in the human subject, much original work on tetanus has been carried out by skilled bacteriologists in military and other laboratories. These observations can further be read in the new light which has been shed on the pathological and bacteriological processes occurring in septic wounds ; it may fairly be said that the pathology of tetanus has now a more secure basis than it had prior to the war. The practical value of this new knowledge has proved very great. It is demonstrated that, while tetanus in war cannot wholly be prevented, its incidence can be reduced to a relatively small figure, and its mortality to less than one-half of that hitherto obtaining. The reduction in incidence and mortality was progressive during the war, and it cannot be doubted that the experience gained holds out the hope of still further reduction in the future.

The Tetanus Bacillus.

The studies which have been carried out on anaërobic bacilli have thrown light on the difficulties which have always attended the cultivation of *Bacillus tetani* in a state of purity. It has been shown that the various anaërobes are prone to live in more or less stable symbiotic associations, which cannot always be dissociated by the ordinary devices of plate culture and picking off from single colonies, however often this is repeated. A subculture may appear pure for several generations, but the latent intruder is apt subsequently to reassert itself. Practically all the tetanus cultures in use at the various serum laboratories have been found thus contaminated, the intruding organism being most commonly *B. sporogenes;* this does not seem to have been detrimental to their usefulness, indeed, it seems possible that such an association yields a more potent toxin than a pure culture of *B. tetani*. It may almost be said that, prior to the war, few cultures of anaërobes were absolutely pure, a fact which largely accounts for the confusion which existed with regard to these organisms. This confusion has in the main been dispelled by the labours of the Anaërobe Committee of the Medical Research Council.* The difficulty of obtaining pure cultures can be overcome by the isolation of individual bacilli by Barber's pipette method or some equivalent technique ; Miss Robertson has employed this method with success at the Lister Institute.

Cultural Methods.—The ingenious apparatus devised by McIntosh and Fildes has enabled anaërobic cultural conditions to be obtained with greater ease and certainty than by previous methods, but the most remarkable discovery during the war has been the fact that artificial exclusion of oxygen is not necessary for the growth of even such a strict anaërobe as *B. tetani*. Anaërobes have been found to grow quite well in open broth tubes provided that the medium contains solid fragments of meat or vegetable tissue. The essential condition is that crevices shall be present in which the bacilli can fabricate for themselves initial foci of anaërobiosis, which are later extended till the growth has spread through the whole medium. Matters are helped, nevertheless, by a surface seal of sterile liquid paraffin ; in the absence of this, though the tetanus bacillus will grow well, it is apt to form little toxin.

When a "meat broth" tube is inoculated with material from a wound containing a mixed anaërobic flora, a certain sequence is observed in the order in which the various species multiply. *B. sporogenes* is the first to develop, but the multiplication of certain oval-spored pathogenic types and of the types with globular end-spores, including *B. tetani*, is delayed till the second or the third day. Guided by this fact, Tulloch succeeded in devising a more or less selective medium of such value in isolating the tetanus bacillus that he not infrequently obtained it in the primary culture from a wound in sufficient purity for purposes of agglutination. The principle adopted was that of preliminary exhaustion of the medium with *B. sporogenes*, and this was attained by trypsinizing meat broth and then allowing it to putrefy naturally in open vessels for five days at 37° C. After filtration through paper, sodium formate was added, the reaction being made neutral to phenol phthalein, and the fluid was then sterilized by passage through a Berkefeld and a Doulton filter in sequence. Before use it was found desirable to add to each culture tube a small portion of fresh aseptic rabbit's kidney. This medium has largely overcome the difficulty of cultivating *B. tetani* from wounds.

* M.R.C. Special Report Series, No. 39 (1919).

Bacilli morphologically resembling B. tetani.—It has long been known that there were anaërobic bacilli resembling *B. tetani* in possessing globular end-spores, but having no toxic properties. Tulloch repeatedly isolated non-toxic bacilli of this type, and found them serologically distinct from *B. tetani*. The Anaërobe Committee of the Medical Research Council has described two such species under the names *B. tetanomorphus* and *B. sphenoides*, and there are others with spores so nearly globular as to lead to possible errors in diagnosis when reliance is placed on morphology alone. In the pure state these species can be distinguished from *B. tetani* either by their sugar reactions or by agglutination, as well as by lack of pathogenic power. The general rule must, however, be laid down that to qualify beyond doubt as *B. tetani*, an organism must exhibit the characteristic toxic' properties of that bacillus.

Serological Races of B. tetani.—Tulloch has proved that there exist at least four distinct serological races, comprised in the species. Each agglutinates only with its own serum and there is some evidence that certain other serological properties, such as antiphagocytic power, may be racially specific in some degree; but all four races produce a common toxin equally antagonized by an antitoxin yielded by any one race. This discovery brings the tetanus bacillus into line with many other pathogenic species, and it is noteworthy that Miss Robertson has found the *Vibrion septique* similarly divisible into serological races, also producing a common toxin. The distribution of Tulloch's types in the wounds of 100 cases of tetanus in English military hospitals, almost all in men who had received a prophylactic dose of serum, was as follows : 41 strains belonged to Type 1, 22 to Type 2, 33 to Type 3, and 4 to Type 4. As regards geographical distribution on the Western front, Type 2 was most prevalent in Flanders and Types 1 and 3 on the Somme, but all four types were encountered in cases receiving their injury in England. The seven strains employed in various serum institutes for the preparation of antitoxin were all found to belong to Type 1, and this accidental circumstance was seized upon by Tulloch to open a new way to the investigation of serum prophylaxis, as will presently be shown.

The Distribution of B. tetani *in Nature*.—The war has confirmed previous knowledge as to the abundance of the tetanus bacillus in soil long cultivated and manured and its absence or paucity in uncultivated lands. Out of 2,549 reported cases of tetanus only 20 occurred in areas of war other than France and Belgium, and of these 20 several were accidental and not due to battle wounds. For reasons which will be considered later, the number of cases of tetanus arising on the Western front gives but a faint idea of the frequency of the tetanus bacillus in wounds inflicted there. Tulloch and Miss Cayley, examining 100 consecutive wounds in cases where no tetanus was present, demonstrated toxic tetanus bacilli certainly in 19 cases and probably in 21.

Tulloch also examined the fæces for tetanus bacilli in a small number of cases. In 21 soldiers returned from overseas he found the bacillus in 7 (33 per cent.), and these bacilli belonged to three different serological types; in 31 British civilians, whose fæces were examined as a control, the bacillus was present in 5 (16 per cent.), and these bacilli were all of Type 1. Although the number of cases is small the figures are suggestive, for it is likely that under the conditions of life in the trenches a good deal of dirt was swallowed. They suggest a possible explanation of the cases of tetanus in unwounded men during the war after abdominal operations. Sir David Bruce records this occurrence after operation for inguinal hernia and for piles, and in no fewer than five instances of appendicectomy; in one of the last-named cases the tetanus bacillus was demonstrated in the fæces. Similar observations were made also in the hospitals in France. Tetanus is of extraordinary rarity after such operations in civil practice.

Tetanus Infection in Wounds.

It has been realized during the war that the tetanus bacillus or its spores may be present in vast numbers of wounds without producing tetanus. Tulloch's actual finding of the organism in at least 19 per cent. of non-tetanic wounds in England must be far below the truth, for he cultivated material from the wounds of 200 cases of actual tetanus and only succeeded in obtaining the bacillus, at least in a pure enough condition for agglutination, in 50 per cent. of them.

It has long been known that when tetanus spores, washed or heated so as to remove all toxin, are injected subcutaneously or intravenously into a susceptible animal, no tetanus as a rule results. Tulloch has confirmed this; he found that a dose of even 1,000 million washed spores failed to produce tetanus in a guinea-pig, and 2,000 million washed bacilli failed in a rat, in the absence of tissue damage. Spores, however, thus introduced, may remain viable for many months, and during this period tetanus may be lighted up by subsequent tissue damage, whether by mechanical injury, by chemical agents, or by infection with other microbes. In spite, then, of its enormous toxicity, the tetanus bacillus posseses little virulence, *i.e.*, little capacity to grow in the body and invade the tissues. In the absence of favouring conditions the spores fail to germinate, and remain in the tissues not even as saprophytes but as inert foreign bodies. It is only on vegetative multiplication that toxin is formed and tetanus set up, and this fact offers an explanation of " delayed tetanus " and of the lighting up of the disease by secondary surgical intervention even after a wound has healed. This consideration also deprives the term " incubation period " of much of its meaning in relation to tetanus, for the incubation period cannot in many cases be dated from the infliction of the wound. The war has shown cases of tetanus arising more than two years after wounding, and to speak of an incubation of two years is a manifest absurdity. The interval after wounding falls into three periods : (1) The period *before germination of the spores* and active multiplication of the bacillus ; in the absence of favouring conditions this period may be indefinitely prolonged and the spores eventually perish, no tetanus arising. This appears to have been the rule during the war, at least under the conditions of serum prophylaxis. (2) The period of *vegetative multiplication* when conditions become favourable for germination, and this may be the case early or late in the history of the wound. This is the period of toxin production, and here serum prophylaxis plays an important part, for if at this stage the body contains sufficient antitoxin the toxin is neutralized as it is formed, or at most only passes up the regional nerves, causing local tetanus. (3) Finally comes the short period of *toxin absorption* and fixation by the nerve cells with the onset of manifest tetanus ; this is the incubation period seen in animals after injection of tetanus toxin. The " incubation period " in human tetanus, in the sense in which the term is used in other infections, should date from the germination of the spores, not from the original implantation, and is probably of only a few days' duration. This detracts in no way from the value in prognosis of the interval elapsing between the infliction of the wound and the onset of tetanus.

It follows that the causes determining germination of tetanus spores and vegetative multiplication of the bacillus are of the first importance, and these causes have received much attention from pathologists during the war. The defence of the body against the tetanus bacillus itself, apart from its toxin, appears to lie in lytic and phagocytic processes, and the predisposing causes of tetanus may be translated into terms of tissue damage sufficient to interfere with these activities. The causes operative in bringing about the rupture of defence may be considered under four headings : mechanical tissue damage, chemical agencies, concurrent infections, and cold.

Mechanical Damage.—This is a primary condition, as providing the necessary nidus for the multiplication of the bacillus. Its extent exercises a powerful influence on the liability to tetanus. It is not merely a matter of tissue laceration, for the area of devitalization may extend, by concussion as it were, beyond the limits of the area mechanically destroyed. It is true that tetanus sometimes arises from very minute wounds, *e.g.*, in some cases of cephalic tetanus, but this does not affect the general rule that the greater the damage the greater the risk of tetanus. Tulloch, working with a chemical agent (saponin) and with *B. welchii* toxin, concludes that when the area of damage is sufficiently great, no amount of antitoxin will ward off experimental tetanus ; this may be one reason for the occasional failure of serum prophylaxis in preventing the early occurrence of the disease. The manner in which mechanical damage acts in favouring tetanus is plain, for in an extensive area of devitalized and weakened tissue the defensive mechanisms of the body are with difficulty brought into play.

There is reason for the belief on clinical evidence that, in wounds containing latent spores of the bacillus, tetanus may be lighted up by the mechanical effects of massage or of muscular exercise when the patient begins to walk. This has been observed even in healed wounds. It must be supposed that such action disturbs the quiet encystment of the microbes and converts the latent sepsis, in which other organisms are concerned besides the tetanus bacillus, into an active process. This is undoubtedly the course of events when delayed tetanus follows secondary surgical intervention ; the occurrence of " septic flares " is notorious in such circumstances. A layer of healthy granulation tissue is well known to be an effective barrier against micro-organisms, and disturbance of this practically renews the conditions obtaining in a recent wound. These facts constitute the strong reason for administering antitoxin before secondary intervention in a wound.

Chemical Damage.—Under experimental conditions, chemical irritants are frequently used to " activate " washed spores which cannot germinate in healthy tissues ; such substances as trimethylamine and saponin cause the necessary tissue destruction, while quinine has also been supposed to act by paralysing the leucocytes. Such chemical irritants cannot be supposed to play any part in war wounds, but a new fact has been discovered by Bullock and Cramer during their work on the pathology of gas gangrene which may be of some importance in tetanus. This fact is the influence of soluble calcium salts in assisting the germination of spores and the multiplication of microbes. Like tetanus spores, those of the chief bacteria of gas gangrene (B. welchii, B. oedematis maligni, B. oedematiens) cannot set up disease in animals when washed free from toxin, but these observers found that the addition of minute amounts of soluble calcium salts (chloride, nitrate, acetate) to the injection always enabled the organisms to set up rapidly fatal gangrene. A suitable dose was found to be 2·5 to 5 mgm. for mice and guinea-pigs. Similar facts were found true for tetanus. Inasmuch as soluble calcium salts are present in varying amount in soil and especially in manured soil, it is possible that they may be of influence in the development of tetanus. Bullock and Cramer suggest that the varying quantity of such salts in the earth of different districts may account for the " patchy " distribution of gas gangrene on the Western front. As regards the lighting up of tetanus, such salts may have not only a direct effect in assisting the germination of B. tetani, but possibly an even more important indirect effect by promoting the growth of B. welchii and other anaërobes, the toxins of which are powerful agents of tissue destruction, and thus of the conditions favourable for tetanus. The mechanism by which soluble calcium salts assist anaërobes in gaining a foothold in the tissues appears from the observations of the writers quoted to be an aseptic inflammation, with endothelial poisoning and interference with the local circulation, whereby the natural means of defence are impaired. Such conditions are possibly operative in other cases of rupture of defence by chemical agencies.

The Influence of Concurrent Infections.—It is probable that " sepsis " takes the foremost place amongst the predisposing causes of tetanus. In the mixed flora of a septic wound there are bacteria with differing properties. The earliest to appear, in less than twenty-four hours after the infliction of a wound, are such anaërobes as B. sporogenes and B. welchii, the latter producing a potent tissue toxin. The anaërobic toxins, apart from their destructive influence upon the tissues, appear to be anti-phagocytic since they damage and destroy the leucocytes also. When after a time the pyogenic cocci begin to multiply, another influence is suggested ; these cocci possess active chemiotactic powers, strongly attracting the leucocytes, and thus, it has been supposed, diverting them from the organisms devoid of chemiotactic influence. The most important influence in a septic war wound, as regards the production of tetanus, is that of the toxins of the anaërobes, and this has been studied experimentally by Tulloch. He found that tetanus toxin itself possessed some anti-phagocytic power, but that this was exhibited in a more marked degree by the toxin of B. welchii, which, as has been said, is also an agent of tissue destruction. In Tulloch's experience the best of all means for "activating" detoxicated cultures of B. tetani was the concurrent injection of B. welchii toxin in a dose small enough to be non-fatal of itself. Such facts are of manifest importance in the production of tetanus in war ; they help us to understand how symbiosis with other bacteria, and especially with B. welchii, which was one of the commonest of wound infections, is the almost universal concomitant of human tetanus.

The Effect of Cold.—Several writers in the past, especially amongst the French, have insisted on external cold as an adjuvant factor in the production of tetanus. The not infrequent occurrence of tetanus in cases of "trench foot" indicates the reality of this predisposing cause. Given a local lesion, in this condition, to which tetanus bacilli have gained access, there are several ways in which cold may affect the development of tetanus, as Vincent has pointed out. Local refrigeration of the tissues impairs natural defence ; below 15° C. no phagocytosis is said to occur ; the hindrance to the circulation due to arterial constriction prevents the access of lytic antibodies ; the œdema which supervenes affords a good culture medium for the bacillus and the subsequent reabsorption of the fluid may suddenly flood the body with toxin. In this way it has been sought to explain the fulminant character of many of the cases of tetanus following trench foot, though it must be remembered that until the danger was realized these cases received no prophylactic dose of serum.

Summary of Evidence as regards Infection with B. tetani.

(1) When the spores have been introduced into the wound, they may remain inert for long periods. Tetanus may arise as late as 891 days after wounding, according to Bruce.

Tulloch cultivated the bacillus from the wound of a man, showing no evidence of tetanus, 882 days after it had been inflicted.

(2) The conditions which enable the bacillus to germinate are of several kinds, but all seem to act in one way, namely by producing tissue damage sufficient in its extent and character to interfere with the natural defence of the body against the bacillus. These conditions constitute the predisposing causes of tetanus and without one or other of them the disease does not arise. The chief are mechanical tissue damage and concomitant infection with other bacteria and especially with other anaërobes; experimentally, and probably in nature, the presence of certain chemical substances acting as tissue debilitants, especially soluble calcium salts, appears of importance, while cold may also be an adjuvant.

(3) It would appear that the necessary conditions for germination were not realized in the great majority of war wounds, or if realized were checked in their operation by serum prophylaxis.

The Absorption of Tetanus Toxin.

The properties of tetanus toxin had been fully studied before the war. Little that is new has been ascertained about the toxin itself or about its mode of action on the nerve cells, nor have any new facts come to light as to the morbid anatomy and histology of tetanus. A subject, however, which has attracted renewed attention has been the path of absorption of the toxin from the site of its production. It has been accepted for many years that it cannot gain access to the motor neurons directly from the capillaries of the central nervous system. In an address at the Royal Society of Medicine in 1916, Halliburton has laid stress on the inaccessibility of the brain and cord tissues to many chemical poisons, while the experimental work of Teale and Embleton has confirmed the fact for tetanus toxin and demonstrated the freedom of the cerebro-spinal fluid from this substance after its intravenous injection. It is generally agreed that the toxin reaches the neurons by passing up the motor nerves and since the work of Marie and Morax and of Meyer and Ransom nearly twenty years ago, almost everyone has accepted the views of these authors that the route is up the axis cylinders of the nerve-fibres. During the war there has been some attempt to challenge the exclusiveness of this route and it has been urged that toxin also passes up the neural lymphatics. The latter view has especially been maintained by Teale and Embleton on the basis of numerous ingenious experiments. They show in the first place that toxin injected subcutaneously into the leg is very rapidly absorbed by the lymphatics and can be demonstrated in the thoracic duct in less than an hour, and that in similar circumstances it can be found in the sciatic nerve, in the lower part in eight hours and in the upper part in twelve hours; in twenty-five hours toxin was demonstrable in the upper end of the opposite sciatic. They claim, further, that tetanus can be delayed or prevented by previous injection of iodine or normal horse serum into the nerve, a proceeding which they consider to operate by obstructing the lymphatics, since it was not found to interfere with conduction of nerve impulses. The defect in such evidence lies in the absence of any proof that lymphatic channels exist capable of conveying toxin up the nerves to the neurons. The only neural lymphatics known to anatomists are those of the epineurium, which do not lead into the central nervous system; all anatomists agree that the central nervous system itself possesses no lymphatics, their place being taken by the cerebro-spinal fluid. It can readily be believed that toxin passes into the lymphatics of the epineurium, but not that these conduct it to the cord. The rest is probably a matter of diffusion along the fluid permeating the tissues of the nerve, and indeed the passage of toxin up the axis cylinders must equally be a matter of diffusion. The importance of the axis cylinders is probably due to the fact that they form well-insulated paths leading direct to the motor neurons.

The war has furnished a considerable mass of evidence as to the diffusion of toxin in the cord of man. In lower animals, spread of toxin in the cord was held by Meyer and Ransom to explain the ascending march of tetanus, but whatever may be true of rodents, the phenomena of human tetanus cannot be thus explained. The order in which the different groups of muscles are affected in the unprotected man has led to the belief that the toxin, absorbed by the lymphatics, passes into the blood stream and is thence taken up by motor nerves remote from the wound. The effect of serum prophylaxis has been to provide a large number of cases of tetanus in which circulating toxin is neutralized, and the only channel of access to the central nervous system has been the regional motor nerves of the wound. Thus has arisen the phenomenon of " local tetanus," and the degree to which toxin spreads in the cord itself could readily be determined by clinical observation.

To some slight extent such spread was witnessed. When a man had local tetanus of the arm, the spasm sometimes extended later to the shoulder muscles; in local tetanus of one leg the opposite leg commonly showed increase in reflex excitability, and not rarely the lumbar muscles shared in lesser degree in the tonic spasm. Cases were indeed described of "general tetanus without trismus," but nothing was seen corresponding to the "ascending tetanus" of lower animals, even when the local tetanus was severe. The observed facts suggest that, in man, diffusion of toxin in the cord is very limited in its extent.

The Mode of Action of Tetanus Antitoxin.

Figures and diagrams have been given in the previous chapter showing beyond a doubt that the routine prophylactic administration of antitetanic serum was followed by a very great diminution in the incidence of tetanus upon the wounded. Roughly, it may be said that with the establishment of this practice the incidence of tetanus fell to about one-sixth of what it had been during the first month or two of the war. More than this, the clinical features of such cases as still occurred were largely modified, while the fatality was reduced to a much lower figure than in any previous experience. As the war went on, serum prophylaxis was more and more efficiently carried out, and corresponding to this the mortality showed a progressive diminution.

When, however, the precise mechanism by which the anti-toxin produced this effect is considered, an analysis of the observed facts presents many difficulties. It has always been supposed that the serum of an animal immunized by repeated doses of toxin was purely antitoxic in its properties and possessed no anti-bacterial powers. It is still undisputed that its main action is antitoxic; not only laboratory experience but also the clinical phenomena of the modified tetanus seen during the war are in harmony with such a view. But Tulloch's discovery of four serological types of B. tetani, possessing a common toxin, enabled him to attack the problem in an entirely new way, and his observations suggest that the prophy-lactic value of the serum does not rest so exclusively upon its antitoxic properties as had been supposed. It has already been mentioned that the antitoxin used during the war was all prepared, so far as known, from Type 1 bacilli, a circum-stance which rendered it possible to compare the effects of a monotypical serum upon those severally infected with all the four types of bacilli. The relative numbers of wounded

originally infected with the different bacillary types are not
known, but it is tolerably certain that Type 1 was by far the
most frequent. Out of 25 strains of *B. tetani* recovered
from wounds in men who had no tetanus, no fewer than 19
(76 per cent.) were of Type 1. As already stated, of strains
recovered from 100 cases of actual tetanus only 41 were of
Type 1, 22 of Type 2, 33 of Type 3, and 4 of Type 4. That is
to say, the incidence of tetanus upon men infected by Type 1
bacillus appears more reduced by prophylaxis with the homologous serum than is the case with men infected with the
remaining types with which the serum was heterologous.
This difference becomes more marked when mortality is considered, for the Type 1 cases had a mortality of 13·1 per cent.,
the Type 2 cases one of 27·7 per cent. and the Type 3 cases
one of 35·5 per cent. None of the Type 4 cases died, but the
numbers are too small to permit of any legitimate conclusion.
If attention is paid only to those cases arising during the first
fortnight after wounding, while the action of the serum may
be supposed to be at its maximum of effectiveness, the figures
are as follows :—

    Type 1   ..   .. 15 cases with 3 deaths : mortality 20 per cent.
    Type 2   8   „   3   „   „   37·5 „
    Type 3   15   „   8   „   „   53·3 „

With the proviso that the figures at his command are comparatively small and admittedly open to certain fallacies,
Tulloch calculates from his data concerning tetanic and non-
tetanic cases that out of three groups each of 160 inoculated
men, one harbouring Type 1, the second Type 2, and the third
Type 3 bacillus, 1 man in the first, 8 in the second and 16 in
the third group will develop tetanus. These observations
seem to permit of only two alternative explanations. Either
Types 2 and 3 are inherently more fatal to man than Type 1,
or the serum exercised some selective influence protecting
more efficiently against its homologous bacillus. The second
alternative would appear the more probable of the two.

If, however, the view of even a partial selection in the protection conferred by a monotypical serum is accepted, this
must involve something more than a merely antitoxic action,
for all the types produce a common toxin. In an elaborate
series of animal experiments Tulloch sought to ascertain what
this other action might be. While no conclusive results
emerge from these experiments, there is much that is
suggestive. His own tentative conclusion is that it would
appear possible that monotypical antitoxic sera may exert

some degree of specific anti-infective influence as regards bacilli of their own type, but that this is quantitative, not qualitative, in character. He was able to produce monotypical anti-bacterial sera which, in addition to their specific agglutinating powers, exhibited also opsonic properties which were in a measure specific to the type.

Certain important suggestions for the improvement of serum prophylaxis against tetanus are pointed out in Tulloch's paper. The first is that all four types of the tetanus bacillus should be employed in the preparation of the protective serum ; the second that the serum should be so prepared as to possess not only antitoxic but also anti-bacterial properties ; the third that it should contain as an additional element an antitoxin against *B. welchii* and perhaps also against the *Vibrion septique*. Attempts were made during the later stages of the war to employ prophylactic sera against gas gangrene itself and not without some success.   Tulloch's work indicates that such sera may also be of value in preventing tetanus, as well as gas gangrene, since the toxins of the anaërobes cause the latter disease to exert a potent effect in promoting the activity of *B. tetani.*

Leaving on one side these indications of a partially selective protection against the homologous type of the tetanus bacillus, it remains to consider the antitoxic action to which the prophylactic effects of the serum are in all probability chiefly attributable. The clinical experience of the war has taught in very emphatic fashion that protection against tetanus in a wounded man, infected with the living germs of the disease, is a very different thing from protection against a single dose of toxin administered to a laboratory animal. In the latter case it is known that protection, complete at first, gradually fades, as always happens in passive immunity, till after a few weeks it has vanished.   There was a temptation to extend this simple conception to the wounded, and indeed cases were observed, as will be mentioned below, in which it explained the course of events.   But in the wounded man the onset of tetanus is determined not merely by the presence of the bacillus, but by the conditions which permit the genesis of toxin in the wound. These conditions, it has been seen, are complex and may arise at any period after wounding ; the toxin may be produced in abundance or scantily ; it may be a potent or a feeble toxin ; the focus in which it is generated may be one convenient for its absorption up the nerves or the reverse.   The extent of the devitalized area, probably, too, the nature of the injury and the presence of favouring conditions, must affect the extent to which the bacillus can multiply and hence the dose of toxin generated, which may be so great that no amount of serum can protect. It is thus easy to understand some of the reasons for the extreme irregularity of the protection conferred by the antiserum on the wounded soldier. Certain of these anomalies must be discussed in the light of the clinical experience offered by the war.

The Effects upon the Incidence of Tetanus.—The statistical figures given indicate that serum prophylaxis prevented tetanus altogether in at least five out of six men who would otherwise have developed it. The sixth man did develop it, and the question arises why the serum here failed. It might be thought that it was because protection had faded, but an analysis of the data shows that such an explanation, though probable enough in some instances, by no means covers all the facts. Amongst some 65 cases in London seen by Sir F. W. Andrewes there were 46 in which the date of administration of the last dose, often the only dose, of serum was accurately known. The dates of onset of these cases, in relation to the last dose of serum, are plotted in Chart I; the fatal cases are indicated by black squares, the shaded ones are cases of non-fatal general tetanus, while the white squares indicate local tetanus. Although the number of cases is not large, it is large enough to

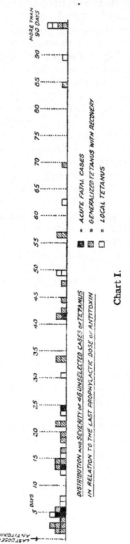

Chart I.

show that the hypothesis of gradually fading protection is inadequate. The maximum number of cases in any one week —more than a quarter of the whole and including half the fatal cases—is seen to occur during the first week after inoculation, when protection should have been at its maximum. Fewer and fewer cases occur as the interval after inoculation grows longer, though the cases of local tetanus are more evenly distributed than those of general tetanus. It might almost be said that the serum had produced no effect were it not for the low rate of mortality in the series (13 per cent.).

The interval between the last date of inoculation and the onset, in the different clinical types of the disease in these forty-six cases, is equally opposed to the idea of a fading protection. The figures are as follows :—

Average Interval after Inoculation.					*Days.*
In 6 acute fatal cases	..	..	..	..	16·1
In 10 severe non-fatal cases	..	..	..	..	29·2
In 17 cases of mild general tetanus	..	..	..	..	38·3
In 6 cases of acute local tetanus..	..	..	..	..	30·6
In 7 cases of chronic local tetanus	..	..	..	..	64·7

It is seen that the clinical type of the disease becomes milder, instead of more severe, as the date of prophylaxis recedes.

The explanation of these facts is obscure. It would seem that there existed a group of cases, small in regard to the whole but conspicuous in the circumstances, in which the expected protection failed, partially or completely, to manifest itself. These cases seem to have obeyed the usual laws, following the general curve of incubation and presenting a higher mortality the earlier they occurred, though a mortality much less than that of pre-serum days. This might almost have been deduced from Chart X in the previous chapter, in which the curves of incubation in the war of 1914–18 and in the American Civil War are contrasted. It is there manifest that the incidence of such cases as still occurred in spite of serum prophylaxis was only deferred by a day or two, and not bodily postponed by some weeks' interval of complete protection.

The reasons for this relatively exceptional failure in prophylaxis must remain speculative. In part it may have been due to the serological type of *B. tetani* concerned, for as already stated, Tulloch's figures indicate a certain degree of selective protection. The serological type was not known in the forty-six cases mentioned above. It is, however, unlikely that this explanation is adequate, for 41 per cent. of the cases of tetanus which did occur were due to Type 1 bacilli. Again, it is probable that in certain cases the amount of tissue damage may be so great, or other conditions may be so favourable to the germination of tetanus spores or to the absorption of toxin, that no amount of antitoxin will protect.

The Duration of Protection.—It is experimentally known that after a dose of antitoxin has been injected into an animal there is a considerable drop in the antitoxin content of the blood after a week has elapsed, and that after a fortnight it is difficult still to demonstrate its presence. In 1916 Dr. MacConkey carried out an experiment on these lines on a number of lady students at the Royal Free Hospital who volunteered for the test. Each received a dose of 1,700 units, and at intervals samples of blood were withdrawn, pooled and tested for antitoxin content. Three days after the injection the blood contained $\frac{1}{8}$ unit per cubic centimetre, after ten days the amount was less than $\frac{1}{10}$ unit, but even after fifteen days it was still more than $\frac{1}{20}$ unit.

Laboratory tests of this kind reveal only such protection as can be measured by comparatively gross methods. The experience of the war has shown that long after such tests are of any avail enough antitoxin may yet remain in the body to modify the severity of the disease, though it may not suffice to prevent it. Doubtless this is not always so, but the phenomenon of local tetanus, known only in protected persons and almost certainly associated with the persistence of enough antitoxin to shield the higher centres, was seen months after the last dose of prophylactic serum had been administered. The figures given above indicate the average date at which local tetanus was seen to commence ; the longest interval after the dose of serum at which it was seen in the series of forty-six cases was 145 days. It may be inferred therefore that in certain favourable cases some degree of protection persists for this period.

Evidence is likewise afforded by cases of recurrent tetanus in which recovery has taken place after large therapeutic doses of serum. Dean was actually able to demonstrate the presence of antitoxin in the blood up to thirty-nine days after intravenous injection of a dose of 30,000 units of serum. In one case seen by Sir F. W. Andrewes, mild general tetanus subsided under treatment in which 48,000 units were given by the intrathecal and a similar amount by the intramuscular route. The disease recurred forty-three days after the last dose of serum, chiefly in the form of local tetanus. In another instance a severe attack of general tetanus recovered under a course of treatment in which some 80,000 units of antitoxin were administered; fifty-seven days after the last dose of serum the disease recurred and ended fatally. Again, an untreated case of local tetanus, which had come on about nine weeks after a single prophylactic dose of antitoxin, passed into general tetanus three weeks later, ninety-two days after the serum had been given. It may be concluded that, in certain cases at least, protection of some kind endures in man for a much longer period than animal experiment would have led one to believe, but it is probable that its duration varies widely in individual cases. In some few cases, as has been pointed out above, it seems to have been practically absent.

The Phenomena of Tetanus modified by Serum Prophylaxis.

The departures from the classical type of the disease which were commonly seen in those who had received serum may be described as quantitative and qualitative.

By quantitative modification is meant diminution in severity without change in the relative prominence of the different symptoms. Although instances were seen in which the violence of the disease appeared unmitigated, the majority of the cases of general tetanus were of a less severe type, responding to serum treatment in a manner rarely observed in the unprotected man. Often the disease was reduced merely to incomplete trismus with some tonic rigidity of the back or belly, or even to trismus alone. The phenomena observed were, in fact, just those which might have been anticipated on the supposition that some antitoxin was still circulating in the blood, but not in sufficient quantity to prevent general tetanus altogether. Some of these mild general cases had, in addition, the local tetanus described below, but this was not always so.

Qualitative modification, involving a change in the customary phenomena of tetanus, consisted in an increased prominence of spasm in the wounded region, which in its most extreme form constituted the sole symptom, a pure "local tetanus." It was often associated with some milder degree of the general disease, but with the increasing mildness of this the local symptoms tended to become more and more prominent. Local tetanus was almost unknown in man before the war, though one or two cases had been described; it was, however, a familiar laboratory phenomenon in such an insusceptible animal as the cat and in more susceptible animals which had been protected by antitoxin. Some degree of local spasm had been sometimes seen in man as a premonitory symptom of general tetanus, but in the unmodified disease any local condition was usually masked by the violence of the general spasms.

The spasms of local tetanus were of two kinds, intermittent local cramps, usually painful, and persistent tonic rigidity which was often painless. Either might occur alone, or the two might be combined. The intermittent spasms often yielded to treatment with antitoxin ; tonic spasm was usually unaffected by such treatment and often persisted for many weeks.

The pathological explanation of local tetanus rests on the assumption of absorption of toxin by two separate routes. It may be taken up by the lymphatics and pass into the blood-stream, whence it is absorbed up motor nerves remote from the wound, thus causing the manifestations of general tetanus. Or it may pass directly up the motor nerves supplying the wounded region, its action being more or less limited to the corresponding neurons. It would seem more easy for anti-toxin to antagonize circulating toxin than to prevent its passage up the local nerves from the wound. In pure local tetanus the absorption of toxin by the latter route seems to proceed unchecked, while absorption by other motor nerves is wholly prevented. Inasmuch as it is the involvement of the pontine and bulbar centres which leads to a fatal issue, pure local tetanus is never fatal. The common combination of local with mild general tetanus is explained by less complete neutralization of circulating toxin. The shielding, complete or partial, of the higher centres allows time for marked absorption up the regional nerves and the effect produced is not masked by general spasm, and thus the clinical picture of the disease is wholly altered. Nevertheless, experience shows that the mitigation of the general symptoms is not necessarily accompanied by local tetanus. Cases were not infrequent during the war in which the disease was of the mildest general type, yet no local spasm was observed. It must be assumed therefore that local absorption of toxin is not an invariable thing though it is a common one. The local conditions in the wound may either favour such absorption or interfere with it.

Serotherapy.

The subject of treatment is fully dealt with in the surgical volumes but it presents certain pathological aspects. The large experience offered by the war has confirmed previous opinion that the curative value of tetanus antitoxin is greatly inferior to its prophylactic power   It is true that in the declared disease it often appeared of service and in a few instances was held to have saved life, but it must be remembered that prophylaxis had in most cases modified the severity of the attack, and it was in such conditions that the successful results of serum treatment were chiefly apparent.   It must be confessed that, when similar treatment was employed in the severe tetanus of uninoculated men, the same success was rarely attained and the mortality of such cases was almost as high as ever.

Two questions aroused considerable discussion during the war ; one was the magnitude of the dose of antitoxin to be employed in declared tetanus, the other the route by which it could most effectively be administered.   More than one writer attempted to find an answer to these questions by an appeal to statistical data, but without convincing results, for it was impossible to obtain " clean " data on which to base an argument.   The cases which lived longest naturally received more antitoxin than those which died quickly, and, on the other hand, there was a tendency to employ more heroic doses in the more severe cases.   In the great majority of cases antitoxin was given by more than one route, thus confusing the issue.

It was admitted on all hands that if a lethal dose of toxin had been anchored to the central neurons there was little possibility of dissociating it by antitoxin in any dose or by any route.   The dosage recommended by the War Office Committee for the Study of Tetanus was 24,000 units in twenty-four hours in acute general tetanus, but larger doses were sometimes given. This Committee consistently advocated the intrathecal route of administration.   The most powerful argument in its favour was found in animal experiment, and especially in the series of tests on upwards of 100 monkeys carried out at Oxford by Professor C. S. Sherrington at the instance of the Committee. The animals were inoculated in a uniform manner with more than eight times the lethal dose of toxin, and no treatment was employed till symptoms of tetanus had developed.   Attempts were then made to save them by administering similar doses of antitoxin by the different routes, with the following results :—

Route of administration of antitoxin.			No. of animals used.	Recoveries.	Deaths.
Subcutaneous	..	..	..	25	2	23
Intramuscular	..	..	..	25	3	22
Intravenous	..	..	25	7	18
Lumbar subdural ..	..	..	25	14	11
Bulbar subdural ..	..	..	20	13	7
Cerebral subdural ..	..	..	10	0	10

These experiments convinced the Committee of the superiority of the intrathecal route and constitute the most important evidence which has yet been brought forward in its favour, though Park and Nicoll had obtained very similar results in guinea-pigs.

On the other hand, good results were claimed for the intra venous route, especially by Professor Dean of Manchester. He treated fourteen severe cases of tetanus with a single dose of 30,000 units administered intravenously, taking the precaution of giving it under deep chloroform anaesthesia in order to minimize the risk of anaphylactic shock. Thirteen out of the fourteen recovered and the fatal case was not due to shock.

Anaphylactic Shock.—The wholesale administration of antitoxic serum as a prophylactic and the employment of serum in the treatment of tetanus in men sensitized by the prophylactic dose, have offered an unexampled opportunity for determining the extent of the risk arising from anaphylactic shock in these circumstances. No very complete data are available, but Sir David Bruce has summarized the facts brought to his knowledge as regards serum treatment in England.

Prophylactic doses of serum were small in volume, usually 3 c.c., and were ordered to be administered at intervals of seven days with the express purpose of avoiding shock ; they were always given subcutaneously, and by this route shock is difficult to produce. It is therefore in no way surprising that shock was hardly ever seen as a result of prophylactic inoculation. Bruce has calculated that some two million prophylactic doses of serum were administered in England alone ; only eleven cases of shock were reported and not one was fatal. Even urticaria and other phenomena of "serum sickness" were seen in only a small proportion of those receiving second and subsequent injections.

On the other hand, anaphylactic shock in some degree was not infrequent in the serum treatment of cases of tetanus, while severe urticaria was common. Forty-nine cases of shock were reported in England with twelve deaths. The observed liability to shock by the different routes of administration, according to Bruce, was as follows : Intravenous 6 per cent., intrathecal 2 per cent., intramuscular 1·2 per cent., and subcutaneous 0·2 per cent.

BIBLIOGRAPHY.

Alcock .. .. Notes on the Medical History   London, 1838, p. 99.
           and Statistics of the British
           Legion in Spain.

Ballingall	..	.. Outlines of Military Surgery.	Edin., 1838, p. 257.
Bruce	..	.. An Analysis of Cases of Tetanus treated in Home Military Hospitals from August 1914 to August 1915.	Lancet, 1915, Vol. ii, p. 901.
,,	..	.. Second Analysis of Cases of Tetanus treated in Home Military Hospitals from 1st August, 1915, to 31st July, 1916.	Ibid., 1916, Vol. ii, p. 929.
,,	..	.. Third Analysis of Cases of Tetanus treated in Home Military Hospitals from August to October 1916.	Ibid., 1917, Vol. i, p. 986.
,,	..	.. Fourth Analysis of Cases of Tetanus treated in Home Military Hospitals from October to December 1916.	Ibid., 1917, Vol. ii, p. 411.
,	..	.. Fifth Analysis of Cases of Tetanus treated in Home Military Hospitals from December 1916 to March 1917.	Ibid., p. 925.
	..	.. Sixth Analysis of Cases of Tetanus treated in Home Military Hospitals from March to June 1917 (Summary only).	Brit. Med. Jl., 1918, Vol. i, pp. 240–324.
,,	..	.. Seventh, Eighth and Ninth Analysis of Cases of Tetanus treated in Home Military Hospitals from June 1917 to April 1918 (Summary only).	Ibid., 1918, Vol. ii, p. 415.
,,	..	.. Tetanus in Home Military Hospitals. Analysis of 1,000 Cases.	Trans. Soc. Trop. Med. & Hyg., 1917–18, Vol. xi, p. 1.
,,	..	.. Note on the Incidence of Tetanus among Wounded Soldiers.	Brit. Med. Jl., 1917, Vol. i, p. 118.
,,	..	.. Importance of Early Prophylactic Injection of Antitetanic Serum in Trench Foot.	Ibid., p. 48.
,,	..	.. Intramuscular *versus* the Intrathecal Route in the Treatment of Tetanus by the Injection of Antitoxin.	Lancet, 1917, Vol. i, p. 680.
,,	..	.. Tetanus.	War Medicine, Amer. Red Cross, 1918–19, Vol. ii, p. 724.
,,	..	.. Tetanus. Analysis of 1,458 Cases which occurred in Home Military Hospitals during the years 1914–1918.	Jl. of Hyg., 1920–21, Vol. xix, p. 1.
Bullock & Cramer	..	On a New Factor in the Mechanism of Bacterial Infection.	Proc. Roy. Soc., Lond., 1919, Ser. B, Vol. xc, p. 513.
Cummins	..	.. Tetanus in the British Army during the European War (August 1914 to November 1918).	Cinquième Congrès, Soc. Internat. de Chir., Paris, 1920.

Cummins & Gibson	An Analysis of Cases of Tetanus occurring in the British Armies in France between 1st November 1916 and 31st December, 1917.	Lancet, 1919, Vol. i, p. 325.
Dean	Report on Twenty-five Cases of Tetanus.	Ibid., 1917, Vol. i, p. 673.
Golla	An Analysis of Recent Tetanus Statistics.	Ibid., 1917, Vol. ii, p. 966.
Halliburton ..	The possible Functions of the Cerebro-spinal Fluid.	Proc. Roy. Soc. Med., 1916-17, Vol. x, Neuro. Sect., p. 1; and Lancet, 1916, Vol. ii p. 779.
Leishman & Smallman	An Analysis of Recent Cases of Tetanus in the British Expeditionary Force.	Lancet, 1917, Vol. i, p. 131
Longmore	Gunshot Injuries.	London, 1895, (2nd Edit.), p. 311.
Marie & Morax ..	Recherches sur l'absorption de la toxine tétanique.	Ann. de l'Inst. Pasteur., 1902, Vol. xvi, p. 819, and 1903, Vol. xvii, p. 335.
Meyer & Ransom ..	Untersuchungen über den Tetanus.	Arch. f. exp. Path. & Pharm., 1903, Vol. xlix, p. 369.
M'Grigor	Sketch of the Medical History of the British Armies in the Peninsula of Spain and Portugal.	Medico-chirurgical Transactions, 1815, Vol. vi, p. 449.
McIntosh & Fildes ..	New Apparatus for the Isolation and Cultivation of Anaërobic Micro-organisms.	Lancet, 1916, Vol. i, p. 768.
Park & Nicoll ..	Experiments on the Curative Value of the Intraspinal Administration of Tetanus anti-toxin.	Jl. Amer. Med. Assoc., 1914, Vol. lxiii, p. 235.
Robertson	Serological Grouping of Vibrion septique and their relation to the Production of Toxin.	Jl. of Path. & Bact., 1919–20, Vol. xx xxiii, p. 153.
Sherrington ..	Observations with Antitetanus Serum in the Monkey.	Lancet, 1917, Vol. ii, p. 964.
Teale & Embleton ..	The Paths of Spread of Bacterial Exotoxins with Special Reference to Tetanus Toxin.	Jl. of Path. & Bact., 1919–20, Vol. xxiii, p. 50.
Tulloch	On the Bacteriology of Wound Infections in Cases of Tetanus and the Identification of Bacillus tetani by Serological Reactions.	Jl. of R.A.M.C., 1917, Vol. xxix, p. 631.
,, ...	The Isolation and Serological Differentiation of Bacillus tetani.	Proc. Roy. Soc. Lond., 1919, Ser. B, Vol. xc, p 145.
,, ...	Report of Bacteriological Investigation of Tetanus carried out on behalf of the War Office Committee for the Study of Tetanus.	Jl. of Hyg., 1919–20, Vol. xviii, p. 103.

Vincent	..	.. Tétanos et froidure des pieds.	Bull. Acad. de Med., Paris, 1917, Vol. lxxviii, p. 492.
Official	..	.. Memorandum on Tetanus.	1918, 4th Edit. War Office Committee for the Study of Tetanus.
,,	..	.. Tetanus.	Memorandum on the Treatment of Injuries in War. Lond., 1919. pp. 16–23.
,,	..	.. The Medical and Surgical History of the British Army which served in Turkey and the Crimea during the War against Russia during the years 1854–55–56.	Vol. ii, p. 279.
,,	..	.. The Medical and Surgical History of the War of the Rebellion.	Part iii, Vol. ii, Surgical History, Washington, 1883.
,,	..	.. Traumatische, idiopathische und nach Infektionskrankheiten beobachtete Erkrankungen des Nervensystems bei den Deutschen Heeren im Kriege gegen Frankreich, 1870–1871.	Berlin, 1885, Vol. vii.
,,	..	.. Report upon Anaërobic Bacteria and Infections.	M.R.C. Spec Rep. Ser., Lond., 1919, No. 39.

CHAPTER IX.

THE ENTERIC FEVERS.

ENTERIC fevers during the war might well have been the subject of the blackest chapter in its medical history. The Army Medical Department has never had any illusions as to the grave potentialities of these fevers in war, only too securely based on the medical records of the British and other armies. This knowledge was shared by the civil population since it had not been forgotten how heavy a toll had been paid to enteric in the South African war. It may therefore be appropriate at the outset to show side by side (Table I.) the total figures for that campaign beside those for the war of 1914–18.

TABLE I.

The Relative Incidence and Mortality from the Enteric Fevers among the British Troops engaged, respectively, in the South African War and in the War of 1914–18.

	Total cases.	Total deaths.	Case mortality per cent.	Mean annual strength.	Annual incidence per 1,000 of strength	Annual death-rate per 1,000 of strength
South African War, 1899–1902.	57,684*	8,022*	13·9	208,226	105·00	14·6
The Great War, 1914–1918.	20,139	1,191	5·9	2,000,000 (approx.)	2·35	0·139

The significance given throughout this chapter to the terms "enteric" or "enteric fever" is the comprehensive one by which it is held to include not only cases of true typhoid fever but also all cases of paratyphoid, whether A, B, or C, and, in addition, all cases diagnosed on clinical evidence alone as "enteric group." In the published literature of the war, and also, unfortunately, in official practice in some of the expeditionary forces, procedure was not always uniform in this respect, and this, in the early years of the war, led to a certain amount of misconception.

* These figures were given incorrectly in Vol. I of Diseases of the War, p. 4 and p. 11, as 59,750 and 8,227. Ed.-in-C.

The conditions prevailing in many of the secondary battle zones were such that the difficulties which arose had to be dealt with on the spot by the men on the spot, and this in matters bacteriological no less than in matters military.   There did not exist till the last few months of the war any central War Office direction in pathology, and its decision when called for had to be given by the overworked head of another branch. So much it is necessary to mention to explain why it is not possible to utilize the massed figures of the whole campaign in discussing certain points of interest.

Notification and Classification.

Precise instructions relating to the notification of infectious diseases were issued to all concerned before the expeditionary force left England, and naturally among these were typhoid and the paratyphoid fevers.   For some years before the war differentiation between " T," " A," and " B," as they will henceforth be termed, had been insisted on, and this remained an ideal throughout the war.   It was one that was realized very thoroughly in France, but in more distant theatres of war, owing to various causes, the word " enteric," or its unpleasing derivative " enterica," was for a time used to cover all cases presenting a symptom-complex suggestive of this group of fevers.   Later, greater uniformity was observed, especially when, in these distant fields, bacteriologists and laboratories increased to numbers adequate for the careful investigation of each case.

In this matter the procedure in France was as follows : Promptness of notification was obviously most necessary, in order that warning might be given to the unit or formation from which the man came, and no attempt was made at this stage to press for any diagnosis beyond that the case was " suspect."   While, however, it was a matter of small importance to the unit to learn that an individual's illness had proved to be paratyphoid B and not typhoid, since the various preventive measures were, of course, identical, this was not so from either the statistical or the scientific standpoint.   From the statistical side it was clear that no figures relating to enteric could have more than a vague and general interest unless every effort had been made to secure a definite diagnosis of the nature of the infecting bacillus ; while, from the scientific standpoint, such accuracy was essential if any progress was to be made.   No valid conclusions could be drawn in regard to such matters as the protective effect of vaccines, the comparative prevalence, severity and mortality of the several varieties in different bodies of troops or in different races, the effects of specific treatment and many other points, unless accurate differential diagnosis had been carried out.

From the first, then, such accuracy of diagnosis of the enteric fevers was aimed at, and if this was not possible at all times and in all theatres of war it was, at any rate, the rule and not the exception, while in the British forces in France itself it was a rule to which there was hardly an exception.

Precise differentiation being frequently only attainable towards the end of a case, for instance, by the final isolation of the bacillus in question from the excreta, or as the result of a series of agglutination tests, any attempts to press for an early verdict might have led to inaccuracies. On the other hand, it was necessary to pass the danger-signal of probable infection back to the man's unit without delay. It was therefore directed that, in the first instance, all cases rousing a suspicion of enteric infection should be notified simply as enteric suspects, and the ultimate diagnosis was not expected until the termination of the case when a final judgment could be passed upon the accumulated evidence.

Information as to a case being an enteric suspect was telegraphed from the hospital to the man's unit, and notification was again sent when the further progress of the case had made it clear that it was typhoid, paratyphoid A, or paratyphoid B, as the case might be ; or that it had eventually proved not to be enteric, but some other affection.

The existence of a third species of paratyphoid bacillus, the so-called paratyphoid C, did not obtain full recognition till after the end of the war, and no cases appear under this heading in the figures under review. It is probable that any which did occur have been included in the enteric group.

Statistical and other Records.

In addition to the notification of suspects and of the final diagnosis to the head of the medical services, further details were sometimes available in the medical case cards, and if the man was invalided, these were included in the transfer documents. These individual case cards, as well as the admission and discharge books of the hospitals, were eventually sent to the statistical department in London, and it is from them that the final analysis of the group of cases should be possible, although the prospects of such an analysis being made are not at present favourable.

Fortunately, such an exhaustive analysis and system of check, though of course desirable, is not really essential to a clear comprehension of the general facts. Indeed, in many respects such an analysis, though no doubt it would be conducted with mathematical accuracy, might in its results lead to erroneous conclusions, for no distinction could be made by the computators between groups of cases of very different value. To the counting machine all cases labelled typhoid and paratyphoid are the same, whether the recorded evidence in support of the diagnosis is sufficient, doubtful, obviously inaccurate, or altogether absent.

The stress and strain of war, the occasional paucity of laboratories or of bacteriologists, the lack of a central co-ordinating direction as to terminology, methods, standards, and so on, have rendered the enteric returns from the different expeditionary forces of very different value, and in some cases these factors bulk so largely that it is difficult to attach much importance to any conclusions founded locally upon them, or to contrast them with any confidence with those reported from other theatres, more fortunately situated in respect of diagnostic facilities.

It is especially unfortunate that the severe conditions ruling throughout the Gallipoli operations made it impossible for those concerned to render or to obtain as accurate information regarding the incidence of enteric as could have been desired, and definite figures as to the relative proportions of T, A and B, their respective incidence among the inoculated and uninoculated, and on other points are lacking. As it was not possible to examine more than a proportion of the cases by laboratory methods, the diagnosis rested in many cases on clinical evidence alone, while another element of confusion was introduced by the wide prevalence of diarrhœa and dysentery, often accompanied by fever. The results of the laboratory examinations made at home on the convalescents invalided from the Mediterranean showed how little confidence could often be placed on the original diagnosis. It was not till conditions became more stabilized and laboratories and skilled bacteriologists more numerous that greater precision was possible.

The force in France was fortunate in being better supplied almost from the first with well-equipped laboratories, both mobile laboratories at the front and those attached to hospitals. On this account, and because of its proximity to England and the comparatively stable conditions of the fighting, it was possible there to approximate more closely to the ideal which was aimed at—that every suspect case should be submitted to a thorough bacteriological investigation, sufficient not only to ensure accuracy of diagnosis but carried out far enough into convalescence to determine the existence or absence of the carrier state. The information thus obtained was, of course, recorded in the laboratory records of the isolation hospitals concerned, and has formed the foundation of many interesting communications to the medical press.

The principal epidemiological and bacteriological facts of each case had also to be entered on a special form, which was sent on completion of the case—by recovery, invaliding, or death—to Headquarters, Lines of Communications. These forms not only served as a check upon the telegraphic information already received there, but every sheet was studied personally by the Adviser in Pathology, who, if need be, returned it to the hospital for completion of details which might be lacking or for further information from the medical officer or from the bacteriologist in explanation of particular points. It is from an analysis of these individual " infectious disease forms," as they were named, that the information relating to enteric in the British Expeditionary Force in France has largely been derived. They have all been carefully preserved.

Disposal of Notified Cases.

Before going further it may be of interest to take an imaginary case of enteric, as it occurred in France, and to follow its course whilst in the charge of the medical services. On reporting sick the man was sent by the regimental medical officer to the field ambulance, where he was either detained for observation for a day or two, if things were " peaceful," or sent at once to a casualty clearing station. On suspicion being aroused that this might be a possible case of enteric, the officer in charge of the nearest mobile bacteriological laboratory was notified by telephone or wire, and he visited the unit and took samples of blood for cultures and agglutination, taking them back to the laboratory for investigation. If a personal visit was impossible, arrangements were made for the samples to be taken by the medical officer and sent promptly to the laboratory. The results of these examinations were reported by wire to the D.M.S. of the army, by whom they were communicated to general headquarters, to the medical unit in which the man was being treated and to his own unit.

In the meantime the man would probably have been sent down to the base by ambulance train, travelling in a special carriage as a suspect of infectious disease, and on arrival at the base would have been sent by special ambulance car to the local isolation hospital. Accompanying him he would have his case card on which had been recorded by the pathologist of the mobile laboratory any results of agglutination or blood culture which had been completed before he left the front area. If, as was often the case, diagnosis was established by these early tests subsequently to his departure down the line, this was communicated to the D.M.S., Lines of Communication, and by him transmitted to the isolation hospitals at each base. This was necessary, since it was usually a matter of uncertainty at which base and at which hospital the man might have arrived, the destination of the ambulance train depending upon the exigencies of the military-medical situation, which often changed from hour to hour.

On reaching the isolation hospital direct from the front, or indirectly through the intermediary of a general or stationary hospital, the patient, if the suspect diagnosis eventually gave place to one of the four, T, A, B or Group, was treated there until his convalescence was far enough advanced to allow of his being sent home. It had been early decided that every case of diagnosed enteric fever should, when fit to travel, be sent home for a change, irrespective of the degree of severity of the attack.

While in the isolation hospital the pathologists attached to the laboratory carried out the series of agglutination and cultural tests, for which a minimum standard had been laid down, and, in consultation with the medical officer in charge of the case, arrived at a definite diagnosis in accordance with the accepted classification.   The officer commanding the hospital eventually transmitted a summary of the details of these tests to the Adviser in Pathology on the form already mentioned.

The patient, supposing him now to be convalescent and able to travel, was sent home to complete his recovery, accompanied by a card setting out all the essential features of his attack and the results of the laboratory tests.   On disembarkation he was sent to a special enteric depôt, of which there were several at first, but later one central hospital and convalescent depôt, situated at Addington Park, near Croydon.   Here he completed his convalescence, and was the subject of systematic bacterio-logical investigation as to the existence or disappearance of the carrier state.   It need hardly be added that the main guiding principle of this machinery was to guard the army, and also the civil population, against the dangers of the enteric carrier through the premature return to duty or to civil life of convalescent soldiers.

After having been proved to be clear of the carrier state at the enteric depôt, and completing his recovery on furlough, the soldier was now posted to an ordinary convalescent camp, where he was " tuned up " to the required pitch of physical fitness, and probably re-drafted overseas.   The medical department, however, was not quite finished with him, but took pains that a notice went with him, and eventually reached his new commanding officer, to the effect that he had recently recovered from enteric fever and that he was on no account to be employed as a cook or on duties in connection with the handling or distribution of food or water.   This final precaution was necessary in view of the possibility that the negative results of the carrier tests, however carefully done, might have failed to detect a case whose excretion of the bacilli was exceptionally intermittent.

Although the above is sketched in relation to the armies in France, the procedure in other theatres of war was approximately the same, allowing for the variations consequent upon local conditions and for the geographical limitations imposed by the greater distances from Great Britain.   In all cases the principal aim was the same, the complete re-establishment of the patient's   health and the vigilance with regard to the possible establishment of the chronic carrier condition.

Incidence and Mortality.

The total figures of incidence and mortality, as far as they could be compiled from the returns in the possession of the War Office, have been given in Volume I on the Diseases of the War.*

It is hardly the part of pathology to deal exhaustively with statistical material, but as pathology bears the responsibility for the preventive inoculation of the armies, for the search for and disposal of carriers, and, very largely, for the accuracy of the differential diagnosis of the disease, figures in relation to these matters and other points of bacteriological and immunological interest not only appear appropriate but are necessary subjects for study if the experiences of the war are to be utilized to the full.

The large majority of the tables given below relate to special points of practical or scientific interest and are, in the main, derived from material collected in France, partly for the reason

---

* Vol. I, Diseases of the War, Chap. II.

that the recorded information on the points in question was here more complete, and partly because of personal familiarity with that theatre of war.   It should be clearly understood that no reflection is implied upon the competence with which the bacteriological work was carried out in other theatres.   The difficult military conditions prevailing in the Gallipoli, Macedonia, Mesopotamia and East Africa campaigns, particularly in the earlier months of these undertakings, are common knowledge, and much of the work which could be and was carried to a successful conclusion by the numerous mobile and fixed laboratories in France, could not, humanly, be undertaken in these more distant zones.

In these circumstances it is no reflection, then, to say that some of the official figures relating to enteric in these campaigns are not free from fallacy.   It cannot, for instance, be seriously questioned that the totals from Gallipoli do not disclose the true incidence of enteric, since this has been abundantly shown in the published work of those who have tested the immunity reactions of men invalided thence to Egypt, to Malta and to the United Kingdom.   For example, in many cases both the history and the blood picture made it clear that the man had had dysentery alone and not enteric, though double infections had certainly occurred.   Again, still greater dubiety attaches to many of the earlier records of the relative incidence of typhoid, paratyphoid A and paratyphoid B, particularly in respect to cases in which the infecting bacillus was not isolated and identified, and in which agglutination standards were adopted which were subsequently admitted to have been inadequate.

On other points of interest to pathologists it is also difficult to contrast the experience of one expeditionary force with that of another since, at any rate for the first three years, each adopted its own standards, and it was not until the closing months of the war that any central co-ordination or control of pathological effort was contemplated by the War Office ; each force was left to work out its own pathological salvation.

Ætiology.

The main facts in connection with ætiology are well established already and have been dealt with in the first volume on Diseases of the War, so only a few points of special pathological interest will be mentioned, in connection chiefly with the experience gained in France.

The enteric fevers are widespread in their distribution, and modern methods of diagnosis are continually demonstrating their frequency in countries which had been supposed to be free. Again, as the war progressed and large bodies of troops were continually being moved from one theatre to another, ambulant cases and carriers without doubt accompanied the forces and provided starting points for small outbreaks which, unless detected, and unless the appropriate measures were taken, might have grown to alarming dimensions.

The elaborate and thorough precautions taken everywhere to ensure a safe drinking water supply to the troops are recounted in the volumes on the Hygiene of the War, and to this, no doubt, is due the fact that no large outbreaks occurred presenting the characters of a water-borne origin. At the same time it must be common knowledge to most of the world, as of course it was to all who were on the spot, that no method of water purification and distribution can be relied upon to safe-guard the troops under the conditions of heavy fighting, and particularly in trench warfare. The many realistic accounts which have been published, such as war diaries and tales of adventure founded on experience, enable it to be readily understood how, given the presence of an ambulant case or a carrier, particularly a urinary carrier, the chances of infection of food of all kinds were enormous. Water could often be obtained only with great difficulty, and the supplies carried up, usually at night, not infrequently failed to reach their destination owing to shell fire or accident. Again, it needs no great imagination to realize that a great thirst will be satisfied at any cost, and officers, even medical officers who were fully cognizant of the danger, have stated that they have been driven to drink obviously filthy water from shell holes or other sources. Shell-hole water was peculiarly dangerous inasmuch as these hollows naturally served to a considerable extent as latrines, from the shelter they gave from fire, and the first rain there-after filled them with water contaminated with urine or fæces.

In these circumstances, aggravated in summer and autumn by plagues of flies, with all their potentialities for disease transmission, the wonder is not that there was a certain amount of enteric fever and other intestinal disorders but that there was so little.

Dust-borne infection probably played a part in the Eastern and tropical theatres of war, but in France, though there were spells of dusty weather in summer, mud was a much more constant condition.

The commonest source of origin was probably through the intermediary of a carrier of typhoid or paratyphoid bacilli, and considering the small number of cases which occurred in France it was remarkable how frequently the bacteriological enquiries in connection with any small group of cases resulted in the detection of such a carrier. This individual was also usually found to be one whose occupation brought him in close contact with others, as, for example, through his acting as a cook or his being concerned in the handling of rations or cooking utensils.

As regards the frequency of the carrier condition a good deal of information was obtained, since the regulations adopted for the segregation and systematic bacteriological investigation of enteric convalescents made it possible to follow up the history of each individual case for several months after subsidence of the symptoms of the acute disease. An arbitrary period of six months from the final decline of the temperature to normal was fixed upon as the period after which a convalescent was classed as a " chronic carrier." Prior to this, if still voiding germs in one or other of his excretions, he was regarded as a " temporary " or " acute " carrier.

The figures which follow show, in a concise form, the most important group of results which it has been possible to study in this connection. They have been obtained by an analysis of the records of the central enteric depôt at Addington Park, Surrey. In this depôt all enteric convalescents were eventually concentrated and the series of bacteriological examinations of the excreta laid down by the Army Council Instruction were carried out. The careful and thorough work of the officers in charge of the laboratories of the depôt make these results very valuable, although it is probable that the figures exaggerate to a certain extent the true percentages of chronic carriers, since it is undoubted that a proportion of mild cases of enteric, especially in the more distant theatres of war, were not invalided to England.

Typhoid.—Of 546 cases shown in the records of the depôt, 16, or 2·93 per cent., went on to the stage of " chronic carrier," *i.e.*, they were still found to be excreting bacilli more than six months after their fever had subsided. Fifteen of them were fæcal and one urinary.

Paratyphoid A.—Of 837 cases, 26, or 3·1 per cent., became chronic carriers. Twenty-five were fæcal and one urinary.

Paratyphoid B.—Of 1,425 cases, 43, or 3·0 per cent., became chronic carriers. Forty-two were fæcal and one was both urinary and fæcal.

In the majority the carrier state eventually cleared up, but unfortunately there is nothing to record in the way of new knowledge on the treatment of the condition. Obstinate cases were invalided, information of their condition being sent to the Ministry of Health and to the medical officer of health of their town. All received careful instruction as to the precautions they should take to prevent their becoming a danger to their relations and neighbours.

Although it is not new, further precision has also been given to the fact that the intermittency of the carrier condition may at times become excessively pronounced. The work of Fletcher at the Southampton War Hospital, although chiefly concerned with carriers of dysentery bacilli, illustrated this as well in connection with the enteric group, and the fact has also been abundantly illustrated in the experience of other laboratories where the same opportunities presented themselves. This intermittency constitutes one of the chief difficulties in connection with the drafting of regulations as to the discharge of enteric convalescents either to duty or to civil life. In general, it may be said that these rules, while giving a large margin of safety, were of intention not framed for absolute safety. Such would not have been practical politics, as it would have necessitated an army of bacteriologists and would also have implied the segregation for very long periods of a number of perfectly healthy men whose services at the front were urgently needed. Even if an occasional carrier escaped back to the army through the extreme degree of his intermittency and the great length of the germ-free phases, this was not regarded as a serious practical danger in view of the orders which followed him everywhere that he had been a carrier and was not to be employed in duties such as cooking, food distribution, water duty, and so forth. This common-sense decision at all events gave rise to no trouble as no outbreaks connected with the return of such soldiers came to notice, at all events in France.

Seasonal Incidence.—The only point to be recorded here is that the incidence showed its highest figures at the times of any combination of the three factors of high temperature, dust, and prevalence of flies, and, above all, when to these was superadded a period of severe fighting, during which it was not possible to enforce all the sanitary rules under which the forces lived at less strenuous periods. At such seasons it was very noticeable in France how great was the disproportion between the small rise in the enteric group of fevers and the considerable rises for other forms of intestinal disease in which the mechanism of infection is the same. This was particularly the case with bacterial dysentery and diarrhœa of non-dysenteric origin. It can hardly be doubted that the determining influence in this disproportionate rise was to be found in the fact that the very large majority of the troops were protected against enteric fevers by inoculation, while there was no special protection against other bowel complaints. Accordingly, when the general and personal measures of hygienic defence broke down, as they tended to do under certain conditions, the diarrhœa and dysentery admissions increased to an embarrassing degree while the rise in enteric remained of relative unimportance.

Race Incidence.—The extraordinary agglomeration of races called from all parts of the Empire to share in the struggle on the Western front might, one would have thought, have given a rare opportunity for observing the relative susceptibility of widely different types of mankind to enteric infections. The point has already been discussed in Volume I of the Diseases of the War, but the evidence in France on this point is practically negative, since they all, to a quite unexpected degree, exhibited a high degree of immunity. It is true that they were almost without exception inoculated, either before or shortly after their arrival in France, and further, with the exception of the Indian divisions, the majority were not as a rule living under the stress of fighting conditions ; still, one would have expected them to have suffered more than was the case. The only other point which should be mentioned in this connection is that in the case of the Indian officers and men of the Indian divisions, inoculations, which were very readily accepted by them, were always carried out with a special T.V. or T.A.B.* vaccine, prepared in such a manner as to free it from all elements which might have conflicted with the observance of their caste principles.

Bacteriology.

It was hardly to be expected, in view of the fairly complete knowledge already on record, that the war would yield much fresh information regarding the bacteriology of the enteric fevers. Nor has it done so, with one important exception, namely, that it now appears that at least one other member of the group, to which the name of paratyphoid C has been given, must be recognized. The name was first used by

---

* T.V. = Typhoid vaccine.   T.A.B. = Mixed typhoid and paratyphoid vaccine. Subsequent to 1st February, 1916, all first inoculations and reinoculations of British troops were done with the latter vaccine.

Uhlenhuth in 1908, but his organism does not appear to be the same as those isolated during the war. Attention was first specifically directed to the subject by Hirschfeld of the Serbian Service who, in 1916, isolated in bile cultures from the blood of suspected enterics strains of an organism closely resembling, both culturally and morphologically, paratyphoid B, but inagglutinable by any B serum at his disposal. The strains, however, were readily agglutinated by the patient's own serum. He found these strains to be more common at the time than strains of genuine paratyphoid B. They sometimes showed a high grade of virulence and they were on several occasions isolated *post mortem*. Similar reports have since been made from war areas so far apart as Salonika, East Africa and Mesopotamia, and a few cases have been identified as originating in England. In all cases the descriptions have been practically identical and since then it has been possible to collect and examine a large number of strains derived from different parts of the world. It may be concluded that the organism in question is specifically distinct from paratyphoid A and B. While only distinguishable from the latter by slight cultural differences it may be sharply differentiated from this organism, and from other members of the Salmonella group by absorption tests. It may be taken as probable that a proportion of cases which have been noted by most bacteriologists on the various fronts as yielding organisms closely resembling paratyphoid B, but failing to be agglutinated by a specific serum, were probably paratyphoid C infections. Their actual number cannot, in any field, have been very high, but they would appear to be fairly widely distributed and of a grade of pathogenicity comparable to the other paratyphoids. Knowledge of a definite nature about paratyphoid C came too late in the war to allow of steps being taken to distribute a specific agglutinating serum suitable for its identification, so that the number of cases cannot be ascertained ; but this cannot appreciably have affected the general statistics of enteric as the great majority of the cases in question would naturally fall into the enteric group, and thus there has been no under-estimation of the total cases of enteric fever through failure to include cases of paratyphoid C.*

The interesting question as to the desirability of adding this element to T.A.B. vaccine and replacing the latter by a T.A.B.C. has been the subject of investigation at the Royal Army

* For further particulars relating to the new species reference may be made to the paper by Professor Sir F. W. Andrewes.

Medical College since the war, and it may be stated that such a quadruple vaccine has been prepared and used in certain parts of the Middle East, still garrisoned by British troops, on account of the occasional occurrence of the strain C. No information of its protective value is yet available, but a satisfactory development of antibodies has been demonstrated in the blood of inoculated animals and men.

Laboratory Diagnosis.

From the first it was decided to spare no effort to ensure that every case of suspected enteric should be investigated thoroughly by laboratory means. This at least was the rule throughout the campaign in France, and also, in the later stages of the war, at home and in the other theatres of war. That the procedure was not uniform throughout from the beginning was one of the consequences of there being no central directing control in the War Office until 1918, when the new Directorates of Pathology and Hygiene were inaugurated as branches of the Director-General's staff.

The following account has chief reference to the experiences of the armies in France. The first aim of the pathologist to whose notice a case of doubtful or suspicious fever was brought was to get a prompt and decisive diagnosis by means of blood culture. This formed one of the most important parts of the work of the pathologists in charge of the mobile bacteriological laboratories which were distributed to each army, and which functioned as close to the front as practicable, keeping touch not only with a group of casualty clearing stations but also with the divisional field ambulances. Each of these officers made arrangements for ensuring that such cases were brought to his notice without delay, and for transporting the samples of blood, or the inoculated medium, to his laboratory as rapidly as possible. As a general rule he found it most satisfactory to see the case and collect the sample himself. The medium employed was usually either pure ox-bile or a solution of taurocholate of soda, to which from 5 to 10 c.c. of blood from an arm vein were transferred directly. After incubation over night at 37° C., sub-cultures were made on plates of one of the media commonly employed for the detection of members of this group. On the whole, that which found most favour among the pathologists in France was McConkey's bile salt, lactose, neutral red medium, though others preferred Conradi-Drigalski's medium or Browning's brilliant green and telluric acid medium. No attempt was made to enforce uniformity in this matter, since it was realized that, as long as one of the well-established methods was used, the pathologist was likely to do best with that with which he was most familiar and which, in his hands, gave him the highest proportion of successes.

Suspicious colonies were fished from the plate and put up in the usual sugars and submitted to agglutination tests with specific sera of known titre, with which every laboratory was provided. These agglutinating sera were obtained from the Lister Institute, the Royal Army Medical College and other sources, and proved, on the whole, very reliable, but instances were not unknown in which apparently anomalous results were eventually traced to the use of an agglutinating serum which was found to have been incorrectly labelled, no doubt in the hurry of preparation. Greater difficulties were encountered in this, as well as in other branches of bacteriological work, through the unsatisfactory nature of some of the sugars supplied for bacteriological work.

If these first culture essays gave a positive result this was immediately communicated by telephone or wire, confirmed subsequently by writing, to the administrative medical officer of the division or corps, and by him transmitted to all concerned locally, as well as to the headquarters of the lines of communication.

If, for one reason or another, the patient in question had not yet been sent down the line to a base hospital, it might be possible for the pathologist to repeat his blood culture, if the first had been negative, or, alternatively, to take samples of the fæces and urine for attempted isolation of the infecting germ. The blood was always tested for its agglutinating power to the various organisms at the time the first blood culture was made, and, before the introduction of T.A.B. vaccine, this frequently gave accurate diagnostic evidence of a paratyphoid infection, even in the absence of a positive blood culture. On the whole, however, these first agglutination records were chiefly of service to the pathologist of the base hospital to which the patient was subsequently admitted, where the quantitative variations in the titre of agglutination to T, A, or B were of great diagnostic importance should all attempts at isolation by culture have failed. Such a comparison was rendered possible by the universal employment of Dreyer's standard emulsions and by adherence to the principles of his agglutination technique, as is mentioned below.

Once an enteric suspect had been admitted to one of the isolation hospitals, whether he had been sent down as such from the front or had been suspected in and transferred from another hospital, he was submitted to systematic bacteriological observation. This included routine examinations of the excreta, a fresh blood culture, unless a positive result had already been communicated from headquarters or had accompanied the patient, and periodic quantitative estimations of his agglutinating power to T, A and B respectively. If the nature of the case was not readily settled by these observations, they were continued until convalescence was sufficiently advanced to allow of his safe transfer to England and an enteric convalescent hospital.

The stress of work which fell on the laboratories of the isolation hospitals was often heavy, but in view of the importance attached to accuracy of diagnosis in the group, every effort was made to provide sufficient skilled assistance, and in France, with the exception of the first weeks of the war, it may be said that every case admitted to one of these hospitals received a searching and continuous bacteriological examination. In other theatres of war the stress of battle conditions, the difficulties of communication and the not infrequent loss of badly needed stores and apparatus through enemy action, all played a part in preventing a similarly thorough investigation of every case, but with rare exceptions the same skill and pains were brought to bear on the cases, once it was physically possible to do this.

Owing to the above difficulties it is now clear that at Gallipoli, and in some of the other Eastern theatres, the diagnosis of enteric fevers had frequently to be based on clinical rather than on combined clinical and laboratory evidence. For instance, it is now fairly generally recognized that the great volume of the sickness which handicapped so gravely the troops in the Gallipoli trenches was dysentery—chiefly bacillary dysentery—and that, owing to the extremely difficult conditions prevailing, an unknown but certainly a large number of the cases recorded in the returns as " enteric " or " enterica " had in reality nothing whatever to do with this group. This was made clear by the results of subsequent examinations, and has also been recorded in current medical literature by some of those who were on the spot and familiar with the local conditions.

It was hardly to be expected that much of genuine novelty would emerge from all this patient laboratory work, however large the accumulated experience, in the case of a group of diseases so long known and so carefully studied in almost every laboratory. The recognition of a paratyphoid C has already been mentioned, but apart from this the chief bacterio-logical interest centres round such matters as the frequency of isolation of the infecting bacillus and the relative frequency of its detection in blood, fæces and urine ; the occurrence of mixed infections or double infections ; the development and persistence of the carrier condition ; and the modi-fying effects, if any, of protective inoculation upon all of these.

The Isolation of the Infecting Organisms.—Careful records have been kept in some theatres of these results, but in others there was little or no attempt to collate the results recorded by the different laboratories. It is doubtful, however, in these cases whether such collated results would have had much value in view of the very different standards adopted, the facilities or difficulties in connection with early blood culture, the climatic conditions, and a host of other variables. These variables make it also difficult to contrast the results obtained in one theatre of war with those in another.

In France, out of a total of 5,939 cases, there have been recorded 2,318 positive cultural successes, or 39 per cent. of the whole. The details are shown in Table II.

The frequency with which the infecting germs have been isolated from the cases is a matter of considerable interest, and it has been possible in connection with the armies in France to get the precise figures through a scrutiny of the Infectious Disease Forms. These forms were carefully kept by the Adviser in Pathology throughout the operations in France and furnish much of the evidence on which the information has been based. A few points require to be made clear for the full comprehension of the table :—

(1) The total number of forms analysed corresponds within a margin of 40 or 50, due to the inevitable spoilt returns, missing sheets, etc., with the actual number of cases of typhoid, paratyphoid A and B which were notified in the British Expeditionary Force from the commencement of operations till the end of 1918.

(2) The return is inclusive as regards all British and Dominion troops, and comprises officers as well as men ; it does not include cases which occurred in the Indian divisions or in the other native contingents or labour detachments. The total number of cases among these units was very small, and even if the information furnished as to the bacteriology of the disease had been more accurate than was the case, their addition could only have modified the figures fractionally.

TABLE II.

The Results of Cultivations from the Blood and Excreta of Enteric Fevers in the Armies in France, August 1914 to December 1918.

	Inoculated					Non-inoculated				
	Cases.	Isolations, all sources.		Isolations from blood.		Cases.	Isolations, all sources.		Isolations from blood.	
		Total.	Percentage.	Total.	Percentage.		Total.	Percentage.	Total.	Percentage.
Typhoid ..	1,553	416	26·7	252	16·2	578	254	43·9	218	37·7
Paratyphoid A ..	438	66	15·0	18	4·1	554	240	43·3	150	27·0
Paratyphoid B ..	863	375	43·4	58	6·7	1,953	967	49·5	387	19·8
Total T+A+B ..	2,854	857	30·0	328	11·4	3,085	1,461	47·3	755	24·4

Total cases analysed .. .. .. 5,939.
Total isolations .. .. .. 2,318 = 39 per cent.
Total isolations from blood .. 1,083 = 18·2 per cent.

(3) Cases of enteric group infection were naturally excluded since in these the bacteriological diagnosis had given no positive evidence of the variety to which they belonged, while, of course, the cultivations made from their blood and excreta were universally negative—otherwise they would have fallen automatically into their proper class.

(4) " Inoculated " includes, in the case of typhoid, all men who had received two doses of T.V. or T.A.B. vaccine within two years of infection, or one dose within one year of infection. In the case of the paratyphoids, " inoculated " includes only men who had been inoculated with T.A.B. vaccine and with the same time limits as given above, namely, two years after two doses, one year after one. All cases in men whose last inoculations were older than this were placed among the non-inoculated.

(5) It will be understood that the bacteriological diagnosis in the cases in which cultural tests proved negative was based upon the agglutination results ; if these, too, were inconclusive the case would not be diagnosed as typhoid or paratyphoid A or B, but, provided the clinical evidence was positive, would have been included among the enteric group cases.

Table II will be of interest chiefly in demonstrating (a) the degree of success which rewarded the persistent efforts of the bacteriologists to obtain a cultural diagnosis ; (b) the relative frequency of the isolations of the three varieties ; (c) the frequency of positive blood cultures in the different groups ; and (d) a comparison between the results in the inoculated and the non-inoculated.

(a) The total positive cultural results, 2,318 out of 5,939, a percentage of 39, may be regarded as satisfactory under the existing conditions. A higher percentage would probably have been obtained if the general character of the infections had been more severe than was the case, through the services of the bacteriologist being requisitioned earlier in the attack, and of their thus being able to carry out more hæmo-cultures during the days in which positive results were more likely to be expected. A further factor is probably attributable to the restraining influence of previous inoculation upon the intensity and the duration of the bacillæmia, as is referred to under (c). On the other hand, a higher percentage of positive cultures from the excreta appears unlikely. The perseverance and skill of the bacteriologists who carried out these tests in the isolation hospitals, frequently making six or more consecutive examinations, could hardly have been greater, and the results here may be taken as fairly representative of the highest figures attainable.

The conditions ruling in the various theatres of war differed too greatly to allow of fair comparison between the percentages of successful isolations, but, on the whole, it may be assumed that the figures given for France are in fairly close correspondence with those obtained elsewhere. For example, although Ledingham quotes higher percentages in connection with individual laboratories in Mesopotamia, where he was consulting bacteriologist—some reaching as high as 80 per cent. —the percentage of positive results which he gives for 1,039 British cases is 36·9, which is in close accord with the similar group in France, which yielded 39 per cent. of successes. Comparisons, however, should not be pressed too closely ; for instance, Ledingham at that time was not a believer in the diagnostic value of agglutination tests in triply-inoculated men and agglutination diagnosis in such cases was not accepted. It is therefore inevitable that an unknown proportion of milder cases which, in France, would probably have been accepted as T, A or B on agglutination evidence, would in Mesopotamia have been called something else, unless the clinician was sufficiently confident of the symptomatology to class them as enteric group cases. Such variations in standards are regrettable since it is unlikely that satisfactory explanations can be given of apparent differences which might be of scientific interest. For instance, in the paper just quoted by Ledingham it appears that cases of enteric in Indian troops—536 in number —yielded 56·8 per cent. of positive cultural results, or 20 per cent. more than was obtained in the British troops. As it is not to be supposed that less skill and patience was brought to bear on the British patient than on the Indian, this would suggest either an increased grade of severity in the Indian cases or a lesser degree of protection by inoculation, which was not the experience in France. As it stands, the query must remain unanswered.

(b) The relative frequency of the isolations made in the three fevers. The table shows an interesting comparison in this respect, isolation being most frequently successful in the cases of paratyphoid B infection—47 per cent. ; less so in typhoid—36 per cent. ; and most difficult in paratyphoid A— 30 per cent. All cases are, however, included here, whether protected by inoculation or not, and the fact of inoculation appears to influence the result to a significant degree. That this is so may be seen by comparing the percentage of total isolations in each of the three diseases in the non-inoculated groups. Here, while paratyphoid B has been recovered somewhat more frequently than the others, the difference is small and the percentage figures in the case of paratyphoid A and typhoid are almost identical. This contrast does not, however, hold in the case of blood isolations, as will be commented on below.

(c) The frequency of positive blood cultures in the three diseases. This is a matter of considerable interest, and although, as has already been explained, the figures given do not represent the highest rates that would have been attained under peace conditions and with repeated examinations, still they are significant from a comparative point of view. Again looking to the non-inoculated group, as giving the fairest material for comparison, it is seen that true typhoid has been isolated most readily, paratyphoid A next, and that the smallest percentage of positive results is in the case of paratyphoid B.

A direct relationship between the severity of an attack of one of these fevers and the occurrence of a readily demonstrable bacillæmia has been generally assumed as the result of individual experiences. Leishman had this brought very prominently under his personal observation on several occasions as Adviser in Pathology in France. Two examples may be given. In the month of October 1914, when typhoid had made its appearance in the armies on the Aisne and was spreading in disquieting fashion, almost entirely among uninoculated men, an exceptionally high percentage of positive blood cultures was reported ; in fact, it was rarely necessary to pursue the bacteriological quest beyond the results given by the first blood culture. These cases were, clinically, the most severe group encountered in British troops and gave a high case mortality. The appearance of a ward filled with them at Versailles recalled vividly the typhoid wards in an Indian Station hospital in the " eighties," when inoculation had not been heard of and where a case mortality of anything below 25 per cent. was considered good. Another example occurred late in 1917, where a series of similarly severe cases of typhoid occurred at one of the bases among the men of a labour company who by some means had evaded inoculation before being sent overseas. In this case attention was actually attracted to the group by noting the unusual frequency with which positive blood cultures were being reported on the case sheets sent to the Adviser in Pathology from the base in question.

As will be seen, the percentage over all of successful blood cultures among the 5,939 cases analysed was 18·2, whereas that of isolation from any source, blood included, was 39 per cent. The lowest figure of blood culture recorded is in that of inoculated paratyphoid A cases, 4·1 per cent., and the highest, 37·7 per cent., is the figure recorded for non-inoculated typhoid cases.

(d) Finally, it is of considerable interest to compare the results of attempted isolation in the three fevers in the inoculated and non-inoculated respectively. The definitions given to inoculation will be borne in mind in this connection. Here again it was assumed by most pathologists and clinicians in France that inoculation having modified the severity of a subsequent attack, this would be reflected in a comparatively restricted multiplication of the causative bacilli in the body, more especially evidenced in a lessened degree and perhaps a shortened duration of the usual bacillæmia. As time went on this anticipation appeared to be verified in the individual experience of most workers in France. Ledingham, however, on the strength of his own observations in Mesopotamia and on the results of a series of careful observations reported by Vaughan of the United States Army, concluded that there was no evidence in support of such a view. It was therefore with interest that the records of the armies in France were studied from this aspect, and it is fortunate that the information available had been recorded in such a form as to make it possible to obtain the requisite details. The figures demonstrate a marked contrast, in the case of each of the three fevers, between the comparative facility of isolation in the non-inoculated and the comparative difficulty in patients who had received protective inoculations within the defined time limits. This comes out in every instance in respect of the column of isolations from all sources, being least marked in paratyphoid B infections, but it is especially in connection with the results of blood cultures that the increased difficulties consequent on inoculation are manifested, and it can hardly be doubted that these figures prove that it is less easy to isolate the causative bacilli from the blood of an inoculated man than from one who has not been inoculated.

Agglutination.

Failing a successful isolation and identification of the infecting germ, the pathologist has to fall back on the evidence obtainable from the agglutinating power of the blood serum. The figures just quoted in connection with the results of cultivation diagnosis (Table II) show that in France approximately two-thirds of the cases finally diagnosed as one or other variety of enteric were so diagnosed on the strength of the agglutination evidence. Had it not been so, this large proportion would either have remained undiagnosed or, if sufficiently typical from the clinical side, would have been placed under the unsatisfactory label of " enteric group." The records from other theatres are not sufficiently detailed to permit of close analysis, but undoubtedly agglutination diagnosis also played a considerable part in most of them. In a few, as for example in Mesopotamia, agglutination evidence was disregarded on the advice of the consulting bacteriologist, and only cultural evidence accepted for precise differentiation.

The history of this part of the subject is interesting, and the divergent views entertained by different pathologists gave rise to considerable debate and to a number of communications to the medical press throughout the war. At first there was little difficulty and little variance of opinion, for, as will be recalled, the armies were, until early in 1916, inoculated only with typhoid vaccine. After this period the increasing use of triple vaccine, T.A.B., through its resultant production of agglutinins to all three organisms, enhanced the difficulties of correct interpretation of the agglutination estimations in cases of continued fever, and there arose the difference of opinion alluded to. On the one hand there were those who considered that these difficulties were too great to surmount, or not worth the trouble of surmounting under service conditions, while on the other were those who took a different view both of the possibilities and of the importance of leaving nothing undone . to secure accurate subdivision of the cases. The history need not be followed in detail, and it will suffice to record here that towards the end of the war the different points of view had been very largely reconciled, and an increasing experience had demonstrated that, within certain limits, agglutination evidence could be relied upon to give a definite diagnostic result even in men who had been inoculated with triple vaccine.

In 1914 and 1915 agglutination evidence was readily interpreted, naturally with greatest certainty in the case of men who had not been inoculated for some years, the demonstration of specific agglutinins to either T, A, or B, in significant dilutions of the serum, being practically as clear evidence as the isolation of the bacillus itself. Again, even in men who had been recently inoculated with T.V., the rise and fall of the agglutination titre to T, as the disease progressed, left no doubt as to the fact of infection, while the appearance of agglutinins to either A or B in a man inoculated only with T.V. was incapable of any other interpretation than that one of these germs was at work.

Even here, however, mistakes might readily be made if reliance were placed on a single estimation, or if the agglutinating power of the serum had not been estimated quantitatively by an appropriate method. Hence it was an instruction in the armies in France from the first that all cases should be tested at intervals throughout the attack, and that the limits of agglutination to each of the three germs should be ascertained and recorded, with the view to the building up of an agglutination curve for each organism. Naturally this could not always be carried out and if, in the meantime, cultural experiments yielded positive results, one could not expect an over-worked pathologist to push on with agglutination work which was no longer essential for diagnosis. Later in the war, however, as the conditions for bacteriological work improved, the majority of such cases were carried through as regards their agglutination history, irrespective of the fact of successful isolation of the infecting germ. This became all the more desirable after the introduction of T.A.B. vaccine, in order that the necessary experience might be accumulated on the behaviour of the agglutination curves in triple vaccine cases whose precise nature had been proved by isolation of the infecting germ.

The importance of such quantitative estimations manifestly made it a matter of prime importance that the methods by which the tests were carried out should be suitable for this purpose, and it became obvious that it would be most desirable that all pathologists should employ the same method and the same standards, if this were found to be possible, in order that the results obtained in a given case in one hospital or laboratory might be comparable with those subsequently obtained in another hospital. It soon became clear that in Professor Dreyer's agglutination method there was available a quantitative method eminently suitable for the required purpose. In this method standardized suspensions of dead bacteria are employed, with a special technique of serum dilution, etc., by which the agglutination titre of a serum is recorded in terms of accurately defined " agglutination units." Professor Dreyer's services were available at Boulogne early in 1915, and he subsequently was attached to the laboratory of the principal isolation hospital at Wimereux for a considerable time. The pathologists charged with the bacteriological diagnosis of these fevers had therefore every opportunity of studying his methods, and the greater their experience the greater became their appreciation of its value as compared with other agglutination methods. It was eventually decided that it should be employed by all laboratories in France, and this was greatly facilitated by the Medical Research Committee making arrangements for the regular supply of the standard emulsions and the necessary equipment from Professor Dreyer's laboratory at Oxford. Careful instructions for use were drawn up by him and were issued to all concerned.

In order that full benefit might be reaped from the general use of such a standard method, directions were given that a summary of the agglutination estimations should be recorded on the infectious diseases form. It was directed that this information should record the limit of standard agglutination to each organism on at least three occasions during the course of the attack. Naturally the pathologists kept the full records in their laboratory notebooks and from such records some have published their results and conclusions. The individual sheets, however, have all been carefully kept and have since been studied closely in the hope that the collected results might yield information of value. The subject does not readily lend itself to analysis, and its full discussion would take more space than is available, so all that will be attempted is to direct attention to the points which throw light upon the extent to which the method can be relied on for a definite diagnosis of T, A, or B.

Dreyer, in his original account of the method and in the printed instructions, and also in a series of papers by himself and Dr. Ainley Walker, written during the war, had described the course which the agglutination curves might be expected to follow in non-inoculated men, in men inoculated with T.V. only, and in those who had had doses of the triple vaccine. The points of diagnostic significance had been indicated and it remained to be seen how these bore the test of experience in the field. As was to be expected of any new method involving, as this did, the strict observance of a somewhat delicate technique, the first impressions of individual workers were not always favourable, but experience rarely failed to convert a doubter into an advocate.

The forms which have been analysed are naturally the records of cases in which a positive diagnosis had been arrived at, and did not include a control group of cases in which the diagnostic verdict was negative. It is true that a partial control series is provided by the cases classed, chiefly on clinical grounds as enteric group, but these do not correspond to the cases of suspect enteric which proved negative on being finally recognized as affections of some nature other than enteric. In France the proportion of such unconfirmed cases to the whole admissions for suspected enteric was approximately 30 per cent. On this matter of control observations mention may be made of a very striking piece of corroborative evidence which occurred in France during the winter of 1915–16. At this period a large number of cases of continued fever were being sent down the line, and others, whose nature was obscure, were also observed in base hospitals. To some medical officers the cases in question presented certain clinical points serving to distinguish them from enteric fever ; to others the cases appeared to be enteric ; they were returned in large numbers as enteric suspects and probably transferred to an isolation hospital. To the pathologist, however, these cases not only failed to give any positive cultures but showed no fluctuations of their T, A, or B agglutination indices when tested at intervals by the Dreyer technique. They were accordingly returned in large numbers by the laboratories as negative to enteric infection and in some localities there was a sharp divergence of clinical and laboratory opinion. It was not long, however, before the suspicions of observers at the front were confirmed, namely, that a new disease—trench fever—had to be dealt with, and it was then evident that the cases in question were, in the large majority, cases of this affection, and had nothing whatever to do with enteric fever. This incident accordingly constitutes a very strong control observation of the reliability of the agglutination tests in experienced hands.

In the majority of the cases the agglutination curves were found to behave in characteristic fashion, the summit of the curve of the " infection agglutinins " reaching its maximum between the sixteenth and twenty-fourth day after the onset, while the sympathetic fluctuations in the titres of the " inoculation agglutinins " of the non-infecting organisms kept within a smaller range and, as a rule, were a little later in reaching their maximum values. A series of observations carried out from a sufficiently early date and maintained over a period of three weeks or more seldom failed to justify a specific diagnosis, the results being checked by a similar study of the agglutinins in cases diagnosed by isolation but in which the full agglutination curves had also been worked out.

There remained, however, a proportion of cases in which it did not appear possible to give a decisive verdict. In many of these this could not be counted to the discredit of the method, being due to such causes as the case being admitted too late for the observance of the critical summit of the curve of the infection agglutinins, or because, for some other reason, an inadequate number of observations had been made. In others, however, the curves proved either irregular or too small in amplitude to justify a diagnosis. Such border-line cases account for a considerable proportion, probably the majority, of the cases included under the diagnosis of enteric group which are analysed below. It must suffice here to indicate what the chief causes of these doubtful results appear to have been, as judged from a considerable personal experience and from the subsequent careful study of several thousands of records. They may be attributed to the following causes :—

(a) Lack of experience of the method, or technical errors.

(b) Inaccurate knowledge of the true " date of onset " of the symptoms.

(c) Incorrect information about inoculation.

(d) High readings of all indices consequent on recent inoculation.

(e) Double infections (proved in a number of cases, probable in more).

(f) Infections by paratyphoid C.

(g) Errors in diagnosis, the fever in reality having been due to some condition other than enteric.

It should hardly be necessary to add that the experience of pathologists in France gave no support to the suggestion, not infrequently put forward, but now with increasing rarity, that the titre of agglutination can be markedly affected by any condition other than inoculation of vaccine or an attack of one of the enteric fevers. Careful investigations directed specifically to this point, for instance in connection with trench fever, yielded in competent hands persistently negative results.

In view of the great trouble taken to ascertain and record the agglutination values in these cases in the armies in France, it has been thought desirable to study the individual case sheets and to extract as much information from them as possible, so that the experiences of the war in this direction may not be lost. The material consists of the case sheets already alluded to from which the analysis of the results of cultivations of the blood and excreta were derived. On these sheets the bacteriologists had been directed to record a summary of the agglutination tests carried out during the course of the disease, the end-point of the agglutination being given to all three organisms on a minimum of three consecutive tests, carried out at intervals of at least four days. The results were expressed either in terms of the highest dilution of serum which gave standard agglutination, or in terms of Dreyer's " agglutination units "—the reduction factor of the emulsion employed being quoted in the latter case.

The recording of these details on the sheets had been asked for in order that the individual diagnosis might be checked at headquarters, and much interesting discussion and correspondence took place in connection with them at the time, helping towards an extended experience of the test itself and especially of the fluctuations which might be expected to occur in inoculated men.

The system followed in attempting this general analysis has been to take the whole of the case sheets of typhoid, paratyphoid A and B for the year 1916, distinguishing those of the inoculated from the non-inoculated and those in which the diagnosis had been confirmed by isolation of the infecting organism from those in which the laboratory diagnosis was based upon agglutination. In addition, a large group of enteric group cases—300 in all—derived partly from the 1916, partly from the 1917 sheets, was closely studied. In each case only those sheets have been included in the analysis in which full details of the tests were furnished and which complied with the minimum standard laid down. Otherwise there was no selection—they were taken as they came.

The numbers analysed are shown in Table III.

TABLE III.

	Agglutination diagnosis.	Isolation diagnosis.	Total.
Typhoid	195	43	238
Paratyphoid A	88	56	144
Paratyphoid B	242	186	428
Enteric Group	300	—	300
Totals ..	825	285	1,110

It was not easy to arrange the mass of figures in relation to each of these 1,110 cases in a manner suitable for comparative study, but this was eventually done by devising miniature agglutination curves combined with a system of code marks relating to the various points which had to be taken into consideration. Nor is it simple, within a moderate compass, to present the conclusions arrived at in anything but a somewhat dogmatic fashion.

In the case of each fever the curves were first studied carefully in the bacteriologically proven cases and then those in which cultures had failed were scrutinized and contrasted, the inoculated and uninoculated groups being studied separately. The following are the principal points brought out in each instance.

Agglutination Tests in Typhoid.

(a) *In men inoculated with T.V.*—In 27 of these Eberth's bacillus had been isolated. The agglutination curves fitted regularly into the expected shape of a definite rise, followed by a fall, the maximum being recorded somewhere between the sixteenth and the twenty-fourth day from the stated date of onset. One case showed a marked secondary rise accompanying a relapse. Three cases showed definite agglutination to paratyphoid B and one to paratyphoid A, suggestive of double infections, but no others showed any such trace throughout the illness. The average maximum height of agglutination (expressed in terms of the highest dilution and not, unless otherwise stated, of agglutination units) was considerable, being approximately 1,000, and one case, in which the bacilli were isolated both from the blood and from the stools, recorded the highest agglutination figure encountered in any sheet, namely 1–1,800,000. Other maxima were 74,000, 25,000 and 20,000, while the lowest figure given was 33 (units) in a case in which the bacilli were recovered from the stools.

Contrasting this series with the 138 cases in which agglutination was the only laboratory means of diagnosis, the curves in general were seen to have the same regular conformation but the average maximum height of agglutination was very definitely lower than in the " isolation " cases, being in the neighbourhood of 500 ; readings below 100 were rare, but the highest figures were 5,200, 5,000 and 3,000. Clinical relapses were recorded in 9 of this series and in all but one this was reflected in a pronounced secondary rise in the agglutination titre.

(b) *In Men inoculated with T.A.B.*—In 16 of these the diagnosis had been confirmed by isolation. The curve of the typhoid agglutinins was here, too, typical in most instances and the average maximum height of agglutination above 1,000, the maximum being 8,000 and the minimum 88 (units) ; but, as in all cases where T.A.B. had been used, chief interest as well as chief difficulty attached to the behaviour and the interpretation of the associated paratyphoid A and paratyphoid B inoculation agglutinins. In the majority the indices to these organisms showed synchronous and sympathetic curves of the same nature but of smaller volume than that of T. To take them separately, A agglutination was unaffected throughout in two cases and, when present, was increased to a maximum, once of a sixfold rise, usually a threefold or twofold rise. The subsequent fall in this associated A index was occasionally pronounced, being sometimes one-quarter or one-third of the figure recorded at the first estimation. Much the same results were noted in connection with the B index ; here also two cases showed no fluctuations, but in general the original figure was raised to a maximum threefold or twofold of the first value, the highest recorded rise being a sixfold one. The subsequent fall, when manifested, reached in one case a level only one-sixth of that first recorded. Two clinical relapses were recorded and showed characteristic agglutination movements, while in three other cases, in which no mention had been made of relapse, the curves suggested that such had probably occurred.

Contrasting the above with 57 cases of typhoid in T.A.B. men in whom the bacilli had not been isolated, the average character of the T curve was normal and characteristic, but the average maximum height of the recorded agglutination was somewhat lower—800—than in the isolation cases. In this group, however, a considerably larger proportion of the cases showed no appreciable fluctuation in the A or B titres, 19 of them being negative in this respect, while in 24 the fluctuations of these A and B indices were identical and similar in volume. In one case the A index rose to a level twelve times as high as the first A reading and in this case a relapse was recorded ; the possibility of this febrile relapse having been due to a superadded A infection appears worthy of consideration. Contrasting the effects on the A and B indices, respectively, the former was unchanged in 9 cases, the latter in 11, and it was notable that, in both, the latest reading was usually a considerably lower one than the first, *i.e.*, the apparent effect of the T infection was to induce a considerable rise in the associated agglutinins followed by a drop to a level lower than the original one. It may be added, however, that this drop was only transitory, and that in the cases which could be followed well into convalescence the original height was recovered and perhaps passed. In several instances both the A and the B indices fell, at their lowest readings, to points one-fifth of the original value ; one of these cases, in which the A index had fallen to this point, proved fatal.

Agglutination Tests in Paratyphoid A.

(a) *In Men inoculated with T.A.B.*—Paratyphoid A bacilli were isolated in 1916 from 19 cases which had been observed for a period sufficient to give agglutination readings before, during and after the critical sixteen to twenty-four days after onset ; the A curve was seen to follow the same regular rise and fall as the T curve in typhoid. The average maximum height—1,800—was higher than that recorded for the typhoid cases, although individual maxima did not occur above 8,000 ; very low readings were rare, 50 and 28 (units) being the lowest. As regards the effect on the other indices the typhoid index was driven up in all but two, in which it remained unaltered, and the highest levels were fivefold increases in the original T values. Terminal falls of the T index were common, sometimes to one-fourth of the first T reading. The B index was less regularly affected, there being no change at all in five cases, while a regular rise and fall was in evidence in only four. One case in which the index of the infecting A showed a steady rise and no fall within the period of observation showed a remarkable stimulation of the B index to a height fifteen times above the first recorded level—very suggestive of a double infection, though no paratyphoid B were isolated. In another case no B agglutinins were found throughout.*

In 50 cases the diagnosis of paratyphoid A in such T.A.B. men rested upon the agglutination, always of course combined with the clinical picture. In these there was the same regular rise and fall of the A agglutinins, reaching their maximum level somewhere about the eighteenth to twentieth day, but in a fair number of them the first observations had not been made early enough to detect the initial rise, and this could only be assumed from the steepness of the fall after the twenty-second or twenty-fourth day. The maximal heights

---

* It was impossible in all cases to be certain that the date and nature of the protective inoculations have been correctly recorded, especially when the information had to be elicited from the man himself, owing to his pay-book being incomplete or having been lost.

of agglutination were seen to show considerable variations, ranging from maxima of 8,000 to such low readings as 15 or 16 units ; the average worked out at 800, being thus less than half that observed in the cases diagnosed by isolation. It will be recalled that the same contrast was seen in the case of typhoid and it will again be manifest, in even more striking fashion, in the case of paratyphoid B infections. It is probably a fair assumption that this is no more than a reflection of the fact that the severer cases yield a higher percentage of positive cultural results and that this severity. is further evidenced by a stronger and more enduring output of the specific agglutinins. The older view, that exceptionally severe cases show a very poor development of agglutinins, is not borne out by the recorded observations of fatal T, A and B cases in France.

Looking to the influence on the other indices it was seen that the T index in these 50 cases was unaffected in 8 cases, but in the others it was, as a rule, greatly disturbed, several cases showing rises up to twelvefold the original height, while others showed falls to one-eighth or one-tenth of the first reading. In 9 cases a definite rise and fall of the T index synchronous with the A was manifest. The B index in these cases remained steady in nine instances, while 6 cases showed no evidence of B agglutination throughout, although they were all returned as having been fairly recently inoculated with T.A.B. Most, however, showed a strong stimulation of B, the two highest readings being, respectively, fourteen times and ten times as high as the first.

(b) *In Men not inoculated with T.A.B.*—The very large majority of these men had been inoculated with T.V. In this group the number verified by isolation—37—happens to be almost identical with that of the agglutination-diagnosis cases—38. In the former the average maximum height of agglutination is high, only 6 cases giving readings under 100, while readings above 1,000 were common. In that which gave the highest figure, 10,000, it was noted that the B index attained simultaneously the high figure of 5,000. This is the sort of thing which is encountered in bacteriologically proven cases of double infection, and it is probable that there were a good many more of these than could be proved conclusively by isolation of both organisms.

The T index in this group was negative in 1 case, unaffected in 5 and showed a regular rise and fall in 9. In most cases the rise averaged a twofold increase, but in 1 case the index was raised sixteenfold, and in another eight. Terminal depression of the T index below the original level was not uncommon, in two instances being one-fifth of the first reading.

As regards the B index there was no trace of B agglutinins in 29 of the 37 cases, and of the 8 in which they were recorded, 2 were so high as to suggest double infections, and in the others it appeared probable that they had really received T.A.B. vaccine and that the fact had been wrongly recorded. There was nothing in the experience of the pathologists in France to suggest that B agglutinins ever make their appearance in the blood from any other source than a B infection or a T.A.B. inoculation.

As to the agglutination-diagnosed cases, 38 in number, the average maximum height of agglutination once more was definitely lower than that in the isolation group, 22 cases having maxima under 100 ; but there were exceptions with very high readings, such as 12,500 and 5,000. It was noticed that the 4 cases which gave strong A agglutination all gave high B readings as well as T, in spite of the supposed non-employment of T.A.B. vaccine. Their T indices were unaffected in 9 cases, absent in 1, and showed a regular rise and fall in 11 ; the rise in 3 cases being of an eightfold order. B was absent in 28 cases, present in 10, usually in low concentration with the exception of the 4 cases noted above.

Agglutination Tests in Paratyphoid B.

(a) *In Men inoculated with T.A.B.*—In this group 64 cases verified by isolation of paratyphoid B are contrasted with 108 cases diagnosed on the agglutination. Taking the isolation cases first, the most striking feature is the great concentration of specific agglutinins which appear in the course of so many of these B infections. In this particular group the average maximum height reached by the curves is no less than 10,000, one case reaching 1,250,000 ; others giving readings of 145,000, 50,000 and 45,000. Occasional low readings are also recorded, such as 50, and in one case no B agglutinins were found at all, although the case was clinically enteric, and paratyphoid B was isolated from the stools. As to the effect on the other indices the typhoid agglutinins remained stationary in 18 cases, many of which gave very high B readings, while in 24 there was a marked rise, some being equivalent to an eightfold rise in the titre. Twelve of the cases showed a marked fall in the T index, either preceded by a rise or starting from the point of the first observation. The A index, on the other hand, was less affected, remaining steady in 12 and being absent altogether in 14. Eleven showed a marked rise in the A agglutinins, and 16 a marked fall. Any rise or fall of more than 100 per cent. of the first reading is considered a " marked " reaction for the purpose of this analysis.

In connection with the extremely high readings of these B agglutinins, it is of interest that there did not appear to be any sign of correlation between such high B indices and the associated A and T indices, e.g., the case in which the B agglutinins reached 1,250,000 showed no appreciable alteration in the T index above or below the height at which this stood to the date of the first examination. This point comes out prominently in connection with each of the three fevers.

Of the 108 cases of paratyphoid B in T.A.B. men, in which isolation of the bacillus was unsuccessful, the average maximum height of agglutination was again remarkably high, in the neighbourhood of 1,500 ; cases with readings no higher than 250 were rare, and several maxima of 25,000 were recorded. As regards the effect on the T index, this showed a regular rise and fall in 18, a marked rise in 23 and a marked fall in 29, while the index remained unaffected in 13 cases. Analysed in the same fashion the A index gave a regular rise and fall curve in 7, a marked rise in 13 and a marked fall in 27, while in 19 cases there was no appreciable change. In this group were 2 cases noted as double infections by the returning officer, in which the A index shot up in one case to 120 times, in the other to 50 times its original height.

(b) *In men not inoculated with T.A.B.*, the majority, however, being inoculated with T.V., 122 had been verified by isolation of the bacillus from blood, stools, or urine, while in 134 the diagnosis rested on clinical evidence and agglutination.

In the 122 isolation cases the typical rise and fall of the B agglutinins was on the whole very regular, though in 8 cases no fluctuations were detected throughout the attack. The outstanding feature as regards the agglutination was the very high dilution in which standard agglutination was often obtained. No fewer than 65 of these cases yielded maxima of or above 5,000, while exceptional cases rose extremely high. The three highest may be specially mentioned from the interesting point of their influence on the associated indices. One gave a figure of 1,125,000 and the T index showed a synchronous eightfold elevation of its original titre ; a second gave 190,000 and the T showed a fivefold rise ; a third gave 100,000 and a fourfold rise in the T index was asssociated with it. But in none of these cases did any trace of agglutination to paratyphoid A appear throughout the attack.

In general, the T index showed a marked rise in 55, a marked fall in 29 and a rise and fall in 26. In 17 it was unaffected and in 5 there was no T agglutination at all. Agglutination in A was absent from all but 15 which showed appreciable but not as a rule high agglutination levels. A few may have represented double infections, but it appeared more probable that in most an inaccurate record of the kind of vaccine employed had been made.

Looking now at the records of the 134 similar cases in which agglutination evidence was all the laboratory could furnish in support of the clinical diagnosis, the general picture is much the same as in the isolation cases, with the usual exception that the average height of the maxima of agglutination stands considerably lower. Still, this average was in the neighbourhood of 2,000 in spite of the fact that a fair number of cases were diagnosed on agglutination curves showing exceptionally low maxima, such as 5, 7, 10 and 12 units. The highest maxima in the group were 80,000, 50,000 and 25,000. The effect on the T index was marked by a sharp rise in 53, by a marked fall in 34 and by a rise and fall in 27, while 26 cases showed no fluctuation of the figure first determined. In 2 no typhoid agglutinins were found. The highest rises of the T index were nearly all associated with definite A agglutination. In all but 16 cases A agglutinins were absent and the remarks made in connection with the preceding group apply here also.

In the above commentary and analysis a group of cases, proved by isolation, has in each instance been examined first in order that a standard might be erected against which to contrast the results in the cases in which sole reliance was placed on the results of the agglutination tests. With the exception, already commented on, that the average height of maximum agglutination to the infecting organism was always considerably higher in the isolation cases it will have been seen that the correspondence is extremely close and it will probably be admitted that there is no justification for the pessimistic view that triple inoculation has rendered the differential diagnosis of the enteric fevers by agglutination tests impossible.

Agglutination Tests in the Enteric Group.

It was natural to attach especial importance to a study of the agglutination records of the cases finally diagnosed enteric group, on the agreement of the clinician and the pathologist that there was no evidence permitting of a more precise differentiation.

It has already been mentioned that about 30 per cent. of all enteric suspects admitted to isolation hospitals in France were eventually discharged as being clearly of some other nature, but there remained the cases which were clinically or bacteriologically suspect but in which no definite laboratory proof could be given. Immense trouble was taken with this class in the laboratories of the isolation hospitals and in addition to repeated attempts at isolation, well into convalescence, agglutination curves were carefully kept.

To examine a large sample of the records three different batches of 100 sheets have been taken dealing with different periods in 1916 and 1917, otherwise they are unselected and taken in order as they came. No very elaborate commentary or analysis need be given, but it was of obvious interest to see upon what grounds the agglutination evidence was considered to have been inconclusive in these cases.

Twenty of the cases had been inoculated only with T.V. while the remaining 280 were said to have had T.A.B. On inspection it was seen that in the great majority of cases the reason for the failure to assign a definite diagnosis of T, A or B was evident and it is possible to group these reasons under four headings, leaving in a fifth class a certain number of cases in which, judging solely from the summary of the agglutination records, it would have appeared possible to have given a diagnosis. The small group of 20 T.V. inoculation cases and the T.A.B. group have been analysed carefully and each may be shown most succinctly in tabular form (Table IV).

TABLE IV.

i. Enteric Group Cases inoculated with T.V.

	Number.
Agglutination indices either unchanged throughout, or showing no fluctuation above 100 per cent.	13
No agglutination, either to T, A, or B	2
Agglutination present to A, B, or both A and B, and indistinguishable in form from the curve of the T agglutinins ..	5
	—
Total ..	20

TABLE IV—*continued.*

ii. Enteric Group Cases inoculated with T.A.B.

	Number.
Agglutination indices either unchanged throughout to T, A and B, or showing no fluctuation above 100 per cent.	79
Number of agglutination estimations insufficient, having been commenced too late or discontinued too soon to include the critical period between the sixteenth and twenty-fourth day	57
Agglutination curves indistinguishable in character and range in the case of all three organisms, or in two with an absence of any agglutination to the third	98
Agglutination curves anomalous (include no doubt some relapse cases, some double infections and probably some cases of paratyphoid C).	21
Cases in which a diagnosis of T, A, or B might, on the agglutination evidence alone, have appeared justifiable	25
Total	280

Before leaving this subject it may be added that each of these cases was studied in the light of such clinical details as were given in the returns and that in a very considerable proportion of them, more than 50 per cent., this was consistent with the view that these were genuine cases of enteric infection. A special group of forty-three of them was picked out for particular attention as being those in which the clinical history was most typical of enteric. They showed no essential difference in the character of the agglutination curves and would have fallen into the same groups as given in the above table and relatively in the same proportions. In two of them only would it have been possible to place them in the last class, those in which a definite diagnosis might have been considered possible.

The importance of the study of the agglutination diagnosis of enteric is obvious. It is hardly conceivable that in future wars the armies will not be protected by a triple, or possibly by a quadruple vaccine and, if accuracy of diagnosis be still desired, agglutination estimations will almost certainly be required. The account given above of the results obtained by Dreyer's method in France should be of service as showing that a very high proportion of cases can, in the absence of positive cultural confirmation, be diagnosed definitely by such a method, even in triply inoculated men.

Protective Inoculation.

The responsibility for the preparation of anti-typhoid vaccine and for all questions relating to its employment in the army rested upon the Pathological Department. The accumulated experience of the pathological laboratories therefore calls for record and comment, while in respect of the actual degree of protection given by the inoculations the personal records accumulated by Sir William Leishman, while Adviser in Pathology to the armies in France during the first three and a half years of the war, furnish information of greater precision in certain directions than that afforded by the other theatres of war.

There is no need to enter at length into the earlier history of typhoid vaccine in the British army ; suffice it to say that, subsequent to the South African war, inoculation in the army was held in abeyance until the results of further experimental work were ascertained. The work of Sir Almroth Wright, as the pioneer of typhoid inoculation, will never be forgotten, and the fact that further experiment and experience led to some improvements on the vaccine first devised by him is but one more illustration of the fact that progress in such matters is continuous. If it is the case that the vaccine used in the war of 1914–18 was superior to that employed in the South African war, it can hardly be doubted that the vaccine of the future will probably leave the present vaccine still further behind in protective value.

The experimental work in question was carried out, after the South African war, at the Royal Army Medical College by Leishman, Harrison, Grattan, Wood and others, under the direction of a War Office Committee presided over by Lt.-Col. C. J. Martin. A long series of reports and papers has placed on record the results of these laboratory researches, as well as of the elaborate statistical test of the vaccine finally selected for general use. It is not proposed to refer to this work further than to point out that it was eventually successful in providing clear statistical proof of the protective effect of the vaccine. With this it was possible, in 1909, to convince the army authorities, both medical and military, that typhoid inoculation was a safe and useful procedure, and permission was accordingly re-granted to its general employment in the troops, but always on a voluntary basis.

The Pathological Department of the Royal Army Medical College gave continual and anxious thought to the application of the method in the army in the event of a great war. With this in view it had, for example, several years before the war, made all arrangements for the maintenance of a reserve of vaccine large enough for the first needs of an expeditionary force, and had worked out in detail the scheme for a great expansion of its manufacture, if this should be called for. Again, experience and military knowledge had shown them that, if inoculation should suddenly be desired on a large scale on a hurried mobilization, they would need to have in their possession accurate information as to the average degree of disability produced by each dose of vaccine, the extent to which this might interfere with the soldier's physical capacity, and the duration of such interference. They had also to know the percentage of men who might be expected to be unfit for full work 24, 48 and 72 hours after inoculation. These points and others were accordingly determined by means of a series of experimental observations carried out at Aldershot about two years before the war, and when the moment came, in August, 1914, they were able to give definite replies on such points to the very natural questions raised at once by staff officers, anxious lest the inoculations should interfere with the smooth working of their mobilization time-tables.

On the outbreak of war the Director-General at once approached Lord Kitchener, whose permission with that of the Army Council was obtained for the carrying out of as many inoculations among the men of the expeditionary force as might be practicable prior to embarkation. Lord Kitchener also issued an order to the effect that he hoped as many men as possible would come forward for inoculation.

It had long been decided that in such an event it would be altogether impracticable to carry out the customary two inoculations at ten days' interval, and it had been determined, from experiment, that the best protection that could be expected in the circumstances was to be got by a single dose of 1,000 million bacteria—in substitution for the usual initial dose of 500 million—followed by a second of 1,000 million. The tests just referred to as to the average degree of disability consequent on the inoculations were conducted on this basis. This single-dose method was accordingly adopted during mobilization, full instructions were circulated to every command and unit concerned, and the machinery for the prompt requisitioning and dispatch of the vaccine was at once set in motion.

The Medical Department laboured under a heavy handicap in lacking compulsory powers in this matter, powers conceded before or during the war to the medical departments of the American, French, Italian and German armies. Bearing this in mind, it will probably be considered no mean achievement that they were able to inoculate with a single dose about 25 to 30 per cent. of the original expeditionary force before they crossed the Channel, and that it was not long before the inoculation strength of the troops in France rose to a figure which fluctuated between 90 and 98 per cent.

The military conditions consequent upon the early battles of the war and the retreat from Mons were such as made any serious attempt at increasing the percentage of inoculation altogether out of the question. It was not until the fighting on the Aisne had been in progress for some time, and until the army had been able to take breath and to make progress in its reconstruction and the incorporation of its reinforcements, that it became possible to press for and to carry out fresh inoculations on any considerable scale.

By this time, towards the beginning of October 1914, the urgent need for this became manifest to those whose duty it was to keep their fingers on the epidemic pulse of the army. Typhoid fever had made its appearance, was showing an alarming tendency to spread in certain units, and was presenting itself, only too often, in the grave form familiar to those who had served in India during pre-inoculation days, and in the South African war. There is little to be gained by attempting to trace out its origins. It is true that some of the earliest cases seen were in German prisoners, but the disease was also present among our allies and close neighbours, the French, both in their fighting forces and in the civil population of the villages in which the British had been billeted. A case or two also joined the force from England in the incubation stage of the disease, while the laws of probability, and later demonstrable proof, made it certain that undetected carriers were amongst the troops. There was nothing to prevent a violent conflagration except general preventive measures and the special protection conferred by inoculation.

Permission was obtained for such inoculations to be carried out, as opportunity offered, and from that time strenuous and unremitting efforts commenced by means of lectures, etc., to persuade the men to be inoculated. Fortunately the task was fairly easy, the position as regards the arguments and proofs which could be brought forward being far more satisfactory than was the case formerly. The percentage of the inoculated rose with remarkable activity, influenced naturally to a large extent by the fact that the reinforcements coming from home and elsewhere presented an increasingly high inoculation strength.

In considering and presenting the figures relating to inoculation it is proposed, as was done in the sections dealing with incidence and diagnosis given earlier in this chapter, to dwell chiefly upon the experiences of the armies in France, and for the same reasons.   Although the total of the available figures of incidence for the war have been quoted in Table I, any close analysis of these in search for particular points relative to inoculation would be misleading since they comprise much material in which the differential diagnosis between typhoid, paratyphoid A and paratyphoid B had not been attempted, while in many cases the information as to inoculation does not pretend to accuracy or is lacking altogether.   The reasons for this have already been considered in connection with the records relating to diagnosis.

Fortunately, the more happy situation of the armies in France, as regards diagnostic facilities and their freedom from any epidemics of such a size as to hamper the work of the laboratories, enabled accurate information to be accumulated on a scale sufficiently large to be worth analysis in connection with most points of scientific interest.

An account has already been given of the system of notification of cases of suspect enteric and of the measures taken to ensure careful record of the final diagnosis, and this only needs to be supplemented in respect of the information relating to inoculation.

Details as to the character, number and date of the inoculations in each case had to be recorded on the infectious disease forms, and were forthcoming in the great majority.   It might be thought that this was simple and should be invariably accurate, but this was not so.   In spite of the circulation of frequent and stringent orders relating to the entry of this information in the soldier's pay-book—the only document which was supposed to attach to him everywhere and always —it was inevitable that this, in times of stress, was often lost. Further, over-driven officers and clerks did not always comply with instructions as to the accurate copying of inoculation details from the old pay-book when a new one had to be issued to the man.   For these reasons, and some others equally unavoidable, it was often necessary to obtain the details of the inoculations verbally from the patient himself, and here one was at the mercy of the man's memory and accuracy. Although this could usually be relied on, there were many proven instances of incorrect information being given in this way.   All that could be done was to record in each case on the return whether the facts of inoculation were obtained from documentary information or from the man's own statement. Nominal rolls of the inoculation of all units might have obviated most of these doubts, but, as the armies grew to millions, this would have involved a colossal amount of clerical labour and would further have necessitated the provision of a large staff and a toil of searching and correspondence out of all proportion to the value of the quest.

In the case of the armies in France the most instructive periods to analyse are, first, those of the earliest months of the war ; second, the period when the very great majority of the troops had been inoculated with T.V. but before T.A.B. had been introduced ; and third, the period when T.A.B. had been in vogue long enough to ensure that the very great majority had either been inoculated or re-inoculated with this vaccine. By presenting tables covering these periods a number of interesting points can be brought out and some useful conclusions appear to be justified.

Table V deals with the number of cases of typhoid fever, paratyphoid fever and enteric group which occurred in the force in France from the commencement of operations in August 1914 till 9th August, 1915.

TABLE V.

Total Cases and Case Mortality from Typhoid and Paratyphoid, British Expeditionary Force, August 1914 to 9th August, 1915.

	Cases.	Deaths.	Case mortality
Typhoid—			
Not inoculated T.V. within 2 years ..	545	111	20·36
Inoculated 1 dose T.V. within 1 year	190	13	6·84
Inoculated 2 doses T.V. within 2 years	236	19	8·05
Totals ..	971	143	Average 14·72
Paratyphoid—			
Not inoculated T.V. within 2 years ..	113	4	3·53
Inoculated 1 dose T.V. within 1 year ..	183	3	1·63
Inoculated 2 doses T.V. within 2 years	423	8	1·89
Totals ..	719	15	Average 2·08
Enteric Group—			
Not inoculated T.V. within 2 years ..	24	—	—
Inoculated 1 dose T.V. within 1 year ..	27	—	—
Inoculated 2 doses T.V. within 2 years	43	—	—
Total ..	94	—	—

In this table, T.A.B. not having yet been adopted, the paratyphoids are grouped together and not differentiated as in subsequent tables, but the fact of inoculation or non-inoculation with T.V. vaccine is, all the same, recorded. Here the chief interest is in the striking contrast between the high case mortality from typhoid among the non-inoculated, 20·36 per cent., as compared with 6·84 per cent. in one-dose T.V. men and 8·05 per cent. in two-dose T.V. men. Comments on the paratyphoid figures will be reserved for the moment.

Such being the general record for the first twelve months of the war, it is worth while to examine the figures of the critical and dangerous first five months ; they are given in Table VI, and their significance may be gathered when it is recalled that this was the period during which the inoculation of the army was being gradually raised from the low level of about 30 per cent. to about 80 per cent.

TABLE VI.

Total Cases and Case Mortality from Typhoid Fever, British Expeditionary Force, August 1914 to 29th January, 1915.

	Cases.	Deaths.	Case mortality
Not inoculated within 2 years	305	34	11·1
Inoculated 1 dose T.V. within 1 year ..	83	1	1·2
Inoculated 2 doses T.V. within 3 years ..	33	—	—
Totals ..	421	35	Average 8·3

Precise information on the inoculation strength was not possible to collect for military reasons, so the incidence per 1,000 is not given here, as in some subsequent tables. All the same, the contrast in the case mortality is dramatic, as is the fact that only one death from typhoid occurred in this period in an inoculated man.

Table VII shows the incidence for typhoid and paratyphoid during the year 1915 among the inoculated and non-inoculated, and is one of great importance, since it deals with a period during which T.V. only was in use, and in which full information was available both in respect of the percentage of inoculation in the force and of the mean strength of the armies. From this information it has been possible to obtain a substantially accurate view of the relative incidence of these fevers in the two groups, and thus to arrive at a statistical evaluation of the protective effects of inoculation.

TABLE VII.

A.—*Monthly Rates of the Incidence of Typhoid Fever among the Inoculated and Non-inoculated during 1915.*

	Percentage of inoculated.	Cases per 10,000.		
		Amongst inoculated.	Amongst non-inoculated.	Amongst all troops.
January	80·0	2·98	9·93	4·37
February	88·3	1·85	17·76	3·71
March	92·0	1·41	21·33	3·01
April	93·0	0·8	8·59	1·35
May	94·0	1·1	8·46	1·54
June	95·0	1·84	2·74	1·13
July	95·8	1·0	2·57	1·06
August	97·1	0·89	4·51	0·99
September	97·5	0·49	4·1	0·58
October	97·5	0·41	1·72	0·44
November	98·1	0·28	2·27	0·32
December	98·5	0·23	5·53	0·31
For the year ..		9·5	103·52	13·78

B.—*Annual Rates of the Incidence of Typhoid, Paratyphoid and Enteric Group among the Inoculated and Non-inoculated (with T.V.) for 1915.*

	Rates per 10,000.			
	1.	2.	3.	1, 2 and 3.
	Typhoid.	Para-typhoid fevers.	Enteric group.	
Inoculated.. .. 614,715	9·5	21·53	2·87	33·91
Non-inoculated .. 29,365	103·52	39·84	7·49	150·85
Total .. 644,080	13·78	22·37	3·08	39·24

The first part of the table (A) deals with typhoid fever alone, and records the monthly rates of incidence per 10,000, in each group throughout the year. These were calculated by the statistical officer of the D.M.S., Lines of Communication, from the monthly returns of inoculation received by the Adviser in Pathology and from the most accurate figures of strength which could be obtained from the military authorities. It will be seen how the percentage of inoculation rose steadily throughout the year from 80 per cent. to 98·5 per cent., also how the relative incidence in every month is in favour of inoculation, usually greatly in favour. The figures for the whole year are very striking—an incidence of 9·5 per 10,000 of strength amongst the inoculated, as contrasted with an incidence of 103·52 per 10,000 amongst those who had not been protected by inoculation. In round numbers typhoid fever had been ten times more common among the non-inoculated.

The second part of the table (B) gives a summary, derived from the same material, to show the comparative annual rates per 10,000 in the two groups of inoculated and non-inoculated, not only for typhoid fever, to which the first portion of the table is confined, but also for the paratyphoid fevers (combined) and for cases classed as enteric group. The results are of interest, and will be discussed in connection with the effects of inoculation on paratyphoid.

Tables VIII and IX give the details of the incidence of the enteric fevers for the two years 1916 and 1917. The facts

TABLE VIII.

Total Cases and Case Mortality of Typhoid and Paratyphoid, British Expeditionary Force, during 1916.

	Cases.	Deaths.	Case mortality.
Typhoid—			
Inoculated T.V. or T.A.B.	739	14	1·89
Not inoculated T.V. or T.A.B.	42	3	7·14
Totals ..	781	17	Average 2·17
Paratyphoid—			
Para: A—Inoculated T.A.B. ..	338	4	1·18
Not inoculated T.A.B.	173	3	1·73
Totals ..	511	7	Average 1·36
Para: B—Inoculated T.A.B. ..	534	3	0·56
Not inoculated T.A.B.	560	7	1·25
Totals ..	1,094	10	Average 0·91
Totals—Paratyphoid A and B..	1,605	17	Average 1·05
Enteric Group—			
Inoculated T.V. or T.A.B.	368	—	—
Not inoculated T.V. or T.A.B.	6	—	—
Totals ..	374	—	—
Totals—Typhoid, paratyphoid and enteric group	2,760	34	Average 1·23

relating to inoculation are duly recorded, but the story now becomes complicated by the introduction of the triple vaccine, T.A.B. This came into use at the beginning of February 1916 in France, and simultaneously in all the other theatres of war. From this time all first inoculations and reinoculations were done with this vaccine and the monovalent T.V. was no longer used. Consequently, from that time the number of men protected by T.V. was a constantly diminishing figure and the number protected by T.A.B. a steadily increasing one until, by the beginning of 1918, when the two years' limit of protection given by two doses of T.V. had expired, the latter would appear no longer in statistical tables.

TABLE IX.

Total Cases and Case Mortality of Typhoid and Paratyphoid, British Expeditionary Force, during 1917.

	Cases.	Deaths.	Case mortality
Typhoid—			
Inoculated T.V. or T.A.B.	217	11	5·06
Not inoculated T.V. or T.A.B.	42	4	9·52
Totals ..	259	15	Average 5·79
Paratyphoid—			
Para: A—Inoculated T.A.B. ..	149	1	0·67
Not inoculated T.A.B.	41	1	2·43
Totals ..	190	2	Average 1·05
Para: B—Inoculated T.A.B. ..	366	2	0·54
Not inoculated T.A.B.	151	2	1·32
Totals ..	517	4	Average 0·77
Totals—Paratyphoid A and B ..	707	6	Average 0·84
Enteric Group—			
Inoculated T.V. or T.A.B.	291	2	0·68
Not inoculated T.V. or T.A.B.	18	1	0·55
Totals ..	309	3	Average 0·97
Totals—Typhoid, paratyphoid and enteric group	1,275	24	Average 2·66

The first thing which strikes one about these two tables is in connection with the total incidence for each year, since it will be noted that the cases diagnosed in 1917—1,275—were less than half the cases notified in 1916, which yielded 2,760.

This, it should be remembered, was in spite of the fact that the strength of the armies in France was approximately doubled in 1917. Obviously the incidence of the enteric fevers was steadily on the down grade.

Separate information as to T.A.B. vaccine is now required, and particularly in connection with the paratyphoid figures. Every effort was made from the moment of introduction of T.A.B. to register the cases, as they were notified, in such a way that they might throw light on the important matter of the influence of the paratyphoid fractions of the mixed vaccine upon both the incidence and the severity of the paratyphoid fevers. The tables in question record the facts but as yet throw little light upon these questions, in the absence of full information as to the strengths and the percentage of inoculation with, respectively, T.V. and T.A.B. Information of sufficient accuracy could not possibly have been obtained on these points during these years on account of the progressive transformation of a T.V.-protected population into a T.A.B.-protected one. The tables, however, bring out many points of interest in connection with the four groups but they must be left to speak for themselves. On the question of the protection of T.A.B. vaccine against paratyphoid fevers they at least show that the number of cases steadily fell during these two years and, further, a point on which anxiety was felt, that there did not appear to be any diminution of the protection against typhoid consequent on the addition of considerable doses of A and B to the same quantity of T as was in the original T.V.

It was commonly held in France, and particularly by those who had advocated the introduction of T.A.B., that the steady drop in the paratyphoid incidence was consequent upon the change of vaccine. The matter, however, is not so simple as it would appear, since it is the fact that the incidence of the paratyphoid fevers had begun to fall in 1915 and continued to fall steadily for some months prior to the commencement of T.A.B. inoculations. This is clearly brought out in Chart I, in which an epitome of the enteric history of the armies in France is well displayed in the form of monthly records of the equivalent annual morbidity-rates per 10,000 for typhoid and the combined paratyphoid fevers.

The chart begins in November, 1914, the earliest date at which the necessary information was available.

On the matter at present under discussion, if one follows the paratyphoid line it will be seen that, from its maximum point in June 1915, it fell steadily to a very low level before the end of that year, while the course of the curve throughout the

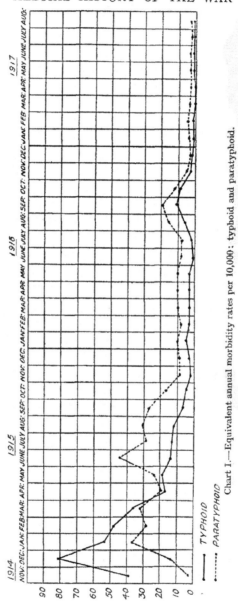

Chart I.—Equivalent annual morbidity rates per 10,000: typhoid and paratyphoid.

following year is remarkably steady, except for a slight autumn rise, which it shared in common with the typhoid incidence line. There is nothing in the paratyphoid line subsequent to February 1916, the date of the beginning of T.A.B. inoculations, to suggest that a new and potent protective factor had come into action.

The chart has not been carried beyond August 1917, but if it had been it would only have shown both the typhoid and the paratyphoid lines to be pressed even more tightly against the zero base line.

It is not suggested that these figures prove that T.A.B. vaccine was not called for, or that it has been shown by them that the paratyphoid fractions were a comparatively inactive addition to T.V., but they do show that it is necessary to search in some other direction for an explanation of the steady decline in paratyphoid incidence which commenced in the middle of 1915.

No one who served in France during that period could possibly claim that the fall was due to any striking improvement of the hygienic conditions, such as the sanitation of the trenches and billets, the water supply, and so on. No important changes of this nature were introduced in the middle of 1915 ; nor were the terribly trying conditions of trench warfare any less rigorous during the second winter in Flanders ; on the contrary, if anything they were harder. Again one must look further afield for the probable cause of the drop.

It was at least possible that the explanation might lie in the fact that typhoid vaccine in spite of what had always been assumed to the contrary, had exercised a measure of protection against the paratyphoid fevers. A strong impression that this was actually the case gradually formed as the war progressed, all the stronger perhaps since such an effect was altogether unanticipated. The years of research work at the Royal Army Medical College, during which constant efforts were made to improve typhoid vaccine, had given no support to the idea that such a result was likely to happen in practice. For instance, no trace of agglutinins or other antibodies to paratyphoid bacteria was ever found to develop in the blood of men or of animals inoculated with typhoid vaccine, although this was carefully looked for, since, in view of their belonging to the same bacterial group, such a development of co-agglutinins or other substances might not unreasonably have been expected.

The impression alluded to was founded in part on clinical grounds, the cases of paratyphoid in non-inoculated men appearing more severe than those in men who had had T.V., and in part by a study of the statistical results of inoculation. An analysis of the returns for the first eighteen months of the war, that is before the story was complicated by the introduction of T.A.B., undoubtedly showed that the case mortality of paratyphoids uninoculated with T.V. was higher than that of inoculated paratyphoids. The point is clearly brought out in Tables V and XI. In Table XI, under heading 2 (a), it will be seen in the first place that there is practically no distinction between the paratyphoid case mortality of men inoculated or not inoculated with T.A.B. vaccine (the " non-inoculated " including a very large majority of men who had been inoculated with T.V. only), the figures, respectively, being 1·25 per cent. and 1·34 per cent. On the other hand, if one turns to heading 2 (b), which shows the number of cases of paratyphoid which occurred in men who were unprotected either by T.V. or T.A.B., the case mortality of 325 cases is seen to be 3·38 per cent.; or, if distinction is desired between paratyphoid A and B, 4·05 per cent. for A and 3·18 per cent. for B. These latter figures may fairly be taken as the normal case mortality of paratyphoid in unprotected men in France and as the figures against which others dealing with inoculated men may be compared. One would have expected that men who had only had T.V. would show the same order of paratyphoid mortality as completely uninoculated men, while, if the addition of paratyphoid elements to the vaccine had been of value in lessening the severity of attacks of paratyphoid and lowering the case mortality—as T.V. clearly does in the case of typhoid fever—this should have been apparent in the figures. As a matter of fact, such a reduction of the case mortality is found and comes out clearly in the tables ; but, and this is the interesting point, it is apparently as marked in the case of men who had only had T.V. as in the case of those who had received T.A.B. The conclusion appears unavoidable that T.V. had modified attacks of paratyphoid fever to such an extent as to reduce the case mortality appreciably, and that in this respect its effects were scarcely inferior to those of T.A.B. itself.

If the above conclusion is correct one would expect to find some evidence of this protective action of typhoid vaccine against paratyphoid fevers in the incidence tables of the year 1915. If Table VII is referred to such evidence will be found in Section B, where the annual rate of incidence of paratyphoid fevers per 10,000 men is recorded as 21·53 among those inoculated with T.V. against 39·84 in those not inoculated. This ratio of approximately one to two, while of much inferior order to the one to ten for the incidence of typhoid fever, appears significant, and supports the hypothesis that was suggested by the observations upon the milder nature and lowered mortality of paratyphoid in men inoculated with T.V.

The point is one of considerable scientific interest and has an important bearing upon the study of immunity in other bacterial diseases due to organisms which, although specifically distinct, belong to the same group.

There would thus appear to be reason for thinking that the Royal Army Medical College typhoid vaccine had given an appreciable degree of protection against paratyphoid fevers, and that the steady fall in the incidence of the latter, which commenced in the middle of 1915, was connected with the steady rise in the percentage of T.V. inoculation in the British armies in France.

From the beginning of 1917 till the end of the war the salient statistical feature is the extraordinarily low incidence of the enteric fevers, the total cases reaching a fresh low level each year until in 1918 the total number of cases was but 376, and this in spite of mobile warfare and of a rise in the strength to two and half million men. The monthly summary of the total cases in 1918 is given in Table X, but it has not been considered worth while to attempt to analyse this from the point of view of the effect of inoculation, since there was such a disproportion between the inoculated and the non-inoculated and so few cases that any comparison would have had little statistical value.

The facts in this connection are, however, incorporated in Table XI, in which are shown the total cases of typhoid, paratyphoid A and B and enteric group, from the commencement of operations until the end of 1918.

In this table, which tells a long story within a short compass, further confirmation will be found of most of the points discussed in connection with previous tables, but its chief interest lies in the study it offers of the total numbers of the various groups notified during the four years four and a half months, and of comparative case mortalities among these groups. Most of these points have been considered elsewhere and comment on the table will be confined to three points.

(1) The case mortality in typhoid is seen to be 18·35 per cent. in the non-inoculated; it is obvious therefore that the type of typhoid fever encountered in France was not one of unusual mildness. The contrast is striking to the case mortality among

TABLE X.

British Armies in France. Total Cases of Typhoid, Paratyphoid and Enteric Group for the year ending 31st December 1918. Table showing the Number of Cases occurring each month.

1918.				Typhoid	Para-typhoid A.	Para-typhoid B.	Enteric group.	Total cases.
January	..	..	..	10	14	7	8	39
February	..	..	..	9	4	7	5	25
March	..	..	..	3	2	6	6	17
April ..	..	..	..	—	2	6	2	10
May ..	..	..	..	11	3	18	3	35
June ..	..	..	..	11	4	14	1	30
July ..	..	..	..	5	3	9	5	22
August	..	..	..	14	4	31	—	49
September	..	..	..	12	2	24	8	46
October	..	..	..	6	1	25	3	35
November	..	..	..	6	—	18	3	27
December	..	..	..	11	6	17	7	41
		Totals	..	98	45	182	51	376

the inoculated, which was only 4·57 per cent.—very little higher than that of paratyphoid A in non-inoculated men, namely, 4·05 per cent.

(2) Under heading 2 (c) a comparison may be made between the ratio of cases of paratyphoid A to paratyphoid B in those inoculated with T.A.B., and the same ratio in the case of those who had not had T.A.B. vaccine. Such a comparison might suggest that a higher degree of protection had been given against paratyphoid B than against paratyphoid A. Whether this was in fact the case, it is at all events in accordance with the experimental observation that the development of B agglutinins following on inoculation with T.A.B. is usually higher and more lasting than that of the A agglutinins. If one could feel certain on this point it would be an argument for increasing the dose of the A fraction of the triple vaccine.

(3) Lastly, attention may also be directed to the case mortalities of the enteric group. The deaths have been too few to allow of any significance attaching to a comparison between those in the inoculated and the non-inoculated, but the figures bear out what has been said elsewhere as to the mild type of the cases falling into this class, and afford some support to the not infrequently heard criticisms upon the very doubtful nature of some of the cases thus diagnosed on clinical evidence alone.

TABLE XI.

Total Cases of Enteric Fever in the British Armies in France, from the commencement of Operations in August 1914 to 31st December 1918.

	Cases.	Deaths.	Case mortality per cent.
1. *Typhoid*—			
Inoculated T.V. or T.A.B. vaccine ..	1,728	79	4·57
Non-inoculated T.V. or T.A.B. vaccine	703	129	18·35
Total ..	2,431	208	8·55
2. *Paratyphoid*—			
(a) Inoculated T.A.B. vaccine ..	1,357	17	1·25
Non-inoculated T.A.B. vaccine ..	2,694	35	1·34
Total ..	4,051	52	1·28
(b) Number of cases from the commencement of operations in men uninoculated with either T.V. or T.A.B.			
Paratyphoid A	74	3	4·05
Paratyphoid B	251	8	3·18
Total ..	325	11	3·38
(c) Number of cases which occurred subsequent to the introduction of T.A.B. vaccine in France, on 1st February, 1916.			
(i) *Paratyphoid A*. Inoculated with T.A.B. vaccine.	463	5	1·08
Paratyphoid B. Inoculated with T.A.B. vaccine.	894	12	1·34
Total ..	1,357	17	1·25
(ii) *Paratyphoid A*. Non-inoculated T.A.B. vaccine.	265	3	1·13
Paratyphoid B. Non-inoculated T.A.B. vaccine.	858	9	1·04
Total ..	1,123	12	1·06
3. *Enteric Group*— (*i.e.*, clinical diagnosis; bacteriological evidence insufficient to distinguish with certainty between typhoid and paratyphoid fever).			
Inoculated T.V. or T.A.B. vaccine	878	4	0·45
Non-inoculated T.V. or T.A.B. vaccine.	63	2	3·17
Total ..	941	6	0·63

Note.—In all instances the "non-inoculated" includes men who had received a single dose of vaccine more than a year before the attack, or two doses more than two years before.

The figures for the whole war relating to the incidence and mortality from the enteric fevers, obtainable from official sources, are quoted in Table I at the beginning of this chapter. These figures, however, are incomplete in detail in the case of several of the more distant theatres of war, and if the blanks can ever be filled it will only be through the arduous and prolonged scrutiny of the admission and discharge books of the various medical units and the other documents concerning the sick and wounded soldier. The blanks in the information relating to these more distant theatres are especially notable in the cases of the two points upon which such stress has been placed throughout this chapter, namely, the laboratory evidence supporting the diagnosis and the particulars of the date and character of the inoculations. In the absence of full information on these two heads no safe conclusions could be drawn, and it has been felt that any attempt to analyse such incomplete records would be valueless. Although this is to be regretted, it will probably be admitted that the experience of inoculation of the armies in France, relating to several millions of men over a period of four and a half years, constitutes a trial on a scale of sufficient magnitude.

CHAPTER X.

DIARRHŒA AND ENTERITIS.

AS a source of temporary wastage and to a lesser extent of chronic invalidity in time of war, " diarrhœa," " enteritis " and " colitis " figure largely in the admission records of military hospitals and medical units, and the very vagueness of all three terms when considered in relation to the bulk of disease they represent must be a source of embarrassment to the medical statistician, the clinician and pathologist alike. The properly directed efforts, however, of pathologists in the war have gone far to elucidate the ætiology of a great mass of the diarrhœal disease which prevailed on all fronts, and it is not to be doubted that, had bacteriological and clinical investigations been more fully co-ordinated, the residuum of unexplained diarrhœal disease might have been still further reduced.

Diarrhœal disease, in so far as this has been a mere phase in the course of specific typhoidal, paratyphoidal and genuine dysenteric infections, is only incidentally part of the subject.

It is, of course, difficult to divorce the data concerned with diarrhœa from those referring to genuine dysentery, and both on epidemiological and ætiological grounds it would be unwise to do so. As, however, dysentery is dealt with elsewhere, only those ætiological factors are considered which play a part in the causation of " war " diarrhœas, so far as they are characterized throughout both clinically and pathologically by the passage of purely diarrhœal motions. Diarrhœa is a symptom, but being frequently the outstanding symptom, is made to connote the disease, in the absence of a specific ætiology. On the other hand, though enteritis and colitis connote inflammatory conditions of the bowel mucosa generally and the large bowel in particular, they have on occasion almost certainly been used indiscriminately with diarrhœa to connote equally unexplained conditions associated with diarrhœa. Doubtless the term enteritis has in recent years come rather to mean a diarrhœal condition accompanied by certain more clearly cut features, such as abruptness of onset, severity of purging, toxæmia and the like. The term colitis, however, has frequently been wrongly employed and has apparently served merely as a cloak for conditions, the dysenteric nature of which was not far to seek.

The fact that *E. histolytica* and *B. dysenteriae* are chiefly concerned in the production of the dysenteric syndrome does not preclude a discussion at some length of the part played by these agents in the ætiology of primary diarrhœas entirely unaccompanied by the passage of blood and mucus or muco-pus. They have been little studied, but epidemiologically they are highly important manifestations of amœbic and bacillary infection.

With regard to *E. histolytica* as a factor in diarrhœa, the real solution of the question as to what extent it can be proved to be a primary source of purely diarrhœal disturbance hinges on the intimate clinical observation of the certified amœbic carrier who in the past has given no history of dysenteric trouble. Wenyon and O'Connor in a tentative discussion of this question remarked in 1917 that while many carriers might show no symptoms of infection for months, others might have repeated attacks of dysentery in the same period. " Between these two extremes there are many intermediate types where infected individuals have mild attacks of diarrhœa, with or without mucus in the stool, which may or may not be the result of *E. histolytica* infection." There is certainly little evidence that the autochthonous cases of *E. histolytica* infection brought to light in this country have ever suffered from definite dysenteric symptoms or even intestinal troubles associated with diarrhœa. Brumpt records the fact that for at least six years he has been a healthy cyst carrier of *E. histolytica* and maintains the view that acute amœbiasis is a relatively rare episode of such carrier infection. It would appear almost certain that something more is required to produce either dysentery or simple diarrhœa than the mere presence of *E. histolytica* in the gut as evidenced by the demonstration of its cysts in the fæces, at least in the case of carriers living in temperate zones. Asylum dysentery in this country has, so far as investigations have gone, been entirely of bacillary type, but in view of the demonstration of *E. histolytica* cysts in a considerable percentage of asylum inmates, it will be of interest to watch whether under the peculiar conditions of asylum life active amœbic dysentery becomes at all a prominent disease. The problem is quite different in tropical and semi-tropical regions where amœbic dysentery prevails, and the missing link in the chain of factors leading to active ulceration of the bowel and consequent dysentery is apparently supplied. It is believed by Wenyon and O'Connor that in all healthy carriers some ulceration of the intestine exists though no symptoms may be apparent. This view is supported by certain *post-mortem* evidence alleging the presence of amœbic ulceration of the gut, sometimes indeed extensive, in persons who have had no history of dysentery during life or have died from other causes. That such cases occur, though rarely, is indisputable. There would appear to be little doubt also that many cases of liver abscess which have come to autopsy have revealed intestinal ulceration associated with *E. histolytica*, though evidence of dysentery during life has not been forthcoming. The problem must be solved by lifelong observation of the autochthonous carrier cases. It has been suggested, indeed, that, in the carrier, *E. histolytica* does not find a nidus in the mucosa at all, but, like *E. coli*, flourishes as a simple saprophyte in the contents of the lumen. Whatever the solution may be, there is no doubt that on eastern fronts the nearer the pathologist is placed to the sick person in the early stage of his infection, the more valid will be the evidence that one seeks to obtain of the part played by *E. histolytica* in primarily diarrhœal disturbances entirely apart from any question of dysentery in the past. Thus, the evidence obtained from examination of diarrhœal motions not containing blood or mucus may be legitimately brought forward in this connection, provided these examinations are made at the earliest possible period in the disease.

The following data have been abstracted from the bacteriological records of the Mesopotamian Expeditionary Force. Of 756 N.B.M.* British cases from the forward area examined at Baghdad during the period April to December, 1918, 52, or 6·9 per cent., contained *E. histolytica :* 18 cases in the active form and 34 in the cyst form. In an Indian hospital dealing with cases from the same area, 1,080 N.B.M. cases yielded 215 (19·9 per cent.) *E. histolytica* infections : 34 in the active and 181 in the cyst form. For the complete year 1918 the figures from all British and Indian hospitals at Baghdad both in B.M. and N.B.M. cases may be entered for comparison :—

Of 1,841 British B.M. cases, 18·1 per cent. contained *E. histolytica*.
Of 2,750 British N.B.M. cases, 12·5 per cent. ,, ,,
Of 1,238 Indian B.M. cases, 46·6 per cent. ,, ,,
Of 1,774 Indian N.B.M. cases, 14·9 per cent. ,, ,,

The percentages of *E. histolytica* infection in N.B.M. cases, both in British and Indian troops, from the forward area agree closely with those obtained from examination at Liverpool of convalescent British dysenteric and diarrhœal cases arriving

---

* B.M. = containing blood and mucus. N.B.M. = not containing blood or mucus.

from Mesopotamia.   Boulenger, in Mesopotamia, examined 200 healthy British and 200 healthy Indian troops with no history of previous dysentery, and found only 5 per cent. of the British and 10·5 per cent. of the Indians infected with *E. histolytica*.   Wenyon and O'Connor's figure for healthy British troops in Egypt with no history of dysentery was 4·5 per cent.

In the great majority of the diarrhœal cases examined at Baghdad, *E. histolytica*, when present, was found in the cyst form only.   In such cases, the diarrhœa may either have been a phase in a primarily dysenteric attack not noted at the time and influenced in all probability by emetin,* or it may have been due to a bacillary superposed on a purely saprophytic *E. histolytica* infection.   A certain small percentage (2·4 per cent. to 3·1 per cent.) of the N.B.M. cases, however, presented *E. histolytica* in the active form and containing red cells.   According to some pathologists, observations of this kind in purely diarrhœal stools have not been uncommon.   Wenyon and O'Connor report the finding in one single instance of a free *E. histolytica* with included red cells in an ordinary unformed stool " which showed no evidence of blood or mucus either macro- or microscopically."   Such cases undoubtedly suggest the inference that *E. histolytica* may be primarily and solely responsible for purely diarrhœal disturbances in a certain small proportion of the great mass of notified cases of diarrhœa and colitis.   Probably, however, by far the greater proportion of such clinical primary diarrhœas are associated with bacillary infections and especially with *B. dysenteriae*.

With regard to *B. dysenteriae* as a factor in the causation of primary diarrhœa, it must be noted that the prevalence of diarrhœa and colitis as diseases subject to notification in a war area follows exactly the seasonal variations of genuine dysentery. To show the relative proportions of such notified cases, those referring to British troops in Mesopotamia during eleven successive four-weekly periods from the commencement of 1918 onwards are given :—

Dysentery : 67, 69, 58, 41, 235, 128, 117, 290, 571, 522, 396.
Colitis : 7, 8, 14, 9, 38, 39, 32, 63, 123, 126, 65.
Diarrhœa : 40, 30, 41, 30, 141, 128, 134, 286, 942, 857, 355.

Thus, for every case of notified colitis 4·7 cases of dysentery and 5·6 cases of diarrhœa are notified on the average.

---

* Many medical officers were in the habit of giving emetin whether absolutely indicated or not.

DIARRHŒA AND ENTERITIS 269

In considering the bacteriological findings as regards *B. dysenteriae* in N.B.M. cases as a basis for estimating the importance of bacillary infection in the ætiology of notified diarrhœa and colitis, these Mesopotamian figures are here compared with those recorded from other fronts on similar material.

Percentage of Cases in which B. dysenteriae *was isolated.*
British and Indian (combined).

	Jan.	Feb.	Mar.	Apr.	May.	June.	July.	Aug.	Sept.	Oct.	Nov.	Dec.	Jan.
B.M. cases	17·3	18·9	28·8	18·5	25	22·7	20·7	28·5	24	35·2	44·9	34·2	40·4
N.B.M. ,,	4·3	5·7	7·0	7·5	8·2	12·0	5·5	6·3	7·8	10·3	11·5	7·3	8·6

British Troops only. (Whole Area.)

	Jan.	Feb.	Mar.	Apr.	May.	June.	July.	Aug.	Sept.	Oct.	Nov.	Dec.
B.M. cases	19·5	29·4	34·2	25·2	33·6	31·7	21	34·5	29·7	43·1	45·4	44·4
N.B.M. ,,	4·2	3·7	5·9	8·2	8·0	12·6	2·7	8·4	14	27·9	13·8	8·5

With the above may be compared the percentage in B.M. and N.B.M. British cases examined at one Baghdad hospital dealing with cases arriving from the forward area in the early stage of the disease.

	Jan.	Feb.	Mar.	Apr.	May.	June.	July.	Aug.	Sept.	Oct.	Nov.	Dec.
B.M. cases	21·2	30	38	23·4	30·1	30·3	24·1	50	48·1	60	53·7	45·6
N.B.M. ,,	3·8	4·5	5·4	6·0	8·6	9·5	4·3	12·5	16·3	32·3	16·4	13·6

These figures show clearly that in epidemic periods, and especially in the autumnal season, it has been possible to demonstrate the presence of *B. dysenteriae* in one-eighth to one-third of the diarrhœal cases submitted to bacteriological examination. The results are of the highest importance both bacteriologically and epidemiologically and place beyond doubt the importance of *B. dysenteriae* in the ætiology of simple primary diarrhœas. Dudgeon, in the course of his survey of dysentery and diarrhœal disease in the Salonika area, remarks that there is abundant evidence that diarrhœa is due to *B. Flexner*, just as is acute dysentery, and notes the fact that *B. Flexner* has been cultivated from patients who have suffered from diarrhœa for twenty-four hours and then rapidly recovered. The Salonika records show a percentage of isolated *B. dysenteriae* in 60·2 per cent. of B.M. cases, 22·5 per cent. of diarrhœal stools containing also mucus, and 3·9 per cent. of purely diarrhœal stools. Ellis made a special study of diarrhœal cases in France, and reported the finding of *B. dysenteriae* in 13 per cent. of 5,332 cases of diarrhœa, and of the 683 positive isolations only 10 were *B. Shiga*. Also, he states that not less than 11 of 13 cases of primary diarrhœa in one unit yielded *B. dysenteriae* (*Flexner–Y*). These diarrhœal cases were not sufficiently ill to warrant their being sent to hospital. As Ellis comments, the importance of regarding these mild cases of diarrhœa as possible Flexner infections, and consequently as indicators or heralds of dysentery prevailing or imminent, cannot be over-estimated. The disappearance of dysentery and diarrhœa from a unit was repeatedly noted by Ellis when steps were taken to evacuate from it all cases of diarrhœa.

It is the invariable experience that in diarrhœal stools, if *B. dysenteriae* is recovered at all,—and there is no doubt that, if diarrhœal stools were submitted to bacteriological examination at the earliest possible period of the diarrhœa and in the freshest condition, the percentage isolated would be considerably higher —it is most usually of the mannite-fermenting type. Of 186 isolations of *B. dysenteriae* in N.B.M. British and Indian cases examined in Mesopotamia, 55 were *B. Shiga* and 131 *B. Flexner*, while of 959 isolations in B.M. cases 422 were *B. Shiga* and 537 *B. Flexner*. At one British hospital in Baghdad dealing with fresh cases from the forward area, 212 isolations in B.M. cases yielded 124 *B. Shiga* and 88 *B. Flexner*, while 77 isolations in N.B.M. cases yielded 26 *B. Shiga* and 51 *B. Flexner*. The preponderance of Flexner over Shiga infections in N.B.M. cases was most marked during the spring epidemic and the months heralding it. It was less marked during the autumn outbreak, when probably a higher proportion of the N.B.M. cases represented really Shiga infections in process of cure. French authors also insist on the importance of recognizing the Flexner origin of mild dysentery outbreaks accompanied by simple diarrhœas. Sacquépée, Burnet and Weissenbach, for example, state that in the French Fourth Army the motions of their dysentery cases were of purely diarrhœal character, and contained neither blood nor mucus. The causative organism in such cases was exclusively a mannite-fermenting *B. dysenteriae*. The dysentery and diarrhœal outbreaks in the Argonne reported by Remlinger and Dumas were due almost entirely to Flexner–Y infections which also, according to Quincke, prevailed among the German troops, at least in the early part of the war.

The occurrence of diarrhœa associated with *B. dysenteriae* raises the question of nomenclature. As the motions are purely diarrhœal, consisting of fluid fæcal matter with catarrhal elements and a few pus cells intermixed (desquamative catarrh), the condition is strictly a simple enteritis of Flexner origin as opposed to a dysenteric enteritis of Flexner origin. In essence, however, these Flexner diarrhœas are almost certainly abortive dysenteries in which the diarrhœal or predysenteric stage is prolonged and constitutes the sole evidence of intestinal disturbance.

There is no doubt that a proportion of the diarrhœas met

with in time of war, which cannot be brought into ætiological relation with *E. histolytica* or *B. dysenteriae* infection, may be due to a variety of other causes not particularly well defined. On evidence of very varying quality, organisms such as *B. Morgan*, *B. proteus* and others have been incriminated as ætiological agents. Whatever be the final conclusion with regard to the ætiological rôle of *B. Morgan* in the summer diarrhœa of children, British, American and Danish evidence all point to the absence of *B. dysenteriae* in that type of infection, provided blood and mucus are absent from the stools. So far as the diarrhœa of adults in war time is concerned, it cannot be held that the occasional presence of *B. Morgan* in the stools of primary diarrhœas or in those of convalescent dysenteries signifies proof of specific infection with that bacillus. The organism has occasionally been found as apparently the sole non-lactose-fermenter in dysenteric stools, but the finding cannot be regarded as signifying anything more than mere commensalism or at the most a secondary infection. The conditions in children may be quite different, and it is not to be doubted that an organism which in the adult plays only a secondary rôle may, when introduced into the less immune intestine of the child, and especially the artificially fed child, produce a primary infection. Logan, in the course of a discussion of the replacement of the lactose-fermenting flora by non-lactose-fermenting types in the diarrhœas of children—a fact which has long been observed—says, " It is doubtful whether the overgrowth of non-lactose-fermenting bacilli initiates the diarrhœa or whether it is a secondary and aggravating factor." The upper part of the small intestine, when empty, has generally been found to be either sterile or occupied with non-lactose-fermenting organisms recalling *B. faecalis alkaligenes* and *Morgan* types possessing feeble fermentative activity in the presence of carbohydrates. In diarrhœal conditions the appearance in the stools of organisms of this class might be expected on mechanical grounds. None the less, the impetus given by favourable intestinal conditions to prolific growth of these organisms, with consequent absorption of their toxic products, may profoundly aggravate a condition due to some other primary cause. Similar considerations apply to many of the paracoli types found in the fæces of chronic dysentery, and the fact that some of these types have been shown to produce filtrates toxic for laboratory animals does not justify a primary infecting rôle being attributed to them. Whether these organisms possess primary infecting powers, at least in adults, must remain for the present undecided.

B. faecalis alkaligenes requires special mention. It has not uncommonly been found in diarrhœal stools, but though evidence of its responsibility for primary diarrhœa is wanting, it cannot be disputed that on occasion it may be responsible for the production of a mild paratyphoid-like fever of short duration, during which the organism in question may be repeatedly isolated from the blood. In 1916 a group of cases of this infection occurred at one hospital in Egypt, which were the subject of papers by Shearman and Moorhead and by Hirst in 1917. In Mesopotamia a similar small group of cases occurred in one unit at Amara, and from four of the ten cases *B. faecalis alkaligenes* was recovered from the blood. That such cases occur in isolated groups is of great interest, and the phenomenon may be brought into relation with those not infrequent saprophytic infections peculiar to institutions where an organism such as *B. pyocyaneus*, or perhaps an intestinal flagellate, appears with regularity over a limited period in the excreta of the inmates or on wounds or mucus surfaces. At one hospital in Mesopotamia the stools of practically all the patients suffering from dysentery or diarrhœa contained over a certain period *B. pyocyaneus*, and during the investigation of a cholera outbreak this same organism very frequently masked the presence of the true vibrio.

It seems possible, therefore, that under such conditions organisms like *B. faecalis alkaligenes*, otherwise devoid of primary infecting power, may through repeated passage acquire a degree of virulence sufficient to initiate a definite infection of a specific nature.

It must not be forgotten that much of the diarrhœal disturbance which prevailed among advancing troops, especially in the early part of the war, but probably to some extent throughout the whole war, was held, and held with some force, to be due simply to intestinal irritation following the consumption of uncooked or improperly cooked food or the ingestion of sand with the food, especially in Gallipoli and Eygpt. Such conditions could not be disputed. In German war articles dealing with dysentery and diarrhœa they are frequently the subject of comment. It was notorious also that fresh arrivals in countries like Egypt and Mesopotamia almost invariably suffered for a time from intestinal disturbance.

Much patient work was done during the war in recording the presence, in dysenteric, diarrhœal and normal stools, of active forms and cysts of flagellates, particularly *Lamblia* (*Giardia intestinalis*), *Trichomonas intestinalis* and *Chilomastix mesnili.* The collected data are recorded in many of the bacteriological reports from various fronts and also in the monographs issued by the Medical Research Council dealing with work done at home in connection with returned cases. There is no definite proof as yet that any of these flagellates can initiate dysentery or diarrhœa. Many writers, however, Escomel, Brumpt, Cade and Hollande, Orticoni and Nepveux, Fantham and Porter and Woodcock, have expressed themselves quite categorically in favour of the view that flagellates such as Giardia and Trichomonas may be responsible for certain forms of chronic enteritis, while Dobell, Wenyon and others take generally the view that their pathogenicity is not proven, and are strongly inclined to regard them as harmless.

In the case of certain flagellates at least, it would seem more probable that the diarrhœa is the cause of the appearance of flagellates in the stools rather than that the flagellates produce the diarrhœa. In the absence of positive evidence of pathogenicity which may be forthcoming from future experimental work, it would seem safer to adopt for the present the middle view, and to regard these flagellates rather as secondary, and possibly aggravating, factors in the ætiology of the particular diarrhœal disturbance with which they happen to be associated. In this connection it has always to be remembered that even *E. histolytica* in the body of the healthy carrier is merely a potential source of intestinal disturbance.

More than fifteen years ago Schmidt and Strasburger, in their classical work on the fæces of men in health and disease, stated that all authors are agreed that the intestinal flagellates have no pathogenic properties, and that they reach the fæces as a rule in the cyst form. In intestinal disturbances, however, accompanied by increased peristalsis, they find a very favourable medium for growth in the fluid fæces. Under these conditions they hold that the prolific growth of flagellates may aggravate and prolong disturbances due primarily to other causes. They also believed that Lamblia when growing profusely over the epithelium of the small intestine might interfere with the absorption of food material. Experience gained in the war does not seem to have materially affected these views.

Little is known with regard to the lesions, if any, which flagellates may produce. Recently Wenyon took the opportunity of examining the intestine in various cases found at autopsy to be harbouring flagellates. In Trichomonas infections he found no lesions in the large intestine that could be attributed to flagellates. Histological investigation revealed the presence of flagellates throughout the mucosa of the large intestine and in the lumen of the glands of Lieberkühn. There was no evidence of proliferative tissue reaction in response to the invasion.

Certain forms of specific infection, associated with enteritis of a severe character, were caused by infected food or drink. Cases of this kind occurred as a rule explosively, and not a few outbreaks have been reported from various war fronts.

The specific ætiology of these outbreaks has not been found to differ from that peculiar to such infections in times of peace. Invariably the organisms cultivated, either from the blood or excreta during life, or from the organs after death, have been found to belong to the Salmonella or Gaertner-paratyphoid group—a group to which much study has recently been devoted in consequence of its wide distribution not only in man but in pigs, in many of the domestic animals, such as oxen and horses, and also in guinea-pigs, rats, mice, and rabbits. These organisms possess all the cultural and biochemical properties of *B. paratyphosus B*. On the other hand, though they may be agglutinated even to high titre by a *Paratyphoid B* serum, they are unable to absorb the specific agglutinins of *B. paratyphosus B* (Schottmüller) from that serum. The *B. enteritidis* (Gaertner) stands apart, and is agglutinated only by its own serum, though in other respects its cultural and biochemical properties are those of *B. paratyphosus B*. By serological tests, involving the employment of the absorption method, it has been possible to divide this great group into various sub-groups. The majority of the food-poisoning outbreaks recorded during the war and accurately investigated from the bacteriological point of view have been found to be due to one serological type, namely, *B. paratyphosus B*, type " Mutton."

The special features, clinical and epidemiological of these outbreaks, are recorded in papers by Perry and Tidy, Sewell, Bellingham-Smith and Priestley, and Comrie and Bird.

One type now referred to as *B. paratyphosus B*, type " Hirschfeld " (or *B. paratyphosus C*), was found in Macedonia, Mesopotamia and elsewhere to give rise to continued fever of paratyphoid character, and in the Middle East, so far as current knowledge goes, it would appear to take the place of *B. paratyphosus B*, type " Schottmüller." Further work will show more precisely the relation of the " Hirschfeld " type to certain Salmonella forms associated with normal or diseased pigs.

An illustration of the wide distribution of the Salmonella group was noted in Mesopotamia. It was found that at one time, while cases of paratyphoid fever associated with the " Hirschfeld " type were occurring in Baghdad, there was an extremely fatal epidemic of enteritis in calves at a Baghdad military dairy, and an epizoötic among stock guinea-pigs, both due to a member of this family, which later investigation proved to be *B. paratyphosus B*, type " Mutton."

BIBLIOGRAPHY.

Brumpt	Protozoaires et helminthes des selles aux armées.	Compt. Rend. Soc. de Biol., 1918,Vol. lxxxi, p. 1044.
Cade & Hollande	Essai de traitement par le néosalvarsan de l'entérite chronique à *Giardia (Lamblia) intestinalis*.	Bull. et Mém. Soc. Méd. Hôp., 1918. Vol. xlii, p. 314.
Comrie & Bird	Epidemic Gastro-enteritis due to Food Poisoning.	Jl. of R.A.M.C.,1919, Vol. xxxiii, p. 374.
Dobell	Amœbic Dysentery and the Protozoological Investigation of Cases and Carriers.	M.R.C. Spec. Rep. Ser., Lond., 1917, No. 4.
Dobell,Gettings,Jepps & Stephens.	A Study of 1,300 Convalescent Cases of Dysentery from Home Hospitals with special reference to the Incidence and Treatment of Amœbic Dysentery Carriers.	M.R.C. Spec. Rep. Ser., Lond., 1918, No. 15.
Douglas, Colebrook & Morgan.	Report upon Combined Clinical and Bacteriological Studies of Dysentery Cases from the Mediterranean.	M.R.C. Spec. Rep. Ser., Lond., 1917, No. 6, p. 27.
Dudgeon	Studies of Bacillary Dysentery occurring in the British Forces in Macedonia.	M.R.C. Spec. Rep. Ser. Lond., 1919, No. 40.
Ellis	Discussion on Dysentery (Bacillary and Amœbic), 19th and 20th April, 1918.	Med. Bull. (Paris), 1918, No. 7.
Escomel	La Tricomonosis intestinale.	Lima, 1919 (Sanmarti & Co.).
Glynn, Berridge, Foley, Price, & Robinson.	Report upon 2,360 Enteritis " Convalescents " received at Liverpool from various Expeditionary Forces.	M.R.C. Spec. Rep. Ser., Lond., 1918, No. 7.
Hirst	Observations on the Pathogenicity and Specific Characters of the *Bacillus faecalis alkaligenes*.	Jl. of R.A.M.C.,1917, Vol. xxix, p. 476.
Ledingham	Dysentery and Enteric Disease in Mesopotamia from the Laboratory Standpoint.	Jl. of R.A.M.C.,1920, Vol. xxxiv, pp. 189, 306.
Logan	The Bacteriology of the Fæces in Diarrhœa of Infants.	Lancet, 1916, Vol. ii, p. 824.
Orticoni & Nepveux	Sur l'étiologie de quelques diarrhées et dysentéries rebelles.	Bull. Soc. Path. Exot., 1916, Vol. ix, p. 293.
Perry & Tidy	A Report on the Investigation of an Epidemic caused by *Bacillus aertryche*.	M.R.C. Spec. Rep. Ser., Lond., 1919, No. 24.

Porter .. .. An Enumerative Study of the Cysts of *Giardia* (*Lamblia*) *intestinalis* in Human Dysenteric Fæces. — Lancet, 1916, Vol. i, p. 1166.

Quincke .. .. Ueber die Wandlungen des Ruhrbegriffs. — Med. Klin., 1914, Vol. x, p. 1679.

Remlinger & Dumas — Sur une épidémie de dysenterie bacillaire, observée dans l'Argonne. — Compt. Rend. Soc. de Biol., 1915, Vol. lxxviii, p. 254.

Sacquépée, Burnet & Weissenbach. — Recherches sur les diarrhées et la dysenterie des armées en campagne. — Paris Méd., 1915, Vol. v, p. 200.

Schmidt & Strasburger. — Die Faeces der Menschen im normalen und krankhaften Zustande. — Berlin, 1903, (Hirschwald).

Schütze .. .. The Paratyphoid B Group. — Lancet, 1920, Vol. i, p. 93.

Sewell, Bellingham-Smith & Priestley. — An Outbreak of Food Poisoning in a General Hospital. — Jl. of R.A.M.C., 1920, Vol. xxxiv, p. 510.

Shearman & Moorhead. — Bacillæmia due to Infection with *Bacillus faecalis alkaligenes*. — Jl. of R.A.M.C., 1917, Vol. xxviii, p. 104.

Thomson, D. & Thomson, J. G. — Protozoological Researches, including Investigations on the Sand in Egypt, undertaken to elucidate the mode of Spread of Amœbic Dysentery with the Flagellate Diarrhœas, with conclusions regarding the Sanitary Measures necessary to prevent these Diseases. — Jl. of R.A.M.C., 1916, Vol. xxvii, p. 1.

Thomson, D. & Mackie — Clinical and Laboratory Researches on Dysentery in Egypt, with some Remarks on Sanitation. — Jl. of R.A.M.C., 1917, Vol. xxviii, p. 403.

Wenyon & O'Connor — Human Intestinal Protozoa in the Near East. — London, 1918 (Bale, Sons & Danielsson).

Wenyon .. .. Histological Observations on the possible Pathogenicity of *Trichomonas intestinalis* and *Chilomastix mesnili*, with a Note on *Endolimax nana*. — Jl. Trop. Med. & Hyg., 1920, Vol. xxiii, p. 125.

Woodcock .. .. Protozoological Experiences during the Summer and Autumn of 1916. — Jl. of R.A.M.C., 1917, Vol. xxix, p. 290.

York, Carter, Mackinnon, Matthews & Smith. — Persons who have never been out of Great Britain as Carriers of *Entamoeba histolytica*. — Ann. Trop. Med. & Parasit., 1917–18. Vol. xi, p. 87.

CHAPTER XI.

AMŒBIC DYSENTERY.

AMŒBIC dysentery is a disease which possesses a particular interest for the British Army. This is not merely because it has played a part in hindering all the many tropical campaigns in which the British Army has been engaged, but because of another historic association with the army. Fifty years ago amœbic dysentery was an unrecognized disorder. To-day our knowledge of its causes, symptoms, treatment and the means for its prevention rests upon a firm scientific foundation ; and this knowledge not only had its beginnings in the investigations of a British army officer, but is due largely to the labours of those who worked in and for the British Army during the war of 1914–18.

Knowledge of the disease dates from the time when Annesley, Parkes, Morehead and the other great Anglo-Indian physicians of last century first learnt to distinguish " tropical " dysentery, with its occasional sequel of liver abscess, from the commoner and long-familiar "epidemic" type. In those days it was not known that the latter disease is a result of bacterial infection, and that " tropical " dysentery is occasioned by the presence of certain protozoa, called amœbæ, in the intestine. Indeed, it was not then known that these organisms can live parasitically in the bodies of other animals · and the first observations which brought this fact to light were actually made upon the amœbæ which live in man.

In the year 1869, Timothy Lewis*—then Assistant-Surgeon attached to the Army in India—was investigating cholera; and in the course of examining the stools of his patients, with the aid of the microscope, he came across certain structures which he cautiously, but doubtless correctly, identified as " amœbæ." In his report published in 1870, he gives a brief account of his findings. After describing many of the objects seen in choleraic evacuations, he proceeds :—

" Frequently a globule has been observed for some time, and finally disposed of as being merely an oil one, when suddenly it is seen to protrude a portion of its substance, retract it, and while doing so another protrusion becomes visible at some other portion of the little mass, and then, perhaps, it will

* The discovery of the intestinal amœbæ of man is commonly, but wrongly, attributed to Lambl (1860).

shift its position exactly after the manner of an amœba. These are frequently hyaline in a fresh stool, but generally granular ; no trace of nucleus or contractile vacuole can be observed ; sometimes they are very numerous, but when there are other corpuscles in the field which act in a somewhat similar manner, it is impossible to say to which class they belong, unless, indeed, they move across the field like an ordinary amœba."

Lewis returned to England from India in 1883, and became Assistant Professor of Pathology at the Army Medical School, Netley : and here he introduced into the course, for the first time, practical instruction in those methods of bacteriological inquiry with which he had become familiar during his work in India. This instruction was continued till the time of his death, at the age of 44, in 1886, and it was subsequently added to by his successors in the post of Assistant Professor.*

D. D. Cunningham, of the Indian Medical Service, who collaborated with Lewis, gave a more detailed account of their amœbæ in papers published in 1871 and 1881. In his descriptions the non-pathogenic organism now known as *Entamoeba coli* is clearly recognizable. Lösch, of Petrograd, was, however, the first to describe (1875) amœbæ from the stools in a case of dysentery. His patient was a young Russian peasant, who had never been out of his native country. The amœbæ observed were undoubtedly those now known to be pathogenic, and called *Entamoeba histolytica*.

Similar amœbæ were found in the tissues of the gut wall by Koch in 1883, in the course of his work for the Cholera Commission in Egypt ; and he also found what appeared to be the same forms in the wall of a liver abscess.

Kartulis, in Egypt, continued the study of dysentery, and published several papers between 1885 and 1891. He maintained that dysentery in general was the result of amœbic infection, and claimed to have produced the disease experimentally in cats—as Lösch had done earlier in a dog—by inoculation of the amœbæ from human stools. These experiments were soon confirmed by other workers, notably by Kovács (1892) and Kruse and Pasquale (1894). The latter investigators also showed that dysentery can be produced in the cat by infecting it with the amœbæ present in liver abscess pus, which is usually, as Kartulis first stated, bacteriologically sterile. Finally, Kartulis showed in 1904 that the amœbæ found in cases of dysentery may give rise to abscesses not only in the liver but also in the brain, and possibly in other organs.

---

* Bruce (1890), Semple (1898), Leishman (1900), Harvey (1903), Harrison (1906), Kennedy (1909), and Cummins (1913).

Considerable advance in the knowledge of dysentery was made in America by Councilman and Lafleur (1891), whose work, from the standpoint of morbid anatomy, must still be regarded as a classic. They were the first to separate " amœbic dysentery "—a name which they themselves introduced—from other kinds of dysentery and to describe in detail its characteristic lesions in the bowel. They were also among the first to suggest that more than one species of amœba may inhabit the human intestine. This was shortly afterwards demonstrated to be true by Quincke and Roos (1893) at Kiel, though the great importance of their observations was not realized at the time.

Further additions to knowledge were made by the Italian workers Casagrandi and Barbagallo in 1895 and 1897. They gave a good account of the non-pathogenic *Entamoeba coli*, and showed how the intestinal amœbæ may be distinguished from free-living species.

By the year 1897 the chief facts about amœbic dysentery and the intestinal amœbæ of man were known. It had been ascertained that there is a special kind of dysentery caused by amœbæ of a particular sort, and it had been shown how it could be distinguished from other kinds of dysentery, and how the pathogenic species of amœba could be discriminated from harmless species associated with it in the bowel, and also from non-parasitic forms. It was also evident, from the work of the Italians, and of Quincke and Roos, that infection is acquired by swallowing the cysts of the pathogenic amœba. But unfortunately the facts were not understood, or were not seen in their true light, at this period ; and for the first decade of the present century knowledge of the subject of amœbic dysentery became chaotic. During this period some good work was done, notably by Dopter (1907) in France, and by Kuenen (1909) in the Dutch East Indies, on the morbid anatomy of the disease ; but on the whole, the large amount of protozoological work done during this time tended rather to add to the confusion than to elucidate matters. A considerable share in causing this confusion must be ascribed to the German zoologist Schaudinn, whose erroneous observations, published in 1903, had a profound influence with his contemporaries and followers. It was not until 1913 that the earlier advances were consolidated and further progress not only made possible but actually effected. This was the result of the admirable researches of an American, E. L. Walker, carried out in the Philippine Islands.

Walker in 1911, and later, in collaboration with Sellards, in 1913, demonstrated by careful observation and experiment that :—

(1) The amœbæ found in water and those cultivable from the intestine of man, are free-living forms incapable of living parasitically in the human intestine. When amœbæ are obtained in cultures from the intestinal contents they are derived from ingested cysts which have passed unchanged through the alimentary canal.

(2) The amœbæ parasitic in man belong to a distinct genus, *Entamoeba*. They are obligatory parasites and cannot be cultivated. At least two species are recognizable—one non-pathogenic (*E. coli*) and one pathogenic (*E. histolytica*). The first forms cysts containing, when mature, eight nuclei, the second cysts containing four nuclei.

(3) The organisms are transmitted from man to man by means of these cysts. Infection results when they are swallowed —as was proved by experiments on human beings.

Walker also accurately defined the " carrier " state. Others had, it is true, previously spoken of amœbic " carriers," but they used the term in a different sense, and without comprehending the facts upon which Walker's conception rests. For example, Martini (1908) and Vincent (1909) both discussed and described " carriers " of *E. histolytica*, but they were ignorant of the life history of the amœba and of the part played by the cysts ; also Harvey* at that time wrote as follows :—

" 1. Chronic carrier amœbic.
"This man had suffered from dysentery before arrival at the depôt and while in residence there had several short attacks easily controlled by ipecacuanha. During these attacks the amœbæ were present in the stools in large numbers. The interesting point was that during the intervals when his fæces were normal, amœbæ were frequently seen."

The carrier of *E. histolytica*, to follow and slightly elaborate Walker's conception, is the person who is infected with the amœbæ, in his large intestine, and who passes their cysts in his stools. He is not clinically a case of dysentery, though he may develop into one in certain circumstances. The amœbæ live upon the tissue lining the bowel, which they erode or eventually ulcerate to a greater or less extent. Dysentery only results when the inroads of the amœbæ become excessive or when the body ceases to tolerate the parasites, becoming abnormally sensitive to their presence and unable to repair the damage done by them. The factors which determine whether an infected person will or will not suffer from dysentery are still imperfectly understood.

---

* *Annual Reports of Sanitary Officers*, India, 1909.

Walker divided carriers into two classes : (1) contact carriers—those who are infected with the parasite but who have never suffered from amœbic dysentery ; and (2) convalescent carriers—those who have had amœbic dysentery, but who have recovered clinically though still remaining infected. The cysts passed by both kinds of carrier are equally capable of infecting other people if they happen to be swallowed ; but whether this other person suffers from dysentery or not depends not upon the source of his infection but upon his own individual susceptibility to the parasite. The carrier is, moreover, typically a " normal " and healthy person, and consequently his danger—as a source of infection—to others, generally passes unperceived. A patient with acute amœbic dysentery, however, is incapable of infecting his fellows at the time when he is actually suffering from the disease ; for he then passes only the active (unencysted) amœbæ in his stools, and such amœbæ, if swallowed, are unable to survive the passage through the stomach, and consequently cannot spread the infection.

It will thus be seen that in 1914 the problem of the causation of amœbic dysentery had already been solved, the mode of infection was known, and the life-history of the parasite had been discovered. Unfortunately this knowledge was not general, and few indeed of those who were called upon to investigate the disease in the early part of the war were familiar with the facts or able to recognize the parasite in the various stages in which it is seen in healthy and diseased individuals.

The morbid anatomy of the disease had also been fully worked out before the war. As long ago as 1846, Parkes, Annesley and others—as can be gathered from their writings and published plates—were familiar with two types of lesion which were to be found *post mortem* in fatal cases of dysentery. These workers were, of course, ignorant of the causes of the differences which they observed, but undoubtedly their descriptions tally with what we now know as the typical lesions of amœbic and of bacillary dysentery. At a later date, the typical lesions of amœbic dysentery were fully and accurately described, and compared and contrasted with those of bacillary dysentery, by Councilman and Lafleur (1891), Dopter (1907), Kuenen (1909), Rogers (1913), and others. Moreover, the earlier workers in India had clearly distinguished the catarrhal or "diphtheritic" (bacillary) from the " ulcerated " (amœbic) type of dysentery, and they were also well aware that the catarrhal (*i.e.*, bacillary) type was the epidemic disease of armies in the field, whereas the other type was the endemic or sporadic "tropical" dysentery which is associated with liver abscess and does not occur as an epidemic. It is unfortunate that these observations were not kept in mind in the earlier stages of the campaign in the Middle East.

Although a great deal of work was done on amœbic dysentery during the war, and the sound part of the older work was abundantly confirmed and considerably extended, yet little that was really new has been added to our knowledge. Before the war it was known that there was one and only one amœba (*E. histolytica*) pathogenic to man. This remains true; but it was formerly believed that man harboured also only one non-pathogenic species of amœba, *E. coli*. It has now been shown, however, by the work of Wenyon and O'Connor, Dobell and Jepps and others, that there are in fact four non-pathogenic species of amœbæ which may be found in the human intestine. There are, in addition to *E. coli*, the species called *Endolimax nana, Iodamoeba bütschlii,* and *Dientamoeba fragilis*. To anyone who proposes to study the excreta in dysentery a knowledge of the appearance of these amœbæ and of their cysts is clearly essential, since they may be confused with corresponding forms of the pathogenic species; but, on the other hand, these non-pathogenic species are only indirectly of medical importance, since they are not concerned in the causation of dysentery or diarrhœa.

Another and a very important point which has emerged from the work done during the war is the discovery that probably a considerable, though still uncertain, proportion—estimated by Dobell at possibly 10 per cent.—of the entire population of the globe are healthy carriers of *E. histolytica*, continually passing the cysts in their fæces. It is now known, chiefly through the work of Malins Smith, Matthews and Mackinnon, who were working during the war at the School of Tropical Medicine, Liverpool, that infection with this amœba is by no means uncommon in healthy British residents who have never been abroad. This conclusion was foreshadowed in the observations of Dobell, who had previously found that the percentage of men passing cysts of *E. histolytica* in their fæces was as great among those who had been invalided from overseas for wounds and other diseases as it was among those who had been invalided for dysentery and bowel complaints. It will be obvious that had knowledge of these facts been available at the outbreak of the war, it would have profoundly altered the policy which was actually pursued in dealing with carriers of *E. histolytica*.

Disposal of Dysentery Cases and Carriers.

It is necessary to consider at this point the organization instituted for dealing with cases of amœbic dysentery and carriers during the war. Almost all the investigations which were undertaken during this period were carried out in connexion with and under limitations imposed by this organization. The two subjects—administrative organization and investigations—may therefore most conveniently be reviewed together. A more detailed account of the chief scientific results will be given in the final section.

The method of dealing with typhoid carriers had been thoroughly worked out in the army in India before the war, and a similar system for dealing with convalescents from the typhoid group of diseases was soon in working order; but as regards bacillary dysentery nothing was done until 1915. The reason for this was that in France the number of cases of dysentery during 1914 and 1915 was practically *nil*. It was not until convalescents began to arrive from the Eastern Mediterranean that it was found necessary to legislate for dysentery.

When these cases first began to arrive in England in 1915, hospitals had already been established in many centres. Each large central hospital was surrounded by an increasing number of auxiliary hospitals, and sick and wounded were distributed to these hospitals according to the accommodation available. The result was that dysentery cases and convalescents from dysentery were scattered about in small numbers—many of them in hospitals where expert advice was lacking, or only obtainable with difficulty.

It was therefore decided that certain specified hospitals should reserve accommodation for dysentery cases, and to these hospitals special laboratory workers were detailed with the object of securing correct diagnosis and treatment. A War Office letter of 10th October, 1915, directed the attention of all officers in medical charge of auxiliary hospitals to the fact that dysentery cases were liable to relapse as the result of dietary indiscretion, and emphasized the necessity of exercising great care in this particular. It was also directed that cases of dysentery, as far as possible, should be separated from other patients in hospital.

On 4th November, 1915, instructions were issued from the War Office to the following hospitals, directing that they should set apart special accommodation for dysentery cases.

2nd Southern General Hospital,	Bristol ..	..	..	500	beds.
1st Western ,, ,,	Liverpool	..	..	500	,,
2nd Western ,, ,,	Manchester	..	..	500	,,
3rd Western ,, ,,	Cardiff ..	..	..	500	,,
3rd Eastern ,, ,,	Brighton	..	..	500	,,
Mont Dore Hospital, Bournemouth		..	..	400	,,

This letter further directed that these cases should not be
transferred or discharged from the dysentery section of the
central hospital until at least three negative bacteriological
examinations of their excreta had been made—the examinations
being spread over a period of one month, during which time the
stools had been normal.

This letter was based on the recommendations drawn up at a
meeting of the Army Sanitary Committee held in October 1915
to consider the question of disposal of convalescents from
dysentery.   At this meeting Dr. J. C. G. Ledingham,
Professor F. W. Andrewes and Lieut.-Colonel D. Harvey gave
evidence.   The recommendations were as follows :—

" (a) All dysentery cases should if possible be concentrated in the Mediterranean. If this were done many men would soon be able to return to duty
and a better selection of men for transfer home could be made. Also a proper
bacteriological examination, on the results of which depended the line of
treatment to be adopted, could be made at an early date.

" (b) That chronic or carrier cases should be sent home and be concentrated
in a hospital or hospitals with a convalescent depot attached.

" (c) That cases now being treated in various hospitals at home should not
be allowed to be discharged to convalescent homes until there had been at
least three negative examinations spread over a period of one month after the
stools had become normal. These instructions should also apply to cases
treated in concentration hospitals when formed.

" (d) If the proposal at (a) can be carried out, it is desirable that arrangement
should be made to establish a hospital centre as early as possible, and until
this centre is ready, cases being sent to England for treatment should be
collected for treatment in one or more centres at home."

In the instructions issued in October 1915 only bacillary
dysentery was taken into account, though they were amplified
later in order to provide for protozoological examinations. As a
matter of fact, if the examinations had been limited to bacillary
dysentery, probably no harm would have been done, in so far as
healthy carriers and the risks arising from them are involved :
but it must be remembered that the majority of men returning
from the Middle East were suffering from dysenteric disorders,
and it was essential that the diagnosis of these cases should be
established, in order that appropriate treatment might be given
at the earliest moment. Overseas the accurate diagnosis of
these cases had not always been possible, owing to the rush of
cases, the limited facilities for clinical and laboratory investigations on the Gallipoli Peninsula and at Mudros, and the shortage
of skilled workers. In many cases which had passed into the
chronic state an accurate diagnosis was difficult even at home,

although some light was thrown on their true nature by the work of Drs. Penfold and Ledingham at the King George Hospital. As a result of agglutination tests on the blood serum of convalescents, they formed the opinion that the majority of cases received from Gallipoli had suffered from bacillary dysentery, and not from amœbic infection. Dr. H. M. Woodcock, acting as protozoologist, agreed with this verdict, although he believed that cases of amœbic dysentery undoubtedly occurred among the patients invalided from the Mediterranean zone. A similar conclusion was also reached by the workers at the London Hospital—Dr. L. J. Rajchman and Dr. G. T. Western, working for the Medical Research Committee under the direction of Professor W. Bulloch. The protozoological investigation of these cases was commenced by Dr. C. M. Wenyon and continued by Mr. C. Dobell and Dr. A. C. Stevenson. Practically the same conclusions were also arrived at by Captain S. R. Douglas and his fellow-workers at St. Mary's Hospital. Rajchman and Western (1917) in their report ultimately reached the conclusion that the Mediterranean dysentery was essentially the result of a mixed infection. This was probably correct, but hardly in the sense intended (*i.e.*, a mixture of amœbic dysentery with paratyphoid or bacillary dysentery). It is known now that the majority of the cases were true paratyphoid fever or bacillary dysentery, and that most of the patients found infected with *E. histolytica* were probably more or less " healthy " carriers of the parasite.

The Medical Research Committee, who had instituted the work at the London Hospital and at St. Mary's Hospital, pointed out in 1915* that grave risks were being run by the release of infective men—risks both to their own health and to that of the community. It was noted at this time, however, that none of these men had developed liver abscess, nor had any of the other patients associated with them contracted amœbic dysentery.

The protozoological investigation of the London Hospital cases showed, finally, that at least 14 per cent. of them were infected with *E. histolytica*; but if those cases with a serological response to dysentery bacilli were excluded, the " true " amœbic cases amounted to only 6·2 per cent. It is now known, however, that if these same men had been examined as carefully and as frequently before embarking for Gallipoli, a like percentage of amœbic carriers might have been discovered among them.

* Letters dated 15th and 16th November, 1915.

In his report on the protozoological findings from 556 of these cases, examined in London between November 1915 and January 1916, Wenyon records that 10·8 per cent. had at that time been found infected with *E. histolytica,* and he expresses the opinion that " the introduction into this country of large numbers of carriers will almost certainly be followed by cases of amœbic dysentery among the general public " ; though he qualifies this by saying that the conditions in England are not favourable for the spread of the disease, and no great outbreak was likely.

The Medical Advisory Committee for Prevention of Disease, consisting of Dr. Hunter and Dr. Buchanan, with Dr. L. Dudgeon, had visited the Gallipoli Peninsula in October and November 1915 and reported that, " it has been ascertained (*vide* previous reports) that the great bulk of the peninsular dysentery has been amœbic." This opinion was based on the clinical and pathological findings of the workers on the Peninsula and at Mudros, and was not the result of any personal investigations in the laboratory. The Committee added, however, in another place, that as regards dysentery, the disease had been " mild on the whole and many cases rapidly responded to treatment with sulphate of magnesia." This would point, of course, to these cases having really been bacillary in origin.

Captain R. G. Archibald, on whose work these opinions were mainly based, and who had had previous experience of amœbic dysentery in Egypt, stated in a paper published with Captain Hadfield and Lieutenants Logan and Campbell in 1916 that " the type of dysentery most prevalent among the troops in the Dardanelles in August, September and October [1915] was amœbic ; only a few cases of bacillary infections occurred during these months. In November, December and January, amœbic dysentery entirely disappeared, and the incidence of the bacillary type of the disease increased." It was further stated that, of the cases of dysentery contracted on the Peninsula, " 70 per cent. were due to amœbic infections and 13 per cent. represented bacillary dysentery infections"—the remainder not being accounted for. In another place the same writers say that most of the dysentery in Gallipoli " was undoubtedly amœbic in type. Almost all the cases represented infections with *Entamoeba histolytica* " ; and they add that in " some cases " there was "*post-mortem* evidence showing either the existence of perforations of one of the multiple amœbic ulcers in the colon or the presence of liver abscesses."

It is clear from these and similar statements made during this period that cases of amœbic dysentery must have occurred in the earlier stages of the campaign in Gallipoli. But in view of the careful work subsequently carried out on convalescents at home, and in the light of present knowledge regarding carriers, remembering also the historical fact that bacillary dysentery is the "bloody flux" of camps and armies, and in view of the small number of cases of liver abscess and amœbic dysentery subsequently reported, only one conclusion can be drawn, namely, that although there were many cases of amœbic dysentery in Gallipoli, the bulk of the dysentery and diarrhœa was due to bacillary infection. Sufficient stress was not laid at the time upon the now well-known difficulty of isolating the specific dysentery bacilli from acute cases, except by direct rectal swab ; and on the other hand, it was not realized that the occurrence of E. histolytica cysts in the stools does not necessarily mean that the patient has suffered or is suffering from amœbic dysentery. Moreover, some of the workers had had little or no experience of the difficulties attending the microscopic examination of a dysenteric stool, and mistakes in diagnosis must frequently have been made.

That the Committee were not satisfied with the accuracy of the diagnosis of dysenteric cases is shown by the fact that on their return to Egypt they recommended in January 1916 to the D.M.S., Mediterranean Expeditionary Force, that a special protozoological investigation of these cases should be undertaken.

This proposed inquiry was carried out by Lieut.-Colonel C. M. Wenyon and Captain F. W. O'Connor, and its results were far-reaching. They are set forth in a series of papers published by these officers in 1917. Wenyon and O'Connor found that, out of 246 men who had come from Gallipoli with a history of dysentery, 6·5 per cent. were carriers of E. histolytica, as shown by the discovery of the cysts in their excreta ; whilst of 1,137 men with no history of dysentery, 4·5 per cent. were carriers. Of 568 men who had never served in Gallipoli, and who had no history of dysentery, 4·5 per cent were likewise found to be carriers.*

An examination of a total of 1,979 healthy men showed 5·3 per cent. of carriers. Included among these were 279 cooks at a camp near Alexandria, of whom 9·6 per cent.

---

* From a statistical standpoint, these percentages cannot be taken to indicate that there was any appreciable difference in the real incidence of infection in these different groups.

proved to be infected. Among 961 hospital cases, mostly suffering from diarrhœa, dysentery, and enteritis, cysts of E. histolytica were found in only 2·2 per cent. Of 168 British military prisoners, 1·8 per cent. were found to be carriers, and as most of these men were suffering from diarrhœa they were comparable with the hospital cases just mentioned. Furthermore, 13·5 per cent. of 524 healthy natives of Egypt were found to be infected with E. histolytica. It should be noted that most of these results were based upon only single examinations of the stools, and therefore represent only the minimum number of infections actually present.

In a series of cases in hospital with acute clinical dysentery (i.e., passing blood and mucus), only 6·1 per cent. showed active amœbæ with contained red blood cells. The remaining 93·9 per cent. were judged to be bacillary dysentery, partly diagnosed by the microscopical appearance of the cellular exudate in the stools and partly by the isolation of the specific bacilli.

Wenyon and O'Connor therefore found that at the time of their investigation—January to August 1916—bacillary dysentery was about sixteen times as common as amœbic. It may be noted here that Captains D. Thomson and T. J. Mackie (1917) found that out of thirty cases similarly examined in Egypt at about the same time, only two were definitely amœbic, i.e., 6·6 per cent. of their cases ; but they arrived at a different conclusion from that of Wenyon regarding the prevalence of uncomplicated bacillary dysentery.

As a result of the findings of Wenyon and O'Connor, the Medical Advisory Committee, consisting of Lieut.-Colonels Andrew Balfour, Buchanan, Ledingham and Wenyon, reported, inter alia, as follows (7th October, 1916) :—

" 1. Healthy carriers of Entamoeba histolytica have been found to be relatively so numerous among British troops in Egypt and among samples of the native population of Egyptian cities as to render it a practical impossibility to adopt, for men in Egypt, any general preventive measures against amœbic dysentery which depend upon the detection of the amœbic carrier and his isolation until cured of his carrier condition.

" 2. For the prevention of the disease in Egypt primary reliance must still be placed on general methods of sanitation . . . .

" 3. Considerations (1) and (2) apply to a large extent also to men who arrive or have arrived in England, France and elsewhere after stay in Egypt. If all convalescents on return to England from Egypt were specially examined to detect entamœbic carriers, the number of carriers so dealt with would still be small compared with the carriers among returned healthy men, who would pass undetected.

" 7. The question arises whether dysentery convalescents in general coming under observation on return to England should, in all cases, be detained in order to sort out for subsequent special treatment all those whose stools show

Entamoeba histolytica cysts or other protozoal infections. The writers of the report, assuming that it is of the greatest importance at the present time to avoid keeping fit men from duty, point out that the above procedure is often not immediately demanded for the men's military efficiency, nor is it indispensable as a measure of prevention. In their view the better practical guide is the clinical condition of the convalescent; those men only being detained for special observation whose stools are abnormal or who are obviously still in bad health."

Whilst the Medical Advisory Committee were engaged in studying the problem in Egypt, a considerable amount of work was also being done in England. Towards the end of 1915 a Committee of the Royal Society, in a memorandum which was forwarded to Egypt by the Director-General, Army Medical Service, insisted on the necessity of providing skilled protozoologists for the work of diagnosis. The number of such zoologists available was very small, and the Royal Society's Committee, in conjunction with the Medical Research Committee, accordingly drew up a scheme for the training of expert workers in England. The Medical Research Committee, by arrangement with the Imperial College of Science, offered the services of Mr. Clifford Dobell for this purpose, and the offer was readily accepted by the War Office. The resources of the Wellcome Bureau of Scientific Research were placed at the Committee's disposal by Mr. Henry S. Wellcome, and here, in co-operation with the two Committees concerned, Mr. Dobell was soon able to organize classes of practical instruction in the special branch of protozoology required. At the outset invaluable assistance was given by Dr. C. M. Wenyon, who had himself begun the training of protozoologists before he left England in January 1916, and who continued to give instruction to medical officers in Egypt during his stay there in that year.

The training of protozoologists was continued, with intermissions, at the Wellcome Bureau from December 1915 until the end of the war. During this period over 100 men and women received instruction. Most of them were zoologists and botanists, with no previous experience of the subject; but many of them became expert, and were eventually allocated to military hospitals, where they did very useful work. Their training was very carefully supervised and no member of the class was allowed to take up work at a military hospital before he, or she, had acquired considerable proficiency. As a result of his experience in instructing these microscopists, Mr. Dobell, in a report published in 1917, came to the following conclusions, which should be borne in mind whenever the records of unskilled or untrained observers come under consideration: " Stool-examinations made by persons . . . . who have not served their apprenticeship to the actual work itself, possess no scientific value whatsoever . . . . and for the average worker a practical training of not less than four to six weeks is, even under the most favourable conditions, requisite."

In May 1916 the first dysentery depôt was opened at Barton-on-Sea, New Milton, under the command of Lieut.-Colonel J. Chaytor White, I.M.S. In November 1916 it was found necessary to open another depôt for dysenteric patients in England, owing to the increasing pressure upon the accommodation at Barton. Accordingly, the Manor (County of London) War Hospital, Epsom, was taken over for this purpose. It was found necessary, at both the dysentery depôts, to take elaborate precautions in collecting specimens of fæces for examination, and a system was finally worked out which made the interchanging of samples practically impossible.

At the request of the Medical Research Committee the results of the work done in the various centres were collected and analysed by Mr. Dobell in October 1916, the results being published later. In this report Dobell discussed at length the question of "negative examinations," and showed that the number of infected persons discovered when only three examinations of the stools are possible, even when the examinations are carefully made by expert workers, represents only about one-half to two-thirds of the true total. At this time the workers at Liverpool under Professor J. W. W. Stephens appeared to be of the opinion that if the three examinations were performed at intervals of a week the great majority of infected cases would be detected. Their subsequent conclusions, however, were in close agreement with Dobell's.

The acting Secretary of the Medical Research Committee had previously reported (9th May, 1916) that " where the official instructions have been interpreted as demanding three negatives at weekly intervals the number of infected men passing out as cured has been relatively small." But there can be no doubt, from the figures in Dobell's report, that if six examinations had been made, a much greater number of carriers would have been discovered. This does not apply, however, to cases of acute amœbic dysentery, where the free amœbæ containing red cells are usually discoverable at the first examination.

A considerable part of this report was occupied with the determination of the true rate of infection with intestinal protozoa, of every kind, in the cases examined up to that time, and also with an analysis of the effects of the various treatments to which the infected cases had been submitted. The incidence

TABLE I.

	Walton-on-Thames.	Oxford.	Manchester.	London; London Hospital.	London; King George Hospital.	London; Endell St. Hospital.	Liverpool.	Hornchurch.	Haslar.	Chichester.	Cardiff.	Bristol.	Brighton.	Barton-on-Sea.
Total number of cases examined.. ..	205	315	439	775	384	135	1,291	522	394	205	495	388	426	1,047
Infected with— *Entamoeba histolytica*	11·0%	7·3%	3·4%	14·19%	2·0%	6·6%	2·09%	10·15%	6·3%	16·9%	6·6%	12·4%	7·5%	10·1%
Entamoeba coli ..	40·9%	20·0%	7·5%	42·58%	14·8%	15·5%	13·0%	38·12%	23·8%	47·8%	45·4%	35·3%	25·8%	23·5%
Giardia (=*Lamblia*) *intestinalis*	19·5%	9·0%	7·9%	17·67%	5·7%	9·6%	16·7%	15·5%	5·6%	14·1%	7·6%	13·1%	19·0%	13·3%
Chilomastix mesnili ..	7·8%	0·3%	3·2%	4·51%	2·8%	9·6%	1 case	3·6%	1 case	"3 or 4 cases"	—	1 case	—	1·7%
Trichomonas hominis..	2·4%	1·2%	1·1%	1·29%	3·6%	11·8%	2 cases	0·76%	—	1 case	—	1 case	—	3 cases
Isospora hominis ..	1 case	—	2 cases	2·06%	2·6%	—	4 cases	—	—	—	—	—	—	—
Eimeria wenyoni ..	—	—	—	1 case	—	—	—	—	—	—	—	—	—	—

of infection with various protozoa, as recorded at different centres, was given in a table which is here reproduced (Table I).

The probable true rates of infection with three of the more important intestinal protozoa were calculated, from the data then available, and shown to be :—

E. histolytica	..	..	..	..	.. 18 to 25 per cent.
E. coli	..	..	..	..	.. 60 to 80 „
Lamblia	..	..	..	..	.. 30 to 45 „

One of the striking points brought out by the analysis of these cases was the fact that " the incidence of infection with *E. histolytica* is approximately the same in all classes of patients examined. . . . There seems to be, on the whole, no conspicuous difference in the incidence of infection among dysenteric cases and those invalided home for other reasons." As an illustration of the frequency with which *E. histolytica* occurred in non-dysenteric cases, the following table (Table II) may be given. It shows the results obtained by Dobell (1916) in examining a series of 200 patients at No. 2 New Zealand General Hospital, Walton-on-Thames.

TABLE II.

Cases.	Number examined.	Percentage infected with E. histolytica.
All cases ..	200	11·0
Dysenteric	90	10·0
Non-dysenteric ..	110	11·8
All intestinal ailments ..	130	8·2
All non-intestinal ailments (wounds, etc.)	70	15·7

On 27th November, 1916, a memorandum, calling attention to the results of the foregoing investigations, was distributed to all the laboratories concerned. The following extracts from this memorandum will illustrate its purport :—

" As regards the routine of examinations for the detection of carriers, Mr. Dobell's analysis shows that this has been altogether inadequate, even where it has been consistently applied, and makes it certain that many carriers, even among the men subjected to examination, must have escaped detection, and have been discharged from hospital as free from infection. The evidence at his disposal indicates, moreover, an important prevalence of the infection among the men of the Mediterranean Force, who, having no history of recognized dysentery or enteric infection, have not been subjected to examination in this country.

" As regards treatment, there were early indications that the officially prescribed course of hypodermic injections [of emetine] was ineffective in eradicating the infection from a considerable proportion of cases of this class. . . . . Evidence is now available, making it clear that a large majority of cases, whether permanently cured or not, fail to show evidence of infection when examined during and immediately after the period of treatment with emetine. From the results obtained . . . . it is now possible to state definitely :—

(1) That negative examinations obtained during treatment or in the week after its conclusion are practically worthless as evidence of cure ;

(2) That the hypodermic course of emetine fails to effect a cure of the " carrier " of infection with *Entamœba histolytica* in a large proportion of cases—at least 70 per cent.

" These conclusions are confirmed by the experience at the convalescent depôts, where it has been found that the proportion of carriers discovered among the patients discharged thither from the hospitals as " free from infection," has been but little below the proportion discovered among the new cases transferred direct to the depôts from the hospital ships, without treatment in this country.

" Meanwhile, ... a trial has been made at a number of centres of the insoluble double iodide of emetine and bismuth, administered by the mouth. . . . . In centres in which the uncompressed powder has been given, under conditions ensuring that the patient received the dose, the therapeutic results have been exceedingly promising. . . .

" On the results of experience thus briefly summarized, the following recommendations may be based. . . . . As regards examination, the needed modifications are as follows :—

(a) For the detection of cases the number of examinations should be increased, when possible, to six. These need not be widely spread, and could, without disadvantage, be made *in the same period as the previously customary three.*

(b) For the control of the effects of treatment, examinations made during the course of treatment, or in the fortnight following its conclusion, should not be counted towards the number of negative findings officially demanded as a guarantee of cure. *The important examinations, as an indication of the success of treatment, are those made at the end of the third week after treatment* . . . .

" The ideal scheme of examinations, for control of treatment, would thus be one at the end of the first week, one at the end of the second week, and three or four at the end of the third week following treatment, if the earlier ones have been negative.

" For treatment of carriers of *E. histolytica* it is recommended that the hypodermic injection of emetine hydrochloride be abandoned in favour of the oral administration of emetine bismuthous iodide. The latter should be administered in daily doses of 3 grains on 12 consecutive days."

The results obtained at the Barton and Epsom depôts during 1916 and 1917 showed conclusively that there were large numbers of carriers of *E. histolytica* among the convalescent dysenteric patients concentrated in these establishments. These patients had, as a general rule, already been examined at a hospital and discharged to the depôt as " negative." Between 20th November, 1916, and 31st August, 1917, over 10,000 cases were examined at Barton, and approximately 5 per cent. found to be carriers (unpublished report by Mr. Redman King). The stools were examined usually only once per case, and this percentage is therefore much below the probable real incidence of infection. On the other hand, the number of carriers of dysentery bacilli proved to be almost negligible.

At Epsom, where 1,300 cases were subjected to a more intensive study, and examined twice per case, the percentage of patients found to be infected with E. histolytica was 12. Only three of these cases displayed any dysenteric symptoms referable to their infections (one acute and two subacute), the rest being carriers. No carriers of dysentery bacilli* were found in this series. (Dobell, Gettings, Jepps, and Stephens, 1918.)

A point of considerable importance which emerged from the work carried out at the depôts was the demonstration that dysenteric convalescents from France, many of whom had never been in the tropics, were frequently infected with E. histolytica. It was known that the great majority of these patients had suffered from bacillary dysentery—not amœbic—in France; and it thus appeared highly probable that they were merely contact carriers of E. histolytica who had at some time acquired infection in France or England, but had escaped detection because their stools had not previously been subjected to microscopic examination. It was found generally, however, that infections with E. histolytica (and other intestinal protozoa also) were much commoner in troops returning from the tropics than in those who had served in France and England only. The following two tables (Tables III and IV) will serve to illustrate the findings in this respect at Barton and Epsom :—

TABLE III.

Barton (November 1916 to August 1917).

Dysentery contracted in	No. of cases examined.	Percentage found infected with E. histolytica.
France	4,718	4·0
Egypt	200	5·5
Salonika	2,065	6·5
Africa (East and West)	238	6·5
Mesopotamia	233	10·0
Gallipoli	68	16·0
India	26	20·0

* It is of interest to note that Dr. Gettings, who was responsible for the bacteriological examinations, found lactose non-fermenting bacilli present in 167, or 12·8 per cent., but no true B. dysenteriae, B. typhosus, or B. paratyphosus. Dr. Gettings had had considerable experience in the study of bacillary dysentery in asylums at home. Unfortunately, he died before this asylum work was completed, but a report on his findings was compiled by Captain S. R. Douglas and is a classical piece of work. (M.R.C. Special Report Series, No. 30, 1919.)

TABLE IV.
Epsom (November 1916 to July 1917).

Dysentery contracted in	No. of cases examined	Percentage found infected with E. histolytica.
France	788	8·4
Egypt	58	18·9
Salonika	333	18·9
Gallipoli	13	23·0
Mesopotamia	39	20·5
India and China	4	75·0

It became clear in 1917 that carriers of *E. histolytica* were very much commoner in all classes of troops than had been suspected before the war. Moreover, the work of Wenyon and O'Connor in Egypt, and of Dobell and his fellow-workers in England, showed that it was not possible to attempt to isolate and treat all such carriers—not only because they were too numerous, but also because their detection would have demanded an altogether impracticable number of stool examinations (namely, something like six examinations of every member of the army, in order to detect about 90 per cent. of the carriers). From the practical point of view it thus became clear that attention ought to be concentrated upon the patients with dysenteric symptoms and upon the convalescent carriers, since all such cases required correct diagnosis and treatment in order to rid them of their infections and permit of their return to the army at the earliest moment.

It also became clear at this time that all the figures relating to the incidence of infection with *E. histolytica*—and other intestinal protozoa also—were more or less untrustworthy as indications of the relative frequency of infection and of the prevalence of amœbic dysentery in the various theatres of military operations. All the figures were derived from the study of the returning convalescents, and no investigation had been made of the intestinal fauna of these patients before they went abroad and contracted dysentery. Many of the carriers detected on their return home were, moreover, almost certainly contact carriers; that is to say, just the class which, if present among the troops before they went abroad, would, as they displayed no symptoms of infection, inevitably have been overlooked. Whenever and wherever dysenteric convalescents were examined by competent protozoologists, carriers of *E. histolytica* were more or less abundantly discovered—even among patients who had never been in any countries save

England and France ; and on the other hand, carriers appeared to exist almost equally plentifully among patients who were invalided home for wounds and non-intestinal diseases, and occurred even among patients who had never suffered at any time from dysentery or any bowel disorders.   Taking all the facts into consideration, it became almost certain, therefore, that carriers of *E. histolytica* must occur, albeit unsuspected, among the normal healthy residents in the British Isles.

It was not until 1917 that the protozoologists in England succeeded in examining a sufficient number of British residents to afford an indication of the proportion of contact carriers among the general population.   The first results were obtained by the group of workers at the Liverpool School of Tropical Medicine and were published in June 1917.   They showed that out of a series of persons (nearly 350) who had never left Britain, about 3 per cent. were infected with *E. histolytica*.   Later work, chiefly carried out by Matthews and Malins Smith, greatly extended these observations and finally placed the matter beyond all doubt.   It will suffice to note here that the results of all the investigations undertaken with a similar object in view (see p. 305 *infra*) have now shown conclusively that *E. histolytica* occurs normally in the population of Britain, and with a frequency which does not appear to be much below that ascertained for the majority of dysenteric convalescents invalided to England from abroad.   These conclusions naturally threw an entirely new light on the previously reported findings.

In May 1918, the Director-General, Army Medical Service, appointed a Committee on Dysentery, " for the purpose of investigating problems in connection with the incidence and segregation of cases of amœbic and bacillary dysentery, more especially with relation to the disposal of carriers, and such other problems as may be placed before it."   The Committee consisted of Sir William Leishman (Chairman), Major F. W. Andrewes, Lieut.-Colonel G. S. Buchanan, Professor C. Dobell, Sir Walter Fletcher and Dr. G. T. Western (Secretary).   They held a number of meetings at the War Office during the rest of the year, and discussed in detail the special problem placed before them, with a view to amending the existing Army Council Instructions relating to dysentery and the disposal of dysenteric convalescents.   Before their proposals could be made effective, however, the war came to an end, and under the new conditions consequent upon the armistice, the reorganization of the machinery for dealing with dysentery in the United

Kingdom ceased to be a matter of urgent military importance. New instructions were, however, issued, and certain improvements thereby effected.

One of the first subjects discussed by the Committee was the question of the occurrence of amœbic carriers among the general population, and it was decided that further investigations should, if possible, be undertaken to determine this problem with certainty. Professor Dobell was invited to institute further inquiries, with the aid of the civilian protozoologists then available, and work was begun immediately at Bristol, Brighton, Birmingham, Reading, Leeds and Sheffield. The results finally obtained, together with those of the Liverpool workers, form the subject of a report issued by the Medical Research Council*. The results were in agreement with those previously obtained, and will be considered in more detail later.

Meantime, much good work was being done in Mesopotamia under the supervision of Lieut.-Colonel J. C. G. Ledingham, Consultant Bacteriologist to the Force, who first visited the country as a member of the Medical Advisory Committee in 1916. The results obtained there by Captains T. K. Boney and L. G. Crossman, with Lieutenant C. L. Boulenger, have been published (1918). These workers were of opinion that in Mesopotamia amœbic dysentery had " been responsible for a great deal of sickness," but they considered that the bacillary form was " of even commoner occurrence."

The Medical Advisory Committee, who had arrived in Mesopotamia in September 1916 from the Mediterranean area, had reported " that bacillary dysentery is the predominant type in Mesopotamia (*as in other war areas*) and there is little doubt that had the cases investigated been in the main local admissions instead of transfers from up river the proportion of bacteriologically proved bacillary cases would have been still higher." Boulenger, who subsequently performed most of the protozoological work, found that out of 890 cases examined, 142 (approximately 16 per cent.) were infected with *E. histolytica ;* but of 309 cases of clinical dysentery, passing blood and mucus, 80 (26 per cent.) showed active amœbæ containing red blood corpuscles in their stools. In 209 of the cases in which no amœbæ were found, the mucus was plated out and dysentery bacilli were found in 101 (*i.e.*, 50 per cent. of the sample or 35 per cent. of the total cases). Boney, Crossman and Boulenger were of the opinion, however, that the remaining 39 per. cent. were also bacillary, in spite of the fact that no *B. dysenteriae* were isolated.

* Special Report Series, No. 59, 1921.

Ledingham has published (1920) an elaborate analysis of these and other laboratory results obtained in Mesopotamia, and has described the laboratory organization in detail. He divides the cases of enteritis into two groups—" blood and mucus " and " non-blood and mucus " ; and by means of tables and charts shows the difference in incidence of the two types of dysentery in British and Indian troops at the front and at the base. He also is of opinion that bacillary dysentery caused the epidemic rises, though amœbic dysentery was responsible for a considerable proportion of the steady admissions all the year round.

From January to December 1918, notifications of dysentery, colitis and diarrhœa numbered 25,642, and the total number of cases examined in the laboratories was 24,667. Table V shows the recorded incidence of amœbic infection.

TABLE V.

	Average general incidence of dysentery per 10,000.	Amœbic general incidence per 10,000.
Last quarter, 1917	83·3	22·00
First quarter, 1918	15·1	5·33
Second quarter, 1918	48·5	10·76
Third quarter, 1918	35·3	10·01
Fourth quarter, 1918	70·03	16·6

Ledingham further concluded that in British troops in forward areas the amœbic incidence was very low, and very clear evidence was available of the negligible part played by *E. histolytica* in the spring and autumn outbreaks of dysentery. Among Indian troops in forward areas amœbic dysentery played a much greater part, but here also Indian epidemic dysentery in the strict sense was not, any more than British, occasioned by *E. histolytica*. Ledingham considered, however, that there could be " no question " that the high rate of " endemic " dysentery among Indian troops was " mainly of amœbic origin in the forward area." Among British troops in Basra base area, the epidemics were also bacillary, though in non-epidemic periods amœbic dysentery is said to have accounted for one-half of the cases.

Captain W. MacAdam (1917) who, with Assistant-Surgeon R. Keelan, examined some 2,000 convalescents from Mesopotamia in India, found that of hospital cases (*i.e.*, men who had been admitted for diseases other than dysentery), 13·6 per cent. were carriers of *E. histolytica ;* whereas among men living in an adjacent depôt, and who had been discharged from hospital, 17·6 per cent. were found to be carriers. These figures were obtained as a result of making only a single examination of each case. An examination of 595 convalescents in this depôt gave the following results :—

TABLE VI.

	Number examined.	Amœbic carriers.	Percentage.
Class A— (No dysentery)	154	19	12·3
Class B— (Remote history of dysentery or diarrhœa.)	246	49	19·9
Class C— (Recently discharged from hospital as " negative " after dysentery.)	195	38	19·4

Twenty carriers were treated hypodermically with emetine and after treatment obtained an average of five negative examinations apiece before being discharged to the depôt. Of these, however, 10 relapsed in one week, 5 relapsed in two weeks, and only 3 remained clear as long as examinations were continued. MacAdam did not consider that these men had been re-infected, and he pointed out that his findings constituted an obvious criticism of the policy pursued at home in regard to the segregation of healthy carriers of *E. histolytica.* At this time, however, everyone was agreed that where the general population of a country was heavily infected with *E. histolytica,* as in India or Egypt, there was little use in segregating healthy soldier carriers, and MacAdam's results with emetine treatment contained nothing novel for the workers in England. Nevertheless, a policy of segregation was still considered advisable under the conditions prevailing at home.

Dr. H. M. Woodcock, Protozoologist to the Mediterranean Expeditionary Force, has published (1917) the results of his work in Egypt. From June to November 1916 he studied 659 cases of dysentery and diarrhœa, of which 378 were in British troops and 281 were Indians. His findings are shown in Table VII.

TABLE VII.

	Total findings of *E. histolytica*.	Percentage of total cases.	Percentage total dysentery.	Percentage of blood and mucus stools.
British (378) ..	7	1·9	2·4	4·0
Indian (281) ..	44	15·7	12·4	26·5

Woodcock gives it as his opinion that " dysentery among the British cases examined was, with few exceptions, *not* amœbic, but due to some bacillary infection." Amœbic dysentery, on the other hand, occurred " far more frequently " among the Indian troops. The stools of 134 normal Indians were examined, and no fewer than 27 (20 per cent.) contained cysts of *E. histolytica*. Woodcock regards it as "probable that . . . . Indian troops were largely responsible for the outbreak of amœbic dysentery among the troops in Egypt and on the Peninsula in 1915," but such a conclusion now appears to be quite unwarranted.

Much work was also done abroad by other workers, whose results cannot be considered here in detail. But the work of the late Lieutenant Bentham in Malta (published in 1920), of Captain F. W. O'Connor in Egypt and Palestine (1919), and of Lieutenant J. Ramsbottom at Salonika may be particularly noted here, in addition to the work of others already mentioned.

During the latter part of the war an immense amount of work was, indeed, done by the protozoological workers both at home and abroad. Records of this work are now for the most part published ; but the published records represent only a fraction of the work actually accomplished. An enormous aggregate of examinations of excreta was amassed, the examiners spending long and laborious days over this very trying task. In addition to the detection of carriers, the examinations were also made with the object of determining the effect of drugs in curing amœbic dysentery and the carrier condition; and it was demonstrated that although hypodermic injections of emetine are useful in controlling actual dysenteric attacks, the alkaloid administered in this form is of far less value for completely eradicating an infection. On the other hand, emetine bismuthous iodide, when properly administered, was found to " clear " a considerable proportion of the cases, although in some instances even three or four courses of this drug failed to cure. The administration of the drug in its

AMŒBIC DYSENTERY 301

most efficacious form was attended by very unpleasant symptoms and was very unpopular with the patients—many of the men, indeed, refusing further treatment after one course.

In view of the fact that there were probably many carriers of *E. histolytica* among the other patients in the hospitals, and, indeed, nearly as many among the population in the towns to which the men would proceed on furlough, the futility of segregating healthy carriers and retaining them in hospital until they had been definitely cleared, is now obvious. This was pointed out by Wenyon and O'Connor in 1916, when they were working in Egypt, where, as they demonstrated, the natives are probably heavily infected with *E. histolytica*—much more heavily, apparently, than were the dysenteric convalescents in hospital. It was also indicated by the experience gained in the hospitals and depôts in England, and by the work of MacAdam in India. The problem of the amœbic carrier has now resolved itself, indeed, into a mere question of expediency. In view of the facts, now ascertained, that epidemics of amœbic dysentery do not occur ; that carriers of *E. histolytica* are present in the population of every country yet examined ; that they occur with a frequency which was formerly quite unsuspected ; that they seldom show any clinical signs of their infection, and that they can be cured only by protracted and carefully controlled treatment ; it can now be definitely stated that the laborious detection, segregation and treatment of amœbic carriers is unquestionably, from the military standpoint, inexpedient.

It cannot, however, be maintained that all the work carried out in this connexion during the war was useless and unnecessary. In 1914 there were, indeed, people who said that carriers could be discharged without risk, but nobody could support such a statement with any cogent evidence or with good reasons for his belief. It was merely a supposition. But the work subsequently done has, for the first time, provided facts which supply a solid foundation for future action. The incidence of amœbic carriers generally is now approximately known ; the protozoal fauna of the human intestine has now been investigated in minute detail ; diagnosis and treatment have consequently reached a degree of perfection quite unattainable in 1914. Whether the matter is considered from the military, the medical, or the purely scientific standpoint, therefore, there can be no doubt that the nation owes much to those investigators who devoted themselves during the war to the study of the problems associated with amœbic dysentery.

Scientific Results of the Investigations carried out during the War.

It has already been noted that the researches carried out in connexion with the study of amœbic dysentery during the war led to no very novel conclusions. The work, as a whole, was rather one of consolidation and further advance from positions already won. Considered from this standpoint, therefore, much of the work accomplished might appear, at first sight, almost superfluous. This, however, is not the case ; for although much of the " new " knowledge can be traced back to remote beginnings, and many recent " discoveries " were made long before the war, it must not be forgotten that the earlier " knowledge " was so embedded in mistakes and misconceptions that its real value has only now become apparent. What is now, in many cases, certain knowledge, established upon convincing and abundant new evidence, was before the war merely one of many different views, none of which could be said with certainty to be either right or wrong. The great value of the recent work, as a whole, consists in the mass of the evidence which it has brought forward—evidence which, when properly interpreted, answers many an old and vexed question, and probably answers it finally.

During the war contributions have been made to our knowledge of the histopathology and morbid anatomy of amœbiasis ; to our knowledge of the distribution and occurrence of the parasite concerned, as already noted ; and more especially to our knowledge of the life and activities of the parasite itself, and of the lives of the other protozoa with which it is so frequently associated in the human intestine. Much information has also been acquired on the subject of treatment.

Histopathology and Morbid Anatomy.—Much work was done during the war in the *post-mortem* examination of fatal cases of dysentery, notably in Egypt by Bartlett and by Manson-Bahr. Some of the conclusions of the former were not, however, supported by other workers, and there is now no doubt that his estimate of the frequency of amœbic dysentery on the Gallipoli Peninsula was a mistaken one. Possibly some of the cases which he described were fatal cases of bacillary dysentery, or paratyphoid B infection involving the large bowel, complicated by the presence of small typical ulcers of amœbic origin—*i.e.*, in carriers of *E. histolytica*.

Bartlett (1917) distinguishes five types of amœbic lesion in. the large intestine :—

(1) *Minute nodules with an injected margin* ; generally about the size of a pin-head. There is no break in the surface of the mucosa.

(2) *Minute nodules with a yellow necrotic or ulcerated centre and injected margin.* Microscopically necrosis of the mucosa and muscularis mucosæ is seen, with slight infiltration with lymphocytes, plasma cells, and neutrophil leucocytes. There is also dilatation of the blood-vessels, with desquamation of the endothelium. The tissues are separated by œdema.

(3) *Larger nodules and " bouton de chemise " ulcers,* varying in size from 0·5 to 1·5 cm. in diameter. Such nodules may be covered by intact congested mucous membrane, and on section gelatinous yellow debris is found in the submucosa. In the more advanced lesions the mucosa, muscularis mucosæ, and the whole thickness of the submucosa may be involved, the ulcer extending laterally beneath the mucosa. Later the muscle coat may be involved in the necrosis. There is gelatinous yellow or grey debris in the base and under the margins of the ulcer. This is the classical " amœbic ulcer." Microscopically the necrotic debris consists of dead tissue cells, fibrils, inflammatory cells, etc. The neighbouring submucous, mucosal, and muscular tissues show serous exudation with fibrin formation and some red corpuscles. The tissue cells are generally swollen and degenerate, and their nuclei show chromatolysis, while the tissues generally show infiltration with lymphocytes, plasma cells, a few neutrophil leucocytes, and some mast cells. Amœbæ are usually present in the submucosa, and may also be seen in the muscle and subserosa ; more rarely they may be found in the mucosa. Moreover, they may be surrounded by intact tissues, showing no inflammatory reaction. The vessels are more or less dilated, and their endothelium damaged and desquamated. The tissues generally are rarefied by œdema.

(4) *Undermined rounded or transverse oval ulcers.* These are larger ulcers found in the latter stages and may be of considerable size. They are merely a further stage in development of the preceding type.

(5) *Confluent ulceration,* which may be of two forms : (a) produced by the coalescence of close-set ulcers of the third type ; (b) produced by confluence of lesions of a more sparsely scattered type.

It must be confessed that these descriptions do not add much to knowledge of the morbid anatomy of the disease, as the typical amœbic ulcerations of the large intestine had already been carefully described by Councilman and Lafleur, Dopter, Kuenen, Rogers and others. Moreover, Bartlett's interpretations of his findings are by no means always above criticism, and may most profitably be read in conjunction with the observations of Manson-Bahr and Willmore (1918).

The old conception of the invasion of the tissues by the amœbæ was that the parasites, by means of their pseudopodia, push their way among and between the body cells ; but recent work has shown that the amœbæ lying in close contact with the epithelial cells multiply by division, secrete a cytolysin which dissolves the cells, and thus come to lie in small pools of histolysed tissue, which they absorb as nourishment. They continue to multiply rapidly, and so make their way into the tissues.*

Bartlett's *post-mortem* examinations have confirmed the earlier work of Musgrave (1910) and others in showing that amœbic ulceration of the gut may be present in the absence of

---

* *Cf.* Dobell (1919).

clinical signs of dysentery. It is now certain, indeed, from what is known of the life of the parasite, that erosion or ulceration of the lining of the large bowel must occur even in the outwardly " healthy " contact carrier.

As Dobell points out, it is not to the advantage of a true parasite to destroy its host, but rather to live in harmony with him. When the amœbæ are carried from the gut to other organs, such as the brain or liver, they cause diseases in their host and also harm themselves; for they are there cut off from the outer world and are unable to complete their life-cycle as they normally do, in the lumen of the gut, by encystation. Only the active forms of the amœbæ are found in liver or brain abscesses—never the encysted forms; and whenever they are found in these situations the parasites have evidently gone astray. It is only in the gut of the more or less " healthy " carrier that they can complete their development.

Cases of liver abscess, due to E. histolytica, have been observed, and some of them have been described, during the war; but on the whole this well-known sequel of amœbic infection has not been frequently seen. A single case of amœbic abscess of the brain has been described by Armitage (1919) and Stout and Fenwick (1918), and at least one other appears to have occurred (Faulds, 1916). This condition had previously been carefully studied by Kartulis (1904), Legrand (1912), and others. It is extremely rare, having been hitherto reported in only about fifty cases, some of which are very doubtful.

Geographical Distribution of Entamoeba histolytica.—Before the war it was generally believed, if not explicitly stated, that amœbic dysentery was a disease of the tropics, and it appeared a natural corollary of this assumption that the parasite responsible for the disease was likewise limited in its distribution. One of the striking results of the work carried out during the war has been the demonstration that both these suppositions were unfounded.

It has already been noted that carriers of E. histolytica were found to exist among non-dysenteric convalescents in the military hospitals as early as 1916, and the findings of Dobell (1916), soon confirmed and extended by those of Malins Smith and Matthews (1917) in England, and of Wenyon and O'Connor (1917) in Egypt, have already been quoted. In many of these carriers it was found that not only were they free from intestinal symptoms at the time of examination, but careful inquiry led further to the conclusion that they had never at any previous period suffered from intestinal disease attributable to their infection. They were, in other words, contact carriers, as defined by Walker. Moreover, while it was natural to suppose that such carriers, when detected among patients from Gallipoli, Egypt, and the tropics generally, had acquired their infections in these foreign parts, yet the whole subject assumed a different complexion when it was found later that similar carriers were arriving in England from France. Most of those detected had, it is true, been invalided from France with dysentery ; but it was already known at that time, from the careful bacteriological work conducted on the Western front, that an overwhelming proportion of the dysentery occurring there was bacillary. At this time Dobell estimated from his own findings, from the medical records of patients, and from information supplied by medical officers at the front, that not more than 2 per cent. of the total dysentery in France was amœbic ; whereas, on the other hand, it was certain that a much larger percentage—of the order of 12 to 20 per cent.—of the dysenteric patients invalided to England were actually infected with *E. histolytica*. The incidence was high—probably not less than 10 to 12 per cent.—even among patients who had never been in any countries save England and France.

These and similar observations showed that it was necessary to obtain more exact information concerning the incidence of infection with *E. histolytica* among healthy troops and among British residents who had never been abroad, and efforts were therefore made to obtain this information. Investigations were begun in Liverpool by A. Malins Smith, J. R. Matthews and Dr. Doris L. Mackinnon in 1917. In conjunction with Professor Warrington Yorke and H. F. Carter, they published a preliminary account of their findings in June of that year. Summarizing their results, they then stated : " Of 344 persons who had never been out of Great Britain at least ten (2·9 per cent.) harboured in their fæces cysts morphologically indistinguishable from those of *E. histolytica*." This work was continued by Matthews and Malins Smith, and is embodied in a series of important reports now published (1919).

It has already been mentioned that soon after the return of Sir William Leishman from France in 1918 a Dysentery Committee was formed at the War Office ; and this Committee recommended that an examination of the excreta of recruits and others who had never been out of England should at once be undertaken with a view to confirming and extending the work of the Liverpool observers. This investigation was accordingly carried out under the supervision of Professor

Dobell at the 2nd Southern General Hospital, Bristol ; 2nd/1st Southern General Hospital, Birmingham ; Reading War Hospital; Leeds and Sheffield Military Hospitals; and the Kitchener Hospital, Brighton.

The results have been fully recorded and analysed by Dobell in Special Report Series, No. 59, of the Medical Research Council, 1921, where the earlier results of the Liverpool workers are also reviewed.

The reports of the Liverpool workers give the results obtained in the examination of a large number of British residents, who had never been abroad, belonging to the following classes: (1) civilians in an infirmary, (2) army recruits, (3) children, (4) asylum patients, (5) university and school cadets. Infections with *E. histolytica*, ranging from 1·5 per cent. (infirmary patients) to 9·7 per cent. (asylum patients), were found in all these series. More than one thousand young army recruits who had never been out of England were examined, and although only one examination per case was possible, no less than 5·6 per cent. were found to be infected with *E. histolytica*.

Goodey at Birmingham examined the excreta of 101 patients undergoing treatment for phthisis in a sanatorium, and found six to be infected with *E. histolytica*. None of these people had been abroad, and none gave a history of dysentery.

At Brighton Thacker found two infected persons in 69 examined. One of these infected persons, however, had been abroad.

Campbell at Bristol examined 178 adults and 49 children who had never been abroad, and found 3·3 per cent. of the former infected with *E. histolytica* and 2 per cent. of the latter.

At Leeds Miss Nutt examined a total of 461 persons—333 adults, of whom 1·2 per cent. were infected, and 128 children, of whom 1·6 per cent. were infected. The same worker examined 168 persons, who had never been abroad, at Sheffield, and found 5·3 per cent. of the children and 1·8 per cent. of the adults infected with *E. histolytica*.

In the course of this work the stools of over 3,000 persons who had never been abroad were examined, and altogether 3·4 per cent. of these people were found to be infected with *E. histolytica*, notwithstanding that most of them were examined only once. From the figures obtained Dobell calculates that probably from 7 to 10 per cent. of the general population of Great Britain are infected with this parasite. It should be added that *E. histolytica* was not the only protozoon studied

during these inquiries. All the other common intestinal protozoa were found, and their frequency approximately determined.
From results published elsewhere, moreover, it appears probable
that Britain does not occupy a peculiar position in respect to
the frequency of infection with intestinal protozoa. Dobell
points out that this means, for one thing, that everyone must
consume food and drink which has been more or less exposed
to contamination with human fæces.

After summarizing the foregoing work and reviewing it from
its various aspects, Dobell emphasizes the following points :
(1) Though *E. histolytica* is, or may be, the cause of human
disease, it is usually comparatively harmless to the persons it
inhabits—at all events in a population in which it has been
long established. (2) The parasite occurs commonly in Britain
in the resident indigenous population, but to the majority of
its hosts it causes little or no inconvenience. (3) It is probably
not a new or recently imported parasite, but at least as old an
inhabitant of these islands as the British nation. (4) As it
has, apparently, caused but little trouble in the past, it is not
likely to cause much in the future. Its prevalence therefore
need not be regarded with alarm. (5) Although *E. histolytica*
is, as a rule, practically innocuous, it is harmful and even
dangerous to certain abnormally susceptible people. Consequently, in the future it will be necessary even in England to
remember *E. histolytica* as a possible ætiological factor when
cases of dysentery, chronic diarrhœa, ulcerative colitis, or
other intestinal ailments are met with, and to remember it
also when patients with hepatitis and similar disorders are
seen.

The foregoing researches, taken in conjunction with others
made in other parts of the world, now make it appear certain
that the " dysentery amœba," *E. histolytica*, is not restricted
to the tropics, but has, in all probability, a geographical distribution co-extensive with that of man. It is not a recent
intruder into Britain or Britons, but an age-long companion
of the human species.

The Intestinal Amœbæ of Man.—During the war the
greatest advances effected in connexion with amœbic
dysentery have been those made in our knowledge of the
protozoa which live in the human intestine. Several new forms
of these have been discovered in the course of the routine
examination of a vast number of stools, and many previously
known species have been restudied in great detail. Much new
light has been thrown upon the morphology and life-histories

of all of them, and the whole subject has been thoroughly
revised and placed, for the first time, on a sound scientific
basis.

About seventeen species of intestinal protozoa are now known
to inhabit the intestine of man, and a full account of them,
based largely upon observations made during the war, has
recently been published by Dobell and O'Connor (1921). One
group of these organisms—the amœbæ—has also been dealt
with recently in a special monograph by Dobell (1919). So
much is now known about all these protozoa that it is impossible to attempt to summarize this knowledge here. Further
information will be found in the two works just mentioned,
and only the main lines along which progress has been made
will be noted here.

Before the war it was generally believed that man harbours
two species of amœba in his intestine—the pathogenic
Entamoeba histolytica and the non-pathogenic *E. coli*. In
reality there are at least five species, but three of these, all
non-pathogenic, were first correctly recognized and described
by British protozoologists during the war. A brief account of
all these forms will now be given, with special reference to
the recent additions to knowledge which have resulted from
these investigations. It is hardly necessary to emphasize
the importance of these investigations: for, quite apart from
their scientific value, all additions to knowledge of the intestinal
amœbæ and other protozoa of man are obviously of considerable
medical importance. Without an accurate knowledge of the
lives and habits of the intestinal protozoa, the diagnosis,
treatment and prophylaxis of a disease such as amœbic dysentery can never be ordered scientifically and effectively.

(1) *Entamoeba histolytica* Schaudinn.—The life-history of this
important species is now known in considerable detail, and
recent work has shown that the account of its development
given by Walker (1911, 1913) was essentially correct. The
parasite lives in the large intestine of man, where it nourishes
itself at the expense of the tissues. After multiplying by
division in this situation, the amœbæ secrete cysts round
themselves and pass out with the fæces. These cysts, when
swallowed, hatch in the intestine, and the amœbæ which escape
from them then establish themselves in the large bowel and so
give rise to a new infection. Neither the amœbæ nor their
cysts are capable of developing outside the human body.

The adult amœbæ (Fig. 1, *1*) have been carefully re-described
by Dobell (1919), who has also given the first detailed

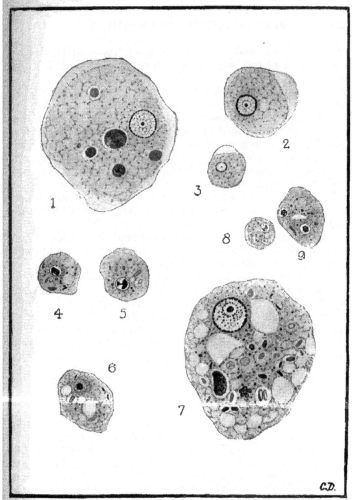

Fig. 1.—1, *Entamœba histolytica*, large active individual from a case of acute amœbic dysentery. Note the clear ectoplasm, the nucleus (with fine beads of chromatin at its periphery, and a small central karyosome), and the remains of several ingested red blood corpuscles in the cytoplasm.

2, 3, Precystic forms (*i.e.*, small individuals about to encyst) of *E. histolytica* belonging to strains forming large and small cysts respectively.

4, 5, Two individuals of *Endolimax nana*. Note the nuclei especially, with their large irregular karyosomes.

6, *Iodamœba bütschlii*. Note the nucleus, containing a large round central karyosome, surrounded by a single layer of minute achromatic granules.

7, *Entamœba coli*. A large individual showing the chief characters distinctive of this species (bulky granular cytoplasm, with many ingested bacteria and other food inclusions; large vesicular nucleus with conspicuous chromatin beads at periphery, and eccentric karyosome, etc.). Compare with 1.

8, 9, *Dientamœba fragilis*, uninucleate and typical binucleate individuals respectively. Note the structure of the nuclei, with their large central karyosomes composed of distinct granules.

description of their method of multiplication in the intestine. Innumerable observations have now established the truth of the contention of Wenyon and others that this species is the only one—of those living in man—which ingests red blood corpuscles. This fact is of great practical importance, since the presence of red corpuscles in the body of the amœbæ constitutes a readily recognizable diagnostic character.

The cysts of this species (Fig. 2, *1–7*) have also been re-described by Wenyon, Dobell and others, and their differential characters accurately determined (*cf.* Wenyon 1915, Wenyon and O'Connor 1917, Dobell 1919, Dobell and O'Connor 1921, etc.). It has also been shown, for the first time, that this species consists of a number of distinct races or strains, which differ from one another by the dimensions of their cysts. Strains have been shown to exist in which the average diameter of the cysts ranges from about 7μ to about 15μ (*cf.* Fig. 2, *1–7*). This is a point of great practical importance; for while the strains forming cysts about 12μ in diameter have long been recognized, those with larger or smaller cysts have often escaped notice, or been referred to other species; and consequently many of the earlier records dealing with the occurrence of *E. histolytica* are vitiated by omissions and mistakes in identification. The smaller-sized cysts were, indeed, universally overlooked until 1916, notwithstanding the fact that they are probably no less common than those of the larger sizes. (*cf.* Wenyon and O'Connor 1917, Dobell and Jepps 1918, Dobell 1919, etc.)

Since the cysts are responsible for the conveyance of the parasite from one host to another, the conditions necessary for their survival and transportation have naturally received considerable attention. It has been established that they are unable to survive desiccation, though they can remain alive and apparently unharmed in water or damp fæces for a period of at least several weeks. Their long survival in water seems to indicate this medium as one of the usual channels by which infection is transmitted. Wenyon and O'Connor studied the effects of various disinfectants upon the cysts, and found, *inter alia*, that chlorine in the strengths employed for the sterilization of drinking water, does not kill—or, apparently, even injure—the cysts of *E. histolytica*. This is obviously a point of considerable interest to the army sanitarian. Wenyon and O'Connor have shown, further, that the cysts of this parasite, and of the other intestinal protozoa, can be dispersed by houseflies. When a fly feeds upon fæces containing living cysts, they pass unharmed through the fly's body, and may be redeposited, still living, with the fly's own excrement upon any object on which it defæcates. How far the fly thus assists in the spread of infection is still disputed, but the observations, which have since been confirmed, are undoubtedly of sanitary importance.

(2) *Entamoeba coli* Casagrandi & Barbagallo.—The large harmless amœba of the human colon (Fig. 1, 7) is now better known from the recent work of Wenyon and Dobell. The characters differentiating it from the preceding species have been more precisely determined, and the general outline of its life-cycle established (*cf.* the drawings on Figs. 1 and 2 with those of the other species). As a specially noteworthy point, it may be added that Matthews has shown that in *E. coli*, as in *E. histolytica*, there are several different strains which can be distinguished from one another by the dimensions of their cysts.

It may also be added that the conditions of survival outside the body, and the method of transmission from host to host, are similar to those noted under the preceding species ; and, further, that the observations on British residents have shown that this organism is very common in people who have never been abroad, of whom some 30 to 50 per cent. appear to be infected.

(3) *Endolimax nana* (Wenyon & O'Connor) Brug.—This is a very small non-pathogenic amœba distinguishable from the species of *Entamoeba* by its nuclear structure and cysts. (See Figs. 1, *4, 5*, and 2, *10–12*). It usually measures 7μ to 10μ in diameter when rounded, with a nucleus usually measuring about 2μ in diameter. The nucleus has a delicate membrane, which is not studded with beads of chromatin, and a rather large and irregularly-shaped karyosome.

The cysts (Fig. 2, *10–12*) are typically oval, measuring 8μ to 9μ in length. They contain, when first formed, a single nucleus, which gives rise to four, by two successive divisions, in the mature cyst. The cysts can easily be distinguished from the small cysts of *E. histolytica* by the structure of their nuclei and the absence of chromatoid bodies.

This species was first distinguished and described by Wenyon and O'Connor, and has also been carefully studied by Dobell and others. It was shortly afterwards—almost simultaneously—rediscovered by workers in the Dutch East Indies. It has also been found by the British workers to occur fairly commonly in the British population.

(4) *Iodamoeba bütschlii* (Prowazek) Dobell.—The amœbæ of this species (Fig. 1, *6*) resemble when alive small specimens of *E. coli* or large ones of *E. nana*. They usually measure

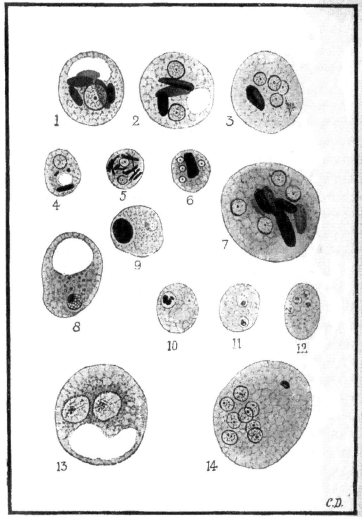

Fig. 2.—1-7, Cysts of *Entamœba histolytica*. 1, 2, 3, uninucleate, binucleate and quadrinucleate (ripe) cysts respectively, belonging to a strain forming cysts of medium size (12μ to 13·5μ). 4, 5, 6, three similar cysts of a strain forming small cysts (7μ to 8μ). 7, 4-nucleate cyst of a strain forming large cysts (*ca.* 15μ). Note the conspicuous chromatoid bodies.

8, 9, Mature cysts of *Iodamœba bütschlii*. These cysts are uninucleate and contain a large mass of glycogen, represented by a space (from which it has been dissolved) in 8, and as a darkly stained inclusion in 9.

10, 11, 12, Uninucleate, binucleate and quadrinucleate cysts respectively of *Endolimax nana*. Note their oval shape, characteristic nuclei and the absence of chromatoid bodies. Compare with 4, 5, 6.

13, 14, Binucleate and 8-nucleate (mature) cysts of *Entamœba coli*. Note the nuclei, etc. The large space in 13 is occupied during life by a large mass of glycogen, very characteristic of the (immature) binucleate cysts of this species. Compare these cysts with those of *E. histolytica* (2, 3, 5, 6, 7).

about 8μ to 12μ in diameter. Their movements are usually feeble, and the organisms quickly die and disintegrate when passed out of the intestine. The most distinctive feature is the vesicular nucleus, which has a delicate membrane and contains a large and rounded central karyosome. Between this karyosome and the nuclear membrane there is always a zone occupied by a layer of fine granules, which stain feebly with chromatin stains but readily with plasma stains such as eosin.

The cysts (Fig. 2, 9) are uninucleate and usually measure from about 9μ to 12μ in diameter, but are very commonly irregular in shape. They usually contain a large sharply-defined mass of glycogen, which stains deep brown with iodine.

The characteristic cysts of this species were described by Wenyon in 1915, who called them "iodine cysts" or "I. cysts" on account of the distinctive staining of their contained glycogen in iodine solution. They were subsequently identified by Dobell and Jepps as the cysts of an amoeba, which was later described by Dobell in 1919 and assigned to a species previously named by Prowazek. This amoeba was discovered and studied independently by Dutch workers in the East Indies at about the same time.

I. bütschlii appears to be relatively uncommon in man, and the recent discovery of a closely similar organism in the pig by O'Connor (1920) and others raises the question whether it may not really be a parasite of pigs, which only occasionally and accidentally occurs in man. The organism has been found in man in England, and is said to occur in the pig in France and Germany.

(5) *Dientamoeba fragilis* Jepps & Dobell.—This is a small and rare species distinguished from the others by being typically binucleate. (Fig. 1, 9). It usually measures from about 5μ to 11μ in diameter. Its movements are snail-like and it is extremely delicate, soon dying outside the body. The organism feeds upon bacteria which are usually present in vacuoles in the endoplasm, and it appears to be quite harmless. The two nuclei are identical in structure, each consisting of a minute vesicle about 1·5μ to 2μ in diameter, with a central karyosome composed of a number of chromatin granules. A clear zone containing no granules lies between the karyosome and the delicate nuclear membrane. In addition to the binucleate forms, uninucleate individuals also occur, their nuclei being structurally identical. (Fig. 1, 8).

The cysts of this species are so far unknown, having been sought for hitherto in vain.

This species was found and first described by Jepps and Dobell in 1918, though it had been previously seen by Wenyon. It has already been found in at least one person who has never been out of the British Isles.

General Conclusions.

From the work accomplished during the war the following general conclusions may be drawn :—

(1) It has been shown that the distribution of the amœba pathogenic to man, *E. histolytica*, is world-wide.

(2) This parasite is readily spread from man to man, even where sanitary conditions are considered satisfactory ; while, where sanitary conditions are unsatisfactory, the rate of infection may be very high.

(3) In the vast majority of cases the infected people become healthy carriers ; it is only exceptionally that they develop amœbic dysentery or an amœbic abscess in any organ.

(4) Amœbic diseases do not occur epidemically, but cases appear to be considerably commoner in tropical and sub-tropical than in cold and temperate countries.

(5) It is obvious, as a result of the work detailed here, that carriers of amœbæ can be set free in a community without grave risk to that community, in spite of the fact that the dangerous person, *qua* infection, is the carrier and not the actual case of acute dysentery.

(6) The detection, isolation and treatment of healthy carriers are, therefore, not essential ; but in future campaigns part of the armamentarium of the medical laboratory worker must be an accurate knowledge of the amœbæ of man, in order that rapid and correct diagnosis and appropriate treatment of acute cases of amœbic dysentery may be assured.

REFERENCES.

Annesley ..	.. Researches into the Causes, Nature and Treatment of the more Prevalent Diseases of India, and of Warm Climates generally.	London, 1828. (2 Vols.).
Archibald, Hadfield, Logan & Campbell.	Reports of the M. and H. Laboratories dealing with the Diseases affecting the Troops in the Dardanelles.	Jl. of R.A.M.C.,1916, Vol. xxvi, p. 695.
Armitage ..	.. Amœbic Abscess of the Brain ; with Notes on a Case following Amœbic Abscess of the Liver.	Jl. of Trop. Med. & Hyg., 1919, Vol. xxii, p. 69.
Bahr & Willmore ..	Dysentery in the Mediterranean Expeditionary Force. (A reply to G.B. Bartlett.)	Quart. Jl. of Med., 1918, Vol. xi, p. 349.

Bartlett	.. ..	Pathology of Dysentery in the Mediterranean Expeditionary Force, 1915.	Quart. Jl. of Med., 1917, Vol. x, p. 185.
Bentham	.. ..	Human Intestinal Protozoal and Helminthic Infections observed in Malta.	Parasitol., 1920, Vol. xii, p. 72.
Boney, Crossman & Boulenger.		Report of a Base Laboratory in Mesopotamia for 1916, with special reference to Waterborne Diseases.	Jl. of R.A.M.C.,1918, Vol. xxx, p. 409.
Casagrandi & Barbagallo.		Ricerche biologiche e cliniche sull' *Amoeba coli* (Lösch).	Bull. Accad. Gioenia Sci. Nat. Catania, 1895, Fasc. xxxix (N.S.), p. 4 and xli, p. 7.
„	„	*Entamoeba hominis* s. *Amoeba coli* (Lösch). Studio biologico e clinico.	Ann. d'Igiene Sperim., 1897, Vol. vii, p. 103.
Councilman & Lafleur		Amœbic Dysentery.	Johns Hopkins Hosp. Rep., 1891, Vol. ii, p. 393.
Cunningham	..	A Report on Cholera.	Ann. Report of Sanitary Commissioner with Govt. of India, 1870, p. 139. (Calcutta, 1871).
„	.. ..	On the Development of certain Microscopic Organisms occurring in the Intestinal Canal.	Quart. Jl. Micro. Sci., 1881, Vol. xxi, p. 234.
Dobell	.. ..	Incidence and Treatment of *Entamoeba histolytica* Infection at Walton Hospital.	Brit. Med. Jl., 1916, Vol. ii, p. 612.
„	.. ..	Reports upon Investigations in the United Kingdom of Dysentery Cases received from the Eastern Mediterranean. 1.—Amœbic Dysentery and the Protozoological Investigation of Cases and Carriers.	M.R.C., Special Report Series, No. 4. Lond., 1917.
„	.. ..	The Amœbæ living in Man : a Zoological Monograph.	London, 1919.
„	.. ..	A Report on the Occurrence of Intestinal Protozoa in the Inhabitants of Britain.	M.R.C., Special Report Series, No. 59. Lond., 1921.
Dobell, Gettings, Jepps & Stephens.		A Study of 1,300 convalescent Cases of Dysentery from Home Hospitals.	*Ibid.*, No. 15, Lond., 1918.
Dobell & Jepps	..	A Study of the Diverse Races of *Entamoeba histolytica* distinguishable from one another by the Dimensions of their Cysts.	Parasitol., 1918, Vol. x, p. 320.
Dobell & O'Connor..		The Intestinal Protozoa of Man.	Lond., 1921.
Dobell & Stevenson..		Reports upon Investigations in the United Kingdom of Dysentery Cases received from the Eastern Mediterranean. Appendix on " The Protozoological findings in 775 Cases."	M.R.C. Special Report Series, Lond., 1917. No. 5, p. 99.
Dopter	.. ..	Anatomie pathologique de la dysenterie amibienne.	Arch. de Méd. Exp., 1907, Vol. xix, p. 505.

Douglas, Colebrook & Parry Morgan.	Report upon a Series of Cases of Dysentery received from the Mediterranean Expeditionary Force.	M.R.C. Special Report Series, Lond., 1917. No. 6, p. 27.
Faulds	Liver Abscess amongst our Soldiers.	Glasgow Med. Jl., 1916, Vol. lxxxvi, p. 337.
Jepps & Dobell ..	*Dientamoeba fragilis* n.g., n. sp., a New Intestinal Amœba from Man.	Parasitol., 1918, Vol. x, p. 352.
Kartulis	Zur Aetiologie der Leberabscesse. Lebende Dysenterie-Amöben im Eiter der dysenterischen Leberabscesse.	Centralbl. f. Bakt., 1887, Vol. ii, p. 745.
,, ...	Gehirnabszesse nach dysenterischen Leberabszessen.	*Ibid.* (Abt. I.), 1904, Vol. xxxvii, p. 527.
Koch & Gaffky ..	Bericht über die Thätigkeit der zur Erforschung der Cholera im Jahre 1883 nach Egypten und Indien entsandten Kommission.	Arb. a.d. kaiserl. Gesundheitsamte, 1887, Vol. iii, p. 1.
Kovács	Beobachtungen und Versuche über die sogenannte Amoebendysenterie.	Zeitschr. f. Heilk., 1892, Vol. xiii, p. 509.
Kruse & Pasquale ..	Untersuchungen über Dysenterie und Leberabscess.	Zietschr. f. Hyg., 1894, Vol. xvi, p. 1.
Kuenen	Die pathologische Anatomie der Amöbiasis verglichen mit anderen Formen von Dysenterie.	Arch. f. Schiffs- u. Tropenhyg., 1909, Vol. xiii (Beiheft) p. 435.
Ledingham	Dysentery and Enteric Disease in Mesopotamia from the Laboratory Standpoint.	Jl. of R.A.M.C., 1920, Vol. xxxiv., pp. 189, 306.
Ledingham, Penfold and Woodcock.	Recent Bacteriological Experiences with Typhoidal Disease and Dysentery.	Brit. Med. Jl., 1915, Vol. ii, p. 704.
Legrand	Les abcès dysentériques du cerveau (amibe encéphalique).	Arch. Provinciales de Chirurg., 1912, Vol. xxi, pp. 1, 75, 212, 625.
Lewis..	A Report on the Microscopic Objects found in Cholera Evacuations, &c.	Ann. Rept. of Sanitary Commissioner with Govt. of India, 1869. Calcutta, 1870.
Lösch..	Massenhafte Entwickelung von Amöben im Dickdarm.	Arch. f. Path. Anat., 1875, Vol. lxv, p. 196.
MacAdam & Keelan	The Problem of the Amœbic Dysentery Carrier in India and Mesopotamia, etc.	Indian Jl. Med. Res., 1917, Vol. v, p. 239.
Matthews	A Mensurative Study of the Cysts of *Entamoeba coli*.	Ann. Trop. Med. & Parasitol., 1919 Vol. xii, p. 259.
Matthews & Smith..	The Spread and Incidence of Intestinal Protozoal Infections in the Population of Great Britain. I–III.	*Ibid.*, p. 349.

Matthews & Smith .. *Idem.*, IV and V.　Ibid., 1919, Vol. xiii, p. 91.

,,　　　,,　　.. The Intestinal Protozoal Infections among Convalescent Dysenterics examined at the Liverpool School of Tropical Medicine. (Third Report.)　Ibid., p. 83.

Morehead .. .. Clinical Researches on Disease in India.　London, 1856. (2 vols.)

Musgrave .. .. Intestinal Amœbiasis without Diarrhœa. A Study of Fifty Fatal Cases.　Philippine Jl. Sci. (B.), 1910, Vol. v, p. 229.

O'Connor .. .. Intestinal Protozoa found during Acute Intestinal conditions amongst Members of the Egyptian Expeditionary Force, 1916–17.　Parasitol., 1919, Vol. xi, p. 239.

,,　　.. .. A Preliminary Note on Two Intestinal Parasites in Pigs.　Med. Jl. Australia, 1920, Vol. ii, p. 337.

Parkes .. .. Remarks on the Dysentery and Hepatitis of India.　London, 1846.

Quincke & Roos .. Ueber Amöben-Enteritis.　Berl. klin. Wochenschr., 1893, Vol. xxx, p. 1089.

Rajchman & Western Reports upon Investigations in the United Kingdom of Dysentery Cases received from the Eastern Mediterranean. II—Report upon 878 Cases of Bacillary Enteritis.　M.R.C. Special Report Series, No. 5, Lond., 1917.

Rogers .. .. Dysenteries, their Differentiation and Treatment.　London, 1913.

Schaudinn .. .. Untersuchungen über die Fortpflanzung einiger Rhizopoden.　Arb. a. d. kaiserl. Gesundheitsamte, 1903, Vol. xix, p. 547.

Smith & Matthews.. The Intestinal Protozoa of Nondysenteric Cases.　Ann. Trop. Med. & Parasitol., 1917, Vol. x, p. 361.

Stout & Fenwick .. A Case of Amœbic Abscess of the Liver and Brain with no previous History of Dysentery.　Lancet, 1918, Vol. i, p. 769.

Thomson & Mackie.. Clinical and Laboratory Researches on Dysentery in Egypt, with some Remarks on Sanitation.　Jl. of R.A.M.C.,1917, Vol. xxviii, p. 403.

Walker .. .. A Comparative Study of the Amœbæ in the Manila Water Supply, in the Intestinal Tract of Healthy Persons, and in Amœbic Dysentery.　Philippine Jl. Sci. (B. Trop. Med.), 1911, Vol. vi, p. 259.

Walker & Sellards .. Experimental Entamœbic Dysentery.　Ibid., 1913, Vol. viii, p. 253.

Wenyon .. .. Observations on the Common Intestinal Protozoa of Man : their Diagnosis and Pathogenicity.　Lancet, 1915, Vol. ii, p. 1173. See also — Jl. of R.A.M.C., 1915, Vol. xxv, p. 600.

Wenyon	The Protozoological Findings in 556 Cases of Intestinal Disorder from the Eastern Mediterranean War Area.	Jl. of R.A.M.C.,1916, Vol. xxvi, p. 445.
Wenyon & O'Connor	Human Intestinal Protozoa in the Near East. An Inquiry into some Problems affecting the Spread and Incidence of Intestinal Protozoal Infections of British Troops and Natives in the Near East, with special reference to the Carrier Question, Diagnosis and Treatment of Amœbic Dysentery, and an Account of three New Human Intestinal Protozoa.	Jl. of R.A.M.C.,1917, Vol. xxviii, p. 1 *et seq.* ; *and* London, 1917, Bale, Sons and Danielsson.
Woodcock	Protozoological Experiences during the Summer and Autumn of 1916.	Jl. of R.A.M.C.,1917, Vol. xxix, p. 290.
Yorke, Carter, Mackinnon, Matthews and Smith.	Persons who have never been out of Great Britain as Carriers of *Entamoeba histolytica.*	Ann. Trop. Med. and Parasitol., 1917, Vol. xi, p. 87.

CHAPTER XII.

BACILLARY DYSENTERY.

OWING to the defective sanitary conditions which are apt to attend the aggregation of large bodies of troops in warfare, especially during active operations, intestinal infections have always occupied a prominent position in military medicine. Enteric fever formerly shared with dysentery this ill repute, but the almost complete control of enteric fever by prophylactic inoculation during the war has left bacillary dysentery as the chief index of defective sanitation, for, except in a small experimental way, no inoculation was practised against this disease. The differences between amœbic and bacillary dysentery have been recognized for many years and it is established that the epidemic dysentery which is so formidable an accompaniment of war is of the bacillary form. In the Eastern theatres of war amœbic dysentery prevailed, indeed, in endemic fashion, but even there it is estimated that 90 per cent. of the dysentery was bacillary, while on the Western front the amount of amœbic dysentery was almost negligible, probably less than 3 per cent. of the whole.

The statistics of bacillary dysentery during the war will be found in the article on this subject in the volumes on the Diseases of the War,* where its morbid anatomy and histology have also been described. The following account is intended to deal with the bacteriological aspects of the disease. Upon this subject much new light has been thrown both by routine laboratory experience and by the special researches which have been carried out at home and abroad.

During the first eighteen months of the war there was so little dysentery on the Western front that there was almost no opportunity for its study. The Gallipoli expedition first furnished an alarming number of intestinal cases. The peculiar conditions of that expedition did not permit of an adequate study of these cases on the spot, though such laboratory work as was possible was carried on at the bases in the Ægean and in Egypt. A vast number of convalescent cases returned to England, and it was hoped that much might be learned from their careful bacteriological study. Large groups of such cases

---

* Vol. I, Chapter III.

were collected at different centres and, under the auspices of
the Medical Research Committee, a number of bacteriologists
and protozoologists set to work upon them. At the London
Hospital, 878 cases were examined by Rajchman, Western,
Collie and Ritchie ; more than 1,300 cases were studied by
Fildes at Haslar ; at St. Mary's Hospital, Douglas, Colebrook
and Morgan examined a small selected group of 29 men with
exceptional thoroughness and detail, while at Liverpool, 2,360
cases of enteritis were studied by Professor Glynn and his
assistants. The elaborate reports sent in by these observers
were published by the Medical Research Council in their
" Special Report Series," and a perusal of these reports reveals
a large number of important and often novel observations.

It must, however, be confessed that the additions to our
knowledge of dysentery were hardly commensurate with the
vast amount of labour bestowed on this work, and for this there
are several reasons. In the first place, an unselected mass of
" enteritis " cases at an advanced stage of convalescence presents very unfavourable material for study. One of the striking
bacteriological lessons of the war has been that it is the acute
case, in the earliest stage,which best repays skilled examination ;
the more nearly the laboratories were pushed up to the front the
more reliable and convincing were the data obtained. In
the second place, at this stage of the war some very important
facts about dysentery had not yet been learned ; it was not
appreciated, for instance, that the presence of cysts of *Entamœba
histolytica* in the stools by no means implied that the patient
had suffered from amœbic dysentery, nor had the various races
of Flexner dysentery bacilli been adequately studied and defined,
while the sero-diagnosis of dysentery was still in the experimental stage. The high degree of intermittence with which
the specific bacillus occurs in the stools in many dysentery
carriers was imperfectly understood ; nevertheless, in spite of,
perhaps even because of, these various drawbacks, the work
done at this stage of the war was of considerable value, less
from the actual knowledge gained than from the revelation of
the imperfection of our knowledge. It served, in fact, as a
powerful stimulus to the more fruitful researches which were
undertaken in the later years of the war.

Bacillary dysentery first appeared in any considerable amount
on the Western front during the fighting on the Somme in the
summer of 1916 and thenceforward was common, occurring
from time to time in more extensive local epidemic outbursts.
Dysentery diagnosis formed a considerable part of the work

in all bacteriological laboratories. The subject naturally engaged the keen attention of the advisers in pathology both in France and in the East. They visited the laboratories from time to time, drew the attention of the workers to new points in technique, strove to secure uniformity in the methods of work, and suggested lines for research. As data accumulated, or when special information was requested, reports were sent in by those in charge of laboratories to headquarters. Papers dealing with bacillary dysentery were also published from time to time in the medical journals.

In the autumn of 1917 Lieut.-Colonel G. S. Buchanan and Major F. W. Andrewes were sent to France on a tour of inspection in relation to dysentery, and furnished on their return a detailed report to the Director-General of the Army Medical Service. In the course of this tour ample opportunity was afforded for visiting laboratories and discussing with the actual workers the various problems connected with dysentery. Partly as the outcome of this tour, arrangements were made for an extensive study of the bacilli of epidemic dysentery in England. Captain E. G. D. Murray was already carrying on an examination of numerous strains at the Royal Army Medical College, in continuation of work already begun in Mesopotamia, and Captain A. C. Inman was detailed to collaborate with Major Andrewes at St. Bartholomew's Hospital in a serological enquiry into the dysentery strains prevalent on the Western front.

At a later date the War Office Committee on Dysentery appointed a small sub-committee to report on the bacteriology of the disease ; the members nominated were Captain S. R. Douglas, Dr. A. Eastwood of the Ministry of Health, Dr. A. D. Gardner of Oxford, Captain E. G. D. Murray, R.A.M.C., and Dr. G. T. Western of the London Hospital, under the chairmanship of Major Andrewes. This sub-committee, after a number of meetings at which all the available evidence was fully reviewed, furnished a detailed report to the War Office Dysentery Committee, which was adopted, printed and circulated for information and guidance to all military laboratories.

Meanwhile in the other theatres of war, where dysentery was vastly more prevalent and more severe in type than on the Western front, the facilities for its bacteriological study had been greatly improved from the chaotic conditions which prevailed during the Gallipoli expedition. Well-equipped laboratories were instituted, staffed by competent workers, and consultant bacteriologists were appointed to supervise the work.

Lieut.-Colonel L. S. Dudgeon served in this capacity in Macedonia, and Lieut.-Colonel J. C. G. Ledingham first in Egypt and afterwards in Mesopotamia. The conditions became such that in these fields of war, no less than in France, a good deal of research work was possible, and the consultants were of the greatest service in stimulating this, as well as in co-ordinating the work of the various laboratories. Such work, conducted on acute cases on the spot, enabled many problems to be attacked which could not effectively be studied in convalescents evacuated to England.

History of Bacillary Dysentery.

The first bacillus to be described as a cause of epidemic dysentery, as distinct from endemic amœbiasis, was that now usually known, after its discoverer, as " Shiga's bacillus." Shiga isolated it in Japan, and published his results in 1898. In Germany, Kruse confirmed this discovery and described the bacillus more accurately. Flexner and other American observers found the same organism in dysentery cases in America and in the Philippines in 1900, but at the same time they found other bacilli which presented certain dissimilarities from Shiga's bacillus. Kruse, too, studying asylum dysentery in Germany, found, as its apparent cause, bacilli unlike Shiga's organism, and he called these " pseudodysentery bacilli." A manifest difference between the two types lay in the fact that Shiga's bacillus was unable to ferment mannite and produced no indol, whereas Flexner's aberrant Philippine types and Kruse's pseudodysentery bacilli readily fermented mannite, and frequently, though not always, formed indol. The distinction was firmly established in 1902 by the serological work of Martini and Lentz. All further work has confirmed the distinctness and importance of Shiga's bacillus, which alone by the ordinary rules of priority is entitled to the name *B. dysenteriæ*, though this is still commonly used for other types of dysentery bacilli with the addition of the discoverer's name to indicate the type.

Flexner's bacillus, which is the same as Kruse's pseudodysentery bacillus, has long been known to present several distinct races, differing slightly and variably in cultural characters and more constantly in serological peculiarities, though evidently related to one another, for the serological races exhibit much group-agglutination amongst themselves. One such race, isolated in 1903 by Hiss and Russell in America, was called by them the " Y bacillus," while another, isolated by Strong in the Philippines, and found to ferment cane-sugar, came to be known as the " Strong type." The classification by fermentation reactions, upon which Hiss chiefly relied, is now recognized as an unsatisfactory one, as the fermentations of cane-sugar and maltose have proved variable and irregular. The only serious attempt at a serological classification previous to the war was that of Kruse, who, with his fellow-workers, published in 1907 a classification of " pseudodysentery bacilli " into eight races, lettered A to H, based on agglutination and absorption tests. This classification, however, valuable as it was, was little known outside Germany.

The evidence connecting Shiga's bacillus and the various Flexner races with the causation of bacillary dysentery was very strong, and twenty years' experience all over the world has served but to confirm their causal rôle. At the same time, there are other related organisms for which similar claims have been set up, though on less convincing evidence. In particular the bacilli resembling Flexner's organism, but differing from it in their ability to ferment lactose (though often very slowly), have been regarded as able to cause the disease ; Kruse, indeed, included these as one of his serological races (Group E). The evidence which has been afforded by the war as to these and other suspect bacteria, will be considered further on. It may be convenient to recapitulate here the opinions of the Bacteriological Sub-committee of the War Office Committee on Dysentery as to the evidence which may be deemed significant as regards the causal rôle of an organism in this disease. They classed the evidence under three heads :—

(1) The occurrence of the organism in fair numbers in the mucus and blood from the colon in the acute stage of the disease, especially when the organism is found in a number of such cases occurring at the same time.

(2) The development in the patient's blood of specific antibodies against the organism, given a sufficient time for their development and a sufficiently delicate technique for their recognition. The development of such antibodies, of which agglutinins are the most readily demonstrated, constitutes practical proof of the relation of the organism to the disease. In the absence of such antibodies the proof must be held lacking in completeness, but the relation of the organism to the disease cannot be regarded as disproved.

(3) Animal experiment furnishing evidence of a selective action of the organism or of its toxin, when injected subcutaneously or intravenously, upon the mucosa of the colon,

constitutes supporting evidence of relation to dysentery. The absence of such selective action does not necessarily disprove the relation of the organism to the disease.

The position at the outbreak of war in regard to the bacteriology of bacillary dysentery may be put shortly as follows. Bacteriologists were fully qualified to recognize Shiga's bacillus, and there was an effective anti-serum against this species. With regard to Flexner's bacillus the position was less certain ; the general cultural characters of the organism were well known, and there were agglutinating sera for the recognition of certain of its races. But the number and the variety of these races were not understood, and there were no examples of Kruse's serological types. There was no such potent therapeutic anti-serum as that against Shiga's bacillus. As regards other species possibly concerned in the causation of dysentery very little was known with certainty. The technique for the bacteriological diagnosis was on the whole adequate though a little weak on the serological side. Sero-diagnosis of dysentery was imperfectly developed, and the difficulties attending prophylactic inoculation with organisms of such toxicity had not been successfully overcome.

The Bacilli causing Dysentery during the War.

The experience of bacillary dysentery during the war differed in two respects from that of all previous wars. Operations were carried on in every kind of climate from the tropics to the Arctic regions, troops were moved from one theatre of war to another, and even on the Western front men were gathered together from almost every part of the habitable globe, dysentery carriers amongst them. The opportunity, therefore, for the study of every type of dysentery bacillus was unrivalled. In the second place the number of skilled men, mostly drawn from civilian laboratories, who were engaged in bacteriological work on the various fronts was very large, enabling good use to be made of the opportunity. Even those who were at first unused to dysentery work speedily became familiar with it and with the problems which it opened up.

In considering the question of the bacteria responsible for bacillary dysentery, it is necessary to bear in mind that " dysentery " is a clinical term and not a sharply-defined disease. On the one hand, it is simulated by any condition producing acute inflammation and ulceration of the colon and rectum, so that certain forms of enteric, notably those caused by *B. paratyphosus* B and C, appeared at times under the clinical guise of dysentery. On the other hand, its milder forms shade off into what is classed as simple diarrhœa ; when dysentery is prevalent diarrhœa also is a prominent affection, and there is no doubt that much of the latter is mild dysentery. Even in England, and much more in the United States, a certain amount of infantile diarrhœa has been shown to be due to true dysentery bacilli. For practical purposes it is necessary to adopt some arbitrary criteria of dysentery, and by general consent these have been diarrhœa with the passage of blood and mucus, with tenesmus, and, in the case of bacillary as opposed to amœbic dysentery, with the presence of an inflammatory exudate manifested by a mingling of pus with the mucus.

The organisms best established as the causes of bacillary dysentery are the bacilli of Shiga and Flexner, and these were the preponderant organisms present in every theatre of war.

Shiga's Bacillus.—It is admitted on all hands that the type of dysentery due to this organism is more severe and has a higher fatality than other types of the affection. In the East it was extremely prevalent. Manson-Bahr estimates that half the total cases of bacillary dysentery were due to Shiga's bacillus, and this is borne out by the reports of other workers there and by the examination of convalescents returned to this country. On the Western front it was fortunately much less prevalent than the Flexner dysentery ; only some 15 per cent. of the total cases were there attributable to Shiga's bacillus. The Germans appear to have suffered heavily from Shiga dysentery, especially on their Eastern front, though much of the disease amongst their civil population was of the Flexner type.

Very little that was new emerged about this bacillus. Its characters have long been well known. It is a sharply defined species and has not been found to present any serological races. No difficulty was found in recognizing it wherever it occurred.

Flexner's Bacillus.—This organism was extremely common as a cause of dysentery in every theatre of war, and on the Western front was responsible for most of the dysentery which was so prevalent from 1916 onwards ; a fact which explains the relatively light mortality from the disease in France. Flexner dysentery seems even more remarkable than the affection due to Shiga's bacillus for its tendency to prevail in epidemics.

Unlike Shiga's bacillus, Flexner's species presents a number of serological races, a fact which soon became apparent from the common failure to obtain confirmation by agglutination of findings which were in other respects beyond reproach. The diagnostic sera with which the laboratory workers were provided came, for the most part, from the Royal Army Medical College, the Lister Institute, and the Oxford Laboratories, or from Messrs. Burroughs Wellcome & Co. They were labelled either " Flexner " or " Y ", for these were the only types recognized; but it was the experience of every laboratory that many strains of Flexner's bacillus from cases of undoubted dysentery failed to agglutinate with these sera. Later in the war the American bacteriologists had much the same experience with their own sera.

It has already been stated that Kruse had worked out a serological grouping of " pseudodysentery bacilli " in 1907. This grouping has been adopted and confirmed by Hutt; but inasmuch as no examples of Kruse's races could be obtained in Great Britain or the allied countries, it was necessary to clear up the confusion which existed by working out a separate classification, for which purpose a superabundance of material existed. The task, which is an exceedingly laborious one, was carried out during the war by three sets of workers. The late Dr. H. S. Gettings had been for some years working at asylum dysenteries; he died before his work was quite completed, but his notes and results, collected and edited by Captain S. R. Douglas, have been published by the Medical Research Council. Captain E. G. D. Murray, himself invalided from Mesopotamia with Shiga dysentery, undertook an extensive investigation at the Royal Army Medical College with the object of selecting suitable strains for the sero-vaccine which was being prepared there. His researches, published in the *Journal of the R.A.M.C.*, embraced, not merely the Flexner group, but the whole range of dysentery bacilli. Captain A. C. Inman, in collaboration with Major F. W. Andrewes, investigated a long series of Flexner strains from all parts of the world at St. Bartholomew's Hospital. Although these researches were independent, the different workers were well known to each other and interchanged cultures, so that their results can be compared. The matter was discussed by the Bacteriological Sub-Committee of the War Office Committee on Dysentery, and, after a full consideration of all the evidence, a fairly complete concordance was found to exist between the three sets of observations. The substance of the sub-committee's findings was as follows :—Excluding the lactose-fermenting types, which they referred to separate species, Flexner's bacillus is to be regarded as a single species comprising at least five serological races. These races present a considerable, though variable, degree of mutual group-agglutination, so that if trust is placed in agglutination alone they will be found to overlap somewhat. They are more sharply separable by absorption tests. It was agreed to label these races with the last five letters of the alphabet. The V race corresponds with original Flexner bacillus, the Y race with the original Y of Hiss and Russell, the W race with the so-called Y of the Pasteur Institute and of the Oxford laboratories and with the Mount Desert strain of American laboratories. The X and Z races are not known to correspond with previously described strains, but it has been impossible to correlate these races with Kruse's types, amongst which they may be represented.*

For purposes of exact diagnosis the sub-committee recommended the use of five monovalent rabbit sera, corresponding to the five races ; for the mere confirmation of a bacillus as a member of the Flexner species they advised the issue of a pooled serum comprising all five types. For sero-diagnosis they suggested the issue of agglutinable emulsions of the five races, while for the preparation of vaccines and therapeutic sera they were of opinion that all the types should be included. The types are preserved in the national collection of cultures at the Lister Institute.

That the recognition of these serological races was of practical importance was at once manifest when some of the above recommendations were put to the test. During the last few months of the war, Captain Inman was sent to France with a supply of agglutinable emulsions and sera corresponding to all the races, except Y, which had not then been fully worked out. Working with Major Perry at No. 14 Stationary Hospital he found that no less than 85 per cent. of the Flexner strains inagglutinable with the Oxford standard sera could now be identified. At the Central American Laboratories at Dijon he had a similar experience, identifying 13 out of 17 strains inagglutinable with the American sera. In sero-diagnosis of convalescent cases the number of positive results was correspondingly increased ; in 43 cases from a single outbreak, sent in as "clinical dysentery," a diagnosis could be made in 77 per cent.

It may be added that as regards the geographical distribution of these races in the different theatres of war, the V, W, X and Z

---

* Since the war, cultures of two of Kruse's types have been obtained from Germany. His race A is found to correspond with the race V of English observers, and his race D with the W race.

races were common on the Western front, whereas the Y race was not recognized there. The Y race was not uncommon in the East, and occurred also in Italy. In Macedonia the V and W races seem to have been predominant. The data are insufficient for a more exact analysis. Nothing is known as to any differences in the clinical character of the dysentery caused by these various Flexner races ; probably none existed.

Gettings' Bacillus.—There exists a type of bacillus similar to Flexner's in cultural reactions and fermentations but altogether dissimilar in serological properties. Whether it should be regarded merely as a race of Flexner's organism or as a separate species is hard to decide, but on serological grounds it would seem best to regard it as a distinct species. It gives, moreover, heavy flocculation with Michaelis' " acid agglutination " test, to which Flexner's bacillus fails, as a rule, to respond. The organism was described by Gettings amongst his asylum strains and forms one of his four Flexner groups ; he informed Major F. W. Andrewes that he had no doubt of its causal relationship to an outbreak of dysentery. It was not recognized in military laboratories during the war, but it may possibly have been present and contributed its share to the "inagglutinable " strains to which reference has been made.

Lactose-fermenting Strains.—The majority of bacteriologists, both on the Western front and in the East, refused to recognize lactose-fermenting strains as having any causal relation with dysentery. While it is certain that such organisms play a part of much less importance than Shiga's and Flexner's bacilli, it is doubtful whether they can be acquitted of any share in the causation of dysentery. The lactose-fermenting power is often overlooked because it is not rarely delayed in its manifestation for two or even three weeks, but the strains which possess this property are always found to present serological unconformity with Flexner's bacillus, and in some cases at least they have a very slow velocity of agglutination, requiring twenty-four hours at 55° C. for the complete reaction. Some degree of co-agglutination with Flexner's bacillus may, however, be present. It is probable that there are several races or even species in the lactose-fermenting group, for they vary amongst themselves in their cultural reactions ; their serological relations are imperfectly known.

Kruse had no hesitation in including these organisms amongst his races of " pseudodysentery bacilli " and in this he was followed by Hutt. Actual epidemics of dysentery due to lactose-fermenting forms have been described. The most convincing evidence comes from Scandinavia. In 1914, Sonne, working at dysentery in Denmark, found that the commonest cause of dysentery there was a bacillus serologically quite distinct from Flexner's bacillus and he included this as Type III in his classification. Later Thjötta found the same species in dysentery in Norway, though many of the cases from which he isolated it were only mild diarrhœa. He found specific anti-bodies in the blood of affected persons. Major F. W. Andrewes had the opportunity of studying a culture from Norway; it fermented lactose on the sixth day and was serologically quite distinct from Flexner's bacillus and from other aberrant types in his possession. In view of such evidence as this, and of the fact that some of the lactose-fermenting strains exhibit a toxicity to the rabbit fully equal to that of Flexner's bacillus, it would seem that British bacteriologists must reconsider their opinions as to the relation of lactose-fermenting species to dysentery, though much more study of these forms is required.

The " Schmitz " Bacillus.—Early in 1916 Schmitz investigated an extensive outbreak of dysentery, with many hundred cases, amongst Roumanian prisoners of war. He found as the cause of this outbreak a bacillus hitherto undescribed and proposed to call it " *B. dysenteriae* (Schmitz)." The evidence connecting the organism with the disease was very strong; it was abundantly present in the blood and mucus of the stools and anti-bodies were found in the blood of affected persons. The bacillus resembled Shiga's organism in its cultural and fermentative properties, except that it readily formed indol; serologically there was no relation either with Shiga's or Flexner's bacillus. On the Western front organisms of this type were not uncommonly found in routine examination of stools, though not in relation with definite epidemics. They were not found to exhibit any notable toxicity and the general opinion of bacteriologists in France was that they were not a cause of dysentery. Andrewes examined a number of strains sent to London from France and, in ignorance of the work of Schmitz, proposed the name " *B. ambiguus* " for the organism. He found it toxic to the rabbit in a large dose, but was not disposed to regard it as a true cause of dysentery. Evidence, however, continued to come in from the East as to its pathogenic rôle. In 1917 it was not uncommonly found in dysenteric cases in Macedonia, where Dudgeon used the term " para-Shiga bacillus " for it; *post-mortem* findings and cultures in fatal cases suggested its causal relation with the disease. The bacillus was found toxic to the rabbit, but anti-sera were successfully prepared. Two distinct races were found, serologically dissimilar, one forming indol and the other failing to do so. Dudgeon termed them " Para-Shiga + " and " Para-Shiga — ", and both were equally separable from the true Shiga bacillus by agglutination and absorption tests. No mention is made in Dudgeon's report of agglutinins in human serum against these bacilli. Fletcher at Southampton, examining convalescent dysentery cases, isolated the Schmitz bacillus from a man whose serum agglutinated the organism from his stools in a dilution of more than 1 : 1,000. In Italy, Broughton-Alcock described two outbreaks of mild dysentery, one an extensive one of more than 350 cases, associated with the Schmitz bacillus ; he failed to find antibodies in the blood.

In the light of all this evidence it would seem that a good case can now be made out for the Schmitz bacillus as a cause of dysentery, especially in Eastern and Southern Europe. It appears to be of much less epidemiological importance than the organisms of Shiga and Flexner, and much of the disease attributed to it, from Schmitz's outbreak onwards, would seem to have been diarrhœal rather than dysenteric in nature ; nevertheless, true dysenteric ulceration occurred and a few cases were fatal.

Several other organisms, such as Morgan's bacillus, *B. proteus* and *B. pyocyaneus*, have at times been credited with a relation to dysentery. That these organisms may be associated with enteritis and diarrhœa is likely enough, but there is not sufficient evidence for including them in the ranks of true dysentery bacilli.

The Laboratory Diagnosis of Bacillary Dysentery.

For practical purposes this subject may be considered under two chief headings—examination of the stools and serodiagnosis. Innumerable cultures were made from the blood and from the urine of acute cases of the disease by many different observers at home, in France, and in the East. In a very few instances the labour was rewarded by the discovery of Shiga or Flexner bacilli in one or other of these fluids, but the overwhelming majority of the examinations yielded a negative result. Thus, during the Somme epidemic in 1916, Captain Wilson cultivated the blood of 88 Shiga cases with three positive results, and that of 70 Flexner cases with no positive result. He examined the urine in 1,113 cases of dysenteric diarrhœa and found Shiga's bacillus three times and Flexner's bacillus eight times. In contrast to the enteric fevers, bacillary dysentery is a local disease of the intestine, and it would seem that any over-flow of the bacilli into the blood or excretion in the urine is a comparatively rare accident. In the well-known arthritis of dysentery, Shiga's bacillus has been found in the joints in ex-ceptional cases, but most observers attribute the condition to toxic causes. It follows that in the diagnosis of this disease, blood culture and urine culture are practically unavailing and attention must be concentrated on the stools. On this subject a vast mass of experience has been accumulated during the war.

Selection of Material for Culture.—It is well established that the prospects of successfully cultivating dysentery bacilli from the stools are greater the more acute the case and the earlier it is examined. Strong evidence on this point has been published by Martin and Williams, based on the examination of more than 1,200 samples of fæces at Rouen, all the samples being from dysenteric cases. From the first to the fifth day after onset the percentage of positive results was 68·0, from the sixth to the tenth day it was only 17·4, and from the eleventh to the fifteenth it had fallen to 6·3 ; later it was lower still. All observers, including the Germans, report a similar experience ; when the mobile laboratories were pushed up to the front so that they could deal with the acute case on the spot, the pro-portion of positive diagnoses obtained was much higher than at base laboratories.

Next, it is established that the material selected for culture should be blood and mucus, or, failing this, mucus freed as far as possible from fæcal matter. This is true also of chronic cases and convalescents in whom well-washed flakes of mucus may yield a positive result when the fæcal material is apparently negative. The large numbers of *B. coli* in the latter overcrowd the plate and obscure the causal organism which is chiefly present in the mucus from the intestinal wall.

Further, all observers are agreed that the more quickly the material is plated out after passage from the bowel, the higher the proportion of positive results. Dysentery bacilli seldom live long outside the body, and cultures made after six hours are commonly negative. Different devices have been employed to overcome this difficulty in cases where material has to be trans-mitted from a distance. One is Teague and Clurman's method of emulsifying the material in double its volume of a 30 per cent. solution of glycerin in 0·6 per cent. saline. If pure glycerin free from acidity is used, this method preserves dysentery bacilli, as it does bacilli of the enteric group, in a viable condition. A second plan, introduced by Dudgeon, is to mix the fresh material with an equal volume of caustic soda solution of a strength of $\frac{N}{33}$; this was found to give a marked increase in the proportion of positive results where plating was delayed.

Direct culture from the dysenteric ulcers after death or when possible by the aid of the sigmoidoscope during life, is usually successful. The latter method is commonly impracticable, but as a substitute the rectal swab is easy to employ An ordinary cotton-wool swab attached to a stout wire some 8 inches long, sterilized and kept in a test tube, is passed high into the rectum beside the finger and rotated against the mucous membrane. This device was given a thorough trial in France and yielded fully as many positive results as material passed naturally. It has the great advantage that material can be obtained at any time convenient to the worker independently of any natural action of the bowels.

Direct Microscopic Examination of material from the Bowel.— Willmore and Shearman have shown that it is easy to distinguish between the amœbic and the bacillary cases by a cytological examination of the discharges from the bowel. Amœbic dysentery is essentially a process of colliquative necrosis, primarily unattended by an inflammatory exudate ; bacillary dysentery is essentially an acute inflammation of the intestinal mucosa with secondary necrosis in severe cases. Corresponding to this difference the cellular exudate in the amœbic form is scanty, and very few polymorphonuclear leucocytes are present, though red corpuscles abound, whereas in bacillary dysentery polymorphs are present in large numbers with or without red corpuscles. These observers draw attention also to the presence of a large type of cell in bacillary dysentery, apparently a " macrophage " of endothelial origin, which may be confounded by the inexperienced with an amœba. In their opinion, based on an immense experience in Egypt, a cytological examination of the intestinal exudate affords not only an easy but the most rapid and the most correct criterion as to the amœbic or bacillary nature of a case of dysentery and is hence particularly adapted to times of stress when the rapid diagnosis of large numbers of cases is urgent. Other observers have confirmed this opinion.

Choice of a Culture Medium.—There is, unfortunately, no known enrichment medium which will favour the growth of dysentery bacilli. Further, these organisms are more delicate than most intestinal organisms, and will not tolerate some of the inhibitory substances which may be added with advantage to the medium in isolating the enteric group of bacilli. As good a medium as any is plain lactose litmus agar with no inhibitory addition. McConkey's bile-salt lactose neutral red agar has been widely and successfully used ; Martin tested it against plain agar both with Shiga's and Flexner's bacillus and found what slight difference there was to be in favour of McConkey's medium. Some have used Endo's medium, while Wilson, comparing a number of media, got the best results from Drigalski and Conradi's medium. Those who have employed the eosin-methylene blue medium of Holt-Harris and Teague as modified by Meyer and Stickel speak very highly of it in dysentery work. It may be concluded that any one of these media in the hands of a worker who is used to it, and has tested the value of his particular formula will yield adequate results.

Identification by Cultural Methods.—There are two ways of examining suspicious colonies on a plate. Some workers think that time is saved by rough preliminary agglutination on a slide, using a 1 : 50 or 1 : 100 dilution of a range of potent sera and afterwards confirming by cultural tests. Should this plan be adopted the preliminary agglutination test must be regarded as a rough orientation only ; the decisive tests lie in cultural reactions and more refined methods of agglutination, and these must never be omitted. Reliance on rough agglutination alone has led to serious errors. The second plan is to begin by submitting any colony found to consist of non-motile, Gram-negative bacilli to preliminary cultural tests, and to confirm the result by agglutination.

The fermentation tests which are of value in the diagnosis of dysentery bacilli are those with glucose, lactose, mannite and dulcite. The saccharose and maltose tests have been found too variable to be of much service. It is advisable to inoculate also a litmus milk tube and a broth tube for indol. No acid should be formed in lactose or dulcite in the case of Shiga's or Flexner's bacillus. Acid formation with dulcite practically excludes any dysentery bacillus, but, as regards acid in lactose, which may be very late in appearing, the remarks already made will suggest caution in diagnosis, though Shiga's and Flexner's bacilli are excluded. Some workers during the war used Russell's double sugar agar (lactose 1 per cent. and glucose 0·1 per cent., with an indicator) ; the medium is so sloped as to leave a deep butt of agar at the bottom into which a stab is made in addition to the surface slope. If the bacillus is a frank lactose fermenter, the whole medium is acid in twenty-four hours ; if only a glucose fermenter the acid is seen around the stab alone, where also, if gas is formed, it will be apparent.   The method seems rapid and economical of medium.   While it is the rule to examine plates as a routine on the day after inoculation it was found expedient to re-examine them on the second day, for it was not uncommon for dysentery colonies to be delayed beyond twenty-four hours in their appearance.

Confirmation by Agglutination.—The macroscopic has been found so superior to the microscopic method of carrying out the agglutination test that it has been employed by the majority of workers.   Most have used saline emulsions from agar cultures of the organisms to be tested ; Dreyer's method, which employs formalinized broth cultures, was little known at the beginning of the war, but those who used it were well satisfied.   It is a fact well attested by many observers that with formalinized broth cultures and an incubation for a sufficient time in a water-bath at 55° C. group agglutination is less obtrusive and cleaner results are obtained than by the more usual technique.   Under the stress of war, however, the necessary apparatus was not often at hand, except in base laboratories.   The velocity of the agglutination reaction is slower with dysentery bacilli than with the enteric group ; even at 55° C. at least four and a half hours are needed for the reaction, while at 37° C. still longer incubation may be given and the final readings should not be taken till the tubes have stood overnight on the bench.   In the case of certain organisms other than Shiga's and Flexner's bacilli, but yet possible causes of dysentery, the velocity of agglutination is still slower and twenty-four hours in the water-bath at 55° C. are required for full agglutination ; this is chiefly the case with certain lactose-fermenting strains.   Inman has pointed out that there is one and apparently only one race of Flexner's bacillus, *viz.*, the W race, which occasionally shows delayed agglutination ; at the end of four and a half hours in the water-bath, the tubes may be practically negative, but after leaving them overnight at laboratory temperature good agglutination may be seen.

During the greater part of the war the range of agglutinating sera available for laboratory workers was not altogether adequate as regards Flexner's bacillus, since, as already explained, the serological races of this organism were only imperfectly known.   Owing, however, to the presence of group-agglutination the sera provided were of considerable utility ; in particular, the Lister Institute Y serum, owing to its wide range over other races, gave a high proportion of positive results. A considerable number of negative results seems to have been due to the lack of X and Z sera. At the close of the war these defects had largely been remedied, especially in France. Where it is merely desired to know whether a given strain is or is not Flexner's bacillus, it suffices to supply a serum pooled from sera of the five known races of that organism. This, with a Shiga serum, would be all that is needed for ordinary dysentery work. But it often happens in tracing the course of an epidemic that more exact information is required, and in such cases the five sera must be used separately.

With regard to the agglutination of Shiga's bacillus little difficulty was experienced, since no serological races appear to exist within the confines of this species. It is probable that some of the "inagglutinable Shiga's" were referable to the Schmitz bacillus.

It may be added that in using agglutinating sera for diagnosis the full titre of the serum by the technique employed should be known. The unknown bacillus should be put up against the serum in three dilutions of the latter, corresponding to a quarter, half and full titre, as advised by the Bacteriological Sub-Committee of the War Office Committee on Dysentery.

Acid agglutination by the technique advocated by Michaelis, a trace of normal serum being added to each tube, was tested by several workers during the war in relation to dysentery diagnosis. Conflicting opinions have been expressed, some regarding the test as worthless, others as having a certain value. Michaelis had asserted that true dysentery bacilli, by which he presumably meant Shiga and Flexner strains, were not flocculated by the range of acid solutions he employed. Nearly everyone who has tried the method agrees that this statement is too absolute, though it is more or less true of freshly isolated strains. Strains long under cultivation not infrequently exhibit flocculation. On the other hand, bacilli lying outside the true Shiga and Flexner groups, such, for example, as the Schmitz bacillus, Sonne's Type III and Gettings' bacillus, commonly but not invariably show gross flocculation with Michaelis' test, which may thus possess some orienting value.

Sero-diagnosis in Dysentery.—Two circumstances during the war have combined to render the sero-diagnosis of bacillary dysentery a more trustworthy diagnostic method than it had previously been. The first was the application of Dreyer's technique with its standardized agglutinable emulsions, and the second the recognition of the various serological races of Flexner's bacillus, enabling a suitable range of emulsions to be provided. The advantages of Dreyer's technique in this connection have been recognized by all who have employed it ; they lie in the sensitiveness of the emulsions to agglutination, in the comparative absence of group-agglutination, and, above all, in the standardized agglutinability of the emulsions. If an object-lesson were wanted as to the confusion which may arise from the absence of standardization, it may be found in the independent efforts made by various workers during the war to determine the lowest serum titre which might be of significance as to the past occurrence of dysentery in a patient. In the case of Shiga infections the discrepancies were not very great, the significant limit assumed ranging from 1 : 40 to 1 : 125 ; but in the case of Flexner's bacillus the limit chosen varied from 1 : 50 to 1 : 2,500. A very agglutinable strain (Dudgeon's " Gallipoli " Flexner) was highly prized in Macedonia because of the large number of positive results obtained with it. Yet these results would not be comparable with those obtained by workers elsewhere who used less highly agglutinable emulsions. On account, therefore, of variations in technique and in the emulsions employed, it is scarcely possible to give more than a few general statements about sero-diagnosis in dysentery until the closing months of the war.

There is a general consensus of opinion as to the value of the method in Shiga infections. The specific agglutinin is known to appear in the blood from the fifth to the twelfth day of the disease, and to rise progressively for a time ; low titres may vanish during convalescence, but the blood commonly shows a definite reaction for months. Rajchman and Western got positive Shiga agglutination in some cases up to ten and eleven months from onset, but it must be remembered that the bacilli themselves may persist in the bowel equally long. In Macedonia, Dudgeon reports the examination of 177 known Shiga cases ; the agglutination reaction was positive in 100, and of the 77 who gave no result, 73 had been suffering from the disease less than ten days. Glynn reports 60 per cent. of positive results in known Shiga convalescents at Liverpool, but the number of cases was small. Similar figures have been found by others in convalescent cases in this country. The results obtained from Flexner cases, if those attained late in the war by Dreyer's method are excepted, were far less satisfactory—many workers, indeed, coming to the conclusion that sero-diagnosis was of little service in this affection. One can now see that there was more than one reason for this, but the chief was undoubtedly ignorance of the number and variety of Flexner strains requisite for the test. A second probably lay in the techniques in common use, which were not of a kind to minimize group agglutination. Most observers report a considerable degree of co-agglutination of Flexner's bacillus in pure Shiga cases. Dudgeon investigated this question with particular thoroughness; he found that out of 177 bacteriologically diagnosed Shiga cases no fewer than 112 gave agglutination also with Flexner's bacillus, although double infections were extremely rare. Moreover, he found that when such human sera were saturated with Shiga's bacillus, not only the Shiga agglutinins but also the greater part of the Flexner agglutinins were removed. In his known Flexner cases, Shiga co-agglutinins were only found to a negligible extent. These findings were such as to lead him to distrust agglutination of Flexner's bacillus except in the absence of Shiga agglutinins. It must be noted that these results were obtained with agar suspensions, formalinized and stored, of an exceptionally agglutinable strain of Flexner's bacillus. Dudgeon was not alone in such experiences, though few have investigated the matter so fully; indeed the facts have long been noted by continental observers. Even when Dreyer's technique is employed, Shiga cases may give some co-agglutination with Flexner's bacillus, but those who have used this method seem to have found no serious difficulty in distinguishing between the two types.

Thus Martin, examining Shiga cases at Rouen, found positive agglutination in every one. Inman also got 100 per cent. of positive results in a Shiga outbreak in England, reported by Buchanan; in all of the 35 actual cases examined more than 10 agglutinin units were found in the serum (12 to 300 units); out of 114 exposed to infection but not known to have developed symptoms, 18 per cent. gave a positive result; whereas in 140 men of another institution, where there had been no dysentery, only a single case was positive.

With Flexner dysentery Martin got 38 per cent. of positive results, while using only two races for his emulsions, but when he added other local strains to his range of emulsions the percentage of positives rose to 72·5. Allusion has already been made to the 77 per cent. of positive results in " clinical dysentery " obtained by Inman in France at the close of the war when four races of Flexner were available for serodiagnosis.

Attention must be drawn to the fact that those exposed to

infection may develop agglutinins against dysentery bacilli without having apparently suffered from the disease ; it must be assumed that a kind of sub-infection occurs, the bacilli being insufficiently numerous to set up actual disease. An example of what may happen is furnished by the observations of Nolf and his colleagues on the Belgian front, where there was an epidemic of dysentery. Amongst orderlies in attendance on the sick or soldiers in the trenches agglutinins were found to develop in certain cases though there had been no intestinal disturbance ; titres as high as 1 in 200 were observed in such persons at the close of the epidemic though absent at its commencement.

Dysentery Carriers.

It has been known for many years that a certain proportion of those who have suffered from bacillary dysentery in any of its forms continue to excrete the bacilli for months or even years after apparent recovery. Such dysentery carriers are analogous to typhoid and paratyphoid carriers except in this respect, that the persistent focus of infection is not the gall-bladder, but, it is conjectured, some small unhealed lesion of the intestine itself ; moreover, urinary carriers are unknown in dysentery. There is every reason for the belief that dysentery carriers are a danger to the community in the same way as enteric carriers.

During the war the authorities were fully alive to this danger and elaborate precautions were taken to detect carriers. The bacteriological investigations carried on at the hospitals where convalescent dysentery cases were collected have revealed a number of important facts concerning carriers. As a convenient classification, the War Office Committee on Dysentery adopted the following terms : " temporary " carrier up to three months from the date of attack ; " chronic " carrier after three months ; " inveterate " carrier after a year or more. It must, however, be noted that in many of the chronic carriers intestinal symptoms were present in some degree ; such cases were often more truly to be termed " chronic dysentery."

Frequency of the Carrier Condition.—Martin and Williams at Rouen paid attention to the date after onset at which dysentery bacilli could be detected in the stools. The proportion of positive cases fell at first very rapidly ; in material embracing more than a thousand cultural examinations, 68 per cent. were positive during the first five days, 17 per cent. during the second five days, 6 per cent. during the third five days. By the fiftieth day only 3 per cent. were positive, and after this only one case was positive (eightieth day).

In home hospitals out of more than 5,000 returned dysentery cases, 3·56 per cent. were found still to harbour the bacillus, but most of these soon cleared up. Glynn reports that out of 265 dysenterics supposed to be cured, 1·8 per cent. were still carriers. Dudgeon states that in Macedonia Lepper found that after three months from onset the number of carriers was 1·5 per cent.

The percentage of chronic carriers is probably somewhat greater than such figures would indicate on account of the difficulty of their detection. This difficulty is not so great in Shiga cases, in which the bacillus is seldom long absent from the stools, as in Flexner cases, in which the bacillus is excreted in a highly intermittent fashion. This has been noted by many observers, but the most exact knowledge is due to the investigations of Captain W. Fletcher at the University War Hospital, Southampton. They constitute the most important study of dysentery carriers made during the war. In place of the small prescribed number of examinations, Fletcher cultivated the stools every day for months in a number of cases, and with the most interesting results. Out of 1,782 convalescents at this hospital, 935 had been diagnosed as dysentery and of these 13 were found to be Shiga carriers and 61 to be Flexner carriers. As regards the Shiga carriers, 11 out of the 13 proved to be inveterate, and special note was made of the physical and mental depression which these men presented ; all passed mucus and sometimes blood in their stools, and there was marked liability to relapse. The stools of these 13 men were examined 469 times and Shiga's bacillus was present 207 times ; the longest negative interval observed was 13 days. Of the 61 Flexner carriers, 13 became chronic and one, at least, inveterate. In contrast to the Shiga carriers these men appeared as a rule in good health and passed natural stools. A striking feature was intermittence in excreting the bacillus ; in some cases the men would go three or four weeks without the bacillus being detected even by daily examination, and then for two or three days it would reappear in the stools, sometimes in large numbers, after which it would vanish for a while. Fletcher justly points out that such intermittence must lead to many failures to detect the carrier condition. His observations led him to conclude that a man who had carried Shiga's bacillus for three months was useless for further military service ; in the case of Flexner's bacillus this is not necessarily true, so far as physical condition is concerned. It may be added that treatment seems to have little or no effect in curing the carrier condition, though it may spontaneously subside with suitable diet or rest.

Modes of Spread.

Bacillary dysentery, like other intestinal infections, is conveyed by the excreta. Experimental work was carried out during the war to determine the channels by which infection occurs.

The dysentery group of bacilli is sensitive to acids, though less so than the cholera vibrio. Dudgeon's observations suggest that the failure to grow them from the stools when these have been kept outside the body for more than a few hours is due to the development of acid ; hence his adoption of alkalies to check this effect. The acid seems at first merely to inhibit growth ; doubtless it ultimately causes death. Mere drying is not necessarily fatal to the bacillus ; Captain Murray stated that he had grown Shiga's bacillus from a powder of the dried organisms preserved in sealed tubes for a year. It would thus appear that the vitality of the organism outside the body, a matter which lies at the root of its ability to spread the disease, may be of considerable duration in the absence of an acid reaction.

Water which has recently suffered fæcal pollution has always been regarded as a possible vehicle of dysenteric infection, although there is no record of the actual recovery of the bacillus from natural water. In the Shiga outbreak in England recorded by Buchanan there was strong reason for the belief that infection had occurred in this way. Several observers have tested the vitality of Shiga's bacillus in water to which it had been intentionally added. Wilson examined forty-two samples of water from shell holes at Bazentin in December 1916 and found evidence of fæcal contamination, but he was unable to demonstrate pathogenic bacteria. In such water, heavily infected with Shiga's bacillus, he was able to recover it after two days but not longer ; Flexner's bacillus in similar circumstances was last recovered after three days. Benjafield added Shiga's bacillus to well water and recovered it after ten days. Dudgeon carried out numerous experiments in Macedonia ; when Shiga's bacillus was added to crude water he failed to recover it after more than four days, but when it was added to the same water, sterilized, the bacillus was recoverable up to twenty-four days provided that the mixture had been kept at room temperature ;

at 37° C. it died out much more quickly. In water which had been chlorinated, but in which free chlorine was no longer present, he found that Shiga's bacillus remained alive for twenty-four hours. The evidence goes to show the possibility of conveyance of dysentery by water, and suggests the importance of preserving chlorinated or boiled water from subsequent infection.

The possibility of persistence of infection in food-stuffs was demonstrated by Inman, who painted portions of bacon and sausage with a suspension of Shiga's bacillus and left them at room temperature for three weeks ; the bacillus was readily recovered at the end of that period.

The part played by flies in the dissemination of dysentery has been confirmed not only by circumstantial evidence but also by laboratory experiment. The association of epidemics of the disease with an excessive prevalence of flies was noted in France as well as in the East, but in Egypt and Macedonia the circumstantial evidence was doubled in force by the fact that there were two periods of fly prevalence, namely, in spring and autumn, the flies disappearing during the very hot weather. Bacillary dysentery similarly tended to disappear during the height of summer. Dudgeon has published curves of fly prevalence and of dysentery incidence, showing a marked correspondence. As regards laboratory demonstration, Dudgeon carried out the following experiments : flies were fed on material contaminated with dysentery bacilli or on blood and mucus in which these bacilli were known to be present and the insects were bacteriologically examined after varying periods. No fewer than 382 flies were thus investigated and positive results were obtained in 79 instances. By the end of twenty-four hours it became difficult to recover the bacilli ; they were more often recovered from the fæces of the fly than from its legs when this interval had elapsed after feeding. Flies were also caught and examined in two hospitals in Macedonia with no artificial feeding ; in one case Shiga's bacillus was obtained from a fly, and in one, Schmitz' bacillus ; a bacillus resembling Flexner's but inagglutinable with the sera available was found on eight occasions. Manson-Bahr isolated Shiga's bacillus from wild flies in Egypt in 1910 ; in 1917 he found this organism in flies caught in the Sinai desert, miles from human habitations. Many observers have obtained *B. coli* and other human fæcal bacteria from flies captured at large. The experimental evidence that flies may convey dysentery infection is thus such as to strengthen the conclusions drawn from circumstantial evidence.

The modes of transference of infection named above, together with other and more obvious ways in which fæcal material may be swallowed, suffice to explain the epidemic spread of bacillary dysentery. They do not, however, touch the initiation of such epidemics and it is in connection with this question that carriers are of such primary importance. When it is remembered that carriers, especially of Flexner's bacillus, are often very difficult of detection, it is plain that under such conditions as those of the war they must have been not uncommon. On the Western front dysentery, practically absent in 1914 and 1915, broke out explosively during the fighting on the Somme in 1916 and this may be associated with some confidence with the presence of troops returned from the East. It was impossible at that time of stress to conduct any comprehensive search for carriers, but the investigations carried out at Etaples during the outbreak of dysentery at that base in 1917 revealed some instructive facts. The bacteriological examination of some 300 healthy men who had suffered from dysentery within twelve months revealed the presence of no fewer than 18 carriers, and of these at least three had passed through dysentery hospitals in England without being detected.

Prophylactic Inoculation.

The high toxicity of dysentery bacilli, and especially of Shiga's bacillus, has proved a serious obstacle to the employment of prophylactic vaccines on account of the severity of the reactions induced. Could this obstacle be overcome it would seem probable that vaccines might exercise a protective effect in dysentery as they do in enteric fever and some other infections.

Early in the war Professor Dean, of Manchester, treated dysentery bacilli with hypochlorites in the form of eusol, and suggested that by this means, although their antigenic power was unimpaired, their toxicity was so reduced as to render them suitable for use as a vaccine. Gibson, however, testing Shiga vaccines thus prepared upon groups of men, found that they developed a high degree of toxicity on storage, and their use was abandoned.

Sensitized vaccine, though the severity of the local reaction is lessened, has not been found to confer satisfactory protection. The Japanese method of giving vaccine and anti-serum simultaneously was tested by Gibson on himself and others; no very severe local reaction was induced, but the production of anti-bodies in the blood was not well marked.

It was concluded that the serum had not only neutralized the toxin but also the antigenic properties of the bacilli. It therefore occurred to Gibson that saturation of the anti-serum with a recent growth of the bacillus might remove the antibacterial substance and yet leave its antitoxic properties sufficiently intact to check excessive local reaction. This principle, when put into practice, was found successful so far as could be judged by experimental data. A vaccine of Shiga's bacillus mixed with a suitable quantity of *absorbed* anti-Shiga serum was well tolerated in doses up to 1,000 million, the reaction being not excessive and the yield of anti-bodies in the blood satisfactory. Flexner and Y strains could be added. The " sero-vaccine " thus devised by Gibson, and issued from the Royal Army Medical College, was sent out in twin-conjoined phials, one containing the vaccine, the other the absorbed serum. The vaccine contained : in 1 c.c. 2,000 million each of Shiga, Flexner and Y bacilli, killed by the addition of phenol. The serum, a polyvalent one from the Lister Institute, was absorbed first with Flexner's bacillus, then with the Y bacillus, and finally with Shiga's bacillus ; it was then centrifugalized and finally passed through a Pasteur-Chamberland filter. Having been tested for sterility and antitoxic potency, it was diluted so that 0·25 c.c. contained 0·1 c.c. of the absorbed serum. The first dose is 0·25 c.c. from each phial, the second, double that amount.

An experimental group of 1,000 men was inoculated with this vaccine, but it was not found possible, owing to war conditions, to obtain sufficient data from them to warrant any conclusion as to the efficacy of the prophylaxis. The matter remains in the experimental stage, but the problem of abolishing excessive local reactions would seem to have been in great part solved.

It may be added that it was also solved in Germany by Boehncke in a slightly different manner. He mixed dysentery toxin with antitoxin in a proportion arrived at by trial, so that the toxin was somewhat under-neutralized, and to the mixture were added vaccines of Shiga's bacillus, Flexner's and other dysentery bacilli. This vaccine, known as " Dys-bakta," was manufactured on a large scale in Hamburg, and widely used as a prophylactic during the closing year of the war ; it is asserted to have been of considerable efficacy.

BIBLIOGRAPHY.

Andrewes ..   .. Dysentery Bacilli   ..   .. Lancet, 1918, Vol. i, p. 560.

Andrewes & Inman | A Study of the Serological Races of the Flexner Group of Dysentery Bacilli. | M.R.C., Special Report Series, Lond., 1919. No. 42.

Boehncke .. .. | Ruhrschützimpfung im Kriege | Med. Klin., Berlin, 1917, Vol. xiii, p. 1083.

Broughton-Alcock.. | Two Outbreaks of Mild Dysentery associated with the Schmitz Bacillus. | Brit. Med. Jl., 1919, Vol. i, p. 666.

Buchanan .. .. | Study of an Outbreak of Bacillary Dysentery. | Lancet, 1918, Vol. ii, p. 166.

Douglas, Colebrook & Morgan | Report upon Combined Clinical and Bacteriological Studies of Dysentery Cases from the Mediterranean. | M.R.C., Special Report Series, Lond., 1917, No. 6, iv, p. 27.

Dean & Adamson .. | A Preliminary Note on a Method of Preparation of a Non-toxic Dysentery Vaccine. | Brit. Med. Jl., 1916, Vol. i, p. 611.

Dudgeon .. .. | Studies of Bacillary Dysentery occurring in the British Forces in Macedonia. | M.R.C., Special Report Series, Lond., 1919, No. 40.

Fildes .. .. | Report upon Recovered Cases of Intestinal Disease in the Royal Naval Hospital, Haslar, 1915–16. | Ibid., 1917, No. 6, iii.

Fletcher .. .. | A Contribution to the Study of Chronicity in Dysentery Carriers. | Ibid., Lond., 1919, No. 29.

Flexner .. .. | On the Ætiology of Tropical Dysentery. | Johns Hopkins Hosp. Bull., 1900, Vol. xi, p. 231. Philad. Med. Jl., 1900, Vol. vi, p. 414. Centralbl. f. Bakt. &c., 1900, Abth. i, Vol. xxviii, p. 625.

Gettings .. .. | An Investigation of the Flexner-Y Group of Dysentery Bacilli. | M.R.C., Special Report Series, Lond., 1919, No. 30. (Edited by Douglas.)

Gibson .. .. | A New Method of Preparation of a Vaccine against Bacillary Dysentery, etc. | Jl. of R.A.M.C.,1917, Vol. xxviii, p. 615.

Glynn .. .. | Report upon 2,360 Enteritis " Convalescents " received at Liverpool from various Expeditionary Forces. | M.R.C., Special Report Series, Lond., 1918, No. 7.

Hiss .. .. | On the Fermentative and Agglutinative Characters of Bacilli of the Dysentery Group. | Jl. Med. Research, 1904–05, Vol. xiii, p. 1.

Hiss & Russell .. | A Study of a Bacillus resembling the Bacillus of Shiga, from a Case of Fatal Diarrhœa in a Child. | Med. News, New York, 1903, Vol. lxxxii, p. 289.

Holt-Harris & Teague | A New Method for the Isolation of B. typhosus from Stools. | Jl. Infect. Dis., 1916, Vol. xviii, p. 596.

Hutt	Neue Beiträge zur Kenntniss der Pseudodysenterie und Para-dysenterie, sowie der sogenannten Mutation.	Zeitschr f. Hyg., 1913, Vol. lxxiv, p. 108.
Kruse	Ueber die Ruhr als Volkskrankheit und ihren Erreger.	Deutsch.Med.Woch., 1900, Vol. xxvi, p. 637.
,, ...	Weitere Untersuchungen über die Ruhr und die Ruhrbazillen	Ibid., 1901, Vol. xxvii, p. 370.
Kruse, Rittershaus, Kemp & Metz.	Dysenterie und Pseudodysenterie.	Zeitschr. f. Hyg., 1907, Vol. lvii, p. 417.
Meyer & Stickel ..	A Comparative Study of the Efficacy of the various Agar-dye-mediums, recommended for the Isolation of Typhoid and Dysentery Bacilli from Fæces.	Jl. Infect. Dis., 1918, Vol. xxiii, p. 48.
Martin, Hartley & Williams.	Agglutination in the Diagnosis of Dysentery.	Brit. Med. Jl., 1918, Vol. i, p. 642.
Martini & Lentz ..	Ueber die Differenzirung der Ruhrbacillen mittels der Agglutination.	Zeitschr. f. Hyg., 1902, Vol. xli, p. 540.
Martin & Williams..	The chance of recovering Dysentery Bacilli from the Stools according to the time elapsing since the onset of the Disease.	Brit. Med. Jl., 1918, Vol. i, p. 447.
Michaelis	Die praktische Verwertbarkeit der Säure-agglutination für die Erkennung der Typhusbazillen.	Deutsch.Med.Woch., 1915, Vol. xli, p. 243.
Murray	An Attempt at Classification of *Bacillus dysenteriæ* based upon an Examination of the Agglutinating Properties of 53 Strains.	Jl. of R.A.M.C.,1918. Vol. xxxi, pp. 257 and 353.
Rajchman & Western	Report upon 878 Cases of Bacillary Enteritis.	M.R.C., Special Report Series, Lond., 1917, No. 5.
Schmitz	Ueber einen bisher noch nicht bekannten Krankheitserreger aus der Dysenteriegruppe.	Münch. Med. Woch., 1917, Vol. lxiv, p. 1571.
,, ...	Ein neuer Typus aus der Gruppe der Ruhrbazillen.	Zeitschr. f. Hyg., 1917, Vol. lxxxiv, p. 449.
,, ...	Abgrenzung des *Bacillus Schmitz* gegenüber den Pseudodysenterie Stämmen.	Centralbl. f. Bakt. &c., Orig., 1918, Vol. lxxxi, p. 213.
Sonne	Giftfattige Dysenteribaciller ..	Copenhagen, 1914.
Shiga	Ueber den Erreger der Dysenterie in Japan.	Centralbl. f. Bakt. &c., 1898, Abth. i, Vol. xxiii, p. 599.
,, ...	Ueber den Dysenteriebacillus (*B. dysenteriæ*).	Ibid., 1899, Abth. i, Vol. xxiv, pp. 817, 870, and 913.
Teague & Clurman..	A Method of Preserving Typhoid Stools for Delayed Examination, etc.	Jl. Infect. Dis., 1916, Vol. xviii, p. 653.

Thjötta	On the Bacteriology of Dysentery in Norway.	Jl. of Bact., 1919, Vol. iv, p. 355.
Willmore & Shearman.	On the Differential Diagnosis of the Dysenteries.	Lancet, 1918, Vol. ii, p. 200.
Official	The Laboratory Diagnosis of Acute Intestinal Infections.	M.R.C., Special Report Series, Lond., 1920, No. 51, Part ii, Agglutination, p. 97.
,, ...	The Bacteriology and Laboratory Diagnosis of Bacillary Dysentery.	Report to the War Office Committee on Dysentery, by the Bacteriological Sub - committee. Published by the War Office, 1919.

CHAPTER XIII.

TYPHUS FEVER.

A T the outbreak of war, knowledge regarding the ætiology and pathology of typhus fever was very defective, although so far as ætiology is concerned important discoveries as regards transmission were made by Nicolle in Algiers in 1909, and his results were confirmed and his observations extended by himself and his colleagues, and by Ricketts, Wilder, Anderson and Goldberger in America. In 1910, Nicolle, Conor and Conseil conducted further useful experiments, although the validity of their deductions from these has been called in question.

Prior to 1914, a great number of different organisms, mostly bacteria, had been described in typhus fever cases, and many of them had been regarded as possessing an ætiological significance. A brief account of them is given by Wilder, but none of them now merit serious consideration except the bipolar organisms found by Ricketts and Wilder during their investigations on typhus in Mexico City in 1909 (a finding confirmed by Gavino, Girard and McCampbell), and the bodies observed in the leucocytes in typhus cases by von Prowazek in 1913. These cannot be lightly discarded, for there is little doubt, at least so far as the organisms described by Ricketts and Wilder are concerned, that they are identical with the Rickettsia bodies discovered at a later date by Rocha-Lima. He found these in lice taken from typhus patients during a prison epidemic, and at the present time these *Rickettsia prowazeki*, as he named them, are regarded by many as being very possibly intimately concerned with the ætiology of the disease.

In 1908, Rabinowitsch had described a bipolar bacillus in the blood of typhus patients, and there are not wanting those who regard his organism as being also identical with *Rickettsia prowazeki*. It would, however, seem that this is not the case, for, as pointed out by Ledingham and others, the fact that the Rickettsia bodies apparently cannot be cultivated seems to distinguish them from Rabinowitsch's organism and also from certain other bacteria now to be mentioned.

Following the work of the American observers there was a number of publications by different research workers, notably Töpfer, Otto and Baehr, announcing discoveries of organisms resembling those they described, but these did not greatly advance our knowledge, though the small anaërobic, pleomorphic, Gram-positive, non-motile bacillus isolated by Plotz in 1915 from cases of typhus in New York, called by him *Bacillus typhi-exanthematici*, and grown at a later date from presumably infected lice, cannot be wholly disregarded, especially as its discoverer considers that it is identical with Rickettsia. As mentioned, however, it can be cultivated, and hence the correctness of his claim is very doubtful. Olitsky, Denzer and Husk, however, consider it valid.

The small cocco-bacilli described by Sergent, Foley and Vialatte in 1914, and found by them in Algiers in lice which had lived on typhus patients, are regarded by these authors as *Rickettsia prowazeki*. The same cocco-bacilli, or similar cocco-bacilli, were found in lice in Tunis shortly afterwards by Nicolle, Blanc and Conseil.

Although the organism now known as *Proteus X 19*, found by Weil and Felix in 1916 in the urine of typhus cases, has, owing to the fact that it has been isolated from the excreta of lice, been looked upon by some as belonging to the Rickettsia, it bears no resemblance to them and it does not appear to stand in any ætiological relationship to typhus. At the same time, as will be seen, it is of great importance from a diagnostic standpoint.

From time to time spirochætes have been found in typhus, and it is not impossible that the malady may yet prove to be a spirochætal disease. Miyashima and his colleagues, however, seem to have conclusively established the non-pathogenicity of the latest spirochæte described, that of Futaki in Japan, who found it in the kidneys and urine of typhus cases.

During the course of the war a great deal of work has been carried out in connection with these Rickettsia bodies, notably by Rocha-Lima himself, but despite his assertions on the subject, and those of Nöller, Töpfer, Schüssler, Otto and Dietrich, who all confirmed his findings, it cannot yet be definitely stated that they are the cause of typhus fever. Indeed, the contrary view is taken by Brumpt, who carried out research in France, and he is supported by Nicolle who, like him, found the bodies so frequently in control lice, which were presumably also clean lice, that he was led to discount their importance.

Nicolle's work on transmission, to which reference had been made, was that which marked a definite stage in advance, for in the first place he succeeded in reproducing typhus in monkeys, and in the second he proved that the virus could be transmitted from monkey to monkey by the human body-louse, *Pediculus humanus*. It suffices here to say that during the war his work has been amply confirmed and greatly extended, in part by himself and his collaborators.

So far as the gross pathology of the disease is concerned, up to the commencement of hostilities but little advance has been made since the days of Murchison. The gross lesions were known and had been fully described, but the histo-pathology had not been minutely studied. Little or nothing had been done as regards the examination of the cerebro-spinal fluid, and in connection with blood reactions the suggestive pioneer work of Wilson in Belfast had not been followed up.

In 1909 he described the presence of heterologous agglutinins in the blood serum of typhus fever cases, and showed that the blood serum often agglutinates intestinal bacilli. At a l ter date French observers in Northern Africa demonstrated the fact that in a certain number of instances typhus blood serum also agglutinates *Micrococcus melitensis*.

It may safely be affirmed of typhus fever that, with the exception of new infectious maladies which have been actually discovered during the war, there is no disease on which so much fresh light has been thrown of recent years.

As stated, the work of Nicolle has been confirmed and extended, considerable progress has been made in elucidating the actual cause of the disease, and an investigation of its histo-pathology has explained much that was hitherto obscure in its clinical symptoms and sequelæ. Moreover, attention was redirected to the question of heterologous or para-agglutination with the result that an important diagnostic test was introduced, while the cytology of the cerebro-spinal fluid was studied and research carried out along various lines which led to the introduction of new methods of prophylaxis and treatment. It must be stated that little of this new work fell to the share of British medical officers, largely no doubt because they encountered typhus for the most part under conditions which were unsuitable for pathological research. In certain cases, however, they have by careful work confirmed or refuted the findings of other observers. So far as ætiology is concerned the French have led the way and the Americans have contributed considerably to our knowledge, though their work has been done for the most part outside the war areas. In certain directions the Germans and Austrians have studied the ætiological problem to good effect, but their chief work has been accomplished in connection with histo-pathology and laboratory diagnosis.

Ætiology.

The virus is transmitted by lice, and in all probability they constitute the only means of spread. *Pediculus humanus* is the vector, and this name includes both the body-louse and the head-louse which Nuttall has shown to be at most merely racial forms of *P. humanus*. Infection takes place both from the bite of the louse and through cutaneous lesions into which the infected excrement of the insect or its crushed body contents have been scratched or rubbed, as has been demonstrated by Nicolle, Mueller, Urizio and other workers.

According to Nicolle, hereditary transmission of the virus in the louse has not been established. It would seem that the blood of the typhus patient is infective for lice only during the five-day eruptive period and that after the infected meal the louse is incapable of transmitting the disease until the expiry of from eight to ten days. This indicates a process of evolution of the virus in the insect host. The louse can be infected from biting a typhus patient on a single occasion.

Children must be regarded as important reservoirs of infection, for they usually take the disease mildly and it is apt to be over-looked in them. Human " carriers " in the strict sense of the word apparently do not exist, for Rocha-Lima has shown that the virus speedily disappears from the patient's blood after defervescence.

It must be admitted that the precise nature of the virus which exists in the blood plasma and also in the serum obtained by centrifuging defibrinated blood is still unknown. It is known that exposure to a temperature of 55° C. for fifteen minutes destroys it, as does drying *in vacuo* over sulphuric acid. It is very sensitive to glycerine and to carbolic acid in 5 per cent. solution. It is resistant to saponin (one hour in 1 per cent. solution), and to the action of normal horse serum, while it can be kept in an active state for two to six days in the ice-chest when blood containing it is mixed with a sterile solution of gelatine in physiological saline or infected organs from a typhus case are placed in this solution.

The actual infective agent does not pass through an efficient Berkefeld filter in sufficient amount to cause infection. In this connection it is interesting to note that Nicolle found that the filtrate from infected lice, even after passage through compara-tively porous bougies, was not virulent, while the merest trace of the deposit on the filter infected a monkey or guinea-pig.

The virus is possibly of a bacterial nature and those who favour this view point to the fact that in centrifuged, citrated blood it is the leucocyte layer which is highly virulent. It is on the surface of this layer that bacteria would naturally be deposited, and they cannot be separated from the leucocytes. Nicolle admits that this is an argument difficult to combat.

Those who do not agree with the bacterial theory advance the argument that none of the organisms isolated has produced the disease when cultures are inoculated. The Rickettsia of which mention has been made have so far proved incapable of cultivation. Although their exact relationship to typhus has not yet been established, the Rickettsia appear at present to have the best claim for serious consideration as the true ætiological factor. They are tiny cocco-bacilli readily coloured a fine ruby red or reddish-purple by Giemsa (one drop to the cubic centimetre used for sixteen to twenty hours), but not easily stained by the ordinary bacterial stains. Loeffler's flagellar stain and carbol gentian violet are, however, effective. They do not retain Gram. Arkwright, Bacot and Duncan of the Lister Institute state that when examining films made from the excreta of lice or the guts of lice containing much fresh or altered blood, they have found it an advantage, in order to remove the debris of red cells, to fix the film in absolute alcohol containing 1 per cent. strong hydrochloric acid. In shape the Rickettsia vary from short elliptical coccus-like bodies to definite rods. There are also biscuit or dumbbell-shaped forms which may possibly represent a stage of division. The two poles, which stain well, are connected by a feebly staining envelope ; thus the bodies often present a bipolar aspect. Short lengths of three to five links placed in a chain or L-shaped have been noted by Arkwright, Bacot and Duncan. The smallest forms are about $0\cdot3\ \mu$ to $0\cdot4\ \mu$, the largest $0\cdot9\ \mu$. The Lister Institute observers give the measurements as being $0\cdot2$ to $0\cdot3\ \mu$ in their shorter diameter by $0\cdot3$ to $0\cdot5\ \mu$ in length, and describe them as being distinctly smaller than *B. influenzae* or *M. melitensis* taken from young cultures. The bodies of Ricketts and Wilder with which Rocha-Lima identifies his Rickettsia are approximately $2\ \mu \times 0\cdot65\ \mu$.

Rocha-Lima now considers the Rickettsia to belong to the strongyloplasmata and has classified them as chlamydozoa. They do not pass through a Berkefeld V filter and will not grow either aërobically or anaërobically on any of the numerous media tried.

They are found, often in large numbers, in the lumen of the gut of lice fed on typhus patients, in the epithelial cells of the mid-gut, where they occur in masses, and in the salivary glands. Sometimes, however, the bodies are present in very small numbers and are difficult to find, a fact which may explain the negative results recorded by some authors. Otto and Dietrich have shown that they are agglutinated by the blood of typhus convalescents and this observation has been confirmed by Ledingham and Arkwright.

It should be noted that Nicolle and Brumpt, who found Rickettsia in lice which had not been in contact with typhus cases and hence discounted their importance, may have been working with pediculi which had fed on trench fever patients, for identical or very similar bodies are now known to be associated with the latter disease. Indeed Jungmann and Kuczynski assert that they have found *Rickettsia prowazeki* in the blood both of typhus and trench fever cases. In the case of typhus it was present during the first days of the rash.

Another significant fact is its reported discovery by Kuczynski in what has been called the " specific nodule " of typhus, *i.e.*, the characteristic lesion of the blood-vessels which is described under " Histo-pathology." He found the Rickettsia bodies occurring in groups in the Kupffer cells of the liver capillaries and illustrates them in his paper. Jaffé says he has been able to confirm this work though he speaks somewhat guardedly. He advances the theory that the Rickettsia is introduced by the bite of the louse into the blood and is taken up by the endothelial cells of the capillaries or smallest arterioles, in which it multiplies and causes a toxic irritation resulting in the formation of the typhus nodule. Necrosis of the cells results and their contents, including the Rickettsia, are discharged into the blood. Fresh infection occurs and the process is repeated. Although the pathological findings and the symptomatology favour this view to some extent, it is at present pure speculation.

The conclusions of Arkwright and his colleagues as a result of their observations may be quoted though they worked chiefly at trench fever. They state that :—

(1) The evidence of the connection of typhus fever with Rickettsia is of the same kind as in the case of trench fever but the presence of the infecting virus can be shown by the inoculation of monkeys and guinea-pigs.

(2) The Rickettsia of typhus does not appear in the excreta of lice with the same regularity as the Rickettsia of trench fever.

(3) Monkey-lice, *Pedicinus longiceps* (?), taken from a monkey infected with typhus on the seventh to the eighth day of the disease, have been shown to contain Rickettsia and probably typhus virus. Pedicini from monkeys which have not been inoculated have never, so far, been found to contain Rickettsia (seventy-five lice examined).

(4) Pediculi fed on typhus patients may contain both the virus of typhus fever and Rickettsia.

Recent work by Rocha-Lima on the persistence of the virus in the louse is of considerable importance. According to him the view held by French and English authors that the louse remains a carrier of the typhus virus for twelve days only is incorrect. He finds that it harbours the virus in an active form for at least twenty-four days and believes that once infected it retains the virus throughout its life. If this is the case—and the frequency with which typhus is introduced into remote districts, and with which persons become infected who have never been in contact with typhus cases speaks in its favour—healthy immune persons must play an important part in spreading the disease by being carriers of virulent lice. In this connection the observations of Lorenz in Roumania may be cited. He found that typhus patients who had not been deloused could still spread infection by their lice three weeks after defervescence. Rocha-Lima having proved by transmission of typhus to guinea-pigs by lice that the patient is not infective once his temperature is normal, it is clear that the disease can be spread only by those lice which have fed on the patient during the febrile period. Lousy patients are not infectious six weeks after defervescence, hence the louse infected with typhus would not appear to live longer than six weeks at most.

There can be little doubt that the various cocci and bacilli, including different strains of *Bacillus proteus*, found in the blood and tissues of typhus cases are of the nature of secondary invaders. Probably, therefore, however important a rôle they may play in the pathology of the disease, they have no ætiological significance. The same cannot be said of the micro-organism recently found by Wolbach and Todd in the vascular lesions of Mexican typhus. It seems to be identical with the parasite discovered by Wolbach in Rocky Mountain spotted fever and has been named by the authors *Dermacentroxenus typhi*. They are inclined to consider it as the cause of typhus, and though, in the absence of any experimental work with it, this suggestion cannot yet be adopted, further research should be conducted in what appears to be a promising field.*

Animal Experiments as regards the Virus.—Important work has been done during and since the war on the transmission of the virus to experimental animals. Nicolle, himself the pioneer in this research, has extended his observations and recounts his findings and the general state of our knowledge on the subject in a recent paper. A brief summary is here given.

The following animals are susceptible : man, the anthropoid apes, monkeys, guinea-pigs, rabbits and rats. The ass, goat, dog, mouse and chicken have proved refractory.

Amongst anthropoid apes and monkeys, the chimpanzee, two species of macacus, *M. sinicus* and *M. cynomologus*, and a New World monkey, *Ateles vellerosus*, are suitable for experimental purposes. The virus is contained in the blood taken from the veins of man or the heart of an infected monkey. Ten to twenty cubic centimetres are usually abstracted. The whole blood is used, 5 per cent. sodium citrate being added to prevent coagulation. Defibrination is apparently detrimental to the virus, and should not be carried out unless the blood has to be transported some distance. Constant results are secured only by intraperitoneal inoculation, and in monkeys 4 to 5 c.c. is a sufficient dose in the case of foreign blood. In passage from monkey to monkey smaller doses can be employed, while if the blood does not seem to be very virulent, the dose may be increased. The infection can be kept going indefinitely and remains constant, neither lessening nor increasing. The weight and temperature of the monkey must be taken twice daily for forty days.

---

* It seems advisable to refer briefly to further important investigations of Todd and Wolbach on typhus fever in Poland. This is the more desirable as, though these were conducted after the period of hostilities, they were a direct outcome of the war and possess great significance. Together with Palfrey these investigators published a preliminary note in the *International Journal of Public Health*, September 1920, but the complete record of their researches is enshrined and beautifully illustrated in the volume entitled " The Ætiology and Pathology of Typhus," which constitutes the main report of the Typhus Research Commission of the League of Red Cross Societies to Poland. This authoritative document was published in 1922 and, in addition to giving an account of the investigations conducted, deals more fully with the recent literature of typhus than it has been possible to do in this volume.

Todd and Wolbach were led to the conclusion that *Rickettsia prowazeki* is the cause of typhus fever, a view based on the result of experiments showing that the virus of typhus and *Rickettsia prowazeki* are inseparable in infective lice and to a less extent on the fact that bodies indistinguishable from *Rickettsia prowazeki* can be demonstrated with great regularity in the lesions of typhus in man.

Given sufficient dosage, intraperitoneal injections and good virus, a reproduction in monkeys of a febrile malady identical, at least so far as the temperature curve is concerned, with typhus in man, results from the inoculation.

As a rule the disease in monkeys is less severe than that in man, but sometimes it is equally grave, and death may occur during the febrile period or during convalescence after a variable period of low temperature and marasmus.

The incubation period, which may be greatly prolonged, is always quiescent, and even during the first days of fever the animal may not appear ill. Abnormal symptoms set in about the third or fourth day and consist in loss of appetite, thirst, fatigue, depression of spirits, the hair standing on end, injection and watering of the eyes, transient facial flushings, mottling of the skin and sometimes an eruption. When the last occurs it is limited to the face and ears, and the spots, which disappear on pressure, occur either isolated or in groups.

Defervescence is nearly always followed by a sub-normal temperature often lasting only one or two days. Marasmus is present during the second part of the febrile period and the beginning of convalescence. Leucopenia precedes and accompanies the cessation of pyrexia. Fever is the main symptom and appears after an incubation period which, following an intraperitoneal inoculation of 4 to 5 c.c. of blood, lasts on an average from six to ten days. The duration of the febrile period in moderately severe and in grave cases varies between five and fourteen days, the average being seven to ten days. The temperature rises rapidly to 104° F. or thereabouts. There are no morning remissions of note, and defervescence is by lysis, which, however, is usually rapid. Relapses have been noted only in the case of monkeys infected by lice. In slight and abortive cases the incubation period is generally prolonged and the fever, of short duration, runs a variable course. Apart from progressive loss of weight, symptoms are not as a rule manifest.

In the case of guinea-pigs, after intraperitoneal inoculation of virulent blood in amounts varying from 2 c.c. to 8 c.c., the animals receiving the larger doses die in a few days, showing wasting, sub-normal temperature and sometimes paralysis. Those given only 2 to 3 c.c. show no symptoms beyond a slight and transient loss of weight. In the majority of cases, however, after an incubation of seven to twelve days a fever of some days' duration is set up. This slight infection is undoubtedly typhus for it is inoculable to monkeys. Without a thermometer the disease would pass unrecognized in guinea-pigs and, having in view the incubation period, any pyrexia occurring before the fifth day after inoculation is not to be regarded as due to typhus. Some animals do not react at all, some very slightly. Guinea-pig typhus can be transmitted from an infected animal to a healthy non-immune by means of the blood or organs. Nicolle has carried out 175 passages during five and a half years, the virulence remaining constant. The technique employed is to remove blood by heart puncture on the second or third day of the fever and to inject 2·5 to 4 c.c. intraperitoneally. The incubation period is not influenced by the day of the fever on which the blood was abstracted. Small doses do not affect guinea-pigs save when the intracerebral route is employed, in which case one drop of blood is sufficient. The resulting infection does not differ in severity from that following intraperitoneal injection. Subcutaneous and intramuscular injections are less certain. Abortion on the second day of the fever is the rule in pregnant females. The organs of the fœtus or new-born pigs are virulent. Temperature should be taken *per rectum*, the thermometer being carefully introduced to a depth of 8 cm., as otherwise damage to the mucous membrane, and possibly peritonitis, may occur. If the virus becomes contaminated it can be purified by passage through the monkey. In guinea-pigs, as in monkeys, the temperature of inoculated animals should be taken for forty days. Absence of pyrexia during this period indicates that no infection has taken place. Some guinea-pigs do not react, but if their blood be taken at the same period as blood from others, inoculated simultaneously with the same virus, it will be found to be virulent. These cases are termed "non-apparent infections."

The rabbit reacts badly, the incubation period being remarkably long, *i.e.*, thirty-three to thirty-five days. Infection is best secured by intravenous inoculation of organs, for example, the suprarenal tissue. The only symptom is fever, which has not yet been fully studied. Rabbit's blood is infective to guinea-pigs, and in the only experiment conducted rabbit to rabbit infection proved successful. The fact that normal rabbit blood possesses considerable toxicity for other animals, notably the guinea-pig, is a serious disadvantage.

Intraperitoneal inoculation of the rat with infected guinea-pig blood produces no symptoms, but the blood of the inoculated rat, taken at the moment when a control-infected guinea-pig shows fever, proves virulent for the guinea-pig in the same quantity as the guinea-pig's blood.

In a few cases inoculations of blood from a typhus patient into a healthy individual, as for example in the case of a medical man purposely infecting himself, or when typhus has been mistaken for some other disease, have proved positive. Under ordinary conditions man to man inoculation is of course inadmissible.

Nicolle has shown that blood is virulent during the whole of the febrile period in man, the chimpanzee, the lower monkeys and guinea-pigs. It is also possibly virulent two days before and the day following the actual fever. The virulence may apparently increase during the course of the pyrexia.

Both in man and in infected animals the virus is found not only in the blood. In guinea-pigs all the organs, even when deprived of blood by injecting the arteries with salt solution, are virulent. The brain and suprarenals are apparently the most virulent.

Moellers and Wolff found that the incubation period in guinea-pigs varied from five to twenty-one days. They recommend for experimental purposes animals of 200 to 300 grm., as, if heavier, they are less sensitive.

Otto and Dietrich in their work on guinea-pigs employed as inoculum defibrinated or citrated blood, serum, washed corpuscles and extracts of organs, all of which proved effective means of transmitting the virus. Clinically they noted fever and malaise. Nicolle finds that washed red blood cells are non-virulent and that the virus is not invariably present in the serum. The leucocytes, however, are always highly infective.

Blanc carried out work at Nish in Serbia, and succeeded in producing typhus in thirteen guinea-pigs out of twenty inoculated. For a " normal virus " he used 1 grm. of guinea-pig tissue emulsified in 1 c.c. of water, and states that 22 c.c. of a decinormal virus was the minimum infective dose. Apparently the Nish virus was weak, for it did not produce abortion in pregnant female guinea-pigs nor were the young born infected. This author states that the cerebro-spinal fluid of human cases with meningeal symptoms proved virulent for guinea-pigs.

A most extensive research on guinea-pig typhus was carried out in Vienna by Doerr and Pick. They confirmed the work of Nicolle and Blaizot, proved that the brain of infected animals is a constant source of the virus, and that from it a "passage virus " can be transmitted from one guinea-pig to another by intraperitoneal inoculation. Heart blood is also effective. Similar investigations were conducted by Landsteiner and Hausmann.

The length of the incubation is largely independent of the dose of the virus or the site of inoculation. The virulence of the " passage virus " as compared with the original virulence was not increased.

Pathology.

Prior to the war the gross pathology of typhus might be summed up in the words of Ker : " There is no pathognomonic sign by which the disease can be recognized after death." During the war, however, and since its termination a flood of light has been thrown on the pathology of the disease, and a large literature has accumulated.

Changes in the Blood and Cerebro-spinal Fluid.—In view of what has been said regarding the virulence of the leucocytes, the fact that they are manifestly altered, as recorded by Nicolle, may be significant. Rothacker states that in toxic cases immature and irritation forms are considerably increased early in the disease, while Schilling asserts that a large proportion of all the neutrophiles possess a pathological character. The inclusions observed in the polymorphs by Prowazek have been mentioned, and they have also been seen by Lipschütz, who recorded them from 18 out of 23 cases examined, noted their size as about $0 \cdot 3 \, \mu$, and did not find them in controls which included cases of enteric, variola and normal blood. Rothacker states that Döhle's inclusion bodies are found as in scarlet fever. The most complete studies of the general blood picture appear to be those by this author and by Daniélopolu. The former says that it is not typical and varies in all three stages of the disease, while even in the same stage it may present entirely different appearances according to the severity of the attack and the reaction of the patient. In what he calls the influenzal stage, occupying the first four days, the blood picture is usually normal in those toxic cases to which reference has already been made. Eosinophiles are scanty. In the eruptive stage, though the total number of leucocytes remains normal, the relative percentage of the polymorphonuclear leucocytes is increased. Eosinophiles are absent. From the tenth day onwards the blood picture entirely changes. The total number of leucocytes varies ; it is usually between 10,000 and 14,000, and often between 6,000 and 8,000, but rarely below 6,000. It is entirely independent of the severity of the disease. From the tenth day onwards the relative number of leucocytes is constant in all cases ; the polymorphonuclears are 95 to 97 per cent., of which often 10 to 15 per cent. are transitional, irritation and immature forms. Myelocytes are scanty. The normal full-grown neutrophil leucocytes remain in about the same number throughout the disease. Lymphocytes are as low as 3 to 6 per cent. Eosinophiles are absent. The red corpuscles often number only two to three million. The hæmoglobin is normal. This blood picture remains about the same until the temperature becomes normal. In convalescence the total number of leucocytes often shows a considerable increase. Eosinophiles reappear, pathological forms disappear and lymphocytosis occurs. By the eighth to tenth day of convalescence the blood picture is normal again. In short, the blood picture has no diagnostic value before the tenth day, and a diagnosis of typhus cannot be made from it alone, as smallpox and many septicæmic diseases present similar appearances.

Daniélopolu, working at Jassy, found the red cell count normal unless there is cyanosis with cold extremities, when the blood is blackish in colour and may show a polycythæmia of 7,500,000. The red cells themselves are normal. As a rule there is a leucocytosis, though there may be an initial leucopenia. The count varies with the severity of the case. In bad cases it may be anything between 20,000 and 128,000. It has a definite prognostic value, and the author correlates it with different types of the disease. He has also investigated the differential leucocyte count, and finds, in contradistinction to the results of others, that there is a mononuclear increase which may be very marked. He states that Türck's cells are constantly present, and more numerous in severe and fatal cases. Myelocytes are rare or absent. Stefanopoulo, who examined cases in Alexandria in 1916–17, obtained very similar results. On the other hand, Schürer states that any neutrophil leucocytosis which has been described is due to complications, especially broncho-pneumonia, and is never seen before the seventh or eighth day of the disease. An increase in the number of leucocytes in the first few days of the fever almost certainly excludes typhus, in which there is a leucopenia or a normal leucocyte count, which is very helpful in distinguishing typhus fever from severe influenza, where there is always a leucocytosis from the first. He considers the blood picture in typhus as very like that seen in enteric fever, only the leucopenia is not so constant and the relative lymphocytosis is less marked.

Weissenbach regards the leucocytic count as of prognostic value, as severe cases, likely to die, exhibit a marked hyperleucocytosis and a high neutrophil polymorphonucleosis.

Fairley, in Egypt, investigated twelve uncomplicated cases. During the first week absence of leucocytosis or a definite leucopenia was the rule with a moderate grade of leucocytosis (10,500 to 14,000 per cubic millimetre) during the second week. The differential leucocyte count in the second week showed an absolute and relative increase of polymorphs and a decrease of eosinophiles, a point noted long ago by Wilson.

As regards the cerebro-spinal fluid, Heuyer, from a study of cases in Albania, states that during the acute stage of the disease and in the forms accompanied by delirium the cerebro-spinal fluid presented the following characters : (1) Increased tension similar to that seen in definite meningitis and cerebral tumour. As the disease subsided, and in very mild forms without delirium or any meningeal reaction, the hypertension was less pronounced. (2) The fluid was clear, but had not the " rock water " appearance of normal cerebro-spinal fluid. (3) Excess of albumin shown by testing with nitric acid, when a thick cloud or flaky deposit was formed. (4) Leucocytosis. This was always very definite and was more intense than was sometimes found in enteric or malaria. In the acute stage, and especially in the forms accompanied by delirium, there was a definite predominance of the polymorphonuclears over the lymphocytes in the proportion of three to one, together with a few large mononuclears and endothelial cells. At the end of the disease or after the fall of the temperature, or in very mild cases, the cellular reaction was chiefly lymphocytic.

Rothacker affirms that in his cases the cerebro-spinal fluid pressure was seldom above 120 mm. of water. He found a slight increase of albumin and a great increase of cellular elements of very varied forms. Monteleone's findings were similar.

The later researches of Daniélopolu have caused him to alter his first opinion that the cerebro-spinal fluid in typhus is always clear. He finds that it may be turbid from a high cellular reaction or a large number of red blood corpuscles, the latter due to hæmorrhagic lesions in the meninges or to excessive engorgement of cerebral blood-vessels. Altered blood pigment may render the fluid xanthochromatic, and this character is associated with increased pressure, a tendency to coagulate and excess of albumin and of cells, these being chiefly mononuclears. Noguchi's reaction for globulin is positive. The colour change was present in 34 per cent. of the 142 cases examined, usually appears during the second week of the fever and is associated with a hæmic leucocytosis. Even in grave and fatal cases the cerebro-spinal fluid may remain colourless. During convalescence the mononuclears and polymorphonuclears disappear and lymphocytes are present.

Devaux, from a study of the cerebro-spinal fluid in two hundred cases of typhus, decided that the virus is essentially neurotropic and that cyto-diagnosis by the method of Widal and Ravaut possesses considerable clinical and prognostic importance. He found that leucocytosis was early and constant, persisting from a minimum of two months to a maximum of eight months. In the first week there was an increase of lymphocytes and mononuclears, in the second a further increase of mononuclears, a diminution of lymphocytes and an increase in polymorphonuclears, at the end of the third a rapid diminution of mononuclears and a persistence of small lymphocytes. His observations, so far as the mononucleosis is concerned, have been confirmed by Tupa, working at Marseilles in 1919, who, however, found in addition an early polynucleosis together with a great number of Türck's mononuclear cells showing an intensely basic cytoplasm.

Morbid Anatomy.—This has been studied by Jaffé, who performed forty necropsies, chiefly on patients dying between the tenth and sixteenth days of the disease and for the most part from complications and not from typhus itself. His description of the macroscopic appearances may be summarized as follows :—

1. Marked tendency to hæmorrhage both subcutaneous and on serous and mucous surfaces.

2. Great dryness of muscles, as observed by Aschoff.

3. Muscles show Zenker's degeneration.

4. Greasy condition of peritoneum.

5. Spleen greyish-red in colour, enlarged and very soft in early stages ; later firmer and somewhat less enlarged. (Bauer found the spleen seldom enlarged but hard with hyperplasia of the follicles.)

6. Nothing characteristic in liver substance. Bile very thick, treacly in consistence and black-green in colour.

7. Punctiform hæmorrhages in the kidneys. Capsules strip readily. Sometimes grey nodules between cortex and medulla due to specific typhus foci.

8. Adrenals deficient in lipoids. (Daniélopolu and Simici mention lesions in the medulla of the adrenals which may even be destroyed by blood-clots.)

9. Brain appears normal. Cerebro-spinal fluid generally somewhat increased.

To sum up, there are no pathognomonic lesions but there are certain changes which, taken together, are highly suggestive. This opinion does not wholly coincide with that of Reynolds, who at Baku early in 1919 had an opportunity of studying *post-mortem* six cases (4 British, 1 Indian and 1 Rumanian) of *uncomplicated* typhus fever. His notes (unpublished) are evidently the result of very careful observation and he states :—

" Our experience, small though it be, has convinced us that the autopsy on a case of typhus fever shows certain characteristics which are not found in other toxæmic or septicæmic conditions and which would cause us to make a diagnosis of typhus fever with a considerable degree of certainty even in cases where the history of the patient prior to the autopsy was unknown, or where the diagnosis of typhus fever had not been established or even considered before death. This opinion is shared by the clinicians who attended regularly at the autopsies conducted by us whilst stationed at Baku.

" The chief appearances seen at autopsy to which we would draw attention as characteristic of the disease are :—

" I. Those associated with a toxæmia of great severity as shown, in particular, by extreme degenerative changes in the heart muscle ; by extensive and profound fatty degeneration of the liver ; by a condition in the lungs indistinguishable to the naked eye from a hæmorrhagic pneumonia ; by great engorgement of the vessels of both systemic and pulmonary circulation ; by the occurrence of petechial hæmorrhages below the pleura, pericardium, capsules of the kidneys ; by great excess of cerebro-spinal fluid ; and by dilatation of the cerebral ventricles.

" II. Those constantly met with in typhus fever and distinguishing it, in our experience, from other conditions, namely, a curious purple colour of the tissues and organs ; very dark fluid blood in which clotting takes place very slowly, or not at all, even after removal from the corpse ; and no naked-eye disappearance of the fat-like constituent of the suprarenal glands."

He comments especially on the curious purple colour seen in all the cases and in many of the tissues and organs and he regards it as pathognomonic of typhus fever. He says that it is difficult to describe but once seen is never forgotten. It is a lighter purple and more glistening than that seen at autopsies of patients who have died of one of the more usual acute toxæmic conditions.

" Sometimes it is a ' sheen ' which may disappear very quickly on exposure to air, being seen in some cases for merely a second or so after the knife has cut the tissues. This characteristic colour is seen usually when first incising the body, being noticed in the subcutaneous tissues and especially in the muscles. We have seen it on exposing the lungs, heart, internal fat, intestines and liver and on the cut surface of the organs when sectioning them. All those who attended any of our autopsies on cases of typhus fever were able to convince themselves of the existence of this curious phenomenon and agreed that it was different to anything observed during the course of *post-mortem* examinations on subjects who had died from conditions, acute or chronic, other than typhus fever."

In no case did he find any naked-eye evidence of the disappearance of the fat-like (cholesterin-ester) constituent of the suprarenal glands, and he regards this as very striking. Unfortunately, he was unable to study sections of the suprarenal cortex.

Histo-pathology.—This is of greater importance than the morbid anatomy. Prior to the war Fraenkel had commenced to examine the cutaneous eruption in typhus, and had found the endothelium and elastic layers of the walls of the skin capillaries affected, so that nodules were produced filled with infiltrating lymphocytes. The prevalence of typhus during the war gave him an opportunity of confirming and greatly extending his observations. It is now known that the eruption consists in a localized necrosis of the walls of the small vessels, with the formation of discrete nodules composed of cells of the adventitia, lymphocytes and plasma cells.

Typhus is essentially a systemic disease of the smaller arteries and capillaries, not only of the skin, as was at first supposed, but of all the viscera, and more especially the brain and upper part of the cord, as has been demonstrated by Jaffé, Jarisch, Ceelen, Nicol and other workers. This important fact explains many of the symptoms of the disease, for the nodules often lead to irritation, stenosis and thrombus formation. Hence the occurrence of the gangrene so often seen in the lower extremities ; hence, as a result of hæmorrhage following the thrombosis, the conversion of the inflammatory roseolæ into petechiæ ; and hence, owing to the involvement of the central nervous system, the diffuse irritative symptoms, the various local paralyses, and the disordered sensations met with in typhus.

According to Jaffé the nodules are found in the greatest numbers in the region of the aqueduct of Sylvius. Jarisch and Nicol found them most numerous in the olivary nucleus of the medulla, and different authors have described them in various viscera, Kuczynski figuring them in the liver and showing the presence of Rickettsia in them. Nicol has summarized recent investigations and has examined a large number of cases in which death occurred at all stages of the disease. He speaks of the condition as a widespread focal arteriolitis and periarteriolitis, in which there is a necrosis and proliferation of the endothelium, together with perivascular infiltration of leucocytes and other cells. He finds that the foci disappear if the patient survives, but that small scars may be left behind.

According to Herzog the perivascular nodules do not occur before the ninth day of the illness, *i.e.*, from seventeen to nineteen days after infection. Parodi, a recent investigator, differs somewhat in his views, which have been summarized as follows :—*

(1) He does not think that the vascular changes observed in the brain are due to a primary lesion of the intima, and in particular to a primary circumscribed necrosis. He does not deny that the virus of typhus may cause changes of a necrobiotic type in the small vessels, but in his opinion they are not constant, and the perivascular changes appear to develop independently of necrobiotic lesions in the vessel walls. (2) He has not hitherto found lesions of a hæmorrhagic type in the brain as described by Jarisch. (3) He has not observed any lesions of proliferative endovasculitis as described by Bauer. (4) Polymorphonuclear leucocytes may take part in the formation of inflammatory foci and are often observed in small numbers in the neighbourhood of an area of encephalitis associated with necrobiotic changes in the corresponding capillaries.

A considerable literature has accumulated on the subject of these nodules. It should be noted that Otto and Dietrich, Grzywo-Dabrowski, Kuczynski, and Doerr and Kirschner have demonstrated their frequent presence in infected guineapigs though they are absent in 15 to 20 per cent. of guineapigs certainly affected with typhus. The lesions occur specially in the brain, notably the medullary region, and appear soon after the onset of fever. They have not been found in rabbits. Controls are invariably negative and there is no doubt that these changes are almost specific.

As regards other features of the histo-pathology in man, it would seem that the most frequent and specific changes occur in the brain, where Grzywo-Dabrowski has found accumulations of cells, together with a diffuse inflammation of the brain substance and meninges. He also describes hæmorrhages and proliferation of the neuroglia cells.

A. C. Stevenson, in an unpublished observation, noted a round-celled infiltration of the walls of the small arteries in the cerebrum and pons, and sometimes a plugging of the vessels with leucocytes, mostly polymorphs.

In the enlarged spleen phagocytosis of red corpuscles and much pigment in the splenic cells have been recorded. The liver, heart and kidney often present infiltration of lymphocytes and plasma cells and a proliferation of the adventitia cells of vessels. Hæmorrhages are common in the kidneys and the heart often shows hyperæmia. According to Grzywo-Dabrowski, the testes, spinal cord, corpora cavernosa, and occasionally the kidneys, exhibit perivascular accumulation of cells like those seen in the brain, while small yellowish thickenings·may be present in the aorta due to proliferation of the cells of the intima.

---

* *Medical Science*, March 1920.

The histo-pathology has also been studied in experimental animals. Thus Neill was led to study the scrotal lesions in guinea-pig typhus owing to the resemblance of typhus to Rocky Mountain spotted fever and the definite scrotal lesions in the latter. He found hæmorrhages in the cremasteric fascia and in the testicle immediately below the visceral laminæ of the tunica vaginalis. They varied from minute petechiæ to large areas, but the lesions, unlike those in Rocky Mountain fever, soon clear up. Twenty-six out of thirty-seven male guinea-pigs were thus affected. The smaller arteries show necrosis of the intima and perivascular accumulation of cells, chiefly mononuclears.

Otto and Dietrich, in addition to the vascular nodules, found moderate enlargement of the axillary and inguinal glands, swelling and injection of the adrenals and small hæmorrhagic infarcts in the lungs and liver. As a rule there was no splenic enlargement.

Doerr and Pick state that no definite lesions occur in the rabbit.

It is specially interesting to note that, in the case of monkeys, Nicolle observed that myocardial degeneration may cause sudden death after the normal health has apparently been recovered.

Laboratory Diagnosis.

One of the most important aids in the laboratory diagnosis of typhus has been the discovery of the so-called Weil-Felix reaction. Reference has already been made to the pioneer work of Wilson in Belfast, which long preceded the discovery by Weil and Felix in 1915 of an organism of the proteus group in the urine of a case proved to be typhus, and which was agglutinated by the patient's serum and by the sera of nine other typhus cases in a dilution of 1 in 200. They named it "X 2." At a later date a second strain of a similar bacillus, christened " X 19," was isolated from the urine. It differed from X 2 in being agglutinated by the sera of typhus patients in a dilution of 1 in 2,000.

Further investigation showed that in 90 per cent. of 500 cases of typhus fever in the German army agglutination of the bacillus was obtainable in a 1 in 100 or higher dilution, whereas it was absent or only present to a feeble extent in an equal number of non-typhus controls. A huge literature has now accumulated on the subject. The following is an account of the work of British medical officers carried out during the war in this direction.

Craig and Fairley tested the reaction in ninety cases in Egypt and Palestine during the early part of 1918. They used a stock culture of the strain X 19, which they describe as a short, Gram-negative, slightly motile and obligatively aërobic bacillus. It throve on ordinary media, liquefied gelatin, produced acid and gas in glucose, saccharose, maltose and mannite, but did not ferment dulcite or lactose. It produced indol freely and acid without clot formation in milk. Subcutaneous inoculation with 2 c.c. of a twenty-four hours' broth culture proved non-lethal to guinea-pigs.

In a few cases they obtained rather anomalous results in the way of delayed agglutination or negative findings but otherwise the reaction was noted in the first examination.

In forty-five British cases examined during the pyrexial period, agglutination titres varying from 1 in 10 to 1 in 2,800 were obtained. In twenty-one native cases, probably all in the second week of illness, the titres were 1 in 10 to 1 in 2,000.

In twenty-four convalescent cases agglutination reactions were also obtained in varying titre. The maximum height of the agglutinin curve was obtained in the second and third weeks of the disease. There were adequate controls which are fully recorded, as are complement fixation and animal experiments. In discussing the significance of the reaction they combat the view which Austrian and German observers held at that time (1918) that the proteus-like bacillus must be regarded as a constant secondary invader in typhus patients, pointing out that such a conception, though explaining the appearance of agglutinin in the blood of typhus cases, is incompatible with the following facts.

" 1. Systematic culture investigations of the urine and blood in cases of typhus fever over all stages of the disease do not yield, except very exceptionally, positive results for this proteus-like organism, and this despite the fact that it grows easily on all ordinary laboratory media, i.e., nutrient broth, agar, etc.

" 2. Serological investigations of typhus cases, while showing the presence of agglutinin for this proteus-like organism, failed to demonstrate the presence of any immune body ; whereas serological investigations of monkeys inoculated subcutaneously yield both positive agglutination and complement-fixation reactions. If the ' secondary invasion ' theory were correct, then inevitably the immune body would be demonstrable in the sera of typhus cases."

They therefore regard the agglutination phenomenon as a pseudo-agglutination and possibly of the nature of a group agglutination. If this be true the typhus virus may be an organism allied to the proteus-like bacillus but incapable of cultivation on ordinary media.

At the same time they regard the test as of the greatest clinical value and conclude their paper as follows :—

" 1. This agglutination test is an invaluable aid in the diagnosis of typhus fever.

" 2. Frequently the reaction appears only in the disease, and as a rule rapidly increases in titre.

" 3. A rapid agglutination in a dilution of 1 in 10 on Garrow's agglutinometer, while not absolutely reliable, is sufficiently suspicious to justify the isolation of the case. This is especially true of individuals uninoculated with T.A.B. or cholera. The serum of fifty uninoculated natives failed to give a reaction even in a dilution of 1 in 10. If the test be repeated at intervals of two days, confirmatory evidence will in the great majority of cases be obtained.

" 4. The test is particularly valuable in the case of natives in whom it may be difficult to distinguish clinically between severe relapsing fever and typhus."

At a later date Fairley carried out a further series of observations which served to confirm these conclusions. Thirty-five cases were examined during the pyrexial period, twenty-five during convalescence, and in four progressive agglutination readings were made.

The complement-fixation reaction was again performed, the antigens used being of two types :—

" *Antigen A.*—This antigen consisted of a fresh saline suspension of a twenty-four hours' growth of *Bacillus proteus* on agar slants (this antigen was the one used in fifty-eight cases of typhus fever, and in animal and human inoculation experiments)."

" *Antigen B.*—In this method the (fresh) saline suspensions prepared from growths of *Bacillus proteus* on agar slopes (twenty-four hours old), were heated to 56° C. for one hour and then carefully centrifuged. The supernatant suspension was utilized as antigen. (This was used to investigate nine cases of typical typhus.) In standardizing the antigen it was found advisable never to use more than one-third the anti-complementary dose."

The serological reactions in inoculated monkeys were also again determined and the results were summarized as follows :—

" 1. The Weil-Felix agglutination reaction has again proved, in a further series of cases, to be a very reliable laboratory aid to the diagnosis of typhus fever.

" 2. Frequently the reaction becomes definitely established during the first week of the disease. The maximum agglutination readings are obtained during the second week of fever and during the first week of convalescence, *i.e.*, eighth to twenty-first day.

" 3. Of sixty-five cases of definite typhus fever, sixty-three, or 94 per cent., yielded positive agglutination reactions.

" 4. Of 120 non-typhus sera no case yielded positive agglutination in a dilution of 1 in 20, utilizing Garrow's method of agglutination. In two cases an agglutination in a dilution of 1 in 10 was obtained. On the Garrow's agglutinometer a positive agglutination of patient's serum in a titre of 1 in 40 may be regarded as diagnostic of typhus fever. A positive reaction in a dilution of 1 in 20 of patient's serum may be regarded as sufficient evidence on which to isolate a case during the first week of illness.

" 5. The appearance of the agglutinin in the sera of typhus cases for the *Bacillus proteus* utilized in the present investigation is not accompanied by the formation of specific immune body. On the other hand, living cultures inoculated subcutaneously into monkeys and man are followed, not only by the appearance of agglutinin, but also by the production of immune body as revealed by the complement-fixation test, utilizing *Bacillus proteus* as antigen.

" 6. The hypothesis that *Bacillus proteus* is a constant secondary invader accompanying the unknown virus of typhus fever lacks confirmation and is incompatible with certain ascertained facts. The Weil-Felix reaction is dependent on the presence in typhus sera of a secondary non-specific agglutinin which has the property of agglutinating this proteus-like organism."

Reynolds, working at Baku from March to July 1919, conducted a similar series of careful investigations on thirty-two acute cases of typhus, twenty convalescent cases and twenty-one diseases other than typhus. The acute cases were studied in No. 40 Field Ambulance, Baku, the remainder in No. 25 Casualty Clearing Station, Baku. The strain of proteus used was X 19. The technique employed is fully detailed and the reaction of the bacillus with normal serum and with normal saline solution is described. The control cases included malaria, enteric fever, acute apical pneumonia, relapsing fever, acute epidemic jaundice, pulmonary tuberculosis with carcinoma and pleural effusion.

In none of these diseases was agglutination obtained in a dilution of serum of 1 in 100, while in one instance only (acute apical pneumonia) was there any agglutination in 1 in 50, and then only a trace. As regards other controls with normal serum in a dilution of 1 in 50, no agglutination was ever obtained nor did auto-agglutination occur when normal saline solution was used in control tests.

In the acute typhus cases high agglutination titres, in one instance up to 1 in 8,000 are recorded, while in the convalescent series, at least early in convalescence, *i.e.*, twenty to thirty days after the onset of the disease, titres varying from 1 in 500 to 1 in 10,000 were obtained.

Captain Reynold's conclusions are as follows :—

(1) Agglutination obtained by serum in a dilution of 1 in 100 indicates typhus fever.

(2) If no agglutination is given by the serum in this dilution after about the eighth day from the onset of the disease, acute typhus fever is excluded.

(3) A positive reaction is given by the serum for a varying number of weeks after an attack of typhus fever. There is no relationship in different cases between the time after the attack and the agglutination titre of the serum.

At the instigation of Lieut.-Colonel J. C. G. Ledingham, Consulting Bacteriologist to the Mesopotamian Expeditionary Force, Capt. L. E. Napier, during 1918 and 1919, investigated the Weil-Felix reaction in a mild epidemic of typhus amongst Armenians in a refugee camp at Ba'qubah, about 30 miles north-east of Baghdad. Of the total 109 cases 102 were amongst Armenians, 5 were British and 2 Indian. The tests were carried out in the case of the Armenians and thus possess a special interest as typhus is more or less endemic in their country.

Indeed, Napier refers to them as a " typhus-ridden people." A
proteus X 19 strain was employed, which gave acid only in
glucose and saccharose with no change in lactose, mannite
and dulcite. Forty definite but mild cases of typhus were
investigated at periods varying from the fourteenth to the
thirtieth day of the disease, and agglutination titres as high as
1 in 10,000 were in some instances obtained. Another group
of eleven cases was specially instructive, inasmuch as the specimens from them were sent to the laboratory " either to confirm
the diagnosis or by a sceptical medical officer who did not
believe in our ability to make a diagnosis in the laboratory
without first seeing the case." They were all positive and all
proved clinically to be unmistakable cases of typhus. In one
instance a titre of 1 in 20,000 was forthcoming on the sixteenth day. It was unfortunately impossible to obtain the
blood earlier than the fifth day.

There were two sets of controls : (a) Fifty normal refugees,
men, women and children, who had not been ill for at least
six months. The highest dilution in which a positive result
was obtained was 1 in 160. Only one gave agglutination
in a dilution of 1 in 100. Four gave it in a dilution of 1
in 50 ; hence for diagnostic purposes Napier considers it is
of little value to start with a dilution lower than 1 in 50.
(b) Twenty-four cases suffering from febrile conditions totally
incompatible with a diagnosis of typhus, and three other
hospital cases. Amongst the febrile cases figure enteric,
paratyphoid, malaria, pneumonia and relapsing fever.

Of the twenty-four febrile cases, two gave agglutination in
a dilution of 1 in 100 and eight in 1 in 50. Excluding four
cases of enteric, no case gave agglutination in a dilution of
1 in 100 while five cases gave it in 1 in 50. It would therefore
seem that the agglutinability of the blood for the organism
tested was increased to a slight extent in any febrile condition
and that the increase is quite marked in the case of enteric
fever. The reverse, says Napier, is also true, i.e., the blood of
a typhus patient will usually agglutinate B. typhosus in a
dilution of 1 in 20 and often in 1 in 100. Apparently the
three paratyphoid cases tested gave no agglutination.

In discussing his results, Napier adopts the view that the
Weil-Felix reaction may be classed with the Widal as merely an
aid, though a very definite aid, to diagnosis. It is unsafe to
make a positive diagnosis unless a higher titre than 1 in 50
is obtained. Agglutination in a dilution of 1 in 100 within the
first six days of the disease is a comparatively trustworthy

indication of typhus, but the most reliable points in diagnosis are the increasing titre in the early and the decreasing titre in the later stages of the disease.

Napier thinks that a disadvantage of the reaction is that in an ordinary severe case by the seventh day, the earliest day on which one can guarantee a definite result, the diagnosis clinically is usually beyond doubt. This, however, does not apply in the milder form of the disease and hence the reaction is of special value in this type of typhus.

Compton, during the typhus season in Syria at the close of 1918 and beginning of 1919, examined fourteen cases in British, Indian and Turkish prisoners of war. His results, which are in accord with those of other workers, need not be detailed, but he thinks that where a feebly positive Weil-Felix reaction is obtained, as in one of his recorded cases, it may be an example of the non-apparent infection described in guinea-pigs by Nicolle and Lebailly.

It is interesting to note that Doerr and Pick failed to isolate proteus X 19 from animals infected with passage virus, nor was such virus neutralized in its effect by potent anti-X 19 serum. Furthermore, the serum of infected animals gave no Weil-Felix reaction. They therefore conclude that the latter has nothing to do with the morbific agent of typhus fever.

Landsteiner and Hausmann conducted cross-immunity experiments with X 19 and typhus virus which, being negative, point to a similar conclusion.

Schilling believes that the blood picture he has described is a great aid in diagnosis, but, as pointed out by Nicolle and others, the only certain diagnostic method is the inoculation of a guinea-pig, unless a monkey is available, by the method already detailed. Several animals should be used and not more than 2·5 c.c. of blood given to each.

Immunization.

As is well known, an attack of typhus almost invariably confers lasting immunity, relapses and second attacks being very rare. The same holds good in guinea-pigs and monkeys if the first attack is a severe one. Nicolle has shown that inoculation with virus heated to 50° C. produces no immunity. Inoculation of the serum of a sick person or that of an animal recovered from the disease or hyperimmunized usually protects from infection by inoculation of virus. Small injections of virus, *i.e.*, too small to cause active disease, may produce a certain degree of immunity.

Immunity acquired by a primary infection is very rapidly established. In animals a test inoculation of virus is inactive on the fourth day after defervescence and immunity in the case of guinea-pigs and monkeys lasts more than one year. It has been proved in the case of the guinea-pig not to be hereditary.

Nicolle states that the normal serum of man, anthropoid monkeys and guinea-pigs contains no protective or neutralizing substance. The serum of convalescent patients and animals often does. Monkeys protected by such an immune serum six and twenty-four hours prior to inoculation of virus are found to have acquired a complete immunity. The serum also contains curative properties, but in a much smaller degree. Nicolle and Blaizot have prepared a specific serum by repeated inoculations of virus into the horse or ass. As an inoculum they used the suprarenals and spleen of " passage " guinea-pigs powdered fine. Intravenous inoculation of this material is well borne by both horse and ass and may be repeated every two or three days for several months. After about thirty inoculations the blood of the ass possesses protective and curative substances similar to those found in the blood of convalescents. Tests of their potency are best made on monkeys as the serum, being prepared from guinea-pig tissues, may be highly toxic to guinea-pigs. Very minute and repeated doses, *i.e.*, $0\cdot25$ c.c. at a time, may, however, be safely employed in the case of guinea-pigs.

Doerr and Pick have confirmed Nicolle's work on immunization and have shown that it follows either a typical or abortive fever course in animals infected with passage virus. Like some other observers, they found that the serum of convalescents, even when injected twenty-four hours after the virulent passage virus, would completely inhibit the pyrogenic power of the latter.

Landsteiner and Hausmann have also demonstrated active immunity in guinea-pigs and have carried out work with attenuated virus, the bare reference to which must suffice. Their paper gives a very full account of laboratory research in typhus.

Serotherapy.

Various attempts at what may be called the " specific treatment " of typhus have been made and a considerable literature on the subject has accumulated, but none of it appears to be of British origin.

The principal measures adopted have been the employment of various sensitized vaccines, auto-serotherapy, the intravenous transfusion of the whole citrated blood from convalescents, the intrathecal injection of blood serum from convalescents, the use of convalescent serum reinforced by virulent blood, the injection of the patient's cerebro-spinal fluid into his own veins or subcutaneously, and the employment of the anti-typhus serum introduced by Nicolle and Blaizot, the preparation of which has been mentioned.

Although it can scarcely be classed as a " specific " treatment, mention may be made of the intravenous administration of typhoid vaccine in Bulgaria. This is said to have done good but the evidence is by no means satisfactory.

It is very difficult to determine the real value of any of the " specific " treatments, for the personal equation cannot be excluded and different outbreaks of typhus vary much in severity. The vaccine methods need not be considered for they are mere " shots in the dark," there being no evidence that the organisms used in their preparation bear any ætiological relationship to typhus.

As regards the blood and blood serum methods, there seems to be a general consensus of opinion that they are beneficial, especially if adopted early in severe cases. The same is true of Nicolle's serum, which has had a fair trial.

Von Zielinski's method of employing the patient's own cerebro-spinal fluid subcutaneously or intravenously is the converse of Orticoni's plan of injecting the patient's own blood serum intrathecally. Its value is not established but it is based on the considerations that, in infectious diseases, antibodies are present in high degree in the cerebro-spinal fluid and that even in mild cases of typhus the quantity of cerebrospinal fluid is greater than in almost any other infectious disease.

Prophylaxis.

Preventive inoculation has to a large extent followed the same lines as the specific treatment, but may be considered in a little more detail. Mention was made of the *B. typhiexanthematici*, and Plotz, Olitsky and Bachr prepared a vaccine from this organism and employed it to a limited extent as a prophylactic agent during the Serbian, Bulgarian, Volhynian and Galician epidemics of 1915–16. They regard the results as encouraging, but unfortunately their report is incomplete as they do not state if any measures were adopted by the staff of the units who were vaccinated against typhus to protect themselves from infected lice.

The other sources of protective substances may be classed as follows :—

1. Infected lice.
2. Whole blood from typhus patients.
3. Blood serum from typhus patients and from infected animals.
4. Organs of infected guinea-pigs.

1. Rocha-Lima and Prowazek showed that the virus in the louse is in much higher concentration than in human blood. Hence it occurred to the former that a vaccine prepared from the tissues of infected lice would be more effective, more uniform and more durable as a preventive agent than human blood from typhus cases.

Experiments were accordingly conducted on guinea-pigs and the conclusion was reached that the vaccine obtained from lice, and concerning the preparation of which full details are given in one of Rocha-Lima's numerous papers, was distinctly promising and was much superior to other methods. It was therefore tried in civil hospitals and caused no ill-effects. Subsequently Martini employed it in a prison epidemic, apparently with good results, but unfortunately the experiment, for several reasons, was not wholly satisfactory. Further experience with this vaccine is required before it can be evaluated, and in any case, owing to the difficulty of obtaining it in sufficient quantity, it is not suitable for " massive " vaccination. It may, however, prove useful in the case of persons specially exposed to typhus infection.

2. The use of whole blood from typhus patients appears to have been first advocated and employed by Hamdi in the Turkish army, and his method has been followed by several observers, i.e., Tewfik Salim, Otto and Rothacker, and others, but as the results were unsatisfactory it need not be considered in detail.

Möllers and Wolff modified it, using defibrinated blood diluted 4 parts to 1 part of normal saline. The blood was taken from patients at the height of the fever, and that obtained from several patients was pooled in order to have it in sufficient quantity and as polyvalent as possible. It was heated to 60° C. and formalin 0·2 per cent. was added as a preservative. Three injections were given at short intervals and beyond a slight local reaction there were no ill-effects. The vaccine was tested on a large scale upon German and Austrian soldiers and Russian and Rumanian prisoners and observations with it were also made upon guinea-pigs. The writers' conclusions are as follows :—

(i) That prophylactic inoculation against typhus with the formalinized inoculum is quite as harmless as that against typhoid or cholera.

(ii) That, although it offers no absolute protection against all possibility of infection, there would appear to be a diminution both of incidence and mortality among those inoculated ; but, even so, no relaxation of the campaign against lice, even among the inoculated, is permissible.

(iii) In certain cases it has been possible to immunize guinea-pigs against inoculation with virulent typhus blood by means of preliminary injections of formalinized typhus blood.

(iv) Of over 650 persons who underwent the prescribed prophylactic inoculation, eleven contracted typhus ; of these eleven, six fell ill with the disease before the lapse of three months, and five between three and eight months from the time of inoculation. Death occurred in one case ; the remainder recovered. Besides the eleven above mentioned, four individuals who had only received two instead of three injections contracted the disease, as well as six others who were inoculated during the incubation period.

3. Nicolle and Neukirch are the chief exponents of the serum method. The former, along with Blaizot, used serum either from typhus cases or from infected guinea-pigs and inoculated thirty-eight persons, chiefly Serbian soldiers. The blood was taken antiseptically during the febrile stage and kept in a cool place. After fifteen hours the vessel containing it was slightly shaken so that the leucocyte layer became suspended in the serum. The latter was then centrifugalized and rendered free of cells and cell debris. Shortly afterwards it was injected subcutaneously, $0 \cdot 5$ c.c. being first administered and seven to nine days later 1 c.c. There was no reaction. None of the inoculated took the disease, but the ordinary preventive measures were so good that the chance of infection by lice was reduced to a minimum. Potel employed Nicolle's anti-typhus serum in an outbreak at Sidi-Abdallah, Tunis, using it in thirty-one cases. The results were on the whole favourable, there being a marked improvement in the general condition, while in many of the cases the disease was aborted from the sixth to the twelfth day. Potel recommends that the injections should be commenced as early as possible, even in

doubtful cases. Subcutaneous inoculation should be employed, the dose being 10 to 20 c.c. per day, repeated for eight to ten days in severe cases.

Neukirch made his investigations in Asia Minor. He used at first blood serum treated with chloroform and then blood serum together with leucocytes, and his results were encouraging.

Lebailly and Poirson in Tunis repeated Nicolle's work and also used anti-typhus serum from a horse, but their observations were on a small scale. Still, they consider that their intervention arrested a limited epidemic, the sera from typhus cases, from guinea-pigs and from the horse being apparently equally effective.

4. Blanc prepared a vaccine from the organs of guinea-pigs and in a few cases endeavoured to protect guinea-pigs from infection by its inoculation. His results were inconclusive and his method does not appear to have been applied in the case of man.

Möllers and Wolff in a recent paper review the whole question of preventive inoculation against typhus fever, and sum up the matter by stating that it is along one of two lines that progress may be expected : either by a combined inoculation with living typhus fever virus and immune serum, somewhat similar to the method employed in rinderpest, or by the use of an attenuated typhus virus, following the procedure adopted in smallpox and rabies.

In conclusion, it should be explained that this chapter deals almost wholly with work done during the war or as a direct outcome of the war. It is not intended to be a complete summary of all the recent work on the pathology of typhus, nor does it deal with researches conducted at a time when general conditions had become more or less normal.

BIBLIOGRAPHY.

Arkwright	Remarks on the Virus of Typhus Fever and the means by which it is conveyed.	Proc. Roy. Soc. Med., 1919–20, Vol. xiii, Med. Sect., p. 87.
Anderson & Goldberger.	Studies on Immunity and means of Transmission of Typhus.	U.S. Hygienic Laboratory Bulletin, 1912, No. 86, p. 81.
Arkwright, Bacot & Duncan.	The Minute Bodies (Rickettsia) found in association with Trench Fever, Typhus Fever and Rocky Mountain Spotted Fever.	Trans. Soc. Trop. Med. & Hyg., 1918–19, Vol. xii, p. 61.

Baehr & Plotz	..	Blood-culture Studies on *Typhus exanthematicus* in Serbia, Bulgaria and Russia.	Jl. of Infect. Dis., 1917, Vol. xx, p. 201.
Bauer	.. ..	Zur Anatomie und Histologie des Flecktyphus.	Münch. med. Woch., 1916, Vol. lxiii, p. 541.
Blanc	.. ..	Recherches sur le typhus exanthématique poursuivies au Laboratoire de Nish d'avril à octobre 1915.	Bull. de la Société de Pathol. Exotique, 1916, Vol. ix, p. 311.
Brumpt	.. ..	Au sujet d'un parasite (*Rickettsia prowazeki*) des poux de l'homme considéré, à tort, comme l'agent causal du typhus exanthématique.	*Ibid.*, 1918, Vol. xi, p. 249.
Ceelen	.. ..	Histologische Befunde bei Fleckfieber.	Berliner klin. Woch. 1916, Vol. liii, p. 530.
Compton	.. ..	Studies on the Weil-Felix Serological Test for the Laboratory Diagnosis of Typhus Fever.	Lancet, 1919, Vol. ii, p. 866.
Craig & Fairley	..	Typhus Fever : Observations on a Serological Test (Weil-Felix Reaction).	*Ibid.*, 1918, Vol. ii, p. 385.
Daniélopolu	..	Le sang et les organes hématopoiétiques dans le typhus exanthématique.	Arch. des Maladies du Cœur, 1918, Vol. xi, p. 49.
,,	.. ..	Le liquide céphalo-rachidien dans le typhus exanthématique.	Ann. de Méd., Paris, 1917, Vol. iv, p. 495. (Rev. in Med. Supplt. Daily Review of the Foreign Press, 1918, Vol. i, p. 91.)
,,	.. ..	Nouvelles recherches sur le liquide céphalo-rachidien dans le typhus exanthématique.	*Ibid.*, 1918, Vol. v, p. 44. (Rev. in Med. Supplt. Daily Review of the Foreign Press, 1918, Vol. i, p. 211.)
Daniélopolu & Simici	Pression artérielle et insuffisance surrénale dans le typhus exanthématique.	Arch. des Mal. du Cœur, 1918, Vol. xi, p. 1.
Devaux	.. ..	Le liquide céphalo-rachidien dans le typhus exanthématique.	Bull. de l'Acad. de Méd. (Paris), 1918, Vol. lxxx, p. 188.
Doerr & Kirschner..	Beitrag zur Diagnose der Fleckfieberinfektion beim Meerschweinchen.	Med. Klin., Berlin. 1919, Vol. xv, p. 894.
Doerr & Pick	..	Experimentelle Untersuchungen über Infektion und Immunität bei Fleckfieber.	Wien. klin. Woch., 1918, Vol. xxxi, p. 829.
,, ,,	..	Das Verhalten des Fleckfiebervirus im Organismus des Kaninchens.	Zeit. für Hyg. und Infektionskrank., 1919, Vol. lxxxix, p. 243.

Fairley .. .. The Laboratory Diagnosis of Jl. of Hyg., 1919,
Typhus Fever. Further Ob- Vol. xviii, p. 203.
servations on the Value and
on the Significance of the
Weil-Felix Reaction.

Fraenkel .. .. Ueber Fleckfieber und Roseola. Münch. med. Woch.,
1914, Vol. lxi, p.
57.

,, ... Zur Fleckfieberdiagnose .. *Ibid.*, 1915, Vol. lxii,
p. 805.

Futaki .. .. (Spirochætes in Typhus Fever.) Lancet, 1917, Vol. ii,
p. 544. (Annota-
tion.)

Gavino & Girard .. Note preliminar sobre el tifo Publicaciones del
experimental en los Monos Instituto Bacte-
inferiores, etc. riologico Nacional
de Mexico, 1910.
(Abstract in Bull.
l'Inst. Pasteur,
1910, Vol. viii, p.
841.) (Ref. in Bull.
Soc. Path. Exot.,
1918, Vol. xi, p.
251.)

Grzywo - Dabrowski Untersuchungen über die Path- Virchow's Arch. für
ologische Anatomie des Fleck- Path. Anat.(Berl.),
fiebers. 1918, Vol. ccxxv,
p. 299. (Ref. in
Med. Supplt.
Daily Review of
the Foreign Press,
1919, Vol. ii, p.
123.)

Hamdi .. .. Ueber die Ergebnisse der Immu- Zeit. für Hyg. und
nisierungsversuche gegen *Ty-* Infektionsk., 1916,
phus exanthematicus. Vol. lxxxii, p. 235.

Hegler & von Pro- Untersuchungen über Fleckfie- Berl. klin. Woch.,
wazek ber. 1913, Vol. l, p.
2035.

Herzog .. .. Zur Pathologie des Fleckfiebers. Centralbl. für Allg.
Path. und Pathol.
Anat., 1918, Vol.
xxix, p. 97.

Heuyer .. .. Quelques recherches cliniques Paris Médicale, 1919,
sur le typhus exanthématique. Vol. i, p. 318.

Jaffé .. .. Zur pathologischen Anatomie Med. Klin., Berlin,
des Fleckfiebers. I. Die makro- 1918, Vol. xiv, p.
skopische Diagnosestellung. 210.

,, ... Zur pathologischen Anatomie *Ibid.*, 1918, Vol. xiv,
des Fleckfiebers. II. Mikro- p. 540.
skopische Untersuchungen mit
besonderer Berücksichtigung
der Frage der Diagnosestellung.

,, ... Zur pathologischen Anatomie *Ibid.*, p. 564.
des Fleckfiebers. III. Mikro-
skopische Untersuchungen mit
besonderer Berücksichtigung
ganz frischer und ganz alter
Fälle.

Jaffé	Zur pathologischen Anatomie des Fleckfiebers. IV. Zur Pathogenese des Fleckfieberknötchens.	Med. Klin., Berlin, 1918, Vol. xiv. p. 1209.
Jarisch	Zur Kenntnis der Gehirnveränderungen bei Fleckfieber.	Deut. Arch. für klin. Med., 1918, Vol. cxxvi, p. 270.
Jungmann & Kuczynski.	Zur Aetiologie und Pathogenese des Wolhynischen Fiebers und des Fleckfiebers.	Zeit. für klin. Med., 1918, Vol. lxxxv, p. 251.
Ker	Infectious Diseases : A Practical Text-book.	1909 Edition, p. 214.
Kuczynski	Ueber histologisch - bakteriologische Befunde beim Fleckfieber.	Centralbl. für Allg. Pathol. und Patholog. Anat., 1918, Vol. xxix, p. 279.
Landsteiner & Hausmann.	Einige Beobachtungen über das Fleckfiebervirus.	Med. Klin., Berlin, 1918, Vol. xiv, p. 515.
Lebailly & Poirson	Essais de vaccination préventive contre le typhus exanthématique.	Arch. de l'Inst. Pasteur de Tunis, 1919, Vol. xi, p. 31.
Ledingham	Bacteriology of Typhus Fever	Lancet, 1920, Vol. i, p. 379. Proc. Roy. Soc. Med., 1919–20, Vol. xiii, Med. Sect., p. 81.
Lipschütz	Klinische und mikroskopische Untersuchungen über Fleckfieber.	Wien. klin. Woch. 1916, Vol. xxix, p. 549.
Lorenz	Beobachtungen bei der Fleckfieberbekämpfung in Roumänien.	Arch. für Schiffs-und Tropen - Hygiene, 1919, Vol. xxiii, p. 157.
Martini	Impfung gegen Fleckfieber mit sensibilisiertem Impfstoff nach da Rocha-Lima.	Deut. med. Woch., 1919, Vol. xlv, p. 654.
McCampbell	Observations on *Typhus exanthematicus* (Tabardillo) in Mexico.	Jl. of Med. Research, 1910, Vol. xxiii, p. 71.
Miyashima, Kusama, Takano, Yabe & Kanai.	Experimental Study of Typhus Fever.	Saikin Gaku Zasshi (Jl. Bacteriol.), 1917, No. 163, p. 613. (Rev. in Trop. Dis. Bull., 1918, Vol. xii, p. 110.)
Möllers & Wolff	Experimentelle Fleckfieberuntersuchungen.	Deut. med. Woch., 1919, Vol. xlv, p. 349.
,, ,,	Die bisher mit der Fleckfieberschutzimpfung gemachten Erfahrungen.	Zeit. für Hyg. und Infektionsk., 1919, Vol. lxxxviii, p. 41 ; and Deut. med. Woch., 1918, Vol. xliv, p. 676.
,, ,,	Zur Frage der Fleckfieberschutzimpfung.	Deut. med. Woch., 1920, Vol. xlvi, p. 484.

Monteleone.. ..	Ricerche sul liquido cefalorachidiano nella febre petecchiale.	Jl. Policlinico, 1919, Vol. xxvi. Sez. prat., p. 1009.
Mueller & Urizio ..	Sulla transmissione del dermotifo mediante le deiezioni dei pidocchi infetti.	Riforma Medica, 1919, Vol. xxxv, p. 734.
Napier	The Weil-Felix Reaction in a Mild Epidemic of Typhus occurring amongst a Typhus-ridden People.	Lancet, 1919, Vol. ii, p. 863.
Neill..	Experimental Typhus Fever in Guinea-pigs. A Description of a Scrotal Lesion in Guinea-pigs infected with Mexican Typhus.	U.S. Public Health Reports, 1917, Vol. xxxii, p. 1105.
Neukirch	Ueber Versuche prophylaktischer Impfung gegen Fleckfieber.	Med. Klin., Berlin, 1917, Vol. xiii, p. 300.
Nicol	Pathologisch-anatomische Studien bei Fleckfieber.	Beitr. zur Pathol. Anat. und Allg. Pathol., 1919, Vol. lxv, p. 120.
Nicolle	Reproduction expérimentale du typhus exanthématique chez le singe.	Compt. rend. de l'Acad. des Sci., Paris, 1909, Vol. cxlix, p. 157.
,, ...	Quelques points concernant le typhus exanthématique.	Bull. de la Soc. de Path. Exot., 1915, Vol. viii, p. 160.
,, ...	Etat de nos connaissances expérimentales sur le typhus exanthématique. (Exposé des méthodes suivies et des problèmes qui restent à résoudre.)	Bull. de l'Inst. Pasteur, 1920, Vol. xviii, p. 1 & 49.
Nicolle & Blaizot ..	Nouvelles recherches sur le typhus exanthématique. (Conservation et siège du virus. Typhus du lapin, etc.)	Compt. rend. de l'Acad. des. Sci., Paris, 1915, Vol. clxi, p. 646.
,, ,, ..	Recherches expérimentales sur le typhus exanthématique pratiquées à l'Institut Pasteur de Tunis pendant l'année 1915.	Arch. de l'Inst. Pasteur de Tunis, 1916, Vol. ix, p. 127.
,, ,, ..	Sur la préparation d'un sérum anti-exanthématique expérimental et ses premières applications au traitement du typhus de l'homme.	Ann. de l'Inst. Pasteur, 1916, Vol. xxx. p. 446.
Nicolle, Blanc & Conseil.	Quelques points de l'étude expérimentale du typhus exanthématique.	Compt. rend. de l'Acad. des Sci., Paris, 1914, Vol. clix, p. 661.
Nicolle, Comte & Conseil.	Transmission expérimentale du typhus exanthématique par le pou du corps.	Ibid., 1909, Vol. cxlix, p. 486.
Nicolle, Conor & Conseil.	Sur quelques propriétés du virus exanthématique.	Ibid., 1910, Vol. cli, p. 685.
Nicolle, Conor & Conseil.	Sur la nature et le siège de l'agent pathogène du typhus exanthématique.	Ibid., 1911, Vol. cliii, p. 578.

Nicolle & Conseil ..	Données expérimentales nouvelles sur le typhus exanthématique.	Compt. rend. de l'Acad. des Sci., Paris, 1910, Vol. cli. p. 454.
,, ,, ..	Propriétés du sérum des malades convalescents et des animaux guéris de typhus exanthématique.	Ibid., 1910, Vol. cli, p. 598.
Nöller	Beitrag zur Flecktyphusübertragung durch Läuse.	Berl. klin. Woch., 1916, Vol. liii, p. 778.
Olitsky, Denzer & Husk.	The Isolation of the Bacillus typhi-exanthematici from the Body-louse.	Jl. of Amer. Med. Assoc., 1917, Vol. lxviii, p. 1165.
Orticoni	Essais de sérothérapie du typhus exanthématique par injections intrarachidiennes de sérum de convalescents.	Bull. et Mém. de la Soc. Méd. des Hôp. de Paris, 1917, 3e. Sér. Vol. xli, p. 827.
Otto..	Ueber den augenblicklichen Stand der mikrobiologischen Fleckfieberdiagnose.	Mediz. Klin., Berlin, 1916, Vol. xii, p. 1143.
Otto & Dietrich ..	Beiträge zur " Rickettsien "-Frage.	Deut. med. Woch., 1917, Vol. xliii, p. 577.
Otto & Dietrich ..	Beiträge zur experimentellen Fleckfieberinfektion des Meerschweinchens.	Centralbl. für Bakt., 1919, Abt. i, Orig., Vol. lxxxii, p. 383.
Otto & Rothacker..	Zur Fleckfieberschutzimpfung..	Deut. med. Woch., 1919, Vol. xlv, p. 57.
Parodi	Note istologiche sulle alterazioni encephaliche nel tifo esantematico.	Pathologica, 1919, Vol. xi, p. 377.
Plotz	The Ætiology of Typhus Fever (and of Brill's Disease).	Jl. of Amer. Med. Assoc., 1914, Vol. lxii, p. 1556. (Preliminary Communication).
Plotz, Olitsky & Baehr.	The Ætiology of Typhus exanthematicus.	Jl. of Infect. Dis., 1915, Vol. xvii, p. 1.
Plotz, Olitsky & Baehr.	Studies in Prophylactic Immunization with Bacillus typhi-exanthematici.	Jl. of Amer. Med. Assoc., 1916, Vol. lxvii, p. 1597.
Potel	Observations cliniques et étiologiques sur les cas de typhus soignés à l'hôpital permanent de la marine de Sidi-Abdallah. Action du sérum anti-exanthématique.	Arch. de l'Inst. Pasteur de Tunis, 1916, Vol. ix, p. 245 ; and Arch. de Méd. et Pharm. Navales, 1917, Vol. ciii, p. 14.
Rabinowitsch ..	Ueber die Flecktyphusepidemie in Kiew.	Centralbl. für Bakt., 1909, Abt. i. Orig., Vol. lii, p. 173.
,, ..	Zur Aetiologie des Flecktyphus.	Arch. für Hygiene, 1909, Vol. lxxi, p. 331.
Ricketts & Wilder..	The Typhus Fever of Mexico (Tabardillo). Preliminary Observations.	Jl. of Amer. Med. Assoc., 1910, Vol. liv, p. 463.

Ricketts & Wilder ..		The Transmission of the Typhus Fever of Mexico (Tabardillo) by means of the Louse (*Pediculus vestimenti*).	Jl. of Amer. Med. Assoc., 1910, Vol. liv, p. 1304.
,,	,, ..	The Ætiology of the Typhus Fever (Tabardillo) of Mexico City. A further Preliminary Report.	*Ibid.*, p. 1373.
Rocha-Lima	..	Zur Aetiologie des Fleckfiebers	Deut. med. Woch., 1916, Vol. xlii, p. 1353.
,,	.. ..	Untersuchungen über Fleckfieber.	Münch. med. Woch., 1916, Vol. lxiii, p. 1381.
,,	.. ..	Beobachtungen bei Fleckthyphusläusen.	Archiv für Schiffs- und Tropen-Hygiene, 1916, Vol. xx, p. 17.
,,	.. ..	Zur Aetiologie des Fleckfiebers.	Berl. klin. Woch., 1916, Vol. liii, p. 567.
,,	.. ..	Zum Nachweis der *Rickettsia prowazeki* bei Fleckfieberkranken.	Münch. med. Woch., 1917, Vol. lxiv, p. 33.
,,	.. ..	Die Schutzimpfung gegen Fleckfieber.	Med. Klin., Berlin, 1917, Vol. xiii, p. 1147.
,,	.. ..	Schutzimpfungsversuche gegen Fleckfieber.	Münch. med. Woch., 1918, Vol. lxv, p. 1454.
,,	.. ..	Die Uebertragung des Rückfallfiebers und des Fleckfiebers.	Deut. med. Woch., 1919, Vol. xlv, p. 732.
	.. ..	Bemerkungen zur Rickettsiafrage.	
Rothacker ..	..	Blut-und Liquorbefunde beim Fleckfieber.	Münch. med. Woch., 1919, Vol. lxvi, p. 1197.
Schilling	.. ..	Das Zusammenwirken von Blutbild und Weil-Felix-Reaktion bei der Laboratoriumsdiagnose des Fleckfieber.	*Ibid.*, p. 486.
Schürer	.. ..	Zur Frühdiagnose des Fleckfiebers.	*Ibid.*, 1918, Vol. lxv, p. 1460.
Sergent, Foley & Vialatte.		Sur des formes microbiennes abondantes dans le corps de poux infectés par le typhus exanthématique, et toujours absentes dans les poux témoins non-typhiques.	Compt. rend. de la Soc. de Biol., 1914, Vol. lxxvii, p. 101.
Stefanopoulo	..	La leucocytose dans le typhus exanthématique.	Bull. et Mém. de la Soc. Méd. des Hôp. de Paris, 1918, 3e Sér., Vol. xlii, p. 323.
Töpfer	.. ..	Fleckfieber	Tr. Kongr. f. Inn. Med. Warsaw, 1916, Vol. xxxi, p. 139. (Ref. in Jl. Amer. Med. Assoc., 1917, Vol. lxviii, p. 1166.)

Töpfer & Schüssler..	Zur Aetiologie des Fleckfiebers	Deut. med. Woch., 1916, Vol. xlii, p. 1157.
Tupa	Sur la cytologie du liquide céphalo - rachidien dans le typhus exanthématique.	Compt. rend. de la Soc. de Biol., 1919, Vol. lxxxii, p. 527.
Weil & Felix ..	Ueber die Beziehungen der Gruber-Widalschen Reaktion zum Fleckfieber.	Wien. klin. Woch., 1916, Vol. xxix, p. 974.
Weissenbach ..	La formule hémoleucocytaire dans le typhus exanthématique. Sa valeur diagnostique et pronostique.	Bull. et Mém. de la Soc. Méd. des Hôp. de Paris, 1919, 3e Sér., Vol. xliii, p. 353.
Wilder	The Bacteriology of Typhus Fever.	Jl. of Amer. Med. Assoc., 1914, Vol. lxiii, p. 937.
Wilson	The Ætiology of Typhus Fever	Jl. of Hygiene, 1910, Vol. x, p. 155.
,, ...	Typhus Fever and the so-called Weil-Felix Reaction.	Brit. Med. Jl., 1917, Vol. i, p. 825.
Wolbach & Todd ..	Note sur l'étiologie et l'anatomie pathologique du typhus exanthématique au Mexique.	Ann. de l'Inst. Pasteur, 1920, Vol. xxxiv, p. 153.
Zielinski, von ..	Ein neues therapeutisches Vorgehen beim Fleckfieber. (Kurze Mitteilung.)	Berl. klin. Woch. 1918, Vol. lv, p. 233.

CHAPTER XIV.

CEREBRO–SPINAL FEVER.

ALTHOUGH cerebro-spinal fever was endemic in England and Wales prior to the war, the cases were sporadic, their number restricted, and the incidence chiefly on young children. From time to time, however, cerebro-spinal fever had shown itself capable of assuming epidemic proportions, as illustrated by severe outbreaks during the present century in Germany, the United States, Glasgow, Belfast and elsewhere. As the result of investigations in these and previous outbreaks the causal micro-organism had been defined, as also the manner in which it is usually conveyed from case to case through a chain of healthy carriers. Accordingly, when in the early months of 1915 cerebro-spinal fever began to spread among troops training in England, the severity of the disease and the mass of susceptible material exposed to it in the shape of recruits called for the immediate application of available knowledge for the purpose of keeping it in check, no less than for close investigation and research with a view to its more effectual control. The medical aspects of cerebro-spinal fever are described in the volumes on the Diseases of the War,* and particulars of the epidemic and of the administrative measures taken to deal with it in the volumes on the Hygiene of the War.† These preventive measures and the machinery set up in order to carry them out led to an extensive study of the pathology of cerebro-spinal fever as it occurred in the military and naval forces of the Crown : that is to say, to an investigation of its causation not only in individuals but in masses ; and the continuance of outbreaks with varying frequency during subsequent years of the war provided numerous opportunities of checking earlier observations and of extending them on a wide scale. As a result of these studies and experiences definite progress has been made in our knowledge of the pathology of cerebro-spinal fever, and already some of the new information thus acquired has proved to have a valuable application for purposes of prevention and specific treatment.

It is desirable to consider what is meant by the term pathology in the present relation. The disease cerebro-spinal

---

* Vol. I, Chapter VI.   † Vol. II, Chapter IX.

fever being the result of an interaction between a recognizable micro-organism and the tissues of a susceptible person, an adequate understanding of its pathology should include, first, knowledge of the biology of the micro-organism in question, of its attributes, of its races, and of the characters which are of value for differentiating these from other micro-organisms with which confusion is liable to occur ; secondly, knowledge of the habitat of this micro-organism, of its frequency, and of the conditions under which it gains access to the body of a susceptible person ; and, thirdly, knowledge of the manner in which, having obtained such access, the micro-organism brings about the symptoms and lesions of cerebro-spinal fever, and the precise nature of these lesions. The preceding problems, however, cover but a portion of the field. To be complete, pathology should also be able to determine the manner in which the body resists this micro-organism, and to indicate features of special value in the defence. Finally, pathology should be able to explain why as a rule out of so many who become infected with the micro-organism in question during an epidemic so few develop the disease ; and, conversely, the reason of susceptibility in others. On analysis, therefore, the pathology of cerebro-spinal fever resolves itself for the most part into a series of problems in bacteriology and immunity, some of which are likely to require for their full elucidation more leisure and opportunities for uninterrupted research than were afforded by an epidemic with a predilection for recruits arising in the stress of a great war in a country where previous experience of this disease in epidemic form was so small that for practical purposes it was a new one.

In order to ascertain the directions in which progress has been made it is proposed, first, to review briefly the state of knowledge of the pathology of cerebro-spinal fever at the point when the outbreak began ; secondly, to describe the procedure employed in the army in the emergency of 1915 for identifying the meningococcus, the differentiation of strains operating in the military epidemic into a number of separate types, the part played by each type in the military outbreak, and the light thrown on the pathogenesis of cerebro-spinal fever by systematic study of the carrier-rate of these defined races of the causal micro-organism. Therapeutic studies with monotypical sera will then be recounted and other observations made while the disease was prevalent among troops. Thirdly, studies of the disease in the naval forces will be mentioned ; and, fourthly, observations in connection with the infection among the civil population. Finally, reference will be made to recent researches during the prevalence of cerebro-spinal fever abroad.

State of Knowledge of the Pathology of Cerebro-spinal Fever at the beginning of 1915.

Since the discovery of the meningococcus by Weichselbaum in 1887 the presence of this micro-organism had been verified in every outbreak of cerebro-spinal fever where adequate investigation had been made, as also had its absence from the tissues of patients suffering from other diseases. When introduced into the cerebro-spinal system of monkeys the meningococcus had been found to be capable of giving rise to the characteristic symptoms and lesions of cerebro-spinal fever. For these reasons, although the proof was incomplete inasmuch as animals had not been shown to acquire meningitis in a precisely similar manner to man, namely, by infection of the meninges from the respiratory tract, the meningococcus had come to be generally accepted as the essential infective agent of cerebro-spinal fever.

The morphological, cultural and physiological characters of the meningococcus had been defined with a moderate degree of precision. A Gram-negative diplococcus, it was known to be a member of a large group which includes the gonococcus, *M. catarrhalis*, and numerous other forms of undetermined significance frequenting the secretion of the upper respiratory passages. On primary culture from the body the meningococcus was known to be very delicate, the medium requiring to be warmed, enriched with blood or ascites fluid, and precautions taken to avoid evaporation, the coccus being susceptible to drying. The meningococcus was known to ferment glucose and maltose, but to leave saccharose unchanged. When injected into laboratory animals it was known to produce death as a rule by septicæmia, but sometimes by toxæmia, its pathogenic action being due to an intracellular toxin or endotoxin in the liberation of which an autolytic enzyme contained within the meningococcus appeared to play a part. It had been shown that the serum of animals prepared against the meningococcus contains a number of specific antibodies of which agglutinin in particular had been found to be of great value for distinguishing the meningococcus from other Gram-negative cocci. There was evidence, however, to show that Gram-negative cocci are particularly apt to stimulate the production of co-antibodies. Thus, when cocci of this group so different in pathogenic action for the human being as the gonococcus and meningococcus were compared serologically, it had been found that the complement-fixation test may fail to differentiate them, and that even when agglutinin is used there might be some doubt, the absorption test being required in order to bring out clearly the fundamental difference between them.

At first it was assumed that meningococci are all alike, but Dopter had shown in the first place that two serologically distinct races exist among them, the meningococcus and the parameningococcus. His later investigations, however, had revealed that strains of the parameningococcus are further differentiated serologically into three distinct sub-groups. The importance of this differentiation lay in the fact that clinical experience indicated that only serum prepared against a strain serologically identical with that infecting the patient is of therapeutic value. As yet, however, the number of meningococci examined serologically had been but small, and there was not sufficient evidence to show either the relative frequency of the various races, or their individual influence in epidemics of cerebro-spinal fever.

It was known that the identification of the meningococcus in nasopharyngeal secretion is a matter of some nicety because of numerous other Gram-negative cocci that frequent this material. Before the epidemic in 1915 began some of these " pharyngococci " had been identified and named, *e.g.*, *M. catarrhalis* and *M. flavus I, II, III.* The morphological, cultural and fermentative characters of the meningococcus had been found to distinguish it from these particular cocci, but the existence of a further group of pharyngococci indistinguishable from the meningoccocus in morphological, cultural and fermentative characters but distinct from it serologically had been indicated by the observations of Lunckenbeim and others who went so far as to call them pseudomeningoccoci. The work of Lunckenbeim, however, was discounted by the fact that he failed to take into account the possibility of there being a number of serologically distinct races of the meningococcus itself, the existence of which had been subsequently established by Dopter.

The observations of von Lingelsheim had indicated that with suitable technique the meningococcus is to be recovered from the nasopharynx of every case of cerebro-spinal fever at the onset. It was well established that during an epidemic of cerebro-spinal fever a proportion of persons in the vicinity of the case, although unaffected by the disease, carry the meningococcus in their nasopharyngeal secretion, the carrier-rate being influenced by time, season and overcrowding (Netter and Debré). The nasopharyngeal spread of the meningococcus was explained by droplet infection, and the carrier-rate had been found to correspond directly with the incidence of the disease. It was found that the duration of carrying varied from a few weeks to many months, and that a residue of the population carried the meningococcus in their nasopharynx in the absence of an epidemic, the normal carrier-rate being apparently in the neighbourhood of 2 per cent.

As meningitis is the chief feature that distinguishes a case from a carrier, the route by which the meningococcus spreads from the nasopharynx to the meninges is of some importance. Two chief hypotheses still hold the field on this point, namely : (1) that the coccus spreads directly through lymphatics, perineural and other, that are known to penetrate the floor of the skull ; and (2) that the vehicle is the blood stream. The well-known immunity of carriers to the disease would appear to indicate that whatever the particular route, the determining factor is the specific resistance of the patient.

The meningococcus had been held by some to be responsible for a certain amount of catarrh of the nasopharynx, and rarely it had been recovered from bronchial secretion. It was known that exceptionally the meningococcus can give rise to a fulminating form of hæmorrhagic septicæmia without involving the meninges.

The morbid anatomy in acute cases of cerebro-spinal fever had not been found to differ materially from that of meningitis brought about by other pyogenic bacteria, the differential diagnosis depending in practice upon the result of bacteriological examination of the exudate. The chief feature is the presence of a purulent exudate which in the cadaver is especially prominent on the posterior portion of the cord and round the base of the brain, though not infrequently the vertex is also involved. In chronic cases the pus may have disappeared, a secondary condition of hydrocephalus being present, due to obstruction to the outflow of cerebro-spinal fluid from the ventricles by adhesions resulting from the preceding meningitis.

With regard to the precise means whereby the body defends itself against the meningococcus, great stress had been laid on opsonin, and there was some evidence to indicate that lysin may also be a factor in the defence. Anti-meningococcus

serum prepared by injecting a plurality of strains of meningococci into horses had been found to possess high therapeutic
value and to lower materially the mortality when adminstered
intrathecally sufficiently early in the disease, and in adequate
dosage. No general agreement, however, had yet been reached
with regard to the standardization of this serum.

Research in connection with Cerebro-spinal Fever during the War.

The routine procedure adopted in the army for dealing with
cerebro-spinal fever was as follows : A memorandum was
issued in which directions were given for the speedy calling in
of the bacteriologist in suspected cases in order to expedite
the diagnosis. Cases of cerebro-spinal fever were to be isolated
and treated with anti-meningoccocus serum, and their contacts
segregated and swabbed. Contacts whose nasopharyngeal
secretion failed to yield the meningococcus were to be returned
to duty as soon as possible ; those found to be carrying
a micro-organism indistinguishable from the meningococcus
were to be kept in isolation until two successive swabs separated
by an interval of several days proved negative. In practice,
therefore, the chief part of this preventive procedure consisted
in identifying and isolating carriers of the meningococcus
amongst the immediate contacts of the case.

The machinery set up for carrying out this routine procedure
consisted of a central laboratory in London to which a travelling
laboratory was attached, and district laboratories throughout
the commands. Where troops were under training and a
military laboratory was not available civilian laboratories
were co-opted, or a special laboratory equipped.

The duties of the central laboratory were as follows : (1) To
supply district laboratories with special materials such as
the covered nasopharyngeal swab of West, media, standard
cultures and, later, suspensions of meningococci, agglutinating
sera and special or selected consignments of therapeutic serum.
(2) To act as a training school for officers proceeding to the
charge of district laboratories. This was desirable at the
beginning because none of these officers had any previous experience of identifying the meningococcus in the nasopharynx,
and later it became still more desirable in order to demonstrate
the technique of meningococcus agglutination and to ensure
that full application should be made of experience gained in
preceding stages of the outbreak. (3) To render assistance to
district laboratories in emergencies and for special service ;
for this purpose the travelling laboratory was indispensable.

(4) To carry out research with a view to the application of the knowledge thus obtained for the purpose of improving the bacteriological procedure in use for the prevention and treatment of cerebro-spinal fever.

The procedure recommended in the emergency of February 1915 for identifying the meningococcus in nasopharyngeal secretion was to swab the nasopharynx with a West swab and and to make plate cultures of the secretion thus obtained on the medium supplied from the central laboratory. After twenty-four to forty-eight hours at 37° C. colonies of Gram-negative cocci resembling those of the meningococcus were to be subcultured on to two slopes of the same medium, one of these being placed at 37° C., the other at 23° C. If in the course of twenty-four to forty-eight hours growth occurred at 37° C. but not at 23° C. the organism could be regarded as the meningococcus, confirmatory evidence being furnished by its ability to ferment glucose and its inability to ferment saccharose. This simple technique had the merit that it could readily be carried out with the appliances then available, and that it did not involve undue delay. As yet no serum was available that would agglutinate the strains of the outbreak.

While this attempt to deal with the disease on bacteriological lines was proceeding, a research was undertaken at the central laboratory for the purpose of obtaining a better medium than the nasgar sent out in the first place. As a result of comparison of various media and forms of enrichment for growing the meningococcus not only from cultures but also from the nasopharyngeal secretion, it was found that agar dissolved in the trypsinized broth of Douglas provided the best basis, and as an extract of peaflour was found to have a pronounced action in stimulating growth of the meningococcus on such medium, this was included. This medium, trypagar, was the standard medium used with considerable success throughout the rest of the outbreak among troops. For primary cultures, enrichment was found advantageous ; and after comparative trials of serum, egg albumen and other materials, a simple dilution of 1 part rabbit's blood in 20 parts of saline was adopted for this purpose with the addition of a little ether to lake the blood and act as volatile antiseptic.

Although the procedure adopted at the outset for identifying the meningococcus worked smoothly and well, it had the grave disadvantage that there was a possibility, and in view of the observations of previous observers a probability, that a proportion of the contacts in isolation as carriers were carrying cocci which, while indistinguishable from the meningococcus in the characters examined, were distinct from it serologically and therefore without the same pathogenic significance. Obviously it was desirable that no man should be kept in isolation unless he carried a micro-organism identical in all respects with that causing disease in his comrades. Accordingly, as soon as a satisfactory medium had been obtained, meningococci from the cerebro-spinal fluid of the cases were collected and submitted to systematic serological investigation. For the present purpose the agglutination test was employed, and in order to exclude error from the action of co-agglutinins the results were checked by the absorption test.

When investigated in this manner meningococci isolated from the cerebro-spinal fluid of thirty-two cases in the military outbreak although indistinguishable in other characters were found by Gordon and Murray to resolve serologically into one or other of four distinct groups or types. Of these, Types I and III appeared to be related because they excited in the rabbit the production of co-agglutinin for each other, and a similar relation was found to obtain between Types II and IV. By simple agglutination, therefore, the meningococci were distinguishable into two chief groups, each of which by the absorption test was subdivided into two separate and individual types. Meningococci from the cerebro-spinal fluid of sixty-three cases of cerebro-spinal fever received at the central laboratory between February and October 1915 resolved as follows when submitted to serological examination.

Type.				I.	II.	III.	IV.
Specimens	..	..	..	..	31	20	10	2
Percentage	..	..	..	..	49	31	15	3

At this comparatively early stage of the epidemic, therefore, the most prevalent meningococcus in military cases was Type I, and the first two types accounted between them for 80 per cent. of the cases. It was found by M. Nicolle, of the Pasteur Institute, that Types I and III represent the meningococcus group of Dopter, and Types II and IV his group of parameningococci.

By the time that the meningococci concerned in the military cases had been defined in this way the great majority of men n isolation as carriers having become free from infection had been returned to duty, but ten men still in isolation as meningococcus carriers were next examined. All were found to harbour in their nasopharynx a micro-organism indistinguishable from the meningococcus in morphological, cultural and fermentative characters. On submitting these ten cocci to examination with the agglutination and absorption test with the sera prepared against the four types of meningococcus, one nasopharyngeal coccus proved to be a specimen of Type I, five were specimens of Type II, and as the four remaining cocci were serologically distinct from any of the four types of convicted meningococci, the men carrying them were released from isolation. Observations with agglutinating sera, prepared against specimens of these nasopharyngeal cocci, confirmed the accuracy of the results previously obtained with the anti-meningococcus sera.

From this experience it was evident that for accurate identification of the meningococcus in nasopharyngeal secretion the agglutination test was indispensable.. For that reason, and also in order to determine the part played by each type individually in the military outbreak, from the autumn of 1915 onwards monotypical agglutinating sera for each of the four types of the meningococcus were prepared at the central laboratory and supplied to district laboratories together with standard suspensions of the homologous meningococci, and directions were issued for carrying out the agglutination test in a standard manner and for the interpretation of results. Throughout remaining stages of the outbreak the principle followed was to admit no meningococcus-like organism from the nasopharynx to the rank of meningococcus unless, when submitted to agglutination with the four monotypical sera, it showed strong evidence of serological identity with one or other of these four types of established meningococci.

The supply of agglutinating sera was undertaken in the first place by Major T. G. M. Hine, who elaborated a quick method of preparing this serum, and subsequently by Major A. S. G. Bell, who introduced further improvements. The preparation of agglutinating serum for Types I and III was relatively simple owing to the good agglutinogenic power of strains belonging to these groups. In the case of Type II, however, and to some extent in Type IV, it was found that the agglutinogenic power of the strains gradually deteriorates —a feature that renders the preparation of standard agglutinating serum of sufficient catholicity somewhat arduous. The means employed to ensure catholicity without loss of specificity have been described by Major Bell, who also succeeded later on in preparing powerful agglutinating sera that would rapidly identify the meningococcus and determine its type within a few minutes, by agglutinating a drop of emulsion on a slide after the well-known method employed for the preliminary identification of the cholera vibrio.

In order to provide for the possible occurrence of further types of epidemic significance, a request was made that any meningococci that failed to agglutinate with the four mono-typical sera should be forwarded to the central laboratory so that, if the need should arise, special agglutinating serum could be prepared for its identification.

The study of the types of meningococcus occurring in the cases was continued by Major W. J. Tulloch who examined 100 further specimens for this purpose with the agglutination and absorption test, and found that 98 per cent. of them were included within the four groups. He found, however, that Type II is complex—at least three sub-groups are included within it—but by selecting a sufficiently representative strain he found that a monotypical agglutinating serum can be prepared that will include practically all of the sub-groups of this type.

At a later date Tulloch also made a special investigation of meningococcus-like organisms of the nasopharynx that form colonies resembling those of the meningococcus, but fail to behave as meningococci when submitted to agglutination with the four monotypical sera. In order to determine the error of the routine serological procedure employed for identifying the meningococcus in the nasopharynx he took forty specimens of these pharyngococci actually rejected by Captain Glover in his routine work, examined their morphological, cultural and fermentative characters, and then submitted them to the agglutination and absorption test with the four monotypical sera. Although the majority of these cocci possessed the fermentative characters of the meningococcus, he found them to be serologically quite distinct from any of the four defined types of that micro-organism. When he proceeded to prepare sera against strains of these pharyngococci, he found that there are so many different antigenic races among them that they do not lend themselves to classification by serological methods. It is interesting to observe that F. Wulff, when studying these pharyngeal cocci during a recent outbreak in Denmark, arrived at a precisely similar conclusion.

Now that an accurate method of identifying the meningo-coccus in the nasopharynx was available, the following memorandum was sent round to district laboratories with the object of obtaining further information concerning the general distribution among the military population of meningococci of established epidemiological significance.

" MEMORANDUM.

(1) *Mode of Spread of Cerebro-spinal Fever. Examination of Controls.*

As part of the investigation of factors governing the spread of cerebro-spinal fever, it is very desirable that, as far as possible, opportunity should be taken of making control observations with a view to ascertaining what proportion of non-contacts harbour the meningococcus in their nasopharynx.

It is suggested that, other things being equal, it would be more useful to examine for this purpose small groups of men from a large number of units rather than a large number of men from the same unit.

Before such investigations are undertaken, a particularly careful enquiry should be made to ascertain whether or no there has been any possibility of recent contact with a case of cerebro-spinal fever or with a carrier from such a case.

No Gram-negative coccus should be accepted as the meningococcus for the present purpose unless it fails to agglutinate with normal serum and at the same time agglutinates to approximately the same titre as the homologous meningococcus with one or other of the anti-meningococcus sera supplied.

In positive cases it will also be valuable to know (1) the relative abundance of the meningococcus in the nasopharyngeal mucus of the person carrying it, and (2) the duration of such carrying.

(2) *Definition of the Relation between Outbreaks of Influenzal Catarrh and Cerebro-spinal Fever.*

In some camps severe outbreaks of coughs and colds have occurred. It is desirable to make observations on the bacteriology of these cases both from the point of view of the presence or absence of the meningococcus, and also for the purpose of determining what are the prevalent bacteria in these cases of catarrh.

Central C.S.F. Laboratory,
16th February, 1916.   Royal Army Medical College, S.W."

The materials supplied by the supply department of the central laboratory between February 1915 and May 1919 were as follows :—

Nasgar bottles (200 c.c.)	1,628
Trypagar bottles (200 c.c.)	35,402
Trypagar slopes and stabs	48,000
Other media bottles	540
Egg medium slopes	2,800
Blood enrichment bottles (25 c.c.)	1,994
Monotypical agglutinating sera (2 c.c.)	5,909
Standard suspensions (25 c.c.)	3,274
West swabs (sterile)	14,334
Levick steam atomizers	273
Hine's jets	1,400

The observations made during 1915 have been summarized in a report by an Advisory Committee appointed for the purpose by the Medical Research Council. The report in question not only consolidated the information available at the time with regard to the bacteriological aspects of cerebro-spinal fever, but also offered valuable suggestions as to directions in which future research might be prosecuted.

Biology and Attributes of the Meningococcus.

A possible explanation of the predilection of the meningococcus for the secretion of the nasopharynx was afforded by the observation of Shearer that this secretion contains an extractive that stimulates growth of the micro-organism in culture. Extractives with a similar action were demonstrated in blood and pus by Miss Jordan Lloyd. The presence in peaflour of an agent with this property has already been referred to, and Flack, who investigated this point at some length, established the presence in wheat germ of another extractive that prolongs the vitality of the meningococcus. On the other hand, it appears that certain bacteria have an antagonistic action to the growth of the meningococcus. This matter came to the notice of Colebrook, who, when a certain carrier became free, observed that a strain of the pneumococcus that replaced the meningococcus in the nasopharyngeal secretion had the effect of inhibiting growth of the meningococcus in culture. Saliva was found by Gordon to have a similar inhibiting effect on growth of the meningococcus, the action being due to streptococci normally occurring in this secretion—a circumstance that explains the relative absence of the meningococcus from saliva even when this micro-organism is swarming in the nasopharyngeal secretion of the same person.

Vines found that while the meningococcus is fairly resistant to light, it is destroyed by desiccation in so short a time as two to five minutes. He also found evidence that this micro-organism possesses an alkali-producing proteolytic capacity in addition to its acid-producing glycolytic power. Although young cultures of the meningococcus fail to hæmolyse blood, older cultures were found by Gordon to possess this property owing to the presence of a thermostable substance that can be extracted by acetone or alcohol, but not by ether. The latter observer also investigated a labile reductase contained by the meningococcus and found that it served as an index to the naked eye of the viability of the coccus and therefore of the suitability or otherwise of its environment.

The pathogenic action of the meningococcus was studied by Gordon who found evidence that the greater portion of its pathogenicity is due to its virulence or power to multiply actively in the tissues. The endotoxin of the meningococcus would appear to be remarkably resistant to heat, since it withstands boiling for thirty minutes, and even 120° C. for a time, but is destroyed within two hours at that temperature. He found that this endotoxin is a true toxin, since the living animal is capable of forming a specific antibody that neutralizes it. The four types of meningococcus are distinct also as regards their respective endotoxins, but it would seem that within a single type as defined by agglutinin and absorption of agglutinin more than one endotoxin may be met with.

The Serological Types of Meningococcus.

Independently of the investigation already described meningococci from military cases during the outbreak were studied by Arkwright and by Ellis. Both employed the agglutination test and found evidence of two main groups. Reference has already been made to the additional information afforded by the absorption test. Between October 1915 and April 1919, out of a total of 526 strains of the meningococcus from the cerebro-spinal fluid of cases examined at the central laboratory 518 were identified with one or other of the four types, 8 specimens being unplaced. Not less than 98 per cent., therefore, of these strains were relegated by the agglutination test to one or other of the four groups.

As regards sources, 462 of these strains came from adults and 29 from children in the United Kingdom; 18 specimens were received from an outbreak in South Africa through Captain E. Douglas Pullon, of Capetown; and 9 specimens were received from the United States through Dr. McCoy, of Washington. The South African strains showed examples of three of the types, the American of all four. It would appear, therefore, that the four types of meningococcus have a wide distribution.

No fewer than 235 of the meningococci placed definitely in one or other of the four groups by the agglutination test were subsequently submitted to the absorption test. The reading previously obtained by agglutination was confirmed in 231 cases, only four exceptions being met with. This experience emphasized the accuracy of the agglutination test for determining the type of meningococcus when carried out in the strictly quantitative fashion and with suitable controls by the standard procedure practised throughout.

The distribution of types during the early part of 1915 has been stated above. Between October 1915 and April 1919 the incidence was as follows :—

Type.				I.	II.	III.	IV.
Specimens	..	..	..	195	218	69	36
Percentage	..	..	..	37·66	44·05	11·38	6·94

Over this latter part of the outbreak, therefore, Type II was in chief abundance, and as before the first two types accounted for 80 per cent. of the cases. While the majority of the outbreaks showed Types I and II in chief abundance, several instances were met with of the local prevalence of an unusual type. Thus Type III was exceptionally frequent at Newcastle, and Type IV occurred in a fair proportion of the cases in an outbreak at Chatham in 1916.

Although specimens of each type of the meningococcus were kept in culture for over four years, being frequently subcultured over this period, no certain instance of mutation was met with. Nor has passage through a series of mice been found to produce any alteration of type. But while no instance of mutation has been observed during a very large number of repeated examinations, several instances have occurred, especially in specimens of Type II, when a coccus on prolonged subculture has become "sub-typical," i.e., has suffered a diminution in its power of evoking agglutinin for some other strains of its own type.

Struck by the coincidence of four serological types of human blood and of the meningococcus respectively, the late Professor L. Doncaster made a special investigation to determine whether any alteration of type could be induced by cultivating various strains of the meningococcus in different types of human blood, but although he made a large number of experiments and continued them for a considerable period, no alteration could be induced in the serological characters of these strains of the meningococcus. The types of the meningococcus therefore appear to be stable and fixed.

It has been found that a specimen of cerebro-spinal fluid from a case of cerebro-spinal fever contains but a single type of the meningococcus, and that the meningococcus present in the nasopharyngeal secretion is serologically identical with that occurring in the cerebro-spinal fluid of the same patient. Not only does this correspondence hold in cases infected with each of the four types, but, according to Gordon, even slight serological peculiarities of the spinal culture are possessed also by the strain from the nasopharynx of the same case. Embleton, who made a careful and thorough examination of over 100 cases during the period of convalescence, found that they continue to carry the meningococcus for an average period of six months, and that a case of cerebro-spinal fever carries the same type of meningococcus throughout. It may be concluded that cerebro-spinal fever is a monotypical infection, a conclusion confirmed by the therapeutic results with monotypical serum so far as that form of treatment has developed. In view of the weight of evidence as to the strictly monotypical character of the infection, the variation claimed by Walker Hall and Peters in the serological behaviour of meningococci isolated from the same case at different stages of the attack requires confirmation. It has been found, moreover, that not only cases but also carriers as a rule carry but a single type of the meningococcus throughout.

When the distribution of types in cases is compared with that found in the nasopharyngeal secretion of carriers in their neighbourhood the correspondence is often very striking. In an outbreak in a large garrison during 1916, 13 cases of cerebro-spinal fever yielded the following types: Type I, 3 specimens; Type II, 5; Type III, *nil;* and Type IV, 5 specimens. Captain R. R. Armstrong swabbed 10,000 men of this garrison and found 410 to be carrying meningococcus-like organisms. When Major Tulloch examined these men later 86 had become free and 324 yielded meningococcus-like organisms. On submitting these to the three monotypical agglutinating sera covering the types present in the cases, 173 of them proved to be epidemic strains of the meningococcus, the distribution of types being Type I, 30; Type II, 72; and Type IV, 71 specimens. This correspondence in cases and carriers is the more striking when it is realized that Type IV has been rare in military cases, and that the proportion of types in the cases was unknown to Major Tulloch when he examined the carriers. The distribution of types of the meningococcus among the military population of London during the war illustrates this correspondence to a remarkable degree. Thus in 1916 Flack found Type II to be six times as frequent as Type I alike in cases and in carriers. The continuous observation of the distribution of meningococci in the military population of Caterham, however, including non-contacts as well as contacts, provided even more striking evidence of type correspondence. There for two years, as

Glover has pointed out, Type II was pre-eminent both in cases and in such of the population as were found to be carriers. By preventive measures to be referred to later the meningococcus was practically banished from this community, but with the influx of a mass of recruits Type I was imported, became the predominant type and gave rise to cases. While this correspondence of type in cases and carriers has been abundantly demonstrated, the wide diffusion of the meningococcus during the outbreak led to the dissemination of various types so that heterologous types were sometimes abundant in later stages of the outbreak.

The observation of Embleton that cases continue to harbour the meningococcus in their nasopharynx for an average period of six months has been referred to. He emphasizes the tendency of these cases to intermit, the probable explanation being that the meningococcus lurks in the deeper layers of the mucosa, since it may be necessary to apply the swab with appreciable pressure in order to obtain a positive result. The majority of persons who become infected with the meningococcus during an outbreak, but do not develop the disease, appear to become free of infection within a few weeks, but some continue to carry for months and exceptionally for over a year. The factors determining the prolonged period of carrying are still obscure. Cleminson, who made a careful rhinoscopic examination of chronic carriers, found evidence that local abnormalities, such as firm mucous contact, play an important part. Neither local disinfectants, nor vaccine, nor attempts to replace the meningococcus in the nasopharynx by other bacteria were successful in clearing up chronic carriers.

The incidence of defined types of the meningococcus in the nasopharyngeal secretion of the military population of Caterham was determined by the London district laboratory by weekly examinations carried on continuously between August 1916 and June 1919, during which period two outbreaks of cerebrospinal fever occurred. This comprehensive investigation, begun by Martin Flack and continued by J. A. Glover, has not only confirmed previous knowledge that factors, such as season and overcrowding, influence the carrier-rate of meningococci, but has measured and defined with a precision hitherto unattained the influence of the carrier-rate in giving rise to the disease, and the effect of overcrowding on the carrier-rate. Furthermore, the knowledge thus obtained has been demonstrated by Glover to be capable of successful application for the prevention of outbreaks of cerebro-spinal fever in future.

At the first stage of the investigation when Flack was in charge, a direct relationship was established between the numerical abundance of carriers of epidemic strains of the meningococcus—chiefly Type II—and the manifestation of cerebro-spinal fever in susceptible men. It was found that during the summer months the carrier-rate of the defined types of the meningococcus did not exceed 2 to 5 per cent. Before cerebro-spinal fever began the carrier-rate showed a warning rise, the danger line being in the neighbourhood of 20 per cent. At the height of the outbreak the carrier-rate of the community reached its maximum of over 60 per cent., after which it fell slowly till in the summer it once more reached the minimal level. This weekly survey of the carrier-rate was continued by Glover who, grasping the all-important influence of overcrowding in producing a high carrier-rate, established the new fact that this rate varied inversely with the distance between the beds in which the men slept at night. So direct was this association that Glover found that he could predict the carrier-rate by measuring the distance between the beds with a foot-rule. His next step was to demonstrate that diminution of the overcrowding by increasing the distance between the beds was followed by a fall in the carrier-rate until eventually it reached the normal level. Glover then proceeded to apply this knowledge to the prevention of cerebro-spinal fever. By preventing overcrowding in the manner described the carrier-rate was kept at the normal level, and as a result during the next epidemic season cerebro-spinal fever was absent at Caterham for the first time in three years. At this point a control observation was afforded by the necessities of war. A large influx of recruits from the mining districts caused overcrowding once more at Caterham. As a result the carrier-rate quickly rose, the type newly introduced and now prevalent being Type I. This warning rise of the carrier-rate was followed by the appearance of cerebro-spinal fever from Type I, but with diminution of the overcrowding the carrier-rate fell and the disease abated. From observations made by Glover it would seem that the carrier-rate is more speedily raised by overcrowding than it is diminished by reduction of this overcrowding.

It was known previously that the manner in which the meningococcus is conveyed is by droplet infection. The observations at Caterham indicate that the striking distance is short, namely, under 3 ft. At the height of one of the outbreaks the distance between the beds was but 6 in. A further point observed was that the higher the carrier-rate the more abundant and nearly pure are the cultures of the meningococcus obtained. Since a high carrier-rate and severe overcrowding are necessary factors in the genesis of an outbreak of cerebro-spinal fever it would appear that, in addition to the susceptibility of the individual, dosage is of first importance. The nasopharyngeal incidence of Gram-negative cocci failing to agglutinate with the four monotypical sera was also observed throughout the Caterham observations, but as, when an outbreak was imminent or in actual progress, the meningococcus showed not only an absolute increase but also a relative increase in comparison with these pharyngeal organisms, it would seem that they are without significance in the pathogenesis of cerebro-spinal fever.

A possible explanation of the mode of internal spread of the meningococcus from the nasopharynx is afforded by the demonstration of Shearer and Crowe that meningococci can survive phagocytosis and presumably therefore are liable to be transported to the blood stream or cerebro-spinal fluid by this means.

The general features of the lesions present in fatal cases of cerebro-spinal fever described in previous outbreaks were confirmed. McLagan and Cooke, however, brought forward evidence to show that in fulminating cases injury to the adrenals may occur as indicated by fall of blood-pressure and the presence of hæmorrhage into these organs on *post-mortem* examination. Embleton has drawn attention to the constancy with which he found empyema of the sphenoid in the fatal cases examined by him. The constancy of this lesion, however, has been disputed by Kennedy and Worster Drought.

Serotherapy.

The capacity of serum from chronic meningococcus carriers, from cases of cerebro-spinal fever, and from cases suffering from other infections to fix complement in the presence of each of the four types of meningococcus was examined by Major Bell. He found serum from meningococcus carriers to contain more amboceptors for these meningococci than did serum from patients suffering from other infections, a probable explanation as to why such carriers escape the disease. Gates has established the presence of agglutinin also in the serum of chronic carriers. After the fourth day of the disease serum from patients suffering from cerebro-spinal fever was found by Bell to contain amboceptors for the meningococcus. Both in patients and in carriers there was evidence in some cases, though not in all, of a predominance of amboceptors for the homologous type of meningococcus.

The epidemic caused a continual demand for more effective therapeutic serum. The therapeutic serum available in 1915 failed to reduce the mortality in military cases below 48 per cent. During the next year, while the general mortality was 44 per cent. a particular consignment of serum used in the London district was found to reduce the mortality there to 18·5 per cent. When a sample of this successful serum was compared in the central laboratory with other sera that had been tried clinically without success the superiority of the former was found to lie neither in its agglutinin content nor in its yield of complement-fixing antibodies, nor in its lysin content, nor in its opsonin content, nor even apparently in its ability to protect mice against the living meningococcus. The sole point of superiority that could be detected was that 0·5 c.c. of the clinically potent serum, when mixed with one minimum lethal dose of the dried bodies of either Type I or Type II meningoccoci and injected into the peritoneal cavity of the mouse, was found to preserve that animal from death, whereas all the other specimens of anti-meningococcus serum that had been found wanting in clinical potency without exception failed to do so.

While its qualities were being analysed in this way the stock of good serum became exhausted and the mortality in the London district with the serum available receded to the neighbourhood of 50 per cent. As soon as the association of therapeutic potency with anti-endotoxic capacity came to light, therefore, samples of all the batches of anti-meningococcus serum in store were tested for anti-endotoxin to Types I and II. A batch of pooled serum was found that neutralized endotoxin in the same manner as the specimen of potent serum. On trial in the London district and elsewhere this new serum proved to be as successful clinically as the best serum previously in use.

At the time that this research was undertaken for the avowed purpose of defining, if possible, the particular constituent of anti-meningococcus serum that determines potency, the Medical Research Committee provided special facilities for the production of anti-meningococcus serum. In view of the uncertainty of the so-called multivalent serum, it was decided to apply the knowledge gained in preceding stages of the outbreak with regard to the races of meningococci at work and to prepare a set of four monotypical sera, each horse being prepared against a single serological type as defined by agglutinin, but employing a plurality of strains. The serum was prepared by Dr. Stanley Griffith at Cambridge and it was not issued for trial until when tested at the central laboratory 0·5 c.c. showed evidence of neutralizing one minimum lethal dose of the endotoxin of the homologous meningococcus. Owing to lack of precise knowledge of the conditions under which anti-endotoxin is formed it was found that serum satisfying this requirement was difficult to prepare, but eventually success was obtained, the neutralizing power of the Type I serum being considerably better than that of the serum prepared against Type II. In order to provide for the treatment of cases before the infecting type of meningococcus had been identified a pooled serum consisting of equal parts of Types I and II sera was sent out.

It should be mentioned that during preceding stages of the outbreak Type I had been regarded as the gravest form of meningococcus infection. Thus in the early months of 1915, when the disease was particularly active and severe, 19 out of 32 meningococci, or 59 per cent., proved to be examples of Type I. Kennedy and Worster Drought also, in comparing the type of disease produced by the several types of the meningococcus, stated that in their experience Type I gave rise to an infection of greater severity and that such cases were more resistant to treatment than others. Fildes also formed the opinion that Type I is the most pathogenic form of the meningococcus, as will be seen later.

The clinical results obtained with these monotypical sera have been collected and analysed by Major Hine. After eliminating obvious sources of error the results were found to be as follows :—

Results of Monotypical Therapeutic Sera.

Infection.					Cases.	Deaths.	Mortality per cent.
Type I	..	..	..	..	65	6	9·23
,, II	..	..	..	..	104	41	39·42
,, III	..	..	..	..	28	7	25·00
,, IV	..	..	..	..	4	3	75·00
Untyped	..	..	..	..	48	22	45·00
			Total	..	249	79	31·07

The outstanding feature of these results is the striking success of the Type I serum. Before the serum was given forty-eight of these cases were reported as either fulminant, very severe, or severe. Five of these Type I cases were children under 15, all of whom recovered.

The result with the Type II serum is far less satisfactory. That this group is complex was known from Tulloch's research with agglutinin. Further definition of this type would appear desirable, employing anti-endotoxin as well as agglutinin for its analysis.

Many of the Type III cases failed to benefit from the pooled Types I and II serum given in the first place, and only improved when Type III serum was administered.

The Type IV cases are too few for remark, save that this group is generally diagnosed late. The single case that recovered was extremely severe with widespread purpuric rash, and had received Types I and II sera without benefit, but recovered with the Type IV serum.

Major Hine found evidence in the reports that speed and accuracy in the diagnosis of the type infecting the patient were rewarded by a higher recovery-rate.

Some experiments made in the central laboratory, in which the capacity of anti-meningococcus serum to protect the mouse against the living coccus was compared with its capacity to neutralize the endotoxin of the same coccus, indicated that the substances in the serum that protect against the virulence and toxicity respectively of the meningococcus are independent. It would seem likely that serum protecting against multiplication of the meningococcus may be of particular value in the treatment of septicæmic cases.

Nasopharyngeal Disinfection.

When, as may sometimes happen under war conditions, overcrowding is unavoidable, a high carrier-rate has resulted, and cerebro-spinal fever breaks out, a procedure that will reduce the abundance of the meningococcus even temporarily in the nasopharynx of a community is likely to be of some value. For this purpose considerable use was made of atomizers worked by steam or compressed air and filling the air of an inhaling room with finely divided disinfectant such as 2 per cent. zinc sulphate. The men were treated in batches and inhaled the spray-laden air through the nose. Although the disinfecting action of the treatment was found to be but temporary, the effect upon the incidence of cases was encouraging. A special jet elaborated by Major Hine was used with success. Gregor has advocated the inhalation of sulphur dioxide or of nitrous oxide gas, and others of chlorine, for this purpose.

Outbreaks of Catarrh.

In order to determine if the meningococcus is concerned in outbreaks of catarrh apart from cerebro-spinal fever, observations were made of the carrier-rate in two large camps during a severe outbreak of influenzal cold. In neither instance was the meningococcus carrier-rate found to be raised either in the patients or in a sample from the rest of the camp population. In a population already infected with the meningococcus, however, the advent of coryza was found by Glover to promote materially the spread of this micro-organism.

Some of the more important points brought out during the military outbreak are as follows :—

(1) Several new facts have been elucidated with regard to the biology of the meningococcus and conditions favourable or otherwise to its growth. By means of agglutinin 98 per cent. of the meningococci examined were referred to one or other of four groups, of which Type I is the most homogeneous and clean cut, and Type II the least. These types appear to be stable and independent entities, to breed true, and to have a wide distribution. There is some evidence that they can be further subdivided, especially in the case of Type II. At the outset Type I predominated in the cases, but later it was superseded by Type II.

(2) With suitable precautions, the agglutination test proved very accurate in practice for identifying the strains of meningococcus concerned in the epidemic. In individuals, the nasopharyngeal infection is monotypical; in masses, it may be either monotypical or polytypical. When carriers are present and the conditions favourable to the transfer of infection by droplets from the upper respiratory passages, the meningococcus spreads. For this reason the carrier-rate of a community is a valuable index to the hygienic conditions observed as regards floor space, and a sensitive measure of the degree of overcrowding, and thus of the danger of the production of cerebro-spinal fever in susceptible individuals such as recruits.

(3) There is evidence that dosage plays an important part in the genesis of cerebro-spinal fever. In cases, as in carriers, the infection is monotypical. Anti-endotoxin would seem to be an important constituent of anti-meningococcus

serum. It is probable that the Type I serum owed much of its success to the circumstance that this group is the most homogeneous and best defined of all the races of meningococcus concerned in the recent outbreak among the military forces. If Dopter's classification is correct, this is the chief epidemic strain of the meningococcus.

Incidence in the Royal Navy.

In a report of their continuous studies of cerebro-spinal fever in the navy between November 1916 and November 1917 Fildes and Baker stated that out of 46 strains of meningococcus isolated from naval cases 45 had been found to conform to one or other of the four types identified in military cases. A large number of new entries were swabbed in order to prevent importation of cerebro-spinal fever into the navy. These men were representative of the general population; their flat carrier-rate was 2·7 per cent., the maximum being under 7 per cent., and the rate showed a seasonal rise. The distribution of types in new entries, cases and contacts was as follows :—

Men.	Number examined.	Types of meningococcus.			
		I.	II.	III.	IV.
New entries	14,618	41	191	12	73
Remote contacts	809	5	32	1	24
Close contacts	297	8	23	—	11
Cases	44	23	11	3	6

The excess of Types II and IV in the new entries is in striking contrast to the predominance of Type I in the cases—strong evidence, as they point out, of the superior pathogenicity of Type I.

Although heterologous types were equally abundant in close and remote contacts, carriers of the same type as that present in the case were double as frequent in the close contacts. While in the vast majority of the 421 carriers examined repeatedly the infection was monotypical, nine instances were observed of change of type from cross-infection. The average period of carrying by 360 carriers was 1·3 months, one-third of the men becoming free in a week. The percentage of chronic carriers (over 1·3 months) with the various types was: Type I, 1·8; Type II, 13·0; Type III, 0·0; and Type IV, 25·9, from which it is seen that Types II and IV were far more persistent in the nasopharynx than the others.

An interesting observation was made as regards antagonism between the types. When cultures of Types I and II were mixed both survived, whereas when Type IV was mixed with Type I or II, Type IV alone survived. As Type IV persisted longest in the carriers, and also replaced other types in seven of the nine carrriers, where a change of type occurred, it appeared that although Type I is the most pathogenic, Type IV possesses the greatest endurance.

A point of much importance was observed with regard to the pathogenesis of cerebro-spinal fever. Twenty-six men who were swabbed before the onset of cerebro-spinal fever were all found to be negative. This indicates that individual cases of cerebro-spinal fever occur shortly after infection with the meningococcus.

Fildes and Baker consider that meningococci consist of two main groups each subdivided into two types, of which in their view Types I and IV are more specialized than Types II and III. They also think that gradations exist between pharyngococci and meningococci. In a subsequent paper Fildes, while reaffirming his view that meningoccoci are subdivided into four main groups, calls attention to the occurrence of intermediate strains that four monotypical sera may fail to identify.

Infection of the Civil Population.

While the preceding observations were in progress Eastwood, F. Griffith and Scott, with whom were associated later Ponder, Lewis and Nabarro, studied the serological characters of meningococci from cases in the civil population of whom a large proportion were children, and examined also the incidence of meningococcus-like organisms in the nasopharynx of non-contacts.

The serological characters of meningococci from cases were investigated independently by Griffith and Scott who both observed two main groups among them, but encountered also a number of intermediate strains, and found a far larger number of sub-groups than had been identified in strains derived from military and naval cases. The recently published observations of Stanley Griffith with strains derived from military and civil cases respectively, including strains received from F. Griffith and Scott, indicate that while the classification of the military strains into four main groups holds good, a considerable proportion of the civil strains cannot be included in these four groups.

The precise significance of the observation of high carrier-rates of meningococcus-like organisms in the nasopharynx of non-contacts by workers in this group is difficult to assess. That season and overcrowding tend to increase the carrier-rate of undoubted meningococci is beyond dispute, and hospital out-patients probably illustrate this as well as troops. The continuous observation of the non-contact carrier-rate at Caterham over a period of three years, during which over 12,000 non-contacts were examined, and the daily examination of new entries to the navy for a year, during which over 14,000 men representative of the general population of the country were investigated, has provided evidence on this matter that may be regarded as convincing.

The differentiation of meningococci by Dopter into four distinct serological groups has been confirmed not only by experience in this country with strains from military and naval cases, but also by later observations at the Pasteur Institute by Nicolle, Debains and Jouan, who designate their types A, B, C, and D.

The strains of meningococcus present during a recent outbreak of cerebro-spinal fever in Copenhagen were investigated by F. Wulff, in the State Serum Institute under the direction of Professor Madsen. No fewer than 76 out of 80 cases, or 95 per cent., were due to a single type of the meningococcus called Type A. Nineteen of the patients developed septicæmia with petechial hæmorrhages without meningitis. Among 215 contacts of cases in the civil population, 8 per cent. were carriers, 6 per cent. being carriers of Type A, and among 328 contacts of military cases the Type A carrier-rate was 7 per cent. Out of 163 soldiers with over a year's service, 33 per cent. were carriers, 15 per cent. being carriers of Type A. On the other hand, out of 565 new entries from different parts of Denmark, although 7 per cent. carried other types of the meningococcus, not one was found to carry Type A. Further points ascertained during this outbreak were the monotypical character of the infection in individual cases, the stability of the serological types of the meningococcus, and the serological diversity of nasopharyngeal organisms with which the meningococcus is liable to be confounded. The type of meningococcus concerned in the Danish outbreak was found to be different from the chief types identified in military cases in this country, but appears to be identical with a sub-group of Type II. A study was made by Thomsen and Wulff of the special susceptibility of recruits to cerebro-spinal fever, and the conclusion reached that, amongst other things, the virulence of the particular strain of meningococcus locally prevalent is a determining factor.

BIBLIOGRAPHY.

Andrewes	Notes on the Bacteriological Examination of Eleven Cases of Cerebro-spinal Fever, etc.	Proc. Roy. Soc. Med. 1915–16, Vol. ix, (Path. Sect.), p 1.
Andrewes, Bulloch & Hewlett.	Report of the Special Advisory Committee upon the Bacteriological Studies of Cerebro-spinal Fever during the Epidemic of 1915.	M.R.C., Special Report Series, Lond., 1917, No. 2.
Arkwright ..	The Serum Reactions (Complement Fixation) of the Meningococcus and Gonococcus.	Jl. of Hyg., 1911, Vol. xi, p. 515.
,, .. ,.	Grouping of the Strains of Meningococcus isolated during the Epidemic of Cerebro-spinal Meningitis in 1915.	Brit. Med. Jl., 1915, Vol. ii, p. 885.
Bassett-Smith ..	Examinations made at the Royal Naval College, Greenwich, for Meningococcus Carriers, with Special reference to Non-contact Cases.	M.R.C., Special Report Series, Lond., 1917, No. 3, p. 66.
Bassett-Smith, Lynch & Mangham.	Carriers of the Meningococcus	Lancet, 1918, Vol. i, p. 290.
Bell	Some Observations on Meningococcal agglutinating Sera and their Production.	M.R.C., Special Report Series, Lond., 1920, No. 50, p. 57.
,, ...	On a Rapid Method of determining the Serological Type of a Meningococcus by the Agglutination Test.	Ibid., p. 63.
,, ...	Complement-fixing Antibodies to the Meningococcus.	Ibid., p. 66.
Bouchet	Désinfection des porteurs de méningocoques et de B. de Löffler par inhalations de chlore gazeux.	Compt. Rend. Soc. de Biol., 1918, Vol. lxxxi, p. 1027.
Canti	A Comparison of Meningococci found in the Cerebro-spinal Fluid and Nasopharynx in Twenty-five Cases.	Jl. of Hyg., 1918, Vol. xvi, p. 249.
Cleminson	Nasopharyngeal Conditions in Meningococcus Carriers.	Brit. Med. Jl., 1918, Vol. ii, p. 51.
Colebrook	Bacterial Antagonism with particular reference to the Meningococcus.	Lancet, 1915, Vol. ii, p. 1136.
Colebrook & Tanner	Meningococcus Carriers ..	Jl. of R.A.M.C., 1916, Vol. xxvi, p. 76.
Compton	Report on Cerebro-spinal Meningitis occurring in the Dorset Military Area during March to July 1915.	Jl. of R.A.M.C., 1915, Vol. xxv, p. 546.
,, ...	Outbreaks of Cerebro-spinal Fever in relation to Atmospheric Humidity.	Lancet, 1919, Vol. ii, p. 151.

Dopter & Koch ..	Sur la co-agglutination du méningocoque et du gonocoque.	Compt. Rend. Soc. de Biol., Paris, 1908, Vol. lxv, p. 215.
Dopter & Pauron ..	Differenciation des paraméningocoques entre eux par le saturation des agglutinines.	Compt. Rend. Soc. de Biol., Paris, 1914, Vol. lxxvii, p. 231.
Dopter	L'infection méningococcique ..	Baillière, Paris, 1921.
Eagleton	The Bacterial Content of the air in Army Sleeping Huts with especial reference to the meningococcus.	Jl. of Hyg., 1919, Vol. xviii, p. 264.
Eastwood, Griffith, F., Scott, Ponder, Lewis & Nabarro.	Reports on Cerebro-spinal Fever	Local Govt. Board, special reports on medical subjects, No. 110, 1916, and No. 114, 1917.
Eastwood	Second Report on Bacteriological Aspects of the Meningococcus Carrier Problem.	Jl. of Hyg., 1918, Vol. xvii, p. 63.
Ellis	A Classification of Meningococci based on Group Agglutination obtained with Monovalent Immune Rabbits' Serums.	Brit. Med. Jl., 1915, Vol. ii, p. 881.
Embleton & Bryant	The Site of Carrying in Meningococcus Carriers.	Lancet, 1919, Vol. ii, p. 679.
Embleton & Peters	Cerebro-spinal Fever and the Sphenoidal Sinus.	Jl. of R.A.M.C., 1915, Vol. xxiv, p. 468.
,, ,,	The Persistence of Cerebro-spinal Cases as Carriers of the Meningococcus during Convalescence.	Lancet, 1919, Vol. i, p. 788.
Embleton & Steven	A Study of 905 Meningococcus Carriers.	Ibid., 1919, Vol. ii, p. 682.
Fildes & Baker ..	A Report upon the Seasonal Outbreak of Cerebro-spinal Fever in the Navy at Portsmouth, 1916–17.	M.R.C., Special Report Series, Lond., 1918, No. 17.
Fildes	The Serological Classification of Meningococci.	Brit. Jl. of Exp. Pathol., 1920, Vol. i, p. 44.
Flack	Report on Cerebro-spinal Fever in the London District, December 1915 to July 1916.	M.R.C., Special Report Series, Lond., 1917, No. 3, p. 31. Also Jl. of R.A.M.C., 1917, Vol. xxviii, p. 113.
Fletcher	Meningococcus Broncho-pneumonia in Influenza.	Lancet, 1919, Vol. i, p. 104.
Flexner	Contributions to the Biology of Diplococcus intracellularis.	Jl. of Exp. Med., 1907, Vol. ix, p. 105.
,, ...	Experimental Cerebro-spinal Meningitis in Monkeys.	Ibid, p. 142.
Foster & Gaskell ..	Cerebro-spinal Fever	Cambridge University Press, 1916.
Gaskell	Report from the Cerebro-spinal Fever Laboratory, Cambridge, July 1915.	Jl. of R.A.M.C., 1915, Vol. xxv, p. 286.

Gates	A Report on Antimeningitis Vaccination and Observations on Agglutinins in the Blood of Chronic Meningococcus Carriers.	Jl. of Exp. Med., 1918, Vol. xxviii, p. 449.
Glover	Military Overcrowding and the Meningococcus Carrier-rate.	Report to M.R.C., printed for official use, March 1918.
,,	Observations of the Meningococcus Carrier-rate, and their Application to the Prevention of Cerebro-spinal Fever.	M.R.C., Special Report Series, Lond., 1920, No. 50, p. 133.
,,	Six Cases of Purulent Bronchopneumonia associated with the Meningococcus.	Lancet, 1918, Vol. ii, p. 880.
,,	Some Deductions from a Series of 243 Military Cases of Cerebro-spinal Fever in the London District with regard to variations in the Therapeutic Potency of Serum.	Jl. of R.A.M.C.,1920, Vol. xxxiv, p. 499.
Gordon & Murray	Identification of the Meningococcus.	Jl. of R.A.M.C.,1915, Vol. xxv, p. 411.
Gordon	Studies of the Meningococcus and their Practical Application.	M.R.C., Special Report Series, Lond., 1917, No. 3 and 1920, No. 50.
,,	The Inhibitory Action of Saliva on the Growth of the Meningococcus.	Brit. Med. Jl., 1916, Vol. i, p. 849.
Gregor	The Scope of certain Gaseous Disinfectants in the Prophylaxis of Influenza.	Ibid., 1919, Vol. ii, p. 523.
Griffith, A. S.	A Study of the Serological Reactions of Meningococci, and an Account of the Method of Preparation of Antimeningococcus Serum.	Jl. of Hyg., 1920, Vol. xix, p. 33.
Hine	On the Rapid Preparation of High-titre Agglutinating Serum for the Meningococcus.	M.R.C., Special Report Series, Lond., 1917, No. 3, p. 99.
,,	An Analysis of the Result of the Therapeutic Application of Monotypical Agglutinating Serum in 267 Cases of Cerebrospinal Fever.	M.R.C., Special Report Series, Lond., 1920, No. 50, p. 176.
,,	Improved Atomizer for Mass-disinfection.	Ibid., p. 173.
Jordan-Lloyd	Chemical Factors involved in the Growth of the Meningococcus.	Jl. of Path. & Bacteriol., 1916–17, Vol. xxi, p. 113.
Kennedy & Worster Drought.	The Relation of the Type of Coccus to the Type of Disease in Meningococcus Meningitis.	Brit. Med. Jl., 1917, Vol. i, p. 261.
Kutscher	Epidemische Genickstarre	Handb. d. pathogenen Mikroorganismen. Kolle v. Wassermann, 2nd Edit., Jena, 1912, Vol. iv, p. 589.

Lieberknecht .. Ueber Pseudo-meningokokken Arch. f. Hyg., 1909, aus dem Rachen gesunder Vol. lxviii, p. 142. Schulkinder.

v. Lingelsheim .. Die bakteriologischen Arbeiten Klin. Jahrb. Jena, der Kgl. Hygienischen Station 1906, Vol. xv, p. zu Beuthen während der Gen- 373. ickstarre-Epidemie in Ober- schlesien im Winter, 1904–5.

v. Lingelsheim & Tierversuche mit dem Diplo- Ibid., p. 489. Leuchs. coccus intracellularis. Men- ingococcus.)

McDonald Stuart .. Observations on Cerebro-spinal Jl. of Path. & Bac- meningitis. teriol., 1908, Vol. xii, p. 442.

Mackarell .. .. Malignant Endocarditis as a Jl. of R.A.M.C.,1915, Complication of Cerebro- Vol. xxv, p. 353. spinal Fever.

MacLagan & Cooke Fulminating Cerebro-spinal Jl. of R.A.M.C.,1917, Fever ; its Prognosis and Vol. xxix, p. 228. Treatment.

Muir.. .. .. Note on the Presence of Men- Jl. of R.A.M.C.,1919, ingococci in the Skin Petechiæ Vol. xxxiii, p. 404. in Cerebro-spinal Fever.

Netter & Debré .. La méningite cérébrospinale .. Masson, Paris, 1911, p. 34.

Nicolle, Debains & Etude sur les méningocoques Ann. de l'Inst. Pas- Jouan. et les sérums antiméningo- teur, 1918, Vol. cocciques. xxxii, p. 150.

Reece .. .. Notes on the Prevalence of Jl. of R.A.M.C.,1915, Cerebro-spinal Fever among Vol. xxiv, p. 555. the Civil Population, 1914–15 ; together with a Short Account of the Appearance of the Disease and of its Distribution among Troops during the same period, and of the Mili- tary Administrative measures adopted to deal with it.

Rolleston .. .. Lumleian Lectures : Cerebro- Lancet, 1919, Vol. i, spinal Fever. pp. 541, 593, 645.

Sellers .. .. Bacteriological Examinations Jl. of R.A.M.C.,1915, at Manchester Cerebro-spinal Vol. xxv, p. 676. Fever Laboratory, 1915.

Shearer .. .. On the Presence of an Accessory Lancet, 1917, Vol. i, Food Factor in the Nasal p. 59. Secretion, and its Action on the Growth of the Meningo- coccus and other Pathogenic Bacteria.

Shearer & Crowe .. The Rôle of the Phagocyte in Proc. Roy. Soc., Cerebro-spinal Meningitis. Lond., Series B, 1917, Vol. lxxxix, p. 422.

Thomsen & Wulff.. Nogle problemer vedrörende Hospitalstidende, meningococinfectionen. Copenhagen, 1921, Vol. lxiv, pp. 17– 28 and 33–45.

Treadgold .. .. Cerebro-spinal Meningitis in the Jl. of R.A.M.C.,1915, Salisbury Plain Area during Vol. xxiv, p. 221. the early part of 1915.

Tulloch	..	..	Report on the Examination of Carriers isolated from 10,000 Men in the Garrison of X, April, May and June 1916.	M.R.C., Special Report Series, Lond., 1917, No. 3, p. 70.
,,	..	..	On the Differentiation by means of the Absorption of Agglutinin Test of the Types of Meningococci obtained from the Cerebro-spinal Fluid of Cases during the Current Outbreak of Cerebro-spinal Fever.	Jl. of R.A.M.C.,1917, Vol. xxix, p. 66.
,,	..	..	A Study of the Mechanism of the Agglutination and Absorption of Agglutinin Reaction, together with an Examination of the Efficacy of these Tests for Identifying Specimens of the Meningococcus isolated from 354 Cases of Cerebro-spinal Fever.	Jl. of R.A.M.C.,1918, Vol. xxx, p. 115.
,,	..	..	A Study of Gram-negative Diplococci of the Nasopharynx resembling the Meningococcus.	M.R.C., Special Report Series, Lond., 1920, No. 50, Pt. III.
Vines	..	..	A Starch Medium for Identification of the Meningococcus by its Sugar Reactions.	Jl. of R.A.M.C.,1916, Vol. xxvi, p. 89.
Walker Hall & Peters	..	..	Changes in the Agglutinability, Fermentation Reactions and Absorption Capacities of the Meningococcus during an Acute Attack.	Jl. of R.A.M.C.,1916, Vol. xxvii, p. 399.
Weichselbaum	..		Ueber die Aetiologie der akuten Meningitis Cerebrospinalis.	Fortschr. d. Med., Berlin, 1887, Vol. v, p. 573.
Wulff	..	..	Undersogelser over Meningococtyper.	Gyldendalske Boghandel, Copenhagen, 1921.
Worster Drought & Kennedy.			Cerebro-spinal Fever	A. & C. Black; Lond., 1919.

CHAPTER XV.

THE epidemiology of the pandemic of influenza of the last year of the war is discussed in Volume I of the Diseases of the War, but in dealing with the bronchitis, broncho-pneumonia and pneumonia among the troops, and more particularly in describing and discussing the morbid anatomy of the fatal cases among them, reference must be made to this subject, because while it is usual to date the pandemic as first revealing itself in May 1918, the fullest studies of the specific gross and microscopical lesions of the air passages among soldiers were made upon material from cases which occurred long antecedent to that month, in the winters of 1916–17 and 1917–18. Admittedly, at the time, the essentially influenzal nature of these cases was not emphasized, even by those who reported the frequent finding of Pfeiffer's bacillus. There was, indeed, great confusion and debate as to how the cases should be classified, and army instructions were conflicting. A careful study of the successive reports and publications can lead to one conclusion only, namely, that the cases of so-called purulent bronchitis, capillary bronchitis, broncho-pneumonia and influenzal pneumonia are members of a single series, and are manifestations of one and the same disease, and this whether they showed themselves in France, in England, in North America, or in the Near or Far East.

It is an interesting chapter of medical history. In July 1917 there was published in the *Lancet* a very full account by Lieutenant J. A. B. Hammond, Captain W. Rolland and Lieutenant T. H. G. Shore, of what they describe as "almost a small epidemic" affecting the troops in the Etaples area. They describe this as first showing itself in December 1916, reaching its height in January 1917, and continuing through February and March. Etaples was a great hospital area with many thousands of beds, with one central "morgue." During the first two years of the war sporadic cases of acute lobar pneumonia had been admitted to hospital both in France and England in moderate numbers. There was seasonal variation in the number of cases but no noticeable frequency in their incidence, and such occasional cases were still admitted to the Etaples group of hospitals during the period under review. But now during February and early March no less than 45 per cent. of all the autopsies were of one nature. In 71 out of 156 consecutive autopsies, on section of the lungs, pus oozed from all the cut smaller bronchi and bronchioles. In 45 of the 71 this bronchitis was the primary condition. This purulent bronchitis caused five times as many deaths as did acute lobar pneumonia.

They give as cardinal symptoms of the condition, tachycardia, dyspnœa and cyanosis with expectoration, which at first slight, frothy and, it might be, blood-stained rather than rusty,

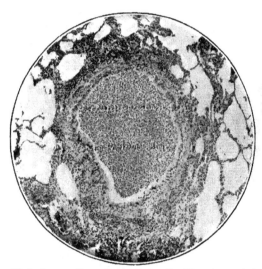

Fig. 1.—Marked congestion of bronchial wall with polymorph infiltration. Mucous membrane well preserved except at one part. Lumen almost completely filled with pus. No peribronchial pneumonia.

accompanied by an irritable and distressing cough, became in a day or two purulent and abundant. Sharp crepitant râles, often first heard in the region of the roots of the lungs, quickly became generalized, and in the majority of cases broncho-pneumonic patches could be made out. In a certain number of cases these spread and became confluent, giving the signs of a lobar pneumonia. A slight pleuritic rub was heard in a few cases. With this the cough became less troublesome and the expectoration easy. There was a high mortality; in the severe cases death occurred on the fifth or sixth day from " lung block."

The less acute cases exhibited a typical purulent expectoration extending from three to six weeks, accompanied by profuse sweats, marked wasting and weakness, with gradual recovery.

Bacteriologically the sputum from 20 cases was submitted to examination. In all but two of these there was present a small Gram-negative cocco-bacillus, afterwards identified as the *Bacillus influenzae*. In 10 out of the 18 cases this was the predominating organism, being present in some in enormous numbers ; in three this was the sole organism visible, and that in abundance.

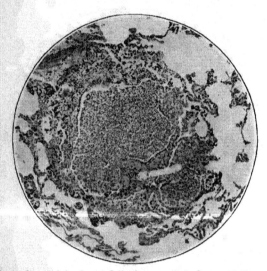

Fig. 2.—A bronchiole almost full of pus. Only here and there can the remains of the mucous membrane be detected. There is a pneumonic condition in the surrounding air vesicles, large pigmented catarrhal cells being present. (x 60.)

Cultures made from these sputa (in blood agar or trypsin-broth-legumin agar) resulted in growths of the *B. influenzae* from 10 of the 18 cases.

What was noticeable was the frequent co-existence of other microbes, and particularly of the pneumococcus. This was isolated or recognized in 13 out of the 20 sputa ; 5 cases yielded streptococci, 5 a form resembling *Micrococcus catarrhalis*. Often several forms co-existed : staphylococci, *M. tetragenus*, or large Gram-negative bacilli, etc., were occasionally encountered.

It deserves note that the two cases in which neither " smears " nor cultures gave *B. influenzae,* both recovered ; of the 20 cases from which the sputum was examined 13 died. It is evident that the very frequency of the pneumococcus led them to the non-committal terminology of ' purulent bronchitis.'

The authors lay stress upon the following conditions found at autopsy :—

(1) The frequency of cyanosis of the face ; (2) the bulky nature of the lungs as a result of an emphysema affecting more particularly the anterior margins ; (3) the general presence of

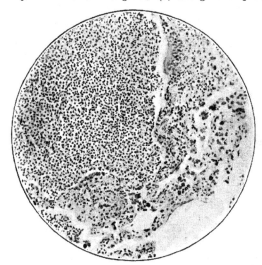

Fig. 3.—A high-power view of part of the preceding specimen. It shows the purulent bronchial contents, the remains of the mucous membrane and the surrounding catarrhal pneumonia.

some degree of pleurisy, plastic in type—in only two of the cases did the amount of fluid exceed a few ounces, while empyema was rare ; (4) the constant appearance of thick yellowish pus in the bronchi ; and (5) the common association of a considerable extent of pulmonary œdema with the above appearance.

Their description of the histology of these lungs is significant :—

" The most striking changes are in the smaller bronchi. Their walls are thickened and the vessels engorged ; the lining epithelium, which is at first intact, is later detached in parts from its basement membrane, and the epithelial cells can be seen lying free in the lumen. In a still more advanced stage the bronchiole is entirely denuded of mucous membrane, and its wall consists of granulation tissue which greatly diminishes its calibre. The bronchi are in the less advanced stages almost completely filled with pus, in which, in some cases, the influenza bacillus was found in appropriately stained sections. Later on columnar epithelial cells in small masses are mixed with the polymorphonuclear pus cells, and by the time the epithelium is entirely shed the amount of pus in the bronchus is greatly diminished. Many of the specimens show marked broncho-pneumonia, but in some there is no great extension of the inflammatory process to the surrounding lung tissue. Indeed, the small extent to which catarrhal pneumonia is often present in the vicinity of markedly involved bronchi would suggest that the pneumonia is due to a local toxic effect rather than to an infection of the corresponding area of lung tissue."

The figures here reproduced from this article in the *Lancet* will illustrate the letterpress. Fig. 3 shows well the swollen and desquamated epithelial cells of the alveoli, and the so-called catarrhal cells of the surrounding " catarrhal " pneumonia.

A greater or less degree of collapse at the vertebral borders of the lower lobes was noted in 15 out of the 45 cases of primary bronchitis ; great enlargement was noted of the lymph nodes at the root of the lung and along the trachea. The spleen was found engorged and firm in many cases, and some swelling and pallor of the cortex of the kidneys was recorded in 25 out of the 45. A distinction is drawn between the cyanosed cases in which the right heart was found dilated though fairly healthy, and the organs congested, and the pallid cases, with organs flabby and soft and heart muscle pale and friable.

In the next number of the *Lancet* following the appearance of this paper, a letter was published by Captain A. Abrahams, R.A.M.C., pointing out that numerous cases of like nature, with a very high mortality, had occurred at Aldershot. The observations there accorded in every detail with those of Hammond, Rolland and Shore. He agreed with them in believing that they dealt with a symptom complex representing a definite clinical entity.

This letter was followed in September by the full study of the Aldershot cases by Captains A. Abrahams and N. F. Hallows, Dr. J. W. H. Eyre, Director of the Bacteriological Laboratory at Guy's Hospital, and Major H. French, Consulting Physician to the Aldershot Command. They described the total cases observed as amounting to scores ; they are unable to give exact statistics since the earlier cases had been diagnosed as pneumonia and broncho-pneumonia. The mortality had been about 50 per cent. The majority of cases had been in men of inferior physique, although occasionally those had been affected who gave no previous history of bad health. It is interesting to observe that neither set of observers makes mention of the prevalence of epidemic catarrh, or of mild transient cases of like type among the troops ; the Aldershot observers, however, note that six out of the eight fatal cases subjected by them to full examination came from one unit.

The pathological details given by them coincide in practically every point with those recorded by the Etaples group. With them, they call particular attention to the involvement of the

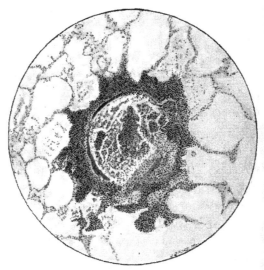

Fig. 4.—Section of lung tissue, under low power of microscope, showing the alveoli to be hardly affected at all, while the bronchiole is filled with cells and debris, and its wall and the immediately surrounding parts are characteristically infiltrated with small round cells.

bronchi and bronchioles and to the peculiar peri-bronchitis and peri-bronchiolitis ; they give an illustration of the specific lesion.

"The condition is not primarily a lobar or a broncho-pneumonia, but a bronchitis, and although a small amount of basal broncho-pneumonia has been present in one or two of our *post-mortem* examinations, in other fatal cases there has been no broncho-pneumonia at all, not even the smallest portions of either lung being found to sink in water.

"Microscopical examination of a section of the affected lung shows blockage of the bronchioles with debris, pus cells and desquamated epithelial cells ; the submucous coat may be laid bare, as though the bronchiole lining has been ulcerated away ; the walls of the bronchiole are infiltrated with small round cells, and this small round-celled infiltration extends a little distance beyond the bronchiole itself into the adjacent lung tissue, forming an irregular ring of small round-celled infiltration more or less uniformly all round the bronchiole, without affecting the alveoli in the form of definite broncho-pneumonia."

Bacteriologically, they subjected eight cases to careful examination. In all the eight, small Gram-negative bacilli predominated in the sputum, these being chiefly intracellular within the polymorphonuclear leucocytes ; but when the sputum was inoculated into three rabbits, they gained from the local lesions in all three animals a mixed growth of *B. influenzae* and the pneumococcus. So also the spleen pulp gave mixed growth of the two organisms. They agreed with Hammond, Rolland and Shore in calling the condition " purulent bronchitis," and, regarding its ætiology, they were of opinion that they dealt with a primary infection of *B. influenzae* with secondary invasion of pneumococci.

The Aldershot observers lay stress upon the fullness and accuracy of the studies of Hammond, Rolland and Shore, and upon the way in which they were able to confirm them. Without question they dealt with the same disease.

There is evidence also that fatal cases of influenza with pulmonary involvement were not uncommon in Northern France during the course of 1916 and 1917, nay, more, that some at least were recognized not as 'purulent bronchitis' but as influenza with influenzal pneumonia. On this point reference is made to the cases reported from No. 3 Canadian General Hospital (McGill), at Boulogne. A full study of these, clinical, pathological and bacteriological, was made by Major L. J. Rhea, C.A.M.C., pathologist to the hospital* and Major T. A. Malloch, C.A.M.C. These observers report nine fatal cases of bronchiolitis and broncho-pneumonia observed in 1916–17, cases characterized clinically by great dyspnœa, marked cyanosis, rapid pulse, irregular temperature, the expectoration of large amounts of nummular sputum, and signs of a generalized bronchiolitis, with or without signs of consolidation. From a study of the details given by them, there can be no question as to their having encountered the same conditions as did the Etaples and Aldershot observers.

" Microscopically there was acute purulent bronchiolitis, peri-bronchiolitis with a formation of minute abscesses where the alveolar walls close to the bronchioles had disappeared. Bacilli like Pfeiffer's bacillus in morphology and staining reactions were seen here. Broncho-pneumonia was present in the alveoli about the bronchioles which were filled with pus. The exudate in the air-sacs contained little fibrin and fewer polymorphs than is the case in lobar pneumonia ; on the other hand, many lining epithelium cells lay free in the alveoli. The interalveolar septa were somewhat thickened, and the alveoli varied very much in size, some being collapsed, and there were also areas of marked emphysema . . . . . The blood-vessels were everywhere much congested, even in the pleura."

The most significant part of Malloch and Rhea's communication is their bacteriological findings.

* Associate-Professor of Pathology, McGill University.

" In the first two cases the sputum was not examined microscopically, but from the results of the *post-mortem* examination of these cases we learned to associate certain macroscopic features of the sputum with the finding of *B. influenzae* under the microscope. In the remaining seven patients *B. influenzae* was found to be by far and away the predominating organism of the sputum."

In all the members of the series, save one where there was contamination with air organisms, *B. influenzae* was grown in pure culture from the terminal bronchi. In the primary and secondary bronchi other organisms were admixed—pneumococcus, *M. catarrhalis*, streptococcus and *Staphylococcus albus*.

Malloch and Rhea note one case of confluent broncho-pneumonia simulating lobar pneumonia both clinically and on first inspection *post mortem*, and call attention to the resemblance of the cut surface of the lung in many cases to what is seen in acute miliary tuberculosis (Huebschmann's influenzal miliary pneumonia). They note, further, that at No. 3 Canadian General Hospital, from 1st January, 1917, to August 1918, 172 cases of lobar pneumonia and 97 of broncho-pneumonia were admitted to the " pneumonia hut," and that in this series they did not find any case of diffuse capillary bronchitis due to any other organism than Pfeiffer's bacillus.

If in one general hospital in France no fewer than nine fatal cases of the condition were recognized in the course of the year, if in every one of the nine cases the *B. influenzae* was gained in pure culture from the purulent exudate in the bronchioles, and if the broncho-pneumonia was of the same unusual type as that described by Hammond, Rolland and Shore in their yet earlier cases, it is evident, in the light of these careful studies, that the frequent presence of the *B. influenzae* noted by the earlier observers was of no little significance, and, further, that influenza existed among the troops prior to the onset of the pandemic, sporadically, it may be, and not of sufficient frequency to cause alarm, but there, nevertheless.

The next full study of these unusual cases of bronchitis and pneumonia—again months before the development of the pandemic—comes from North America. This was the elaborate and conscientious investigation made by W. G. MacCallum, Professor of Pathology at Johns Hopkins University, upon an epidemic affecting the camp of recently recruited soldiers of the United States army during the winter of 1917–18.

As with other troops so with the American, recruits brought into camp from remote country districts succumbed readily to the exanthemata of childhood. While rubella was, in the main, the bane of the British troops, and this and mumps of the Canadian, in the United States measles was at first by far the most prevalent condition. To anyone reading MacCallum's monograph it is abundantly evident that it was written under the primary belief that he was dealing with a pneumonic condition, or conditions, secondary to measles, and that while he records the presence of influenza bacilli in a certain number of his cases, he laid special stress upon the presence of a hæmolytic streptococcus. In 34 out of 38 cases of interstitial and lobular pneumonia he isolated this form of micro-organism, and in two of the seven cases in which he did not gain cultures he recognized it in sections of the lungs.* Only at a later stage, during the revision of his proof was it brought home to him that the lesions he described are those typical of the influenza which in the latter half of 1918 had become pandemic.

" Since this paper was sent to press another and much greater epidemic has occurred with appalling mortality from pneumonia. . . . . The invention of a new stain for Gram-negative bacteria by Dr. Goodpasture . . . . made it possible to re-study the tissues from the epidemic described above with the assurance of being able to demonstrate influenza bacilli in the tissues whenever they were present. . . . . I have therefore taken the opportunity afforded in the correction of the proof to introduce notes on the presence of these organisms, although the general discussion is left unchanged. . . . . It is now proved that the bacilli can be demonstrated in the bronchioles and occasionally in the alveoli of the lungs in 16 of 48 acute cases, while in at least 6 other cases they were present in the sputum.

Type of pneumonia.	Total number of cases.	Influenza bacilli present in
Interstitial broncho-pneumonia	16	5
Interstitial and lobular pneumonia	9	4
Lobular pneumonia	7	—
Interstitial broncho-pneumonia and lobar pneumonia	5	2
Lobar pneumonia	11	5

" It may be said that they tend to be associated with the interstitial and organizing process, since even some cases of lobar pneumonia show a tendency to organization of the exudate and thickening of the interstitial tissue. . . . It is even suggested in the face of the obvious influence of the epidemic of measles that during the whole period of the winter epidemic there may have

---

* It may be suggested that the striking frequency with which MacCallum records the presence of hæmolytic streptococci in his series of cases is to be associated with the fact that the majority of his cases were secondary to measles, rubella, scarlatina and diphtheria. Now in all these diseases hæmolytic streptococci become the dominant members of the flora of the pharynx, being present in great abundance. It is noteworthy that not one of his negative cases is recorded as having been affected with measles or other exanthem, as also that the two of his series of 11 cases of lobar pneumonia from which he isolated *Streptococcus hæmolyticus* as well as the pneumococcus were the two in which there had been antecedent measles.

been influenza which predisposed to secondary streptococcus infections. But there remain the facts that most of the cases show no influenza bacilli, and that in those which are most typical of the form of interstitial broncho-pneumonia . . . . . the most painstaking search through many sections has failed to reveal any of these organisms. It is true that Case **37** shows relatively few streptococci and great numbers of influenza bacilli. . . . . But in all the others the streptococcus is the predominant organism, if we except Case 196, in which there were no streptococci and in which the lesion seems to have been caused by pneumococci.

" I think it must be recognized that the insterstitial form of broncho-pneumonia can be produced by various organisms . . . . . it appears in spite of the frequent presence of the influenza bacillus this was essentially an epidemic of streptococcal pneumonia."

While he leaves the matter open his description and his abundant microphotographs make it absolutely certain that from January to March 1918 influenza was raging at Fort Sam Houston in Texas, and at Camp Dodge, Iowa. At this stage the epidemic was in what may be termed its first phase ; MacCallum makes no reference to cases of non-fatal three-day fever and catarrh affecting those previously in sound health (*i.e.*, to what may be termed the second phase, so characteristic of the May and June epidemic of 1918), his cases with scarcely an exception occurred among men weakened by previous disease, most often measles.

As showing that he dealt with the same characteristic lesion as that described by the Etaples and Aldershot observers, it is as well to give his description of the characteristic lesion :—

" In all the later stages this change in the connective tissue, elastic tissue and musculature which make up the wall of the bronchus is striking. The normal elements are spread apart by great numbers of mononuclear cells which intercalate themselves between the fibres and often form a mass which lifts up and dislodges the epithelium. Most of these cells are small like lymphoid cells, but many are larger, occasionally assuming the character of plasma cells or the various types of larger mononuclear wandering cells. Œdema accompanies them and aids in the spreading apart of the connective tissue. The blood-vessels are distended with blood and evidently new ones are formed with associated fibroblasts, for in many cases the wall assumes the appearance of a highly vascular granulation tissue in which the blood-vessels come to be radially placed. In some cases the bronchi become dilated, occasionally to a marked degree as in Case 181, and to a less extent in Cases 41 and 184. In the most advanced conditions as in Case 41, the walls of the bronchioles become enormously thickened and form a compact tube of infiltrated tissue, but in most instances the wall is rather relaxed and loose in texture. With dilation the epithelium may be stretched and flattened or it may disappear by being desquamated, leaving the surface of the new granulation tissue exposed.

" The normal wall of the smaller bronchi contains only a relatively small amount of lymphoid tissue scattered in thin strands in its outer layers, except at certain places such as the points of division where somewhat more compact masses often occur. About the same may be said of the adventitia of the blood-vessels and the interlobular septa. It seems possible, however, that much of the infiltration which has been described, and a part of the thickening of the bronchial wall may be due to the swelling and spread of the lymphoid tissue all along the wall of the bronchus, and its appearance of being a new

PLATE I.

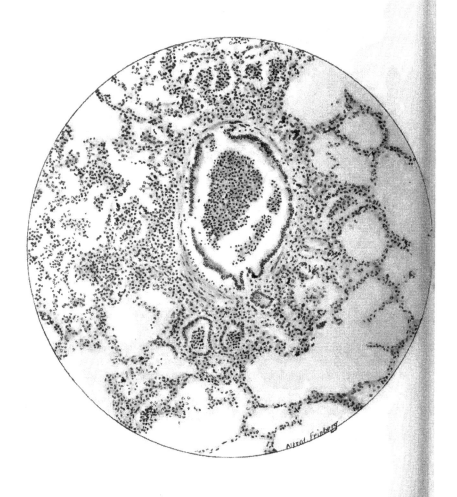

Interstitial broncho-pneumonia.　Early bronchial and peribronchial lesion.

Note the thickened and infiltrated alveolar walls and proliferation and desquamation
of the alveolar epithelium.

growth of granulation tissue with radially arranged and abundant blood-vessels may well be explained in the same way, since with a greatly thickened mantle of lymphoid tissue there would arise a more conspicuous vascular supply for that tissue.

"The lymphatics which run in the bronchial wall are distended with leucocytes, mononuclear cells and blood, and usually thrombosed with great quantities of streptococci entangled in the thrombus.

"In the later stages a uniform process appears which is a combination of these. The alveolar walls contiguous to the bronchi become widened and thickened by an invasion of mononuclear cells just as in the bronchi wall itself. The alveoli are partly filled with fluid and with desquamated alveolar epithelium. Many of them a little farther removed are quite filled with red corpuscles and all contain dense masses of compact fibrin in which cells are partly entangled. Mononuclear cells escape into the alveoli but in small num-bers. It is strange that although streptococci are found in the lumen of the bronchus among the polymorphonuclear cells which persist there, and in still greater numbers in the thrombosed lymphatics of the wall, they are not to be found in these distended alveoli, which seems to show that this process has a certain protective influence."

From his description and from his plates, of one of which Plate I is a reproduction, it is absolutely clear that MacCallum dealt with the same basal and, if it may be so expressed, underlying condition as that present in the Etaples, Aldershot and Boulogne cases. The relations of the hæmolytic streptococci to his and similar cases will be discussed later on.

If, therefore, on the one hand, morbid anatomical studies are of any value, and if on the other any stress is to be laid upon the presence of the *B. influenzae* in association with this group of cases, then the study of the pathology of fatal cases demonstrates strikingly the existence of three phases in the development of the pandemic—a first phase, December 1916 to May 1918, so mild in its manifestations as not to cause comment, during which with rare exceptions only those already weakened succumbed ; a second phase, May to August 1918, with acute onset, high fever and short duration of the attacks, definitely epidemic but with relatively few fatal cases ; and the third virulent phase, late autumn 1918, affecting all ages and conditions, those in previous robust health equally with those weakened by previous disease, and characterized by longer continuance, great frequency of pulmonary disturbance and high mortality.

It will be demonstrated that the main features, clinical and pathological, which characterized these cases among the troops from the winter of 1916–17 onwards were also the main features of the pandemic in May 1918.

All who have investigated this pandemic, while they may still remain divided as to the essential primary cause, recognize the frequency of secondary invaders, so that it is impossible to proceed without constantly endeavouring to distinguish between the essential and underlying, and the secondary and superposed disturbances. If the primary cause is left an open matter, at least there must be frequent reference to, and differentiation of the lesions set up by the secondary invaders, by streptococci, pneumococci and staphylococci. This being so, it is impossible to deal with the pathology of the disease without referring to its bacteriology. It is necessary, therefore, to distinguish between lesions common to all fatal cases, which, as being common, may be regarded as due to the one common primary cause, and other lesions which, while perhaps common to a particular group of cases, have been absent from other cases and groups of cases. These other lesions, it is found, can in most cases be referred to secondary bacteria.

There are, admittedly, three dangers in this course :—

(1) Strains of the same species of micro-organism according to their previous history may set up different lesions. As regards influenza, it is a generally accepted observation that successive epidemics have varied in the extent to which one or other system has been affected—the respiratory, the gastro-intestinal, the nervous, etc. Reference has already been made to the different phases of the pandemic. It is quite possible, therefore, that differences should exist in the lesions currently observed in, for example, different camps, differences not due to the presence of other secondary invaders but to altered properties of the primary causative organism.*

(2) Individual human beings may vary in their reaction to one common order of pathogenic micro-organisms and as a consequence there is the danger that an unusual reaction may be ascribed wrongfully to the presence of some other microbe.

(3) The same order of lesion may be set up by different species of microbe.

Upon fuller consideration the first two dangers are found not to be serious. The procedure employed is to compare, for example, a series of affected lungs. If they are affected by the same disease, although the virulence of the causative microbe may vary, the order of lesion tends to be the same. So, too, in individuals of different orders of susceptibility, if the one organ is affected it will tend to show grades of the same lesion, not lesions of different order.

The third danger is more difficult to overcome, especially in connection with the lung, and the type of lesion found in

---

* As regards *B. influenzae,* since the war evidence has rapidly accumulated of the existence of multiple strains of this organism.

influenza. During the last two generations observer after observer has described this peculiar type as supervening after whooping-cough, measles and diphtheria, drawing attention to its interstitial character and the lateral involvement of the alveoli surrounding the affected bronchi as contrasted with pneumonia of the true lobular type. Yet this deserves note that, save where associated with influenza, this condition is almost entirely recorded as met with in children. Delafield appears to be the only observer who laid emphasis upon the fact that it is met with in adults, but this at a period antecedent to the discovery of Pfeiffer's bacillus. What is a greater stumbling-block is that two capable and well-qualified groups of observers have induced these peculiar lesions experimentally; the one, Cecil and Blake, by inoculation of animals of the laboratory with cultures of the influenza bacilli whose virulence had been exalted by passage ; the other, Nicolle and Lebailly, Gibson, Bowman and O'Connor and Rose Bradford, Bashford and Wilson, by inoculations of filtrates through porcelain filters of the body fluids of influenza patients.

On general principles it is difficult to accept that two widely different orders of microbe, the influenza bacillus and a filterable virus, should set up the same unusual reaction in the lungs ; namely, this striking form of peri-bronchitis and purulent bronchitis which has characterized the pandemic. MacCallum, however, would add yet another, namely, the streptococcus, to the list of organisms capable of setting up this particular lesion, and herein he has the support of Blake and Cecil and of Gay. The way in which a conscientious observer may for years devote himself to a particular study and never recognize some feature in his material until some other observer calls his attention to it, when to his confusion he finds that feature present with extraordinary frequency, is a familiar phenomenon. It is difficult, however, to believe that with streptococcus infections of the lungs relatively common before the war, this remarkable lesion should have been overlooked, the more so as, with the beginning of the epidemic there were four sets of observers in Etaples, Boulogne, Aldershot and the United States, all independently noting this as the particular feature in their cases, and three of the four giving illustrations to demonstrate how the presence of this lesion differentiated their cases from the usual run of pneumonic cases. It is difficult, therefore, not to conclude that one common agent was responsible.

Until the next acute epidemic of influenza manifests itself

and the observations are repeated, no further progress is possible. In the meantime, one must suppose that either the cultures and material of the American army observers were contaminated with a filterable influenza virus, or that the material of British army observers was similarly contaminated with influenza bacilli; or, thirdly, that filterable virus and influenza bacillus are two phases of one pathogenic microbe. These, however, are and remain suggestions; the difficulty remains.

The difficulty can only be temporary, and is not one incapable of eventual solution. For the present, therefore, the following will be accepted as postulates: (1) That one agent and one only was primarily responsible for all the cases of the pandemic; (2) that in its most virulent form, or, where not in its most virulent form, when attacking those specially susceptible, this agent, whether the influenza bacillus itself or, most often, in intimate association with that bacillus, was responsible for the fatal issue; and (3) that in the majority of fatal cases other pathogenic agents infected the lungs and became factors causing death. There is, it is true, one outstanding difference between the pre-pandemic cases and those from the height of the pandemic, namely, that the former are characterized by a profuse purulent bronchitis, a condition wholly absent from the latter, its place being taken by a yet more profuse serous and blood-stained discharge in which pus cells were as infrequent as red cells were common. This, it will be shown, indicates a difference in degree and not in kind.

Morbid Anatomy of Influenza.

In the pandemic of 1918 the lesions of the respiratory system were constantly in the forefront, as regards the fatal cases and the conditions found at autopsy. The lesions of other systems were of secondary importance.

The Upper Air Passages.—In the ordinary routine of *postmortem* examination the base of the skull and the nasal passages are not subjected to examination. There are, therefore, unsatisfactory records of the condition of the uppermost respiratory tract. The clinical records of the army cases in general note that the nasal discharge was comparatively slight. Nevertheless, if there was not actually coryza, the frequency of early "nose-bleed" was noted by several observers; Colonel French describes this as a phenomenally frequent early symptom. Major Cooper Cole, C.A.M.C., describing the epidemics of the autumn of 1918 at Bramshott Camp, reports that epistaxis, often recurrent, was present in one-third of the 2,247 hospital cases. Clearly, therefore, there was a congested state of the nasal mucosa, while several observers note that the pharynx was red and angry.

In the pre-pandemic cases Abrahams, Hallows, Eyre and French found yellow pus in the sphenoidal sinuses in nineteen out of twenty cases. Referring evidently to this same outbreak at Aldershot, Colonel French, in his report to the Ministry of Health, states that in twenty-two consecutive autopsies the sphenoidal air cells were opened up. Only one looked normal. The remaining twenty-one exhibited a lining membrane which was congested and red. In six cases there was definite pus, opaque and yellow, which filled the air cells ; in the other fifteen there was present a turbid fluid which yielded the same organisms as were found in the lungs. The first focus of growth of the primary infecting agent appears therefore to have been in the nasal passages. Eventually, also, it manifested a special liability to spread thence into the nasal sinuses. In the pandemic cases Captain R. H. Malone notes that out of fourteen autopsies, nine gave pus from one or other of the nasal sinuses. The smears from this pus invariably showed *B. influenzae* as the predominating organism in far greater number than pneumococcus. Cultures made from those samples of pus in two cases yielded colonies of *B. influenzae* only ; one gave pneumococcus growths, but no influenza bacilli ; the rest yielded mixed growths.

Lieut.-Colonel E. W. W. Greig gives similar figures for the Indian troops at Karachi in the autumn of 1918 and beginning of 1919.

Wolbach, dealing with the pandemic as it affected the troops at Camp Devens, Massachusetts, an outbreak noticeable for the large percentage of pure influenzal pneumonia, after a careful study of 28 cases found :—

Inflammation of the sphenoidal sinus		..	20	cases.
,,	,, middle ear	..	13	,,
,,	,, frontal sinus	..	7	,,
,,	,, ethmoidal cells	..	8	,,

His figures harmonize with those of E. Fraenkel in Germany, who in an examination of 60 cases obtained 45, or 75 per cent., with sinusitis. In this association it will be noted that several observers call attention to the involvement of the middle ear. In his series of 2,247 cases at No. 12 Canadian General Hospital, Bramshott, Major Cooper Cole reports 40 cases of acute otitis ; 10 of these had mastoid involvement. The same observer mentions 4 cases of frontal and 10 of maxillary sinusitis.

It is not a little interesting to note that Majors Blake and Cecil, of the United States Army Medical Corps, in their successful series of inoculations into monkeys of influenza bacilli whose virulence had been maintained and exalted by passage, when they set up the disease by introducing a swab saturated with a recent culture or by spraying the pharynx with blood broth culture, found that constantly in killing the animals there was a sphenoidal sinusitis, and they were able to gain cultures of the bacilli from these regions.

It may safely be concluded that *congestion of the nasal pharynx was a primary lesion in practically every case.* The frequent involvement of the nasal sinuses noted by these observers above quoted is of importance as indicating evidence of continued growth of the infecting organism and the source of recurrent infection of the lower respiratory tract.

But whether primary or secondary there was one lesion, tracheitis, affecting all fatal cases in the pandemic of 1918 and apparently affecting the majority of non-fatal cases. The pharynx might be dry and exhibit congestion, but the secretions were slight. So also involvement of the larynx was uncommon. A few complained of hoarseness, and occasionally on autopsy the vocal cords were found congested, as was also the under aspect of the epiglottis. In a few cases this congestion was intense, but in the majority of cases the larynx showed no abnormality. While, exceptionally, the whole trachea showed intense congestion, in general the upper third was not inflamed. According to Sundell, the region of the fourth ring might be regarded as a frequent upper limit. In a few fatal cases the congestion only affected the lower third, but always this lower third exhibited intense congestion, and always it extended into the main bronchi. It may indeed be laid down that *the one invariable lesion encountered in the fatal cases of the 1918 pandemic of influenza was a tracheo-bronchitis involving the region of the bifurcation of the trachea and spreading both upwards to a variable extent and downwards into the main bronchi and their ramifications.* And this was present in the pre-pandemic cases. Its existence is recorded, or indicated, by all military observers, in Mesopotamia, Macedonia and the United States, as well as in France, Italy and England. It preceded the bronchial and bronchiolar conditions. Thus, Abrahams, Hallows, Eyre and French, in their singularly full study of the Aldershot cases, referring more particularly to the pneumonic type, observe that this began with a short, dry, hacking cough—the cough, it may be emphasized, that is characteristic of tracheitis. Regarding the milder epidemic of May and June 1918 affecting the troops in France, Major McNee notes that there was always sore throat, tracheitis and laryngitis, and that the expectoration only shows itself on the third or fourth day.

Similarly, Captain F. H. Kitson, reporting upon the epidemic at Faenza, Italy, which began in May 1918, notes that the larynx, trachea and bronchi are always congested.

Describing the epidemic in Macedonia, which reached its height in September 1918, coincident with the military operations which led to the capitulation of the Bulgarians, Major-General Phear, R.A.M.C., states that it usually began in an intense tracheitis spreading to the bronchial tubes, with abundant thin purulent sputum tinged with red.

Describing the first cases of the pandemic, Colonel French, in his report to the Ministry of Health already quoted, refers to the husky voice with hawking and throat clearing, less often actual cough being present ; and as regards the main wave in the autumn of 1918, he states : " In practically every case there was also cough, not always severe, but sometimes in itself distressing, short, dry and hacking to begin with, looser and associated with frothy or blood-stained or purulent sputum within a few hours or the next day."

In the United States the same state of affairs is dwelt upon by several observers. Thus, Lieut.-Colonel Eugene L. Opie, Major Allen W. Freeman, Captain F. G. Blake, and others, in their report to the Surgeon-General, United States Army, upon pneumonia following influenza at Camp Pike, Ark.—a report based upon a detailed study of 11,725 cases of influenza occurring between 20th September and 14th October, 1918, with 200 autopsies—note that " coryza, pharyngitis and tracheitis with a harassing cough have been almost invariable ; epistaxis and slight hæmoptysis are frequent."

Professor O. Klotz, reporting upon the pathology of the disease as it showed itself in two military camps at Pittsburgh in October 1918, states : " In all of our cases the trachea showed definite inflammatory reaction. Of the 32 cases, studied at autopsy, there were 26 having an acute tracheitis, 5 with an acute muco-purulent inflammation, and 1 with a reaction in the subacute stage."

Lieut.-Colonel Greig, in 60 autopsies at Karachi, states that the trachea was congested in 52, normal in 8. Regarding these figures, Colonel Adami is inclined to think from his own observations that they refer to the more generalized tracheitis ;

when the lung is so intensely congested if the upper two-thirds of the trachea are not involved, one is apt to overlook even pronounced injection in the region of the bifurcation.

The tracheitis manifested itself as an intense purplish congestion with loss of lustre of the surface. That surface was frequently covered by a thin greyish exudate which, however, was easily removable. Abrahams, Hallows, Eyre and French note that by a glancing light multiple minute depressions might be made out. Adami did not himself observe these depressions. They dealt, it must be remembered, with the milder pre-pandemic cases. Possibly in these the process was not so acute, and there was not the complete erosion of the mucosa which became the rule in the fatal cases of the autumn of 1918. These depressions may have represented small areas of vesiculation followed by necrosis and dissociation of the epithelium. It was a rarer event to encounter yellowish patches of false membrane here and there standing out against the purple background. Under the microscope the false membrane was thin, formed largely of desquamated epithelial cells, and unlike the diphtheritic false membrane, it exhibited little fibrin. Smears from these false membranes showed abundant diplococci and streptococci. Similar yellowish false membranes might be present in the under aspect of the epiglottis and in the bronchi. Frequently small darker areas of hæmorrhage into the submucosa were to be seen.

More common than false membrane were occasional small deposits of hyaline material resembling that which will be described later as occurring in the alveoli.

Major T. R. Little, C.A.M.C., describing the fatal cases at Witley Camp in the winter and spring of 1919, states that "sections of the trachea and bronchi showed an almost complete loss of the epithelial surface with a marked infiltration of leucocytes into the submucous coat." Major Little, indeed, was the first to draw attention to the extent and constancy of this lesion. It was found by Colonel Adami to be invariably present in the fatal cases seen by him at the other Canadian camps and hospitals.

The fullest microscopical study of the tracheal condition has been made by Professor O. Klotz, of Pittsburgh, his material being obtained from thirty-two autopsies upon those dying during the first five weeks of the acute pandemic in October and November 1918, and comprising both soldiers and civilians. According to his findings the first striking feature is the response of the vessels of the submucosa, both blood-vessels and lymphatics; the process is sharply limited by the cartilage. With this intense engorgement there are not a few hæmorrhages with escape of the blood on to the surface or into the interstitial tissue. Accompanying this congestion there was a pronounced serous exudate.

But what has caused this intense congestion? It is most significant that, as Klotz points out, and as Adami confirms,

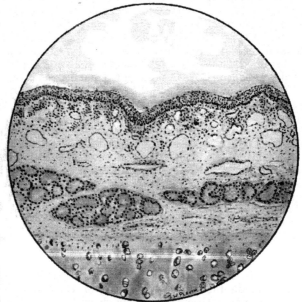

Fig. 5.—Trachea from one of Professor E. Glynn's Liverpool cases, 1919, to show earliest stage of reaction in influenza. Epithelium intact, but basement membrane slightly swollen and recognizable, with congestion and some small celled infiltration of submucosa. Hyaline deposit over epithelium. (Low power, x 64.)

the submucosa is free from bacteria in this early stage despite the intense reaction. It is not set up by the active entrance or growth of bacteria into the submucous tissues. Strongly localized as it is in the trachea, not extending beyond the cartilage, the only explanation—unless the action of invisible, ultramicroscopic microbes is invoked—is that it is of toxic origin, due to the action of toxins elaborated by the growth of bacteria upon the surface and very possibly dissociated in consequence of the rapid destruction of the same by the reactive exudate.   The whole picture, indeed,—the rarity of polymorphonuclear leucocytes, and the later accumulation of lymphocytes and plasma cells,—is of the toxic, rather than the invasive, type. One is inclined, therefore, to predicate that the first lesion originates through the growth of the specific bacteria upon the epithelial surface of the trachea.

If Pfeiffer's bacillus is the essential and primary pathogenic organism, it is at least suggestive that the other definitely pathogenic micro-organism of the influenza group of minute Gram-negative bacilli, namely, the Bordet-Gengou bacillus of whooping-cough, has, as shown first by Mallory, its habitat upon the tracheal epithelium.

Fig. 5 shows the earliest stage, namely, that of great congestion of the submucosa, with exudate on to the surface between the epithelial cells. That exudate, even at this early stage, as shown in the figure, favours the formation of a hyaline deposit, which is one of the specific features of influenza.

Not merely is there this inflammatory œdema, but so abundant is the outpouring of fluid that, as Klotz points out, failing to escape in sufficient quantities between the cells of the columnar epithelium it accumulates beneath them here and there, forming a series of vesicles or blebs, thereby favouring an extensive and early desquamation. In the height of the pandemic it was rare to encounter a case in which there was not complete desquamation of the epithelium of the lowest third of the trachea, the mucous glands being the only epithelial elements left unaffected. From these, in non-fatal cases, must proceed the regeneration of the epithelial coat. The basement membrane, it is true, was left behind, and this subsequently became swollen and degenerated. It exhibited no evidence of retained "mother cells" from which regeneration might proceed.

As a result of this desquamation it is singularly difficult to demonstrate the first phase above predicated, of surface growth of bacteria. By analogy with what had been seen on studying Rhea's preparations from whooping-cough, one expected to find a dense proliferation of the fine bacilli, forming a superficial layer clogging the cilia, but so far neither in the trachea nor in the larger bronchi was this appearance seen. Klotz, who has had the same possibility before him, writes :—

"In those specimens in which the mucous membrane was still intact we attempted to demonstrate the clustering of the micro-organisms about the ciliated cells, as was described by Mallory in whooping-cough. Although the organisms, and particularly small Gram-negative bacilli, could be demonstrated lying about these cells, no characteristic arrangement was found. Furthermore, when the mucosa was still attached to its basement membrane we were never able to demonstrate organisms below the surface of the epithelial layer."

These findings, it may be urged, do not prove that the small Gram-negative organisms are not responsible. They may indicate that the *B. pertussis* is more nearly parasitic, whereas the *B. influenzae* growing on the surface of the tracheal mucosa elaborates substances so much more toxic that the epithelium is as a result cast off before any abundant local multiplication has taken place.

It is rarely that unmistakable evidence of this process of vesiculation described by Professor Klotz is encountered,

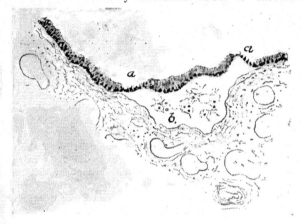

Fig. 6.—Vesicle formation between epithelium and submucosa in a large bronchus. The columnar-celled epithelium is in part eroded (at *a, a*) leaving only the basement "mother cell" layer. Submucosa œdematous and greatly congested. *b*—Vesicle containing delicate coagulum, enmeshing wandered in small round cells. (Free hand sketch, low power. From one of Colonel French's Aldershot cases, 1919.)

because the outer wall of the vesicle is so extraordinarily delicate that in handling it undergoes rupture. Even in the larger bronchi it is, for the same reason, rarely encountered. Fig. 6 is from a bronchus of good size, the preservation of the vesicle being due to the fact that the bronchus was filled with clotted blood and was hardened and cut in this condition.*

It must be pointed out, however, that this is only one of the processes leading to desquamation. The indications are that

---

* This sketch was made without a camera lucida. It was made by employing the method of observing with the left eye and using the right to project the image on to a sheet of paper at the level of the stage of the microscope—a method that only suffices for a rapid sketch of the outlines of the right half of the field of vision. Not to complicate matters, the blood which filled the lumen of the bronchus has been omitted.

an equally frequent, or more frequent, process is that indicated in the following figures, namely, of rapid degeneration with swelling of the fully formed cells of the columnar epithelium (as shown in Fig. 7 (A)), followed by desquamation of the same, there being left behind *in situ* only the undifferentiated " mother cells " adherent to the basement membrane, forming a *chevaux de frise*, swollen, but with nuclei still deeply stained (as shown in Fig. 7 (B)). Eventually these become affected and break away, all that is left being a notably thickened and hyaline basement membrane.

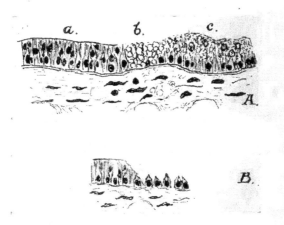

Fig. 7.—A. Columnar-celled epithelium of large bronchus. At *a* epithelium relatively unchanged save for slight thickening of basement membrane. At *b*, minute hæmorrhage with destruction of epithelium. At *c*, basement cells of epithelium intact with well stained nuclei; outer cells swollen and undergoing necrosis with pale staining nuclei.
B. The same, another area. To show necrosis and desquamation of outer fully formed cells of columnar epithelium, leaving a *chevaux de frise* of swollen basement " mother cells," with deeply staining nuclei.
(Freehand sketch, high power. From one of Colonel French's Aldershot cases, 1919.)

Following upon the denudation, the interstitial exudate in the submucosa becomes more cellular, lymphocytes predominating, with a noticeable frequency of plasma cells, and, save immediately beneath the swollen basement membrane, *polymorphonuclear leucocytes are conspicuous by their infrequence*. With this, while at first the lymphatics were distended with clear lymph now they become packed with lymphocytes. Occasional venules and arterioles are seen to be thrombosed. It is, moreover, striking that while on the denuded surface there may be abundant bacteria, there is singularly little carriage of these into the inflamed submucosa; one may encounter a rare organism in the distended lymphatics, but little beyond this. So also there is peculiarly little tendency to fibrinous deposits; there may be a slight homogeneous hyaline deposit here and there upon the denuded basement membrane, but extensive deposition of a fibrinous false membrane is characteristically absent.

The Main Bronchi.—These presented constantly a picture

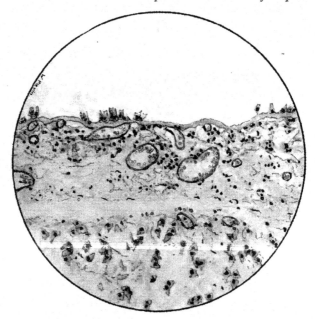

Fig. 8.—Main bronchus from one of Professor E. Glynn's Liverpool cases, showing congestion, œdema, moderate small round-celled infiltration in upper layers of submucosa with plasma cells in deeper layers, pronounced thickening of basement membrane, and *chevaux de frise* of "mother cells" of epithelium. (x 250.)

of the same order as that seen in the lower trachea—intense congestion and swelling of the submucosa with dilatation of both the blood-vessels and lymphatics, and denudation through desquamation of the mucosa. This denudation is not in general so complete as that seen in the lower part of the trachea, occasional islands being left of intact epithelium. The impression gained was that the larger bronchi were more affected

than those of medium size, but again that the smallest bronchi
were so constantly involved, denuded of their epithelium and
distended or dilated as to make it difficult to determine whether
one dealt with small bronchi or bronchioles. Occasionally in
the larger bronchi, as in the trachea, areas of necrosis and
yellowish false membrane were noticeable.

Progressively, in descending the branches, hoops give place to
plates and smaller masses of cartilage, with coincident relative

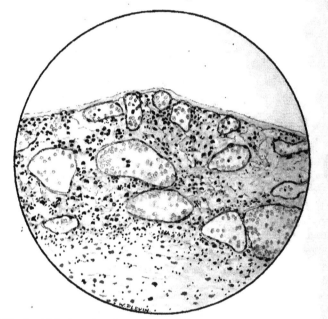

Fig. 9.—Main bronchus from one of Colonel H. French's specimens of
influenza lungs in the museum at Guy's Hospital, showing complete denudation of epithelial coat with great hyaline thickening of basement membrane
and congestion of outer layers of submucosa. (x 250.)

increase in the muscular layer. This does not interpose the
same barrier to the extension of the inflammatory process, so
that the terminal bronchi and bronchioles through their vessels
and lymphatics become involved in continuity, with similar
secondary infiltration with lymphocytes. Whether through the
action of the toxins or the infiltration, the involuntary muscle
fibres may show indications of degeneration and atrophy, with
resultant diffuse dilatation of the bronchi. While it is true

that there are few records of pronounced generalized bron-chiectasis,* the impression gained was that a moderate grade of bronchiectasis was distinctly common, an impression which will probably be confirmed by all who have studied micro-scopical sections of the lungs in which the relatively large size of the bronchi and bronchioles is a noticeable feature. The fullest note encountered upon this bronchiectasis is by Lieut.-Colonel Opie and his colleagues, who state : " Further evidence

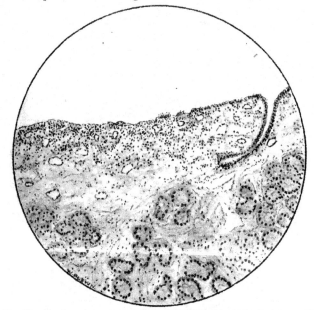

Fig. 10.—Trachea from one of Colonel H. French's Aldershot cases, 1919. To show more particularly retention of epithelium by, and in the neighbour-hood of, a duct of one of the mucous glands. (x 64.)

of profound injury to the bronchial wall is the dilatation that these small bronchi undergo. Bronchiectasis is most con-spicuous in this basal part of the lower lobes, and is usually more advanced on the left side than on the right. Small bronchi with no cartilage in their wall may reach a diameter of 0·5 cm. More advanced bronchiectasis is found in autopsies performed late in the outbreak."

* Klotz, for example, refers to only one case of pronounced bronchiectasis among his thirty-two cases, and Goodpasture and Burnett to four out of thirty cases.

Note may here be made of the occasional presence of small saccular bronchiectases to which Boggs, in Osler's service at Johns Hopkins Hospital, drew attention as associated with the presence of Pfeiffer's bacillus, dilatations of about the size of a pea filled with pus containing influenza bacilli and lined by a pyogenic membrane. Malloch and Rhea record three cases of this nature.

An equally or even more noticeable feature is the extraordinary thickness of the submucosa and its intense vascularity. Devoid of epithelium this is indistinguishable from granulation tissue.

This desquamative tracheitis and bronchitis has not hitherto received the attention it deserves. It is in the main responsible for the protean aspects of influenzal pneumonia. Physiologically the moistened ciliated epithelium lining the trachea and bronchi is a factor of prime importance in maintaining the sterility of the air gaining entrance to the lungs. That sterility is brought about in the first place by the inhaled air passing over the moistened epithelium of the turbinated bones of the nasal passages, and next by impinging upon, and being reflected from the moistened wall of the pharynx. But these upper mechanisms do not surely arrest all the bacteria. The final phase of abstraction occurs in the trachea and by impingement of the divided current of air at an angle upon the walls of either main bronchus. Once the bacteria fall upon the ciliated surface they, along with the mucous fluid discharged from the mucous glands, are borne upwards, away from the lungs. It is not necessary here to dilate upon the auxiliary action of wandering leucocytes or the strategic position of the cluster of lymph nodes in the angle of bifurcation. The essential point is that, *remove the ciliated epithelium, and there is removed also what ordinarily is the effective barrier to entrance of bacteria into the lungs by means of the air passages.* Such removal, it is true, is followed by discharge of serous fluid from and into the injured surface and this serum is known to be bactericidal for many species of bacteria. But not for all. It is not a little interesting that in influenza it is just those bacteria least susceptible to the destructive action of serum—the streptococci, pneumococci and staphylococci—which most commonly are found invading the lung along with, or following upon, the organism which, as has been pointed out, finds a *locus minoris resistentiae* in, and favourable site of growth upon the tracheal and bronchial mucosa.

The Lungs.—An elaborate statistical study and a description of the manifold lesions met with in the influenzal lung are unnecessary. Such now, as in the past, would only cause confusion. It has been attempted conscientiously by many writers, notably with regard to the British army and expeditionary forces by Abrahams, Hallows and Colonel French (Aldershot cases), by Tytler, Janes and Dobbin (Boulogne cases), and in less detail by Patterson, Little and Williams (cases in No. 5 General and No. 25 Stationary Hospitals, at Rouen), and Shore (cases in Etaples), with regard to the Canadian troops in Canada by Cole, and to the American troops by MacCallum and Cole, Klotz, and others. Further, a complete study of the lung lesions has been done well and thoroughly for the pandemic of 1889–1890 by Leichtenstern, whose description of the morbid anatomy of the lungs in Nothnagel's Cyclopedia might have been written upon material from the pandemic of 1918. What is more, Leichtenstern realized, as fully as did the later generation of observers, the mixed bacteriology of these influenza lungs.

But what is of use will be the differentiation of the influenzal lesions proper, disentangling them from the other lesions due to the secondary invaders. It is true that there is no absolute certainty as to the essential pathogenic agent. But from a study of the trachea and bronchi, there are clear indications as to its mode of action. That action is quite different from anything set up by streptococci, staphylococci and pneumococci. By its toxins, without apparent primary entrance into the tissues, it causes intense dilatation and engorgement of the vessels (lymphatic as well as blood-vessels), of the submucosa, with pronounced local œdema, desquamation of the epithelium and tendency to the development of hæmorrhages, followed by lymphocytic and some plasma cell infiltration. Leucocytes in the restricted sense, *i.e.*, polymorphonuclears, while not absent were, with exceptions to be presently noted, relatively few and far between. If lesions are found within the lung, which *mutatis mutandis* are of the same order, they may safely be ascribed to the primary irritant. Such lesions are undoubtedly encountered, for recent observers are virtually unanimous in calling attention to the peri-bronchitis and peri-bronchiolitis of the influenzal lung.

In the normal lung as one passes from the larger to the smaller bronchi the walls become progressively thinner. All traces of cartilage and of mucous glands disappear, until the smallest bronchi are merely rather delicate muscular tubes with an inner lining of mucosa and submucosa whose vessels and lymphatics communicate freely with those of the alveoli in immediate apposition. Following Klotz's description, these smallest and simplest bronchi may be spoken of as the bronchioles, the distinction drawn in sundry text-books of histology not being practical. While in the trachea and larger bronchi the cartilaginous rings and plaques and the thick muscular walls form a barrier arresting the extension outwards of the inflammatory process, there is no such arrest in the bronchioles. The result is very evident. In influenza there is striking evidence of this diffusion outward of the inflammation and consequent development of what MacCallum quite rightly terms an " interstitial pneumonia," in contradistinction to the more familiar " lobular

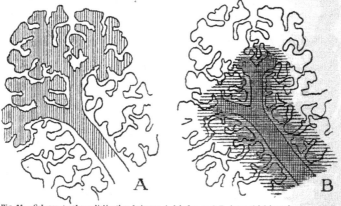

Fig. 11.—Schema to show distinction between A, lobular, and B, interstitial broncho-pneumonia. In A the air sacs belonging to the affected bronchioles are heavily involved; surrounding air sacs belonging to other bronchial systems are not affected. In B the bronchi and bronchioles are primarily affected; the inflammation spreads to the surrounding air sacs, those of the particular bronchial tree not being more affected than the others, and is most intense in the immediate neighbourhood of the bronchiole and bronchus.

broncho-pneumonia," in which the infective agent gaining entrance to a bronchus extends down it, and sets up an inflammation which is limited to that bronchus and its bronchioles, and the alveoli derived therefrom. By the diffusion of the influenza toxin through the walls of the smaller bronchi and bronchioles the immediately surrounding alveoli become involved—alveoli derived from other bronchioles and belonging to other bronchial systems. The only criticism that might be made to the use of MacCallum's term, as applied to the influenza lung, is that it emphasizes the lung condition to the exclusion of the earlier and equally characteristic tracheo-bronchitis, and doing so gives a wrong mental picture of the sequence of events. More correctly *the specific influenzal condition is a tracheo-bronchitis (and bronchiolitis) with interstitial pneumonia.*

To understand clearly the features of the influenzal lung it is well to follow the development of this specific lesion.

(i) The primary seat of election involving always the bifurcation of the trachea and the main bronchi, it follows that in fatal cases both lungs have been constantly involved. Not a single record of unilateral involvement has been recorded.

(ii) As already noted, the extension of the infection along the secondary bronchi has been irregular ; some are found deeply involved with epithelial desquamation and great congestion and thickening of the submucosa, others with epithelium intact and little congestion. It is this irregular extension that explains the patchy character of the lung lesions. As a result, probably, of the more direct air current, the bronchi of the lower lobes were more apt to be involved, and the pneumonic and other disturbances were more constant and more extensive in the lower than in the upper lobes, in the right lung rather than in the left.

(iii) The brunt of the infection fell upon the bronchi and bronchioles, and not upon the air sacs. If the lesions are associated with the presence of *B. influenzae* the above statement is confirmed by bacteriological examination of the affected lungs. These Gram-negative bacilli, whenever encountered, were found in abundance in the exudate within the smaller bronchi and bronchioles, but most often scattered sparsely in the contents of the alveoli. It is a condition the reverse of that which is found in lobar pneumonia ; there the pneumococci are abundant in the air sacs, while the bronchioles and bronchi are little involved and the pneumococci not specially noticeable within them.

(iv) The reactions accompanying the influenzal bronchiolitis varied, and this, apparently in the main, according to the grade of virulence of the infective agent in the successive phases of the pandemic. Thus, in the cases seen in England, France and the United States in the early part of 1918, the outstanding feature was the bronchitis and bronchiolitis, and the bronchioles were distended with pus, so that on section of the lung, and pressure, pus was expressed like worm casts from the divided tubules. This pus, as noted by Malloch, often afforded pure cultures of *B. influenzae*. Opie and his colleagues also call attention to the fact that *B. influenzae* could be grown with few exceptions from the muco-purulent material that wells out of the cut bronchi, or from material scraped with a platinum loop from the main branches.* The cellular infiltration of the submucosa and

---

* It deserves note that Pfeiffer, the discoverer of the *B. influenzæ*, from the first noted the abundance of his bacillus in the purulent contents of the bronchioles.

muscularis was so considerable as to lead to pronounced thickening of the tubes with extension of the cellular infiltration along the walls of the immediately surrounding air sacs, or more accurately along the lymph spaces between the alveoli. When the lung was felt between the fingers the thickened branching tubes gave an impression not unlike that of a collection of small tubercles, and on cross section the appearance was not unlike that of tubercles, save that on pressure pus exuded from the centres. In this mild form the congestion was not so pronounced nor was the œdema* and exudation into the alveoli. The lungs in these earlier cases were not particularly wet, nor were hæmorrhages, although present, a marked feature. The outstanding lesion of the lung substance proper was a bronchitis, bronchiolitis and peri-bronchiolitis (or zone of interstitial pneumonia immediately around the bronchioles). Owing, evidently, to the blockage of the bronchi the lungs in those cases of purulent bronchitis differed in appearance from those met with in the more acute pandemic disease. As noted by several observers they were characteristically voluminous, showed rib-markings, and preserved the shape and size of the chest cavity save here and there where retracted in consequence of atelectasis; further, they showed little tendency to collapse, even when cut.† It deserves note, as supporting this view that there is one common underlying disease, that even in the earliest pre-pandemic cases in which " purulent bronchitis " was the outstanding feature, observer after observer called attention to the presence of a certain amount of œdema, and the tendency to hæmorrhage around the affected bronchi. On the other hand, it is equally interesting that as cases of the purulent bronchitis type continued to present themselves at the height of the epidemic, time and again one noted the oozing of pus from cut bronchi and bronchioles in lungs that were waterlogged and hæmorrhagic.

Next to the bronchitis and bronchiolitis it was this acute

* It must be remembered that employing the ordinary definition of œdema, as the collection of serous fluid in the interstices of a tissue, the only true pulmonary œdema is that brought about by distension of the lymph spaces of the alveolar walls by serous fluid. When the air sacs become filled with this fluid it is, strictly speaking, wrong to describe the condition as pulmonary œdema, for that fluid is outside the tissues and in free communication with the exterior.

† In these respects they were curiously reminiscent of the lungs of the guinea-pig that has died of acute anaphylaxis. Indeed, as Rosenow has pointed out, many findings in influenza—the expanded, hyper-resonant, relatively immobile thorax, the cyanosis, sharp leucopenia, delayed coagulability of the blood and the voluminous lungs—might be the expressions of an anaphylactoid intoxication.

alveolar emphysema which, more particularly in the earlier wave of the pandemic and in the pre-pandemic cases, was a striking feature of the disease. It involved all the lobes, showing itself most markedly beneath the pleura and in those alveoli adjoining the interlobular septa, *i.e.*, in the peripheral portions of the lobules, and here it led to atrophy and rupture of the alveolar walls and pallor of the lungs.

But evidently, also, the causes leading to this diffuse emphysema were also operative in the early stages of the later more virulent cases, although in these the condition was rapidly masked by the hæmorrhages and abundant development of serous exudate, while again, accumulation of fluid in the pleural cavity might lead to partial compression and collapse of the lung substance. Yet even in the most acute cases of the main wave of the pandemic, under the microscope the contrast between the more compressed alveoli in the neighbourhood of the inflamed bronchi and bronchioles, with their swollen and infiltrated walls, and the widely distended more peripheral alveoli, with their thin walls, was most striking.

To it was due the not infrequent interstitial emphysema, whether involving the lung and mediastinal tissues alone or spreading upwards to the subcutaneous tissues of the neck and upper thorax. Wolbach in 28 autopsies at Camp Devens in the height of the pandemic encountered 11 cases of mediastinal and 6 of subcutaneous emphysema. According to British army experiences these are remarkable figures. The lungs of the trained soldier at the front appear to have been of a tougher, more resistant nature. But such interstitial emphysema is an evidence of alveolar emphysema, and one agrees with Wolbach in recognizing that it occurred during the most virulent stage of the pandemic, *i.e.*, that alveolar emphysema characterized all stages. The heaviest figures encountered are those of Major T. R. Little, who in 73 autopsies at Witley Camp, Surrey, upon Canadian soldiers in the autumn of 1918, found interstitial emphysema in " 17 per cent.," *i.e.*, in 12 cases. Major Cooper Cole similarly records 12 cases of extensive interstitial emphysema extending up to the malar eminences, at No. 12 Canadian General Hospital in Bramshott Camp. Of these 12, only 1 recovered.

Oedema and Hæmorrhage.—But even at the beginning of the pandemic the milder forms of uncomplicated peri-bronchitis and purulent bronchitis were rare ; commonly the greyish tubercle-like thickenings with opaque yellowish centres were each surrounded by a hæmorrhagic zone, outside of which was a diffuse zone of " œdema " in which the air-sacs were filled with serous fluid. And, passing to the most rapidly fatal cases, progressively the zone of intense congestion with accompanying hæmorrhage around the affected bronchioles became more and more the main feature ; the distension of the lymphatics and the serous exudate into the surrounding alveoli occupied a still wider surrounding area ; hæmorrhages were apt to become massive, the cellular infiltration became less and less marked and whereas in the milder cases polymorphonuclear leucocytes were abundant, not only in the purulent contents of the dilated bronchioles but also in the submucosa and the interalveolar tissue and the distended lymph channels around the affected bronchioles, now this order of leucocytes was relatively rare and what leucocytes were present were of the lymphocytic type, with, in cases of more than four days' duration, a considerable admixture of " plasma cells."

Leucocytic and Serous Reaction.—To explain these variations one may recall Metchnikoff's classical observation upon inoculating into the ears of the rabbit, on the one side a small amount of a culture of attenuated, on the other side an equal amount of a culture of fairly virulent anthrax bacilli, and his demonstration that with the attenuated virus there is not nearly the same amount of swelling and serous exudation. But the region of the inoculation is more opaque and solid, and, upon examination, exhibits an abundant aggregation and infiltration of polymorphonuclear leucocytes ; whereas the fully virulent organisms induce a serous exudation and swelling that affect the greater part of the ear, so that the skin is raised from the subjacent tissues by clear reddish fluid containing very few leucocytes in suspension, a fluid which also infiltrates the deeper tissues. *The more powerful toxins set up a characteristically serous type of inflammation with but slight migration of leucocytes ; the less powerful induce a characteristically leucocytic type of inflammation.* MacCallum, indeed, evidently inclines to the opinion that the preponderance of lymphocytes and plasma cells in this type of bronchiolitis and interstitial pneumonia is not due to a selective migration but to proliferation of the lymphoid tissue pre-existing in the walls of the smaller bronchi and bronchioles.

Thus, next to the specific involvement of the bronchioles and the above-mentioned alveolar emphysema, the outstanding feature of the pure influenzal pneumonia is the intense congestion spreading outwards from the affected air tubes, and the serous type of inflammation induced. The congestion is most

marked where the toxins are most concentrated, *i.e.*, in the
immediate neighbourhood of the affected bronchi and bronchioles, and here in consequence hæmorrhages are most marked.
The escaping blood is apt to fill and distend the air-sacs of
this zone and in them to undergo clotting with a moderate
deposit of fibrin. Outside this zone intense congestion without
hæmorrhage is seen, and as a result of that congestion, great
thickening of the alveolar walls with abundant exudation of
an inflammatory serous fluid into the alveoli, distending them
and giving to the influenzal lung its striking wetness and
waterlogged appearance. So abundant is the discharge that
the alveolar epithelium tends to become loosened and individual
cells or collections of cells cast off lie free in the serous contents
of the air-sacs. The epithelial cells which have not become
detached are apt to show swelling and enlargement and signs
of proliferation. To this abundant serous exudate was due the
abundant watery sputum noticed in the earlier pandemic cases.
There was thus intense congestion and filling of many of the
alveoli with serous fluid, but not a true consolidation. In the
majority of cases, owing to the patchy nature of the process,
with intervention of alveoli that were still air-containing, the
affected areas of the lung when cut out did not sink, or at most
remained floating, suspended below the surface, when dropped
into water.

The Air-Sacs.—In what were regarded as uncomplicated
cases it has not been possible to distinguish any difference
between the reactions seen in the air-sacs directly communi-
cating with an affected bronchiole and those belonging to
surrounding systems which have become affected in continuity.
The affection is primarily of the air passages, the involvement
of the air-sacs is secondary. It is true that, as Pfeiffer originally
noted, there may be relatively abundant influenza bacilli in
the contents of the air-sacs. There has, however, been no
evidence that where present they set up any specific local
lesion, unless, as some authorities hold, the desquamation of
the epithelium is regarded as brought about by a selective
toxic action on the part of the specific influenza virus.

Hyaline Deposits.—There is, however, one specific lesion
seen in the alveoli of the influenzal lung although this is not
associated with the presence of influenza bacilli in them. It is a
lesion which is quite distinct, unlike anything seen in the lung
of acute croupous or lobar pneumonia. This is the frequent
presence of homogeneous transparent hyaline material in small
clumps attached to, or in some cases, as a definite layer lining

the alveolus. Ordinary fibrin forming a dense network, as in lobar pneumonia, was rarely encountered; while this ordinary fibrin might be present it was distinctly scanty. These deposits recall the similar clear homogeneous material sometimes seen in the early stage of development of the diphtherial false membrane, and there regarded as a modified fibrin. Like that, this does not have all the staining reactions of fibrin proper.

The Lymphatics.—Another feature of the influenzal lung deserves notice, namely, the coincident remarkable distension of the lymph channels. In no other pulmonary condition in man has anything comparable been seen. The only parallel condition is in the contagious pleuro-pneumonia of cattle, in which the patchy involvement of the lung bears not a little resemblance to that seen in influenza, and in which the large size of the lymph vessels in the interlobular septa is even more striking. It is worthy of note that, as shown by Nocard and Roux, this form of pneumonia in cattle is due to a filterable virus.*

The Lymph Nodes.—Associated with this affection of the lymphatics, a constant feature of the influenza lung is the great congestion and swelling of the lymph nodes of the hilus of the lung and at the bifurcation of the trachea; these are always reported as enlarged and reddened. The chain of super- ficial and deep cervical glands was also involved. Cooper Cole notes that in serious cases the axillary glands showed " almost constantly " a like enlargement. The chain of glands in the neck up to the cricoid cartilage is reported as presenting similar changes. On section, in addition to the congestion of these organs, the main feature is the distension of the sinuses, which are packed with lymphocytes, erythrocytes and large epitheloid phagocytic cells, so packed that the structure of the glands tends to be obliterated. Hæmorrhages were rare, as are records of suppuration. In one of Colonel French's cases, in the museum at Guy's Hospital, there are areas of necrosis in the bronchial glands—apparently secondary to thrombosis and arrest of the circulation. It is not certain, however, that such thrombosis is a feature of uncomplicated influenza. As MacCallum points out, when there is a superposed streptococcal infection, the streptococci swarm in the distended lymphatics of the lung, and these, rather than the influenza bacilli, are probably responsible for the frequent development of thrombosis and a fibrinous network in the lymphatics.

---

* It is not, however, yet clear that this is a lesion of uncomplicated influenzal pneumonia ; it appears to be most pronounced in the streptococcal cases.

Pleurisy.—To this implication of the lymphatic system may well be ascribed the concomitant pleurisy, which had a character of its own. In general the amount of fluid was not great. Kitson reports that in his series of 842 admissions for influenza at Faenza, little over 5 per cent. (5·42) gave clinical signs of pleurisy, while only three of the series had recognizable effusion. But at autopsy it was uncommon not to find a small amount of pleural fluid, 50 c.c. and more, and this fluid was thin and clear or a little turbid, often blood-stained or brownish, and containing shreds of fibrin. In some few cases the amount of fluid was so considerable as to bring about a partial collapse of the lung. Tytler, Janes and Dobbin in their Boulogne series of 86 fatal cases obtained a non-purulent effusion varying in amount from 50 to 100 c.c. in 40 per cent. of their cases ; in 8 per cent. the quantity was 500 c.c. or more. In 20 per cent. the fluid while thin is described as slightly purulent. All British observers agree that empyema was uncommon ; Kitson had only one case, Tytler, Janes and Dobbin, three. It was so infrequent that it may safely be ascribed to secondary infection. Indeed, every case of empyema complicating influenza that has been studied bacteriologically has yielded either pneumococci or pyogenic cocci.

With the presence of this fluid exudate the visceral pleura showed signs of inflammation, the pleurisy, to use the phrase employed by Abrahams, Hallows and French, being typically of the lack-lustre variety with sparse scattered deposits of fibrin ; 60 per cent. of the Boulogne cases showed a fibrinous or fibrino-purulent deposit on the pleural surfaces. Routine examination would probably have revealed this in a yet higher percentage. In the same group 68 per cent. presented sub-pleural hæmorrhages ; Tytler, Janes and Dobbin note that routine examination would in their opinion have raised this percentage materially.

There is in the lung a close superficial network of pleural lymph vessels, and from this there dip at right angles larger vessels which, passing down in the interlobular septa, join with similar vessels and eventually open into the sinuses of the lymph nodes at the hilus of the lung. Occasional valves are to be detected along the course of the septal lymphatics. In whichever direction these valves are operative, and there is debate upon this point, the excessive distension of the septal lymphatics seen in influenza must put these valves out of action, and what with the obstruction to the flow of lymph inwards, whether through the cellular blockage of the sinuses of the bronchial lymph nodes, or through local thrombosis in the channels passing through the lungs, there is evidently set up some regurgitation of lymph from the septal vessels into the pleural or subpleural network. To this in the main may be ascribed the increased amount of pleural fluid. It is uncertain how far the scanty fibrinous deposit on the surface was of mechanical origin, secondary to desquamation of the pleural endothelium, or how far of infective origin. But it is remarkable how few observers record either the presence of influenza bacilli in smears from the surface of the lung or the development of cultures of the same from the pleural fluid. Of British observers, Tytler alone records obtaining cultures of *B. influenzae* from this source.

Collapse.—Localized lobular areas of collapse were more common in the early less acute cases, marked by purulent bronchitis, and, in these, were ascribable to the closure of individual bronchi and subsequent atelectasis of the associated systems of air-sacs. In the later, very acute and highly œdematous cases these areas of collapse were not so noticeable. Reference has already been made to the more generalized compression and partial collapse secondary to the presence of fluid in the pleural cavity.

How far the massive hæmorrhages, and the infarcts which were not uncommon, are to be ascribed to uncomplicated influenza, how far to the action of the secondary invaders must be left an open question.

Secondary Invaders and their Influence upon the Pulmonary Conditions.

Up to this point an attempt has been made to distinguish those lesions which, present in the majority of fatal cases and characteristic, may well be regarded as induced by the primary agent, whether this agent be Pfeiffer's bacillus pure and simple or some agent not as yet surely distinguished which acts in conjunction with Pfeiffer's bacillus. In the majority of cases other micro-organisms gained entrance into the pulmonary exudate and lung tissue.

Of these, those most commonly encountered were pneumo-cocci, streptococci and staphylococci. One or other of these might predominate so as to give the impression that it alone was responsible for the lesions; indeed in several localized epidemics, while the common lesions of tracheitis, bronchitis, interstitial pneumonia and hæmorrhagic œdema were duly present, one or other secondary invader has been so constantly present and so frequently gained in pure culture that observers have come to regard it as the *causa causans*. More commonly there was an admixture.

Pneumococcus lesions.—The existence of an epidemic of influenza did not cut out the existence of ordinary lobar pneumonia. In other words, cases of typical and uncomplicated acute lobar pneumonia were admitted to the army hospitals during the prevalence of the pandemic. Thus among the admissions at Faenza in the spring of 1918, Captain Kitson had as many as 2·3 per cent. of true lobar pneumonia cases ending by crisis. At Aldershot, on the other hand, in the autumn epidemic in the same year, one case only with the typical consolidation came to autopsy, with two-thirds of the lung substance involved.

At the beginning of the war, the late Sir William Osler, basing his statement probably on the experiences of the American Civil War in the "sixties," mentioned pneumonia as one of the three great scourges to be feared. If thereby he meant pneumonia of all orders, then the terrible fatality accompanying this influenzal pandemic has proved him a true prophet. If, however, he had in mind the ordinary acute lobar pneumonia, it is interesting to note that, despite the almost unexampled exposure of the troops through four winter campaigns in wet and muddy trenches, lobar pneumonia was strikingly infrequent. It was not more frequent in the base hospitals in France and Macedonia than it is among young adults in general hospitals at home. Indeed, evidence is accumulating that acute croupous pneumonia is of the nature of a house infection and that open-air life is a preventive rather than the reverse.

More frequently the pneumococcus took on the rôle of a secondary invader, and from individual army hospitals came reports that the pneumococcus was the main organism concerned. It may be the case that in the absence of full bacteriological study there was at times considerable confusion between the *Diplococcus pneumoniae* and streptococci, the other common secondary invaders, since the latter in fresh exudate are present more often as diplococci than in chains. But there are abundant observations by expert bacteriologists demonstrating the presence of pneumococci in large numbers. Where the combination was present it is interesting to note that the antagonistic action of the influenza toxins (acting on the bronchi and leading to a serous exudate with little attraction of leucocytes), and of the pneumococcus toxins (acting on the alveoli and powerfully attracting the leucocytes), led to a mixed picture.

A full description of this group of cases is given by W. G. MacCallum. It was the prevalent form in Baltimore, and at Camp Lee in Virginia, a pneumonia which was sometimes very sharply lobular in its distribution. In many cases the consolidated lobules stood out with extreme distinctness, separated by air-containing or collapsed lobules, so as to present—

" A checker-board (chess-board) appearance over the pleura and even on the cut surfacè. But in most instances the areas of consolidation were not so limited, but became confluent through several lobules, ultimately involving the whole of a lobe. This was clearly a very rapidly produced condition to be found only in those who succumbed after a short illness. There was no effusion of fluid into the pleural cavity, the surfaces were smooth except for patches of opaque blood stain like dull red paint on the surface. The bronchi contained only a brownish frothy fluid and their mucosa was pale. The lung was evidently consolidated and airless in part, especially in the posterior and lower portion of its lobes, and on section these areas were found to be swollen, firm and elastic, but smooth, moist, dark red and elevated above the surrounding surface into which they sloped off through an œdematous zone. No plugs of rigid exudate were to be seen in alveoli or bronchioles. . . . . The whole area oozed bloody viscid fluid. . . . . Microscopically, the alveoli are found to be filled with the finest possible network of fibrin entangling red blood corpuscles, leucocytes and mononuclear cells, many of which are desquamated epithelium. . . . . The bronchioles and ductuli alveolares are filled with fluid which gives with the fixing fluid only a delicate fibrillar reticulum. The walls of these bronchioles and ductules are overlaid with a curious hyaline material which is not fibrin and which extends down into the mouths of the atria."

This, especially in its microscopical picture, might be taken for that almost mythical stage of congestion leading up to early red hepatization described in the text-books; a stage in which true lobar pneumonia is evidently very transient, lasting but a few hours, whereas apparently in these cases it may last for days. The pneumococci evidently have played an active part in its production—" scattered through all the exudate, whether in the bronchioles or in the alveoli, are pneumococci, sometimes fairly numerous, sometimes in incalculable numbers, so that every phagocytic cell is loaded with them, and there are millions free in the alveoli. In a great many cases there are absolutely no other organisms in the lungs—culture, mouse inoculation, smears, and best of all, careful stains of the sections for bacteria showed this."

But there is clearly something more here than a pure pneumococcus infection. The " hyaline " deposits, the patchy nature, the peripheral hæmorrhagic œdematous zones, all are of influenzal type. MacCallum would explain the divergence from the pure lobar pneumonia type by postulating that the unknown cause of the pandemic, which he holds was not the influenza bacillus, induced a general infection, and that this underlay and modified the secondary pneumococcus infection.

What appears to be an equally possible explanation is that the primary cause, whether influenza bacillus or not, induced in the first place a tracheitis and in this way favoured the entrance of the pneumococci into the lungs, where, finding themselves in their tissue of election, they over-ran and overwhelmed that primary cause, gaining a footing and multiplying to the practical exclusion of other forms.

Adami does not recall cases or their description which conformed quite to MacCallum's type. Nor does MacCallum's description entirely conform with that of other leading patholo-·gists in the United States. All, it is true, admit a frequency both of pneumonia of the lobar type and of findings of pneumococci far in advance of anything seen among British troops. This is to be expected. It must be remembered that during this century, either the inhabitants of the United States have shown themselves more susceptible to the pneumococcus of various strains than Europeans, or they have become infected by strains that are more virulent. This is certain, that the mortality from lobar pneumonia in the great cities of America far exceeds anything known in Europe. Opie in his Camp Pike report states that typical lobar pneumonia occurred in about one half of the cases coming to autopsy. He describes lobar cases as exhibiting clinically apparent recovery from influenza, as evidenced by the fall of temperature to normal. After from one to three days of normal temperature, typical lobar pneumonia with characteristic rusty sputum developed suddenly. He distinguishes another group exhibiting purulent bronchitis and presenting the picture of both lobular and lobar pneumonia in the same individual. A group of 36 cases of fatal lobar pneumonia taken in sequence and examined bacteriologically gave pneumococcus in 33 cases (91·7 per cent.), *B. influenzae* in 31 cases (86·1 per cent.) and *S. haemolyticus* in 13 cases (36·1 per cent.). The strains of pneumococcus were not those usually met with in severe uncomplicated lobar pneumonia (types I and II)—in nine out of ten cases the forms isolated were those common in the mouth and throat of healthy men, most often type IV.

Klotz takes a view that is strongly opposed to this last :—

" It is incorrect in influenza pneumonia to speak of the lesion as lobar pneumonia or broncho-pneumonia if by these terms we have in mind the pathological characters observed in the pneumococcic pneumonia with its lobar or bronchial distribution. Influenza pneumonia appeared with both lobar and lobular characteristics. Nearly every case had both types of lesion present, but the nature of the inflammatory process is so decidedly different from that of the ordinary endemic pneumonia (croupous pneumonia) that a confusion in the interpretation is likely to arise and in fact has already raised a considerable polemic. Influenza pneumonia is commonly lobar, lobular or bronchial in distribution. It is, however, not of the characters that are associated with the lesions designated under these terms. When, therefore, we here used the term ' lobar ' we mean lobar in distribution and not lobar in type. . . . . Even within the same lobe a variety of types was present."

It may be noted that in Klotz's material, out of thirty-two cases examined and submitted to full bacteriological examination by Holman, pneumococci were isolated in twenty cases, mainly from the bronchi and lungs.

MacCallum, Opie and Klotz may justly be described as among the four leading pathologists of North America. It will be observed that the descriptions of Klotz and MacCallum are not of necessity opposed, as also that Opie's group of mixed lobar and lobular pneumococci tacitly admits Klotz's contention, which is in harmony with the main body of British observations.

In other words, while in these influenza cases the pneumococcus was frequently present in large numbers, it did not give rise to croupous pneumonia proper, but what reaction was present was profoundly modified by the existing action of the influenza virus. There was not the true dry homogeneous hepatization, the intense massing of polymorphonuclear leucocytes in the air sacs, nor again the abundant network of fibrin.

Often again where empyema developed, pneumococci were present in the pleural pus. They and not the influenza virus proper were responsible for the pus production.

The cases seen by Colonel Adami have shown a combination of the specific influenza peri-bronchial type of lesion with a more diffuse partial consolidation, merging into zones of hæmorrhagic œdema, with abundant pneumococci in the alveoli, and in place of the absence of pleurisy they have manifested a distinct tendency to show fibrinous purulent pleurisy, if not a frank empyema. This differed from the empyema of streptococcus cases in the greater deposit of fibrin. Nor has there been any question as to the existence of a very definite bronchitis and bronchiolitis. Admittedly they have not been of the early and rapidly fatal type noted by MacCallum.

Hæmolytic streptococci were not infrequent secondary invaders, but in the British army cases could, in general, scarcely be described as common. In their most careful differential study at No. 3 Canadian General Hospital, at Boulogne, in cultures from the lungs of 67 cases, Major Tytler, Captain Janes and Captain Dobbin isolated these from only 5 cases (7·5 per cent.). Streptococci of the nature of *S. viridans* producing a green colour on blood agar, without capsules and not fermenting

inulin, were much more common (25 per cent.), while similar
forms not fully differentiated, which might be either pneumococci or S. *viridans*, were recognized in 34 per cent. of the cultures,
and pneumococci fully differentiated were present in 25 per
cent. of the cultures, and were the predominant organisms in
7·5 per cent. of the plates, as compared with predominant
hæmolytic streptococci in 4·5 per cent., predominant *Staphylococcus aureus* in 21 per cent., and predominant *B. influenzae*
in 45 per cent.

In the navy, on the other hand, according to Surgeon-
Lieutenant-Commander P. Fildes, R.N.V.R., Surgeon-Lieutenant
S. L. Baker, R.N., and W. R. Thompson, hæmolytic streptococci were as common as they were in the United States.
This, at least, was their experience at Haslar. In the spring
outbreak they rarely recognized or isolated *B. influenzae*.
From the trachea, lungs and blood they gained almost exclusively hæmolytic streptococci resembling *S. pyogenes*. With
this they call attention to the relative frequency of tonsillitis,
of empyema, and of pyopericarditis.

But here is their most significant and frank admission ; when,
with the onset of this main wave in the autumn of 1918, they
began to employ for cultures a modified Matthews' and a modified Levinthal medium, they recovered growths of Pfeiffer's
bacillus from so many patients not suffering from pneumonia
and from the lungs of so many men dying from pneumonia that,
to quote their statement :—

" We are of the opinion that it is unnecessary to look further than this
organism for the cause of the epidemic, the streptococci and other organisms
which have been mentioned being only secondary infections upon lungs
already infected by *B. influenzae*.

" The difference in the bacterial flora obtained by the use of these media
is so remarkable that we are prepared to admit that our earlier conclusions
were incorrect."

And they state : " At the present time we are obtaining
cultures of *B. influenzae* from every *post-mortem* upon these
pneumonia cases."

But with this there was no diminution in the incidence of
hæmolytic streptococci. Pyopericarditis remained frequent,
empyema very common, while sections of the lungs showed
streptococci in enormous numbers, and they were present in the
pleural cavity and pericardial exudate.

The capacity to set up the specific pulmonary lesions of
the pandemic, therefore, is ascribed by some, like Professor
W. G. MacCallum, to hæmolytic streptococci, allied to
S. pyogenes; and by others, like Mather and Rosenow, to

non-hæmolytic streptococci, allied to *S. viridans* and the forms common in the normal throat. Little isolated from 62 out of 73 fatal cases at Witley a small Gram-positive diplococcus, the only organism which he was able to gain in pure culture. He found it slightly hæmolytic and intermediate in character between the pneumococcus and streptococcus (*pyogenes*). He regarded it as probable that the initial infection of the upper air passages was due to *B. influenzae,* and that the grosser complications were caused by this organism. Inoculation of animals with Pfeiffer's bacilli gained from his cases led to no fatal results, whereas combined inoculations with the two organisms brought about death in many animals.

It is impossible to accept the conclusions of MacCallum, Mather and Rosenow. As has been shown, there is a respiratory disease, with specific pathogenic features, in which *B. influenzae* alone is found, and it may be added that Blake and Cecil, of the Army Medical School at Washington, employing cultures of that bacillus in which virulence had been maintained and exalted by passage, have reproduced these specific features in a long series of monkeys. We cannot bring ourselves to believe that pure cultures of organisms of a totally different order can reproduce these same lesions in their entirety, namely, the characteristic combination of sinusitis, tracheo-bronchitis, bronchitis and peri-bronchiolitis, hæmorrhagic œdema, alveolar emphysema, and hyaline deposits in the alveoli.

It is impossible to discuss the pathology of these lung conditions without constantly referring to their ætiology and so to their bacteriology. Our conclusions are : (1) that there is one common and original microbic cause of influenza ; (2) that if this be not the *B. influenzae* of Pfeiffer, it is in the earliest cases constantly associated therewith ; (3) that, as shown by Blake and Cecil in their experiments upon monkeys, the influenza bacillus, while setting up the characteristic lesions, may in many cases become disintegrated and disappear by the third or fourth day of the disease, the liberated toxins continuing to act upon the tissues—a condition similar to that met with in some cases of cerebro-spinal meningitis ; and (4) there is, lastly, the remote possibility that in the later phases of a pandemic a phenomenon similar to paragglutination is encountered. In paragglutination, organisms themselves non-pathogenic, living in the body in association with organisms which produce agglutinins, eventually themselves undergo agglutination by relatively high dilutions of the serum of the

specifically infected animal. The possibility is that streptococci, living in body fluids containing the influenza toxins,
may take up and eventually themselves elaborate these toxins,
thus in their growth within the body reproducing the lesions
of influenza. Adami is led to make this suggestion by a vivid
memory of his first encounter with the phenomenon of
paragglutination in a chronic cholera carrier, in which a
coliform bacillus present in the stools was agglutinated by
high dilutions (1 in 2,000) of a specific serum. Now MacCallum,
who may be regarded as the leading upholder of the streptococcus theory, himself admits that the pneumonia set up by
S. haemolyticus exhibits lesions which are not those present in
what has been described as uncomplicated influenzal pneumonia.
He describes a profuse growth of the streptococci in the
lymphatics of the lung, with marked thrombosis of the same
and of the capillaries of the alveolar walls. In his case 55 :—

" Extensive areas of necrosis occur in which the lung substance is converted
into a soft yellow opaque material. Those areas look like abscesses as they
project under the pleura . . . . . but they are really pretty firm opaque
necrotic patches of consolidated lung swarming with streptococci. . . . .
Microscopically the lesions just mentioned are the outcome of the filling of
alveoli with streptococci and an exudate of leucocytes and fibrin. . . . .
In Case 187 in which the consolidation is almost lobar in appearance, the
capillaries of the alveolar walls are widely thrombosed with hyaline strands
of fibrin which completely occlude them. The exudate and even the tissue
of the lung becomes necrotic under these conditions.
" In the more hæmorrhagic consolidation, such as is seen in Case 20, great
stretches of lung substance simply become necrotic and filled with blood
without any infiltration of leucocytes. In such places the streptococci in
long chains form a tangled matted growth as though they were growing in
the most favourable culture medium."

These are not the lesions seen in uncomplicated influenzal
pneumonia, but lesions characteristic of streptococcus infections
in general, i.e., extension of the growth along the lymphatics and
blood capillaries with thrombosis and necrosis.

Another feature of the streptococcus cases which is not
typical of what may be termed uncomplicated influenzal pneumonia is, to quote MacCallum, " the extraordinary frequency
of pleurisy with fibrino-purulent effusion. At first a thin
watery brownish turbid fluid with a granular sediment and
floating shreds of fibrin, if the patient survives long enough
the exudate becomes distinctly purulent." Now this thin
watery fluid here described is that seen in ordinary influenzal
pneumonia ; but it is limited in amount. In MacCallum's
cases even after resection of a rib and drainage, thirteen cases
together yielded more than 28 litres of fluid at autopsy ; 1,000
to 1,500 c.c. were commonly found. Again, uncomplicated
influenzal pleurisy does not go on to empyema proper. There

was a special tendency for streptococcus empyema to be localized by adhesions, when the pus was found thick and of a whitish green colour yielding abundant colonies of streptococci. Such empyema might also be set up by the pneumococcus, but here a difference was recognizable, there being a greater deposit of fibrin and less tendency to localization.

One further point deserves note, namely, the frequent association of hæmolytic streptococci with tonsillitis. Now, while acute congestion of the nasopharynx was one of the prime symptoms of the pandemic cases, it was striking how rarely either pseudo-membranous or ulcerative tonsillitis showed itself. Richey, of the United States Naval Medical School at Washington, reports that medical officers of the United States Navy and Public Health Service during the course of experiments upon human volunteers at San Francisco and Boston saw developed six cases of tonsillitis following upon the transferring of crude naso-pharyngeal washings and bronchial secretions from influenza patients into the nose and throats of sixty-one different men. The highest number of cases occurred in a group of men who a month previously had received a mixed vaccine (*B. influenzae*, pneumococci of various strains and *S. haemolyticus*). None of these men developed influenza. The tonsillitis was typical and in the purulent exudate of all the cases a hæmolytic streptococcus was the predominating organism, the colonies being similar to those gained from the donors of the respective groups. These experiments alone oppose the view that hæmolytic streptococci are the cause of influenza.

Staphylococcus Pneumonia.—In some areas, notably, according to Major Tytler, in the Boulogne area, cultures from the lung yielded abundant colonies of *Pyococcus albus*. Where this was the case more than one observer has noted that they were particularly associated with abscess formation, either multiple and small, along the course of the affected bronchioles, or larger and lobular, probably from coalescence of numerous bronchiolar abscesses in one or more adjacent lobules. These abscesses, according to Major-General Phear, were also relatively common in Macedonia.

After-results.—A study of the more slowly fatal cases of uncomplicated influenzal pneumonia, of cases that had survived ten days or more indicated that the toxic effects were most manifest in the early days of the attack, for in these cases of long continuance there were clear evidences of repair, as indicated by the frequent evidences of organizing fibrosis and cicatrization, with thickening of the interlobular septa. This cicatrization led to localized contraction and consequent distortion, most marked in cases that had survived three weeks and more.

The " Gassed" Lung.—But if the influenzal lung was in these many respects unlike either that of the familiar acute lobar pneumonia or of ordinary lobular pneumonia there was one other condition, and one first recognized as an entity during the course of the war, to which it presented many resemblances, namely, the lung of acute " gassing." Poison gas led to the same necrosis and desquamation of the mucosa of the trachea and bronchi, the same congestion and swelling of the submucosa, the same congestion, hæmorrhages and œdema of the lung tissues proper and to similar mingled areas of emphysema and consolidation. Only the peri-bronchiolitis and interstitial pneumonia and the hyaline deposits were lacking.*

Other Lesions.

Comparing the pandemic of 1918–1919 with its predecessors, the remarkable feature has been the predominance of the respiratory type of the disease, a predominance so great as to amount to the virtual exclusion of the gastric and intestinal, and the nervous forms. These were singularly rare. A few isolated cases have been recorded of influenzal meningitis with isolation of Pfeiffer's bacillus, as also of acute gastric and intestinal disorder.

In this latter connection, attention may be directed to Lowe's series of cases of acute ulcerative colitis.

The Skin.—Of the skin lesions, herpes, labialis and facialis, was not sufficiently common to be attributed to the action of the primary toxic agent. With the extreme toxæmia and the hæmorrhagic lesions in the lungs so commonly present, it might have been expected that purpura and localized subcutaneous hæmorrhages would have been frequent ; they were, however, distinctly rare. In the many thousands of cases that came under his notice as consultant, Colonel H. French only met with four cases, all fatal. He calls attention to two other cases, both fatal, of multiple purpuric spots upon the feet and ankles, associated with œdema of the lower extremities and

---

* For fuller details of the morbid anatomy of the gassed lung *see* Reports of the Chemical Warfare Medical Committee, Nos. 1, 2, 9 and 17, published by the Medical Research Committee.

progressing to the development of hæmorrhagic bullae undergoing ulceration. The "heliotrope cyanosis," which was so
grave a portent, persisted after death.

Muscle.—A frequent, and evidently frequently overlooked,
lesion, one, that is to say, recorded from those hospitals in which
autopsies were performed with known thoroughness, was
hyaline degeneration, or more accurately, coagulation necrosis
(Zenker's degeneration) of the striated or voluntary muscle.
As in typhoid fever, the site of election for this lesion was
the lower segment of the rectus abdominis, *i.e.*, below the
umbilicus. Professor Wolbach, of Harvard, encountered the
condition in over 25 per cent. of his autopsies in Camp Devens.
Where this was present, careful examination revealed that
other muscles were apt to be involved, also in part, in the
form of localized patches of degeneration and necrosis—the
diaphragm, internal and external oblique, latissimus dorsi,
intercostal, and pectoralis major muscles. To this list Klotz
adds two cases of degeneration affecting the sternomastoid and
gluteal muscles. While degeneration might show itself in
cases dying on the fourth day, hæmorrhage and rupture
occurred in his cases most often between the eighth and tenth
days of the disease, although in one case it was found on the
twenty-third day. Colonel Adami suggests that it is probable
that similar localized areas of degeneration account for the
acute pains and subsequent weakness in, more particularly,
the muscles of the trunk and lower extremities reported by
more than one observer.

Little is known as to the primary cause of this lesion, whether
it is due to a selective toxic action or to localized thrombosis.
Under the microscope individual muscle-fibres and groups of
the same are seen to be greatly swollen, to have lost their
striation and to have become curiously translucent and hyaline.
More often, in the influenza cases they had passed beyond this
stage to rupture with accompanying and often extensive
hæmorrhage. In the more extreme cases the rupture with
hæmorrhage involved the whole body of the rectus from
side to side. Associated with the fragmentation of the
muscle-fibres in parts, proliferation of the sarcolemma
nuclei was very noticeable, along with some small cell
infiltration.

With these figures those of Major W. J. Wilson, R.A.M.C.,
and Sergt. P. Starr, R.A.M.C., for the main wave of the disease
in France 1918, tally very closely ; 92 autopsies yielding 23
cases of hyaline degeneration of the rectus abdominis. They

report the commonest site as being situated 2 in. above the pubic rim, but note existence of hyaline fibres near both origin and insertion of the muscle.

Among the Canadian soldiers at Witley Camp in the main year of the pandemic, Major T. R. Little, C.A.M.C., records seven cases of rupture of the rectus abdominis, exclusive of the milder cases, in 73 autopsies.

Circulatory System : Heart.—Several observers emphasize the singularly slight involvement of the heart muscle in the fatal cases of influenzal pneumonia. At most they record distension of the right side, but the muscle was found in general firm and of good colour, with at most, as might be expected, a moderate grade of cloudy swelling. In the prepandemic cases, Abrahams, Eyre, Hallows and French draw a distinction between the pallid cases, in which they found the muscle pale and friable (*i.e.*, fatty degeneration), and those with heliotrope cyanosis in which the muscle appeared normal.

The endocardium was rarely involved. Malloch and Rhea have reported two cases in which they gained pure cultures of *B. influenzae* from cases of vegetative endocarditis and there are one or two similar records. More often the vegetations, when present, have yielded cultures of pneumococci and streptococci. Possibly endocarditis, whether primary or secondary, was more common in non-fatal cases. Colonel French has called attention to the increase in cases of chronic and subacute endocarditis following upon the pandemic of influenza.

The same is true of the pericardium. At most, in uncomplicated cases, as so often with the pleural fluid, there might be a slight increase of pericardial fluid with turbidity and rare shreds of fibrin, and smears from such might show *B. influenzae* and no other organism. Where there was any obvious purulent pericarditis, there, always, other secondary organisms were present, pneumococci or streptococci, with occasional admixture with influenzal bacilli.

As indicated by the state of the lungs, the distension of the right heart with cyanosis, and engorgement of the venous system was a common finding. There have been few studies upon the effects of the influenza toxins upon the smaller arteries and capillaries, although there is little doubt that these would throw considerable light upon the hæmorrhagic and œdematous state of the lungs. It deserves note that Rose Bradford, Bashford and Connor, in their study of the lesions of the monkey's lung following inoculation with their filterable virus, lay stress upon the lesions encountered in the smaller vessels in the form of proliferation of the endothelium with heaping up and apparent disintegration of certain of the cells, accompanied by the formation of localized thrombi. In the influenza lung, Adami encountered occasionally similar appearances and imagined that these have borne some relationship to the thromboses and hæmorrhages. Here attention may be called to the fact that while the formation of fibrinous threads within the alveoli is so slight in uncomplicated cases of influenzal pneumonia, typical fibrin formation is seen in the vessels and lymphatics.

Alimentary Canal.—A rare complication, little noted, is one referred to by Cooper Cole, amongst Canadian troops at Bramshott in the autumn of 1918. He reports more than thirty cases of swelling of the parotid gland and its capsules. This swelling was occasionally bilateral, and in some cases associated with swollen testicle. These cases were not clinically mumps. The swelling allowed free movement of the jaw, while little change was observable at the mouths of the ducts. Reference has already been made to the infrequent records of gastric and intestinal lesions in the pandemic. It is possible that slight vascular lesions along the course of the alimentary canal were moderately frequent, for those observers who apparently made full routine examinations called attention to them. Thus Wilson and Starr refer to the frequency of sub-mucosal ecchymoses of the stomach.

Captain F. Armitage, N.Z.M.C., records two cases of bowel hæmorrhage unaccompanied by ulceration of the ileum, or large bowel, or colon, such ulceration being found in none of his autopsies. Captain E. Cronin Lowe, N.Z.M.C., has reported three unusual cases of extensive membranous colitis, occurring at No. 2 New Zealand General Hospital, Walton-on-Thames. They were all cases in which an initial influenzal attack developed a rapidly progressive broncho-pneumonia, ending in septicæmia, with streptococcal cultures from the heart, blood and spleen. In the lungs, pneumococci and streptococci pre-dominated; few Pfeiffer's bacilli were present. There were occasionally small superficial ulcers in the stomach, submucous hæmorrhages in the duodenum of two of the cases and conges-tion of the ileum in all three; in two, extensive submucous hæmorrhages. The cæcum in all cases showed intense sub-mucous injection and small hæmorrhages in one of these. The whole submucosa consisted of a mass of diphtheritic necrosis of a slate-green colour, with here and there small areas of intense congestion; the lymph follicles were greatly swollen.

This condition extended for 3 to 4 in. up the ascending colon. The congestion affected also the transverse and descending colon.

In Klotz's series of thirty-two cases these also were frequent ; he found petechial hæmorrhages in the stomach fifteen times, in the intestines four times.

"Often we could observe the presence of free and more or less altered blood in the stomach and intestines, and in twelve cases the amount was considerable, sufficient to be spoken of as melæna. It is probable that the oozing of the blood takes place not only from the areas visible to the eye, as petechial hæmorrhages, but also from the more normal-looking mucosa of stomach and bowel. The tendency to hæmorrhage was not necessarily accompanied by visible alterations in the epithelial layer of the mucosa. . . . . The lesions were isolated and sporadic, but always about small capillary loops. It appeared to us that the damage was always primarily upon the vascular tissues and particularly upon the endothelial walls of the small channels."

Multiple erosions appeared to arise in a process of bland necrosis, limited by healthy tissue and not tending to enlarge. These were found ten times in the stomach and twice in the intestine.

Here attention should be drawn to the singular infrequency of acute peritonitis as a complication in the British army cases. This is in striking contrast to MacCallum's record ; he found that " acute peritonitis seemed to be a not infrequent accompaniment of the streptococcal pneumonia."

Liver.—Beyond a slight amount of swelling and pallor, *i.e.*, cloudy swelling, in general little was to be noted in this organ. Nevertheless, several observers call attention to the occasional presence of jaundice indicating a graver disorder of this organ.

Spleen.—Several observers, more particularly in the early cases, call attention to some swelling of the spleen, the organ being found engorged but still firm. In general, this swelling was slight.

Kidneys.—More frequent was a swelling of the kidneys, with pallor and cloudy degeneration of the cortex. On section there was found a moderate grade of parenchymatous nephritis and a slighter grade of glomerular nephritis, with occasional small hæmorrhages into the cortical tissue. There was little cell infiltration, the appearance being of a more toxic than infective type.

Bladder.—Klotz cites two cases of hæmaturia supposed to be renal, found at autopsy to be due to a hæmorrhagic state of the submucosa of the bladder, and non-infective. In these two cases there were associated ecchymotic foci in pericardium, pleura, stomach and intestines.

Adrenals.—Occasional cases have been recorded of extensive hæmorrhage. Wolbach ascribes these to secondary infection with hæmolytic streptococci. As in other acute infections, localized areas of necrosis of the cortex were apt at times to be encountered.

Testes.—MacCallum, Klotz and Wolbach have laid stress upon the cessation of activity in the seminiferous tubules and absence of spermatids, spermatocytes and spermatozoa with rarer complete degeneration and atrophy of the tubules. The spermatogonia are present and the Sertoli cells most conspicuous, so that with only these left the structure of the tubule becomes very simple. The condition is evidently toxic, for it is accompanied by little or no cellular infiltration. It is probable that careful examination will show a like condition in other infections accompanied by acute intoxication. Indeed, Cordes some years ago called attention to the cessation of spermatogenesis in many acute infections. In more chronic cases there was to be seen a beginning replacement fibrosis.

Summary.

(1) Surveying the data brought here together, one cannot fail to be impressed by the fact in the first place that the small epidemics and sporadic cases of purulent bronchitis and broncho-pneumonia of 1916 to 1918 were histologically and bacteriologically of the same order as the first and main waves of the great pandemic of 1918–19. It is true that the outstanding feature of the pre-pandemic cases was profuse purulent expectoration and that at the height of the pandemic this in most cases was wholly wanting, being replaced by an equally abundant sero-sanguineous discharge. This difference, however, is explicable as a matter of degree and not of kind—the serous and hæmorrhagic reactions being set up by organisms and toxin, of high virulence, the purulent reaction by the same organisms when of lower virulence. As a matter of fact, purulent bronchitis was common in fatal cases of the first wave of the pandemic, and was still encountered during the height of the pandemic. Similarly, pulmonary œdema and hæmorrhages around the affected bronchi were noted not infrequently in the pre-pandemic cases. To explain this " over-lapping," another factor has to be taken into account, namely, the grade of reacting or resisting power on the part of the individual.

(2) It has been repeatedly stated in the past that so many and so varied are the lesions encountered in the " influenzal " lung that it is impossible to distinguish any specific lesion. The data here brought together show that these earlier views

are erroneous. On the contrary, a succession of lesions of the respiratory tract is recognizable in these influenza cases that is in itself absolutely specific. The individual lesion may not be specific, but the succession and association are such as are peculiar to this one disease and as have been encountered in none other. These are :—

i. Acute congestion of the posterior nares and pharynx leading to inflammation of the accessory air cells of the nose, more particularly of the sphenoidal sinuses.

ii. Acute tracheitis, affecting particularly the lower third of the trachea and the region of the bifurcation, characterized by desquamation of the epithelium and intense congestion of the submucosa.

iii. Acute bilateral desquamative bronchitis and bronchiolitis with an intensive purulent exudate in the less acute cases and a sero-sanguineous discharge in the more acute.

iv. Associated with this a peculiarly characteristic peribronchitis and bronchiolitis with interstitial pneumonia.

v. Hæmorrhages into the tracheal, bronchial and bronchiolar submucosa, which in the most acute cases may be very extensive, involving several lobules, and leading to hæmoptysis.

vi. The combination of generalized emphysema, affecting the periphery of the lobules, with congestion and sero-sanguineous exudate, the two together rendering the lungs large and moist.

vii. Relatively slight involvement of the air sacs, with characteristically slight formation of fibrin ; swelling and desquamation of the alveolar epithelium with frequent presence of delicate hyaline deposits on the alveolar walls. Similar hyaline deposits might be present in the bronchial tubes from the trachea downwards.

(3) With swelling and congestion of the bronchial and cervical lymph nodes and a slight (? mechanical) pleurisy the above are the characteristics of uncomplicated influenzal pneumonia. But such uncomplicated cases were rare. Even in the less acute pre-pandemic cases a most prominent feature was the frequent complication set up by the growth within the lungs of other organisms, notably pneumococci (of the types met with in the normal throat), streptococci, both hæmolytic and " green-producing," allied to *S. viridans* and *Staphylococcus*

albus. Other forms such as *M. catarrhalis, B. mucosus* and *B. septus* were encountered less frequently. The pneumococci, streptococci and staphylococci set up modifications in the appearance of the lungs, but in the presence of the emphysema, hæmorrhages, bronchiolitis and interstitial pneumonia, could only be regarded as secondary and not primary invaders.

BIBLIOGRAPHY.

Abrahams, Hallows, Eyre & French.	Purulent Bronchitis : its Influenzal and Pneumococcal Bacteriology.	Lancet, 1917, Vol. ii, pp. 377–382.
Adami, Vallée & Martineau.	A Chronic Cholera Carrier	Can. Med. Assoc. Jl., 1911.
Armitage	Note on Influenza and Pneumonia.	Brit. Med. Jl., 1919, Vol. i, pp. 272–274.
Bartels	Bemerkungen über eine im Frühjahre 1860 in der Poliklinik in Kiel beobachtete Masernepidemie, mit besonderer Berücksichtigung der dabei vorgekommenen Lungenaffectionen.	Virchows Arch. f. Path. Anat., 1861, Vol. xxi, p. 65.
Blake & Cecil	Studies on Experimental Pneumonia. Production in Monkeys of an Acute Respiratory Disease resembling Influenza by Inoculation with *Bacillus influenzae.*	Jl. Exper. Med., 1920, Vol. xxxii, pp. 691–719.
,, ,,	Studies on Experimental Pneumonia. Experimental *Streptococcus haemolyticus* Pneumonia in Monkeys.	*Ibid.,* 1920, Vol. xxxii, p. 401.
Boggs	The Influenza Bacillus in Bronchiectasis.	Amer. Jl. Med. Soc., N.S., 1905, Vol. cxxx, pp. 902–911.
Burnford	Further Notes on the Epidemic (Influenza), with Special Reference to Pneumonia, in Macedonia.	Proc. Royal Soc. Med., 1918–19, Vol. xii, Med. Sect., p. 49.
Cole	Preliminary Report on Influenza Epidemic at Bramshott in September–October 1918.	Can. Med. Assoc. Jl., 1919, Vol. ix, p. 41 ; and Brit. Med. Jl., 1918, Vol. ii, p. 566.
Cordes	Untersuchungen über den Einfluss acuter und chronischer allgemein Erkrankungen auf die Testikel, specielle auf die Spermatogenese, sowie Beobachtungen über das Auftreten von Fett in der Hoden.	Virchows Arch. f. Path. Anat., 1898, Vol. cli, p. 402.
Delafield	Studies in Pathological Anatomy	New York, 1878–91.
Fildes, Baker & Thompson.	Provisional Notes on the Pathology of the Present Epidemic.	Lancet, 1918, Vol. ii, pp. 697–700.
Gibson, Bowman & Connor.	The Etiology of Influenza.	M.R.C. Special Report Series, No. 36, London, 1919, p. 19.

Goodpasture & Burnett.	The Pathology of Pneumonia accompanying Influenza.	U.S. Naval Med. Bull., 1919, Vol. xiii, p. 177.
Greig	Observations on the Pathology and Bacteriology of Influenza.	Ind. Jl. Med. Res., 1920–21, Vol. viii, p. 326.
Greig & Maitra ..	Bacteriological Examination of the Accessory Sinuses of Nose, etc., in Cases of Influenza.	Ibid., 1918–19, Vol. vi, p. 401.
Hammond, Rolland & Shore.	Purulent Bronchitis	Lancet, 1917, Vol. ii, pp. 41–45.
Hecht	Die Riesenzellenpneumonie im Kindesalter.	Ziegler's Beitr.,1910, Vol. xlviii, p. 263.
Klotz	Studies in Epidemic Influenza	Publications from the University of Pittsburgh School of Medicine, 1919, p. 223.
Little	Chief post-mortem Findings and Bacteriological Examination of Material collected from Seventy-three Cases of Pneumonia Supervening on Influenza.	Bull. Can. Army Med. Corps, 1918–19, Vol. i, pp. 117–118.
Lowe	Three Cases of Influenzal Pneumonia with Septicæmia and Extensive Membranous Colitis.	Lancet, 1921, Vol. i, pp. 112–113.
MacCallum	Pathology of Epidemic Pneumonia in Camps and Cantonments in 1918.	Trans. Assoc. Amer. Physic., 1919, Vol. xxxiv, p. 169.
,, ...	The Pathology of the Pneumonia in the United States Army during the Winter of 1917–18.	Monographs of the Rockefeller Institute for Medical Research, No. 10, 1919, p. 139.
Malloch, T. A. ..	Discussion on Influenza ..	Proc. Roy. Soc. Med., 1918–19, Vol. xii, Gen. Reports, pp. 45–50.
Malloch, A., & Rhea	Fatal Bronchitis and Bronchopneumonia caused by Bacillus influenzae of Pfeiffer during an Inter-pandemic Period.	Quart. Jl. of Med., 1920–21, Vol. xiv, pp. 125–138.
,, ,,	Two Cases of Endocarditis due to Bacillus influenzae.	Quart. Jl. of Med., 1918–19, Vol. xii, pp. 174–182.
Malone	A Bacteriological Investigation of Influenza.	Ind. Jl. Med. Res., 1919–20, Vol. vii, p. 495.
Opie,Freeman,Blake, Small & Rivers.	Pneumonia following Influenza at Camp Pike, Ark.	Jl. Amer. Med. Assoc., 1919, Vol. lxxii, pp. 556–565.
Patterson, Little & Williams.	Report on the Bacteriology and Pathology of 46 cases of Influenza.	M.R.C. Special Report Series, No. 36, London, 1919, p. 88.

Phear	Medical Experiences in Macedonia and the Caucasus.	Proc. Roy. Soc. Med., 1919-20, Vol. xiii, Occasional Lecture, 57-100.
Richey	Experimental Streptococcic Tonsillitis. The apparent inefficacy of Streptococcic Vaccine as Prophylactic.	Jl. of Inf. Diseases, 1919, Vol. xxv, pp. 299-305.
Rosenow	Studies in Influenza and Pneumonia.	Ibid., 1920, Vol. xxvi, p. 469.
Shore	Report on the Morbid Anatomy of Influenza.	M.R.C. Special Report Series, No. 36, London, 1919, p. 96.
Steinhaus	Histologische Untersuchungen über die Masernpneumonie.	Ziegler's Beitr., 1901, Vol. xxix, p. 524.
Sundell	Studies of Influenza in Hospitals of the British Armies in France 1918.	M.R.C. Special Report Series, London, 1919, No. 36, p. 65.
Tytler, Janes & Dobbin.	Pathological and Bacteriological Findings in Fatal Cases of Pneumonia during the Influenza Epidemic of October and November, 1918.	M.R.C. Special Report Series, No. 36, London, 1919, p. 77.
Wilson & Starr	Bacteriological and Pathological Observations on Influenza as seen in France during 1918.	Brit. Med. Jl., 1919, Vol. i, pp. 634-635.
Wolbach	Comments on the Pathology and Bacteriology of Fatal Influenza Cases as observed at Camp Devens, Mass.	Johns Hopkins Hospital Bull., 1919, Vol. xxx, p. 104.

CHAPTER XVI.

TUBERCULOSIS.

IT will be some years before the investigation into the official records of the war can afford full statistical data as to the incidence and mortality from tuberculosis amongst the British troops during the years of the war, and it is safe to assume that, even when the records have been completely sorted out and analysed, much of the truth will still be hidden. In no disease are statistics more liable to error than in tuberculosis. Figures based on death-rates may perhaps be reliable within certain limits because the cases tend to become more typical shortly before the end and the true nature of the malady is usually apparent ; but where notifications of cases form the basis of statistical investigation, the vast possibilities of error that lie behind clinical diagnosis have to be taken into account.

In the American Civil War, for instance, the official records disclose a total of 13,499 cases and 5,286 deaths attributed to tuberculosis amongst the white troops engaged on the Federal side. The author of the Medical History of that war, however, finds reason to place the total at 17,476 cases, and taking into account various sources of error concludes that even this figure by no means indicates the " extent to which tubercular disease prevailed " in the Federal armies. He points out that " tubercle was frequently found in the lungs of men who died from other diseases." Thus, 30 out of 435 cases dying from pneumonia, 16 out of 330 cases of paroxysmal and continued fevers and 106 out of 667 cases of diarrhœa and dysentery were found on *post-mortem* examination to show tuberculosis of the lungs. He remarks that in view of the latter observation there should have been 6,000 cases of tuberculosis amongst the 37,000 deaths from intestinal disorders that occurred in white troops during the war. These extracts from the history of a previous war serve well to illustrate the sources of error that must always be taken into account in evaluating statistical records of tuberculosis. It may be assumed that all these factors will bring their element of fallacy into the interpretations to be placed on the records of the war of 1914–1918, even when these are complete. Only figures compiled by the A.D.M.S. (Sanitation), G.H.Q.,

France, from intercurrent reports are at present available, and the possibilities of error are therefore considerable. But even when full allowance is made for inaccuracy of diagnosis under the stress of war, it may be assumed that this error is more or less comparable as between the records of different military formations and racial groups. Hence extreme differences in incidence and mortality between such formations and groups are worth serious consideration with reference to such phenomena as relative susceptibility and the like. It is for this reason that the available figures, partial and incomplete as they are, have been reproduced in tabular form to illustrate this brief account of tuberculosis in the British armies during the war.

Troops should have gone overseas practically free from tuberculosis if infection with this disease had been capable of accurate diagnosis by clinical examination. From 1st August, 1914, to the end of 1917, it was laid down in Army Orders that men showing any signs of tuberculous disease should be rejected on enlistment. From the end of 1917 onwards it was considered necessary to lower the standard in some measure and to pass for Grade III men who showed signs of past or suspected tuberculosis but who gave a history of two years' good health. It is certain that these regulations were carefully applied by recruiting medical officers. The rejections for tuberculosis were numerous. In London, for instance, of 160,545 men examined during the period January to October, 1918, no fewer than 3,874, or 2·3 per cent., were rejected for tuberculous disease, 3,328 of these, or 2 per cent., of the total number examined being cases of pulmonary tuberculosis.* These stringent regulations, applied with vigour, as can be seen from the high percentage of rejections, must have been very effective in diminishing the number of " open " and infective cases of tuberculosis amongst the troops, a matter of great importance in view of the conditions of close contact in crowded billets and ill-ventilated dug-outs in the area of active operations. The type of recruit from the end of 1916 onwards was poor and the standard fell with each successive year of the war. These points are well brought out in the Report of the Ministry of National Service,† which shows graphically the percentages of " units of fitness," according to Keith's standard, actually found in 2,425,184 recruits examined, as compared with that which should be yielded by a normal community of young

---

* Report of the Ministry of National Service, Vol. I.
† Figs. 2 and 3, p. 12 of Vol. I.

TABLE I (A).

Incidence, Mortality and Incidence-rate per 100,000 in British and Dominion Troops in France and Flanders.

	1916.			1917.			1918.			1919.		
	Cases.	Deaths.	Rate.	Cases.	Deaths.	Rate.	Cases.	Deaths.	Rate.	Cases.	Deaths.	Rate.
January ..	41	5	4·11	125	10	7·18	157	8	8·31	28	6	1·72
February ..	62	3	5·99	132	6	7·11	117	7	6·23	30	7	2·51
March ..	128	6	11·15	143	5	7·24	96	7	5·05	—	—	—
April ..	102	3	1·42	119	8	5·86	107	14	5·28	—	—	—
May ..	140	1	10·47	168	13	8·27	125	6	6·13	—	—	—
June ..	118	7	8·08	206	10	9·95	135	9	6·68	—	—	—
July ..	99	—	6·40	156	4	7·39	117	4	5·48	—	—	—
August ..	108	—	6·83	167	11	7·89	124	6	5·85	—	—	—
September ..	31	3	1·95	130	5	6·14	62	2	3·10	—	—	—
October ..	97	5	6·10	104	7	4·92	71	3	3·65	—	—	—
November ..	69	4	4·30	111	4	5·47	62	2	3·28	—	—	—
December ..	139	4	8·42	99	8	5·15	48	6	2·57	—	—	—

TABLE I (B).

Incidence and Mortality in Indian Troops, Indian Native Labour Corps and Portuguese Troops.

	Indian Troops								Indian Native Labour Corps				Portuguese Troops			
	1916.		1917.		1918.		1919.		1917.		1918.		1917.		1918.	
	Cases.	Deaths.	Cases.	Deaths.	Cases.	Deaths.	Cases.	Deaths.	Cases.	Deaths.	Cases.	Deaths.	Cases.	Deaths.	Cases.	Deaths.
January	18	1	2	—	21	—	13	3			13	1			29	4
February	22	1	15	—	15	3	26	1			10	—			14	5
March	17	—	20	3	10	3					25	6			7	2
April	18	1	42	1	3	3					30	9	6	1	—	—
May	39	—	37	—	7	2					45	10	6	—	4	—
June	31	1	16	2	13	2					9	16	6	—	15	—
July	21	—	20	20	15	1			3	2	7	6	5	2	3	2
August	7	—	30	11	13	1			11	6	2	1	2	7	2	7
September	4	—	22	—	8	1			5	—	3	3	10	—	—	—
October	2	—	12	3	11	—			1	1	2	1	10	3	—	—
November	—	—	8	3	8	3			2	—	2	—	10	5	—	—
December	1	—	11	1	12	5			6	1	1	1	15	3	—	—
Average Annual Strength	12,298		11,531		14,551				18,436		10,490		16,500		33,000	

TABLE I (c).

Incidence and Mortality in Kaffirs, Cape Boys and Chinese Labour Corps.

	Kaffirs.				Cape Boys.						Chinese Labour Corps.					
	1917.		1918.		1917.		1918.		1919.		1917.		1918.		1919.	
	Cases.	Deaths.	Cases.	Deaths.	Cases.	Deaths.	Cases.	Deaths.	Cases.	Deaths.	Cases.	Deaths.	Cases.	Deaths.	Cases.	Deaths.
January	7	1	18	15	1	—	1	—	3	3	—	—	29	4	3	8
February	4	2	11	11	—	—	3	—	4	2	—	—	13	9	57	4
March	4	4	18	11	—	—	3	—	—	—	—	—	26	11	—	—
April	14	—	14	13	—	—	5	—	—	—	1	—	21	8	—	—
May	12	7	14	15	1	1	7	3	—	—	2	—	44	19	—	—
June	19	7	13	13	—	—	7	—	—	—	4	1	28	8	—	—
July	15	8	5	11	—	—	7	1	—	—	5	—	36	18	—	—
August	15	5	13	5	1	—	4	3	—	—	—	2	30	8	—	—
September	16	14	5	—	—	—	4	1	—	—	6	1	29	8	—	—
October	11	7	—	—	—	—	4	1	—	—	4	3	34	14	—	—
November	9	7	—	—	3	—	8	1	—	—	18	5	25	6	—	—
December	18	13	—	—	5	1	7	3	—	—	16	7	26	10	—	—
Average Annual Strength	11,308		5,948		966		1,351				31,935		93,797			

and middle-aged British males. The actual findings fell short of the normal by 18·4 per cent., the equivalent of a loss of 446,225 men.

Armies levied from an industrial population of poor physique and subjected to a severe strain under conditions calculated to facilitate the spread of " respiratory infection " might have been expected to show high rates of incidence and mortality from tuberculosis, and it might have been anticipated that the rates would have increased each year as the physical standard fell and the regulations for the rejection of tuberculous recruits became less stringent. The monthly incidence and mortality, together with the case-rate per 100,000 from January 1916 to the end of February 1919, for the British armies in France and Flanders, are given in Table I (A),* and it will be seen at a glance that both incidence and mortality were very low. Further, the remarkable fact comes to light that the incidence-rate per year per 100,000 of strength falls instead of rising from 1917 to 1918, at a time when the standard of recruiting was lowered.

It is of interest to consider the clinical type of tuberculosis amongst those cases that were diagnosed as suffering from this disease in the British medical units in France and Flanders. An investigation into this question was carried out by the A.D.M.S., (Sanitation), at G.H.Q. in 1917 and the results for British troops are given in Table II (a). It will be seen that 91·3 per cent. of all the cases notified were pulmonary. On consulting the Eighty-Second Annual Report of the Registrar-General (1919), it will be found that the mortality from pulmonary cases amongst males of age groups 20 to 45 amounts to 12,356, while the total number of deaths from tuberculosis of all kinds is 13,484. Thus, the mortality from pulmonary tuberculosis in the male population of England under home conditions amounts to 91·6 per cent. of the total, a figure corresponding closely to the incidence ratio in France. It would therefore seem that the elimination of infective individuals by careful medical examination and rejection of clinically recognizable cases had but little effect in altering the proportion of cases of tuberculous disease of the respiratory tract. This raises the interesting question as to whether the cases diagnosed as pulmonary tuberculosis in France were mainly the result of infection contracted while on active service or due rather to

* All the statistical tables in this chapter are compiled from information supplied by Major-General W. W. O. Beveridge when A.D.M.S. (Sanitation), G.H.Q., France.

TABLE II.

Table of Incidence by Clinical Types in various Age Groups, British Expeditionary Force, France and Flanders, 1917.

Variety.	Age Group.							Age not stated.	Total cases.	Percentage.
	-20.	21-24.	25-29.	30-34.	35-39.	40-44.	45-			
(a) British Troops—										
Pulmonary (T B +)	126	276	284	198	146	97	30	23	1,180 }	91·3
Pulmonary (Clin.)	43	76	72	56	55	12	9	13	336 }	
Glandular ..	5	8	4	4	2	1	—	—	24	1·4
Meningeal ..	10	8	4	1	—	—	—	1	24	1·4
Bones and joints..	5	4	2	2	—	—	—	1	14	0·84
Abdominal ..	16	11	6	4	2	—	—	3	42	2·5
Testicle	2	5	7	5	3	2	—	—	24	1·4
Miliary	3	6	5	—	1	—	—	1	16	0·96
Totals ..	210	394	384	270	209	112	39	42	1,660	—
(b) Indian Troops—										
Pulmonary (T B +).	14	7	10	12	4	3	—	—	50 }	44·6
Pulmonary (Clin.)	9	10	18	13	4	—	1	—	55 }	
Glandular ..	19	29	26	17	5	4	3	—	103	43·8
Meningeal ..	1	—	—	1	—	—	—	—	2	0·85
Bones and joints..	2	—	—	1	—	—	—	—	3	1·28
Abdominal ..	4	4	8	4	1	1	—	—	22	9·3
Totals ..	49	50	62	48	14	8	4	—	235	—
(c) Indian Labour Corps—										
Pulmonary (T B +).	1	2	4	1	2	—	—	—	10 }	78·6
Pulmonary (Clin.)	2	2	4	2	2	—	—	—	12 }	
Glandular ..	—	1	1	1	1	—	—	—	4	14·3
Meningeal ..	—	—	1	—	—	—	1	—	2	7·1
Totals ..	3	5	10	4	5	—	1	—	28	—
(d) Portuguese Troops										
Pulmonary (T B +).	—	35	17	2	1	—	—	1	56 }	97·2
Pulmonary (Clin.)	—	9	1	1	—	—	—	1	12 }	
Meningeal *..	—	1	—	—	—	—	—	—	1	1·4
Abdominal ..	—	1	—	—	—	—	—	—	1	1·4
Totals ..	—	46	18	3	1	—	—	2	70	—

TABLE II.—contd.

Variety.	Age Group.							Age not sta-ted.	Total Cases.	Per-cent-age.
	-20.	21-24.	25-29.	30-34.	35-39.	40-44.	45-			
(e) *Cape Boys*—										
Pulmonary (T B +).	2	1	—	—	—	—	—	—	3 } 58·4	
Pulmonary (Clin.)	1	2	1	—	—	—	—	—	4 }	
Glandular ..	—	1	—	2	—	—	—	—	3	25·0
Bones and joints..	—	1	1	—	—	—	—	—	2	16·6
Totals ..	3	5	2	2	—	—	—	—	12	—
(f) *Kaffirs*—										
Pulmonary (T B +).	5	8	15	6	18	13	8	4	77 } 91·5	
Pulmonary (Clin.)	6	4	18	5	9	3	8	—	53 }	
Glandular ..	—	1	—	1	1	—	—	—	3	2·1
Abdominal ..	—	—	2	2	1	—	2	—	7	5·0
Miliary	—	1	—	—	1	—	—	—	2	1·5
Totals ..	11	14	35	14	30	16	18	4	142	—

the lighting up of old latent infections under the stress of war conditions. It is difficult to obtain good evidence upon this point, but one fact at least points strongly to the conclusion that the majority of cases were due to the re-activation of latent tuberculosis. This fact is that no less than 77·8 per cent. of all the pulmonary cases were found to have tubercle bacilli in the sputum. In the rapid and acute parenchymatous tuberculosis of freshly infected adults free from previous tuberculous disease, there is less time for cavitation and less tendency to a " positive " sputum in the early stages. In Indian troops in France, for instance, the positive sputa only amounted to 47·6 per cent. of the pulmonary cases and in Kaffirs to 59 per cent. A similar observation has been made by Ch. Roubier in a paper entitled " Les Formes Cliniques de la Tuberculose thoracique chez les troupes exotiques importés en France pendant la guerre." This author calls attention to the relative rarity of tubercle bacilli in the sputum in the pulmonary tuberculosis of Senegalese troops. It is almost certain that a high proportion of positive sputa recorded shortly after admission to hospital—and it must be remembered that British soldiers diagnosed as tuberculous were rapidly trans- ferred to home territory—is an index of relative chronicity of clinical type, the type that is characterized by pulmonary ulceration with well-marked cavities opening into bronchioles and bronchi. That some such factor was operative amongst the British soldiers found suffering from tuberculosis in France is further supported by the fact that the percentage of positive sputa was lower, 74 per cent., in the cases under 20 than in the aggregate of all age groups.

It may be assumed that a large proportion of the British soldiers passed for service had already been exposed to tuberculous infection. Von Pirquet tests carried out by Cummins on military patients at Netley Hospital in 1909 showed as high a proportion of positives amongst patients clinically free from tuberculosis as amongst those actually suffering from the disease, and similar investigations on a large scale throughout Europe have established the fact that the adult population of large cities shows from 80 to 90 per cent. of positives to this test. *Post-mortem* examinations point to the same conclusions. Captain T. H. G. Shore, who was in charge of the mortuary at Etaples during the war, has supplied some notes of the *post-mortem* results recorded by him, and these are reproduced as Tables III and IV. These tables have reference to thoracic and

TABLE III.

Tuberculosis of Thoracic and Abdominal Glands.

Total P.Ms.*		Thoracic.		Abdominal.		Both.	
1,579	British　　.. 　　..	36	*10*	46	*5*	1	*3*
220	Canadian　　.. 　　..	3	*2*	3	*2*	..	*1*
93	Australian　　.. 　　..	1	*1*	2	*1*	..	*2*
56	New Zealand　　..	1	*3*	1	*2*	..	*1*
17	South African　　..	..	..	1			
4	Newfoundlanders　　..	..	*1*				
13	British West Indians	..	*1*	..	..	..	*3*
7	South African Native Labour Corps.	..	*2*				
10	Portuguese　　.. 　　..	..	*1*				
16	U.S.A.　　.. 　　..	1					
31	German Prisoners of War.	1	..	1			

Figures in italics = cases dying from tuberculosis.
Other figures = cases dying from some other cause.
* Total P.Ms. are the totals in which anything approaching a complete *post-mortem* examination was made. Many others were only partial and done for some other particular reason, tuberculosis being disregarded.

TABLE IV.

Tuberculosis of Thoracic Glands in British Troops.

P.M. No.			
17	Bronchial glands ..	<——	Cavities in both apices. Broncho-pneumonia.
*185	Bifurcation gland ..	——>	Broncho-pneumonia. Laryngitis. Enteritis. Peritonitis.
362	Bronchial glands ..	——>	General miliary tuberculosis.
*494	Mediastinal glands..	——>	Miliary tuberculosis, left lung. Meningitis.
807	Mediastinal gland ..	<——	Old lesion, right base, lighted up by wound of same lung. Miliary tuberculosis.
882	Mediastinal gland (calcified).		Caseous kidney. Cystitis. Miliary tuberculosis.
1,726	Bronchial gland ..		Peritonitis.
*1,751	Bronchial gland ..	——>	Broncho-pneumonia. General miliary.
(?)2,073	Mediastinal gland ..	——>	Broncho-pneumonia. Pneumothorax.
2,401	Mediastinal gland ..	<——	Caseous right apex. Recent pleurisy (also non-tuberculous nephritis).

Deaths from tuberculosis = 10.
Deaths from other causes = 36.
* Possibly acute hilus infections.

abdominal glandular lesions only and so do not indicate the total number of *post-mortem* examinations in which traces of tuberculosis might have been found, but they show that of 101 cases of thoracic and abdominal tuberculous adenitis in British soldiers, 83 were found in patients dying from some other cause than tuberculosis. Opie, in an analysis of 66 *post-mortem* examinations on British soldiers who died in France, records the findings of 18 cases with caseous or calcified mesenteric glands, no less than 27 per cent. of the total. British troops suffered but little from manifest tuberculosis while on active service and the deaths from this cause overseas were inconsiderable. There was but little evidence of fresh exposure to infection while on active service since the proportion of pulmonary to other forms remained the same as at home. The high percentage of positive sputa points rather to the lighting up of old foci than to the acquisition of new infection while on service. There is every reason, therefore, to suppose that a large proportion of British soldiers possessed latent foci of tuberculous infection when they entered the army.

If one were to take into consideration only the figures collected in France and Flanders for British troops, one might arrive at the conclusion that tuberculosis mattered but little as a disease of armies. But there is another side to the picture. While the total number of cases of tuberculosis recorded amongst British troops in France was only 4,184 during the whole period from August 1914 to February 1919, the numbers of invalided and discharged found by the Pensions Boards to be suffering from tuberculosis were very large. It is impossible at the present time to obtain the exact figures, but the following facts have been obtained from the Ministry of Pensions.

Up to March 1920, all cases of tuberculosis were classified under "chest complaints" except in the case of officers who were shown as suffering from tuberculosis. From 1st April, 1920, to 31st March, 1921, the Ministry of Pensions awarded 2,641 pensions for pulmonary tuberculosis, 306 for non-pulmonary and 1,494 for tuberculosis "not differentiated," making a total of 4,441 awards for this disease. The total new awards for all causes during that period were 95,836, so that awards for tuberculosis represented 4·53 per cent. of all new awards. Prior to April 1920, all that can be said for certain is that 2,957 pensions were given to officers suffering from tuberculosis and that pensions were given to 95,132 "other ranks" for "chest complaints." A total of 1,182,000 new awards had been granted up to 31st March, 1920, and if the same proportion holds as between tuberculosis and other causes, then 4·53 per cent. of this total, or 53,544 cases, must have been tuberculosis. Adding to this the 4,441 cases pensioned between 1st April, 1920, and 31st March, 1921, a total of 57,985 cases of tuberculosis pensioned up to that date is arrived at. There is no record of the total deaths that should be added to this number.

The figures, then, must be admitted to be very defective, but yet they give a fairly clear picture of tuberculosis as a military disease under the conditions of modern warfare amongst European troops. It is not the fulminating and fatal type of phthisis popularly known as "galloping consumption" neither is it a disease of small importance that can be ignored by the army medical authorities. Rather is it the slow and relentless progression of an invasive process, held latent at first by the resistance acquired through the constant small infections incident to modern industrial life, but finally prevailing when the hardships and privations of war are thrown into the balance. The story is told not so much in the number of deaths as in the loss of industrial efficiency, the sinking of the individual life from an active self-supporting one to an existence depending upon state aid and requiring the sheltered conditions of a sanatorium or colony.

Stated briefly, the tuberculosis of the British and Dominion troops during the war showed the characters of an environmental rather than of an infective disease. It seemed in the majority of cases rather the upsetting of a balance between pre-existing infection and acquired resistance than the inception of an acute infective process in soil hitherto unassailed by the tubercle bacillus.

A point which might be quoted as evidence against this conclusion is the undoubted fact that penetrating gunshot wounds of the chest led to little or no tendency to the reawakening of old tuberculous infection. Captain J. B. McDougall has recorded a series of 139 cases of chest wound traced by him after recovery from their wounds. In only one case was it possible to associate a subsequent tuberculous process with the chest injury. Similar conclusions were reached by Bernard and Mantoux in the French army from an investigation of 475 cases of chest injury. Observations to the same effect were made by E. Sergent. But while penetrating wounds of the chest are clearly negligible as a factor in lighting up old infection, except, as pointed out by Sergent, when the wound actually involves a "latent" focus directly, the same is not true of contusions of the chest. Here the injury, being of a kind to compress quiescent foci and perhaps distribute their contents into the surrounding healthy tissues, might be expected to do more damage, and as a matter of fact Bernard and Mantoux found that no less than 6 per cent. of the cases with chest contusion developed tuberculosis as a result. Here there could be no question of fresh infection and the theory of the "upsetting of a balance between pre-existing infection and acquired resistance" receives strong confirmation.

When one examines the manifestations of the same disease amongst "exotic" troops and labour corps, recruited from races less urbanized than those of Europe, a totally different clinical and epidemiological picture is found. Tables I (B) and I (C), illustrating the incidence and mortality from tuberculosis amongst Indian troops, the Indian native labour corps, the African and the Chinese labour units, speak for themselves and serve to illustrate the contrast between the phenomena of this disease in relatively "virgin soil" and its manifestations in the already infected soil of Europeans.

It may safely be said that the physique of the Indian divisions was of the highest order. Sikhs and Gurkhas, hill-men bred far from the deleterious conditions of industrial and town life, members of military races inheriting the tradition of war, such were the men who came to France in 1915. To what extent had these soldiers been previously exposed to infection? An exact answer is hard to find, but it is certain that their exposure must have been far less than that of British troops. The following quotation from a recent work by Dr. A. Lancaster gives an accurate idea of the conditions obtaining in that country : " In India, as in all parts of the world, there is a remarkable degree of variation in the prevalence of consumption in different regions. There are some more or less isolated areas where even yet tuberculosis appears to be almost non-existent ; others where it certainly was so within the memory of reliable observers who have watched the disease spreading widely as communication with more populous regions has become more free." It would appear that the degree of previous exposure amongst Indian troops must have varied widely according to race and locality, but in the aggregate it was probably slight. A glance at Tables I (B) and V will show that both incidence and mortality were very much greater than amongst British troops, though not quite so high as amongst Africans. But the tuberculosis of Indian troops and Indian labour units in France and Flanders possessed one character which differed not only from that of the British soldiers but also from the African labour units. Table II (b) shows that there was a remarkable increase in the " glandular " and " abdominal " cases as compared with the records of other races. The tuberculosis of bones and joints was also higher, but such lesions develop slowly after infection and the records of one year are likely to understate the true degree of surgical tuberculosis. Here there is a phenomenon which at once recalls the characters of tuberculosis in childhood as it is known in England, though the almost complete absence of tuberculous meningitis constitutes a point of difference. This observation raises many interesting questions. It is well known that glandular and abdominal tuberculosis in childhood in Great Britain is closely associated with the drinking of infected milk, a large percentage of glandular lesions being due to bovine tubercle bacilli.

The Indian races drink large quantities of milk, but it is generally recognized that the cattle of India are practically free from tuberculosis. The evidence cited to prove this point by Dr. Lancaster in the work already quoted is conclusive. It would appear that the Indian soldiers in France purchased large quantities of milk in the villages in which they were billeted, and it cannot be doubted that this milk was frequently infected. It is tempting to speculate as to whether their marked liability to glandular infections was not connected with the ingestion of infected milk by adults who were hitherto " virgin soil " to the bovine bacillus. It is interesting to note that the tuberculous meningitis of childhood in England is chiefly human in origin. It is to be hoped that light may yet be thrown upon this point by the search for bovine strains amongst glandular cases returned to India from the European theatres of war. Colonel Glen Liston and his assistants have examined many strains from tuberculous adenitis arising in natives in India without finding any instance of bovine infection, and the discovery of a large proportion of such strains amongst men returning from France would be of great interest in this connection.

In Table V the incidence and mortality per annual average strength of 10,000 for 1918 is set forth in such a way as to illustrate in a striking manner the differences between the racial groups that were mingled together in the zone of the British armies in France and Flanders. It will be noticed that the mortality and, as a rule, the case incidence is lowest amongst the more urbanized and highest amongst the more isolated and scattered peoples.

TABLE V.

Annual Incidence and Mortality from Tuberculosis per 10,000 *of Average Annual Strength in Seven Racial Types of the British Expeditionary Force, France and Flanders,* 1918.

	Cases per 10,000.	Deaths per 10,000.
British and Dominion Troops	6·056	0·398
Portuguese Troops *	33·636	9·242
Chinese Native Labour Corps	36·355	13·433
Indian Troops	93·464	17·249
Indian Native Labour Corps	142·040	53·384
South African Native Labour Corps (Kaffirs) † ..	290·665	221·923
Cape Colony Labour Corps (Cape Boys) ..	444·115	103·627

* On a basis of eight months.
† On a basis of nine months.

The number of cases amongst the African native labour units is exceedingly high. Unfortunately adequate *post-mortem* records of tuberculosis amongst them are not available. The

TABLE VI.

Fatal Tuberculosis in Native Races.

	P.M. No.	Lungs.	Pleura: Actual Tubercles.	Periton-itis.	Liver.	Spleen.	Kidney.	Glands.	Larynx.
Maori	1,752	Cavity right apex; caseous deposits; miliary.	+	+	+	++	+ and right supra-renal.	..	+
	237	Fibroid apex; cavity; broncho-pneumonia.	Left effusion, 3 pints. +	−	−	−	−	Pulmonary on both sides.	
	423	− (Tubercular pericarditis).	Bilateral effusions. ++	−	−	−	−	Mediastinal massive.	
South African Native Labour Corps.	521	Left, extensive caseous pneumonia (tubercular pericarditis).	Right only. +	+	++	+	+		
	892	..	..	..	..	+ Calcified.	..	Shot by sentry.	

TABLE VI—*continued*.

P.M. No.	Lungs.	Pleura: actual tubercles.	Peritonitis,	Liver.	Spleen.	Kidney.	Glands.	Larynx.
1,135	(?)	++ Bilateral effusions.	+	+	−	−	Mediastinal.	
1,424	—	+ Left effusion, 1½ pints.	++	+	+	+	Neck; pulmonary, abdominal.	
1,671	Left, cavity due to extension from mediastinal glands; rupture into bronchus, miliary, right lower lobe.	++	++	+	++	+ Tubercular abscess, right.	Mediastinal. +	
1,945	— (Tubercular pericarditis).	++ Bilateral fibro-caseous.	+·	+	++	+	Pulmonary.	

British West Indian

records of Captain Shore contain a few notes which are of great
value in this connection, and it is from them that it has been
possible to furnish the information set forth in Table VI.
Here it will be seen that the tuberculosis was generalized
throughout the organs in the majority of his cases. In one
instance only is there a record of fibrosis, and there is one case
of a calcified gland in a man shot accidentally by a sentry.
The impression gained is that in these cases the disease ran an
acute and untrammelled course to a fatal issue, and this
impression is strengthened by the fact that the disease was, in
Kaffirs especially, almost invariably fatal within a few months
of its onset.

In the Portuguese troops, coming from a country where
industrialism is less developed than in England, both incidence
and mortality were much higher than amongst the British. In
the Chinese labour units the number both of cases and of
deaths was greater than amongst the Portuguese though less
than amongst the East Indians.

While our records are far less thorough than those kept for
their " exotic " troops by the French army medical authorities,
it may be safely stated that the conclusions to be drawn are
the same as those brought so clearly to light in the reports of
A. Borrel, Ch. Roubier and others. Amongst these primitive
races, gathered from remote countries, tuberculosis was not a
slow or chronic process, not an "environmental" disease, but
an acutely infectious and rapidly fatal malady recalling in its
clinical manifestations the progress of tuberculosis as produced
in susceptible laboratory animals by massive inoculations with
the germ. This marked contrast between the behaviour of a
pathogenic agent amongst races bred up under totally different
conditions though comparable in age, in the calorie value of
their food and in their conditions of housing or shelter while in
France, is an important fact for consideration in the epidemiology of tuberculosis.

BIBLIOGRAPHY.

Bernard & Mantoux	Traumatismes de guerre et tuberculose pulmonaire.	Bull. et Mém. Soc. Méd. des Hôp. de Paris, 1917, 3ᵉ Sér., Vol. xli, p. 683.
Lancaster	Tuberculosis in India ..	Lond., 1920 : Butterworth & Co.
McDougall	Traumatic Pulmonary Tuberculosis.	Tubercle,1920,Vol. i, p. 353.
Opie & Anderson ..	First Infection with Tuberculosis by way of Lungs.	American Review of Tuberculosis,1920, Vol. iv, p. 629.

Roubier	Les formes cliniques de la tuberculose thoracique chez les troupes exotiques importées en France pendant la guerre.	Gaz. des Hôpitaux, 1920, Vol. xciii, p. 1333.
Sergent	L'Influence des traumatismes sur les épanchements pleuraux.	Jl. de Méd. et de Chirurgie Pratique, 1916, Vol. lxxxvii, p. 163.

CHAPTER XVII.

TRENCH FEVER.

THE disease now known as trench fever was recognized first in Flanders in the spring of 1915, and was already well established amongst the British armies by midsummer of that year. The earliest published description was that of Graham, who noted in two cases the characteristic tendency to relapse. Hunt and Rankin followed shortly afterwards with a more complete clinical account, and also gave the results of some bacteriological examinations. It was in their paper that the name " trench fever " first was seen in print. The initial work attempting to deal with the essential pathology of the disease, and also the first account in which two clinical types were distinguished, was that of McNee, Renshaw and Brunt, which did not appear until February 1916. Their work had been begun in the early summer of 1915, and the successful transmission of the disease from man to man was accomplished in September 1915.

The name trench fever came into use among the soldiers themselves and was adopted directly from them. It was only after a long time that it was accepted in the official nomenclature of diseases, and in the interval was subjected to much criticism. It was pointed out, for example, in the later years of the war that the disease occurred in men who had never been near the trenches, and even in men who had never left England. The name can be defended, however, by those who early investigated the disease from the fact that the fever undoubtedly first made its appearance in the trench zone. During 1915 it was confined to men in this zone, and to the personnel of field ambulances and casualty clearing stations who by reason of their duties came into close contact with sick and wounded men direct from the trenches. Later, with the great mixing of troops and the prevalence and mixing of lice, the disease became widespread along all the lines of communication.

It is of some interest to attempt to trace the origin of the disease in the armies. This point has been entered into in considerable detail in the report of the American Commission on Trench Fever, but without any noteworthy conclusions being arrived at. McNee towards the end of 1915, in an attempt to trace the history of the disease, made extensive personal enquiry, and received verbal and written reports both from doctors practising in Flanders and from some of the local landowners whose ancestors had lived for many years in the area. Nothing, however, suggesting the clinical picture of trench fever was contained in their reports, and almost all the accounts of the fevers of Flanders dealt with typhoid and malarial infections.

It is quite impossible to know now whether the disease first commenced and assumed epidemic proportions in British or French troops. Certainly it was widely recognized and studied on the British side long before notice was taken by French writers of this peculiar fever. It is of interest in this connection to mention the fact that McNee saw a French soldier on leave from the trenches in a typical relapse of the fever as early as the end of July 1915. Unfortunately no record was kept of the sector of the French front in which he fell ill, but he had been mobilized at the outbreak of war and had never been in contact with British troops until he was given leave of absence after his first bout of fever.

At the time when trench fever was first noticed among the British troops, the variety of races holding the trenches on the allied side was already considerable. Along with the British troops was the whole Indian Corps. On the British left, between them and the Belgians, the French troops included many colonials, Turcos, Senegalese, and so on. Many of the Belgians, moreover, had already served in their African possessions. Knowing how long a patient with trench fever may remain a carrier of the disease in his blood, who can say what little known tropical or sub-tropical disease may have been spread broadcast among the virgin population afforded by the troops, and where or in what race of soldiers in Flanders the earliest cases of the fever arose?

The disease was confined to France at first, but the movements of troops gradually extended it to many of the other scenes of British military operations. It seems certain that the fever was carried east by the 27th and 28th Divisions when they were transferred from France to Salonika in the autumn of 1915. From available accounts, however, this fever does not appear ever to have occurred among British troops in the East in epidemic proportions, except perhaps in Salonika. In Egypt it was only met with late in the war and was never serious.

As regards trench fever among French troops, the first written account appears to be that of Beauchant, published in

November 1916, but French medical officers had been discussing the disease long before that date. It is curious to find how few investigations of the disease are described in French medical literature, where, however, the same nomenclature as the British—*fièvre des tranchées*—is employed.

On the German and Austrian fronts the disease was quickly recognized, being described by Werner in March 1916 and by Hiss in July of the same year. In German writings the fever is known under a variety of names—*Febris Wolhynica, Febris Quintana, Fünftagefieber, Werner-Hissche Krankheit, Maas Fieber*, etc.

In 1917 Sisto and Pari described the same fever as occurring among Italian troops.

Although no attempt will be made to give a systematic clinical account of the fever, certain points in the history of the epidemic evolution of the disease are both interesting and important.

In all the early cases of the disease, seen before July 1915, the fever was a short one, lasting as a rule five to seven days and followed in the majority of cases, but not in all, by a single short relapse. Once the relapse was over the patient felt well immediately and returned to duty almost at once. The invaliding from trench fever at this period was therefore *nil*.

In July 1915 was seen the first of what was described by McNee, Renshaw and Brunt as the long or relapsing type of fever, where the initial period of pyrexia was shorter and the relapses more frequent and severe. The first case of this kind, observed by Sir Wilmot Herringham and Major McNee, was very puzzling at the time and was thought at first to have no relationship with the shorter type of febrile disease. Up to December 1915, when the paper referred to above was completely written, about twenty similar cases had been seen. It was eventually concluded, following the experimental transmissions from man to man by the blood, that both the long and short types of fever were one and the same disease. This has been accepted by all subsequent writers, but later it became obvious that all kinds of intermediate types existed, so that the above classical types could not be closely upheld. In the summer of 1916 Hunt and McNee were astonished to find that nearly all their new cases fell into the long category, and this continued for the remainder of the war in casualty clearing station work. It was evident, however, that as the disease rapidly assumed epidemic proportions and medical officers became aware of its characters, the short types of the fever were retained with their units and treated there. Only the long relapsing fevers required evacuation, and as these increased in number with the growth of the epidemic, the medical wards of the casualty clearing stations soon became full of them. Even then it is impossible to think that during 1916 the invaliding rate of such cases was the same as later. Many if not all of them were retained and returned to full duty, without ever again becoming casualties from the disease. In fact, McNee is strongly of opinion, founded on a very wide experience of the disease from its first recognition until the end of the war, that as the epidemic developed the severity of the disease and its virulence gradually increased, so that in the later years of the war the disease was very much more serious for the individual than it was at the beginning.

Another clinical point is of interest in the same connection. During the first year after the disease was recognized the spleen was never found to be enlarged, although this point was investigated by many observers fully competent to detect the presence of this sign. In the later years enlargement of the spleen was a feature of the majority of cases. This also may be taken as an indication of the gradual evolution in the severity of the disease as the epidemic progressed.

During the early part of the war none of the exhaustion sequelæ of trench fever, such as neurasthenia, tachycardia and so on, were ever observed. Towards the end they were unfortunately a source of great trouble. The chronicity of the disease at this period may also be accounted for by the increased virulence of the infection, and perhaps also in part by the exhaustion of the troops by the long campaign.

With regard to the history of the various investigations on trench fever, carried out during the war among British troops, at first all the work done was carried out by isolated individuals, chiefly because of its scientific interest. As the epidemic progressed, its importance as a source of wastage was only slowly recognized, and it was not until 1917 that a Trench Fever Committee was appointed by the Director-General of the British armies in France. Soon afterwards, at the end of the same year, the American Red Cross Society was instrumental in forming an American Commission to investigate the disease, and by agreement the British and American work was concentrated in the same British hospital at St. Pol. About the same time, the War Office in London appointed a Commission to investigate the cases invalided to England, and here again a fortunate arrangement enabled the patients to be collected together at Mount

Vernon Hospital, Hampstead, while the resources of the Lister Institute of Preventive Medicine were also available for special parts of the work.

The important results obtained by these organized commissions in so short a period of time provide a lesson to be borne in mind for any future investigations of a similar nature.

Pathology.

General Bacteriological Investigations. — Since at first a strong suspicion arose that the cases of trench fever belonged in some way to the enteric groups of fevers, much of the early work in pathology was directed towards proving or disproving this hypothesis. During 1915 this task was relatively simple, since the troops were only inoculated against *Bacillus typhosus*, the triple vaccine containing also *B. paratyphosus A* and *B. paratyphosus B* not having been introduced at that time. Hence agglutination tests were of great service in definitely excluding the two last infections. For the exclusion of a true typhoid infection, blood cultures in bile-salt broth, and bile were much in use by different observers, but all were negative. Examination of fæces and urine in the later stages of the disease by the usual plating methods were also fruitless. In addition, a number of blood cultures were made on a wide variety of media in the general search for a bacterial cause in the blood, but no positive results were obtained.

After the formation of the British and American commissions at the end of 1917, a further complete investigation of the disease in British troops was undertaken, on general bacteriological principles, in which the possible connection of the disease with the enteric group of fevers was not lost sight of, in spite of the large amount of evidence already accumulated against it. By this time the troops were almost universally inoculated with the triple vaccine, so that the ordinary Widal reaction was impossible. On this account, the agglutination methods introduced by Dreyer for the detection of typhoid and paratyphoid infections in inoculated individuals were adopted, and given a considerable trial. Here again no evidence supporting a typhoid basis for the disease could be discovered. Workers with the American Red Cross Commission also took the opportunity of completely re-investigating the disease by general bacteriological methods, using culture media of various kinds, under both aërobic and anaërobic conditions. Their results were also completely negative.

Positive results from blood cultures have been recorded by very few observers, but their results, although well controlled by others, have been confirmed by none.

Riemer found a short spirochæte, with four spiral turns, present in very scanty numbers in blood films. In anaërobic cultures in serum, he claims to have obtained cultures of this organism. Control experiments by Sundell and Nankivell, using Riemer's own cultural technique, gave no confirmation of his results.

Houston and McCloy cultivated an enterococcus from the blood of three cases of trench fever, and the same organism from the urine and sputum of other cases. In view of the multitude of sterile cultures by other workers this finding must be considered accidental.

Hæmatology.—From the beginning much attention was paid to the examination of blood films in the new disease, both in the search for a parasite and to discover any alterations in the blood counts and morphological appearances of the cells, which might be of diagnostic value.

It may be said at once that the great majority of the many workers at this disease have failed to detect a parasite of any kind, using wet and dry films, diverse methods of staining and fixation, dark ground illumination, and so on.

A variety of parasites have, however, been written of by others. Some of these findings can be definitely excluded by subsequent work, while the remainder have received no uniform confirmation. A few examples may be quoted.

In 1916 Hiss, Zollenkopf, Töpfer, and in 1917 Jungmann and Kuczynski, all describe in blood films bodies which appear from the descriptions to be of similar nature. These bodies are dumb-bell-shaped, measure 1 or 2 microns in length and resemble diplococci or bipolar-staining short bacilli. Hiss describes them as free in the plasma, and more rarely within the red blood corpuscles. Zollenkopf found them in the interior of the red blood cells, and notes that they are most numerous during the attacks of fever.

In view of the discovery of closely similar bodies in blood films from cases of typhus fever and Rocky Mountain spotted fever, the search for these bipolar structures must be continued in any future work.

Riemer has, as already stated, claimed to have found a spirochæte in blood films, and to have cultivated the organism in an anaërobic medium.

Dimond described a protozoan, of the nature of a hæmo-gregarine, in blood films and in material obtained by puncture of the lungs and spleen. It was shown by Henry, however, that an error had been made in that the same flagellate could be obtained from filter candles through which distilled water had been passed, the organism being evidently a contamination in the distilled water used by Dimond for laking the thick films employed.

The earliest description of the blood picture in trench fever was given in the paper by Rankin and Hunt, who noted the average leucocyte count in twenty-four cases to be 10,500, with variations ranging between 4,700 and 22,000. The number of the leucocytes was not found by them to vary with the tem-perature to any great extent. Morphologically the only real abnormality found was a slight relative increase in the lympho-cytes. No mention is made of morphological changes in the red corpuscles.

McNee, Renshaw and Brunt also investigated the hæmatology of the fever, and found leucocyte counts varying from 5,200 up to 18,200. In differential counts a slight relative increase in the lymphocytes, both large and small, was observed. As regards the red cells one morphological change was met with very frequently. This was the presence of polychromatophile cells above the normal in size, and especially in the relapsing cases well-marked punctate basophilia. In several instances this latter change was so well marked as to require very careful examination to exclude an intracorpuscular parasite. An explanation of these changes was found on making blood counts, since all the men showed a definite defect in the amount of hæmoglobin, the average colour index of this series being 0·8. The finding of punctate basophilia must not, however, in the light of subsequent work by the same authors and others, be taken as a constant feature in the disease, although it was of such frequent occurrence during the course of the work in 1915. During that year the men served for long and continuous periods in the trenches, and the anæmia was evidently a result of these trying circumstances. This view was confirmed during an investigation for quite another purpose in the winter of 1915–16, when the blood counts of samples of men from various regiments were examined in an enquiry into the nature of "trench foot." It was found, during the winter referred to, that the average hæmoglobin percentage of the men in the trenches was little over 70, when tested on an instrument giving a reading of 90 to 95 per cent. with various medical officers who were not in the trenches. It is obvious that the presence of punctate basophilia was accidental, and not an essential feature in the blood picture of the disease.

Later in the war the hæmatology of trench fever was very fully investigated by Perkins and Urwick, whose conclusions were as follows :—

(1) There is no appearance in blood films which is characteristic of the disease.

(2) A single enumeration and differentiation of the leucocytes is often of value as a means of diagnosis from enteric, but cannot afford any reliable evidence that the disease present is trench fever.

(3) Repeated counts carried on through the various phases of the disease produce a composite picture which, though not without exceptions, is so constant that it may be considered characteristic. It consists in a combination of the following features : (a) A marked rise of leucocytes of all three kinds (polymorphs, lymphocytes and large mononuclears) at the time of the febrile relapse. (b) A gradual relative rise in the lymphocytes during the period of convalescence.

Perkins and Urwick also refer to morphological changes in the red corpuscles. As one of the most striking characteristics they note the occurrence in great numbers, especially during a relapse, of the so-called "corps en demi-lune," which had previously been described in association with trench fever by Renaux. This phenomenon was also noted by McNee in the blood films from many cases. As pointed out by Perkins and Urwick, however, these bodies are in no way specific, and are very commonly found in films taken during a malarial paroxysm, and in other conditions associated with very high pyrexia. They noted punctate basophilia in a few cases only, and point out rightly that as a diagnostic feature it has little value. Although they did not attempt to enumerate the blood platelets, they formed the impression that these elements are increased both in number and size, especially during the febrile periods.

Tate and McLeod have studied especially the changes in the white blood corpuscles. While they agreed with the counts of most previous observers they considered that an error was made in interpreting the findings as evidence of a slight relative lymphocytosis. They state that the results published have suffered from insufficient control, chiefly because the normal differential count of the soldier in France cannot be accepted as the normal of the same man at home. They have concluded that under the conditions of war a relative lymphocytosis must be taken as the rule, and that the only essential and in any way characteristic feature of the blood in trench fever is a moderate polymorphonuclear leucocytosis.

Cerebro-spinal Fluid.—In several cases the onset of the fever so closely resembled that of cerebro-spinal meningitis that lumbar puncture was performed. This gave an opportunity of examining the cerebro-spinal fluid in the disease, when it was found that no excess of cells existed and that no other abnormal constituent was present.

Urine.—As regards all ordinary bacteriological examinations the urine was completely negative in the disease. In no case did signs of nephritis develop during the fever, although in severe infections albuminuria, of transient duration and ordinary febrile type, was met with. It must be pointed out, however, that Lloyd, Day, and others, have brought forward what they consider to be evidence that trench fever infection causes damage to the renal tissues, which may be followed at a later date by the onset of "war nephritis." The value of their evidence is difficult to assess, especially as their work was done in the later years of the war, when trench fever was so common. It would be strange, to say the least, if some cases of other infections, such as nephritis, did not give a history of trench fever or suffer from relapses of their former disease during the course of their later malady.

In 1917 Sundell and Nankivell described the occurrence in urine from trench fever cases of a spirochæte, which could be found most easily at the end of the second week of the disease. Patterson also obtained a similar spirochæte in centrifugalized urines. It was soon established, however, by many laboratory workers that these spirochætes could be easily found in the urine of many normal men, being evidently saprophytes growing in the glans and anterior part of the urethra.

Morbid Anatomy.—Fortunately the disease was never fatal, so that no one has ever recorded *post-mortem* findings in a recent or old infection. During the later part of the war, when the disease was so prevalent, McNee began to investigate histologically the spleens of any soldiers dying from wounds, where the organ was found to be notably large. No abnormalities were, however, found, nor was anything suggestive of a parasite ever detected.

Experimental Pathology.

Infectivity of the Blood to Animals.—In the summer of 1915, as soon as McNee and his colleagues began to recognize that this was probably a new disease in no way related to the enteric group of fevers, animal experiments were begun along with the other general pathological investigations. At the time rabbits, white mice and rats were the only animals available, but at a later period guinea-pigs were also used. In none of these experimental animals did pyrexia develop, or any other signs suggestive of a positive inoculation. At autopsy no abnormalities were found.

Similar animal inoculations were repeated later by the members of the American Commission, who used again guinea-pigs, rats and mice. Their results were also negative.

Various observers have, however, reported positive inoculations of animals with the blood of trench fever patients. Their experiments require mention for future reference, even although the results remain unconfirmed.

Hiss has described diplococci or short bipolar-staining rods in the blood of inoculated guinea-pigs.

Da Rocha Lima also states that guinea-pigs can be inoculated with the disease, but that mice are insusceptible.

Jungmann and Kuczynski claim to have produced a fatal infection in wild mice by the intraperitoneal inoculation of whole blood. They give an account of bipolar-staining bodies, which they found both in the inoculated animals and in the blood of the patients as well.

Couvy, Dujarrac and de la Rivière affirm that they obtained positive results with guinea-pigs, and were successful in transmitting the infection from animal to animal. When such animals were killed during the period of pyrexia, spirochætes were found in the liver and kidneys, which they believe can be differentiated from the organism causing spirochætal jaundice, and have a causal relationship to trench fever.

Infectivity of the Blood to Man.—Since animal experiments had proved a failure, and the disease was obviously not dangerous to life, McNee, Renshaw and Brunt resolved in the summer of 1915 to attempt to transmit the disease to man. At first owing to difficulties in collecting volunteers and patients under the same roof the pooled serum from several acute cases seen in the field ambulances was used for an experiment, but without result. Finally it became possible to carry out an inoculation with " whole blood," taken from the vein of a patient directly into a syringe which had been washed out with a solution of sodium citrate and injected forthwith into the vein of a volunteer. This experiment was completely successful, the volunteer passing through a severe and typical attack of the fever. As this was the very first successful transmission, the whole case may be reported in full.

On 2nd September, 1915, a R.A.M.C. orderly, who had been on duty in the ward in which the " trench fever " cases were being kept, was in the middle of a brisk and typical attack of the disease.

At a time when his temperature was 101·4° F., 5 c.c. of his blood were taken into a syringe, previously washed out with citrate solution, and transferred immediately into the veins of Private W. Private W. remained well until 11th September, nine days after the inoculation. On the evening of the third and fourth days his temperature reached 99° F., but he felt perfectly well at the time. On the morning of 11th September he awoke at daybreak, feeling unwell. He had a slight headache and his temperature at 6.45 a.m. was 99·2° F. He got up but could not remain out of bed for longer than an hour, as the headache became more and more severe and he felt cold and " shivery." He returned to bed at 9 a.m. and soon after was attacked by pain, chiefly in the thighs and small of the back. Unlike other cases, he had no pain below the knees. By evening he felt very ill, and at 6.30 p.m. his temperature was 103·8° F. and pulse 88. Next morning he was rather better, the pain being easier, although the headache remained severe. His temperature, too, had fallen, being 99·8° F. in the morning and 100° F. at night. On the third morning his temperature was normal, but the headache remained and the pain did not entirely pass off. The same evening, however, he was perspiring profusely, and felt just as ill as on the first day of the attack. His temperature on this occasion was 100·8° F. The following morning there was again a slight remission, but only for a short time, and during the next few days he was very ill, until the temperature reached normal once more on the seventh day after the onset.

Immediately the temperature became normal he felt comparatively well, and was able to sit up for a short time. His headache was completely relieved, but he still had slight pain in the thighs. Thereafter two definite relapses occurred, the one reaching its acme on 19th September and the other on 23rd September. During these relapses headache and pain in the thighs and back returned with considerable severity, without being, however, quite so severe as at the beginning. It will be observed that one relapse was at its height about four days after the temperature fell to normal on the seventh day, and that the other followed after a precisely similar interval. The subsequent course of the case was towards complete recovery, but it is a noteworthy fact that whenever the temperature rose in the least degree above normal, as, for example, on 15th October, thirty-five days after the initial fever, pain in the thighs returned with severity.

Seven experiments in all were performed with the whole blood, and all of them were successful, whether the intravenous or subcutaneous methods of inoculation were employed. In these experiments the incubation period varied between six and twenty-two days, being shorter when the intravenous method was employed. The blood was shown to be still infective on the twenty-second day of the disease at a time when pyrexia was absent.

The infectivity of whole blood was fully confirmed by the American Commission, who in a series of sixteen cases had only one unsuccessful result. In these experiments the incubation period varied between five and twenty days.

The British Commission also established the constant infectivity of whole blood in a series of six experiments, and were, moreover, able to show in a convincing way that blood from a patient was still infective three hundred days after the onset of his fever.

In further work on the experimental pathology of the disease, the results obtained have been less uniform. It will therefore be best to give a short account of the results in the chief sets of experiments, and then to point out the essential differences between them.

McNee, Renshaw and Brunt, after proving the infectivity of the blood, continued their investigation on the question of what part of the blood contained the virus. These experiments could only be carried out on a very small scale, since the work was in no way aided officially, and volunteers had to be sought for under very restricted conditions by the workers themselves. One man was inoculated intravenously with clear serum. He did not develop the disease, although watched for a long time. Another volunteer was inoculated with serum which owing to a fault in technique was deeply tinged with hæmoglobin. He acquired the disease in typical form. A third man was inoculated with plasma, which was prepared at the same time as the previous experiment and was also hæmoglobin-tinted. He also became infected. Six men were inoculated with serum which had been passed through Berkefeld filter candles, but all of these experiments were quite negative. Two volunteers received injections of red blood corpuscles which had been washed several times in normal saline solution. One of these gave a positive result, the other negative. Two men were inoculated with an extract of ground-up red corpuscles subsequently filtered through Berkefeld filters, with negative results in both cases. One volunteer also gave no reaction after inoculation of filtered blood plasma. As a result of these experiments, the following conclusions were arrived at with regard to the presence of the virus in the blood.

(1) The disease is transmissible in every case by the whole blood, whether injected intravenously or intramuscularly.

(2) The disease is not transmissible by the serum. In the one instance in which the serum proved infective, hæmolysis of corpuscles had occurred before injection.

(3) It follows as a corollary to the preceding statement that the virus is not a " filter-passer " in the serum, as from analogy was thought might be the case. All the experiments with filtered serum were negative.

(4) The plasma was infective in one experiment, but hæmolysis of red cells had occurred so that the plasma was hæmoglobin-tinted. The filtered plasma in another test was not infective.

(5) The above results seemed to point to the virus being contained within the blood corpuscles themselves, whether leucocytes or red cells.

(6) Blood corpuscles, after washing five times in saline to remove the plasma, were still found to be infective. This further supports the view that the virus is intracorpuscular.

(7) Blood corpuscles were broken down, and the hæmoglobin-tinted fluid passed through a filter in an attempt to prove the virus an ultramicroscopic one confined to the corpuscles. The fluid when injected, however, was not found to be infective.

These experiments, carried out in 1915, remained quite uncontrolled and unconfirmed until the American commission took up the same problems in January 1918. In their experiments the plasma, injected in amounts ranging between 6 c.c. and 13 c.c., was found to be infective in all of five experiments. A single experiment with 5·5 c.c. of serum was negative. Three out of four injections with red blood corpuscles, washed in normal saline solution to remove the plasma, gave positive results. Eight filtration experiments were carried out, but the filters were only tested to hold back B. *typhosus*. In spite of that, however, five experiments with centrifugalized filtered plasma, and one with centrifugalized filtered serum, were all negative. In two instances, filtrates of ground red corpuscles were used for injection. One of these gave a definitely negative result ; the other was regarded as a doubtful positive ; but a study of the protocol of this experiment shows that a febrile attack, lasting only four days, began fifty days after the inoculation. Moreover, blood taken at the end of the short period of pyrexia was not infective when injected into another volunteer.

The main difference, therefore, in the findings of the American commission, when compared with those of McNee, Renshaw and Brunt, is that the commission believe that the virus exists free in the plasma, and is not intracorpuscular. They consider that the positive results with washed blood cells are accounted for by the cells carrying down with them, during the centrifugalization, sufficient virus to bring about infection. Like the British observers, the commission was unable to establish the filterability of the virus from any of the constituents of the blood.

The British commission was quickly led away by the interesting developments in other directions from investigating the infectivity of the various blood constituents. They confirmed the infectivity of whole blood, but carried out no experiments with serum, plasma or washed cells.

Infectivity of the Urine.—To test whether the virus of the disease was contained in the urine, eight experiments were carried out by the American commission. In all of these the inoculation was made on to a scarified area of the skin with the dried centrifugalized urinary sediment. Five of the volunteers developed the disease, showing that the virus may be present in the urine. The incubation period in these cases was from six to thirty days. The virus is apparently not present in sufficient quantity to infect at all stages of the disease, since in one positive case three separate inoculations from different sediments were necessary to infect, and in another case two inoculations were required.

Having established the presence of the virus in the urine, it seemed obvious to continue filtration experiments with the virus in this non-albuminous medium. The American commission therefore carried out the following experiments. The urine from several cases of trench fever was collected and centrifugalized, the supernatant clear fluid poured off and the residue evaporated at 30° C. to a gummy mass. This sediment was then ground up in a mortar with normal saline, and the resulting suspension was passed through a Chamberland L. filter. The filter had been tested to hold back *B. typhosus.* Two volunteers were inoculated intravenously with one portion of the filtrate, and three others were inoculated by scarification of the skin with the unfiltered sediment, which was thus shown to contain the virus. One of the men who received part of the filtrate intravenously developed the disease, and from him the infection was carried on to another man. The other volunteer injected with the filtrate remained perfectly well.

It is important to draw attention here to the fact that this single positive case, out of two experiments, represents the only work with human material supporting the idea that the virus of trench fever is a " filter-passer."

Infectivity of the Fæces.—Three experiments were carried out by the American commission to test this point, dried fæces being rubbed into scarifications on the skin. All gave a negative result.

Infectivity of the Sputum.—Clinically it is rare for trench fever to be associated with even a slight degree of pulmonary catarrh, but during the winter months catarrhs of the ordinary infective kinds may be encountered during the disease. The American commission carried out five experiments with dried sputum on three volunteers, one of whom became infected in this way. Apparently the virus, therefore, may pass out in the sputum if bronchitis be present, but as a source of infection in ordinary epidemic circumstances it must be of very minor importance.

Method of Transmission of the Disease.

The early work on this problem, as in the case of all new diseases, was beset with difficulties, the extent of which cannot easily be appreciated now. In the early account of McNee, Renshaw and Brunt, founded on work carried out in 1915, the question had to be left open. It was then merely stated that the disease might be either contagious from man to man, or, what seemed much more likely in view of the successful transmission experiments with blood, might be carried by some of the common flies or parasites found in the trenches. Since the disease continued, and indeed increased rapidly during the winter of 1915–1916, it was obvious that flies could not be the agents concerned. As a result of further enquiries during the spring and summer of 1916, Hunt and McNee were able to bring forward much inductive evidence in favour of the transmission of the disease by the body-louse. The evidence available at this time was founded chiefly on outbreaks of the fever among the personnel of medical units, and may be briefly quoted.

"First of all with regard to the outbreaks in casualty clearing stations. I. It is noteworthy that in a small ward containing ten beds, three orderlies who have been attending cases of the disease for many months have never become infected. Thus close personal contact alone appears insufficient for infection. II. In another casualty clearing station, where four of the ward orderlies had typical attacks, the conditions were different. The ward was a large one and often contained over a hundred patients, mostly slight cases of illness, and some of whom were certainly lousy when admitted. The men with trench fever were kept more or less together on one side of the ward. III. Other men of the personnel of clearing stations affected by the disease have included : (1) the attendant of the Thresh disinfector, (2) the attendant of the incinerator, (3) a stretcher bearer, and (4) the man who had charge of the removal of soiled blankets. These four men were never in contact with patients, but always in proximity to the clothes or blankets of cases admitted, and therefore very liable to infection with lice. IV. Of thirteen men in a clearing station who developed the fever, seven admitted they had seen lice from time to time on their clothes."

Hurst, working in Salonika in 1916, brought forward equally suggestive evidence in favour of louse transmission.

The authorities in France were unwilling in 1916 to recognize officially experiments on soldiers in order to confirm or refute the theory of louse transmission, and nearly two years elapsed before the systematic experiments of the American commission in France, and the British commission in London, showed conclusively that the body-louse transmitted the disease in nature.

Before, however, the work of these commissions had commenced, a few experiments had been done by British medical officers on themselves. Such experiments were necessarily few and uncontrolled, and therefore valueless for absolute conclusions, but in face of the opposition to a properly conducted set of experiments, these workers are due every credit. The most suggestive of these experiments was carried out by Davies and Weldon, who after collecting lice and starving them for three days, allowed them to feed on two patients suffering from trench fever. Thereafter, after an interval of fifteen minutes, a pair of lice was fed on each observer, and on the following day one of these officers again allowed two of the lice to feed on his blood. Twelve days later he developed a very typical attack of the disease.

It will be necessary to refer in some detail to the brilliant work of the British and American commissions, both of which came into being in December 1917. Both commissions independently studied what were essentially the same problems, and both showed quite conclusively, in a long series of experiments, that the body-louse transmitted the disease. The independent and successful experiments of each entitle them to equal credit for the results obtained.

It will be best to give shortly a summary of the conclusions arrived at by the two sets of workers before discussing certain differences in detail. The technique adopted will also be briefly commented upon for the help of those to whom the original accounts may be inaccessible.

The findings of the American commission have been published in the form of an elaborate report. No complete report has so far been issued by the British commission, but the main results have been incorporated in a book by Lt.-Col. W. Byam, who was one of its members.

Byam gives the conclusions with regard to the infectivity of trench fever, and its method of transmission, as follows :—

"We are of opinion, therefore, that trench fever is conveyed by the excreta of infected lice ; that the excreta may enter through the broken skin or unbroken conjunctiva ; that rubbing and scratching promote infection, but that the bites of lice may possibly cause a sufficient lesion to enable the virus to enter the body."

The findings of the American commission with regard to transmission are incorporated in the following way in their report :—

" That the disease is transmitted naturally by the louse, *Pediculus humanus,* Linn., var. *corporis,* and that this is the important and common means of transmission. That the louse may transmit the disease by its bite alone, the usual manner of infection, or the disease may be produced artificially by scarifying the skin and rubbing in a small amount of the infected louse excrement."

It will be observed that, while there is complete agreement on the fundamental point of louse transmission, there is some difference of opinion as to the way in which the louse plays its part. The American commission believe that the virus is conveyed to the new host by the bite of the louse, and that this is the common method of infection. The British commission, on the other hand, are of opinion that the usual method of natural infection is by the excreta of infected lice entering through an abrasion of the skin. They admit that the puncture caused by a bite may possibly be sufficient to allow the entry of the infected excreta, but do not think this can often occur.

These differences in the findings of the two commissions are interesting but not fundamental, and it is best at the present time to leave them as they stand. From both of them the main important prophylactic conclusions can be drawn. Attention should, however, be drawn to one essentially practical point. It is obvious that if the results of the British commission be accepted in full, a man with abrasions of his skin might be infected by sleeping in blankets previously contaminated with infected louse excreta, in the absence of lice and bites.

Apart from the two methods of entry of the virus dealt with above, there would seem to be no other probable means of spread of the disease in nature. Certain other possibilities have been considered and have a scientific, although not a great practical, interest. It has been shown, for instance, by the British commission that infection is possible through the unbroken conjunctiva, after instilling an emulsion of infected louse excrement. Further, as has already been described, the American commission established the fact that the urine and sputum may contain the virus. For practical purposes, however, it is certain that infection by the mouth can never occur, since the British workers found it impossible to transmit the disease to volunteers by feeding them on louse excreta known to be actively infective.

Technique of Experiments on Louse Transmission.—The American report points out that in planning the experiments three considerations were involved : First, the employment of clean lice ; second, the preliminary treatment of the lice to render them infective ; and third, the exposure of the volunteers to the lice under as natural conditions as possible. The strain of lice was a laboratory strain which had been kept going by Bacot, of the Lister Institute, London, for over two years. This was the known "clean" stock. Other experiments were carried out for definite purposes with lice hatched out from eggs found on verminous shirts in France. Others, again, were performed with live lice taken from the clothing of soldiers admitted as cases of trench fever. Of twenty-six louse transmission experiments, fourteen were successful. Eleven of these positive results were obtained when using Bacot's clean strain of lice, and two with lice taken direct from trench fever patients.

The lice were infected by allowing them to follow their natural customs as far as possible. They were allowed to feed for thirty minutes, three times a day, and in the intervals were kept at a temperature of about 80° F.

The insects were allowed to feed on the forearm of the experimental subject by the "cell" method, in practically every case, the lice being enclosed in a small box or cell fixed on to the skin of the arm by some form of bandaging or strapping. In the first set of experiments, sixteen in all, no attempt was made to prevent the deposit of louse fæces on the skin. Hence, although they proved conclusively that the louse had to do with the transmission of the infection, they gave no clue as to the relative importance of the bites *per se*, and the introduction of louse excrement into punctures or scratches on the skin. In a second set of experiments a definite attempt was made to exclude contamination of the area of infection with fæces, and to estimate the importance of the mouth-parts of the insects in carrying the disease. The technique adopted was the following. After the insects had had their last feed, by the box or cell method, on a trench fever patient, they were carefully picked off the cloth on which they lived, and placed in a new box containing fresh strips of flannel. At each feeding-time on the experimental subject, a clean chiffon cover was placed over the box and held in position by an elastic band. The box was then tied on *underneath* the flexor surface of the forearm, so that the chiffon cover was uppermost and against the skin. The box thus hung down and was never tilted during the course of the experiment. The lice fed by climbing to the chiffon and biting through the interstices. In this way contamination of the skin area by fæces was reduced to a minimum. The bitten areas were, moreover, carefully cleansed in various ways after each feeding, so as to remove the few small specks of excrement which could generally be found on search with a hand-lens. Two men were exposed to experimental infection in this careful way. Both of them developed trench fever, one after twenty-seven days and the other after thirty-eight days. No scratching or abrading of the skin, apart from the bites, was possible in these cases.

The technique of the British commission was influenced by their very first experiments, so that they approached the problem from rather a different angle. In their first two experiments two men were allowed to be bitten by lice over periods of two and three months. These lice fed first on trench fever patients and were transferred thereafter to the volunteers. During these periods the volunteers were bitten 9,500 and 13,224 times respectively. In one of these experiments, in order to avoid mere mechanical transmission, the lice were never allowed to feed on the man until at least three hours after they had bitten the infected host. In the other case the lice were transferred at all times, and even before their first meal was complete, so as to induce them to feed again at once. Neither of these two men developed trench fever. While carrying out these experiments an important observation was made, namely, that neither volunteer was seen to scratch himself or to show evidence of having done so. It was therefore at once determined to see if failure to infect was due to this cause. For the next experiment the excreta from nearly 600 lice, which had fed for twenty-seven days on many cases of trench fever, were collected and dried. A small area of skin on the upper arm of a volunteer was scarified lightly so that blood was just drawn, and then a portion of the dry powdered excrement was dusted into the blood and rubbed into a paste with it. The paste was then allowed to dry in the air. Eight days later the man developed trench fever. This experiment was the starting point of all the subsequent work of the commission, Bacot's clean laboratory strain of lice being again used for all the critical experiments. In addition to transmitting the disease by scarification and rubbing in infected excreta, success was also obtained in an experiment by squashing eleven lice over a scarified area of skin. To complete the experiments it was shown that real trench fever was being produced in this way, by carrying on the infections to new volunteers by injecting whole blood. Control experiments, in which the fæces of normal lice from Bacot's strain were rubbed into scarified areas of skin, were always unsuccessful.

Other important experiments were carried out to show that even in the dried condition, infected louse excrement remains potent for a long period. In three experiments, all of them fully successful, the dried excreta had been kept before use for 16, 60 and 120 days, a fundamental point in connection with the prophylaxis of the disease. The incubation periods in these cases were 8, 7 and 13 days. Further experiments by this commission showed that infection could occur by instilling an emulsion of excreta into the conjunctival sac, but that feeding men on heavily infected excrement produced no effect. They also showed, as did the American commission, that lice infected with trench fever do not transmit the disease by the ova to their offspring.

They also set out to discover by experiment whether the louse is merely a mechanical transmitter of the virus, or whether a developmental stage, or a stage of multiplication of the causal organism, occurs in the insect. These experiments showed that lice excreta do not become infective for some days after the feed on a trench fever patient, the minimum time in the experiments being five days. It thus seems probable that time is necessary for multiplication of the virus, or for some developmental cycle to occur, within the insect host. Further important points elucidated went to show that lice, once infected, continue in this state up to their death, and that a very high proportion of the insects finally become infected after feeding on a trench fever patient. In two experiments the commission was able to prove that the excrement from a single infected louse, collected for a period of five days and then inoculated in the usual way, brought about typical attacks of the fever after eight and nine days' incubation.

Nature of the Virus.

It will be evident, from what has been written, that the virus of trench fever is constantly circulating in the peripheral blood during the course of the disease, and according to the work of the American commission is chiefly present in the plasma.

No means have so far been discovered of demonstrating the causal organism to the eye, and the conclusion has been drawn that it is ultramicroscopic. It must be pointed out again, however, that this view has not been arrived at from experiments with the virus in human blood, since all filtration experiments with different blood constituents have been negative, or at least inconclusive. These remarks, moreover, take no account of the bipolar-staining bodies which have been described in blood films by some observers, but which have not been found by many.

The conclusion that at one stage at least the virus is a " filter-passer " rests on experiments carried out by the American commission, both on filtered urinary sediments and on filtrates of infected louse excrement. With filtered urinary sediment a single experiment was successful, while the filtrates of infected louse excreta produced the disease in two out of three attempts. In both sets of experiments the filters had only been tested to hold back *B. typhosus*, and might quite possibly allow the passage of a very small organism, still within the bounds of visibility with a good microscope. It is interesting to find that the British commission was unable to confirm these results, all filtration experiments with emulsions of fæces of infected lice being negative, except in two cases where the filters also allowed the passage of *B. prodigiosus*.

It is evident, in view of the difficulties which arise in all filtration experiments through porcelain candles, that absolute reliance cannot be placed on this method of investigation.

It was only after the infectivity of the excreta of lice fed on sufferers from the fever was fully recognized by the British commission, that further progress in this country with regard to the nature of the virus became possible.

It had been found in 1916 by Töpfer, to whose work reference has already been made, that in the fæces of lice infected with trench fever abundant masses of small particles, closely similar to those originally described by Ricketts in Rocky Mountain spotted fever, were present. The history of these particles, now generally called " Rickettsia," is briefly as follows.

Ricketts, in 1909, while investigating Rocky Mountain spotted fever, found minute bodies which he came to believe had a causal relationship to the disease. They were first observed, which is interesting when their minute size is considered, in small numbers in blood films from cases of the disease. Later they were found abundantly present in the fæces of the tick, known to be the carrier of the fever. These results have more recently been fully confirmed and extended by Wolbach. In 1910 Ricketts and Wilder found very similar bodies in the intestinal contents of the louse concerned with the transmission of Mexican typhus fever. Sergent, Foley and Viallatte confirmed the observation with regard to these bodies in lice from typhus fever patients shortly before the outbreak of the war, and da Rocha Lima, Töpfer and others have continued the work on typhus-infected lice during the war period.

Töpfer's first paper on trench fever appeared in 1916, and he claimed to be able to distinguish trench fever Rickettsia from typhus Rickettsia in the lice. In trench fever he found the Rickettsia bodies developed on the fifth day after the first infecting feed and were present abundantly on and after the eighth day.

Jungmann and Kuczynski, in 1917, claimed to have infected wild mice with the blood of trench fever patients, and in the course of their work found bipolar bodies, similar to those described by Töpfer in human blood, in the blood of the mice and in the excreta of lice fed on the patients. They regarded the bodies as identical in all three situations.

Munk and da Rocha Lima, in 1917, again confirmed the presence and multiplication of Rickettsia in the intestinal contents of lice fed on men suffering from Wolhynian, or trench fever.

Arkwright, Bacot and Duncan, since the end of the war, have continued work on the relationship of Rickettsia to trench fever. In a communication published in April 1919, they give an account of their own experiments. They have found in the fæces of infected lice abundant bodies apparently identical with the Rickettsia described by previous workers in this field. The technique used by them is important and requires description. In preparing films from the intestinal contents so as to get rid of granules of altered blood, the thick film method recommended by W. M. James for malaria work was adopted. The films, after drying, were fixed for one or more hours in absolute alcohol containing 1 per cent. of strong hydrochloric acid. The films were then stained by Giemsa's method. Sources of error in the technique are pointed out—granules of debris, disintegrating nuclei of leucocytes and certain bipolar-staining bacteria which resemble Rickettsia very closely. The criteria adopted in deciding the presence of Rickettsia have been :—

(1) Its minute size, smaller than $M. melitensis$ or $B. influenzae$, usually about $0 \cdot 3 \mu$ by $0 \cdot 3 \mu$, or $0 \cdot 3 \mu$ by $0 \cdot 5 \mu$.

(2) Its irregularity in shape—round, oval, diplococcal or bacillary with stained poles.

(3) Its occurrence in very large numbers or even in masses, especially on flakes of solid matter in the excreta.

(4) Its well-stained appearance when coloured by Giemsa's stain, the colour being purple like that of the nucleus of a leucocyte.

The lice used were again Bacot's laboratory strain, which had then been maintained for over three years in the laboratory. They showed that these lice, when fed on seven healthy men, never developed Rickettsia. On the other hand, feeding on trench fever patients, both in the febrile and apyretic stages, led to the development of Rickettsia in the fæces after an incubation period of four to twelve days.

A point in the technique of the work requires mention. It was found necessary to keep the experimental lice at a temperature of 27° to 30° C. between the times of feeding, this being essential for the full multiplication of the Rickettsia bodies in the gut of the insects.

The relationship of Rickettsia bodies in louse excreta to trench fever infection is thus abundantly proved to be close.

What is the nature of Rickettsia? This remains so far unknown, since no one has been able to cultivate the bodies on any form of artificial medium. It is possible that they are not micro-organisms at all, but their appearance certainly suggests strongly that they are of bacterial nature. In 1920 Ledingham published experiments showing that their injection into laboratory animals gives rise to agglutinins, which is again so far in favour of a bacterial origin.

Powers of Resistance.—This is obviously a point of great practical importance in the prevention of the disease, and occupied the attention of both the British and American commissions during their work. In practice, of course, the problem narrows itself down to effective methods of sterilizing blankets, clothing, and so on, so as to destroy the virus of the disease.

It was found by the American commission that the virus, as present in louse excreta, resists a temperature of 60° C., moist heat, for thirty minutes, and is fully virulent after such treatment, but is destroyed by a temperature of 70° C., moist heat, for the same period. They conclude, therefore, that a temperature of 55° C. for thirty minutes, which destroys the louse and its ova, does not suffice to kill the virus of trench fever which may be present on the underclothing of trench fever patients.

The British commission proved that dried infective louse excrement was still virulent after keeping for one hundred and twenty-one days, a fact of much practical interest. They showed that simple washing of infected blankets or underclothing is inefficient, since immersion of the virus in hot soapy water for twenty minutes does not reduce its potency. Fluid disinfectants, such as 2 per cent. cresol of lysol, were found satisfactory, the virus being destroyed in twenty minutes. Their experiments with the common form of sterilization by moist heat give different results from those of the other commission. In the British tests a temperature of 60° C., moist heat, was found sufficient to destroy the virus in twenty minutes, or 10° C. less than the limit of safety indicated by the American experiments. The effects of dry heat were also investigated, the virus being found to resist a temperature of 80° C. for twenty minutes, but to succumb at 100° C. in the same time.

Immunity to Trench Fever.

It is evident, from the constancy with which the disease could be transferred to volunteers, that as far as the British races are concerned natural immunity to trench fever must be very rare. Age, moreover, appears to be without influence. In France young and middle-aged soldiers fell victims with equal readiness, while the experiments of the British commission were carried out on elderly people. Sex, too, is unimportant, since numerous nursing sisters suffered from trench fever. Unfortunately, the opportunity seems to have been missed of noting the incidence in foreign races, and no records are available, for instance, to show whether, or to what extent, the Chinese coolies employed in labour corps contracted the disease in France at the time when it was so rife.

With regard to acquired immunity, there is experimental evidence from the British commission pointing to the conclusion that a certain degree of immunity, which may persist for six months or longer, follows an attack of the fever. Trench fever is, however, so notoriously liable to relapses over periods of many months that it is extremely difficult in the natural disease to differentiate relapses, occurring after long periods of well-being, from a completely new infection with the virus. This difficulty had been already discussed by Hunt and McNee in 1916.

General Summary.

The extent of existing knowledge of the pathology of trench fever can be summarized as follows :—

(1) The exact nature of the infecting virus is as yet uncertain.

(2) The means of transmission of the disease in nature is the body-louse.

(3) The blood of a trench fever patient may contain the virus for many months, even in the absence of all pyrexia.

(4) In the louse, the presence of the infection is closely bound up with the appearance of so-called Rickettsia bodies in the intestinal canal of the insect.

(5) There is an incubation period of about five days in the louse, after feeding on a trench fever patient, before the excreta become infective.

(6) Once infected, the louse remains in this condition until its death, but the virus is not transmitted by the ova.

(7) The virus of trench fever remains virulent in dried louse excreta for a long time ; there is experimental proof up to one hundred and twenty days.

(8) The virus is destroyed by 2 per cent. lysol or cresol, and by a temperature of 70° C., moist heat, in twenty minutes.

(9) The prophylaxis of the disease essentially depends on the destruction of lice, and on effective disinfection of all clothing.

BIBLIOGRAPHY.

Arkwright	Discussion of Byam and Lloyd's paper on Trench Fever.	Proc. Roy. Soc. Med., 1919 – 20, Vol. xiii, Epid. Sect., p. 23.
Arkwright, Bacot & Duncan.	The Minute Bodies (Rickettsia) found in association with Trench Fever.	Trans. Soc. Trop. Med. & Hyg., 1918–19, Vol. xii, p. 61.
,, ,,	The Association of Rickettsia with Trench Fever.	Jl. of Hyg., 1919–20, Vol. xviii, p. 76.
Beauchant	Fièvres des tranchées	Paris Médical, 1916, p. 641 ; and Presse Méd., Paris, 1916, Vol. xxiv, p. 493.
Brasch	Contribution à l'étude de la " fièvre de Volhynie " (fièvre de 5 jours).	Bull. Internat. d'Hygiène Publique, 1916, Vol. viii, p. 1219.
Brumpt	Au sujet d'un parasite (Rickettsia Prowazeki) des poux de l'homme.	Bull. Soc. Path. Exot., 1918, Vol. xi, p. 249.
Byam, Dimond, Sorapure, Wilson & Peacock.	Trench Fever. A Preliminary Clinical Report.	Jl. of R.A.M.C.,1917, Vol. xxix, p. 560.
Byam, Carroll, Churchill, Dimond, Lloyd, Sorapure & Wilson.	Trench Fever	Trans. Soc. Trop. Med. & Hyg., 1918, Vol. xi, p. 237.
Byam & Lloyd ..	Trench Fever	Proc. Roy. Soc. Med., 1919 – 20, Vol. xiii, Epid. Sect., p. 1.
Byam & others ..	Trench Fever : a Louse-borne Disease.	London, 1918.
Coombs	Trench Fever in Mesopotamia ..	Lancet, 1917, Vol. i, p. 183.
Costello	Trench Fever—mainly its Clinical Manifestations.	Practitioner, 1917, Vol. xcviii, p. 456.

Couvy, Dujarrac & de la Rivière.	Note sur l'étiologie de la fièvre des tranchées.	Compt. Rend. Soc. de Biol., 1918, Vol. lxxxi, p. 22.
da Rocha Lima ..	Zur Aetiologie des Fleckfiebers	Berlin klin. Woch., 1916, Vol. liii, p. 567.
Davies & Weldon ..	A Preliminary Contribution on P.U.O. (Trench Fever).	Lancet, 1917, Vol. i, p. 183.
Day	War Nephritis	Ibid., 1918, Vol. ii, p. 660.
Dimond	Trench Fever	Ibid., 1917, Vol. ii, p. 382.
Drummond ..	Trench Fever	Quart. Jl. Med., 1917–18, Vol. xi, p. 363.
Graham	On a Relapsing Febrile Illness of Unknown Origin.	Lancet, 1915, Vol. ii, p. 703.
,, ...	Trench Fevers	Ibid., 1918, Vol. i, p. 482.
Gratzer	Ueber eine Erkrankung des Schützengrabens.	Wien. klin. Woch., 1916, Vol. xxix, p. 295.
Grieveson ..	On Trench Fever	Lancet, 1917, Vol. ii, p. 84.
Henry	The "Hæmogregarene" of Trench Fever.	Brit. Med. Jl., 1917, Vol. ii, p. 739.
Herringham ..	Trench Fever and its Allies ..	Quart. Jl. Med., 1915–16, Vol. ix, p. 429.
Hiss	Ueber eine neue periodische Fiebererkrankung.	Berlin. klin. Woch., 1916, Vol. liii, p. 738.
Houston & McCloy	The Relation of the Enterococcus to Trench Fever and Allied Conditions.	Lancet, 1916, Vol. ii, p. 632.
Hughes	Trench Pyrexias : their Prevention and Treatment.	Ibid., 1918, Vol. ii, p. 474.
Hunt & McNee ..	Further Observations on Trench Fever.	Quart. Jl. Med., 1915–16, Vol. ix, p. 442.
Hunt & Rankin ..	Intermittent Fever of Obscure Origin.	Lancet, 1915, Vol. ii, p. 1133.
Hurst	Trench Fever	Ibid., 1916, Vol. ii, p. 671.
,, ...	Medical Diseases of the War ..	London, 1917.
Jungmann	Zur Aetiologie des "Febris Wolhynica."	Berlin. klin. Woch., 1916, Vol. liii, p. 323.
Jungmann & Kuczynski.	Zur Klinik und Aetiologie der Febris Wolhynica.	Deut. med. Woch., 1917, Vol. xliii, p. 359.
Korbsch	Zur Kenntnis der Febris Wolhynica.	Ibid., 1916, Vol. xlii, p. 1217.
Ledingham ..	Agglutination Experiments with Trench Fever Rickettsia.	Lancet, 1920, Vol. i, p. 1264.
Lloyd	Trench Fever and War Nephritis	Ibid., 1919, Vol. ii, p. 640.
Macgregor	Case of "Trench Fever" contracted in England.	Brit. Med. Jl., 1917, Vol. i, p. 221.

McNee, Renshaw & Brunt. — Trench Fever .. .. .. — *Ibid.*, 1916, Vol. i, p. 225 ; *and* Jl. of R.A.M.C., 1916, Vol. xxvi, p. 490.

McNee .. .. — Trench Fever .. .. .. — Med. Bulletin : Review of War Med., Surg. and Hyg., Paris, 1918, Vol. i, p. 146.

Muir.. .. .. — Pyrexia or Trench Fever .. — Brit. Med. Jl., 1916, Vol. ii, p. 641.

Munk & da Rocha Lima. — Klinik und Aetiologie des sogenanten " Wolhynischen Fiebers." — Münch. med. Woch., 1917, Vol. lxiv, p. 1422.

Nankivell & Sundell — Presence of a Spirochæte in the Urine in Cases of Trench Fever — Lancet, 1917, Vol. ii, p. 672.

,, ,, — Source of Spirochætes in Urine — *Ibid.*, 1917, Vol. ii, p. 836.

Pari .. .. — Febbre quintana o volinica .. — Gazz. degli Osp. Milano, 1917, Vol. xxxviii, p. 849.

Patterson .. .. — Spirochætes occurring in the Urine of Cases of " Pyrexia of Unknown Origin." — Brit. Med. Jl., 1917, Vol. ii, p. 418.

Perkins & Urwick .. — The Hæmatology of Trench Fever. — Quart. Jl. Med., 1917–18, Vol. xi, p. 374.

Ramsey .. .. — Notes on so-called " Trench Fever " as seen in England. — Brit. Med. Jl., 1917, Vol. i, p. 222.

Renaux .. .. — " Fièvre des tranchées " .. — Compt. Rend. Soc. de Biol., 1917, Vol. lxxx, p. 404.

Ricketts .. .. — A Micro-organism which apparently has a Specific Relationship to Rocky Mountain Spotted Fever. — Jl. Amer. Med. Assoc., 1909, Vol. lii, p. 379.

Ricketts & Wilder .. — Ætiology of the Typhus Fever (Tabardillo) of Mexico City. — *Ibid.*, 1910, Vol. liv, p. 1373.

Riemer .. .. — Beitrag zur Frage des Erregers des Fünftagefiebers. — Münch. med. Woch., 1917, Vol. lxiv, p. 92.

Sergent, Foley & Viallatte. — Sur des formes microbiennes abondantes dans le corps de poux infectés par le typhus exanthématique. — Compt. Rend. Soc. de Biol., 1914, Vol. lxxvii, p. 101.

Sisto.. .. .. — Un caso di febbre considdetta " Volinica " fra i nostri combattenti. — Riforma Med. Roma, 1917, Vol. xxxiii, p. 953.

Stintzing .. .. — Ueber Febris quintana .. — Münch. med. Woch., 1917, Vol. lxiv p. 155.

Sundell & Nankivell — Trench Fever .. .. .. — Lancet, 1918, Vol. i, p. 399.

Tate & McLeod .. — Trench Fever .. .. .. — *Ibid.*, p. 603.

Töpfer .. .. — Zur Aetiologie des " Febris Wolhynica." — Berlin. klin. Woch., 1916, Vol. liii, p. 323.

,, ... — Zur Ursache und Ueberträgung des Wolhynischen Fiebers. — Münch. med. Woch., 1916, Vol. lxiii, p. 1495.

Töpfer	Der Fleckfiebererreger in der Laus.	Deut. med. Woch., 1916, Vol. xlii, p. 1251.
Werner	Ueber rekurrierendes Fieber, mit Fünftageturnus, Fünftagefieber aus dem Osten.	Münch. med. Woch., 1916, Vol. lxiii. p. 402.
Werner, Benzler & Wiese.	Zur Aetiologie des Fünftagefiebers.	Ibid., p. 1369.
Werner & Benzler ..	Zur Aetiologie und Klinik der Febris Quintana.	Ibid., 1917, Vol. lxiv p. 695.
Wolbach	The Ætiology of Rocky Mountain Spotted Fever.	Jl. of Med. Res., 1916, Vol. xxxiv, p. 121 ; 1916–17, Vol. xxxv, p. 147.
Wright	Some Notes on Trench Fever ..	Brit. Med. Jl., 1916, Vol. ii, p. 136.
Zollenkopf	Eine neue dem Wechselfieber ähnliche Erkrankung.	Deut. med. Woch., 1916, Vol. xlii, p. 1034.
—	Preliminary Report of the Committee upon Trench Fever and Pyrexia of Unknown Origin.	Brit. Med. Jl., 1918, Vol. i, p. 91.
—	Second Report of the Committee upon Trench Fever and Pyrexia of Unknown Origin.	Ibid., p. 296.
—	Trench Fever : Report of the American Red Cross Commission.	Oxford, 1918.

CHAPTER XVIII.

SPIROCHÆTAL JAUNDICE.

IN 1914 knowledge of spirochætosis ictero-hæmorrhagica was mainly derived from the study of certain outbreaks of a fever, which was accompanied by jaundice, occurring in small localized epidemics and very accurately described by many of the observers.

The history of the disease is traced by Martin and Pettit. They mention a long series of French authors who described the clinical and pathological picture during the nineteenth century. In spite of these excellent and accurate descriptions it was left for Weil to attach his name to the disease. Weil, in 1886, described its main characteristics—jaundice, pyrexia and a tendency to hæmorrhages—and pointed out its infectious character.

An excellent account of the condition, both from the clinical and pathological aspects, was published by Widal and Abrami in 1908. The causal organisms had not been definitely identified, and although many organisms had been suggested as the cause of the disease, none of them stood the test of time and experimental investigation. Weil's disease was known as a comparatively rare condition which generally occurred in epidemic form. The epidemics were sometimes of considerable extent, three hundred cases having been reported in one outbreak in Alexandria, although sometimes they were more in the nature of local outbreaks in a household, four or five members of the same family being infected.

The main clinical symptoms at the onset were gastric, accompanied by fever, and later jaundice ; albuminuria and hæmorrhages were the outstanding features.

In 1914, Inada and Ito reported the discovery of a spirochæte in the liver of a guinea-pig, which had been inoculated with the blood of a patient suffering from Weil's disease. These authors were able to repeat the finding, and to demonstrate the main features of the disease, as they occur in man, in guinea-pigs which had succumbed to infection with material containing the spirochætes. They further succeeded in passing the infection from animal to animal for over fifty generations, and were constantly able to demonstrate the presence of the spirochæte in the blood and tissues of the animals infected. They finally succeeded in demonstrating the same organism in the blood of patients, and in the tissues of those who had succumbed. The demonstration of immune substances in the blood of convalescent patients by means of the Pfeiffer reaction, and the protection of guinea-pigs from fatal doses of the organism, were taken as the final proofs of the causal relation-ship of the spirochæte.

In so far as the British army was concerned there were three definite epidemics of jaundice during the war. The first of these occurred during the occupation of the Gallipoli peninsula. Its ætiology is uncertain, but from verbal accounts it does not seem to have been what is now called spirochætosis ictero-hæmorrhagica. From numerous enquiries it would appear to have been very widespread and not at all fatal, and rarely accompanied by high temperatures or hæmorrhages. The second epidemic occurred in 1916 on the Ypres front. There were some cases of jaundice at other times. In 1915 cases were seen at the base, and other cases were reported during the later stages of the war, but the great majority of cases of spirochætosis occurred in the summer months of 1916. The epidemic was singularly localized. Individual cases occurred all over the area occupied by British troops, both in the trenches and on the lines of communication, but the only region from which there was a continuous series of cases was the left sector of the Ypres salient, during the months of May, June, July, August and September 1916.

The third epidemic of jaundice occurred in the British army in Italy and was also spirochætal in type.

Ætiology.

The mode of transmission of the parasite is not definitely settled, but an animal host which, itself unharmed, harbours the parasite in a virulent state has been found in the common rat. The Japanese authors first demonstrated this in wild Japanese rats in 1916, and it was soon found to be true in many parts of the world. In France, Flanders, England and America, confirmation was soon forthcoming. About 30 per cent. of rats have spirochæta in their urine, and by making an emulsion of the kidney of the rat or by collecting the urine it is possible to transmit the spirochæte to the guinea-pig and reproduce the same disease as occurs when blood from a case of spirochætosis is inoculated.

The route of infection is still unsettled. Inada and his collaborators thought that, as they were able to infect animals through the unbroken skin, the same channel might account for human cases, possibly through some abrasion or scratch. Infection through the intestinal canal is also easy experimentally. No insect has been incriminated, though lice, ticks and fleas have all been suspected. There is therefore no definite knowledge of the common mode of infection. In Japan it was found that the disease most frequently occurred in mines which were constantly wet and ill-drained, and that the draining of these mines materially reduced the incidence of the disease. The organism is delicate and will not long survive inimical conditions, though it will live at low temperatures. It does not long survive admixture with mud, sewage or excreta. Contamination of food by rats would seem the most probable source of human infection, but the cutaneous route cannot be eliminated. The possibility of human carriers must also be considered, as one is able to demonstrate live spirochætes in the urine in cases during the convalescent stage. These have indeed been found up to three months after the illness.

Bacteriology.

The organism was first described by Inada as a spirochæte, but for excellent reasons Noguchi has placed it in a new class of organisms and named it the *Leptospira icterohaemorrhagiæ*. Its morphology is such as to warrant a separate class.

The organism as seen in stained preparations differs in many ways from that seen in dark field illumination. When stained by Giemsa in fixed preparations from the blood or from culture, one sees a slightly undulating organism which often has a fairly wide hook at each end. The undulations are irregular but the hook at the end is almost constant. The length varies but the majority of leptospira are from 9μ to 12μ in length and 0.5μ in width. With osmic acid fixation and Giemsa staining, Noguchi has demonstrated the spiral, which is so fine that at first it was not recognized. With dark field illumination the most striking appearance is the spiral, which is extremely fine and regular and extends to the tapered extremities of the organism.

The spiral is 0.5μ in width, that is, a leptospira of 10μ will show twenty spirals, about six of which are in the " hook " portion of the organism. The hook is often turned to the same side at each end, but sometimes there is only a hook at one end. The living leptospira, seen by dark field illumination, is actively motile ; it may move indifferently in any direction with regard to its long axis. The movements when the organism is seen working through a jelly are slowed and it is often more easy to see the structure of the spiral. A very characteristic movement both in animal fluids and in culture is a rapid rotation around the long axis of the organism which, on account of the hooks, gives the impression of watching a motile, refractile figure of eight.

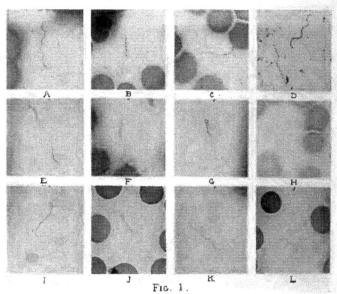

Fig. 1.

Fig. 1.—Photomicrographs of *Leptospira icterohæmorrhagica* in blood films from infected guinea-pigs. D. shows *S. pallida* and *S. refringens* for comparison. Giemsa stain. (x 1,000 D.)

The organism has been cultivated by many workers. Inada obtained cultures in Noguchi tubes in his early work. It has been shown that the leptospira grows well in conditions of partial anaërobiosis. In deep tubes of medium prepared of diluted rabbit serum and a small percentage of agar, cultures are prolific in seven to ten days at a depth of about 1 cm. from the surface. A superimposed layer of liquid paraffin may be used but is not necessary. Most workers are agreed that rabbit serum is the most suitable medium. Noguchi uses the

serum diluted 1 in 10 with normal saline, with the addition
of 10 per cent. of a 2 to 3 per cent. nutrient agar the reaction
of which is PH 7·4. The addition of the agar makes the
medium semi-solid and in this the leptospiræ grow well. The
addition of 0·5 per cent. of hæmoglobin procured from rabbit
blood cells by the mixture of equal parts of distilled water
and defibrinated blood seems to enhance the richness of the
culture. The organism grows at 37° C. rapidly, but the viability

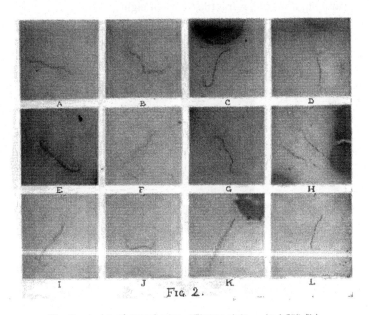

Fig. 2.—*L. icterohæmorrhagica.* Giemsa stain. (x 1,500 D.)

of the cultures is greater when the incubation takes place at
26° C. Such cultures will live for some months. The pathogenicity of the leptospira is gradually lost in culture. The
organism can be stained by all the usual Romanowski stains.
Probably the most efficient of these is the Giemsa method.
Although it is easy to recognize the organism when it is stained,
it is difficult to see the spirals in stained preparations. Noguchi
states that with osmic acid vapour fixation and prolonged
staining with Giemsa it is possible to demonstrate this characteristic feature. The most useful stain for general purposes has

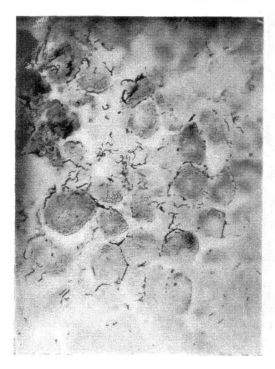

Fig. 3.—Section of guinea-pig liver. Levaditi.

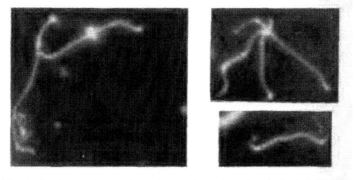

Fig. 4.—Dark ground stage photomicrographs to show the spiral. (x 3,000 D.)

been Fontana's stain without any modification. In tissue the organism can be demonstrated by the original Levaditi process.

The life-cycle of the leptospira has not as yet been fully investigated, but there seems to be some evidence of a granular stage in its life-history. The facts that the organism is filterable, that the filtrates fail to show leptospiræ, and that in spite of this cultures and animal inoculations demonstrate that the virus has passed the filter, suggest that possibly there is a stage during which the organism is present in the form of granules. Suggestive granules can be seen in cultures and sometimes in animal tissues.

Pathology.

The incubation period of the disease has been fixed by an accidental infection which took place in Martin's laboratory and which left no doubt that the period was six to eight days. The Japanese workers had already placed the incubation period at about ten days, but this unfortunate accident settles the point. The infection is ushered in by fever, nausea, faintness and headache, or some combination of these, and the onset is generally sudden. There may be hæmoptysis, epistaxis or hæmatemesis at an early stage. Malaise is common, and the sensation of having been beaten is often mentioned by the patient. Pains in the muscles, conjunctival injection and headache are almost constant early symptoms. Jaundice does not often occur before the fourth day and increases rapidly until the seventh day, when it tends slowly to retrogress. Many cases occur in which jaundice is of slight degree, and in some instances it is never apparent. A striking symptom, when it is present, is the hæmorrhagic herpes labialis. Although this is sometimes trivial, it is occasionally very widespread.

The route of invasion is still unsettled, but the evidence given above points to either an intestinal or a cutaneous channel. On the whole the intestinal route seems the more probable.

The leptospiræ are present in the blood at the early stages of the disease, but they gradually disappear and after the sixth day are in most cases absent. They can rarely be demonstrated in the blood by direct examination. Inada found the organisms in the blood fairly frequently and in considerable numbers, but the disease in Japan is much more severe than that seen during the war in Europe. The death-rate in Japan was about 35 per cent., whereas in the epidemic which occurred in Flanders it was less than 10 per cent. This fact may account for the difficulty experienced in finding the leptospiræ in the blood, either by staining methods or dark ground illumination. Stokes only once found leptospiræ in the blood by dark ground illumination. Dr. A. C. Coles examined six films taken from a case on the second day and after an exhaustive search was able to find two examples of the organism in one film. It is stated by Japanese workers that if the patients die in the acute stage of the infection it is relatively easy to find the leptospiræ in the tissues. The liver shows numerous organisms, and they have been demonstrated in the kidney, intestinal wall, adrenal organs and heart in various cases. All the cases examined by Stokes died after the seventh day, and the kidney was the only tissue in which the organisms were found. They were found by the Levaditi method in three out of seven cases examined. They occur in small localized groups in the cells and interstitial tissue of the convoluted tubules; they were never seen in the glomeruli. The disappearance of the organisms from the blood stream is probably accounted for by the appearance of immune substances in the blood. These can be demonstrated after the sixth day and are in measurable quantities after the eighth day.

The leptospiræ are excreted in the urine, sometimes in a viable and virulent state, and they have been found up to the sixtieth day of convalescence. They have also been shown to be present in the stools by inoculation experiments.

The changes produced in the tissues are those of degeneration. The degree of the changes is in proportion to the severity of the infection. The lesions are well marked in the liver, but it is in the kidney that the most constant and most advanced changes are seen. The importance of the kidney lesions must be emphasized. They appear to be one of the most important causes of death. Suppression of urine and a condition resembling uræmia are common terminal occurrences. At autopsy the most striking change is seen in the kidney; in fact, it is the only viscus which constantly shows a definite naked-eye pathological change.

Relapses are not uncommon and may occur at any time, but most commonly about the fifteenth day. Stokes failed to infect animals with blood taken during a relapse on several occasions, and in a small series of about five cases which relapsed the patient did not seem gravely ill, but merely showed a recurrence of an irregular temperature. The following temperature charts show fairly well the types of temperature met with.

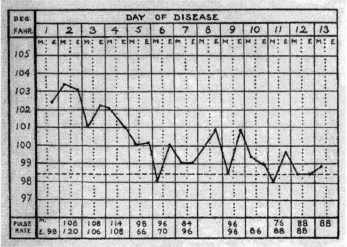

Chart I.

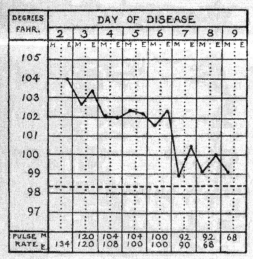

Chart II.

Morbid Anatomy.

The outstanding feature at autopsy is the extreme degree of jaundice. The organs are deeply stained and the fluids in the cavities are of a bright yellow colour. The only notable exception is the brain, which does not show coloration with bile.

The liver sometimes is enlarged, but generally the organ shows no macroscopic change other than the staining with bile common to all the organs. There is no evidence of fatty change. The spleen is described as being frequently enlarged, and this point is emphazised by the Japanese investigators. They also have described enlargement of the axillary and inguinal lymph glands.

The kidneys show marked naked-eye change. The organ is swollen, filled with blood and with numerous petechial hæmorrhages ; the appearance of the swollen, congested, hæmorrhagic, bile-stained organ is very striking.

Hæmorrhages may occur in any viscus or in any of the serous cavities or membranes.

Stokes never saw any marked change in the liver, the spleen was always normal in size, and no enlargement of the lymph nodes was detected. The hæmorrhages have been marked in some of the cases. In one case the cause of death was a hæmorrhagic diarrhœa ; in another continuous hæmorrhage from the mucous membrane of the bladder. Another case showed very remarkable hæmorrhages in the lung. In nearly all cases it is easy to find subperitoneal, subendocardial or subpleural hæmorrhages. These have been seen all along the length of the intestine, generally submucous, but occasionally into the mucous coat.

The liver is remarkable in the extreme variation of the changes found in different cases. In some cases very advanced lesions are found ; the cells in the central zone may show swelling, absence of the nucleus, and in more advanced specimens complete necrosis. The lesions are generally central. There is also dissociation of the cells and considerable infiltration with leucocytes. There is no evidence of massive bile obstruction. The bile canaliculi are sometimes infiltrated with leucocytes but they have never been seen filled with bile. In other specimens little or no change has been observed. In most cases there is evidence of active regeneration ; mitotic figures are easily found and there are often cells with multiple nuclei.

The cause of the jaundice which is so marked has been investigated by many workers. In the absence of any evidence of obstruction in the bile ducts, it was suggested that possibly the leucocytic infiltration around the bile capillaries might account for the cholæmia. A more probable explanation is given by Brulé, who believes that it is the inflammatory disturbance of the liver cell which impairs its function of excretion of the bile pigments.

No evidence of active destruction of blood cells has been forthcoming. The fact that the stools are not markedly pale makes it probable that some bile is formed, possibly by the more healthy cells.

It would seem that the changes in the liver depend on the period of the disease at which the patient dies. In the early deaths among the more acute cases, there are several degenerative lesions, and in the later deaths very little may be found.

The findings in the kidney are more uniform. There is almost invariably a very marked degeneration of the tubular epithelium, most evident in the proximal convoluted tubules and the ascending loops of Henle. The distribution is diffuse, every tubule is more or less involved, the lumen is obliterated and the nuclei are shadows. Diffuse infiltration with leucocytes is usually present, and often hæmorrhages. The picture is that of an acute degenerative nephritis.

In other organs the occasional incidence of hæmorrhages does not call for comment.

Laboratory Diagnosis.

When the clinical symptoms and signs are typical it is not difficult to arrive at a diagnosis. When jaundice is absent, and when the characteristic clinical signs are not present, the diagnosis must depend on laboratory methods.

The diagnosis should depend mainly on the result of animal inoculation in the early stage of the disease. Before the sixth day a very high proportion of successful inoculations in guinea-pigs can be looked for. About 75 per cent. of positive results are obtained from inoculation on the fifth day, and higher figures when the blood is taken on earlier days.

It is also frequently possible to infect an animal with the urine from patients in the later stages of convalescence. Some guinea-pigs are comparatively immune, and it is wise to use two or three animals for an experiment. Five to ten cubic centimetres of blood taken from a vein and distributed in three guinea-pigs should give a positive infection, if the blood is taken before the sixth day. If amounts of blood greater than 4 or 5 c.c. are injected the animal sometimes dies outright. It is rarely possible to find the leptospiræ in blood films, and it is rarely worth while spending time in this search as a method of diagnosis. When urine, in the convalescent stage, is used for animal experiments it should be used in large quantities, 200 to 500 c.c. being very thoroughly centrifuged and the deposit inoculated intraperitoneally. The deposit may also be examined microscopically, either by dark ground illumination or by staining methods.

The serum of the patient in the convalescent stage shows very marked immune properties, and it is often possible to confirm a clinical diagnosis by protection experiments in an animal. Stokes found 1 c.c. of serum from a convalescent patient sufficient to protect an animal against a massive dose of culture, or liver emulsion rich in leptospiræ. Agglutination reactions with cultures can also be tried, but considerable care should be exercised in using this method as the cultures were found to be readily agglutinable by normal serum, and also to show considerable auto-agglutination.

In some cases it is possible to obtain a direct culture from the blood. A good medium is rabbit serum, 10 c.c., 2 per cent. nutrient agar, PH 7·4 10 c.c. and saline solution 80 c.c. The agar should be added to the mixture of serum and salt solution while still very hot. A trace of rabbit hæmoglobin may assist the culture. A few cubic centimetres of blood are added to 100 c.c. of the medium in a flask, and then it is gently mixed with the medium. The culture may appear in four to twelve days. It is probably better to incubate at 28° C. than at a higher temperature. In the event of organisms not being found microscopically, it is sometimes worth while injecting a quantity of the culture into an animal, as, though it may be difficult to find the organism, they may have multiplied sufficiently to give a positive result by inoculation. The organisms may be looked for in the urine in the convalescent period; they generally appear from the twelfth day onward. Examinations should be made at frequent intervals. Stokes found leptospiræ in large numbers on one day and failed to find any on the next. The leptospiræ are said to be present in the fæces and have been demonstrated by inoculation experiments, but this could not be a reliable means of diagnosis. They have also been found in the cerebro-spinal fluid.

When an animal is inoculated with blood from a patient in the early stages of the disease, there is generally an initial fever of slight degree, possibly caused by the injection of foreign protein. This passes off and is succeeded by a definite rise in temperature on or about the seventh day. The second rise is sharp and definite ; the temperature often reaches 105° F., and then there is a sudden fall, the temperature becoming subnormal when the animal has collapsed and is dying. The rise and fall of the temperature may take from three to four days. Animals were often seen to develop a temperature on or about the eighth day and to show no further symptoms. These animals are often immune to further inoculations with virulent strains. It is possible that if the animal was killed at the time of the rise of temperature, and the blood and emulsion of the liver injected into a second animal, a positive result would be obtained. The *post-mortem* findings are very typical. Hæmorrhages may be found in any of the organs and are constant in the skin and lungs ; there is jaundice and a very obvious inflammation of the kidneys.

The leptospiræ can be easily found in the blood, an emulsion of the liver, or the kidney. They are easily found with a dark ground illumination or by staining by Fontana's stain. A strain of the leptospiræ can be made more virulent for guinea-pigs by passage. An emulsion of the liver or the heart's blood of the dead animal can be used. After three or four passages the strain is very virulent, and the animals die in three to four days. When the strain has become virulent very large numbers of the leptospiræ are present in the blood, and it is less difficult to obtain cultures of the organism.

Serum therapy has been recommended by the Japanese workers and excellent results have been reported in reducing the late mortality of the disease. In the acute cases it is found that it is rarely possible to treat the patients in time, death occurring on the fourth or fifth day.

In tropical countries, where yellow fever, a disease caused by an almost identical leptospira, may occur, the question of diagnosis will depend on the isolation of the leptospira and comparative immune reaction with monovalent sera prepared from known strains of the two leptospiræ. Pfeiffer's reaction and agglutination tests should be carried out. The two organisms are identical except in their immune reactions.

Prophylaxis mainly depends on measures to ensure that rats do not have an opportunity of infecting food with their excreta, and on measures to ensure drainage and to minimize the possibility of skin contamination with rat's urine. There is a possibility that prophylactic inoculations of dead cultures of leptospiræ may confer immunity, but this point has not at the moment been definitely settled. The possibility that human carriers exist cannot be lost sight of, the organisms having been found in a viable state in human urine sixty days after the onset of the disease.

Bibliography.

A very large and complete bibliography is given by Martin and Pettit in their monograph " *La Spirochétose Ictérohémorragique*," published by Masson & Cie, Paris.

CHAPTER XIX.

ACUTE INFECTIVE POLYNEURITIS.

THE material available for the study of the pathology of this disease consisted of that obtained from six fatal cases where a *post-mortem* examination was performed. In a series of thirty cases observed by Sir J. Rose Bradford, mainly in 1917, death occurred in eight cases, in one of which no *post-mortem* examination was possible and in another only the naked-eye appearances could be noted. In the other six cases the material obtained was handed to Captain E. F. Bashford, who carried out the microscopical and experimental observations. The full details are published in the *Quarterly Journal of Medicine.**

The clinical picture of so-called acute febrile or infective polyneuritis is peculiar and characteristic, and although it presents some resemblance to that seen in other well-recognized varieties of neuritis, yet the differences are so striking that it is not surprising that the experimental and histological study of the disease revealed that the lesions are widespread and not confined to the peripheral nerves. The malady is in reality a diffuse affection of the nervous system, affecting especially the spinal cord, spinal ganglia and peripheral nerves, and only slightly the cortex cerebri. The onset of the disease is accompanied with fever and a moderate leucocytosis, the blood count yielding from 12,500 to 19,000 white cells per cubic millimetre, with no special increase in the large mononuclear cells, and no notable change in the eosinophiles. These facts suggested the possibility of the malady being really an infection and allied to such diseases as poliomyelitis and encephalitis. It is, however, very remarkable that in 1916 and 1917, when these cases of polyneuritis occurred in the British Expeditionary Force, poliomyelitis was very rare and no case of encephalitis lethargica came under the notice of Rose Bradford until the end of 1918. Further, polyneuritis has perhaps some resemblance to certain cases of acute ascending paralysis, inasmuch as it is not uncommon for the palsy in cases of acute infective polyneuritis to be of the ascending type.

* *Quarterly Journal of Medicine*, Vol. 12, Nos 45 and 46.

Morbid Anatomy.

No gross lesions of the nervous system were present in any case, but some œdema of the brain together with some congestion of the vessels were sometimes observed and the spinal veins between the dura mater and the vertebral column were frequently greatly distended. The lungs showed great congestion, and subpleural petechial hæmorrhages were not infrequent; bronchitis, lobular pneumonia and plastic pleurisy were sometimes present. No general glandular enlargement was observed, but the mediastinal glands were sometimes swollen and soft. The viscera and more especially the liver and spleen were generally markedly congested, but no other lesions were found and the kidneys showed no naked-eye changes suggestive of nephritis.

After hardening in formalin and in Zenker's solution, minute petechial hæmorrhages may be visible to the naked eye in the cross-section of the spinal cord, together with great engorgement of the meningeal vessels. There may also be some irregularity in the size and shape of the grey matter of either side of the cord, varying in degree at different levels in the cervical and lumbar regions.

Histology.

Peripheral Nerves.—All the nerves examined, *e.g.*, sciatic, anterior and posterior tibial, radial, musculo-cutaneous, vagus and phrenic, showed similar features, varying in intensity in the six cases and always most marked in the nerves of the lower limbs. The lesions were most readily found in the sciatic and in the anterior and posterior tibial nerves and were also well marked in the phrenic. In purely sensory nerves the lesions, although present, were not so obvious, inasmuch as they were more scattered, and often many sections had to be examined before their presence could be demonstrated. Wallerian degeneration was always present together with proliferation of the cells of Schwann; this degeneration was never massive, isolated fibres or groups of fibres were affected and other neighbouring fibres were unaffected. In addition, well-marked lesions of acute neuritis were present, such as inflammatory exudate of round cells together with small hæmorrhages. This neuritis is not uniformly distributed throughout the nerve, small areas here and there in the course of the nerve are involved, and this is so even in the case of the sciatic nerve where the lesions are most easily found.

Spinal Cord.—Minute and widely diffused hæmorrhages are present in the grey matter but are very rare in the white matter. The grey matter also shows an excessive cellularity, especially marked in the cervical and lumbar enlargements ; the excess of small round cells was not, however, accumulated around either the meningeal or intraspinal vessels even when these were markedly congested. In polyneuritis the accumulation of these round cells takes place around the nerve cells, whereas in anterior poliomyelitis the cellular infiltration is in definite association with the blood-vessels, thus making a distinct contrast between the two conditions. There is also a considerable proliferation of the ependymal cells of the neural canal.

The nerve cells of the cord present very definite changes, widespread and irregular in their distribution and affecting not only the anterior horns but also the posterior horns and the tract cells. At different levels of the cord, in one and the same case, there may be considerable differences in the degrees to which one or other horn is affected ; for instance, in the cervical region one horn, say the left, being more involved than the right, and in the lumbar region the converse being the case. In all cases the cells affected seemed to be picked out irregularly and in varying groups, so that a much degenerated cell might be in juxtaposition to a group of healthy cells. In the earliest stages the nucleus is excentric and swollen ; later it is markedly excentric and shrunken, and the nuclear membrane may not be visible. The cell bodies lose their angular outline and become rounded, sometimes with the loss of the dendritic processes, and the cytoplasm may show one large or several small vacuoles.

The tigroid substance, both in the cell bodies and in the dendritic processes, becomes clumped or powdery and may disappear from the periphery of some cells and from the centre of others. Fat-like yellowish pigment, staining brown with Marchi's method, may be present in the cells ; the axis cylinder may be swollen, but often shows no obvious change. The pericellular spaces are unusually large and the small round cell infiltration is often especially marked round the nerve cells, so that the latter are closely invested and appear to be undergoing absorption. Notwithstanding the accumulation of small round cells around the nerve cells, there is no such accumulation in relation to the blood-vessels. The white matter of the cord showed few changes beyond the presence of Wallerian degeneration. The nerve cells of the posterior root ganglia showed excentricity of the nucleus and sometimes some vacuolation of the cytoplasm ; occasionally this was very marked. The tigroid substance was clumped and finely granular and some cells contained an excess of pigment. A patchy accumulation of small round cells between the nerve cells was also present. The changes in the posterior root ganglia were irregular in their distribution and might be well marked in some ganglia, *e.g.*, the lumbar, and absent in others, *e.g.*, the cervical, in one and the same case.

Brain.—A slight degree of round-celled infiltration was present in the cortex, most marked around the larger antler cells of the motor cortex, but the nerve cells showed very little change, except possibly some slight excentricity of the nucleus. Slight changes of a similar character were present in the nerve nuclei of the pons and medulla.

Muscles.—Degenerative changes were present in the voluntary muscles, individual fibres and groups of fibres being affected in the midst of healthy unaffected fibres.

Viscera.—The liver showed slight infiltration of small round cells in the large and small portal tracts, and the kidneys showed early patchy parenchymatous and glomerular nephritis.

Experimental Transmission of the Disease.

The spinal cord obtained from human cases was preserved in 50 per cent. glycerine and an emulsion of this was injected subdurally under complete ether anæsthesia in monkeys (*Macacus rhesus*). The material used was derived from three fatal human cases and the spinal cords had been preserved in glycerine for twenty-five days, three months and seven months respectively. The emulsion of spinal cord was, at the time of inoculation, sterile as tested by all ordinary aërobic and anaërobic methods. In all three cases positive results were obtained, and the monkeys developed symptoms resembling clinically those seen in man, and similar lesions to the human ones were found in the nervous system of the monkeys on *post-mortem* examination. The monkeys showed no alteration in their behaviour nor any symptoms of ill-health after recovery from the anæsthetic for about a week. At the end of this period they apparently suffered from some malaise, as they remained quiet and lost their appetite and some developed a nasal discharge. It is uncertain whether any significance is to be attached to these early slight symptoms, but it is quite possible that they are analogous to the initial and more or less trivial symptoms that may be present in the human cases some weeks before the onset of the definite paralytic phenomena. These possible prodromal symptoms in the experimental monkeys soon pass off and the animal regains its usual activity and vigour. About a month after the inoculation, well-marked lassitude with loss of appetite appears and the animal shows distinct unwillingness to use the hind limbs for jumping. One hind limb may be obviously weaker than its fellow, and one or both hands may be used to enable the animal to sit securely on its perch. There may be definite trailing of one limb. Within a week to a fortnight from the onset of the weakness in the hind limbs, the arms became similarly involved, sometimes bilaterally, so that food is taken by being seized by the mouth instead of being carried to the mouth by the hands ; wrist-drop may be present. In two cases the muscles of the jaw were also affected, so that only soft food could be taken. Neither the eyelids nor the pupils were affected in any case, but weakness of the neck muscles was sometimes present so that the head could not be held up. In one case œdema of the face occurred, most marked after sleep, and disappearing during the course of the day. The respiratory movements may become very shallow, but even in the cases where the general weakness was very marked improvement might set in and a gradual and slow recovery take place. Whether the recovery would be complete or not it is not possible to say, as such animals were killed in order to determine whether any lesions of the nervous system were present. Similar results were obtained by the subdural inoculation of material obtained from the experimental monkeys into healthy monkeys and thus the disease was transmitted from monkey to monkey as well as from man to monkey.

The onset of the disease in all but one of the monkeys inoculated (nine in number) was insidious, and although its progress was very gradual, nevertheless it was well developed in all cases in five to six weeks from the date of inoculation. In one case no symptoms developed after the subdural inoculation, but there was some doubt in this case as to whether the operation had been carried out successfully. In one case only was the illness fatal and here death occurred suddenly eleven weeks after subdural inoculation ; in all other cases the animals were killed when the symptoms had become marked.

In all cases on *post-mortem* examination no intercurrent disease, tuberculous or other, was found, and no gross lesions of the nervous system were present except some hyperplasia of lymphatic glands and some congestion at the bases of the papillæ of the kidneys and possibly some congestion of the vessels of the meninges. On histological examination lesions were found in the nervous system similar to those described in man. Although by the use of ordinary aërobic and anaërobic cultural methods no growth is obtained from material derived from the nervous system, yet by the adoption of a special method, *e.g.*, the Noguchi method, bodies similar to those obtained by other observers in poliomyelitis are obtained. There is, however, doubt as to the nature of these bodies and hence at present there is no proof of the culture of a living virus, although the experimental transmission of the disease suggests strongly that the malady is due to a living virus, probably a filter-passer.

CHAPTER XX.

GINGIVITIS AND VINCENT'S ANGINA.

THE condition of the gums known as gingivitis is a disease which is common amongst the civil population of the British Isles and other countries, and during the war it was in evidence to a certain extent amongst soldiers at home and overseas.

It may be either acute, subacute or chronic. The acute form when it takes on the ulcerative condition is a painful disease with well-marked local and constitutional symptoms. In the subacute and chronic forms the symptoms are not as a rule of a painful nature, and the patient may go on for months without drawing attention to the condition of his gums. All forms of the disease are more prevalent in those who have defective teeth, and who neglect the elements of oral hygiene, and for these reasons the dentist very often meets with it in the ordinary routine of his practice, and treats for both conditions, namely, gingivitis and decayed teeth.

Acute Ulcerative Gingivitis.

This is a spreading inflammation of the margins of the gums, resulting in sloughing and ulceration of the inter-dental papillæ and the gums around the necks of the teeth. The onset is gradual, commencing in a small area of the gum which extends to adjacent areas, and in some cases to the mucous membrane of the mouth. After a week or ten days, in the absence of treatment, a sloughy and ulcerated condition of the inflamed areas sets in, accompanied with severe pain, constitutional disturbance, offensive breath, difficulty of mastication, hæmorrhage from the gums either spontaneous or on the slightest pressure ; the teeth are painful, and some may be loose.

The disease most frequently commences around the upper incisor teeth or lower molars, but it may commence at any part of the gums, and spread from one jaw to the other, to the adjacent mucous membrane of the mouth or to the tonsils and fauces. In severe cases and in those which become chronic, a rarefying osteitis and destruction of bone around the teeth in the affected area sets in, causing the periodontal membrane to become involved and eventually leading to pyorrhœa alveolaris.

According to reports from dental officers with the troops in France, gingivitis in the acute ulcerative form was present in about 0·7 per cent. of patients seeking dental treatment, and in about 0·3 per cent. of soldiers living under various conditions but not reporting sick on account of dental disease. From these reports it would appear that the disease was not at any time a formidable source of sickness amongst the troops at the front.

Subacute and Chronic Gingivitis.

This is a swollen or inflamed condition of the gums, and may be local or general. The gums bleed readily on touch or pressure, or there is a history of bleeding extending over some time. Pain may or may not be present and in some cases the patient may be unaware of the condition. These forms are often associated with pyorrhœa alveolaris, and in all probability they are the starting point from which the periodontal membrane becomes involved.

Soldiers rarely report sick on account of subacute or chronic gingivitis, and the condition is generally met with only as a side issue when men are admitted to hospital for other diseases, or when mouth inspections are carried out for its detection. All conditions of teeth may be present; they may be clean and sound, dirty and decayed, and periodontal disease may also be present. The disease is more prevalent in civil life than in the army and this was also the case during the war. It is more in evidence as age advances and as the teeth become decayed, and it is more frequently found in those who neglect cleanliness of the teeth and mouth.

In an investigation of gingivitis and Vincent's disease carried out by Sir David Semple, Captain Price-Jones and Miss L. Digby for the Pathological Committee of the War Office during the autumn of 1918 on men in military hospitals in England on account of wounds and diseases other than gingivitis, it was found that, in 3,000 soldiers of all ages from 18 to 35 years and upwards who were examined, there were 359 cases of gingivitis, or 11·9 per cent. Of these 359 cases, 354 were either subacute or chronic and 5 were of the acute ulcerative type. With the exception of the five acute cases, none had been admitted for gingivitis. Many of these men had been serving in one or other of the theatres of war, and over 700 of them were examined within four days from the time they left the trenches.

Men under 25 years of age furnished the lowest percentage of cases, namely, 6·7, and those over 35 years the highest, namely, 19·2 per cent. in one unit and 33 per cent. in another unit. When a comparison was made between those who had been overseas and those who had not been out of England, the percentage was considerably less among the former.

During the war the experience of army dentists with the troops at the front was that subacute and chronic gingivitis and periodontal disease were common amongst men who neglected to keep their teeth clean, and they give figures varying from 12 to 20 per cent. in patients who came for dental treatment.   In civil life civilian dentists give figures varying from 20 to 30 per cent.

Vincent's Angina.

This is an acute ulcero-membranous tonsilitis or pharyngitis which is almost invariably preceded by one or other of the forms of gingivitis described.   The gum condition may be present for days, weeks or months before infection of the tonsils or pharynx takes place, or it may be of such a mild form as to escape notice, but when investigated it will be found that in every case of Vincent's angina either gingivitis is present or there is a history of recent gingivitis.

Taylor and McKinstry made a systematic examination of the gums in 70 cases of Vincent's angina and found them infected in every case.   The same authors, out of 150 cases of fuso-spirillary gingivitis, found the characteristic lesions of Vincent's angina present in the pharynx and tonsils in 70. It would thus appear that Vincent's angina is always preceded by gingivitis, but that gingivitis is not always followed by Vincent's angina, facts which point to the causal organisms being the same in both cases.

There are two recognized forms of Vincent's angina, namely, a diphtheroid type in which there is a firm yellowish-white false membrane and the ulceration is superficial, and an ulcerative type where the membrane is soft, greyish and foul-smelling, and the ulceration deep.   In both forms the constitutional disturbance is severe, the breath offensive, and the neighbouring glands may be enlarged and painful.   The disease is comparatively rare in the army, and was not much in evidence during the war.

Bacteriology.

In all forms of gingivitis and Vincent's angina fusiform bacilli and spirochætes are present in large numbers, especially in those cases in which there is an acute ulcerative and sloughy

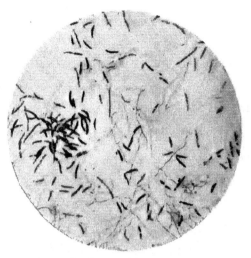

Fig. 1.—Photomicrograph of a direct film from a case of Vincent's angina showing *B. fusiformis* and spirochætes, stained carbol-fuchsine. (x 1,000.)

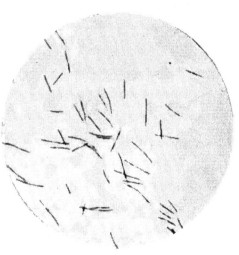

Fig 2.—Photomicrograph of a pure culture of *B. fusiformis* from a case of gingivitis, stained carbol-fuchsine. (x 1,000.)

condition of the tissues, where they are found in almost pure cultures.   Fig. 1 is a photomicrograph of a direct film from a case of Vincent's angina, showing *Bacillus fusiformis* and spirochætes, stained carbol-fuchsine (×1,000). Fig. 2 is a photomicrograph of a pure culture of *B. fusiformis* from a case of gingivitis, stained carbol-fuchsine (×1,000). Fig. 3 is a photomicrograph of a congo-red film from a culture of spirochætes from a case of Vincent's angina (× *circa* 1,000).

In the diseased conditions described the *B. fusiformis* and spirochætes are in all probability the causal organisms ; they

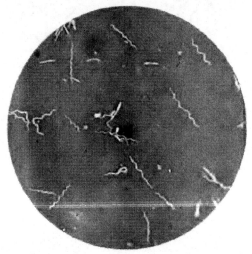

Fig. 3.—Photomicrograph of a congo red film from a culture of spirochætes from a case of Vincent's angina. (x *circa* 1,000.)

are invariably present and in enormous numbers. On the other hand, they are invariably present, but generally few in number, on the gums, and frequently also on the tonsils and fauces of all those who have teeth.

In the investigation already referred to, in the case of 512 soldiers of all ages from 18 to 35 years and upwards whose gums were bacteriologically examined, fusiform bacilli were present in 489 cases, or 95·5 per cent., and spirochætes in 488 cases, or 95·3 per cent. In 234 of these 512 soldiers the tonsils and fauces were also examined, and fusiform bacilli found to be present in 78 cases, or 33·3 per cent., and spirochætes

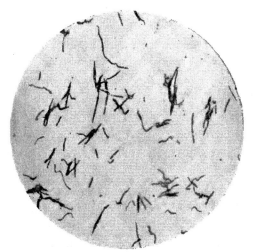

Fig. 4.—Photomicrograph of a carbol-fuchsine stained film from a six days old colony grown on serum agar.   (x 1,000.)

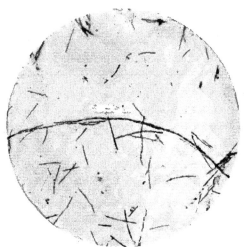

Fig. 5.—Photomicrograph of a carbol-fuchsine stained film from a six days old colony grown on serum agar.   (x 1,000.)

in 108 cases, or 46·1 per cent.   Eight of the men were without teeth, and their gums and tonsils were free from *B. fusiformis* and spirochætes.

It would thus appear that *B. fusiformis* and spirochætes are normal inhabitants of the human mouth, and that in cases of gingivitis and Vincent's angina they are enormously increased.

In the absence of direct experimental proof it is highly probable that they are the causal organisms of these diseases.

The *Bacillus fusiformis* (Vincent's bacillus) is anaërobic and when grown in artificial media may assume pleomorphic forms.   In pure cultures, in addition to typical bacilli (slightly curved and with pointed ends), leptothricial forms and wavy intermediate forms may be found.   These forms are shown in Figs. 4 and 5, which are photomicrographs of carbol-fuchsine stained films from a six days old colony grown on serum agar (×1,000).

In the mouth both in conditions of health and disease, *B. fusiformis* is always associated with spirochætes.   At least three varieties of spirochætes are to be found, namely, *Spironema buccale, Spironema medium* and *Spironema dentium* (see Fig. 3). These three forms are recognizable in congo-red films from the gums or fauces, or from anaërobic cultures from the same sources.

Prevention.

The basis of prevention may be summed up in two words, oral hygiene, that is, cleanliness of the mouth and gums, cleanliness of the teeth and cleanliness of the throat.   Where these three elementary points are attended to gingivitis and Vincent's disease are seldom found, and the onset of dental caries is diminished and retarded.   When the gums and necks of the teeth are kept clean, there can be no marginal gingivitis, and as gingivitis almost invariably precedes pyorrhœa alveolaris and Vincent's disease, these two diseases are also prevented, and so is the formation of tartar, masses of bacteria hardened by the deposition of lime salts from the saliva.   The only equipment necessary is a tooth-brush and cold water, an equipment which is within the means and reach of everybody and should be used morning and evening, if not after every meal.   Tooth powders and various other preparations sold as washes for the mouth and teeth answer no more useful purpose in keeping the gums and teeth clean than cold water.

Acute ulcerative gingivitis and Vincent's disease being

infectious diseases, steps should be taken to prevent others becoming infected from using .the same drinking vessels, and by other means which would suggest themselves.

Treatment.

Acute ulcerative gingivitis and Vincent's disease require rigorous treatment. When sloughs are present they should be carefully removed before applying local remedies. Various local remedies have been found useful, such as liquor arsenicalis in combination with ipecacuanha and glycerine, also mouthwashes of hydrogen peroxide, eusol, carbolic acid, and so on. When tartar is present it should be removed as soon as the condition of the gums permits of this being done. When all sloughs have disappeared and the gums begin to heal, glycerine or tannic acid is a useful preparation to harden them. As soon as the acute symptoms have subsided and the mouth is clean, the condition of the teeth should be attended to.

In the case of Vincent's angina the applications mentioned will also be found useful, and these may be followed by gargles of hydrogen peroxide and other antiseptics. Dubreuil speaks highly of the local application of a saturated solution of chromic acid on a swab, followed by gargling with hydrogen peroxide (1 in 10) so as to prevent swallowing of the chromic acid in the saliva. He states that the ulcerated condition rapidly becomes clean and heals up, and that a second application on the fourth or fifth day is rarely necessary.

Similar treatment may be supplied to any fuso-spirillary infection of the gums.

BIBLIOGRAPHY.

Bowman	Ulcero Membranous Stomatitis and Gingivitis among Troops on Active Service.	Brit. Med. Jl., 1916, Vol. i, p. 373.
Colyer	Acute Ulcerative Gingivitis ..	Brit. Med. Jl., 1918, Vol. ii, p. 396.
Dubreuil	Traitement de l'angine de Vincent et des infections fusospirillaires par l'acide chromique.	Journ. de Méd. de Bordeaux, 1920, Vol. xci, p. 153.
Semple, Price-Jones & Digby.	A Report for the Pathological Committee of the War Office of an Inquiry into Gingivitis and Vincent's Disease occurring in the Army.	Jl. of R.A.M.C.,1919, Vol. xxxiii, No. 3, p. 217; No. 4, p. 282.
Taylor & McKinstry	The Relation of Peridental Gingivitis to Vincent's Angina.	Brit. Med. Jl., 1917, Vol. i, p. 421.

CHAPTER XXI.

WAR NEPHRITIS.

THE ultimate cause of war nephritis has not been discovered, and in dealing with its ætiological aspect it will consequently be necessary to discuss all the factors which may possibly play a part in its causation. In the first place, there is the outstanding fact that acute nephritis attacked relatively large numbers of the troops, especially those engaged in trench warfare, and hence the disease is often called "trench nephritis." The disease appeared in the early months of 1915, there being few cases before February of that year, and steadily increased in frequency in the following months. In July there were over 50 cases per 100,000 troops, and the maximum of a little over 100 per 100,000 troops was reached in December, 1916. The figures pertaining to the earlier months show clearly that the occurrence of the disease was not related to the cold weather. As just noted, nephritis occurred especially among men in the trenches, though cases were also met with among men at the base who had not been at the front. It is, however, noteworthy that very few cases occurred among officers ; and further, Dunn and McNee failed on enquiry to find cases in the civilian population in areas where the disease was prevalent amongst the troops. The disease appeared in the German and Austrian armies about the same time as in the British troops, and presented closely similar features. In the French army the affection appeared somewhat later, and the case incidence of nephritis was less than in the British, and the proportion of cases in the Belgian army was smaller still. It is noteworthy that there were practically no cases amongst the Indian troops, although the disease was occurring amongst the British troops operating with them in the same divisions. There is thus the picture of nephritis appearing as a common disease among the various troops on the Western front about the same time and without relation to locality. As regards the latter point, it may be noted that when a division in which the disease was occurring shifted its locality, the incidence of the disease remained pretty much the same in the new locality ; and further, a division in which previously the disease was rare, did not show any marked increase after taking over an area in

which it had been common.   In other theatres of war, notably
in Gallipoli, where trench warfare prevailed, war nephritis was
not met with.

No similar occurrence of nephritis in conditions of civil life
is known, and history does not show that nephritis has been of
sufficient frequency in previous wars to attract attention, with
the exception of the American Civil War.   This exception is,
however, of considerable importance, as the disease then corre-
sponded with the recent outbreak in two particulars; it occurred
after the establishment of trench warfare, and it was not related
to cold weather—on the contrary, the maximum incidence
among the troops was reached in the middle of summer.

Whilst the affection presented the usual features of nephritis,
some points call for separate reference.   The patients were
usually young men previously healthy, and apparently exposure to the conditions at the front for some time was necessary
before the disease appeared.   This was specially noticeable
when fresh divisions were going out to France, as usually two
or three months elapsed before the appearance of the disease
amongst them.   Rose Bradford met with very few examples of
the disease in men who had been less than a month at the front.
The onset was usually rapid, with albuminuria, often pyrexia,
facial œdema, and so on, and a very common symptom was
dyspnœa, which occurred at an earlier stage and was more
severe than in the nephritis of civil life.   In the great majority
of cases the affection was mild, and recovery occurred rapidly
under hospital conditions.   Nevertheless, relapses were not
uncommon, and some cases passed into the stage of subacute
nephritis.   Death in the early stages was of rare occurrence,
but there were quite a number of fatal cases, and the *post-mortem*
examinations on a number of these have supplied the facts as
to the essential lesion of the kidney.   A description of these
will apply chiefly to the cases where death took place early.
It is, of course, well recognized that a primary lesion of one part
of the kidney may give rise later to changes in the other constituents, and thus the original lesion becomes obscured.

Pathological Anatomy and Histology.

The question as to the essential and primary lesion in the
kidneys underlying the clinical phenomena of war nephritis, is
one of prime importance, and requires a study of the changes
present where death has occurred in the early stages of the
disease.   The description given by Shaw Dunn and McNee was
based on an examination of the kidneys from thirty-five cases

with a fatal result in each within a fortnight, the shortest duration being within forty-eight hours. Keith and Thomson give an account, which is essentially in agreement, of the changes found in two cases where death occurred at the end of the second week. Herxheimer communicated to the German Pathological Society, at a discussion on war nephritis, the results of his examination of seven cases of duration not exceeding three weeks, and his conclusions were supported by Benda, Aschoff, Merkel and others. Jungmann and more recently Gross also gave descriptions which correspond in essential particulars. The accounts of all these writers are in wonderful harmony. The earliest lesion is in the glomeruli—a glomerulo-nephritis—and in them the capillary endothelium is the first to show evidence of lesion. At a later stage changes spread to other parts of the kidney and there is then produced the complicated picture of a subacute nephritis.

The account of the histological changes given by Ameuille, is, however, different. He describes the changes as chiefly interstitial, consisting in an œdema of the connective tissue with much infiltration of polymorphonuclear leucocytes, these often forming clumps or aggregations. This picture had not been met with in any of the early cases examined by Shaw Dunn and McNee.

The Renal Lesions.—In the cases where death has occurred within the first fortnight, the changes visible to the naked eye are very slight. Usually the kidneys are of normal size, but occasionally some enlargement is present. The capsules are non-adherent and when stripped, leave a smooth and usually pale surface. The cortex is generally pale and presents a contrast to the medullary pyramids which are congested. Hæmorrhages are usually absent at this stage, but they have been observed in one or two cases. Slight œdema of the kidney substance has also been described by Herxheimer. The naked-eye appearances are thus far from being characteristic, but on examination of the cortex with a hand-lens, the glomeruli are seen to project from the cut surface as pale translucent globules, this appearance indicating their enlarged and relatively anæmic condition.

As regards the microscopic changes, the following extract from a paper read by Dunn and McNee contains all the facts recorded by them.

" On histological examination the most prominent abnormality in all cases is found in the glomeruli. These appear, on low-power examination, to be somewhat enlarged and more cellular than normal, while they contain little or no blood (Fig. 1). In many instances a rounded projection extends from a swollen glomerulus into the opening of the convoluted tubule. The details of the glomerular changes can be made out only by the aid of special staining, and on close examination with an oil-immersion lens, but as they appear to be of cardinal importance they will be fully described.

" Many of the capillary loops forming the tuft have their lumina dilated, and contain numerous nucleated cells, but few or no red blood corpuscles (Fig. 2). These cells have oval or flattened nuclei, like those of endothelia, and fairly abundant protoplasm, which frequently shows a very indefinite margin. Where they are numerous and closely packed together they resemble a syncytium. In several of the cases mitotic division is observed in a few of the nuclei, but long search for this feature in the others has yielded a negative result. Granules of fat are occasionally present in the protoplasm, and fatty

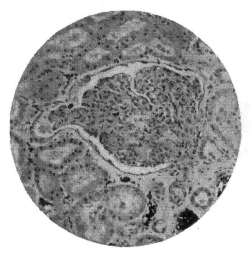

Fig. 1.—A glomerulus in an acute case of nephritis, exhibiting slight enlargement and pouting into the opening of the convoluted tubule. The tuft is excessively cellular and contains very few red blood corpuscles. Note the absence of inflammatory exudate or adhesion. (x 125.)

change is sometimes very marked in the cells occupying loops of capillaries which project into the mouth of a tubule. Polymorphonuclear leucocytes and lymphocytes accompany the endothelial cells in the lumina of the capillaries in varying numbers, but they are never very abundant. Search has been made for hyaline thrombi in the same situation, but with negative result. In many of the kidneys, especially where the disease has been rapidly fatal, the accumulation of abnormal cells in the glomerular capillaries is very marked and widespread, so that in any section of a tuft not more than one or two loops contain red corpuscles and have a normal lining. The degree of blockage is less pronounced on the whole in cases of older standing. In view of the considerable vascular disturbance which must ensue from occlusion of capillaries, it is remarkable that exudative phenomena are almost entirely absent, and degenerative changes are only slight. The epithelial cells covering the tufts generally show only slight catarrh ; their protoplasm is thickened and of degenerate appearance, while discarded cells, which are sometimes caught around the projection in the tubule mouth, may exhibit fatty degeneration. Crescent-shaped accumulations of cells in the capsule are seen only in one case, and are there very scanty. There is no exudate of fibrin or leucocytes inside or around the capsules, and intracapsular hæmorrhage is rarely seen. The tufts show no appearance of patchy fibrosis or of adhesion to the capsules, such as occur so commonly in glomerular nephritis. The greatest degree of degenerative change is limited, as a rule, to some hyaline thickening of capillary walls, and of the fibrous tissue of Bowman's capsule. The capillary blood-vessels in the cortical labyrinth and in the medulla show no change comparable to that found in the glomeruli.

" An additional form of lesion has been observed in only three cases, and in these only rarely. This is a condition of total infarction of certain glomeruli.

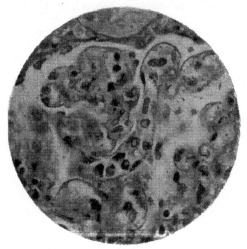

Fig. 2.—High-power view of a portion of a glomerulus in acute nephritis, showing accumulation of excess endothelial cells in the lumina of the capillaries. (x 400.)

The capillaries in these are dilated and engorged with red blood corpuscles, and excess of endothelium is present only in a few loops. These glomeruli exhibit catarrh and hernial protrusion like the others. In serial sections it is determined that the infarction is due to the presence of hyaline material in the afferent arteriole, and in some instances the wall of this vessel shows evidence of necrosis and slight leucocytic invasion. No micro-organisms are recognizable in the hyaline material, or in the glomeruli generally, by any staining method.

" The conditions in the convoluted tubules show less uniformity, and in most cases are much less easy to valuate ; the renal epithelium so quickly develops autolytic change that no absolute reliance can be placed on the appearance of breaking down of cell protoplasm, unless it is known that the tissue has been suitably fixed very soon after death. In some of the cases, however, there is certain evidence of catarrh ; thus, in addition to fragmentation of protoplasm and loss of nuclei, some cells show well-marked fatty degeneration, while in others the nuclei exhibit various stages of karyokinetic division (Fig. 3). Even where these phenomena are noted there is seldom much

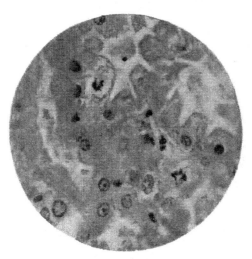

Fig. 3.—Mitotic division of highly specialized secreting cells in convoluted tubules in a case of acute nephritis. Two mitotic figures are visible. (x 400.)

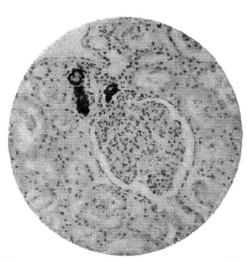

Fig. 4.—Calcified cast, densely black, in the junctional tubule beside a glomerulus; from a case of acute nephritis. (x 125.)

desquamation of whole cells, and never any loss of all the cells from one section of a tubule. The epithelial casts, which are rarely seen in lower segments of tubules, are evidently made up by agglomerations of cells which have desquamated separately.

"Tubular hæmorrhage is present to some extent in every case, but is not abundant, and is sometimes found only with difficulty. It is seen either in the first convoluted tubules, in which case the blood is fresh and the blood corpuscles are well preserved and lie free, or else in the ascending limb of Henle's loop in the form of a brown-coloured cast, with the corpuscles packed together, lysed and misshapen.

"In most of the kidneys there are some long hyaline casts in the upper part of the ascending limb of Henle's loop, and especially in the junctional tubules leading from these. In three of the cases, in which the known duration of the disease was from six to fourteen days these hyaline casts are very numerous and elongated, and in a considerable number of them the upper or peripheral end contains calcified debris in the form of granules or small concretions. The calcified material occurs most frequently and characteristically in the junctional tubule, which winds round the arterioles of the glomerulus from which that tubule has originated (Fig. 4).

"The interstitial connective tissue of these kidneys is, on the whole, of the delicate consistence seen in the normal organ. In all of them there are present some sclerosed glomeruli, with accompanying patches of slight fibrosis of the interstitial tissue of the cortex, but these are not more numerous than may be found in the kidneys of healthy men of military age who have died of wounds. They are evidently of no significance for the existing acute disease.

"Brief reference may be made to an alteration which is not infrequently observed in the medullary pyramids ; this is a condition of œdema and hyaline swelling of the connective tissue fibres which surround and support the groups of straight arterioles. The descending limbs of Henle's loops, which are embedded in the same tissue, sometimes contain dense hyaline material, staining strongly with eosin ; occasionally this is accompanied by leucocytes. The significance of these appearances is unknown, and they require further investigation."

Whilst the primary and essential lesion is in the glomerular capillaries, evidence of damage soon appears in the other structures of the kidney. Such extension of lesion is usually manifest in cases where death has occurred after four weeks, and the general result may be summarized by saying that there follow the usual changes met with in subacute glomerulo-tubular nephritis. The kidneys present varying degrees of enlargement, pallor and mottling of the cortex, leading to a "large pale kidney." Kidneys in this latter stage have been met with and described by Andrewes, Keith and Thomson, Shaw Dunn and McNee, Herxheimer, Beitzke and others. In a proportion of cases a hæmorrhagic condition appears before death, and the kidneys assume a red mottled appearance ; hæmorrhages may also be present in the pelvis. There is evidence that the supervention of hæmorrhages is specially related to the occurrence of complications elsewhere, such as various "septic conditions," severe broncho-pneumonia or influenza.

Microscopic examination in the later stages has in certain cases shown a continuance of the original glomerular lesion and extension to the parts around. The enlarged glomerular tufts are the seat of connective tissue overgrowth, and become adherent to the capsules at places in varying degrees. There is sometimes proliferation of the subcapsular epithelium with the formation of a laminated mass of cells, not infrequently accompanied by hyaline material, and later an ingrowth of connective tissue into the mass. The tubules also become markedly affected, catarrh and secondary fatty degeneration being present. The epithelium of many becomes cubical or flattened in type, and while many are dilated with casts of various kinds, others show atrophic change. There also occurs marked increase of the interstitial tissue, with lymphocytic infiltration. It is, however, unnecessary to go into details, as there is nothing characteristic in the changes, and they vary in different cases. There is no definite information with regard to a stage of contraction, as it is very difficult to exclude the existence of a previous lesion. That such a stage will follow in some cases is practically certain, and the further history of cases of war nephritis, when worked out, will probably yield facts of importance on this point.

The general conclusion is that the primary lesion in the kidneys is in the capillaries of the glomeruli and is characterized by swelling and proliferation of their endothelium; it may be called an intracapillary glomerulitis. Subsequently there is an extension of pathological change to other parts. Such a lesion is in no way peculiar to war nephritis; in fact, it is already recognized as the earliest occurrence in glomerulo-nephritis. It is met with especially in diseases where streptococci are present—scarlet fever, angina, erysipelas, and less frequently in pneumococcal infections. It is without doubt to be interpreted as the result of excretion of toxic substances, and not produced by the actual presence of organisms. In conformity with this view, the kidneys in war nephritis have been carefully searched for bacteria with negative result, as has also been the case in the glomerulo-nephritis of civil life. Moreover, it is to be noted that the lesion is of a general kind, all the glomeruli being implicated, though some to a greater degree than others. In this respect the lesion differs from the embolic type of glomerulo-nephritis occurring in streptococcic endocarditis, where the glomeruli are affected quite irregularly, both as regards the distribution of the change and the parts of individual glomeruli affected. It must be kept in view that the lesions described are those in early fatal cases and therefore severe. In the ordinary type of case with recovery, the lesions must be of slighter degree, and it is readily conceivable how the condition of the endothelium may pass off, and complete restoration to normal result. Nevertheless, the clinical facts indicate that the slight initial lesion may become progressive and lead to a fatal result at a later stage, though the proportion of such cases has not been great.

The Urine and Functional Disturbances.—One cannot say that there is any special feature in the character of the urine in war nephritis as compared with other forms. The amount in the early stages of the disease is usually diminished to a varying degree, but not infrequently it is normal; in fact, in certain cases even at an early period it has been increased. Ameuille found that in early cases with œdema the amount was rarely under 500 c.c. per day. Anuria has been observed to occur for a short time, or to be present before death, but such an occurrence has been proportionately very rare. There is, however, a distinct increase in the amount of urine during the process of diuresis, which usually accompanies the disappearance of œdema. Albumen is usually abundant, and an indication of the amount may be given by the following figures taken from a report by Shaw Dunn and McNee. Among 38 cases examined in the early stages, they found the amount to be over 8 parts per 1,000 (Esbach) in 3 cases, 5 to 8 parts in 12 cases, 1 to 4 parts in 18 cases and below 1 part in 5 cases. Mackenzie Wallis found the proteins to be the usual serum albumen and serum globulin in a proportion of from 5 to 1, to 6 to 1, as in other forms of nephritis; no other proteins were detected. Casts are usually present and often in large numbers. In the early stages hyaline and granular casts tend to predominate, whilst later, epithelial and fatty casts become more abundant, though the latter are often scanty or may be absent. Red corpuscles in varying amount are also to be found on microscopic examination, and the presence of blood may be visible to the naked eye. Ameuille states that the presence of blood could be detected macroscopically in 6 per cent. of the cases. Bruns, on the other hand, found hæmaturia to be of more frequent occurrence. A hæmorrhagic nephritis with abundant blood in the urine, seems to be due to the addition of some infective complication. The presence of leucocytes in the urine has been recorded by most observers, but there have been differences of statement as to their amount. Mackenzie Wallis found the presence of a considerable number of polymorphonuclear leucocytes in the urine to be a marked feature in war nephritis, as it is in scarlatinal nephritis, and Ameuille also states that these cells were abundant in his cases. Ullmann, on the other hand, remarks on their scarcity in those he examined, and Bruns states that they are scanty at first and become more numerous about the time of disappearance of the œdema. This discrepancy, as well as many others, probably depends in part at least upon the different stages at which the examinations have been made. Certainly the changes in the kidneys in the earliest stage do not seem likely to lead to the presence of many leucocytes in the urine at that period.

The condition of the urine in the early stages indicates a general interference with the kidney functions. In accordance with the nitrogen retention which is the rule in the acute stage, the amount of urea in the urine usually shows diminution, which is sometimes marked, but in connection with the functional inadequacy of the kidney the amount of urea in the blood is the more important indication. Retention of chlorides is also generally distinct in the acute stage, and in cases with marked œdema the reduction in the urine is often great. In some instances chlorides have been found to be absent. During the period of diuresis in the course of recovery, the output of chlorides increases and often exceeds the normal, as does also the amount of urine. It is to be noted that albuminuria and some hæmaturia may persist after the phases of retention of nitrogen and chlorides have passed off.

In relation to the question of renal sufficiency, estimations of the amount of urea in the blood have been carried out on a fairly extensive scale. The general result has been to show that the urea is increased in amount, and with it other nitrogenous bodies of non-protein nature ; so that there is a nitrogen retention. Mackenzie Wallis found that in acute cases the normal amount of urea, $20 \cdot 50$ mgm. per 100 c.c. of blood, rose to 100 or 150 mgrm., and that this retention was usually accompanied by a diminution in the amount of diastase in the urine. He examined also the urea content of the cerebrospinal fluid in a number of cases, and found it to be distinctly raised in all the cases with uræmia. In the early stages of all cases, both with and without œdema, Ameuille found an increase of urea in the blood, this being never less than 70 mgrm. per 100 c.c. whilst in unfavourable cases it might be much higher. With improvement in the general condition the amount rapidly fell. Keith and Thomson found slight increase of the blood urea only in some acute cases of the resolving type, whilst in the non-resolving there was a definite rise of urea up to 158 mgrm. According to the results of MacLean and

De Wesselow, there is generally some retention of urea in early acute cases, whilst in severe examples as much as 600 mgrm. of urea per 100 c.c. of blood may be present. A fatal result was in every case observed when the amount exceeded 300 mgrm. They consider that the estimation of the urea in the blood affords valuable information as to prognosis. In some cases where the blood urea is normal, a certain degree of kidney insufficiency may still be present, and may be shown by the want of power to concentrate urea in the urine, when 15 grm. of urea is given by the mouth.

It is well known that the salt content of the blood plasma, as indicated by estimations of the chlorides, is comparatively constant, and that when chlorides are retained this is compensated for by retention of water, the excess of fluid tending to pass into and accumulate in the tissues. Accordingly, chlorides do not accumulate in the blood as urea does. Estimations of the chlorides in the plasma in war nephritis have been carried out by MacLean and De Wesselow, and by Keith and Thomson. The former found very slight changes in the chlorides of the plasma, while some distinct variations were observed by the latter. Trevan found the amount of chlorides in the blood to be above the normal in four cases examined.

The diastase test has been applied to war nephritis in a fairly large number of cases. Mackenzie Wallis examined the diastase output in the urine in fifty cases, and found marked diminution or absence in thirty-one ; eight of these had no diastase in the urine at all. On the other hand, those with normal output were all convalescent. The results as regards the amount of diastase were not in relation to the duration of the disease but to the severity of the case, that is, to the damage to the kidneys. He notes that where low values persisted, patients showed tendency to relapse. MacLean and De Wesselow obtained results which also confirm the value of the test as an indication of the condition of the kidneys. They found that a low diastatic value was associated with nitrogen retention ; in fact, they did not meet with a single case where a high value was present along with the latter condition. Patients in the early acute period of the disease with a very low diastatic value as a rule did not do well. Adler employed the diastase test along with the phenyl-sulphone-phthalein test, and found them of great value in prognosis. The two tests were generally in agreement, but sometimes the latter was the more helpful of the two, occasionally showing the approach of uræmia even in the absence of ordinary clinical symptoms.

Bruns found a diminished excretion of chlorides during the stage of œdema, though they never disappeared from the urine, and an increase of urea in the blood in about half the cases, the highest figure being 150 mgrm. per 100 c.c. He notes that uræmic symptoms are fairly common at this stage, and that eclamptic convulsions may occur without increase of urea in the blood. MacLean also records two cases of fits with recovery, in which the blood urea was not appreciably raised. Zondek gives the result of observations on cases which he examined some weeks after the commencement of the nephritis, and these showed a satisfactory excretion of chlorides with a distinct nitrogen retention in the blood. He notes that a complete restoration of the kidney function may occur as regards these points, whilst there is still a distinct amount of albumen and even blood in the urine. Functional tests have also been carried out by the administration of urea and chlorides by the mouth, by the injection of phenyl-sulphone-phthalein, but these though of use in individual cases have not added materially to the main facts.

Œdema.—Whilst the presence of some œdema in the early stages of the disease may be said to be the rule, nearly all writers mention the occurrence of cases without œdema. Ameuille and Parisot, however, have insisted on the importance of distinguishing such cases, and have put them in a separate class, which they call pure azotæmic cases. The initial symptoms are rather more severe than in the cases with œdema. There is more pyrexia, and severe headache and vomiting are often present ; hæmaturia is not infrequent. Owing to the absence of œdema they consider that the true nature of the affection may be overlooked. In relation to this subject, some interesting facts are recorded by MacLean and De Wesselow with regard to functional deficiency in the later stages of the disease. They find that, while in the early stages all the functions of the kidney are more or less affected, cases in which convalescence does not soon occur often assume the characters of either of two types, to which they apply the terms azotæmic and hydræmic. The types are fairly distinct, though mixed forms also occur. In the former there is nitrogen retention in the blood, with low concentration of the urea in the urine and with low diastatic value, and there is evidence of involvement of the cardio-vascular system. There is no œdema, and albuminuria is moderate or slight in amount. In the latter type œdema is present, and there is retention of chlorides, and a large amount of protein is present in the urine. There is, however, no nitrogen retention, the diastatic reaction is high, and there is little or no affection of the cardio-vascular system. It would be interesting to know the histological changes corresponding with those two functional types, but data on these points are not available.

Acidosis.—Observations with regard to acidosis in war nephritis have been comparatively few in number. Trevan, as quoted by Langdon Brown, estimated the alveolar CO_2 in five cases during the dyspnœa, and found it normal in three, whilst in two there was slight reduction. Keith and Thomson carried out a series of tests both in resolving and non-resolving cases, estimating the alveolar CO_2, the alkali reserve of the blood and the combined CO_2 of the plasma. In the resolving group there was, in nine cases out of twelve, distinct evidence of slight acidosis, which passed off as improvement of the kidney condition occurred. In the non-resolving group it was rather more marked and more persistent, and sometimes required alkali therapy for its removal. They consider that the acidosis is closely related to impaired renal function, and appears to depend on the degree of damage to the kidneys. There is, however, no evidence that the marked dyspnœa, which has been so prominent in war nephritis even at an early stage, is due to acidosis.

Numerous observations show that some elevation of the blood-pressure is of common occurrence in the acute phase of war nephritis, though here, again, there is some discrepancy in the account. For example, Abercrombie, as the result of numerous observations, states that the blood-pressure seems to be always raised at some period of the disease ; he found in acute cases of moderate severity that the systolic blood-pressure was usually 135 to 180 mm. of mercury. According to Langdon Brown, the blood-pressure is variable but usually raised, and the most favourable condition is a moderately raised pressure at the outset, falling fairly quickly to normal. Abercrombie agrees with him on this point. Bruns states that in all cases before the œdema began to disappear there was increased arterial pressure, the readings being 140 to 210 mm. of mercury. MacLean records a closely similar result. On the other hand, Ameuille found that in 90 per cent. of cases with œdema, the blood-pressure did not exceed normal limits from beginning to end, and that of the cases with high tension some had this condition at the onset, whilst in others it developed at a later period. Writers are in general agreement that in favourable cases the blood-pressure falls as the œdema disappears, and this is often followed by a subnormal value.

It is thus seen that all the important results of kidney insufficiency, and the associated functional disturbances recognized as occurring in the acute nephritis of civil life, have been found to be present in war nephritis.

Lesions in other Organs.—The records are insufficient for a statistical account of the lesions in other organs associated with war nephritis. A general picture may, however, be presented by a summary of the chief findings in sixty cases collected by Shaw Dunn,* though even in these the records are not complete. In all of them the kidneys were examined microscopically and the lesions conformed to the description given above. Some clinical facts are also given.

The ages of the patients obtained in 33 cases were :—

20 years and under in		..	..	..	1 case.
20–25 years	,,	..	..	..	5 cases.
26–30 ,,	,,	..	..	..	7 ,,
31–35 ,,	,,	..	..	..	8 ,,
36–40 ,,	,,	..	..	..	S ,,
41–42 ,,	,,	..	..	..	4 ,,

The mortality appears to be definitely higher among the older men. The duration of the illness in 52 cases was :—

" A few days " in		..	..	..	8 cases.
2–7 ,,	,,	..	..	..	21 ,,
8–14 ,,	,,	..	..	..	19 ,,
About 3 weeks ,,		..	..	..	3 ,,
,, 5 ,,	,,	..	..	..	1 case.

Thus in nearly fifty of the cases death occurred within a fortnight.

In cases dying at these early periods, uræmia appears to be an important factor. Uræmic convulsions were present in 14 cases, absent in 37, while there was no note in 9. Other uræmic symptoms, such as coma, drowsiness and mental confusion (in cases where there were no convulsions) were present in 24, absent in 14, and there was no note in 8. Thus symptoms apparently of uræmic nature occurred in 38 cases in all. The temperature was referred to in only 24 cases. Hyperpyrexia (107° F.) was present in one case, pyrexia (100° or over) in 17 cases; the temperature was normal in 5 cases and subnormal in 1 case.

As regards the occurrence of œdema, this condition was present in 41 cases, absent in 6, not noted in 13. The œdema, though quite definite, was not usually very severe.

Kidneys.—The condition of these has been fully described above, but the following notes from *post-mortem* records may be of interest. They were described as of normal size in 26 cases, enlarged in 21. The degrees of enlargement in 8 of the latter are indicated by the weights of both kidneys as follows : 390, 420, 440, 450, 475, 500 and 550 grm. Thus in a small proportion a considerable degree of enlargement was present. The appearances of the kidneys were described in 49 cases as follows : normal in 12, congested in 11, pale in 13, blurred in 3, and faintly granular in 3 ; hæmorrhages visible to the

---

* The notes and tissues from many of these cases were sent in to No. 3 Mobile Laboratory by various medical officers, largely at the instigation of Sir Wilmot Herringham.

naked eye occurred in 7 (abundant in 2 of these). In relation to these facts it may be noted that hæmaturia, visible to the naked eye, was present in 16, absent in 21, while there was no note in 21 ; anuria was present in 2 cases.

Respiratory System.—The lungs were œdematous in 23 cases, œdematous with broncho-pneumonia in 15, the seat of broncho-pneumonia in 5, congested in 8, normal in 1 case. In 8 cases where the *post-mortem* examination was made by Shaw Dunn, the following were the conditions : In 4 cases œdema was present, usually in all the lobes, distributed in lobular fashion like a broncho-pneumonia and alternating with over-distended areas ; in 3 cases broncho-pneumonia with œdema, and in 1 case broncho-pneumonia alone.

The *bronchi* were the seat of bronchitis in 6 cases and of purulent bronchitis in 4 ; congestion was present in 4 and frothy secretion in 4 ; the condition was normal in 1 and not noted in 41.

The Pleuræ.—Effusions were noted in 29 cases ; pleurisy in 2 ; the condition was normal in 10 ; no note in 19.

As regards associated symptoms, dyspnœa was present in 43 cases and absent in 2 ; no note in 15. Cough was present in 27 cases and absent in 2 ; no note in 31.

The *spleen* was described as normal in size in 10 cases, and enlarged in 21 ; no note in 29. The degree of enlargement in 7 cases is indicated as follows : 210, 210, 210, 240, 550 grm., "2½ times normal," and "three times normal." In 5 cases minute hæmorrhages were noted.

In this connection it is noted that Herxheimer found the spleen swollen and soft in all his fourteen cases of war nephritis, and regarded it as supporting the view that the disease is an infection.

The *brain* was examined in 32 cases. It was described as normal in 15 cases, congested in 7 and œdematous in 6. Multiple minute hæmorrhages in the white matter were present in 2 cases, and a local softening in 1 case. In 1 case meningitis was present.

The *retinæ* were examined in 8 cases and hæmorrhages were present in 3 of these ; the condition was normal in the others.

Shaw Dunn and McNee examined microscopically various organs, and found lesions in the lungs and brain. In the lungs a change was often present in the infundibula and small bronchioles (Fig. 5). These were dilated and had lost their epithelial covering ; their walls were swollen and hyaline-looking, and were covered by material resembling fibrin. In many of the capillaries of the damaged infundibula, minute hyaline thrombi were present. This lesion does not correspond with any usual type of bronchitis, and rather resembles that produced by an irritant gas such as chlorine, though the action of gas as the causal agent could be excluded in most instances. That the changes described were comparatively common, was shown by the fact that out of 23 cases examined they were well marked in 8, and present in less degree in 8 others. They seem to be of some importance, as, if war nephritis is due to an infection, they may indicate the site of entrance of the infective agent ; and in any case they may be related to the occurrence of dyspnœa, which is so marked a feature in the disease. In the brain small capillary hæmorrhages were found in 2 out of 12 cases in which a thorough examination was possible, and were confined to the white matter of the cerebrum. On microscopic examination the hæmorrhages were often found to be ring-shaped on section, there being a central vessel surrounded by necrosed tissue, with a zone of effused red corpuscles at the margin (Fig. 6).   Hyaline thrombi were present in the central vessels in several instances, and the lesions are probably to be interpreted as minute infarcts with hæmorrhagic margin.   It may also be added that the retinæ were examined in 8 cases, and minute hæmorrhages of similar character were found in 3 of these.

Herxheimer, having in view the possibility that the œdema might be due to damage of the capillary endothelium throughout the body, examined carefully the capillaries in skin, subcutaneous tissue and various internal organs, but failed to find any change.   Lesion was present in the kidneys alone and was confined to the glomeruli.   He records, however, a case which is of some interest in this connection.   The patient was a young man in the third week of the disease, who was suddenly seized with difficulty of breathing followed by coma, death resulting on the day after.   In the roof of the fourth ventricle there were numerous small hæmorrhages of capillary origin.   At that stage of life such an occurrence suggests some toxic damage of the capillary walls, though no change could be detected in the vessels in other parts of the brain.   The lesion found in this case is of interest in relation to the results of Shaw Dunn and McNee given above.

Ætiology.

As the real cause of war nephritis has not been discovered, one has to consider in what direction the evidence points as to the nature of the disease, and what factors may play a part. The central fact is that the disease suddenly attacked a large number of comparatively young and healthy men, and cases with previously damaged kidneys, which formed a small proportion of the total number of cases of war nephritis, must be excluded.

Even if it were the case that exposure to wet and cold could cause the lesions of the disease, the established facts do not lend much support to the view that exposure is concerned in its origin.   As has been pointed out by various writers, the disease became common only in the late winter months, and steadily increased through the summer, a similar occurrence being noted in the case of the American Civil War.   In other wars, too, there was equal exposure without its occurrence.   No doubt, in the two years after the disease had started there was a slight increase

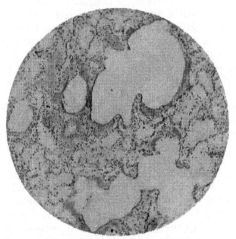

Fig. 5.—Section of œdematous lung in a case of acute nephritis. Of the two large cavities one, the more rounded, is a terminal bronchiole; the other, irregularly V-shaped, represents two infundibula. The former shows loss of epithelial lining and deposition of fibrin-like exudate on its walls. In the infundibula fibrin layers are present, especially on the ridges, and give the appearance of a thick wall, which is quite abnormal. (x 60.)

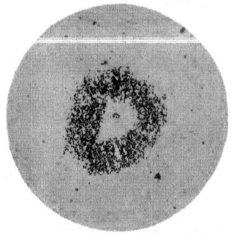

Fig. 6.—Minute hæmorrhage in cerebral white matter in a case of acute nephritis. The pale area in the centre of the hæmorrhage is necrosed nervous tissue. Near the centre of the necrotic focus there is seen the transverse section of a minute blood vessel filled with red corpuscles. (x 125.)

during the cold winter months; but the important figures
are those which pertain to the establishment of the disease, and
here there is no relation to severity of weather. The question
of exposure to cold and wet in individual cases has also been
investigated, but there is considerable variation in the results.
Bruns, for example, obtained a history of such exposure in
70 per cent. of his cases, fully two hundred being examined, but
this result is rather exceptional. On the other hand, Langdon
Brown obtained a history of exposure in only twenty out of
fifty-eight cases, and the experience of most observers with the
British and French troops corresponds with this. And, as
Ameuille remarks, " the feeling of chilliness at the onset of the
disease may be readily assumed to be the result of exposure."
Apart, however, from these facts, there is no evidence that
a glomerulo-nephritis can be produced by exposure alone;
in fact, many authorities deny that any form of nephritis is
produced in this way. While putting aside exposure as the
cause of war nephritis, in certain instances it may have been a
predisposing condition, as it may be to almost any acute
disease.

The question of water and food supply has also been carefully
considered. There is no evidence that water supply was in any
way related to the outbreak. The water taken by those who
contracted the disease was obtained from different sources and
in different districts, some of it being chlorinated and some not.
To the food supply, however, considerable importance has been
attached by various investigators. McLeod and Ameuille
consider that excess of protein diet along with deficiency of
fresh vegetables brings about a sort of scorbutic or fragile condition of the kidneys with albuminuria, and that this apparently
functional albuminuria passes by stages into nephritis of
mild degree. They bring forward the somewhat significant
facts that the excretion of urea by healthy British soldiers was
much higher than in the case of the French, that albuminuria
was much more frequent in the former, and that nephritis
appeared later and was less severe in the French than in the
British armies. It may be admitted at most that an excess of
protein might make the kidneys less resistant to any superadded
toxic or infectious condition, but it has been pointed out* that
the officers had as much protein in their diet as the men, and
that in the later period the proportion of protein in the ration
was considerably diminished. McLeod and Ameuille failed
to obtain any evidence that the incidence of nephritis was

---

* M.R.C. Report, 7th June, 1918.

higher among those with albuminuria than among those with healthy urine. In connection with this question of albuminuria, it may be noted that MacLean found a similar high frequency of occurrence among British troops in training, a little over 5 per cent. in 50,000 men examined. He found, however, that it showed no tendency to increase on service, or to be followed by injurious effects on the kidneys, and he came to the conclusion that war nephritis is not the result of any condition present during training, but is due to some cause which is chiefly operative in the fighting area. Several German writers, *e.g.*, Hirschstein, Albu and Schlesinger, and Neuermann, lay stress on the importance of diet in connection with the origin of war nephritis, holding that the taking in excess for a prolonged period of concentrated protein, salted meat and so on, with deficiency of vegetables, may lead to damage to the kidneys. Instances might, however, readily be adduced where such a diet has not produced any tendency to the occurrence of nephritis. In relation to this aspect of the subject, it is interesting to note that Mackenzie Wallis found, on examination of the urine, no evidence of intestinal toxæmia in cases of war nephritis; there was no increase of the ethereal sulphates as a whole, and indican was not found in more than normal traces. The urobilinuria often associated with intestinal putrefaction was not observed.

Anti-typhoid inoculation has also been brought up as in some way related to the outbreak, but for this there does not appear to be any evidence whatever. Seeing that the procedure was universal throughout the army, and that the inoculated were subjected to exposure in other spheres of war, and in fact also at home, any tendency of it to lead to nephritis could not have escaped notice. No such tendency has been observed, and there is also the fact that nephritis was a rare affection in the South African war. The suggestion may thus be dismissed as without any foundation. Cases have been recorded where albuminuria has been artificially produced by men taking chromic acid, cantharides and so on, but these have, of course, no bearing on the question at issue. It may also be stated that any metallic poisoning, (*e.g.*, lead from tinned food has been suggested), may similarly be excluded; and, in fact, the lesions found in the kidney are not such as can be produced in that way.

Langdon Brown found a positive Wassermann reaction in 18 out of 56 cases, a higher proportion than in the army generally. Ameuille, on the other hand, found no difference in the French army between nephritic patients and other men examined, as regards frequency of a positive reaction. It does not appear that there is sufficient evidence that previous syphilis acts as a predisposing condition; but if it does so it does nothing more.

Infection.—Whilst at first various theories were put forward as to the causation of war nephritis, as the disease progressed and cases became more numerous, the view that it was due to an infection received more and more support. And this view, based initially on the facts with regard to incidence and the main clinical features, appeared to be strengthened by pathological results. In considering the question, it will be well to discriminate as to what may be included in the term, and there seem to be at least three different possibilities. In the first place, there might be a true bacterial infection of the kidneys and urinary passages, with bacteria in the urine, and so on; in the second place, the urinary tract might be free from bacteria and the nephritis be produced by a bacterial infection in some other part of the body, as a result of the elimination of toxins; and in the third place, the infection might not be of bacterial nature, but be produced by some other kind of organism, most probably a filter-passing virus.

The first of these possibilities may be definitely set aside. The examination of catheter specimens of the urine has not revealed the common presence of any pathogenic organisms. In examinations carried out at St. Bartholomew's Hospital, the urine was generally found to be sterile, and while Shaw Dunn and McNee obtained streptococci in a fair proportion of the urines examined, they found similar organisms in control catheter specimens in non-nephritic cases; they considered that no importance was to be attached to them. Wilson also failed to find any evidence of a specific organism in the urine. It appears quite unnecessary to quote the various negative results given by others. Andrewes was unable to detect any organisms in sections of the kidneys, and this has been the general result. Furthermore, the lesions in the kidneys are not such as are recognized as being produced by any known bacterial infection of the organs. It may also be mentioned that blood cultures made from cases of war nephritis have practically always failed to yield any bacterial growth.

As has been mentioned above, the initial kidney lesion resembles that met with in scarlet fever and in certain bacterial infections, especially streptococcal. Whether any of the established findings are related to this fact has to be considered. One naturally thinks first of all of affections of the fauces. There is no evidence that tonsillitis has been associated with the nephritis ; in fact, various writers, for example, Rose Bradford and Abercrombie, remark on the rarity of this affection. Sore throat was more common, and Langdon Brown found it to be an early symptom in 17 out of 58 cases ; but according to the records generally, it was not a frequent or prominent symptom, and certainly nothing like a distinct epidemic of sore throat was observed. Canti, as quoted by Langdon Brown, made cultures from the throats of nephritic patients who had complained of sore throat, using other soldiers and civilians as controls, and failed to find any special features in the former, either as regards the number or the characters of the bacteria. He also failed to find any anti-bodies to streptococci in the blood of several cases of war nephritis examined. Rose Bradford, as a result of analysis of a large number of cases of war nephritis, found that bronchitis was present in 30 per cent., and states that bronchitis was the only frequent illness prior to the onset of dropsy. He remarks, however, that bronchitis was common amongst the Indian troops, whereas nephritis did not occur. Abercrombie also found bronchitis to be so frequent in association with war nephritis that he was doubtful whether it ought to be considered a complication or one of the phenomena of the disease. Herxheimer, who has made an important contribution to the pathological anatomy of the disease, considers that the glomerular changes are secondary to coccal infections, and from the frequent presence of tracheitis, laryngitis and bronchitis, that the path of entrance is the upper respiratory passages. It is difficult, however, to accept such a view as satisfactory. Bronchitis, with such a coccal invasion of the bronchial tubes, is of common occurrence, and it has no special tendency to be associated with the onset of nephritis. Further, if it were correct, one would expect to find a close relationship between influenza, where secondary infection with streptococci was common, and nephritis, and this was not observed. Further, the seasonal incidence of nephritis, the increase while the temperature was rising, does not harmonize well with such a view. Another theory is possible, namely, that the unknown virus producing nephritis entered by the respiratory passages, and that either it tended to lead to bronchitis, or was aided in gaining a foothold by the presence of bronchitis ; but this would be pure speculation. The peculiar lesion observed by Shaw Dunn and McNee in the pulmonary infundibula may, however, be of considerable importance in this connection.

The suggestion was put forward at a comparatively early period that war nephritis was due to suppressed scarlet fever, but this seems to be quite without support, and also to be negatived by various facts. An epidemic of scarlet fever without any non-suppressed cases is an unknown phenomenon, and in addition there was an absence of characteristic throat affection and of desquamation. Kayser speaks of the disease as a " scarlatinoid nephritis," and considers it an independent infective disease, which he thinks is probably louse-borne He mentions the occurrence of a fine desquamation of the face and hands in the third week of the disease, but, so far as we know he is the only writer who records such an occurrence. In connection with the subject of infection, it is interesting to note that Shaw Dunn and McNee could find on enquiry no evidence of the occurrence of war nephritis amongst the civilian population, though the troops mingled freely with them. On the other hand, some cases occurred amongst orderlies at the base. This would suggest that, if the disease be an infection, it is carried in some special manner obtaining amongst the troops, possibly that it is vermin-borne, in a manner analogous to trench fever; but of this there is no definite evidence.

Mackenzie Wallis drew attention to the close similarity in certain points between the nephritis of scarlatina and war nephritis, not as implying the identity of the two, but merely as indicating that the latter might be due to some specific infection. He found that both the blood serum and the sterile urine from cases of war nephritis were markedly toxic when injected into rabbits. The toxicity of the urine was higher than that of normal urines, 5 c.c. of the former being sufficient to kill a rabbit in a few minutes. Further, when small quantities of urine or serum, sufficient to produce only transitory toxic phenomena, were injected into rabbits and monkeys, illness developed about the eighth day, and in two cases a fatal result preceded by albuminuria followed. No distinct lesion, however, could be found in the kidneys. The toxic agent passed through a Berkefeld filter and was destroyed by half an hour's exposure at 55° C., apparently being either a labile toxin or a filter-passing virus. These results are suggestive, but do not permit the drawing of a definite conclusion.

In this review of the evidence bearing on the ætiology of war nephritis, it must be admitted that its exact causation has not been satisfactorily determined. Two main possibilities appear to emerge from the discussion. The first is that the disease is the result of concomitant factors—bronchitis or other bacterial

infections aided by the diet, exposure and so on. The second
is that it is the result of a specific infection of unknown nature
and origin, though possibly a filter-passing virus. It is difficult
to regard the first as satisfactory, when all the facts regarding
war nephritis in relation to nephritis in general are considered.
The second would accord better with the definite clinical characters, the incidence of the disease and the early lesions in the
kidneys, but cannot be regarded as much more than a probability.

BIBLIOGRAPHY.

Abercrombie	Acute Phase of Five Hundred Cases of War Nephritis.	Jl. of R.A.M.C.,1916, Vol. xxvii, p. 131.
Adler	Epidemic Nephritis	Practitioner, 1917, Vol. xcviii, p. 130.
Albu & Schlesinger	Ueber Nierenerkrankungen bei Kriegsteilnehmern.	Berlin. klin. Woch., 1916, Vol. liii, p. 130.
Ameuille	Les néphrites de guerre	Revue Générale de Pathologie de Guerre, Paris, 1917, No. 5, p. 559.
,,	*Ibid.*	Annales de Méd., 1916, Vol. iii, p. 298. Presse Méd., 1916, Vol. xxiv, p. 489.
Ameuille & McLeod	Le fonctionnement rénal chez les troupes en campagne et des rapports avec les néphrites de guerre.	Bull. de l'Acad. de Méd., 1916, Vol. lxxvi, p. 103.
Beitzke & Seitz	Untersuchungen über die Aetiologie der Kriegsnephritis.	Berlin. klin. Woch., 1916, Vol. liii, p. 1313.
Bradford, Rose	Nephritis in the British Troops in Flanders.	Quart. Jl. Med., 1915–16, Vol. ix, p. 125.
,,	Nephritis in British Troops in Flanders. A Preliminary Note.	Jl. of R.A.M.C.,1916, Vol. xxvii, p. 445.
Brown, Langdon	Report on Fifty-eight Cases of Acute Nephritis occurring in Soldiers of the Expeditionary Force, investigated at St. Bartholomew's Hospital for the Medical Research Committee.	*Ibid.*, 1915, Vol. xxv, p. 75.
Brown, Langdon & others.	Discussion on Trench Nephritis.	Proc. Roy. Soc. Med., 1915–16, Vol. ix, Med., Ther. and Pharm. Sect., pp. i–xl.
Bruns	Klinische Erfahrungen über die akute Nierenentzündung der Kriegsteilnehmer.	Zeitschr. f. klin.Med., 1916, Vol. lxxxiii, p. 233.

Dunn	.. ..	Epidemic Nephritis	Practitioner, 1917, Vol. xcviii, p. 126.
Dunn & McNee	..	The Study of War Nephritis ..	Brit. Med. Jl., 1917, Vol. ii, p. 745.
Gross	.. ..	Frische Glomerulonephritis (Kriegsniere).	Ziegler's Beitr. z. path. Anat., 1919, Vol. lxv, p. 387.
Herxheimer	..	Ueber das pathologisch-anatomische Bild der " Kriegsnephritis."	Deut. med. Woch., 1916, Vol. xlii, pp. 940 & 969.
Hirschstein	.. ..	Zur Entstehung der Nierenerkrankungen im Felde.	Berlin. klin. Woch., 1916, Vol. liii, p. 1045.
Hogarth	.. ..	Report on Cases of Albuminuria amongst British Troops in France.	Jl. of R.A.M.C.,1916, Vol. xxvi, p. 372.
Jungmann	.. ..	Ueber akute Nierenerkrankungen bei Kriegsteilnehmern.	Deut. med. Woch., 1916, Vol. xlii, p. 965. Zeitschr. f. klin. Med., Vol. lxxxiv, p. 1.
Kayser	.. ..	Beiträge zur Kenntnis der Kriegsnephritis.	Berlin. klin. Woch., 1916, Vol. liii, p. 1043.
Keith & Thomson	..	War Nephritis	Quart. Jl. Med., 1917-18, Vol. xi, p. 229.
Löhlein	.. ..	Bemerkungen zur sogenannten " Feldnephritis."	Med. Klin., Berlin, 1916, Vol. xii, p. 922.
MacLean	.. ..	Albuminuria and War Nephritis among British Troops in France.	M.R.C. Reports, 1919, London, No. 43.
MacLean & de Wesselow.		Effects of War Nephritis on Kidney Function, etc.	Quart. Jl. Med., 1918-19, Vol. xii, p. 347.
McLeod & Ameuille		The Effect of Trench Warfare on Renal Function.	Lancet, 1916, Vol. ii. p. 468.
Neuermann	.. ..	Eine Mitteilung über akute Nierenentzündung mit Oedemen.	Münch. med. Woch., 1916, Vol. lxiii, p. 1134.
Parisot & Ameuille	..	Les néphrites aigues cryptogénétiques observées chez les troupes en campagne.	Bull. de l'Acad. de Méd., 1915, Vol. lxxiv, p. 516.
Pick	.. ..	Akute Nierenentzündung im Kriege.	Berlin. klin. Woch., 1916, Vol. liii, p. 173.
Teissier	.. ..	A propos des néphrites de guerre.	Bull. de l'Acad. de Méd., 1917, Vol. lxxvii, p. 806.
Tremolières & Caussade.		Etiologie évolution et pronostic des néphrites aigues de guerre.	Annales de Méd., 1917, Vol. iv, p. 73.
Ullmann	.. ..	Ueber die in diesem Kriege beobachtete neue Form akuter Nephritis.	Berlin. klin. Woch., 1916, Vol. liii, p. 1046.
Wallis	.. ..	An Investigation of Acute Nephritis : the so-called " Trench Nephritis."	Jl. of R.A.M.C.,1916, Vol. xxvi, p. 259.

Zondek	..	..	Funktionsprüfungen bei der hämorrhagischen Nierenent-zündung von Kriegsteilneh-mern.	Zeitschr. f. klin. Med., 1916, Vol. lxxxiii, p. 185. Berlin. klin. Woch., 1916, Vol. liii, p. 451.
Official	..	..	Reports on War Nephritis ..	M.R.C., London, 1918.

CHAPTER XXII.

ENCEPHALITIS LETHARGICA.

PRESENT knowledge of encephalitis lethargica* is due entirely to observations made during and after the period of the war. There is evidence that in several countries a disease of the same nature may have occurred in the past, perhaps as long ago as 1685 in England, 1745 in Germany and 1800 in France and Italy, but its first definite recognition and description as a separate clinical and pathological entity are due to von Economo and von Wiesner, who made a detailed study of thirteen cases which occurred in Vienna in 1917. Early in 1918, before the observations made by those workers had become generally known, a number of cases of an obscure disease with cerebral symptoms were reported in London, Sheffield and other towns in England. At first they were regarded as cases of " botulism " and later as cases of the cerebral form of acute poliomyelitis, but a systematic investigation carried out by medical officers of the Local Government Board and the Medical Research Committee proved that the affection, in its clinical, anatomical and epidemiological features, was distinct and independent, and could be identified clinically as being the disease, new to medical knowledge, which had been described a few months earlier in Vienna. A little later it was described in France, and towards the autumn of 1918 in the United States of America. It is now generally known and recognized, and its distribution has been found to be almost world-wide.

It may be defined as a general infectious disease presenting a group of cerebral or cerebro-spinal symptoms of which the most distinctive are a condition of increasing languor and drowsiness passing into lethargy and stupor, associated usually, though not invariably, with a combination of various cranial nerve palsies, of which ptosis, squint and nystagmus are characteristic signs. Mild or so-called abortive cases, presenting.

---

* The name "encephalitis lethargica" (von Economo) has the right of priority and is now in general use, but the disease has also been described under the following terms :—" acute infective ophthalmoplegia or botulism " (Harris), " toxic ophthalmoplegia " (Hall), " epidemic stupor " (Batten and Still), " l'encéphalite épidémique " (Levaditi and Harvier), etc.

only slight lethargy or stupor, mental apathy, headache and lack of facial expression are also recognized. The disease is caused by a living virus which appears to be filtrable and presumably enters through the naso-pharynx and passes up along the nerves. The virus produces in the nervous system definite inflammatory lesions which are most conspicuous in the upper part of the pons and the basal nuclei, the site of election being the region of the nuclei of the third nerve. The degree of infectivity from person to person is of a low order, and although there are occasional occurrences in the same family or institution, cases of the disease usually happen singly in a sporadic manner. The cases reported in the army both during the war and subsequently have been few in number and quite without discoverable relation to one another. In England and on the Continent the disease has definitely a maximum seasonal incidence in the winter months. Most cases have been reported in persons during the middle period of life, but all ages are attacked and both sexes nearly equally. The case mortality may be given as between 20 and 50 per cent. ; it varies usually with the extent to which mild or abortive cases are included in the figures.

As to the nature of the disease, present opinion tends to support the view put forward in 1918 by Lt.-Col. S. P. James that it is one of a group (including cerebro-spinal fever and acute poliomyelitis) in which the pathological agent is much more frequently present in the human organism than the clinical evidence implies ; and that an attack of the disease is the result either of a breakdown in the immunity to the effects of the virus which the individual who harboured it had up to that time enjoyed, or of a non-immune person becoming freshly infected with a strain of the virus which has attained the degree of pathogenicity that can be considered as " specific." This view best explains the irregular, widespread, sporadic distribution of the disease, and the fact that it is seldom or never possible to trace a case to any known source of infection except the patient himself. It emphasizes the rôle of the individual in the origin and progress of the illness, and implies that the key to the problem rests not in the purely bacteriological view of the causation of disease, but in the wider view that disease results from the interaction of several factors of which changes in the vital and chemical properties of the tissue cells, on the one hand, and in the provoking stimulus or pathogenic agent, on the other, are the chief. It is not possible to say what influence, if any, adverse conditions, both mental and physical arising out of the war, may have had in relation to some of these factors ; but MacNalty has pointed out that in Vienna, Paris and England the disease first appeared at the time when individuals were exposed to the mental strain of several years of war ; that the cases occurred chiefly in large urban centres of population where such strain may have been more acutely felt ; and that a disease is prone to attack an individual at the most fatigued point of bodily resistance. Parsons has ascertained that in 117 out of 488 cases the predisposing cause adduced was a condition (*e.g.* overwork, worry or shock) leading to, or symptomatic, of psychic disturbance.

No direct relation between encephalitis lethargica and influenza has been established, nor has it been found that any close relation exists between the local prevalence of the disease and the occurrence of cases of " epidemic hiccup."

Ætiology.

Research by animal experiment indicates that the causal organism of encephalitis lethargica is a living virus present in the tissues of the central nervous system ; that the virus is filtrable through Chamberland filters ; that it can be preserved for some time in glycerine ; and that it can be transmitted experimentally in series to monkeys and rabbits. J. McIntosh, working on behalf of the Medical Research Committee, was the first to succeed in transmitting encephalitis lethargica to an animal. The material used was a filtered emulsion in saline of small portions of the cervical cord, pons and basal nuclei from a fatal case occurring during an outbreak in an institution at Derby in August 1919. A *Patas* monkey inoculated intracerebrally with the filtrate which had been drawn through a Berkefeld filter, developed signs of encephalitis lethargica and died, the brain showing characteristic lesions similar to those present in fatal cases in the human subject. The disease produced in this monkey was then successfully transmitted in series to other monkeys and to rabbits. In February 1920 Levaditi and Harvier confirmed these results and isolated from the nervous system of rabbits inoculated with material from human cases a virus which is filtrable through Chamberland filters Nos. 1 and 3, and which preserves its virulence for at least forty-eight hours after the death of the animal. The virus is killed at 56° C. and by prolonged contact with phenol, but lives a considerable time in glycerine and preserves its virulence in an artificial medium containing cells of the testicle of the rabbit and kept at a temperature of 37° C. When dried *in vacuo*, or when mixed with milk, and kept at room temperature the virus was found to be pathogenic for as long as forty days. Levaditi and Harvier regard this virus as the causal agent of encephalitis lethargica. In cases of the disease in the human subject it is present in the central nervous system and the spinal cord, but not in the blood, the cerebro-spinal fluid or the organs of the body. It can be transmitted to rabbits intracranially, intra-orbitally, or by inoculation into a peripheral nerve, but not subcutaneously, intravenously, or intraperitoneally. In these animals both the symptoms and the anatomical lesions produced by successful inoculation are said to be identical with those found in the human subject.

The usual avenue of infection in the naturally acquired disease is considered to be the naso-pharynx, and perhaps inflammation or abrasion of the mucous membrane is necessary for entry of the virus. It is thought that ordinarily the virus passes along the olfactory nerves to reach the brain. Netter found histological changes in the salivary glands of infected animals and suggested that the virus may be present in the saliva. Mild, so-called abortive or " transient " cases must be regarded as capable of spreading infection, and failure to recognize them may account in part for the apparently sporadic occurrences usually reported. It is held that the symptoms in some of these cases may be limited to soreness or dryness of the throat, naso-pharyngeal catarrh, headache, vomiting or diarrhœa, with perhaps transient loss or dimness of vision or transient diplopia.

Morbid Histology.

As a rule the *post-mortem* examination of a fatal case of encephalitis lethargica reveals no noteworthy macroscopic change either in the internal organs or in the central nervous system. But on microscopic study of suitably prepared sections of the brain substance, it can be seen that there is a definite inflammatory lesion consisting of a cellular infiltration of the perivascular lymphatic sheaths and of certain areas of grey matter. This perivascular infiltration is the characteristic feature of the lesion in true cases of the disease. It affects chiefly the small or medium-sized veins and in some areas of the grey matter it may be so dense as to form definite foci. It is most extensive in the basal nuclei of the brain, nearly equally so in the upper part of the pons, much less extensive in the medulla, absent or very slight in the spinal cord. The cellular exudate consists chiefly of large and small mononuclear leucocytes, some polyblasts and a few plasma cells. According to

McIntosh, polynuclear leucocytes are rare. In addition to the perivascular infiltration, changes due to a slight degree of interstitial inflammation may be present, but according to most observers there is usually almost complete absence of degenerative nerve cell lesions. The ganglion cells are still present in considerable numbers and are usually well defined and with the Nissl granules present ; neuronophagia is therefore very rare and when present is not marked. On this point, however, not all observers are in accord, and recently Da Fano and Ingleby have reported that, in the cases which they examined, the nerve cells showed changes, ranging from slight chromatolysis to complete disappearance of Nissl granules and atrophy of the nucleus. Da Fano also reports finding in the nerve cells a granular pigment-like material, and " minute bodies " which appeared to consist of a central basophil particle surrounded by a delicate stained area. Marinesco, Netter and others observed hæmorrhagic foci in the grey matter, but von Wiesner and McIntosh state that they are rare and when present are of microscopic size. To explain the differences in morbid histology recorded by various workers MacNalty has suggested that the inflammatory manifestation may be slow to appear. In some cases which appeared clinically to be quite typical, and were fatal within a few days, careful microscopical study of the parts of the brain usually affected failed to show any abnormal change.

Besides the central nervous system the salivary glands in some cases are stated to be affected with foci of round-celled infiltration.

Pathology.

The pathological process by which the serious symptoms of this disease arise can only be conjectured, and the problem is the more obscure from the not infrequent failure, which has just been mentioned, to correlate the clinical signs and symptoms with noticeable changes in the brain substance or other organ or fluid of the body. MacNalty has advanced the suggestion that the process mainly involves the afferent nerve-fibres streaming towards the thalamic region, neo-pallium and so on, in such a manner as to interfere with or block entirely the normal afferent stimuli from the environment by the perception and appreciation of which the conduct of the individual is guided and controlled. The result is that the patient lapses into a state of drowsiness, lethargy, stupor or coma corresponding in degree to the extent to which there is inhibition of environmental stimuli. The nucleus of the third nerve and certain of its emerging fibres are in intimate relation to the afferent paths referred to, and the known anatomical relationships of other areas to which the usual lesions are localized enable a similar explanation to be applied.

Laboratory Methods of Diagnosis and Immunity Reactions.

Despite the claims made by several observers in different countries that they have been successful in cultivating an organism from the cerebro-spinal fluid, the blood, naso-pharyngeal washings, or various tissues in cases of encephalitis lethargica, it is now held by British and French workers who have given most attention to the subject that in cases of true encephalitis lethargica uncomplicated by other diseases, no specific change in the cerebro-spinal fluid can be detected microscopically or by bacteriological methods, that no positive result follows the application of the Wassermann test, and that no organism can be cultivated from that fluid, from the blood or the naso-pharyngeal mucous membrane, either on ordinary media or on the special media perfected by Noguchi. For this reason the present application of laboratory methods of diagnosis is confined to tests for excluding other diseases with similar symptoms. Tuberculous meningitis is the disease most frequently overlooked or unrecognized in arriving at a diagnosis of encephalitis lethargica, and as a general rule (in the absence of a positive finding of tubercle elsewhere) the cerebro-spinal fluid should be thoroughly searched for tubercle bacilli before a confident diagnosis of encephalitis lethargica is given. Cerebro-spinal meningitis and cerebral syphilis are other diseases which in some cases can be excluded only by examining the cerebro-spinal fluid. Pathological and chemical tests or culture methods may also have to be employed to exclude typhoid fever, diphtheria, septic meningitis, and renal disease ; and although " botulism " is rare, it may have to be excluded by bacteriological examination of food which patients have taken. If the patient is not seen until the stage of coma, the blood may have to be examined to exclude malaria and the urine to exclude diabetes. The question of examination for suspected narcotic poisoning may also arise.

Rabbits and other animals successfully infected by intracerebral inoculation with the virus of encephalitis lethargica invariably die, so that it has not been possible to carry out immunological observations similar to those reported by Landsteiner and Levaditi as regards the refractory stage of experimentally produced acute poliomyelitis in animals. Levaditi and Harvier report, however, that by subcutaneous inoculations with virus dried *in vacuo* or previously treated with ether they have succeeded in conferring some degree of active immunity on rabbits. The immunity is not complete but is said to be sufficient to render the animals refractory to infection by the ocular and nasal routes. The serum of these vaccinated animals does not destroy the virus of encephalitis lethargica *in vitro* and has no protective action. The same workers have ascertained also that the serum of human subjects recently convalescent from the disease, when mixed with virus and kept several hours at 37° C., does not protect rabbits against the effects of intracerebral inoculation. Nevertheless, they find that when the mixture of human serum and virus is inoculated on the scarified cornea, instead of intracerebrally, an inactivating effect is apparent. They prepared a mixture containing two volumes of convalescent serum and one volume of virus, and another containing two volumes of normal serum and one volume of virus, and kept them in an incubator at 37° C. for five hours. Rabbits inoculated on the scarified cornea with the mixture of virus and convalescent serum did not develop keratitis and survived, while rabbits inoculated in the same manner with the mixture of virus and normal serum developed keratitis and died of encephalitis. They suggest the possibility of using a " kerato-diagnostic test" based on this observation.

Cross-immunity experiments have shown that the procedure for immunization with the virus of encephalitis lethargica does not protect monkeys against the virus of acute poliomyelitis, and that the same procedure with the latter virus does not protect rabbits against the former. Amoss has shown also that the serum of convalescents of encephalitis lethargica does not inactivate the virus of acute poliomyelitis *in vitro*. These results, in addition to well-established clinical, epidemiological, histological and experimental differences, justify the conclusion that encephalitis lethargica and acute poliomyelitis, though closely related, are independent, and that each is due to a distinct specific virus.

Serotherapy.

No specific treatment is available and the lack of evidence of immunity in the serum of convalescents is unfavourable to trial of the method which is reported to have been used with some success in cases of acute poliomyelitis.

Prophylaxis.

As the infectivity of the disease is of a low order it is not usual to take special precautions to isolate patients and contacts. In the household and neighbourhood of patients search should be made for persons suffering from sore throat or other symptoms suggesting an " abortive attack," and if any are found they should be treated with that probability in mind.

Bibliography.

The literature dealing with the disease is already very voluminous and is continually being augmented. A useful summary by Dr. A. S. MacNalty of pathological work up to April 1921, in which about forty recent references are indexed, is contained in the *British Journal of Experimental Pathology*, Vol. ii, No. 3, June 1921. The work of French pathologists is fully detailed and indexed in a summary by C. Levaditi in the *Bulletin de l'Institut Pasteur*, Vol. xix, Nos. 9 and 10, of 15th and 30th May, 1921. The original reports by C. von Economo and R. R. von Wiesner are found in the *Wien. klin. Wochenschrift*, 1917, Vol. xxx, pp. 581 and 933, and " *Die Encephalitis Lethargica*," by C. von Economo, published by Franz Deuticke, Leipzig and Vienna, 1918. The English " Report of an Enquiry into an Obscure Disease, Encephalitis Lethargica," is No. 121 of the Reports to the Local Government Board on Public Health Subjects, 1918. The most recent English publication on the disease is No. 11 of the Ministry of Health Reports on Public Health and Medical Subjects, 1922, by Dr. A. C. Parsons, with contributions by Drs. A. S. MacNalty and J. R. Perdran. The bibliography in this volume contains references to the writings of about 1,200 authors.

CHAPTER XXIII.

THE WAR OFFICE COLLECTION OF PATHOLOGICAL SPECIMENS.

THE collection of the War Office pathological specimens is not yet complete, nor arranged in the room which is in course of preparation for its display at the Royal College of Surgeons, London. A record of its origination and growth is, however, of interest.

Although no particular references to the specimens it contains are at present practicable, a description of the specimens of especial interest has already been published in various periodicals and journals before they were incorporated into the collection, and many have been referred to in the volumes of the Diseases and Surgery of the War.

One of the first objects of the committee appointed in 1915 to collect material for a Medical History of the War * was to obtain from all military hospitals such specimens as would help towards the understanding and illustration of the nature of the wounds, injuries and diseases from which soldiers suffered during the war.

At the beginning of May 1915 Sir Walter Fletcher approached the Council of the Royal College of Surgeons of England, when the Council placed the work-rooms and store-rooms of the museum at the disposal of the Royal Army Medical Corps, and agreed to preserve, classify and register all specimens forwarded from military hospitals for the use and disposal of the Medical History Committee.

The number of specimens received at the College rapidly increased as a result of the efficient service which was eventually established between the pathological laboratories attached to base hospitals and casualty clearing stations in France and the museum of the College. At a later date a similar service was arranged between the pathological departments of military hospitals at home and the museum. The services of Lt.-Col. T. R. Elliott in France, and of Lt.-Col. Sir John Bland-Sutton in England were of the greatest value in connection with this organization.

In December 1916 the Army Council requested the Council of the College to suggest a means for displaying the specimens

---

* See Vol. I, General History of the Medical Services, p. x.

received. As they were prepared, therefore, they were exhibited in the museum, each with a brief description and history attached, the latter being drawn up from the rough notes that accompanied nearly all the specimens received.

Material was moreover systematically forwarded under proper official arrangements by the Canadian and Australian contingents, but was afterwards trans-shipped to Canada and Australia without its being incorporated into the National Collection, with the exception of a few specimens which were presented through their respective Governments.

In its final form the collection will comprise the following sections :—

(1) 2,000 wet specimens illustrating the nature and sequelæ of the wounds and the diseases to which soldiers are liable under modern conditions of warfare.

(2) About 600 dried preparations illustrating injuries of the bones.

(3) Drawings made by artists of clinical and pathological subjects, particularly those made by Mr. A. K. Maxwell with the army in France.

(4) X-ray plates and skiagrams received from various military hospitals, such as Queen's Hospital, Sidcup, and the Military Orthopædic Hospital, Shepherd's Bush.

From Sidcup a group of wax models and casts illustrating the plastic surgery of the face and numbering about 150 has been furnished.

The pathological series of wet specimens comprises not only examples of recent injuries, and their later results, in all the organs of the body and the bones, but likewise numerous examples of the diseases which arose during the course of the war, such as dysentery, typhoid and paratyphoid.

The results of infection with *Bacillus aërogenes* and the effects of noxious gases (" gassing ") on the respiratory organs are also illustrated.

The work of preparing, arranging and describing the pathological material was entrusted by the Council of the College to Professor S. G. Shattock, the Pathological Curator, and Mr. C. F. Beadles, the Assistant Pathological Curator. The preparation of the material was carried out by the latter, and the descriptive catalogue drawn up by the former ; each description is, with few exceptions, accompanied by a clinical history. The specimens are nearly all of excellent natural colour, and the technique exercised in their preparation of the highest kind.

Professor Sir Arthur Keith undertook the description of the bones, which were excellently prepared by Mr. F. A. Izzard, partly in France and partly at the Royal College of Surgeons. The collecting of these particular specimens was mainly due to the labour of Captain T. H. G. Shore.

In the creation of the collection the cost of the glass jars and of the preservatives used was borne entirely by the War Office, which granted certain sums of money, moreover, towards the work carried out in the Royal College of Surgeons.

Without exception the method adopted has been: (a) the fixation of the material in a formaldehyde solution; (b) its dissection or section; (c) its immersion in methylated alcohol to restore the natural colour; and (d) its final mounting in 50 per cent. glycerine.

In the arrangement of the wet specimens the different organs injured in individual cases will be kept together, the grouping adopted being as far as possible regional. In regard to the bones, these will be arranged in the usual anatomical way.

The following conditions were agreed to by the Council of the Royal College of Surgeons, on 13th October, 1921, and the agreement was signed on 11th November.

"Conditions on which the Army Medical War Collection of Pathological, Orthopædic, etc., specimens are entrusted to the care of the Royal College of Surgeons of England.

1. His Majesty's Secretary of State for War (hereinafter called the Secretary of State) shall hand over for custody to the Royal College of Surgeons of England the Army Medical War Collection (hereinafter called the Collection) of specimens, including pathological preparations, models, drawings and photographs, at present kept at the Royal College of Surgeons, and of such other specimens as the Director-General Army Medical Service may hereafter with the approval of the Royal College of Surgeons add thereto, also such orthopædic and facial exhibits as are judged by the representatives appointed by the Royal College of Surgeons and the Director-General Army Medical Service respectively to be of permanent value, and the Royal College of Surgeons shall accept the custody of the same, subject to the terms and conditions hereinafter contained.

2. The Royal College of Surgeons shall distinguish the specimens comprised in the said collection by a special mark or letters on the label of each specimen or exhibit and by conspicuously displaying the title " Army Medical War Collection " at the entrance to the room or rooms in which the Collection is exhibited.

3. The Royal College of Surgeons shall suitably house, maintain and exhibit the said Collection in its Museum and shall provide such additional glass, preservatives, labels, catalogues, and other appliances and materials as may be required for the further preparation, exhibition and maintenance of the Collection without any charge whatsoever.

4. The Royal College of Surgeons shall insure the Collection against fire in the same manner as the contents of the remainder of the Museum are insured.

5. The Collection shall be open at the times during which the rest of the Museum of the Royal College of Surgeons is open, and the Royal College of Surgeons shall, in addition, afford all reasonable facilities for officers of the Royal Army Medical Corps to visit the Collection at other times.

6. The Royal Army Medical College shall have power to select from the Collection type or duplicate specimens to be kept at Millbank for teaching purposes and to exchange such specimens for others in the Collection from time to time.

7. The Royal College of Surgeons shall remount and maintain such specimens as may be sent to it for the purpose from the collection of type or duplicate specimens kept at Millbank.

8. The Secretary of State shall appoint in such manner as he shall think fit three to five Trustees, who shall be at liberty to inspect the Collection from time to time and confer with the Museum Committee of the Royal College of Surgeons in reference to matters concerning the Collection.

9. The Royal College of Surgeons shall exercise the same care and supervision over the Collection as over the rest of its Museum. The Conservator of the Museum of the Royal College of Surgeons shall be responsible for the maintenance and care of the Collection, and shall see that suitable assistance is provided for the purpose, subject to the supervision and control of the Museum Committee of the Royal College of Surgeons.

10. The Royal College of Surgeons shall complete the preparation and mounting of such specimens as have not yet been so dealt with and may be considered by the Conservator and Director-General Army Medical Service to be suitable for exhibition, and shall care for, maintain and arrange for the suitable display of the entire collection for so long as the Secretary of State may desire, the Collection remaining the property of the Secretary of State.

11. The Royal College of Surgeons shall carry out the several undertakings herein set forth to the satisfaction of the Trustees appointed under Clause 8 of this Agreement.

12. The Secretary of State shall have the right to remove the entire collection at any time should he consider this desirable for any reason whatsoever, but the Royal College of Surgeons shall not have the right to terminate the arrangement.

13. In consideration of the foregoing the War Office shall pay to the Royal College of Surgeons the sum of £7,500, which sum shall be held to cover all future costs in connection with the housing, displaying, care, maintenance, preparation, mounting, etc., of the Collection and the provision and payment of the necessary personnel so long as the Collection remains in the custody of the Royal College of Surgeons."

The following publications have been made in connection with material after its incorporation into the War Office Collection :—

Bland-Sutton	.. Missiles as Emboli	Lancet, 1919, Vol. i' pp. 773–5.
Keith & Hall	.. Bones showing the Effects of Gunshot Injuries in the Army Medical Collection.	Brit. Jl. Surg., 1919, Vol. vi, pp. 537–65.
,, ,,	.. Specimens of Gunshot Injuries of the Face and Spine contained in the Army Medical Collection.	Ibid., 1920, Vol. vii, pp. 55–71.
,, ,,	.. Specimens of Gunshot Injuries of the Long Bones, to show the Type of Posture produced, contained in the Army Medical Collection.	Ibid., pp. 149–67.
,, ,,	.. Specimens of Long Bones showing the Processes of Infection and Repair, contained in the Army Medical Collection.	Ibid., pp. 302–19.

Makins .. .. Gunshot Injuries to the Blood-vessels. 1919.

,, ... Specimens showing the Effect of Gunshot Injury on the Heart and Blood-vessels, now on exhibition in the Museum of the Royal College of Surgeons of England. Brit. Jl. Surg., 1921, Vol. viii, pp. 107–32.

Shattock .. .. Disruptive Phenomena in Gunshot Injuries. Proc. Roy. Soc. Med., Path. Sect., 1918, Vol. xi, pp. 47–118.

Thorburn .. .. The Pathology of Gunshot Wounds of the Spinal Cord, as illustrated by the Specimens in the War Office Collection. Brit. Jl. Surg., 1921, Vol. viii, pp. 202–18.

INDEX

Flexner's Bacillus: *See* Dysentery, Bacillary.
Flies: as carriers of dysentery, 341.
Fraenkel, E.: his statistics of influenza cases, 427.
Franco-German War: 166; statistics of tetanus in, 164, 165, 168, 182; *marked local variations of*, 165; *reasons for this, ib.*; mortality from tetanus in, 169.
Freeman, Maj. A. W.: his report on influenza at Camp Pike, Ark., 429.
French, Col. H.: his records of the influenza epidemic at Aldershot, 417–9, 427, 439; *illustrations regarding*, 433, 434, 436; his observations regarding influenza symptoms, 426, 429; his case of necrosis in the bronchial glands (influenza), 446; his cases of skin lesions in connection with influenza, 457–8.
French Army: 249, 486, 560; the first to equip casualty clearing stations as surgical hospitals, 36; use of anti-gangrene sera in, 73; trench fever in, 486–7; war nephritis in, 541; *appeared later and was less severe in, than in British army*, 558.
Fry, Capt.: death of, 7.

Gardner, Capt. A. D.: his work on the preparation and standardization of agglutinable cultures, 19; member of the sub-committee of the W.O. committee on dysentery, 321.
Gas Gangrene: 7, 17, 33, 98, 131, 170; forms of, in wounds, 34–5; consideration of, in the physiology of wounds, 67–73; requirements and condition of life of the, microbe, 67; growth of pathogenetic microbes in the blood fluids, 67–71; *research regarding*, 68–9; problems of, infection, 69–70; conditions favouring the establishment of a local acidosis, 70; growth of the microbe without assistance from myogenous acid, 71; symptoms produced by action of the microbe, *ib.*; treatment of, 71–3; *local surgical*, 71–2; *general constitutional*, 72; *results of intravenous injections of 4 per cent. bicarbonate of soda*, 72–3; *use of anti-,sera*, 73; development of knowledge regarding, during the war, 78; high incidence of, during Marne and Aisne fighting, *ib.*, 80; definition of, 79; ætiology of, 79–81; importance *of local conditions of the soil*, 79; *of weather, ib.*; *of the condition of the man, ib.*; *of the type of wound and the missile causing, ib.*; sites for occurrence of, 79–80; importance of surgical factor, 80–1; incubation period, 81; varieties of the disease, *ib.*; pathology of, 81–6; progress of, 81–2; production of œdema, 82; changes in the muscles and skin, 82–4; *illustrations of*, 83–94; distribution of the organisms in the body, 84–6; laboratory diagnosis, 86–90; *by inoculation of animals*, 87–9; *by examination of films*, 89–90; *by clinical examination*, 90; serotherapy, 91–5 (*see* Sera); prophylaxis, 95–6 (*see* Sera); occurrence of many cases of, in 1914 leads to renewed study of anaërobic infections, 97; list of organisms immediately concerned with, 98; list of anaërobes infecting wounds whose action may be contributory to, 99; highest titres in anti-, sera, 117.
German Army: 165, 249; incidence of tetanus in (Franco-German war), 168; trench fever in, 487; war nephritis in, 541.
Gettings, Dr. H. S.: his investigations regarding dysentery, 294 n, 326.
Gibson, Capt. Graeme-: appointed assistant to the Adviser in Pathology, 8–9; dies of influenzal pneumonia at Abbeville, 1919, *ib.*
Gingivitis: incidence of, 533; forms of, *ib.*; acute ulcerative, 533–4; *statistics regarding*, 534; sub-acute and chronic, 534–5; statistics of an investigation regarding, 534, 537–9; statistics regarding age incidence, 534–5; experience of army dentists regarding, 535; in connection with Vincent's angina, *ib.*; prevention, 539–40; treatment, 540.
Glover, Capt. J. A.: his routine work regarding pharyngococci, 392; his investigations at Caterham regarding cerebro-spinal fever, 398–400.
Glynn, Prof.: his work regarding enteritis cases at Liverpool, 320; illustrations of his work regarding influenza, 431, 435.

Golla, Capt. F.: his records of the inverse relation between mortality from and incubation of tetanus, 176-7; *charts illustrating*, 177.

Goodpasture, Dr.: invents new stain for Gram-negative bacteria (influenza), 421.

Gordon, Lt.-Col. Mervyn-: vi.; his work at the cerebro-spinal fever laboratory at the Royal Army Medical College, 28.

Gray, Lt.-Col. A. C. H.: his description of the growth and development of mobile bacteriological laboratories, 9; in charge of " Princess Christian Motor Laboratory," 10.

Greig, Lt.-Col. E. W. W.: his observations regarding an influenza epidemic among Indian troops at Karachi, 427, 429-30.

Griffith, Dr. S.: 406; his work at Cambridge on the production of anti-meningococcus serum, 402.

Griffith, F.: his study of the serological characters of meningococci, 406.

Hadfield, Capt.: collaborates with Capt. Archibald in a report regarding the type of dysentery prevalent among troops at Gallipoli, 286.

Hallows, Capt. N. F.: his records of an influenza epidemic at Aldershot, 417-9.

Hammond, Lt. J. A. B.: his records of an epidemic of influenza at Etaples, winter 1916-17, 413-7; *illustrations regarding*, 414-6.

Harvey, Lt.-Col. D.: vi; advises on technical matters relating to hospital laboratories, 24; in charge of Army Vaccine Department at the Royal Army Medical College, *ib.*, 30; his recommendations regarding the disposal of dysentery convalescents, 284.

Health, Ministry of: 321, 427, 429; co-operation with W.O. regarding the prevention *of enteric fever*, 27, 221; *of bacillary dysentery*, 27.

Herringham, Sir W.: 554; his observations on a case of trench fever, 487.

Hine, Maj. T. G. M.: 403; his work of supplying agglutinating sera for research regarding meningococci, 391; his analysis of clinical results obtained with monotypical sera (cerebro-spinal fever), 402-3; designs special jet for naso-pharyngeal disinfection, 404.

Hospital, King George: research work at, regarding amœbic dysentery, 285.

Hospital, London: 321; work at, regarding *amœbic dysentery*, 285, 285-6; *bacillary dysentery*, 320.

Hospital, Mount Vernon, Hampstead: observations made at, regarding trench fever cases, 488-9.

Hospital, Royal Free: experiment at, regarding tetanus antitoxin, 203.

Hospital, Royal Herbert, Woolwich: investigations at, regarding latent infection in wounds, 161, 163.

Hospital, St. Bartholomew's: serological enquiry at, regarding the dysentery strains prevalent on the Western front, 321, 326.

Hospital, St. Mary's: inoculation department of, supplies typhoid vaccine, 30; work at, *on amœbic dysentery*, 285; *on bacillary dysentery*, 320.

Hospital, Southampton War: work at, regarding the carrier condition in enteric fever, 221; work at, regarding the bacteriology of bacillary dysentery, 339-40.

Hospitals: statistics regarding general and stationary, during the war, 14; system of organization of pathological work in T.F. general, 23-4; condition of wounds at base, in early days of the war, 33-5; no cases of tetanus in Paris, during insurrectionary outbreak of 1848, 165; analysis of tetanus cases in French, 1918, 174; arrangements made at certain, in 1915 for dysentery cases, 283-4.

Hospitals, Convalescent (Dysentery): arrangements made for, 1915, 283-4; first, opened at Barton-on-Sea, May 1916, 290; Manor War Hospital, Epsom, opened, Nov. 1916, *ib.*; results of investigations made regarding amœbic dysentery at Barton and Epsom, 293-5.

Hunter, Dr.: visits Gallipoli as a member of the Medical Advisory Committee, 286.

Imperial College of Science : 289.

Influenza : 17, 21, 359, 547, 561, 568 ; conclusions regarding types of, 413 ; records of an epidemic at Etaples, winter 1916–17, 413–7 ; *illustrations regarding*, 414–6 ; records of Aldershot epidemic, 417–9 ; *illustration regarding*, 418 ; records of cases at No. 3 Canadian General Hospital, Boulogne, 419–20 ; records of an epidemic among American soldiers in the United States, 420–3 ; three phases in the pandemic of, 423 ; main features of, of winter 1916–17 similar to those of the pandemic of 1918, *ib.* ; theories regarding the importance of secondary invaders, 423–6 ; *summary*, 426.

Morbid Anatomy, 426–48 ; the upper air passages, 426–35 ; *reports of various observers, ib.* ; *illustration* showing earliest stage of reaction in influenza, 431 ; *illustrations of bronchi*, 433–434 ; the main bronchi, 435–8 ; *illustrations regarding*, 435–7 ; the lungs, 438–48 ; *illustration regarding*, 440 ; differentiation of influenzal lesions, 439–40 ; development of the specific lesion, 441–8 ; *involvement of both lungs*, 441 ; *extension of infection along the secondary bronchi, ib.* ; *brunt of infection falling on the bronchi and bronchioles, ib.* ; *variation of the reaction accompanying the influenzal bronchiolitis*, 441–6 ; *œdema and hæmorrhage*, 443–4 ; *leucocytic and serous reaction*, 444–5 ; *the air sacs*, 445 ; *hyaline deposits*, 445–6 ; *the lymphatics*, 446 ; *the lymph nodes, ib.* ; *pleurisy*, 447–8 ; *collapse*, 448.

Secondary Invaders and their Influence upon the Pulmonary Conditions, 448–57 ; pneumococcus lesions, 449–52 ; hæmolytic streptococci, 452–6 ; staphylococcus pneumonia, 456 ; after-results, 456–7 ; the " gassed " lung, 457.

Other Lesions, 457–62 ; the skin, 457–8 ; muscle, 458–9 ; circulatory system—heart, 459–60 ; alimentary canal, 460–1 ; liver, 461 ; spleen, *ib.* ; kidneys, *ib.* ; bladder, *ib.* ; adrenals, 461–2 ; testes, 462. *Summary*, 462–4.

Inman, Capt. A. C. : collaborates with Prof. Andrewes in a serological enquiry into the dysentery strains prevalent on the Western front, 321, 326 ; his work in France with agglutinable emulsions and sera (dysentery), 327.

Italian Army : 249 ; trench fever in, 487.

Italian Campaign, 1859 : *incidence of* tetanus during, 164 ; *mortality from*, 169.

Izzard, Mr. F. A. : his work on the preparation of museum specimens, 576.

James, Lt.-Col. S. P. : his opinion regarding the nature of encephalitis lethargica, 567.

James, W. M. : his thick film method for the elimination of altered blood granules in malaria work, 506.

Janes, Capt. : his bacteriological investigations at No. 3 Canadian General Hospital (influenza), 452–3.

Jaundice, Epidemic : 368.

Jaundice, Spirochætal : 494 ; knowledge of, in 1914, 513 ; early history of, 513–4 ; three epidemics of, during the war, 514 ; *at Gallipoli, ib.* ; *at Ypres, ib.* ; *in Italy, ib.* ; ætiology, 514–5 ; theories regarding mode of transmission of the parasite, 514 ; rats as transmitters, *ib.* (*see* Rats) ; theories regarding the route of infection, 515 ; *possibility of human carriers of, ib.*, 526 ; *bacteriology*, 515–9 ; *illustrations regarding*, 516–8 ; description of *Leptospira icterohaemorrhagiae*, 515–6 ; *cultivation of*, 516–9 ; *life-cycle of*, 519 ; pathology, 519–21 ; *incubation period*, 519 ; *course of infection, ib.* ; *route of invasion, ib.* ; *movements of leptospirae*, 519–20 ; *changes in the tissues*, 520 ; *relapses, ib.* ; temperature charts regarding, 521 ; morbid anatomy, 522–3 ; laboratory diagnosis, 523–6 ; *importance of animal inoculation in*, 523 ; *procedure regarding*, 523–5 ; serum therapy, 525 ; prophylaxis, 525–6.

Lightning Source UK Ltd.
Milton Keynes UK
UKOW05n1345240217
295267UK00001B/117/P